Schooling

Learning

Teaching

Nancy Diekelmann and John Diekelmann

iUniverse, Inc.
New York   Bloomington

Schooling Learning Teaching
Toward Narrative Pedagogy

iUniverse books may be ordered through booksellers or by contacting:

iUniverse
1663 Liberty Drive
Bloomington, IN 47403
www.iuniverse.com
1-800-Authors (1-800-288-4677)

ISBN: 978-1-4401-1338-3 (sc)
ISBN: 978-1-4401-1339-0 (ebk)

Printed in the United States of America

iUniverse rev. date: 3/3/2009

To Pamela M. Ironside PhD, RN, FAAN, ANEF, Professor and Director of the Institutes for Heideggerian Hermeneutical Studies, Indiana University School of Nursing for her inspired support and indefatigable assistance in making this book possible.

To the Aoteoroa New Zealand midwives and nurses, who are called to hermeneutic phenomenology by their own practices, for their generosity and caring as they co-responded to this call by letting us converse with them.

Contents

Foreword

Pamela M. Ironside, PhD, RN, FAAN, ANEF
Director, Center for Research in Nursing Education
Indiana University School of Nursing

These are times of relentless change in higher education. Calls for reform across the political, social, and theoretical spectrum have become commonplace. The research literature of education, as well as nursing education, abounds with a cacophony of voices centered on educational reform through concretizing, standardizing, critiquing, or deconstructing extant pedagogies. Outside educational circles, calls for change also emerge, with the state of education frequently conceptualized as a crisis brought about by the lack of accountability of faculty or lack of motivation of students. In other words, the problems necessitating reform are problems with faculty, with students, or with both rather than with the underlying pedagogy being used.

In health professions in general, and nursing education specifically, these calls for reform are intensified by the persistent need to prepare more practitioners in a shorter time and to prepare them to deliver healthcare that is safer and of higher quality than that currently experienced by many recipients of health services. Shortages of faculty, particularly those prepared for teaching, further exacerbate concerns. What has become clear is that neither simply doing more of the same (more content, more skills, more experiences) nor pressuring faculty and students to *do* more will address these concerns in a substantive way. Indeed, if these challenges were amenable to "more," they would not persist as problems to be addressed! Rather, new approaches are sorely needed—approaches that rethink the nature of schooling learning teaching amid the complexities and demands of both educational and clinical environments.

This book describes such an approach. Narrative Pedagogy emerges from listening to the shared stories of students, teachers, and clinicians. Narrative Pedagogy enacts hermeneutic phenomenology as it gathers students, teachers, and clinicians in communally interpreting the narrative tellings of their experiences in nursing education and participation in nursing practice. As such, Narrative Pedagogy is a recovery of the often overlooked understanding of schooling learning teaching as a phenomenon from the simplistic reduction of schooling to a production of competency outcomes, of learning to the achievement of a set of pre-specified competencies, and of teaching to a particular set of strategies. Drawing on over 20 years of scholarship, the authors have listened to, interpreted, and learned from these narrative tellings. As a nursing scholar, Nancy Diekelmann conducted a series of hermeneutic phenomenological studies in nursing education and identified the Concernful Practices of Schooling Learning Teaching. The Concernful Practices describe the shared experiences of teachers, students, and clinicians as they gather for learning and provide a new language to articulate what matters in their experiences. During the course of her research it became apparent that as teachers, students, and clinicians at pilot schools attended to the Concernful Practices in their pedagogical encounters, Narrative Pedagogy as a phenomenon became sighted (showed itself). Since that time, schools of nursing and midwifery around the globe have worked in concert to enact Narrative Pedagogy in order to transform their schools through attending to how Concernful Practices show up. Publicly sharing and interpreting stories of their experiences, as well as thinking together about both how these experiences are understood and what possibilities can show up through thinking from a different place, have enabled a richer way of letting the phenomena of sighting and listening disclose and beckon themselves.

The narrative excerpts threaded through this book reflect the wisdom of years of listening to and interpreting stories of these experiences juxtaposed to and enriched by hermeneutic phenomenological thinking. The conversations provided in this book are fictive—each a compilation of many experiences shared by participants over the course of this research and placed into conversation illuminating richer ways of thinking and comportment and concomitant possibilities for reform. These converging conversations reflect shared concerns and insights of both authors and participants and deepen the collective disciplinary understanding of the possibilities emerging from enacting Narrative Pedagogy. The converging conversations provide the reader with a glimpse of the phenomenon of schooling teaching learning as it shows up in nursing education, although the insights proffered resonate far beyond the health professions and human sciences disciplines.

John Diekelmann, in his readings of Heidegger, Gadamer, and Jean-Luc Nancy, contributes to a regional ontology of schooling learning teaching that reveals how this co-occurring, invisible phenomenon is the always already experience of being human. Bringing the literature of nearly a century of phenomenological thinkers to bear on explicating schooling learning teaching, he offers a rich and complex exegesis of these experiences, inviting the reader to see the limitations of predominant realist or idealist explanations. Mining these phenomena hermeneutically, he guides readers to challenge their presuppositions and to deepen and add complexity to their understandings of how it is with schooling learning teaching.

Yet it would be a mistake to see Narrative Pedagogy as standing over and against realist or idealist pedagogies. Clearly teachers, students, and clinicians cannot escape or overcome the claims that operate within language systems and the traditions and contexts within which they practice. But they can seek poetic understandings through working with the free play of words and meanings that emerge as shared experiences are philosophically explicated. The authors hold open and problematic the commitment to the language of schooling learning teaching that arises from a particular approach (metaphysical) to language and how language speaks. They acknowledge that while metaphysics must be a part of the dominant scientific, technical approach to education, it need not dominate or silence other ways of thinking and acting. Narrative Pedagogy, while offering a place for the converging conversations of teachers, students, and clinicians, listens for possible richer "saying-ways" of thinking and the essential engaged openness of the context of nursing education and practice.

This book is at once practical and compelling—a "must read" for practicing teacher-scholars as they seek to address the complexity, fragmentation, and isolation in contemporary schools. Such readers will find this book compelling and intellectually challenging. The first of its kind, the book provides a rich, complex explication of schooling learning teaching as a phenomenon that exceeds a human-centered experience or pointing. Rethinking schooling as attending, learning as listening, and teaching as co-responding—all communal experiences—offers a substantive alternative to the learner (individual)-centered, conventional ways of viewing schooling, teaching, and learning as merely institutionalized cognitive gain and skill acquisition with reified roles for teachers and students.

Equally important, this book makes an invaluable contribution to teacher preparation courses. The novice teacher-scholar will certainly encounter complex philosophical ideas and an accompanying language that can initially be intimidating. The authors attend such readers as they journey to the margins of their understanding, supporting their quest for comprehension with short descriptions of salient philosophical ideas in a glossary and frequent endnotes to direct the novice to where in the volume or in the larger literature an idea can be further explored. The converging conversations offered in Chapters 12 through 14 serve to show practically how these philosophical ideas can be sighted in nursing education. These sightings provide the novice reader with glimpses of how a regional ontology of schooling teaching learning compels teachers, students, and clinicians to enable a richer nursing education. In this way, this book does more than improve pedagogical literacy; it becomes a catalyst for changing the field!

Narrative Pedagogy researchers will be similarly served by the play of language, philosophy, education, and nursing presented in a format that makes this play readily apparent for consideration. In this book, Narrative Pedagogy attempts to open possibilities for a richer array of listening (interpreting) than that allowed by the usual application and presentation of disciplinary epistemologies. "Walking the talk" of method as way *(È méthodos)*, converging conversations resist the linear, sequential presentation of "findings" familiar in the research literature. Rather this book draws together narrative tellings, themes, and patterns identified in other hermeneutic phenomenological studies, Concernful Practices, and questionings in groundbreaking ways.

The language of this book will invite the reader to return to these pages again and again. As one listens to language speaking anew with each reading, the deceptively simple is seen in its complexity, and the complex (even the tautological) is seen as resonating deeply and clearly in sensed familiarity. The insights offered by the authors are subtle and nuanced and simultaneously revolutionary. This book goes to the heart of schooling learning and teaching as a matter of concern and tenders openings and overtures that will fascinate and captivate pedagogical and philosophical scholars alike.

Preface

Narrative Pedagogy is committed to a practical discourse that describes the wisdom gained through the dialogical experience of schooling, learning, and teaching. In our explications of narrative tellings, the insights of science and its systematic approach to understanding schooling, learning, and teaching are kept in sight. These are interpreted (read) for the dangers hiding in the closures of their objectification and their succumbing to the claim of a will to will or power. Narratives or stories are described as narrative tellings in order to show how narratives and telling are inextricably connected to language. We present insights gleaned from the shared dialogical experiences of narrative tellings as converging conversations that reveal practical comportment as prudent and knowledgeable. A converging conversation is an approach to presenting hermeneutic phenomenological scholarship as retold conversations in which themes and patterns (gleaned from narrative tellings) are kept in motion such that *thinking is free for the dismissal of the narrative tellings as fictive and unreliable or free for listening to the hints they offer.*

Shared practices are interpreted in order to reveal any privileging of the closed systems of language and experience in the use and abuse of language as power. Within this circulation, there are shared background practices initially seen by us as the Concernful Practices of schooling learning teaching. These are listed below. But we must call the reader's attention to the fact that these have been illuminated through explicating our narrative tellings of nursing education and should not be considered as a final closure. Concernful practices are always already underway.

Concernful Practices of Schooling Learning Teaching

Presencing: Attending and Being Open

Assembling: Constructing and Cultivating

Gathering: Welcoming and Calling Forth

Caring: Engendering of Community

Listening: Knowing and Connecting

Interpreting: Unlearning and Becoming

Inviting: Waiting and Letting Be

Questionings: Sense and Making Meanings Visible

Retrieving Places: Keeping Open a Future of Possibilities

Preserving: Reading, Writing, Thinking-Saying, and Dialogue

As the interpretations and explications of these shared dialogical practices emerge, the movement is toward a hermeneutic phenomenology that reveals schooling, learning, and teaching as a co-occurring, invisible, intra-related phenomenon.

The questions that guide this hermeneutic phenomenological reading in the context of nursing education include "What is learning?" and "How do schooling, learning, and teaching belong together?" Our current thinking is that schooling, learning, and teaching are seamlessly intrawoven and that they co-found one another. It appears, for example, that teaching as dialogically experienced *lets* the uncovering of learning. Learning is always a past teaching. It is the locus of sense from which teaching arises; and as such, learning can grant teaching its co-responding essence such that learning and only learning can occur. Questions present themselves as most meaningfully explored in the narrative tellings of students and teachers as they are in attendance with schooling's necessary situatedness. As the presencing of narrative tellings, the implications of teaching *as* uncovering learning are revealed in a way that evokes further thinking-saying and proffers suggestions and possibilities for schooling, learning, and teaching. Thinking is described in this book as thinking-saying in order to show how thinking inextricably belongs to language.

Questions that turn on "What is learning?" are frequently encountered in higher education. There are many paths to approaching learning, including defining learning as cognitive gain and changes in behavior—a familiar and common understanding held by many disciplines in contemporary higher education. Modernity's claim on higher education disposes conceptions of learning as represented, ordered, and measured. This approach to understanding learning with its accompanying critiques is helpful. The post-positivist commitment to embracing learning theories and their various forms of cognitivisms reveals predominant pedagogical approaches. In this book, we refer to these pedagogies as conventional pedagogies.

Narrative Pedagogy does not seek to consign conventional pedagogies to oblivion, but rather includes them in never-ending converging conversations that highlight contributions, limitations, and dangers. When large amounts of information need to be learned, conventional pedagogies such as outcomes or competency-based education are useful. But they are not without their limitations and dangers. For example, when humans reduce schooling, learning, and teaching to a "usefulness" or "utility," there is a concomitant practice of assigning values to the types, kinds, conditions, and ways in which schooling, learning, and teaching are measurable, effective, and efficient. Scienticism, as a belief, becomes the *center and measure* of all schooling, learning, and teaching. Learning becomes an object of study and is separated from schooling and teaching. Learning loses its sense of exigency—specifically, the disclosing and beckoning mystery that dwells within schooling and teaching, which shows humans as finite mortals.

Perhaps what matters about asking the question "What is learning?" is not that there are answers. Perhaps what matters is taking seriously how forgetful humans have become of the worthfulness and meaningfulness of questioning-as-thinking: not questioning that seeks answers, but questioning-as-thinking for its own sake. Care must be taken, however, in how thinking as retrieving questions as rejoinders are questionings and not necessarily related to seeking answers. We hope to point to how asking the question "What is learning?" is itself an on-coming converging conversation—a listening dialogue with the conventional practices, which humans conduct because they always already understand.

Narrative Pedagogy obtains as the on-coming of ongoing converging conversations. It calls into question the seemingly self-evident assumptions or presuppositions of all pedagogies. While Narrative Pedagogy always includes self-mindfulness, it seeks richer understandings of schooling, learning, and teaching. *Narrative Pedagogy is a recovery of the embodied and dialogical experiences of schooling learning teaching as an intra-related phenomenon rather than a series of unrelated neutral activities.*

Concernful practices are explored herein through both the empirical and dialogical experiences of students, teachers, and clinicians as they relate tellings of nursing education. The conversations that presence themselves as historically situated are constituted by the historical pre-understandings of schooling, learning, and teaching which are always already embedded within current pedagogies. In this book, our dialoging partners show up or announce themselves in contemporary learning theories, as well as in the play of given critiques and deconstructions of these theories. It is important not to forget the play of philosophies of science as they situate themselves. Conversations are such that all voices of the difficult rock-strewn paths to wisdom and truth belong to the on-coming/ongoing of converging conversations.

This book arises out of conversations (interviews) with nursing students, teachers, and clinicians. The narrative tellings of their personal experiences are listened to such that familiar and identifiable themes and patterns are set forth. In selecting narrative tellings that embrace the familiar or the everyday, we do not attempt to demonstrate one correct interpretation among the many offered. We do not try to clarify and evaluate already known interpretations, but neither do we discard them out of hand. We seek rather to reveal hidden meanings in order to bring them to light—not stopping at what the authors of the narratives tell, but going behind the text to ask what is not being said and perhaps what the narrators could not, would not, or do not say.

The interpretations of any narrative telling are never final, but always underway. They are not meant to be the innermost revelations of a conscious ego-subject but rather are the tension and contending that show up in any narrative telling. Interpretations are not merely a return to some current and past understandings that obtain as sedimented in familiarities. In our explications of schooling learning teaching, retrieving of the unsaid is a sustaining aspect of hermeneutic phenomenological interpreting.

If our efforts bear fruit, schooling learning teaching will let its own retrieval (ripening) of itself show itself as itself. We seek to open layers of interpretations and misinterpretations to sight in order to let them shine through; in this way we are letting ourselves stand in the difference between what is said and what is unsaid. Interpretations are never a simple return to some romanticized past of the projection to an idealized future but obtain as a unique event of disclosure. Every interpretation disrupts explicit formulations in a given narrative telling. The refusal to go beyond the explicitness of a text is a harboring of idolatry as a closure, as well as a historical naiveté.

The question arises: Can one understand the narrators better than the narrators understood themselves? In this book, we attend to history as students, teachers, and clinicians tell of practices that they found meaningful and helpful but that may currently be lost, overlooked, or forgotten. These shared practices are not brought forward as a return to a previous kind of schooling. Rather they are brought into play as tellings that unveil the always already presenting of preserving, overcoming, and extending the shared practices of human comportment in the context of schooling learning teaching.

Primary narrators have their ownmost traditions that claim them. It is when another participates in their narrative tellings that the traditions become a new tradition. The play of traditions, in their narrowest (personal) sense and in their widest historical sense, is such that they are always already re-forming themselves. There is always the possibility that in any play of tradition there is the unthought, namely, the unsaid as an unsighted backdrop of understanding. Traditions appear (come to presence) in various ways, but these ways are always temporal and therefore historical. They offer hints; they say something. They let themselves be sighted.

We seek in this book to uncover richer understandings—"new takes"—on the familiar practices or dialogical experiences of schooling learning teaching. This interpretation offers a never-ending conversation through evoking a kind of "thinking-saying" that prepares us to think anew: What is learning? This transformation that we seek is reflected in a shift from asking "What is learning?" to "How is it with learning?" The shift is away from objectifying and quantifying learning toward explicating how learning reveals itself. For example, is learning prior to thinking? Is learning hermeneutic (constitutively interpretive)?

We embrace the situation of conversation as a fertile model, even where silent narrative telling shows itself only by the question of the listener. Interpretations (readings) are *always on the way.* They are attempts at uncovering understandings as plausible and fruitful but never as definitive. Complete understanding is a possibility only for God. If humans were all-knowing, all speaking and writing would be absolutely correct. The eloquent, passionate art of speaking with another would not be needed. If humans existed as absolute knowledge, language in any form would be unnecessary. There would be no eloquent (or otherwise!) poetry, music, debates, arguments, or historical narrative. The limit that unfolds for all of us mortal humans is what calls (invites) us to eloquent passion.

Understanding is a sojourn and, like any sojourn, is risky. Dwelling within the uncertainty of the narrative tellings' situatedness of schooling learning teaching, human beings always already belong to phenomena. This is the intrinsically linguistic condition of hermeneutic phenomenology. Humans shape and are shaped by the situations of both their empirical and their dialogical experiences. The reciprocity of the dialogical experience of understanding and the practices ordered by understanding are inseparable.

Embedded in our hermeneutic phenomenological approach to scholarship is a unique but risk-laden opportunity. A commitment to revealing the unitary essence of schooling learning teaching, how this unitary essence co-occurs and belongs together, can be an adventure which contributes to a richer understanding of the open essence of what it means to be human. Is schooling the topos—a place of clearing—that possibilitizes all modes of learning and teaching? How have schooling, learning, and teaching become sundered such that teaching is appropriated by concerns of "the teacher" rather than co-occurring dialogical experiences that belong to learning and schooling? Dialogical experiences as concerns are central to the story we are attempting to tell. We seek to disclose what is hidden, remains unspoken and concealed in our understanding of schooling, learning, and teaching. But this is always done through a questioning that is situated and open. Our position within the text is on the borders between what is concealed and what is revealed. Questioning is always central, not as a mere cross-examination, but in a way that keeps open the possibility for anything to emerge.

An example of this kind of questioning is asking "What should *never* be taught in the nursing curriculum?" It is a common practice in nursing education for teachers and students to spend a great deal of time and effort in determining what content (subject matter) *should* be taught and learned. Through rethinking the question in the negative, the issue of content as the enclosing of the discipline and of how closely enclosure issues are associated with learning is made evident. For example, the nursing curriculum becomes de facto human centered by keeping out required content on the nonhuman world. That is, the practice of nursing is framed by a schooling, learning, and teaching that is claimed by a singular attention to a narrow conception of world as only a human world and indeed, we would argue, is enclosed in the short-sighted centrality of the human as the *only* significant concern.

Many cancers are enabled via pesticidal assaults on certain plants and animals. For example, some chemicals used in large-scale agribusiness have been shown to be carcinogenic as well as detrimental to non-targeted species. If nursing is committed to prevention of illness and disease as a shared ethic, how does including or excluding conversations about the nonhuman sphere and the human practices that change the mien of that collocation influence schooling, learning, and teaching in nursing? However, this questioning might open up exploring how course work related to the nonhuman sphere also reproduces the very kind of thinking that contributes to the unbridled use of the planet as nothing but a convenience store by making the physical world *merely* a field of scientific study of nonhuman concerns with no attention to human practices. In traditional nursing curricula, humans matter more than the planet's biota. We are not arguing here for a change in values or proposing that educational content should be added or deleted, though that conversation is a worthful one. We seek rather to show how questioning can guide possibilities for sighting, listening, and thinking anew in nursing education.

Further questioning could lead to exploring the belongingness of content or subject matter and learning. That is, how do learning and subject matter belong together? This question emerges out of how humans are appropriated, in conventional pedagogies, by a kind of learning that is singularly shaped by cognitive gain or skill acquisition. Understanding this is both revealing of what is already known of contemporary nursing education and suggestive of what is yet to be explored. That is, can there be learning without measurable cognitive gain? Is learning constitutively a cognitive experience? Through these kinds of questionings, Narrative Pedagogy shows itself as the play of converging conversations that are thought evoking and also practical and risky as they suggest more open and inclusive possibilities for pedagogies.

In this book, we risk a reading of philosophers, Martin Heidegger, Hans-Georg Gadamer, Jean-Luc Nancy, and others, that grows out of our practical everyday world rather than out of the hermitic characteristics inherent in the technical worlds of various disciplines. We have endeavored to do justice to these thinkers and the many capable translators and commentators who have influenced and informed the world of readers with their interpretations. Reader-interpreters are urged to explore the glossary in order to introduce themselves to the rich complexity of hermeneutic phenomenological translating. In addition, we have followed a number of conventions frequently used in philosophical writing, including the following:

1. Hyphens, commas, or slashes are not used to separate "schooling learning teaching" and certain other groups of words in order to maintain these terms as a nonlinear but intra-related, conjoined phenomenon.

2. Hyphens are used to connect seemingly disparate words in order to indicate meanings that would otherwise not occur. For example, "thinking-saying" is intended to express thinking as inextricably connected to language and not exclusively the property of an isolated, cognizing ("blank slate") ego-subject. In hermeneutic phenomenology, thinking is constitutively a language experience; thinking and saying belong to each other and co-found each other.

3. Slashes are used in expressions such as "world/clearing/openness" when a single word does not seem to suffice. The words in "world/clearing/openness" call forth the single but resonating phenomenon of a locus of meaning that humans cannot control or produce.

4. Quotation marks are used to call attention to a concept that belongs to an incommensurable paradigm. For example, the term "blank slate" belongs to the scientific paradigm, to disciplines like developmental and cognitive psychology that have varying scientific theories on language and knowledge acquisition. The use of terms in this way is kept to a minimum.

5. A string of words is sometimes presented in parentheses following another word, as in "dwelling (abiding/whiling/sojourning)." This practice lets words show how they simultaneously can say many disparate and yet similar things and thus cannot be restricted to a single meaning when one is seeking richer understandings.

6. Abbreviations are used for frequently cited philosophical texts in order to effect a smoother read.

In this book, the reader-interpreter will be introduced to a way of thinking that listens to the saying of discursiveness. Words, grammar, and syntax do not admit of univocal meanings. They are historically situated. *Words, grammar, and syntax presence as paratactic rather than as an enforced syntax.* For the reader-interpreter, then, the trustworthiness of the text or text analog dwells in calling into question the taken-for-granted practices in its conversation.

One aspect of trustworthiness and the level of scholarliness in hermeneutic phenomenological scholarship is the ability to *extract or identify* from a rich array of interview transcripts, narrative tellings, or accounts of students, teachers, and clinicians that are complex and that reflect at least one person's meaningful experience or persons' experiences-in-common. Those presented in this book reflect a 20-year hermeneutic phenomenological study of the experiences or narrative tellings of students, teachers, and clinicians in nursing education. Throughout the book, the names used are pseudonyms, and all identifying data in the narrative tellings have been removed. In the interpretations of the study of narrative tellings, it is the researchers' ability to stay close to the texts, as a committed faithfulness, that *results in* the trustworthiness and high level of scholarship attributed to a research report. This approach does not privilege the scientific view of the researcher as identifying a basis for measuring objectivity in the study using preestablished standards. Rather, trustworthiness and worthfulness emerge through description of cycles of interpretations, the inclusion of other participants (both research team members and study participants), and the use of welded quotes to make clear and visible the thinking reflected in the interpretation. All these attend, in one way or another, to the scientific concerns of validity and reliability. Interpretations reveal the thinking of the researchers such that readers are free to agree or disagree with the interpretations being offered. The intent in explicating narrative tellings is to engage readers and offer a wider array of interpretations in a manner that evokes thinking-saying. Opening up more nuanced interpretations is sought in order to free thinking as thinking-saying as called forth by narrative telling.

In this book, we are showing how converging conversations move beyond the methods commonly used in narrative research. The converging conversations as presented here are retold stories that keep themes and patterns in motion. This movement is one of becoming open in which narrative tellings as converging conversations move beyond scientistic conceptualizations of method.

Hermeneutic phenomenology is *about* Narrative Pedagogy. The word "about" here should be considered in *all* of its senses, including the following:

1. Situatedness. In the phrase "to be about," the word "about," as a preposition, is taken in its simplest sense. For the sake of readability, we will not risk the use of the ponderous term "arounding" even though this is what we mean. Therefore we use the term "circulating" to refer to the human being placed in attendance. The issues that turn on the who, what, when, and where of this placing cannot be included within the scope of this book. The questions that are the turnings of these phenomena do come-to-fore — are with (of) human beings, are about (of) human beings either as assertions, as questioning, or as moving from one neighborhood/region to another. To be about is to be *of* something.

2. Aboutness. The verbal or temporal sense of the noun "about" is captured by "verging on," "living with," or "nearing" such that readiness, frequenting, and approaching cannot be disengaged from each other. *To be about is meaningful, linguistic comportment.*

3. Relating. The adverbial sense of "about" resides in belonging to the nighness of the face-to-face. Relating brings about points of view or matters which are always already as they historically come to presence. There is no isolated or isolatable *about* which can be hypostatized. The "about" is offered as modifier, that is, difference.

The *about* is about living with the play of differing wherein apartness can only be neared asymptotically but never reduced to a *pure* fusion. The hermeneutic reading of phenomena as outlined above is not explanatory, theoretical, or rule governed.

Hermeneutic phenomenology, as philosophically thought, is the historically situated listening and sighting of messages as they bring tidings. Listening and sighting become thought-said when the human being is first thematized as (thought of as) an open sojourning in a temporal world, rather than a giving of priority to the human being as a self-contained entity. Human beings find themselves called to temporally unique encounters and involvements wherein the latter are sighted as historically freed up for listening. For phenomenology in its hermeneutically thinking-saying encounters and involvements-with, matters of concern show themselves as themselves and are never to be taken exclusively as the productions of an absolutely self-knowing (transcendental) ego-subject/s.

The messages that show up as encounters and involvements need to be received to be messages at all. They are receptions as always already in place as sense. The task of phenomenological hermeneutics as thinking and co-responding to/with is to let possibilities obtain such that they can always already be understood anew as they self-reveal. There is never a complete self-revealing of any phenomenon, and there is never a perfect hearing of any message. There are only showings and tidings.

Describing or labeling these messages as showings and tidings hold in themselves at least two dangers: (1) They can close off the possibility of other meanings, and (2) they can become so solidified that they lose all significance. With both of these dangers, time and historicality can be thought as frozen in place. The danger of dangers is in this freezing: Time and history cannot be halted. The especially salient danger is forgetting or overlooking that language as discursive saying and sense qua sense possesses humans, not the other way around.

In this book, we risk naming the pathway that draws us along our way as the play of hermeneutic phenomenology and Narrative

Pedagogy. We open a meeting place for the thinking-saying of philosophers whose narrative tellings are part of our interpretive reading. We will comport ourselves along the way such that the significant insights of feminist, critical, and postmodern thinkers are not overlooked or passed by. Our own sojourn will offer a sharing of voices—recognizing that there is no voice, whether silent or uttered, that is not sighted as a sharing in one way or another.

We begin our journey with Part I, "Retrieving Origins: Adventures and Arrivals," as a description of our path of hermeneutic phenomenology. Explicating the presuppositions of our work toward converging conversations as crossings that gather and assemble, we offer the possibility for catching a glimpse of the roadblocks in modernity's quest for certainty. Laying bare the theoretical surround of our work includes discussions of transposition, nearness, and temporality as well as the reciprocal play of clearing and presencing. Starting from another place, thrownness, language, and understanding are highlighted in order to show the hermeneutic phenomenological path toward boundary, articulations, and the nearness of the near as the always already. All of these show themselves under the aegis of the necessary enacting circulation of participation. Part I, "Retrieving Origins," ends with a sighting of method as *È méthodos:* method as being on-the-way.

In Part II, "The Narrative Turn: Pedagogies of Possibility," schooling as attending, learning as listening, and teaching as co-responding are explicated as co-occurring, invisible, ontological phenomena. Attending as thrown open, exposed having to-be-in-the-world, listening as attending to the call of finitude, and responding as co-responding is the towards-which of *enacting hermeneutic phenomenology in order to enable Narrative Pedagogy*. Exemplars of how enacted conversations, narrative telling, and dialogue shape and are shaped by the way of *È méthodos* are offered for the reader-interpreter's consideration. Narratives are presented in order to show schooling learning teaching as a co-occurring, invisible phenomenon in the context of nursing education. The

Concernful Practices of Schooling Learning Teaching are pointed at as pedagogical wayfarings.

The conversations in Part III, "Converging Conversations of Schooling Learning Teaching," offer a variety of glimpses into the enacting of hermeneutic phenomenology. Narrative Pedagogy is shown as it resonates in the stories of students, teachers, and clinicians in nursing education. Themes and patterns from a 20-year study of how Narrative Pedagogy is enacted in schools of nursing are thereby put into motion, letting understanding show itself as open and problematic but replescent with possibility.

Part IV, "Toward Narrative Pedagogy: Openings and Overtures," is the end of this book. But it is not an end as a preestablished goal or the completion of a project. End is thought here as a place of unfolding of limit. Limit here is the place where matters of concern begin their essential unfolding.

Our return to our beginnings is our attempt to be open to what might have been otherwise overlooked on our way. Overlooking is not an overseeing in the sense of a subordination of one matter of concern to another. Overlooking can show itself as openings and overtures. The fact that this book is written in English reveals our personal thrownness and our historicality. The associated fact that we have significantly relied on continental European philosophers of an interpretive bent demonstrates our judgment that analytic philosophies of mind are incapable of dealing with the human situation as a historically and temporally involved and distributed here, now, and mine.

Openings and overtures may here be taken in both their passive and active sense. As with disclosing and beckoning, as well as with bearing and gesture, openings and overtures need the engagement of the ones engaged. This book opens and makes an overture to those reader-interpreters who will be part of an overture that opens itself onto its themes.

We could have not been drawn into the overture of this book without the generous gestures of family, friends, and colleagues; we wish to acknowledge their kindness, hospitality, and support. First and foremost we thank Professor Pamela M. Ironside, for her untiring dedication in making this book a reality. Her excellent final reviews and her readings of our beginning primitive, disjointed, and often incoherent attempts were sustaining. Without her caring and commitment to helping us put our thoughts into a thinking-saying that attempted to present matters which hinted, disclosed, and beckoned, we could not have written this book! To Gloria Barsness, who fed our souls, our thankful appreciation for her diligence, speed, and expertise in preparing our manuscript. To Joyce Sexton, our excellent copy editor, our gratitude for her wise counsel in copy editing and manuscript preparation. To Timothy and Tinney Heath, who helped in so many ways. The reader will note that the cover photograph by Tim is of a council ring. The council ring as a signature was adapted from First Nation kivas by the Danish-American landscape architect Jens Jensen and was meant by him to be a locale where converging conversations could take place. And to David and Barbara Underland, who offered shelter as only family can do.

In addition, the Aoteoroa New Zealand nurses and midwives were called to hermeneutic phenomenology by their own practices. They co-responded with that call by inviting us to converse with them. In particular we thank Julie Boddy, Alison Dixon, Andrea Gilkison, Jackie Gunn, Margaret Idour, Rose Mc Eldowney, Margaret Martin, Louise Rummel, Phillipa Seaton-Sykes, Liz Smythe, Deb Spence, and Australians Jill White and Cheryl Moss. In the United States, we thank Pamela Brown, Christine Dinkins, Margaret Douglas, Frances Henderson, Diane Heliker, Katherine Hopkins Kavanagh, Fred Kersten, Mary Layoun, Mary Lebold, Kenneth Maly, Marie Miles, Rita Monson, Richard Palmer, Donald Polkinghorne, Maude Rittman, Thomas Sheehan, Sherry Sims, Melinda Swenson, Jeanne Sorrell and Sharon Wyatt. We thank the many doctoral students we have been privileged to study with, who have shaped our scholarship with their thinking and insights. To them, we give our heartfelt appreciation. To the Institute for Heideggerian Hermeneutical Studies participants, we offer our thanks for their generous gifts of wisdom and insights during our sojourn. And our gratitude to the teachers, students, clinicians, and schools for their enthusiasm in taking on Narrative Pedagogy over the past decades and for consistently sharing stories of their experiences with us. These tellings helped us learn about and see more clearly how enacting hermeneutic phenomenology enables Narrative Pedagogy. The way calls on us to risk the way we were borne unto.

Abbreviations for Works Cited

Works by Gadamer

AH   Gadamer, H-G. (1992). *Hans-Georg Gadamer on education, poetry, and history: Applied hermeneutics* (D. Misgeld & G. Nicholson, Eds.; L Schmidt & M. Reuss, Trans.). Albany, NY: State University of New York Press.

COP   Gadamer, H-G. (2004). *A century of philosophy* (R. Colman, Trans.). New York: Continuum.

D&D   Gadamer, H-G. (1980). *Dialogue and dialectic* (P. Smith, Trans.). New Haven, CT: Yale University Press.

DD   Gadamer, H-G. (1985). *Destruktion* and deconstruction (G. Waite & R. Palmer, Trans.). In D. Michelfelder & R. Palmer (Eds.), 1989, *Dialogue and deconstruction: The Gadamer-Derrida encounter* (pp. 102-113). Albany, NY: State University of New York Press.

F   Gadamer, H-G. (1994). Foreword. In J. Grondin, *Introduction to philosophical hermeneutics* (J. Weinsheimer, Trans.). (pp. ix-xi). New Haven, CT: Yale University Press.

GIC   Gadamer, H-G. (2001). *Gadamer in conversation* (R. Palmer, Ed. & Trans.). New Haven, CT: Yale University Press.

GR   Gadamer, H-G. (2007). *The Gadamer reader: A bouquet of the later writings* (R. Palmer, Ed.). Evanston, IL: Northwestern University Press.

HL   Gadamer, H-G. (1987). Hermeneutics and logocentrism (R. Palmer & D. Michelfelder, Trans.). In D. Michelfelder & R. Palmer (Eds.), 1989, *Dialogue and deconstruction: The Gadamer-Derrida encounter* (pp. 114-128). Albany, NY: State University of New York Press.

HOP   Gadamer, H-G. (1994). Martin Heidegger's one path. In T. Kisiel & J. van Buren (Eds.), *Reading Heidegger from the start* (P. Smith, Trans.) (pp. 19-34). Albany, NY: State University of New York Press.

HR   Gadamer, H-G. (2005). Heidegger as rhetor: Hans-Georg Gadamer interviewed by Ansgar Kemmann (L. Schmidt, Trans.). In D. Gross and A. Kemmann (Eds.), *Heidegger and rhetoric* (pp. 47-65). Albany, NY: State University of New York Press.

HW   Gadamer, H-G. (1994). *Heidegger's ways* (J. Stanley, Trans.). Albany, NY: State University of New York Press.

PH   Gadamer, H-G. (1977). *Philosophical hermeneutics* (D. Linge, Trans. & Ed.). Berkeley, CA: University of California Press.

RAS   Gadamer, H-G. (1981). *Reason in the age of science* (F. Lawrence, Trans.). Cambridge, MA: MIT Press.

RJD   Gadamer, H-G. (1989). Reply to Jacques Derrida. In D. Michelfelder & R. Palmer (Trans. & Eds.), *Dialogue and deconstruction: The Gadamer-Derrida encounter* (pp. 55-57). Albany, NY: State University of New York Press.

RMC   Gadamer, H-G. (1990). Reply to my critics (G. Leiner, Trans.). In G. Ormiston & A. Schrift (Eds.), *The hermeneutic tradition: From Ast to Ricoeur* (pp. 273-297). Albany, NY: State University of New York Press.

RPJ   Gadamer, H-G. (1997). Reflections on my philosophical journey (R. Palmer, Trans.). In L. Hahn (Ed.), *The philosophy of Hans-Georg Gadamer* (pp. 3-63). Chicago: Open Court.

TI   Gadamer, H-G. (1989). Text and interpretation (D. Schmidt & R. Palmer, Trans.). In D. Michelfelder & R. Palmer (Eds.), *Dialogue and deconstruction: The Gadamer-Derrida encounter* (pp. 21-51). Albany, NY: State University of New York Press.

TM Gadamer, H-G. (1990). *Truth and method* (2nd rev. ed.) (J. Weinsheimer & D. G. Marshall, Trans.). New York: Crossroad.

Works by Heidegger

4S Heidegger, M. (2003). *Four seminars* (A. Mitchell & F. Raffoul, Trans.). Bloomington, IN: Indiana University Press.

BC Heidegger, M. (1993). *Basic concepts* (G. Aylesworth, Trans.). Bloomington, IN: Indiana University Press.

BH Heidegger, M. (2007). *Becoming Heidegger: On the trail of his early occasional writings, 1910-1927* (T. Kisiel & T. Sheehan, Eds.). Evanston, IL: Northwestern University Press. [Note: Some of the material referenced in this publication was not authored by Heidegger.]

BPP Heidegger, M. (1982). *Basic problems of phenomenology* (A. Hofstadter, Trans.). Bloomington, IN: Indiana University Press.

BQP Heidegger, M. (1994). *Basic questions of philosophy* (R. Rojcewicz & A. Schuwer, Trans.). Bloomington, IN: Indiana University Press.

BT Heidegger, M. (1962). *Being and time* (J. Macquarrie & E. Robinson, Trans.). New York: Harper & Row.

BW Heidegger, M. (1993). *Basic writings* (A. Hofstadter, Trans.; D. Krell, Ed.). New York: Harper & Row.

CP Heidegger, M. (1999). *Contributions to philosophy (from enowning)* (P. Emad & K. Maly, Trans.). Bloomington, IN: Indiana University Press.

DT Heidegger, M. (1966). *Discourse on thinking* (J. Anderson & E. Freund, Trans.). New York: Harper & Row.

EF Heidegger, M. (2002). *The essence of human freedom* (T. Sadler, Trans.). New York: Continuum.

EGT   Heidegger, M. (1975). *Early Greek thinking* (D. Krell & F. Capuzzi, Trans.). New York: Harper & Row.

EHP   Heidegger, M. (2000). *Elucidations of Hölderlin's poetry* (K. Hoeller, Trans.). Amherst, NY: Humanity Books.

EP   Heidegger, M. (2003). *The end of philosophy* (J. Stambaugh, Trans.). Chicago: University of Chicago Press.

FCM   Heidegger, M. (1995). *Fundamental concepts of metaphysics* (W. McNeill & N. Walker, Trans.). Bloomington, IN: Indiana University Press.

HCT   Heidegger, M. (1985). *History of the concept of time* (T. Kisiel, Trans.). Bloomington, IN: Indiana University Press.

HHI   Heidegger, M. (1996). *Hölderlin's hymn "The Ister"* (W. McNeill & J. Davis, Trans.). Bloomington, IN: Indiana University Press.

ID   Heidegger, M. (2002). *Identity and difference* (J. Stambaugh, Trans.). Chicago: University of Chicago Press.

IM   Heidegger, M. (2000). *Introduction to metaphysics* (G. Fried & R. Polt, Trans.). New Haven, CT: Yale University Press.

M   Heidegger, M. (2006). *Mindfulness* (P. Emad & T. Kalary, Trans.). New York: Continuum.

N4   Heidegger, M. (1982). *Nietzsche volume IV: Nihilism* (F. Capuzzi, Trans.; D. Krell, Ed.). New York: Harper & Row.

OBT   Heidegger, M. (2002). *Off the beaten track* (J. Young & K. Haynes, Trans.). New York: Cambridge University Press.

OEL   Heidegger, M. (2004). *On the essence of language* (W. Gregory & Y. Unna, Trans.). Albany, NY: State University of New York Press.

OHF   Heidegger, M. (1999). *Ontology—the hermeneutics of facticity* (J. van Buren, Trans.). Bloomington, IN: Indiana University Press.

OTB Heidegger, M. (2002). *On time and being* (J. Stambaugh, Trans.). Chicago: University of Chicago Press.

OWL Heidegger, M. (1971). *On the way to language* (P. Hertz, Trans.). New York: Harper & Row.

P Heidegger, M. (1992). *Parmenides* (A. Schuwer & R. Rojcewicz, Trans.). Bloomington, IN: Indiana University Press.

PLT Heidegger, M. (1971). *Poetry, language, thought* (A. Hofstadter, Trans.). New York: Harper & Row.

PM Heidegger, M. (1998). *Pathmarks* (W. McNeill, Ed.). New York: Cambridge University Press.

POR Heidegger, M. (1991). *The principle of reason* (R. Lilly, Trans.). Bloomington, IN: Indiana University Press.

PT Heidegger, M. (1976). *Piety of thinking* (J. Hart & J. Maraldo, Trans.). Bloomington, IN: Indiana University Press.

QCT Heidegger, M. (1977). *Question concerning technology and other essays* (W. Lovitt, Trans.). New York: Harper & Row.

ST Heidegger, M. (1985). *Schelling's treatise on the essence of human freedom* (J. Stambaugh, Trans.) Athens, OH: Ohio University Press.

TDP Heidegger, M. (2000). *Towards the definition of philosophy* (T. Sadler, Trans.). New York: Continuum.

TL Heidegger, M. (1998). Traditional language and technological language (W. Gregory, Trans.). *Journal of Philosophical Research, 23,* 129-145.

WCT Heidegger, M. (1968). *What is called thinking?* (F. Wieck & J. Gray, Trans.). New York: Harper & Row.

WIP Heidegger, M. (1958). *What is philosophy?* (W. Kluback & J. Wilde, Trans.). New York: Twayne.

WT   Heidegger, M. (1967). *What is a thing?* (W. Barton & V. Deutsch, Trans.). Chicago: Regnery.

ZS   Heidegger, M. (2001). *Zollikon seminars* (F. Mays & R. Askay, Trans.). Evanston, IL: Northwestern University Press.

Works by Kisiel

GBT   Kisiel, T. (1993). *The genesis of Heidegger's "Being and Time."* Berkeley, CA: University of California Press.

HGH   Kisiel, T. (1985). The happening of tradition: The hermeneutics of Gadamer and Heidegger. In R. Hollinger (Ed.), *Hermeneutics and praxis* (pp. 3-31). Notre Dame, IN: University of Notre Dame Press.

HWT   Kisiel, T. (2002). *Heidegger's way of thought.* New York: Continuum.

RHT   Kisiel, T. (2006). Recent Heidegger translations and their German originals: A grassroots archival perspective. *Continental Philosophy Review* (formerly *Man and World*), *38,* 263-287.

Works by Jean-Luc Nancy

BP   Nancy, J-L. (1993). *The birth to presence* (B. Holmes & others, Trans.). Stanford, CA: Stanford University Press.

BSP   Nancy, J-L. (2000). *Being singular plural* (R. Richardson & A. O'Byrne, Trans.). Stanford, CA: Stanford University Press.

EF   Nancy, J-L. (1993). *The experience of freedom* (B. McDonald, Trans.). Stanford, CA: Stanford University Press.

FT   Nancy, J-L. (2003). *A finite thinking* (S. Sparks, Ed.). Stanford, CA: Stanford University Press.

GT   Nancy, J-L. (1997). *The gravity of thought* (F. Raffoul & G. Rocco, Trans.). Atlantic Highlands, NJ: Humanities Press.

IC Nancy, J-L. (1991). *The inoperative community* (P. Connor, Ed.; P. Connor, L. Garbus, M. Holland, & S. Sawhney, Trans.). Minneapolis: University of Minnesota Press.

L Nancy, J-L. (2007). *Listening* (C. Mandell, Trans.). New York: Fordham University Press.

SV Nancy, J-L. (1990). Sharing voices (G. Ormiston, Trans.). In G. Ormiston & A. Schrift (Eds.), *Transforming the hermeneutic complex* (pp. 211-259). Albany, NY: State University of New York Press.

SW Nancy, J-L. (1997). *The sense of the world* (J. Librett, Trans.). Minneapolis: University of Minnesota Press.

WOT Nancy, J-L. (2008). The being-with of being-there. Continental Philosophy Review (formerly Man and World) 41, 1-15.

Works by Sheehan

COF Sheehan, T., and Painter, C. (1999). Choosing one's fate: A re-reading of *Sein und Zeit* §74. *Research in Phenomenology, 28,* 63-82. *(COF)*

DG Sheehan, T. (1995). *Das Gewesen:* Remembering the Fordham years. In B. Babich (Ed.), *From phenomenology to thought, errancy, and desire* (pp. 157-177). Boston: Kluwer Academic.

DH Sheehan, T. (1985). Derrida and Heidegger. In H. Silverman & D. Ihde (Eds.), *Hermeneutics and deconstruction* (pp. 201-218). Albany, NY: State University of New York Press.

ETT Sheehan, T. (1990, Autumn). Everyone has to tell the truth: Heidegger and the Jews. *Continuum 1*(1), 30-44.

GTT Sheehan, T. (1978). Getting to the topic: The new edition of *Wegmarken.* In J. Sallis (Ed.), *Radical phenomenology:*

Essays in honor of Martin Heidegger (pp. 299-316). Atlantic Highlands, NJ: Humanities Press.

HMT Sheehan, T. (Ed.). (1981). *Heidegger: The man and the thinker.* Chicago: Precedent Press.

HNA Sheehan, T. (1995). Heidegger's new aspect: On *In-Sein, Zeitlichkeit* and the genesis of *"Being and Time."* Research in Phenomenology, 25, 207-225.

HPM Sheehan, T. (1983). Heidegger's philosophy of mind. In F. Floistad (Ed.), *Contemporary philosophy: A new survey* (pp. 287-318). Boston: Martinus Nijhoff.

KE Sheehan, T. (2001). *Kehre* and *Ereignis:* A prolegomenon to introduction to metaphysics. In R. Polt & G. Fried (Eds.), *A companion to Heidegger's introduction to metaphysics* (pp. 3-16, 263-274). New Haven, CT: Yale University Press.

N Sheehan, T. (1999). Nihilism: Heidegger/Junger/Aristotle. In B. Hopkins (Ed.), *Phenomenology: Japanese and American perspectives* (pp. 273-316). Boston: Kluwer Academic.

ND Sheehan, T. (2002). Nihilism and its discontents. In F. Raffoul & D. Pettigrew (Eds.), *Heidegger and practical philosophy* (pp. 275-300). Albany, NY: State University of New York Press.

OWE Sheehan, T. (1983). On the way to *Ereignis:* Heidegger's interpretation of *Physis.* In H. Silverman, J. Sallis, & T. Seebohm (Eds.), *Continental philosophy in America* (pp. 131-164). Pittsburgh: Duquesne University.

PS Sheehan, T. (2001). A paradigm shift in Heidegger research. *Continental Philosophy Review, 34,* 183-202.

Glossary and Interpretive Commentary

Typically a glossary presents a list of words, defined in order to enclose a particular saying-showing. But, as we attempt to make clear in this book, hermeneutic phenomenology is not a pathway that admits of any finalities. Therefore the words listed in this glossary turn on our reading of their proper historical essence. That said, one is drawn into the understanding of historicality as an always already on-coming rather than a registering of past events.

Any word shows itself as translation in the co-occurring senses of temporal-historical passage, mutability, diffusion, transposition, reading, and retrieval. In this transmission, the spoken word, in the purview of hermeneutic phenomenology, "is already an answer" (*DT,* 129). As the disclosing and beckoning of historical moments, the spoken word "carries with it the unsaid to which it is related by responding and summoning" (*TM,* 458). See also *WCT,* 174.

A word (or two) must be given in regard to translation. Gadamer has written that all interpreting, translating, and understanding occur in language (*TM,* 384-389). To read Heidegger in translation is to be thrown into the thick of the struggles by various translators to render "Heideggerianisms" into other languages, in our case English in all of its geographical variations. The same is true for Gadamer and Jean-Luc Nancy, but currently to a much lesser extent.

For this reason we are including a list of our selected translations of pivotal Heideggerian terms and their sources. Although we have settled on certain translations, often overlooked is the conversation that takes place around the process of translating itself. The play of various translations, albeit separated by time and space, enables richer understandings of often vague and hermetic terminology. We will mostly restrict ourselves to terms found in Heidegger's work because an understanding of these texts is necessary for an adequate grasp of hermeneutic phenomenology.

In this work we will commonly follow the translations articulated by Thomas Sheehan and to a lesser extent Theodore Kisiel. Other important translators are listed below. Our listing cannot pretend to be inclusive. It almost goes without saying that *all* translators' introductory notes and footnotes are productively read and in one sense or another serve to illuminate. For instance, reading the Macquarrie and Robinson translation of *Being and Time* benefits from reading the thoughts of the translators mentioned above and others. It should be noted how the footnotes in the Macquarrie and Robinson translation often reveal their thought processes and are often more revealing that the actual terms they use. The task of pinning down to a single meaning any term used in hermeneutic phenomenology verges on compromising the task of this pathway itself. For Heidegger, "Meanings grow into words. It is not the case that word-things are invested with meanings" (*BT,* 204). Meanings are shared if they are meanings at all. We offer the following discussions as an introduction to the play of readings surrounding translations of Heidegger's works, including these:

Emad, P., & Kalary, T. (2006). Translators' foreword. In M. Heidegger, *Mindfulness* (P. Emad & T. Kalary, Trans.) (pp. xiii-xlii). New York: Continuum.

Emad, P., & Maly, K. (1999). Translators' foreword. In M. Heidegger, *Contributions to philosophy (from enowning)* (P. Emad & K. Maly, Trans.) (pp. xv-xliv). Bloomington, IN: Indiana University Press.

Kisiel, T. (2002). The new translation of *Sein und Zeit:* A grammatological lexicographer's commentary. In T. Kisiel, *Heidegger's way of thought* (pp. 64-83). New York: Continuum. *(HWT)*

Kisiel, T. (2006). Recent Heidegger translations and their German originals: A grassroots archival perspective. *Continental Philosophy Review* (formerly *Man and World*), *38,* 263-287. *(RHT)*

Lilly, R. (1991). Translator's introduction and Notes on the translation. In M. Heidegger, *The principle of reason* (R. Lilly, Trans.) (pp. vii-xxi, 135-138). Bloomington, IN: Indiana University Press.

Sheehan, T. (1997). Let a hundred translations bloom! A modest proposal about *Being and Time. Continental Philosophy Review* (formerly *Man and World*) 30, 227-238. *(LHT)*

Sheehan, T. (2001). A paradigm shift in Heidegger research. *Continental Philosophy Review* (formerly *Man and World*) *34,* 183-202. *(PS)*

Sheehan, T., & Painter, C. (1999). Choosing one's fate: A re-reading of Sein und Zeit §74. Research in Phenomenology, 28, 63-82. *(COF)*

van Buren, J. (1999). Translator's epilogue and Endnotes on the translation. In M. Heidegger, *Ontology—the hermeneutics of facticity* (J. van Buren, Trans.) (pp. 91-125). Bloomington, IN: Indiana University Press.

Gadamer calls our attention to a thinking in which "every translation is at the same time an interpretation" (*TM,* 384). Therefore every reading of the thought-dense prose of thinkers such as Heidegger, Gadamer, and Jean-Luc Nancy presents the reader with difficulty. In the case of Heidegger, translations into English resonate with the range of understanding of what he was attempting to say, or what he meant, by using language in his particular way. Also, especially in the case of Heidegger, the debate on what constitutes a proper translation from the German has been marked by contentiousness. Perhaps more important, especially in the world of hermeneutic phenomenology, is the debate and conversation surrounding the above matters of concern. It has been very productive for us to give thought to the thinking-saying that has emanated from the swirl of controversy on how to properly translate from the German. The questions (not *the* answers) lie in rejoining play and not in any absolute, fixed ground.

We also offer our readings of some key terms in order to bring them into nonphilosophical English. Our aim has been not to simplify them but to render them in such a way that they "say" the matters that this book is concerned with. The question arises, Does translation impoverish a thought? Although he was writing about popular language versus philosophical languages, Jean-Luc Nancy asks the question, Can there be a complete homology of signification—in sense and structure—between two language traditions? (*GT,* 41).

The terms in this glossary offer hints for ways on how this book may be read (interpreted). Our best counsel is for the reader to develop a working familiarity with the conversation suggested by the glossary in order to participate in the narrative telling that will ensue.

Our glossary shows itself thus:

apposition—We think appositions as the side-by-side togetherness of the belonging together of phenomena that disclose and beckon as paratactic before they are syntactic. Examples: being singular plural, thrownness understanding language, building dwelling thinking, schooling learning teaching.

appropriation—See *disclosing and beckoning.*

bearing and gesturing—See *disclosing and beckoning.*

being—See *engaged openness.*

beings—See *matters of concern.*

clearing of openness, the—See *open clearing, the.*

Dasein—See *human being of openness, the.*

disclosing and beckoning—Our reading of interpretive practices under the rubric of hermeneutic phenomenology calls for a term of art that can properly articulate the heart of our discussions. These discussions turn on the narrative tellings that belong to (are engaged with) language as the showing of discursive involvements (dialogical experience). That said, we have decided to risk Heidegger's term *Ereignis* (appropriation, enowning) as disclosing and beckoning. The play of disclosing and beckoning can be found on page 94 of the lecture "The Nature of Language" (*OWL,* 57-108). It is fitting that this term is part of a lecture on language as showing and calling (*OWL,* 91, 93, 107). In terms of hermeneutic phenomenology, beckoning does not stem from a determinable place or time, and disclosing does not occur as an act of a human agent or a transcendent phenomenon. Beckoning beckons (hints) toward the way humans are drawn onward unto. Disclosure offers the enabling of enacting. Disclosing and beckoning are presented here as guide words meant to call readers on their way.

We justify our appellation of *Ereignis* by offering that disclosing and beckoning essentially fulfills Heidegger's thought of this term as "the openness opened up" by human beings' essential finitude (*PS*, 18). Disclosing and beckoning is appearance (presencing) as having been opened up "in conjunction with intrinsic concealment" (*PS*, 16). Disclosing and beckoning exigently needs the presence of historical humans but can never be a product of human willing. Disclosing and beckoning can also be sighted and listened to as bearing and gesturing (*OWL*, 16-19, 26-29). Because disclosing and beckoning can never be *an* object, it shows as the silence and invisibility of hinting.

discursiveness—For Heidegger the human being does not possess but belongs to language as saying. Saying as showing is letting appear that which can be sighted and listened to as the setting of all present matters of concern "free into their given presence. Showing-saying brings what is absent into their presence" (*OWL*, 126). The hermeneutic phenomenological task is to listen to the co-responding of a discursiveness that can be neither willed nor created ex nihilo. (See also *DG*, 157-158; *BH*, 220-226.) Discursiveness includes but is not restricted to everyday practical conversance with matters of concern.

engaged openness—The philosophical term "being" has been seen to be plagued in the secondary literature on Heidegger by "much confusion and absurdity" (*PS*, 5-6).

What, that, and how a matter of concern *is* alludes to its temporal presencing as available for concernful human use. There is no "being" that is independent of the open discursive, historical engagement of human beings (*PS*, 187-192). The human being is *engaged* (has exigent need of what lets itself be usable) *and belongs to* the open clearing of open engagement (*4S*, 63). (See also *BH*, 227; *N*, 282-283, 301-303.) Being can also be thought as "an entity's givenness [to/for] possible human engagement" (*KE*, 5-7). We will use the term "engaged openness" in order to mark "being" as the play of the availability of entities/matters of concern to/for possible human engagement. One must always be mindful that human beings do not control or produce engagement but can be free for engagement with the play of interpretation. Engaged openness is at once question, answer, and rejoinder.

enowning—See *disclosing and beckoning.*

entities—See *matters of concern.*

facticity—The temporal-historical movedness of the passivity and activity of the human being of openness. The self-gathering of past (as alreadiness) and future (as becoming, on-coming) in the present (as presence-to) enable what can act and what can be acted on. Matters of concern constitute and are constituted by the human being of openness. See also *BT, OHF,* and *TM* for the hermeneutics of facticity.

finitude—That condition by which the human being of openness is fated to be incomplete—both in its self-knowledge and its ownmost knowledge of the moment of its mortality.

historicality—The carrying forth of the past. Historicality (historicity) is "lived out of the past" into the future (*BH*, 271). One *is* one's own generation as it "precedes the individual" as "the *historical* being-with-one-another" (*BH*, 272). Historicality is the movement of what happens. (See also *BT,* 41; *HWT,* 184; *COF.*)

historiography (historiology)—The reporting of what has happened as the knowledge and the ascertaining of history (*BH*, 271) such that the past is considered as merely a determinable series of events.

human being of openness, the—Heidegger appropriated the German word *Dasein* (existence) in his attempt to come to grips with a human way of being that was other than the modern one of a biologically or theoretically autonomous, willful, cognizing subject. To be sure, the human being is all of the above. But for Heidegger, this was only an unwarranted distillation of the story. Openness can be thought-said as the possibility of engaged openness that abides as the emergence/elusion of the unconcealedness of the truth of engaged openness (*PM*, 283-285). The human being of openness is not the location of some object in quantitatively determined space and time, but is first and foremost how it can care to be (*BT*, 418). (See also *BH*, fn. 2, 485-486; *BH*, 431; *ZS*, 225; *PS*, 11-12; *N*, 288-298; *ND*, 279-280; *KE*, 8-16.) In order to retain the belonging of human beings to their temporal-historical ways of engaged openness we will use the somewhat clumsy, but we believe necessary, term "the human being of openness" when we deem it appropriate.

idealisms—Those positions which assert that truth is located in the essence of objects. Matter is reduced to mentally determined concepts. The mind as an idealized assumption is the seat of all reason and logic, that is, truth. "The primary and most unshaped elemental matter" (*N*, 299) is the transcendental ego-structure or God (*N*, 308-312).

language—See *discursiveness.*

matters of concern—The play of matters, topics, things, beings, and entities is the emergence/elusion of the question of precise definitions (*PH*, 69). Heidegger has shown that there can be no such thing as isolated matters or entities. These are always already a context (world) before they are willfully reduced to theorizable or mathematically determined objects (*BT*, 95-107). As its dealings, the human being is dispersed (thrown) into "manifold ways of concern" (*BT*, 95). Matters/entities do not appear "*by means of human making.* But neither do they appear" removed from the care/

concern of finite humans (*PLT,* 181). Matters, entities, and care/concern conjoin out of word as play of meanings (*PLT,* 182). For these reasons we have been drawn to designate the above as matters of concern. (See also *BH,* 227.)

meaning—See *sense.*

metaphysics—For Heidegger, "Metaphysics grounds an age, in that through a specific interpretation of what is and through a specific comprehension of truth it gives to that age the basis upon which it is essentially formed" (*QCT,* 115; *OBT,* 57). (See also *ID,* 58; *4S,* 46; *PM,* 280, 284.)

modernity—This Pan-European position was formalized in the mid-17th century as René Descartes' *cogito ergo sum:* "I think, therefore I exist." The absolutely self-certain human cognizing subject rationally and willfully could establish itself as the central producer of the objectivity of objects via logical, technical, and mathematical procedures. Binary oppositions such as mind-body, subject-object, nature-nurture, and fatalism–self-determination were to be resolved via enlightened rational thinking as opposed to theological beliefs. Any matter of concern could be nothing other than neutral objects represented in advance by a conscious subject. Modernity has become expressed as a global phenomenon. (See *QCT,* 148-153.)

narrative telling—The term narrative telling is our attempt to focus on the conversational aspects of narratives. It is to be mindful of and to embrace narratives' telling (in all the senses of telling) as the loci of matters of concern. The reader should be mindful of "narrative" as this term belongs to relating as belonging-to and telling. Telling, in its own turn, is relating as the pivotal turning of the timely, the notable, and the weighty where these have no fixed point (*GT,* 75-85). Narrative tellings gather the human being of openness as the call to the saying of conversation.

ontic—Relating to (belonging to) the presencing of entities as matters of concern; enabled by engaged openness (*ZS,* 187). Death is the *must-be* nondeterminable phenomenon for each human being as finite and thrown. The human being "bears its thrownness without mastering it"(*PM*, 93) as nondeterminable determinations of its "partially known past and the plurality of expectations about the future" (Nelson, 2000, 156). Death is ontic in that it can be seen. (See also *BT*, 32-35.) The factical human being is ontic.

ontological—Relating to (belonging to) an existential possibility; a "can-be" (*GBT*, 432) wherein an ontic "have to be" can be acknowledged as a have-to-be (*GBT*, 435). Ontological phenomena are invisible—they show themselves prior to visible (perceived by the senses), ontic phenomena (*ZS*, 6-8, 187). Being toward death is invisible but is always already understood. (See also *BT*, 293-311.) The human being of openness as possibility is ontological.

open clearing, the—The non-passive stillness of active always already on-coming drawing of the nonperfectible/noncompletable human being of openness as its ultimate possibility (mortal finitude) (*OWL*, 106; *WCT*, 8-10). Hermeneutic phenomenology accepts the possibility of absence of perfectibility as *the* privative presence that enables the exigent need of phenomena to show themselves as the presence of absence: the absence of presence. Hermeneutic phenomenology thereby lets phenomena call themselves forth as a surplus over mere facultative apprehending. The reaching-out-for of the open clearing lets/frees/releases/engages the human being for reaching what it is freed to reach, via touching it with matters of concern (*OWL*, 91-93; *BW*, 441-449). The open clearing is not a location; it is a sojourn that gathers.

realisms—Those positions which assert that reality is exclusively given through observation of the physical world. For these positions the brain must be merely a physiological, cognizing, functional entity. Experiments on objects are necessary to compel/provoke reproducible results. "The primary and most unshaped elemental matter" (*N*, 299) is the much-sought-after grand unification formula.

saying—For Heidegger the saying of language is its showing, letting appear, its being seen and heard (*OWL,* 93).

sense—Often translated as "meaning." In Jean-Luc Nancy's writings, "sense" points to a possibility of meaning, not to a discrete, significant meaning.

temporality—See *historicality.*

things—See *matters of concern.*

thinking-saying—Meant to convey the inseparability of language as a saying call and the practice of thinking as it co-responds to the call.

understanding—For Heidegger, understanding is a can-be, which gives the human being of openness its possibility. Understanding must be sharply distinguished from the knowledge and epistemology attributed by modernity to a cognizing subject (*BT,* 182-195). Understanding is neither a gift of empathy nor something that can be possessed. Understanding is "co-original with one's existing and is present in every act of interpretation" (Palmer, 1969, 31). First and foremost, one always already sights something as something. Knowledge as culturally determined and epistemology as a theoretical-metaphysical determination are only possible because there is thrown (temporal-historical) understanding (*ZS,* 139).

The completion of our glossary does not give it an end. Its end is always already yet to come. Any attempt at a glossary is weighed down with thought that cannot "complete the meaning (of what) it thinks" (*GT,* 79). Such thinking-saying lets matters of concern have the weight that carries them away from totalized meanings to meaning which is excessive to itself. The weight of meaning without end is the disclosing and beckoning finitude of exposed openness-to-meaning.

The open, poetic saying of Emily Dickinson (1960) offers a hint that gathers thinking-saying into a moment of insight that asks after the divination of mortal speaking as:

The undeveloped Freight
Of a delivered syllable ...

Poetic bearing and gesture need thinking-saying to be weighed upon. The engaged openness of the slightest matter of concern always already overflows, outweighs its limit—its weight, however miniscule, lets it force its way forward.

There will be moments other than this glossary in which matters of concern are given names. We call on the reader-interpreter to let these names speak for themselves as they offer hints to their own context. Our index attempts to provide additional glimpses into their discursive play.

The way of this book includes the pedestrian elements of glossary and index as well as the telling of narratives. A way allows a nearing-to/reaching-for a matter of concern. The saying-showing of matters of concern allows reaching the utterance of discourse (*OWL,* 126). Our utterance/writing of discourse is the way we call forth as our own being-called-to.

Introduction

The open clearing calls as the poet offers a story that tells of the wonder that belongs to the everyday. There is a sojurn that all are allowed to be over and on wherein:

> *you find yourself, once over, sinking at every step*
> *into a luscious mess—. . .*
>
> Amy Clampitt, "The Outer Bar"

Often when one goes to tell a story, one finds that the story as a sojurn is already there. One can learn to see that stories disclose and beckon themselves as themselves: They show up. They can be sighted and listened to. They surprise.

To be human is to be learned: not in the historically situated sense of what it means to be erudite, but in the sustaining sense of being enabled to listen to the listenable. As listenables, stories offer themselves, but they correlatively need understanding listeners in order for both the stories and the listeners to be engaged/belonged to. Human beings are ineluctably exposed/opened up, not as the enclosed consciousness of modernity's metaphysics, but as a crossing singular-plural texture. Humans can encounter and participate with matters of concern in the back-and-forth play of their shared practical immediacy. Learning as learnedness shows itself as the telling of narrative—the offering of stories.

The stories of learning disclose themselves because they have to. Learning as such is not the provable product of inanimate nature or an achievement of perfect self-presence as the metaphysics of modernity believes. By its very nature, learning reveals itself: (1) It cannot be the possibility of complete ignorance, for then it would be impossible; and (2) it cannot be perfect knowledge, for then it would not be present as a necessity. Learning is the mark of human finitude as it shows itself as its own lack of "perfect presence-to-itself" (*KE,* 11) as incompletability. The openness of what it means to be human plays forth somewhere between the incapacity of total ignorance and the impossibility of omniscience.

Learning obtains as a locus of meaning where, as possibility, it is co-related to schooling and teaching. Schooling as attendance is where and when the apprehending-receptive human must be in residence. Learning needs a temporal-historical place *of* which to play. Teaching belongs to co-responding in order to offer/allot the calling forth of thinking-saying as it belongs to schooling and learning. Without teaching there would be no historical traditions as sense/meaning for the human being to apprehend-receive, which as they disclose and beckon draw the human of openness into the future as it becomes (on-comes).

Hermeneutic phenomenology as sighting (perhaps even as poesy) is the sustaining possibility that enables the human being to risk enacting the traversal of an open expanse in order to reach matters of concern. One can risk losing one's warm and comfortable dry shoes as these are drawn into that "luscious mess." To risk such a traversal is to attentively keep alive the notion that by letting what one is sighting and listening unto come near to one, there can be surprise—both as moments of insight and as the emergence/elusion of errancy.

The story that this book offers turns on narrative telling as a pathway wherein stories of schooling learning teaching are listened-to and sighted as they disclose and beckon. Human beings of today's modernist tradition can learn only if they let learning be an unlearning. As this enacting listens to the call of matters of concern before it, the human being can learn only if it unlearns what something "is" in terms of the historicality of modernity's mission to close its self-enforced subject-object gap. To learn the fit of the understanding of engaged openness to the understandability of engaged openness, as a matter of concern not available to or establishable via measurement or mere empirical cognition, is the task that silently calls the human being to thinking-saying.

The human being is the entity who *is* its opened, receptive mode, manner, or way such that it points to what is. Particular entities show up when they become available to such pointing. That which is thought-said to be subject to actualizing does not complete and exhaust itself in what is actual and factual at any given historical moment. The play of world continues to be offered by engaged openness such that there belongs the future as an on-coming, forerunning can-be, the present as what has to be presence-to, and the past as an alreadiness that is always already in play as aheadness. The human being as an exposed out-in-the-open openness points toward engaged openness-as-can-be insofar as the former is always already and at each place attends itself to possibilities of engagement. The human being of openness attends to the call to attention (compelling summons) as listening.

The "luscious," as being mired in mud, can also call forth angst, profound indifference, terror, startled dismay, reverent awe, and steadfast composure. As well, it can dispose itself as richness, wondrousness, melodiousness, and enchantedness. All of these are possible ways of disposedness—they cannot be switched on or off by dint of the willful activity of a lone ego-subject. The way of the ensuing chapters will point to the unlearning of what has been rather loosely called metaphysical thinking. The metaphysical, as the word stems from the Greek, literally means beyond the physical or supra-sensual (*WCT,* 58). For modernity, the assumed hegemony of absolute human reason is a position claimed by a metaphysic. Humans have assigned pure reason to themselves as they claim to be the absolute ground of all that is. This assignation turns on an assumption that assumes itself.

Narrative Pedagogy and Metaphysics

The metaphysics of modernity as an "all-highest first cause" (*ID,* 60) reduces matters of concern to mere entities which are "indifferently valid everywhere" (*ID,* 58). Metaphysical thinking cannot let go of its self-arrogated grip on its own metaphysical notion of concretizing the reality of the real. The real thought in terms of the metaphysics of modernity is that which is brought (provoked) into presence *by* the metaphysics of modernity (*QCT,* 158-174). Metaphysics cannot appeal to its own logical structures to effect an escape from its own tautology.

It is only with great difficulty that the hidden power of metaphysics can be sighted. Thinking must first be sighted as the listening of thinking-saying. Before thinking as a taking cognizance of something, there is practical comportment. The immediacy of practical, involved understanding is prior to its verbal expression. Language in its widest sense *exigently needs* the not said in order to be said. Heidegger has written that practical comportment runs "everywhere through language precisely when [humans speak] by being silent. Only when [humans speak do they] think—not the other way around, as metaphysics still believes" (*WCT,* 16). Practical comportment is first and foremost to be involved with entities of one sort or another as matters of concern. The human being can listen to matters of concern as they present themselves in their difference from historically situated, engaged openness. Thinking can be thought of in Plato's sense, as the soul's infinite dialogue with itself, but thinking-saying takes place as a surplus to that overly restrictive metaphysical conception of its ideality.

Thinking-saying in its widest sense cannot take place without language being listened to in its widest sense, that of its self-showing. Thinking-saying belongs to the showing of language—its saying. Thinking-saying belongs together with engaged openness (*ID,* 57). There is a circling, differing holding apart and holding together (*ID,* 68), whereby thinking-saying "is free either to pass over the difference without a thought or to think it specifically as such" (*ID,* 63). The belonging together of engaged openness and matters of concern is an open region (clearing) which opens itself (*ID,* 67). The always alreadiness of this open cannot be closed by metaphysical thinking.

The task of hermeneutic phenomenology is to catch sight of and listen to the open clearing as the open. Thinking-saying is free for the ontic have-to-be of finitude and the ontological can-be of the always already lack of closure. The on-coming of the human being of openness is one's ownmost possibility—the *same* for each, but never reducible to an indifferent identity. Narrative tellings offer the nearness of death as a life possibility.

The following narrative tells of a nurse educator, a nursing student, and a nurse clinician. Anka, an experienced nurse teacher, and Kevin, a senior student, watched on the sidelines as the nurse, Naomi, took the hand of a mother and accompanied her from the foot of the bed up to the head, where her comatose daughter lay dying. Death in the ICU is an event in which families spend their last moments together. Here students and teacher witness the nurse attending both the dying daughter and her mother. Later, outside the room, Anka reflects with Kevin and Naomi on what they have all experienced.

Anka: *Did you notice, Kevin, how the nurse brought the mother to the head of the bed and encouraged her to speak to her daughter, even though she is comatose? Families often have difficulty speaking to a comatose member. Naomi was a role model for the mom as she talked to the patient about what day it was and how long she had been in the ICU. And when we left, the mother was conversing with her daughter. Here's the nurse now—let's ask her about this. Naomi, what do you plan to do today with the patient and her mother?*

Naomi: *For two days now, I have looked into this young woman's eyes and I "see" no one in there. She is not responding, and we [other clinicians on the unit] are beginning to think she needs to be allowed to die. But head injuries are difficult and unpredictable; you never know. Clearly these patients can suddenly turn the corner and wake up. But as nurses, we often get a sense of "when there is no one there." We are working hard to reconnect the mother with her daughter because I think their time together is short. This mom is helping us bathe her and she's talking to her more and more, encouraging her to open her eyes or squeeze her hand. My experience in situations like this is often the family also begins to understand their family member has left them. They know when their loved one is no longer there. Getting them involved in caring for their loved one seems to help. This young woman has been coded [resuscitated] five times now and I am wondering if it is time to make her a DNR [do not resuscitate] so her life can complete its journey. The doctor is very close to this family, and he will need a lot of time to get ready for this decision. We will follow the family's lead, if we can, but I am feeling it is time to at least start the conversation; all the while we are doing our very best for her. I plan to talk with the mother today about "What would it mean to you if you took your daughter off life support?" It's a question everyone is thinking but no one wants to speak. Nurses maybe live in these silences as we attend families with a dying member.*

Kevin: *It's easy to think of death in the ICU as a sort of a symptom. You know, just a heart that stops and needs to be restarted. But it is also sometimes, like here, a life event.*

Anka: *And maybe the hard part for all of us is knowing when to treat death as a symptom and when to respond to death as a life event. This can be especially hard because in the ICU, everyone is there to survive—we even use the term, "life support."*

Naomi: *Death in the ICU is difficult, and we know that families will spend the rest of their lives reliving it. We try our best to know when to treat and when to begin to talk with the family, and sometimes the docs, about letting a life complete its journey. There are no hard-and-fast rules or tests to tell you what to do.*

As this narrative telling shows, the journey out of metaphysical thinking is not to be guaranteed in the sense of the certainty of a mental representation (*EP,* 88). The certainty claimed by metaphysical thinking cannot be overcome by a mere act of will, for that is metaphysical thinking itself. However, it can be caught sight of and listened to and thereby left to itself. The practice of hermeneutic phenomenology is claimed by the invisible rather than by the certainty of mathematical calculation or empirical observation. As well, it is claimed by the aphonic of what is listened to rather than the measurability of what is detected by acoustic equipment. Hermeneutic phenomenology is a path of the inapparent where one risks a sojourn that "lets that before which it is led, show itself" (*4S*, 80).

Being singular plural, thrownness understanding language, building dwelling thinking, schooling learning teaching: These series of "three apposite words" mark an equivalence of apparent and inapparent appearance.

In this book we will attempt to let the words schooling learning teaching speak paratactically, but not as a "not-yet syntactic" (*WCT*, 183-186). The disclosing and beckoning open between, where there are no words, speaks as "nearness, in the sense of the radiance issuing from unconcealedness into unconcealedness" (*WCT*, 237). As this way, the above triads, as matters of concern, belong to each other in their concealed moments of possible elusion as they suddenly add, mix, and join with/to each other as possibilities.

Appearance as appearance is herein a thinking-saying of disclosing and beckoning as "not brought about by anything beyond itself and not bringing about anything as its consequence" (*QCT*, 171, Translator's fn. 25). Disclosing and beckoning as the appearing (presencing) of appearance (presence) shows and opens as the play of engaged openness. The play that belongs to these terms is a co-implication of the sharing of the world—the world as "the coexistence that puts these existences together" (*BSP*, 29). None of the four sets of three terms should be taken as idealized entities that proceed from or ground the others. As we work to extend the projects of Heidegger, Gadamer, and Jean-Luc Nancy we say, along with Nancy, that "each designates the coessence of the others" (*BSP*, 37). "Being-many-together is the originary situation; it is even what defines a 'situation' in general" (*BSP*, 41).

Our way will be marked by a step-by-step series of presupposed openings and overtures as antecedent calls-to-attention. We will present our sightings and listenings as matters of concern disclose and beckon such that they enable us to enact our own being "passible" to sense, that is, of being enabled to (disposed to) receive and welcome disclosing and beckoning of sense (*GT*, 69).

Part I

Retrieving Origins: Adventures and Arrivals

Chapter 1

The Path of This Work: Hermeneutic Phenomenology

Home is where one starts from.
T. S. Eliot, "East Coker"

> *. . . a path that leads*
> *away to come before . . .*
> *lets that before which*
> *it is led show itself.*
> 4S, 80

Everyone who reads this book is already schooled, learned, and involved in the reciprocity of teaching. This does not mean that "the everyone" must have attended an institution, must have committed skills to memory, and thereby must have submitted to teachers' dictates. In an originary and in the widest sense, schooling is what each human is always already attending; learning is what takes place as the listening play of what is seen and heard, and teaching is the gathering of the first two in conversation and dialogue as co-responding. Our intent in this book will be to show the converging conversations that turn on schooling learning teaching as an ontological phenomenon. This intra-related phenomenon is invisible and silent but is an involvement just as real as that which is seen and heard.

Rather than establishing a system of correct and normative educational standards, processes, and outcomes, we will challenge the claim of modernity's science to truth wherein it subordinates "education" to one neutral category among others.

Our response to our self-imposed challenge will be to demonstrate that the irresolvable lacunae of fact-value distinctions overlook the essence of what it means to be human: to be always already finitely opened up as a historically particular engagement with matters of concern. Human beings always already find themselves as a presence-to necessary participation with others, an understanding play of matters of concern as they take place in conversation and dialogue. This includes but is by no means restricted to mundane activities, usage, writing, reading, and talking. A surplus obtains wherein humans are drawn as an open becoming that is in excess to mere sense perception or measurements.

Matters of concern, conversation, and dialogue always already appositionally mix as a swirl of possibilities. The appositive or paratactical is the between of conversation and dialogue in a play of the face-to-face. Can a possibility arise out of this thrownness wherein it is possible for a book about the limits of education to mark out a way that cannot be a guaranteed application? Can a publication that pretends to the methodical be bereft of any traditional sense of method? Does a writing that must participate in a given logical, grammatical structural tradition fail to eliminate any ambiguities that, as their own turnings, serve to generate seemingly irresolvable misunderstandings?

Throughout this book we will maintain that we are not renouncing the correctness that scientific practices have to offer. There exist necessary relationships that turn on their being quantifiable, calculable, and predictable. Our presentation will work to show that science is about reductive practices that science, in itself, cannot get itself around (*QCT,* 155-182). By naming and presenting schooling learning teaching as a co-occurring intra-related phenomenon, we are not attempting to glimpse these moments as quantifiable equivalents. Rather we seek to pursue this phenomenon in such a way as to let it become unfolded from the contexts of its taken-for-granted concrescence. We shall undertake an endeavor wherein phenomena can show themselves as "grantings." Our task vis-à-vis hermeneutic phenomenology will be an attempt to reveal how the disclosing and beckoning movement of schooling as attending, learning as listening, and teaching as co-responding all belong together and with each other as the engagedness of their always already circulation.

What is the place of the play of hermeneutic phenomenology, "education," art, and science? Should all thinking be merely interpretive to the exclusion of attempts to establish facts via observation, logic, and mathematics? Has modernity become trapped in incommensurable paradigms? Dogmas? Power relationships? Does the work of art occur only as mere personal experience or as some political-economic propaganda vehicle? Does skill acquisition end only in the search and consequent discovery of immutable knowledge? For example, does "higher learning" imply that there is "lower learning"? How does the strife of ideological betweens show itself? Arrive? Are these gaps unbridgeable, or is another way possible wherein detours may be undertaken in order to unveil closedness that seems to be transparent and self-inflicted? Must absolute certainty obtain in the conceiving of play and is there a danger in only viewing play as a series of mere dichotomous or binary oppositions to be worked out and settled once and for all as the ground of reductionist proclivities?

In speaking to the risky and tumultuous terrain of such questions, Gadamer warns,

> There is a danger . . . of limiting ourselves to a theory
> of science which, in the name of methodological rigor,
> robs us of certain experiences of other people, other
> expressions, other texts and their claim to validity. (*F,* x)

The naming of phenomena, as well as the naming of dangers, entails risk. Risk is inherent in any opening of other pathways of thinking. Any opening that gives thinking can hide within it the possibility of going astray. But in a putative going astray there also resides the possible disclosure of the heretofore unrevealed as it is forgotten or passed over. Perhaps the adherence to a risk-free lack of risk is the greatest risk of all.

Presuppositions

One presupposition for conversation is language.

ZS, 214

We begin this book with our own presuppositions. In our best judgment these grow out of our conversations with and about the work of Martin Heidegger and Hans-Georg Gadamer. To a lesser extent, we will draw on the no less contributory work of Jean-Luc Nancy and others who either expand or call into question the work of the other two. Thus our presuppositions include the following:

1. There is an always already delivered-over-to situatedness that one both can and cannot do something about. Human beings have to act and be acted upon; the active and the passive fundamentally belong to each other.
2. Making sense of the delivered-over-to situatedness comes as the allotment of language, which is prior to any cognition, representations, or quantifications.
3. Discursiveness around the basis of the belonging together of the first two presuppositions enables matters of concern to show up as possibility.

The reading of converging conversations among schooling learning teaching as an invisible phenomenon is other than establishing a system that pretends to instantiate institutionalized, correct, and normative educational standards, processes, and outcomes. Herein lies a danger. The reading of a thinking that claims itself as an "access," as some sort of ultimate system, traps itself into the ultimate system it labors to overcome (*CP*, 42). Thinking-saying as jointure is a possibility wherein letting the play of taking something as something is seen. In this attempt it has to be clear that both the jointure and the access remain an endowment of engaged openness.

The historical-temporal worlding of the world is other than a mechanical apparatus or system: "Systems, like screwed-on pieces of apparatuses, can be unscrewed and replaced again by others" (*PM*, 303-304). World as an inapparent joining together of an appearing exceeds every empirical ordering (*4S,* 8). The receiving or the receivable as the understanding of matters of concern turns on the emergence of matters of concern (*ZS,* 185). The coming to pass of the temporality belonging to the ability of matters of concern "to be engaged is always correlative to the human ability to have access" to them. Otherwise understanding and engaged openness, lacking any intrinsic connection, would merely bump up against each other, only occasionally and always accidentally, as they go their separate ways" (*N,* 302).

The hint and withdrawal of truth is something that cannot be forced (*CP,* 56). The sense of "givenness" residing in hermeneutic phenomenology transposes the a priori from mathematical, immanent knowledge deduced from established principles to being exposed to an ineffable always already wherein "knowledge" is taken away (*HWT,* 187-199). Despite what seems to be a paradox, in hermeneutic phenomenology understanding as immediate experience is freed from the shackles of epistemology's prejudgments about itself, to a pathway wherein understanding offers itself in order to be interpreted as matters of concern.

The As-Structure

> *The as-structure is grounded ontologically in the temporality of understanding.*
>
> *BT,* 411

In *Being and Time,* Heidegger explicates the interpretive "as" as being grounded in taking something as something (*BT,* 188-189). Taking here entails the understandability of the available (*KE,* 5-12). Elaborating on this thematic, von Herrmann (2001, 121-124) submits that availability as accessibility "does not mean having something at one's disposal and doing with it as one pleases. Involvements are always already 'disclosed in our understanding of the world' as 'a totality of involvements.'"

The telling, saying, hinting dialogical "as" of interpretation simply stands in/whiles in/sojourns with the openness of "an open field of sense-making relations" (*PS,* 193): the open clearing. If one pays heed to the granting of the interpretive as-structure, one can see that it harbors within itself the possibility of revealing as well as the possibility of covering-up (concealing). The as-structure focuses not on the matter at hand as such, but on the play of its ownmost situatedness. The understanding of engaged openness as the play of involved bestowals cannot be pinned down as a reproducible object or as a universal verity.[1] As a "heeding, the hermeneutical as, of duly 'letting something be seen *as* something,'" is a reading which "elicits what is already understood by diverting attention away from it to the inaugural place of its disclosure" (Schalow, 1992, 233). Taking something as something does *not* generate meanings as fixed and privileged possessions. Rather there is an untangling of always already differing relationships whose interplay lets presences as takings-as. These recede (absence) into past and future as unfoldings. Unfoldings, as such, are always already present as historically particular phenomena. Glimpses are enabled, which, as always already unfoldings, call forth the as-structure that enables the enacting of hermeneutic phenomenology. Disclosing and beckoning is the letting forth (offering) of meaning.

Possibly includes but is not exclusive to some present matter of concern and is inclusive of the possibility of absence as incompletability and finitude. Made thematic in this way, absence is privative presence, presence is privative absence. Hermeneutic phenomenology lets absence and presence exigently need and belong to each other. They are "engaged" in *all* senses of the word "engaged."

The hermeneutic "as" obtains as reciprocity. The boundaries offering its intelligibility are emergent and are concomitantly fading contours of that which any interpretation trails after. The as-structure moves along as retrieval whereby it participates in an "open expanse within which the hermeneutical as can trace the lines of intelligibility and thereby satisfy a more original requirement for uncovering" otherwise covered-over notions of existence that otherwise obtain as mere materiality or monothematic idealism (Schalow, 1992, 234). The "as" points to phenomena as something other than fixed or atemporal notions. A letting be becomes possible such that the relation of engaged openness and temporality comes to fruition as it lets the discursive essence of the "and" hold sway (Schalow, 1992, 234). That taken note of, one must not let the connective "and" as a binary opposedness become hypostatized into an eternal or discrete now.

The understanding of humans as a subjective and objective genitive always already takes place through *language* within a tradition (*HWT,* 193). Any given specific moment is prepositioned to experience matters of concern in certain ways. These are experienced as the discursive (linguistic) play of sense as significance and meaning. Hermeneutic phenomenology turns on the assumption that if "intentional or existential structures are first found in the thick of experience, they then must first be uncovered *from* it before they are projected *upon* it" (*HWT,* 192). Hermeneutic phenomenology is a pathway of mutually revealing possibilities in order to be free for what withdraws or emerges. Because hermeneutic phenomenology *must* emerge as the freeing up of historicality and temporality, it is not grounded in a methodology that dictates connections or imperatives, permanent appearance or disappearance.

Hermeneutic phenomenology is bound to, is claimed by, finitude. First and foremost, the finitude of each human being is never lost sight of. This moment of finitude guarantees that each particular human can never be complete. Another moment of finitude turns on the always already particular/temporal historicality of matters of concern and their current meanings. The human being is bound to incompletability. Thus, it can be seen that binding is about belonging-to, not connections. For example, Heidegger's *Being and Time* is not about being and time as tangible entities; it is about the "and" or the connective as possibility. The same holds true for Gadamer's *Truth and Method,* where the subject matter turns on the connectings of traditions of various conceptions of truth and their concomitant claim of/by method. Another view of nonconnected connecting is taken in Jean-Luc Nancy's *Being Singular Plural,* wherein he lets the titled phenomena disclose and beckon paratactically or side by side such that these are never without each other but are not bound together as sense-less isolated and neutral identities. Binding is belonging together, not submission to ultimate categories.

Possibility

> *Dasein [The human being of openness] is in every case what it can be, and in the way in which it is its possibility. The being-possible which is essential for Dasein [the human being of openness], pertains to the ways of its solicitude for others and of its concern with the "world."*
>
> BT, 183

Connectedness is the possibility *of* possibility. This jointure is not the "co- or ad-herence" of putative actualities but is inclusive of them. The historical how of possibility, via exposition of particular/historical presence-to, is *"the first principle of hermeneutics"* (*BH,* 212). It is the understanding of understanding as originary nonfoundational ground wherein the movement of hermeneutic phenomenology may be pursued.[2] The temporal-historicality of the human being of openness (Da-sein[3]) is its ownmost meaning. We submit this exposition as an other pathway in order to facilitate an opening unto the emergence of the phenomena we are putting in question and concomitantly as questions for us as interpreters. Our title, *Schooling Learning Teaching: Toward Narrative Pedagogy,* carries no connectives or connecting punctuation within "schooling learning teaching" such that as an intra-related phenomenon it may serve as a pointer in our attempt to let it show itself *as* co-occurring.

The always already self-emerging of phenomena as they are present to hermeneutic phenomenology are what offers choice and decision as possibilities. Unlike some putative ideal theory or grand unification formula of mathematized physics, possibility is not an eternal, perpetual emptiness. Possibility discloses and beckons as possibility, the possibility of humankind as the human being of openness of retrieving and being retrieved by the already as not-yet always already infinite becoming.[4] This is the ontic starting point of where we have to be in our hermeneutic phenomenological understanding.

The pathways that interpretive thinking must follow cannot be dictated by rigidly controlled road maps. On the other hand, as the reader will see, the pathway followed herein entails risk. One must dare to question presuppositions as they appear in their play of presencing and disappearance. Thus, if one asks what gives any principle its "unshakable right," one finds that its circulatory system of rightness (certainty) is rooted in its presuppositions (*BW*, 440-445). Matters of concern turn on the ownmost presencing of any particular historical unfolding of originary engaged openness. Whence and with regard to what does mutual presencing bind itself as a phenomenon? Is binding as such presupposed by the play of engaged belonging, attracting, holding, disclosing, and beckoning? Can these be demonstrated according to the tenets of scientific methods as they have come down to us? Or is another pathway called for?

The response of hermeneutic phenomenological thinking is to say that a historical period that has allowed a central place to be occupied by technology-based science can never deal with the social with-world. That with-world is world wherein sense obtains as a spatial-temporal passage such that it is plural and shared (James, 2006, 108). The with-world is not some enclosure one enters and exits from time to time but always already obtains as open becoming (*BSP*, 97). World in this sense is not graspable via "neutral" observations or idealized mathematical constructions.

Heidegger adds to our conversation as we accept the limitation to respond to the following question: "Is the manifest character of what *is* exhausted by what is demonstrable? Does not the insistence on what is demonstrable block the way to what is?" (*BW*, 448). In one way or another human beings are abandoned to the question, "What is the 'is'?" This question obtains as a worrisome "tautological abstraction." Jean-Luc Nancy avers, "Our task is to break the hard shell of this tautology" (*BSP*, 35). Human beings are served by (in both the accusative and the dative case of serving) asking after the "is" as engaged openness, being-with.

World in the sense of hermeneutic phenomenology is the "confluence of self, time and language" (*HWT,* 100). Therefore world is to be taken as calls to which we are delivered over, joined, and held as the "conjoining that enjoins the call and thus grounds" the human way of being of openness (*CP,* 57). The open ground calls us such that it "draws us along by its very withdrawal" (*WCT,* 9). Heidegger points to the givenness of the open which we always/ already are and to the granting of openness as openness (Zarader, 1986, 20). Human beings exist somewhere between the holy and the mineral inert. Jean-Luc Nancy rather provocatively has written, "We would not be 'humans' if there were not 'dogs' and 'stones'" (*BSP,* 18). Human beings are a part of what truly is "neither one nor the other, but the co-belonging as the concealed middle," whereby an exposed, ownmost place of sense comes to pass (*4S,* 4).

The on-coming of coming to pass offers the hint "that everything is comprehensible, except the comprehensibility of everything" (*N,* 313). It follows from the above expositions that the human situation is more than the observable and quantifiable systematized corporeality of modernity's technoscientism. It now becomes fair to say that it is incumbent upon us to follow these statements with a cogent exposition of the neighborhood (open clearing) schooled human beings are let into.

Converging Conversations as Crossings

> *Thinking must first learn what remains reserved and in store for thinking to get involved in. It prepares its own transformation in this learning.*
>
> *OTB,* 60

The path of this work is already determined by its subject matter. Our path will lead the reader to certain places, which will in turn open up paths to other places. The always already is "the crossings through of presence" (*BSP,* 5). The meaning of "in circulation" goes in all directions at once such that "all the space-times opened by presence to presence . . . all things, all beings, all entities, everything past and future" (*BSP*, 3) are co-constitutive. Humans "expose sharing and in circulation as such by saying 'we'" (*BSP*, 3). But as Heidegger reminds us, saying-we engages the human being of openness "taken as time-space, not in the sense of the usual concepts of time and space" but as the place for the free-play of time-space as it grounds the clearing of the engaged openness of matters of concern (*CP*, 227).

One of the major tasks of this book is to make thematic the thought of converging conversations as crossing. Our path in crossing will attempt to be one of genuine questioning. We interpret questioning as proper (or open) if it is led to see that which *enables* its answer. Enabling lets possible clarifications show how questioning proceeds. What is trailed after is the play of enabling itself. Questions and answers need (belong to) each other; one articulates the other— they are rejoinders (Fynsk, 1996b, 41-42, 76).

Enabling as play is what one comes across. Crossing as the rhetorical trope, "crossroads," has occurred in Greek tragedy (Sophocles), African American blues music (Robert Johnson), and American poetry (Robert Frost). These point to crossings as ways or paths of movement to decisive rejoinders, which are not ultimately or even provisionally answerable. Influenced by the German poet Hölderlin, Heidegger explicated thinking of crossings as the mirror-play of the fourfold of earth, sky, divinities, and mortals (*PM*, 310-311).[5] Crossings are the nondimensional open of the between where the appositive issues forth as a side-by-side removal unto face-to-face nearness.

In hermeneutic phenomenology, crossings are thought as a historical play of intersecting regions wherein seemingly incommensurate practices or otherwise isolated modes of thinking are seen as permeating each other. This permeating is as multiplicity rather than as a removal into a predetermined unity. Heidegger outlines the dilemma *of* modernity as "standing at the methodological cross-road which will decide on the very life or death" of thinking. According to Heidegger, "We stand at an abyss: either into nothingness, that is, absolute reification, pure thingness, or we somehow leap into *another world,* more precisely, we manage for the first time to make the leap into the world as such" (*TDP,* 63).[6] Heidegger used the image of wood paths as a title for a collection of his essays. He wrote of wood paths, "Each goes its particular way, but in the same forest. Often it seems as though one were identical to another. Yet it only seems so" (*BW,* 34).[7]

Crossings as pathways, which are an always already arriving at, are movement rather than crossroads, which mark arrival. As such, crossings can indicate a stable place or relationship and are often marked or labeled as such. An inconspicuous state of affairs takes place when crossings aren't noticed. Rather than stopping to decide this way or that, as one can do in a crossroads, the human being can overlook crossings because everything seems to be a clear pathway, especially as experienced in everyday comings and goings. Crossings as regions intersect and separate as the interplay of difference enables the open of the always already site of dialogue and conversation, which in turn may or may not be listened to or for. Each human being and each crossing belong together as they go their mutual ways, their every moment (*WCT,* 175). These can never be traversed via the mere stand-alone decision of an ego-subject in relation to the choice of way. Past ways traversed are never simply behind, but always already obtain as a calling ahead by the future as an on-coming becoming (*WCT,* 175). Crossings cannot be taken as a once-and-for-all-time event; they advene as a unique each time.

Crossings disclose and beckon such that "whatever happens with historical human beings always derives from a decision about the essence of truth that was taken long ago and is never up to humans alone" (*PM,* 182). For Heidegger, truth self-discloses as "the essence of unhiddenness" (*PM,* 182). This unique essence, as the presence of an impassable crossing, can call forth a thinking conversation that lets the absence of a grounded presence always already obtain as a possible "wrong way" (*WCT,* 175).[8] The always already historically situated possibility of crossing as a wrong way shows itself as "the inconspicuous state of affairs . . . which is inaccessible and not to be gotten around" (*QCT,* 177). Crossings are offered (allowed) as varied and "yet convergent paths of access to the *question* of" disclosing and beckoning as the emergence/ elusion of disclosive forerunning (*4S,* 60).

In order to deal with the crossings of schooling learning teaching, we choose to reach back into present traditions and at the same time reach forward into possibilities' forerunning. Reaching obtains as a play wherein phenomenology and hermeneutics in a seeming paradox reach the reached as the unreachable. According to Kisiel, Heidegger asserted that "The self-world in which I originally have myself understandingly is not a thing nor even an I in an epistemological sense, but a meaningful context. Its concepts are expressions of sense and not of an order of objects to which they must be brought into coincidence" (*HWT,* 178). The project of pure transcendental (eidetic) phenomenology was to reach a secured and thus ahistorical ego-subject. But taken in a different light, "phenomenological concepts never assume the fixity and definition of scientific concepts, they cannot be defined by being ordered and classified with an objectively formed materials context, they are always plurivocal and subject to vacillation and variation with the uniquely original situation in which they are actualized" (*HWT,* 178).[9]

If the rational, knowing subject of modernity cannot be ultimately grasped, what belongs to hermeneutic phenomenology, if it is neither direct observation/measuring, mathematical/formal logic, nor psychology? In order to glimpse the unfolding play of this manner of questioning we will turn to a path that crosses from phenomenology to hermeneutic phenomenology.

Gathering and Assembling:
Catching a Glimpse of the Roadblocks

> *What is given to thinking to think is not some deeply hidden underlying meaning but rather something lying near. . . .*
>
> QCT, 111

A question implicit in any interpretative thinking regards a road not taken. If an apparent roadblock is set up such that a route must be followed that leads to a seemingly insurmountable barrier, the alternate way arrives as a possible turning point, a cul-de-sac (*BW,* 34). For Gadamer, the proper experience of a barrier is not one of imprisonment but is one of a turning, wherein the human being is opened to its essential finitude (*TM,* xxiv, 357). Human beings cannot master their separation from the divine, the future, or certainty. These absolutes cannot be gotten around via the methodological procedures indebted to certainty. The ego-subject, mythologically certain of itself, contributes to a play of barriers that foreclose on the possibility of essential questioning (*4S,* 70).

Holding understanding as understanding, open and problematic, serves to keep thinking pathways in play. Encountering this play allows for the possibility of the corrections that history as historicality and temporality offer to understandings. Inherent in holding understanding open is to put at risk one's pre-understanding. Hermeneutic phenomenology turns on a mindfulness wherein the problematic is held apart from mere problems. In science, the problematic and problems are held together; that is, the solution is to make them both merely a pregiven context. In hermeneutic phenomenology, the problematic as the situation of the problem is held to be apart but situation and problem belong to each other; that is, context is not to be solved for. Context/situation is allowed to emerge as a questioning call, inseparatable from the rejoining-saying of the call.

Does there exist a sense of barriers, which call individual human beings to a foreshortening, such that they become aware that in their finitude they can't get "farther" than they are? Is the attempt to establish a risk- and danger-free firm footing another sense of roadblock? Humans run into the fact that they can't eternally go farther in order to connect with all time. At this point, finite understanding runs into questionings, which do not and cannot guarantee solutions. Problems, if "solved," can only pretend to be the way to something universal. The naïve utopianism of nanotechnology[10] promises to eliminate any and all roadblocks to the human control of the production of anything. Is the task of human beings to find ways around or move roadblocks in order to clear the way in pathway? Or is the task offered to human beings the risking inherent to becoming what all humans are already?—that is, risking the finitude of the individual and the unknowability of the future as an always already open becoming.

Let us hear how questioning roadblocks and barriers can show up. Lena, an experienced teacher, describes her concerns. As she relates her own concerned experiences, she shows Gadamer's thought of the belonging together of experience and question (*TM*, 362).

Lena describes her questionings.

> *We never think about or question things that stand right in front of our eyes . . . like how learning is invisible. Sometimes teachers think they see learning when a student's eyes light up but mostly we know it's totally invisible. Instead of talking about the problems created because learning is invisible, we skip over the issue and just go about trying to make it visible. Teachers are nervous talking about teaching something invisible, even though we do it all the time. It's too uncertain. So we come up with definitions and ways to "observe" learning so we can measure it objectively. That way, we've removed any uncertainty . . . we know exactly what learning is and how to assess or measure it.*

Human beings understand that they cannot master uncertainty. Understanding that learning is invisible, teachers act as if it is visible through their observational claims made for the efficacy of empirical observations.

Next Lena raises doubts about universal absolutes.

> *But measuring learning really doesn't work. Students who have never seen the skill or procedure done before have teachers demonstrate it to them; they do a successful return demonstration, and Bingo! We say the students have learned it! They get full credit for learning and you are a successful teacher. Yet the next day on the clinical unit, the students may forget entirely*

what they demonstrated to you so successfully the day before. So have they learned it? Did you teach it? We think we are making learning with our definitions, competencies, and checklists more certain, but we are not. Instead of talking about learning as invisible and the problems it creates for measuring or assessing it, we never admit to this uncertainty in what we do as teachers! We bypass thinking about trying to assess something that is basically invisible, by making it into a problem to be solved.

> The modern quest for certainty can create an obsession among teachers for better testing and evaluation of student learning, though there is rarely such concern about evaluating teaching and its relation to learning in students. Simulations, clinical checklists, written tests, and a host of other competency evaluation strategies take on ever more significance.

Lena continues.

When students fail to exhibit behaviors (competencies) that indicate they have learned, teachers make this kind of "failure" into a problem, like "low learning retention" or insufficient practice time for "transfer of learning" from the learning lab to the clinical units. Or teachers come up with explanations for why failure happened. Maybe the student was anxious on the clinical unit and not in the safe learning lab. This explanation, of course, justifies learning labs and all the investments schools make in technology. And this is necessary as patients become more acute and students' "use" of patients to learn on becomes more dangerous for both. I am not arguing here for or against learning simulation labs. Only that we change or stop ignoring the uncertainty of assessing something that is invisible like learning and by making it into an explanation or problem to be solved. Complex and persistent questions go unasked.

> It is easy for teachers to forget that a test made of valid and reliable items is basically a valid and reliable experience of the items merely chosen by the teacher.

Questions show themselves to Lena as rejoinders.

I keep asking myself questions like, Has the student learned the skill if it was only measured in a context in which it will never be practiced? But teachers always assess [measure] skills and procedures in the clinical context too, just to be sure. But do we? It's impossible to have every student do every skill on the clinical units. Oftentimes we don't have enough patients needing these procedures when the students are there. When the end of the course comes and every student has not demonstrated their competencies [skills or procedures] but they have been checked off as being successful in the learning lab, what does the teacher do? Fail the students, give them an incomplete or pass them on, so long as a certain percentage of the competencies are achieved, hoping the next instructor will provide the experience to demonstrate the missing competencies to be evaluated? What if this happens to senior students? Do they not graduate? Of course not! Students graduate with never applying many of the skills they learned in the learning lab in real patient situations. So did they learn it? Teachers give tests, yet if we were honest, we know some students pass exams because they are lucky and guess correctly. Others just memorize answers and within no time, they forget. So did they learn, but only for a day or a week? How long does learning have to last "to count" as learning? It is amazing how often we fool ourselves even though we know better.

> To involve oneself in the give and take of rejoinders is to risk a pathway, a pathway populated with the pendant ambiguity *of* questioning others. Questionings and answerings as rejoinders do not ultimately define the questioner or the answerer.

Otherness and uncertainty call to Lena.

In our rush to develop competencies that all students have to meet, we run away from the ambiguousness of the problem of everything being different from everything else that stands right in front of us. In ignoring it, we have made it invisible. For example, what if a student fails to demonstrate a procedure successfully, like catheterizing a patient? Imagine giving every student time to repeat these procedures until they can successfully demonstrate their learning. We are lucky if we can provide one clinical experience for a student, let alone several. Do we just accept the simulation lab as an acceptable acontextual alternative, lower the students' grades, and pass them on to the next course with these deficiencies? Sort of like, "You did some things wrong but it was good enough so we pass you on"!

> Certainty is its own two-sided releasement. Is the task offered to human beings to be resolutely certain or resolutely uncertain? Or can human beings let the play of the certain/uncertain be the encountering of a countering call for meaningful conversation? The dance around binary oppositions hobbles that which gives, lets the human being of openness to thinking-saying.

Lena expresses her position in a nutshell.

This is where competency-based nursing gets us into trouble. How many and what part of a skill or procedure can you get wrong and still get credit; what percentage of competencies do you need to achieve? Now there is something we never talk about because we know we would never agree. We know catheterizing is a risky procedure and no matter how good the learning simulation is, we know testing learning by asking students to do the procedure on a live person is difficult. The procedure when simulated is similar but never identical to the range of human anatomy students encounter. However, if a student does not learn to do this skill, the risk to the patient of developing an infection is high. This is just one way that competency based education just doesn't work and we know it, but we refuse to see it or even talk about it. We just say, "Well, nothing's perfect" and go on our merry way. All the while this approach to teaching and learning is like a big invisible elephant in the background waiting to stomp on us.

When schooling learning teaching is sighted as an invisible co-occurring phenomenon, different pathways to thinking-saying show themselves. The certainty afforded by a tradition, which passes over learning as an invisible phenomenon, gathers and engages Lena as she listens to the silent call inherent in the present absence of certainty. This narrative telling allows reader-listeners to sight and participate in Lena's risking the thought that the perfectly obvious is not so obvious after all.

What are the consequences to students and teachers of the nonmeasurability of invisible phenomena? Can such phenomena even be considered and explored? In this narrative, phenomena such as time, space, and measure answer that they are self-evident until they are questioned after. All of these seemed to be available to mere sensory perception. The persistence of questioning the answers enables the place where problems as mere abstractions let a richer sense of understanding show itself (*TM*, 376).

How can a glimpse be caught of something that cannot be seen, like love or intent? How can something be listened to that cannot be heard, like silence? How can something be measured that has no extent, like gentility? The image or metaphor of a roadblock is a convenient one, but does an image or a metaphor reasonably initiate or lead meaningful conversation? Images and metaphors can serve to block hermeneutical explication as they harbor a propensity to contribute to the freezing or abstracting of thought (*POR*, 46-49). We have implied that humans are not the master of the giving, granting, and bestowal of everything that is. But in this claim, mastery lurks and thinking is claimed by the illusion wherein humans, as defined by modernity, everywhere and always encounter *only* themselves (*QCT*, 27).[11]

The Time *of* Hermeneutic Phenomenology

> *True time is the nearness of presencing out of present, past and future—the nearness that unifies time's opening threefold extending.*
>
> OTB, 16

Hermeneutic phenomenology marks finitude as the always already underway. For Heidegger, finitude shows up as the necessity of being-toward-death, wherein the human being can never be complete, or willfully complete itself. To be the open clearing is to be exposed to the on-coming of temporality's historically situated always already. Gadamer takes up this thought by trying to "hold fast to the inexhaustibility of the experience" of sense (*TI*, 24). Jean-Luc Nancy contributes to the conversation by pursuing sense as finite in terms of his rejection of the logics of transcendence or immanence (James, 2006, 95). Finitude is shared; it is the infinite sharing of human beings as singular plurals. It always already gives/lets/discloses itself as the sense of excess: the excess of meaning.

Ontologically, being unto death is the nearness of the far. Death as becoming is the ontic possibility of the impossibility of being at all. The past is always already in front of the human being, as the alreadiness of its being delivered over to being-in-the-world and being-of-the-world (*BT*, 41). There is an always already presence-to that cannot escape the withdrawal of future and past. The disclosure of sense is "a coming that is *neither immanent nor transcendent*" (*SW,* 17). "The now" becomes an enigmatic paradox such that it sends out an invitation for the presence of its own absence.

For Heidegger, "there is obviously something necessary about the belonging together of time and of the human being's unfolding essence" (*ZS,* 38). The belonging-to-task of hermeneutic phenomenology is to always already let the retrieval of sense, such that this letting-retrieval does not depend on establishing the clarity of the putative "difference between psychic particularity and historical significance" (*TM,* 513). In this sense hermeneutic phenomenology is a prudent practice belonging to a time-space whose self-retrieving movement is always yet to come. Retrieval does not exist as repetition but as a phenomenon of historicality.

The positivist view that knowledge is the universal, as established by the principle of empirico-calculative science, is hereby called into question. Any claim to calculative finality depends on predetermined problems but is undermined by the mystery of time. Mystery and time belong to each other such that "it is precisely finitude that comes to view—not only [human] finitude, but the finitude of [disclosing and beckoning] itself" (*OTB,* 49). [12] Disclosing and beckoning (*4S,* 60-61) is hereby seen as the "mysterious temporal structure of [retrieval], whereby the same text always says something different in different contexts and at different times" (*HWT,* 195).

The significance that belongs to time is that time is always already time-for. Divorced from an ego-subject's act of intending doing something, the "for" of time is something other than that act, a comportment to something, or even a directedness toward something. Time does not admit of being added to such that "it is subsequently related to something else" (*ZS,* 43). When the attempt is made to add to time, the infinite character of time presences itself.

The measurement of time as a neutral, undifferentiated sequence of now points is not to be presupposed as the "authoritative form of knowledge" (*ZS,* 50). Time is other than a matter of measurement or indifference. This indifference, in the guise of objectivity as it is "paradigmatic to natural sciences, hinders the way in discussing the relationship between humankind and time, thus blocking proper questions about the peculiar characteristic of time" (ZS, 58). This peculiarity obtains "as the human being's sojourn temporalizes itself in it" (ZS, 66). Time gives itself "as disposable and disposed of for something, emerges as such in expecting [the future as on-coming becoming], retaining [the past as alreadiness], and making present [as presence-to]. This is the temporizing of the time we 'have' and 'do not have' in its threefold unity" (ZS, 67).

The attempt to hypostatize time is further complicated by the necessity of adding presence to time. An eternal verity needs constant presence to enable it to be itself. The only recourse here is to look to the necessary infinite regression of some theory of theories or to adhere to the necessity of an all-knowing infinite wisdom (God). Measured time requires a "now" that is exactly like any other "now." That reduced "now" needs a discrete event or occurrence of some fixed something somewhere.

The enigma of time offers a hint when humans attempt to resolve the putative gap between psyche and soma. The precise point where and when a specific neurotransmitter molecule is between a vesicle and a postsynaptic receptor is necessary to complete at least a tentative working model of a brain. Of course, this is only another necessary step on the path of the science of small things. The question still remains: Where is intentionality as well as meaning, sense, and significance located, if all there is is merely the conceptualization of an isolated ego-subject, putatively trapped in the tautology of a conscious awareness that is merely aware of consciousness?

Gadamer addresses time as historically effected consciousness (TM, 341-379). For him, consciousness is not a discrete quantifiable phenomenon but obtains as the readiness to accept that the human being cannot possess perfect enlightenment. The rejoining give and take of question and answer anticipates answers that acknowledge that questions are themselves part of a tradition and that they take themselves as addressed by it as an experiencing of its conversation (TM, 378-379).

Jean-Luc Nancy offers (articulates) that the temporal play-space wherein "the opening of a space-time for the distribution of singularities, each of whom singularly plays the unique and plural role" is a worlding of a co-existing self (*BSP*, 66). The self "is each time at a remove from immanence or from the collective, but is also each time co-essential to the coexistence of each one" (*BSP*, 66). Time as each time or this time "is not the time of an origin, nor the origin of time: It is the spacing of time, the opening up of the possibility of saying 'we' and enunciating and announcing by this 'we' the [historicality] of existence" (*BP*, 163-164).

Space: Granting Something Its Place

> *What is germane to the time-space of true time consists in the mutual reaching out and opening up of future, past and present.*
>
> OTB, 14

Can space have a whereabouts? An answer to asking, "When is time?" is as incorrect as is the question "Where is space?" (*ZS*, 33). According to science, space is a homogenous system of points, as indifferent locations or as an indifferent occurrence. But space is first and foremost what grants something its place (*ZS*, 32). Space in this sense is other than an a priori condition "for the possibility of sensory perception of an object" (*ZS*, 114). In order for space to co-determine, in the same way that any object of science requires, time must be frozen into the *nunc stans* of one unchanging present and such that space can be reduced to a universalized abstraction (*ZS*, 30-33).

Prior to its being abstracted, the spatial is the open of engaged encountering. The open as the open clearing engages the human being such that "time is not the product of [human beings], [human beings are] not the product of time. There is no production there. There is only giving in the sense of extending which opens up time-space" (*OTB*, 16). Time-space is thought of as "the openness which opens up in the mutual self-extending" (*OTB*, 14) of becoming, alreadiness, and presence-to (*HNA*, 215). Engaged openness as the crossing "passage from one place to another *needs time*" while concomitantly and "reciprocally, originary time, appearing as such, *needs space*" (*BSP,* 61).

Time as a span "is *significant for* something and is *datable for* something. Thus, simultaneously time is *extended* in its way and is not an isolated now-point" (*ZS,* 59-60). Space is provided, not by dimensional calculations, but as the self-extending of the three moments of time, as the interplay of each toward each (*OTB,* 15). What is proper to time can be neared only via denying time as a present now and letting time withhold itself. Spanning and stretching are not the ordering act of any given individual or individuals cohering in supposed identical moments "but just the reverse: the character of the continuity and spannedness of time, in the common sense, has its origin [incipience] in the original [incipient] stretch of temporality itself as ecstatic" (*BPP,* 270).[13] The bridge in the essay "Building Dwelling Thinking," is a span belonging to, engaged by disclosing and beckoning that cannot obtain without banks supporting, and carrying matters of concern which always already must gather (*PLT,* 151-159). The bridge gathers that which articulates the dynamic nearness of openness as "attentive belonging, mutually tractive draw, persisting hold," and disclosing and beckoning (*HWT,* 180).

The question arises as to whether the stretch of life's course can be stilled without being disrupted (*HWT,* 176-177). An additional question arises that turns on the questionableness of any assertion that claims to bring time to a stand. Time is not an isolatable phenomenon: "Every now, then, and at-the-time, not only has a date but is spanned and stretched within itself" (*BPP,* 264). Therefore, "Time is no longer primarily a gulf to be bridged because it separates; it is actually the supportive ground of the course of events in which the present is rooted" (*TM,* 297). Time sustains human beings as what they are already. The human being belongs to time. The human being of openness can let itself belong to time.

Modernity: The Quest for Certainty

For modernity the presupposition of measurability is the homogeneity of space and time.

ZS, 213

The self-imposed roadblocks inherent in the subject-object paradigm of modernity consist of the compelling need for measurability in order to establish proximity. In that modernity is based on various conceptions of consciousness, it traps itself in its own barrier to any unfolding of the question of the historical-temporal offerings of matters of concern. After all, what could be nearer to me than—me? As a starting from the *ego cogito* (I think, therefore I am), modernity's basic self-constitution is "to have no windows from which something could either enter or exit. In this way, the *ego cogito* is an enclosed space" (*4S,* 70). As a self-imposed, self-enclosed space, modernity became faced with the need to deal with the problem of discrete enclosures. The subject-object paradigm of modernity struggles with how to link enclosed objects with enclosed (pure) ego-subjects.

Human beings of openness are historically-temporally disposed (opened) in their dealings with matters of concern. In *Basic Questions of Philosophy,* Heidegger explores fundamental disposedness[14] in terms of the Greek sense of wonder and its play in terms of not knowing. In contrast, as he reads the historicality of openness, modernity came to be claimed by another path: "The primordial questioning knowledge and the holding firm before the concealed, have been replaced by a domination over everything, since everything has become obvious" (*BQP,* 168). When everything becomes obvious, questioning that resides in the giving of the unconcealed as such becomes "a sign of a lack of the power to act" (*BQP,* 169).

The sighting of hermeneutic phenomenology is "compelled by the most hidden and consequently the deepest need of the age, and by that alone" (*BQP,* 170). In other words, "the semblance of obviousness" is exigency as the most uncanny "need arising from the lack of need" (*BQP,* 171). Need here is not a fundamental lack or the misery of impoverishment. Rather, need is the incompleteness that resides in exigency as possibility, wherein an abundance can arise to counter the restrictions of "the field of view of calculating reason" (*BQP*, 132). Thus for Heidegger, the engaged openness of subject matter to questioning as the play of enjoining offers ways of inquiry (*ZS*, 132). The immeasurable (love, hate, mourning, happiness) cannot be scientifically objectified. They can only be thematized via hermeneutic practices. The human being is transported to themes by their ownmost compelling exigency—it is disposed to deal with them (*BQP*, 134-135).

Human dealings-with are "the sharing of a simultaneous space-time" (*BSP*, 65). This is the presencing-crossing of absencing origins of sense such that sense advenes "mutually and only mutually" (*BSP*, 83). Sense is the fullest measure of the meanings of space-time. There is no speaking of the meaning of space without time; there is no speaking of the meaning of time without space. Thoughts that turn on any notion of sharing put themselves at risk of being dismissed as mere sentimentality or romanticism. On the other hand, if there is a together, what does together consist of— if it consists of anything? Space-time takes place essentially as discursivity; the saying-showing of language.

A nursing student, Latraya, shares her dealing-with experiences.

> *I'm a senior and it worries me that so many nurses have an attitude problem . . . too many are selfish, uncaring and insensitive. And when you get down to it, nursing students are no different. Has this always been the case? You can always hope they will change, but I sure would not want some of them taking care of me when I am sick. I see both nurses and nursing students who are rude, disrespectful and they ridicule patients behind their back. Our nursing instructors talk about caring and being nonjudgmental, yet they do not walk the talk. This is not what we see when we sit in on faculty meetings! At the end of the semester we evaluate teachers,*

and once a group of us wrote how disrespectful this particular teacher was and gave actual different examples. Nothing happened. She treated another group of students the same way the next semester! At the end of the term when we go over our clinical checklist with our teachers, we get rated on "caring" and on being "nonjudgmental" on a scale of 1 to 5. What a farce! No one ever fails a course because they are judgmental or uncaring!

In its widest sense care is shared as a common lot. Heidegger opened up a reading of care such that even Latraya's "uncaring" individuals are claimed by care. One way of caring is to be uncaring. Caring and uncaring are not without each other; they dwell together. Without care, caring humans could not recognize uncaring.

Latraya goes on to expand on her singular-plural sojourn.

Most of the time our teachers have so much to worry about in supervising us that they don't have time to listen to us talking with our patients or checking out whether our thinking is judgmental or respectful or not—they only see us when we are performing some skill or doing a procedure or giving medicines. When one of us brings up how a nurse treated a patient disrespectfully, it's like the teacher is afraid to talk about it. We only hear how we might have misunderstood what was happening or what we heard. . . . When one of the students brought up labeling a patient a "frequent flier" as an uncaring thing to say, our teacher minimized this label as a common one and just a way nurses have of venting their frustrations. Students are bad too. And I think most teachers either ignore students with attitude problems or they try to catch them on other things, and deduct points from their care plans or clinical papers so they get a lower grade. They avoid entirely any discussion of caring and incivility on anyone's part. It's like it's too subjective or the teachers can't agree on what uncaring really is. I thought objectivity was the main point of our time. But then why can they be so secure in what caring is, that they can grade us on it! And take up a whole part of the course with content on caring.

> The binary oppositions of good care/bad care or empathetic caring/indifferent caring forget or overlook the unity of care. The engaged openness of the human being of openness is to be claimed by and addressed by the quickening of care as it belongs to disclosing and beckoning.

When interpreted in terms of Latraya's situatedness, care shows itself as a listening-sighting "as."

Even when they observe behavior by a nurse that is uncaring or disrespectful, they say nothing and when I challenged my instructor once and said, "Shouldn't we say something to that nurse?" she said, "We're guests on this unit and we need to keep this as a clinical site for students. She's just having a bad day."

> World reveals itself as matters of concern addressed by engaged openness. One is at-tuned and re-attuned by the historicality of each new calling.

World is not an abstract dimension; world and Latraya are always already with each other.

It's really discouraging because I think we should work harder on understanding caring, and being open, respectful and inclusive. We should talk about civility in nursing practice, even if we can't teach it or measure it. I mean, these are difficult things, but important things, and we should pay more attention to them as nurses! They matter! Even if we can't always agree on what was or was not disrespectful in a particular situation, it's good to even talk about that . . . that we can't agree and why. I think it would be great to discuss "What does it mean to NURSES when a patient or students are disrespectful?" Patients call nurses bad names and students label teachers. It is such a common uncaring and hurtful practice, yet we all think of ourselves as caring. Can nothing be done? How can teachers think that by talking about all the kinds of caring and how to be culturally sensitive and non judgmental, students are going to become caring? Using competencies to evaluate us on caring, when we think the teacher is uncaring towards us, is the height of hypocrisy! One nursing student told me she has never felt so "beaten up" and "uncared for" in her life. And I suspect some patients, nurses, and teachers feel the same way.

How are we to think the moments of learning and nursing such as solicitude, inclusiveness, respect, and civility that cannot be measured? Do they not matter? How are these being taught and learned? Engaging oneself, in this case as dealing-with, reveals the ineffability in Heidegger's notion of care. Solicitude as a moment that belongs to care cannot be required, measured, predicted, or assured. It can only be freely given as a reciprocal possibility (*ZS*, 110, 224).

Thinking as it is claimed by the securing of calculatable magnitudes or extents is reduced to "nothing more than a manipulation of operational concepts, representational models, and models of thinking" (*ZS*, 107). It follows then "that the absolute self-certainty of the human being as the subject asserting itself, contains and [takes] standards [as] the possible determination of the objectivity of objects" (*ZS*, 107). The necessary endgame of technoscientism must be "to so objectify experience that it no longer contains any historical element" (*TM*, 346). With the attempted removal of anything other than a putative historical and temporal objectivism, methods insofar as they pretend to objectivity "are concerned to guarantee that . . . basic experiences can be repeated by anyone" (*TM,* 347).

For epistemology, "with its confident aspirations of achieving a rationally grounded certainty and comprehensive conceptual mastery," the needless as the nonexigent is morally the unnecessary (Hogan, 2002, 215).[15] But for Heidegger, "experience of the lack of exigency as such is a necessity" (*N4,* 250). The will to incontrovertible evidence dismisses "anything less than certainty as a deficiency that must be eradicated" (Hogan, 2002, 218). The immeasurable is devalued into a value (*N4,* 250) whereby "anything less than an all-inclusive account marks a failure" of the application of method (Hogan, 2002, 219).[16]

Any questioning can become "entrapped in a desire for having direct mastery over its subject matter by accepting the self-absenting of its own presuppositions," a stance that inhibits any attempt to place an inquiry into a more originary pathway (Schalow, 1992, 41). A first step is to accept that there is absence that gives presence—there is a play of mutual releasement that belongs to and claims thought as practical *and* as an ethos practically and prudently opened to that which is questioned. Human beings "are always already there at each instant" such that they must participate "each time, each time making their entrance anew" (*BSP,* 71).

Entrance is arrival and departure at once. The opened open; openings' movement "as *sense* is always a movement to, onto, or a passage and spacing of sense, which is irrecoverable and ungraspable, but which nevertheless *is* the space of the world as meaningful, intelligible, and experienceable as such" (James, 2006, 102). World arrives around sense but never admits itself of *the* right answer which could serve to identify the efficacy of judging. As its own origin world is the mysterious wonder of "the *being-with of each time with every time*" (*BSP,* 83). World is the mutual as the opening of intelligible space and is "always presupposed whenever we experience anything at all" (James, 2006, 103). Engagement as place, sense, and world discloses and beckons as other than the consciousness defined by the Cartesian tradition of thought. The rationales of transcendence and immanence as given by philosophies of consciousness wander about in an ambit, which cannot have meaning, sense, and significance at any place outside of the ego-self. The world, as a with-world, is here first: "it worlds" (*HWT,* 130-132).[17]

The place of Latraya's story is engaged space and time such that it is its own opening-up. Spaces as opened up "can occur only as temporality, and temporality can occur only as the historical opening up of spaces, that is, space-time" (James, 2006, 105). Modernity's distinctions of mind and body, the ideal and the real, and what cognition is per se belong to the prior "passage of sense as a bodily event, as an opening up of meaningful spaces and a meaningful world" (James, 2006, 107).

The question that calls forth thinking is, Can any forced removal of historical tradition, the inherent fluidity of language and the future as possibilities, obtain as a finality? We now propose to explore how hermeneutic phenomenology attempts to present a transposing step back. The disclosing sense of *theōrein,* as participatory openness, will be retrieved from the attempt at closure, which is and must be the hallmark of modernity's conceptualization and appropriation of "theory" as *the* conclusive answer. When there is asking, there is a richness that dwells in experiencing, as the way human beings are already engaged.

Chapter 1 Notes

1	See also *BT*, 188-195, and section 63.

2	See also *GBT*, 319.

3	See J. Diekelmann, 2005, fn. 53, for explication of Dasein.

4	See J. Diekelmann, 2005, 3-57, for a further discussion of retrieving.

5	See also *PLT* and *OWL*.

6	See also *HWT*, 128.

7	See also *OBT*, v.

8	See also *PM*, 150-154.

9	See also *GBT*, 121-123, 152, 180.

10	See Glazer, 2007, 44-45.

11	See also *TM*, 376.

12	See also *ZS*, 179.

13	See also *BT*, 426-427.

14	For further explication of disposedness as "the structure of having been already addressed by what is to be taken into the question," consult von Herrmann, 1996, 187.

15	For further discussion of the claims of epistemology on nursing education see N. Diekelmann, 2002d, "Too much content . . . : Epistemologies' grasp and nursing education," *Journal of Nursing Education, 41*(11), 469-470.

16	See also Thompson, 2002, 142, and Bonnett, 2002, 231-234.

17	See also *TDP*, 59-61, and *RHT*, 276-277.

Chapter 2

Getting Around the Theoretical Surround

> *What inconspicuous state of affairs conceals*
> *itself in the essence of science?*
>
> *QCT,* 171

In tracking the historicality of "theory," as this term is laid claim to by theory-driven science, one is struck by what the modern sense of theory does not say. The inconspicuous state of affairs that theory turns on is marked by modernity's rule of the theoretical as a fundamental principle that orders the cutting off of any and all further questioning (*PM,* 133). The task of hermeneutic phenomenological thinking is to ponder the silence residing in such putative obstacles in order to arrive at a richer and more appropriate way of asking after the showing of a phenomenon. Each question "that does justice to its issue [issuing forth/generation, emergence/incipience] is already a bridge to its answer" (*PM,* 232). The inconspicuous obstacle to thought, hidden in the modern practices of science, equates theory with intuitive comportment such that presencing and presence are placed "more at the finished end of science rather than at its interrogative beginnings" (*GBT,* 277).

Science as theory emerges as the enclosure of matters of concern such that these are allowed no escape. Theory, thought in this sense, admits of no connection to practical concerns but must obtain as "a 'pure' looking around" (*BH,* 260). Theory as such is "ordered to the eternal and unchanging" separatable from the practical as "ordered to the changeable" (*HPM,* 299). Science cannot answer, cannot get around, the question: "Is the supreme mode of going along with the matter called *[theōria]*, by leisurely lingering with it, really without care or a particular escalation of its movement?" (*GBT,* 240).[1]

How does thinking get around a theoretical surround that obtains as the pure beholding of pure movement? A hermeneutic phenomenological reading of theory is thinking that disturbs the "undisturbed leisurely lingering" (*GBT,* 268) of "theory as a position that takes matters of concern lightly and makes them 'easy.'" The historical saying-showing of *[theōrein]* cum theory reveals a more or less continuous progression of observing from the direct cognizance and initial orientation of *aesthesis* [sensory apprehension/perception] to the pure beholding *[theōrein]* of the Greco-European tradition of philosophical thinking (*GBT,* 239), especially as it occurs in its Anglo-American variants. The task of hermeneutic phenomenology is to retrieve theory such that it can be released from the varieties of "stable self-fulfillment of [perfect presence to itself]" (*GBT,* 243) back to a sighting, which sights that which lets itself be sighted as the engaged openness of matters of concern.[2]

Consciousness

The possibility that the universal world formula will enable the human being to be produced, just like any other object, trips up on the enclosed space (immanence) of conceptualizations of consciousness (*4S,* 68-72). Consciousness, as an issue for variants of analytical philosophy, psychology, and neuroscience, arrived as a foregrounded problem only with the advent of the Cartesian *cogito ergo sum* as modernity's "invention of the mind" (Rorty, 1980, 17-69).[3] Moreover, the advent of consciousness (mind) as a doctrine presented its own set of predetermined requirements. First and foremost among these was the necessity for somehow establishing pure consciousness in order for philosophies of consciousness/mind to be considered a valid science.

Heidegger's erstwhile mentor, the philosopher Edmund Husserl, provided an important clue for interpretive thinking when he uncovered the phenomenon of categorial intuition. Kisiel avers that in opposition to Kant, Husserl maintained that both sensed objects and judgment forms obtain in observations by subjects. This is looked on as a co-presentation, wherein "categorial intuition accompanies every sense intuition. Apperception [co-perception] is there with every perception, appresentation [as making things present, co-presentation] with every presentation. There is 'more' to seeing than meets the eye" (*HWT,* 45). But for Heidegger, Husserl's relational structure of the meaning of meaning-bestowing acts was a mere construct that served to block access to meaning as such (*ZS,* 208).

In Kantianisms, the primary assertion is that sense data are a given. Husserl called this into question by arguing that any "is," insofar as it pertains to meanings, harbors within itself a surplus or excess that calls for a different act. Kant's reading of the philosophical problem of being wherein one immediately understood entities in their contextualized *thats, whats,* and *hows,* was not to be derived from his tabulated categories of judgments, but rather from self-presences as phenomena. Husserl read the correlation of objects and ego-subject as other than a concrete instance or moment of "a corporeal individual" (*HPM,* 296). In his own way, Husserl was also denied access to the temporal-historical structure of engaged openness and the possibility of the human being of openness by "his self-restriction to the issues of consciousness and objectivity" (*HMT,* xiv). The question that ensues is whether any putative isolatable consciousness and unconditioned objectivity are the stuff of truth as both eternal and free of time.

The project of modern science is to proceed toward the goal of valid, repeatable experiences. "Experience is valid only if it is confirmed; hence its dignity depends on its being in principle repeatable" (*TM,* 347). For Gadamer, "Husserl projects the idealized world of exact scientific experience into the original experience of the world, in that he makes perception, as something directed toward merely external physical appearances, the basis of all other experience" (*TM*, 347).

The articulation of the human being as intentional called into question the mixtures of logical-theoretical and natural-scientific abstractions as they were thought to manifest themselves in psychophysical and neurological processes. Mere sense perception cannot take into account the surplus of meanings that accompanies any seeing.

For example, a newly diagnosed Type II diabetic patient can be merely a diagnostic category that reflects a particular metabolic condition. This patient, experienced categorially, can be appreciated as an ego-subject rather than treated as a mechanism. As a mother living in poverty, with three children, no health insurance, and a possible future of compromised access to anticipated healthcare needs, she *is* as a historical context. In this example, techno-medicine would end its client involvement with the treatment of the quantifiable manifestations of the disease. Transcendental-eidetic phenomenological thinking would bracket out the historically particular world of the patient and treat her, medically speaking, as primarily an isolated instance of an absolutely certain ego-subject. This could obtain as the monitoring of her compliance with preestablished dietary restrictions and her acceptance of the installation on her body of an insulin pump. Deviation from these procedures shows up in her records as merely noncompliance. Her individual situation need not be taken into account if she is treated according to nationally established treatment protocols. These protocols can deal only with idealized abstractions.

Husserlian phenomenology turns on the performance of "the absolutely self-positing transcendental ego" in order to fulfill pure intentionality or constitution. Therefore the putative necessity of theoretical disengagement is a closure, which brackets the entire "natural attitude" from any always already understanding world as engaged openness of matters of concern. The natural attitude of Husserlian phenomenology is claimed by a prior theoretical attitude wherein the conscious human being as the primary phenomenon is seen as something present: composed of mere perception and self-constitution as "purely ideal essential content" (*GBT,* 394-396). Mere objects (real or not) of consciousness are intended by a theoretically informed pure consciousness as a phenomenological-transcendental reduction such that in their essential or ideal whatness they are freed from any extraneous individuating characteristics (*HPM,* 296).

Disengaged looking away hereby becomes read by Heidegger as the forgetting or overlooking of the historicality and the particularity of worldly contexts of meaning. In contrast, he posited that every intending already understands engaged openness and therefore any phenomenological method must simply be the *practice of thematizing of everyday life.* This entailed a step back from thematic objects as "the purely ideal essential content" (*GBT,* 395) of intentional acts. This is not a looking back to a pure consciousness, reflecting only its ideal self. Rather it is a thematic retrieving of the realm of possibilities taken as possibilities, which are the practical, prudent, already involved engaged openness dimension of matters of concern: their way of presencing. Phenomenological thinking for Heidegger was not grounded in the reduction of phenomena to mere entities. The task for phenomenology, as it is hermeneutic, was to let be seen "a simple and direct leading to" (*BH,* 178) what one's radically open understanding is: that which was enabled, by what "makes possible [enables] all understanding of things [matters of concern] as this or that" (Thomas Sheehan in *BH,* 305)—their engaged openness (*HPM,* 296-297). Therefore, *first and foremost the human being of openness is always already becoming the moment of its mortality, such that the presence of its possible absence is concomitantly the absence of its possible presence. This lack of perfect self-presence is what enables finite understanding and precludes the perfect understandability of any entity.*

Despite the nature of Husserl's intellectual breakthrough, a question remained: How could something unperceived by the senses be intuited (*HWT,* 45)? The issue turns on the enabling of the enabled, that is, the possibilizing of the possibilizing loci of meaning (*GT,* 308). The human being catches sight of entities immediately but it does not sight their immediate existing (presencing) as such. *Existing as such is the invisible historical-temporal how.* Heidegger, in contrast to Husserl, asserted that the *originary* work of phenomenology is hermeneutic, such that any "how" rests in "a prior gathering of any thematic ontological concern into a question" (Schalow, 1992, 85). The questions of questionings are an always already give and take underway toward co-responding with the call that calls the human being of openness into question. The silent call that calls forth thinking is the very what that calls the human being of openness to thought: finitude.

Hermeneutic phenomenological questioning turns on the emergence (issuing forth) of a "how" becoming present-to the always already play of sense. This emergence discloses and beckons as the living presence of facticity (*GBT,* 260) such that "ontology gathers momentum from itself to gain sufficient 'leverage' to achieve entryway into its 'subject matter,' to arrive at the 'phenomenon' under scrutiny" (Schalow, 1992, 85). Matters themselves as matters of concern are the task of hermeneutic phenomenology. Sense as articulation and prefigurings, which call the human being of openness forward to itself, show themselves as the meaning and significance of factical life. Phenomenological listening obtains as the categorial seeing and hearing of prefigured meanings, which call the human being into the finite future.

The ties to the Cartesian conception of consciousness leave Husserl's thought at a disadvantage. First and foremost, "factic life is not an object but a situation" (*HWT,* 177). Factic life is immediately present and given, not as theorizable objects and isolated things, but as sense and world (*HWT,* 181). Thus, for Heidegger the human being of openness is, in each temporally particular instance, the matter of concern "which is not yet but can be" (*Logic,* lecture course of Winter Semester 1925-1926, 234f, cited in *HWT,* 183). Thought this way, the constant present is not a stasis but an always already thrown open, kinetic on-coming, dependent on its very absence, in order to be what it is.

The Transposition of Sense: The Sense of Transposition

The realm from which one leaps first becomes surveyable in a different way than before. The leap of thinking does not leave behind it, that from which it leaps; rather it assimilates it in a more original fashion.

POR, 60

The enacting of hermeneutic phenomenological thinking-saying is an assembling of moments of insight, which self-emerge/issue forth as a pathway. To be underway, one can choose to undertake the risk of a leap onto a path that guarantees no outcome, but lets possibility *as* possibility arrive. To be dependent on the richness of possibility is the freedom of thought (*EGT,* 55).

Listening is not the product of human willing but obtains as the self-gathering of questions. Transpositions from the closed domain of theory to the open clearing of the matter of concern's lucidity call forth provocativeness. These transpositions, as their calling, invite questioning. Responding to this inviting is only a first step. The incipience of any invitation lies in the play of emergence/elusion (presence/absence, revealing/concealing). Therefore, there is danger in the apparent security of the closure involved in a merely descriptive announcement, which locks matters of concern into unquestioned and preconceived patterns.

Transpositions that are moments of hermeneutic phenomenology, are not determined by set programs, which set up walls between the physical and the nonphysical (the sensible and the nonsensible) such that belonging together as engagement is lost (*POR,* 48). There are puzzling, seemingly random plays that govern the formulations of questioning. Rather than being denied, this seemingly overwhelming randomness must be affirmed in its play as the introduction to interpretive readings that offer thought. True thought, following Heidegger, places the thinker in the phenomenology (saying) of the inapparent, wherein disclosive encircling unconcealment, prior to any possible distinction between theory and practice, lets disclosing and beckoning as that which thinking is led show itself as itself.

Whenever interpretive reading cum conversation/dialogue occurs, matters of concern emerge. These matters are identical neither with concrete topics nor with the register (scope/enclosure/circumscription) into which matters of concern find themselves transposed. One finds oneself as interpreter, drawn into end conditions, which are responsible for the emergence of interpreting. The register engaged in interpreting "is marked by a basic duality: (a) it is meant to provide a means of access to what is interpreted, but (b) it is also the framework into which the subject matter is translated. These two functions of the register are interdependent, and this holds true—at least up to [a] point—even if the register is more or less superimposed on the subject matter. In this case, the framework nevertheless functions as a means of access" (Iser, 2000, 151).

Any pathway as access or passage entails risking a movement, which as a leap from where one finds oneself sees one's former realm in a richer light but also cannot leave it behind as if one were merely changing clothes. Risking the leap "looks back into the leaping-off realm in order to hold it in view" (*POR*, 75). Realms as regions or neighborhoods give hints, but hints and only hints. In any leap of thought one must be prepared to risk a leap. Therefore it is necessary "to make the realm from which one leaps visible and make the relationship one sustains with this realm clear" (*POR*, 93).

Transposing here is not to be taken in the metaphorical sense of abstracting or separating such realms as "the real" and "the ideal" into self-contained frames (*POR*, 47-48).[4] It must not be confused or equated with psychologistic conceptualizations of empathy. Transposing is akin to translating wherein "it is not only a matter of what one is translating at the moment; rather, it is a matter of which language into which language" (*POR*, 97). *Language cannot be separated from its realm, region, or neighborhood.*

Transposing in a discursive sense is taken as a way to move *up* in register or to modulate in a new key. Interpretations thereby introduce thoughts to the always already understood (Groth, 2004, 129). Transpositions, thought as enabling, show as a retreating leap, "the gathering of thinking upon itself, a glance ahead to what comes." As such, "thinking begins anew" (*4S*, 61). Taking our hint from Heidegger, we offer "a few indications that could help us discern various and yet convergent paths of access to the *question* of" disclosing and beckoning (*4S*, 60) as it shows itself in hermeneutic phenomenology and transcendental-eidetic phenomenology.[5]

Hermeneutic phenomenology	Transcendental-eidetic phenomenology
Presuppositions	
• One sights what one says.	• One says what one perceives.
• One can be called away from entities to sense.	• One habitually must go from meaning to entities.
The primary givens	
World-as • Open future—time as the generative source, self-movement of self-understanding from initial absences. Ecstatic emergence/elusion, reference.	*Entities-as* • Constant presence; presence and absence are synthesized into stable stases, totality.
• Understanding of engaged openness. Meaningful whole-pre-predicative, "handy," practical, prudent.	• Categorially intuited predications of perception as manifold.
Temporality-as • Kinetic structures of worldly existing—disclosing as disclosing-nonstatic play, historical openness, possibility.	*Time-as* • Constant, immanent structures of intentional consciousness/transcendental subjectivity, certitude.
• Situated and exposed existence (openness). Meaningful context, situated significance involvements—sense.	• Oriented self-consciousness, pure, pointillistic ego, absolute self-position.
• A way to be, the prepositional nexus of practical and prudent alreadiness.	• A what, a nonnecessary adjunct to pure consciousness.
The primary presence	
• Meaning as possibility—what is immediately present in concerned preoccupation; matters of concern.	• Bodily givenness (actuality) as presence given by cognition—what is perceived, intuited.
• Inconspicuous nonobjective presence of worldliness in its correlative concernedness.	• Overt bodily presence correlative to perceivedness as psychophysical and neurological processes.

Human situatedness	
• Always having to become nonpossessable time and history.	• Absolute consciousness present to itself.
• Dynamically ontological, self-referential, situational (temporal) individuality as singular plural being-with-openedness.	• Epistemologically self-reflective.
• Can become nonhabitual, proper possibilities, not as finished "product"; mortal becoming as the "same-as," but not as an "identical-to."	• Authentic possibilities are possessed by ego—each is theoretically identical with regard to every other ego.
Language-as	
• Plurivocal and subject to vacillation and variation; the possibility of correctness and incorrectness, saying as sense, un-sense, and no longer sense.	• Fixed and defined.
• Humans ordered (claimed) by the saying-showing of discursiveness.	• Ordering of objects according to subsumptive generalizations.
• Concrete historical sense, belonging to dwelling as abiding-with.	• Generic universals.
The exposition of sense as situated	
• Expository interpretation.	• Ideation, intuition.
• Preconscious realm of engaged openness, disclosing and beckoning.	• Acts of consciousness; logical theoretical and natural-scientific abstraction.
• Open finitude, the always already nonpossessable incessance, disposed, finite.	• Possessed by the willful possession of absolute self-presence to itself.
• Already-involved-with structure of care.	• The structure of reason and logic.
• Concerned preoccupation of getting around, interpretation of the as-what.	• Perception of a thing as free-floating and isolated.
• Exigently becoming the enactment character of what presences, absences.	• Finished, complete, constant presence, the ideal essence of what presences.
• Kinetic confluence of the world, the self, time, and dialogic experience.	• Static union between expression and intuition.

Transposing is hereby taken as the venturing steps, into the emergence/elusion of the occurrence of occurring, the reciprocal play of taking something as something. Taking-as obtains, shows up, as the engaged play of being taken by an encountering that is not in one's absolute possession and accepting it, as a being open for reciprocal showing (*ZS*, 5, 223-224). The play of taking something as something transposes the human being of openness into the possible. Practical and prudent comportment always already enables the human being of openness to enter into the open clearing of whatever is possible (*FCM*, 364). The nominal and verbal senses of *taking-as* raise the human being of openness away to possibilities, in the sense of the possibly actual wherein the human being of openness is transposed, such that its infinite finitude delivers it over to its presence/absence as possibility. The human being of openness can "constantly *be mistaken* concerning what is actual" (*FCM*, 366).

Finitude enables the human being of openness to sight actuality as historically situated. If for the Greeks, things simply appeared, and for Kant, things appeared to the ego-subject (*4S*, 36), it can be asserted that modern humans only talk to themselves (*4S*, 37). In modernity's view, everything obtains as "the persistent standing-at-one's disposal" (*4S*, 62) as orderability (*QCT*). Sighting and listening receive their definiteness from the possibility that is historically granted to them.

Nearness and Temporality as Absence and Presence

> *Nearness brings near—draws nigh to one another—*
> *the far and, indeed, as the far.*
>
> *PLT,* 178

The historically particular always already gives a temporal, meaningful, intimate con-tension.[6] This con-tension holds the between of that which comes into view (nearness) and the how of its coming into view. The difference between the absence, out of which matters of concern come to presence, and that which is present is *temporality as the dialogical experience of the nearness of absence and presence.*

Deferral and distance as matters of concern do not appear by means of human fabrication. But neither do they appear without the active involved attendance of the human being who belong to them (*PLT,* 181). Thought and thinking-saying, as we have attempted to let them show themselves, need responding and re-calling in order to be a conjoined thought-of-thinking-saying. Distance is nigh, not as a neutral measurement, but as the always already asymptotic play of historical time-space. Nearness as the asymptote of never getting to the point of some ideal identity comes about (takes place) as a play of disclosing and beckoning (*OWL,* 94).

It is critical for hermeneutic phenomenology to think absence *as* absence. Absence is not the mere ontically determined nonpresence of some formerly present and/or expected presence of person, entity, or matter of concern. Ontic absence turns on something that is physically or ideally merely missing. The privation of what is present is the possible absencing of a matter of concern, as the concomitant moment of remembering and anticipating. Humans understandingly find themselves exposed as a meaningful context that is temporally and historically given (*HWT,* 178). Each human being as a mortal is involved with death as "never something that merely exists, but which nevertheless presences" as possibility (*PLT,* 178). Mortality cannot be thought as a momentary event, which can be dealt with as a biological or technological phenomenon. All human beings arrive in an already historically particular world, only to be commended to/as the mutuality of their ownmost departures. When thought in this way, human finitude obtains as the simplicity of the complex, the complexity of the simple. "The splendor of the simple" (*PLT,* 7) calls to the human being as always underway, wherein the luminosity of death, as being called into darkness, outshines the pointillist illuminations of/by finite humans (*DT,* 89). The variegated play of presence/absence offers and calls such that "somewhere between arrivals and departures" lies the temporal-historical place of sense (Diekelmann, J., 2005, 47).

Time as always already presencing/absencing is not the production of human beings, and human beings are not the output of time. The "scientific model" that makes time a measurement or variable can be forcibly applied to measured time but cannot be applied to temporality. There is only offering "in the sense of extending which opens up time-space" (*OBT,* 16). Time-space obtains in thought, as the open clearing that opens up, in the reciprocal self-extending (giving, offering) of becoming, alreadiness, and presence-to (*HNA,* 209-220). Therefore incipience always already is origin (issuing forth) *as* the always already. The work of interpretive thinking is not to be absorbed in the futile effort to hypostasize time into a static "now" but to let historical time as temporality circulate as an on-coming future becoming, which is lived out of the past, such that the human being bears and is borne by its past is into its on-coming future (*BH,* 271-272).

Temporality arrives from absence and departs to absence such that there dwells in incipience/elusion, "not the poverty of any half- and one-sidedly grasped relation whatever, but an unmined wealth of relations" (*BC,* 94). The incipience of the incipient obtains as attentive belonging which is other than the mission of permanent closure claimed by the will to freeze time into the sameness of an undifferentiated now or an infinite eternity. Temporality is its own transposing play whose call engages human beings as they are, only insofar as they live in nearness to death. As the ultimate possibility of life, human finitude offers the capability "of bringing what is most elevated to the clearing and lighting" to the truth of engaged openness (*POR,* 112).

The truth of temporality dwells (sojourns/whiles/abides) in its denying of its presence. The emergence/elusion of temporality obtains as an offering-gathering of nearness which must include the intimacy of the remote as the noncalculatable nearness of the near (*OTB,* 10-17; *PM,* 286, fn. a).

World/Clearing/Openness

> *. . . where does the clearing come from and how is it given?*
>
> BW, 449

Hermeneutic phenomenology participates as a granting of an open clearing, wherein the human being finds itself "under the control of something beyond [its] ken, where the paths 'to the [matters of concern] themselves' sometimes abruptly trail off into obscurity," and in which thoughts come to all individuals rather than originate in them as ego-subject (*HWT,* 198). Humans can choose to listen or flee and be absorbed (entangled) into a seemingly secure familiarity. *First and foremost hermeneutic phenomenology is a carrying/bearing of a call, an unsettling call.*

The open clearing is not singularly a human creation. Assigning-to, addressing-to, and destining-to self-present as openness, wherein "the human only exists in coming from itself to what is wholly other than itself" (*4S,* 73), that is, temporal play-space as the engagement of matters of concern. The primacy of theoretical notions of self-productive consciousness and its necessary consequence, the primacy of the human, can be left to itself, attenuated, or perhaps even abandoned, in order to more clearly discern that "there is a fated correlativity between the human ability to know and the ability of entities to be known" (*N,* 294). Engaged openness obtains as a play of access and relatedness, such that dialogical experience and understanding co-occur, only as there is something offered, albeit as possibly something that is a material absence (*BPP,* 10-11). World as this play presents itself "as a totality of references rather than a totality of things" (*GBT,* 375).

World/clearing/openness is historical-temporal such that, as an always already, each human being is responsible for owing a debt to engaged openness. The latter receives what is owed to it as an offering from humans such that they are reciprocally called and enabled to accept participation in engaged openness and thereby cannot disown or deny it. The human being of openness is free for making sense of prudent and practical action (*FT,* 178-179).

The ontological sense of freedom discloses and beckons as the opened clearing that is prior to the historically situated oppositional, irresolvable, and causal determinations of "free will" (the absolute and arbitrary spontaneity of subjective choice) versus "determinism" (the absolute fatalism of external fate).[7] We will touch on "freedom-for" as a moment of the heart of the human being of openness later in this book. The human being of openness is always already free for taking engaged openness as a theme but can never be free of the claim of engaged openness' disclosing and beckoning.

The gift/offering of exposed, open, engaged openness is the yet-to-be of a possible can-be (*GBT*, 434). Finite (mortal) human beings are on the way, as they are drawn along by their very lack of final, full self-presence. This lack possesses/claims/calls each human being and defines its proper and unique historical essence. Human finitude is the offering that is conjointly responsible for/to the various dispensations of engaged openness (*PS*, 199).

These dispensations are offerings, historical givenness, conditionedness, and hints: They are that which is open to be thought, such that thinking is engaged as thinking-saying. Thinking-saying gives (shows) itself as being discursively engaged "by the human being's having to do with it" (*ZS*, 8). The human being is endowed with thought such that it is "at once enabled and enacted by [engaged openness] itself" (*RHT*, 264). Thoughts qua thoughts presuppose world/clearing/openness but cannot create (produce, fabricate) it (*OTB*, 64-66). The open clearing allows (offers/gives/admits) passage. Thinking stems from the passage of thoughts, not the other way around. Thoughts and their thinking-saying are dispensed as a gift (offering); they are passed on to the human being of openness as its ownmost passage.

Hermeneutic phenomenology reads the human being such that its capacity to be affected *as* sense touches it both as passivity (receptive of "the givenness of what is given") and as activity (reception as the "'active' participation in givenness itself") (Raffoul, 1997, xviii). The human being is indebted to (liable for) sense. To be indebted to (liable for) sense is to be capable "of receiving and welcoming it" (*GT,* 69).

Thinking as thanking (acknowledging, accepting) opens as a possibility wherein the debt of the human being, to the dispensation (givenness) of matters of concern as they while (abide/dwell/sojourn) sense, is paid off, but never settled, as the proper catching of what is thrown. Catching (listening) is brought forth as a possibility of performing and executing (enabled and enacted), origination and accomplishment "only in the moment of response" (Richardson, 1974, 602). Human beings stand (while/sojourn/dwell) and endure (undergo dialogical experience) as openness in the open clearing wherein the latter is given (commended to) thinking. The conversation/ dialogue of thinking-saying cannot be let into (released to) the open clearing by some diffuse (eternal) unboundedness. Thinking as thinking-saying is freed for the open clearing as incipience (presence/absence, emergence/elusion), which abides (sojourns/ whiles/dwells) as the temporal-historical play-space of sense. Thinking's essential unfolding limit is a telling of the dependency that tells dependent human beings of their finitude as it properly binds (calls) them to their belonging to it (*WCT,* 142, 146).

The call is a pointing, offering an abode "which in calling to and upon, in reaching out and inviting, directs" (*WCT,* 124) the human being in its practical and prudent comportment. More essentially, "in every calling, a call has already gathered. The calling is not a call that has gone by, but one that has gone out and as such is still calling and inviting; it calls even if it makes no sound" (*WCT,* 124). Heidegger realized the dangerous, enigmatic way of this traversal. His task was an odyssey that took him into the midst of unsettling questions. Heidegger's questioning asked after (pursued) the incipience and disappearance of calling such that in its provenance dwell possibilities that "still [direct] even today's thinking on its way" (*WCT,* 167). There is a calling to attention that enables questions such as these (*WCT,* 124-125) to be enacted:

- "Where does the calling come from that calls" on the human being to think?
- "In what does this calling consist?"

- "How can it make its claim on" the human being?
- "How does the calling reach" the human being?
- "How does [the call] reach down into the [human being's proper essence (the human being of openness)] in order to demand from" it that its proper essence be one of thinking?
- "From what source could the calling into thought come than from something that in itself [exigently] needs thought, because the source of the calling wants to be thought about in its very [essence], and not just now and then?"

The human being is called on to think and appealed to to think, such that thought is claimed for itself by the calling as belonging to that which proffers food for thought. For Heidegger, the proffering call that commends the opened human essence to thought is not a forced containment. It sets free a mutual belonging to the finite decisiveness that the human being of openness is such that to think in this way "establishes the free scope of freedom" in which the proper, unique human essence may sojourn (*WCT*, 132-133).

The clearing is the open region of space-time, which infinitely grants (offers) unconcealment as finitude. As an offering, the play of granting remains concealed. The open clearing obtains as possibility and not as correctness and dependability. The closure of thinking—thought as mere representation, ideation, view, hearing, opinions, and notions—elides the simple acknowledgment (acknowledging/accepting/thanking) of thinking-saying as an offering (gifting). The givenness of entities/matters/issues/world belongs to the open clearing; the open clearing exigently needs matters of concern to be itself. The open clearing sets one "the task of learning from it while questioning-it, that is, of letting it say something" (*BW*, 442).[8] The open clearing is to be simultaneously taken-as in its nominal and verbal sense. But the open clearing is not any entity and possesses no time. The open clearing has a listening-for that possesses no ears. The open clearing can receive because there is an open sending/sender who neither produces nor fabricates.

The engaged openness of matters of concern "is neither a hypostatized 'subject' nor something that stands opposite to and independent of human beings, but refers to the worldly horizon or field of presencing the open expanse, in which [matters of concern] first show themselves and appear as such" (McNeill, 2001, 134).[9] Engaged openness as understood here is not engagement for consciousness (sense data) (*RAS*, 153), protocol statement (*RAS*, 154-155, 163), or mathematical abstraction (*RAS*, 156), which are all forms attributed to the indubitability of self-consciousness (*RAS*, 157). The leaving of the subject-object duality to itself allows thinking-saying the alreadiness of human ends, as the complex play of the interlocking practical, prudent, purposive directions of human social existence. The practical essence of human comportment is sustained as that which enables and claims the everydayness of the prudent social conduct that determines human beings (*RAS*, 165). Historicality as alreadiness allows (gives) presence-to to the receptive human being of openness such that historicality is involved with its possible becoming (*RAS*, 166).

As drawn into the open future, the human being comes across questions that emerge as rejoinders as they ask for their own direction. For metaphysics, defined as absolute presence, the terms incorporated in questions must be thought in their nominal, determinable "reality." If thought in a hermeneutic phenomenological way, the words in questions are thought temporally, or verbally. Terms herein are not fixed or fixable entities, but are thought as modes of revealing. What does this mean? Where does this get the practitioners of Narrative Pedagogy?

Narrative tellings call forth surprise:

> *Roger, an experienced nurse educator practicing Narrative Pedagogy, starts his lecture with the question, "How are we to think schizophrenia?" Suddenly there is silence in the class. Students look at one another as he repeats the question. They become attentive as they are held in suspense by this question.*

This short narrative lets questions be a sighting. If questions are asked properly, they are meant to hold questioners and listeners in suspense (*RAS*, 53). To allow oneself to be suspended over the measureless is to see and hear that "the hermeneutic standpoint has nothing to do with the establishment of the correct meanings of words, as if meanings were firm or possessed a firmness that could be grasped" (*HL*, 125). Difference is movement issuing forth as the play of identity. Identity and difference self-disclose as the joining and distinguishing of matters of concern as the discursive saying of temporal-historical engaged openedness (*DH*, 211). Thinking-saying turns on the issuing forth of distance. Otherwise, the saying of thought would not be a responding.

Dialogical Experience

> *To put oneself on a journey to experience means to learn.*
>
> OWL, 143

Coming into nearness with disclosing and beckoning obtains as dialogical experience, such that going along a way is always already being underway. The way is always ahead of each human being as a belonging-to, concernedness, and the aheadness of language. Paradoxically, the way to the way needs a stepping back in order to be in con-tension with what is already the case, whiling as a given state of affairs (*OWL*, 67, 75). The human being of openness is gathered into thought such that thinking-saying already occurs "where a language holds sway" (calls). A richer thinking-saying that can issue forth from earlier thinking (*HW*, 109) is allowed as possibility.

The way back to the calling of language takes the human being of openness forward to a retrieval of discursiveness. Discursiveness is neither reasoning, judgment, definition, concept, ground, or relationship; nor is it speech or writing. Although discursiveness cannot do without any of the aforementioned, it also needs and belongs to thought and thinking as a response of resaying and voicing of "saying" (Ziarek, 1994, 35). Saying becomes thought here as showing, letting appear, being seen and heard (*OWL*, 122).

In this way discursiveness does not convey guaranteed overt or covert significations. It rather always already delivers matters of concern *as* matters of concern into the open clearing for the first time, each time (*OBT,* 45-46).

Readings, which turn on first time, each time as a unique essence, raise the spectre of a nonscientific relativism. Integral to the task of hermeneutic phenomenology is the explication of modern science as a technoscientism, which has arrogated to itself the last word on truth as it obtains as the correctness or certainty of epistemology. Scientistic thinking, whether in the guise of idealism (where matter is reduced to mind) or realism (where mind is reduced to mere matter), claims that its methods are foolproof and will eventually be able to establish the efficacy of reality once and for all time. For science to give up this claim to absolute certainty would be for it to cease to be itself as a will to will. Scientism must choose to give way to interpretation in one form or another or to remain in the grip of certainty as a project.

The major claims of science-as-truth can be subjected to the scrutiny of hermeneutic phenomenology. Idealism turns on the imposition "of categorial forms upon the matter of sensation" (*HWT,* 192). This requires that the manifold of intuition (sensory perception) be subsumed under concepts. For Kant, pure reason gave the meaningfulness of any particular experience its structure. Intentionality, as it became claimed for consciousness by Husserl, softened this claim somewhat, but still gave primacy to the grounding of truth in epistemological certainty. The assertion of certainty overlooks the possibility that the meaningful context is the world in which the human being finds itself thrown (*HWT,* 192-193).

Empiricism is held in a circular reasoning, by which it attempts to convert experience into an a priori condition of possibility that resides in the experience itself. In order to avoid the charge of relativism, empiricism must establish experience as a phenomenon that has "the same qualities" or "the same distributions" everywhere (*L,* 11). Husserl attempted to escape this logical tautology by converting experience "ahead of time into the object of an intention that configures it" (*L,* 20) via "reconstructing the originally intending I" (*TM,* 473). The problem arises when the certainty of the originally intending I, viewed as an absolute, cannot escape from its self-imposed enclosure.

Even though certainty implies the capacity to make comparisons, comparing in this sense calls for some criterion of perfection, according to which some thing of interest is differentiatable (*TM*, 439). The variant of realism known as utilitarianism attempts to "do away with qualitative distinctions of worth on the grounds that they represent confused perceptions of the real bases of [human] preferences which are quantitative" (Taylor, 1985, 17). The belief inherent in an approach of this sort is that once science has reduced noncalculatable phenomena to mere values, progress will be enabled via practices that accept only correct calculation as the true.[10] Significance is to be imposed from the self and not drawn "from the situation in which the self finds itself" (*HWT*, 192).

Mathematically determined nature is an attempt to construct an objectified ensemble of entities that can be put at the limitless disposal of an ambiguous "anyone" via calculation (*TM*, 457).[11] The methodological ideal of modern science must ensure "that every one of its steps can be retraced to the elements from which its knowledge is built up, while the teleological units of significance such as 'thing' [matter of concern] or 'organic whole' lose their legitimacy" (*TM*, 459). For example, the approach to language as mere sound units cannot come to grips with the problem of building meaning out of these isolated physical inputs. Scientistic thinking finds itself depending on the constructing of meaning out of the very phenomena it dismisses as valueless (Dreyfus, 1991, 219). Mathematically determined correctness is correct because it is correct.

Logically speaking, it can be asserted that a consequence (correctness) cannot take into view its governing principle (mathematics). Governing principles can determine consequences but the reverse is not possible (*4S*, 24-25). Static measures of space and time, despite their accuracy, cannot take into account matters of concern as an "open face-to-face encounter with another" (*OWL*, 104). The practice of reducing spatiotemporal phenomena to mere mathematically calculated parameters is a sending of engaged openness. Reductionism's inherent closing off (refusing) of itself renders it incapable of determining itself, as the very closure it is (*OWL,* 101-108).[12] Appeals to some preexisting standard as absolute knowledge show themselves as the commandeering orders that they are (*OWL,* 132-133).

The human being of openness is herein challenged forth by the paradigm of technoscientism to commandeer the planet for complete domination. This "can be met only by occupying an ultimate position beyond the earth from which to establish control over the earth" (*OWL,* 105). Paradoxically the ontic viewing of the earth from outer space has not produced absolute control over the earth. Rather it has led to an ontological awareness among some that any pursuit of control runs up against human finitude. To the best of established knowledge, time as eternity has not been experienced from a given absolute vantage point (*BT,* 269-270). Knowledge as eternal cannot self-establish as eternal without this supreme vantage point. This holds for locating truth in cosmic outer space as well as in the nano-space belonging to small things.

Modern science, as all-calculating, overlooks matters of concern. The dissolution of their whiling (abiding/sojourning/dwelling) is such that these are passed by in favor of forcing them into the nothing of mere calculated elements (*HW,* 108). What is forgotten here is that when sense advenes it can never be "a neutral colorless, or aphonic sense: even when written, it has a voice" (*L,* 34).

Discursiveness is voice in excess to vocalization as it ranges over a wide field. It passes from one place to another in the aheadness of its on-coming digressions. The forms of discursiveness and its freeing up of traditionary content (alreadiness) "cannot be separated in the hermeneutic experience" (*TM,* 441). Artificial or invented languages have no meaningful basis in the community of life (*TM,* 446). Narrative telling cannot be secret or artificial, nor can it be some system of mathematical symbols. The latter are always presupposed as the disclosure and beckoning of discursiveness. Science cannot escape from "a particular world orientation and cannot at all claim to be the whole" (*TM,* 449). Absolute objectivity needs an objectifier to objectify objectivity. How does this play obtain? How can the complete self-presence of total abstraction be achieved? Discursiveness as a mediating call offers its infinite whole as dialogical experience. Hermeneutic phenomenology is both called on and allowed to unfold (*TM*, 457).

If each "mind" were taken to be infinite, there would be no hermeneutical experience available (*TM*, 486). Discursiveness is a sharing wherein worlds appear. Therefore the finite sending/appearing of messages to be interpreted, as well as their concomitant ambiguity, is where strength, not weakness, resides (*TM*, 488). The strength of hermeneutic phenomenology lets the human being of openness put itself at the point where it does not know where it is going (*DH*, 217). For the human being to be where it is already, thinking-saying is the play of disclosing and beckoning, as disclosing and beckoning offers itself to the self-resonating heart and core of dialogical experience of the human being of openness (*RHT*, 265).

The "game of interpretation" that humans "are engaged in every day" is not a historiographical enumeration of objectivations present to an observing measuring gaze (*PH*, 32). The game that plays, plays because the human being of openness is always already possible as "interpretation *(logos)*"[13]; matters of concern are available as texts (*DH*, 213).

Exposure and Risk

> *We are exposed to the risk of no longer being able to understand or interpret ourselves—but also, we are thereby exposed once again to ourselves, and once again to one another, to our language and to our world.*
>
> *GT,* 65

The danger that conceals itself in texts is their need to be interpreted/ translated/read. Interpretations can serve to flatten out phenomena or to open them up. Earth, for example, can be read as "the serving bearer, blossoming and fruiting, spreading out in rock and water, rising up into plant and animal" (*PLT,* 149); as that "which 'stirs and strives,' which assails us and enthralls us as landscape" (*BT,* 100); or as merely just another location to be subjected to efficiently managed strip mining. Flattened readings risk missing the saying /showing sense of phenomena as being built up in their range of meaning. If readers, translators, or interpreters attempt only to copy saying/showing, they overlook the mutual engagement of world origin and saying—being-together in its richest sense.

For Heidegger, the human being is let into a world of an elaborate play of other humans and matters of concern such as utensils, theories, and, above all, ontologies and the determinations of metaphysics. A truism close to each human is the fact that one does not pick one's parents. Also not to be forgotten is that children participate in child-rearing based on their given factical historical situation. Facticity is the wherein as humans are delivered over to what they are by the "it gives" to the "there is." These terms are not meant to establish some mystical or religious belief. Heidegger's thinking was an attempt to release humankind from the metaphysical determination of the human as a homogenous, determinable, autonomous subject, which is in turn thought to be *the* sole determining agent for the unconditioned presence of everything that is. His work was meant to let the phenomenon of the human being of openness show itself as comportment, characterized as "*being-in-the-world,* determined by the bodying forth of the body" (*ZS,* 91). His work enabled the further contributions of Gadamer, Jean-Luc Nancy, and a host of other thinkers and poets.

To be a thinking-saying human is to be enclosed in a corporeal body that is, for the most part, capable of self-induced movement. Being set in motion is akin to quickening and indeed grows out of quickening. But setting in motion cannot be determined in a hermeneutic phenomenological way as a ground or a cause-effect relationship. Bodying-forth is not the mere perambulation of a psychologically or biologically discrete determined object.

A pivotal moment of the world that each human is let into is the openness of "originary being-with-one-another" (*ZS,* 116). Others are always already a concern for each human being, one way or another. This aspect of Heidegger's thought has been largely overlooked by his interpreters. An exception has been the French philosopher Jean-Luc Nancy. He avers, "Only the community can present me my birth, and along with it the impossibility of my reliving it, as well as the impossibility of my crossing over into my death" (*IC*, 15). The human situation does not admit of a static temporality of constant presence. Therefore, to be human is not to have absolute possession of the future, but to be possessed by an ever unfinished becoming, to be finite. *The question of that finitude cannot be settled; it never goes away, it goes its own way.*

The finite community of finite human beings co-reveals the presenting to one of one's birth and death as one's existence outside of one's self (*IC*, 26). The temporal with-world is a nonaccessible multiplicity of origins that carries us into a future (*BSP*, 10). It is a co-appearing, co-appearance given "well in advance of all our projects, desires, and undertakings; it is impossible for us to lose community" (*IC*, 35). According to Jean-Luc Nancy, "Being modern means the following: taking note of an exposed, 'unpresentability' as such, but which nothing other than the very presentation of our co-appearing, of 'us' co-appearing, and whose 'secret' exposes itself and exposes-us to ourselves without our even beginning to penetrate it—if it is a matter of 'penetrating' it at all" (*BSP*, 73). As this journey, humankind is "given and abandoned to the community: a gift to be renewed and communicated" (*IC*, 35) as the disposedness essential to participation (*BSP*, 93-99). Gadamer articulates the task of the interpreter (reader, translator) as never falling prey to mere imitation or entanglement in the rote repetition of a seemingly obvious truth. Humans must listen-to, placing themselves "in the direction of what is said (i.e., in its meaning) in order to carry over what is to be said into the direction of [their] own saying" (*PH*, 68).

A paradigm case that haunts hermeneutic phenomenology turns on Heidegger's political involvement. Heidegger overlooked the nearness of his ownmost near and its facticity such that he was blind to his own situation. In Heidegger's writings, being together with others is far more implicit than explicit (*WOT*, 3-5). Perhaps one reason this aspect of his thought has been overlooked is his now infamous political involvement. Although he was punished for it, he has never been forgiven by many for his comportment and errors in judgment. His silence on the specific actions of Nazi terror has been and will be a shadow that dogs his thought forever. On the other hand, do his silence on the "bloody terror," as he described the Nazi regime in a letter to his ex-student Herbert Marcuse,[14] and his "But how?" comment to Elisabeth Hirsch[15] reflect the fact that human comportment in certain human horrific practices is beyond language and philosophical reflection? Does Heidegger's self-admitted "failure of thinking" and his silence call forth an unfolding boundary of philosophical thought? If so, practices that labor to preclude the horrors of fascist regimes can claim (call) human dialogical experience such that "In the danger lies the saving power" (QCT, 28-35, 42-44).

Heidegger himself participated in the unsettling, bounding captivation of the abyss of fascism. Despite his "understanding of the people as 'voice' and not as 'race'" (WOT, 12) he was drawn into believing that German National Socialism was a reasonable alternative to the materialisms of Marxist-Leninism (Bolshevism) and the corporate capitalism exemplified by certain economic practices in the United States. When it became clear that Nazism was part and parcel of the "gigantic,"[16] it was too late for Heidegger and Germany to take corrective steps.

An even-handed account of the enigma named "Heidegger" is presented by Miguel de Beistegui (2005, 155-179). In the chapter on Heidegger and National Socialism, de Beistegui presents an outline of factual materials and possible motivations. He closes his thoughts on Heidegger with a series of questions that present the spellbound credulity inherent in any uncritical espousing of political fascism. For de Beistegui, Heidegger at that time firmly believed that German National Socialism was the answer to overcoming the forgetting of the calling play of historical unfoldings of engaged openness: a "reawakening to the sense of wonder and awe before the essence of truth" (de Beistegui, 2005, 175). Further, "to believe, if only for a second, that Hitler and his 'movement' may have had the slightest intention of realizing such an ideal, amounts to an obvious and particularly worrying form of blindness" (de Beistegui, 2005, 175). *Heidegger's compromise with his own thought shows itself not only as enigma but more trenchantly as a warning.*

On a personal level, Heidegger was never able to come to grips with his own banal stereotyping. Gadamer relates that Heidegger never gave up the thought that there was a worldwide conspiracy by Jews to control information (*AH,* 11-12).[17] On the other hand, the unqualified assertion can be made that there is *nothing* in Heidegger's philosophical writings that in any way justifies the systematic extermination practices of the Nazi regime aimed at European Jews, Roma, gays, disabled persons, and political opponents. Perhaps more importantly, the modern world has never been able to come to grips with the failure to prevent the use of the rational to effect the ruthless perfection of effectiveness and efficiency—genocidal practices that continue to be perpetrated to this day.

Heidegger has presented two gifts: one positive and one negative. The negative "gift" was his political involvement; the play of his xenophobic "Germanness" and the banality of his anti-Semitic stereotyping.[18] The words "in the danger lies the saving power" resonate from his comportment such that they are made available for listening and co-responding. A positive gift is the pall cast over any and every mode of thinking such that the question always to be asked is, Where are current practices of fascism to be found?

The danger harbored in the confident refusal of questions of malice, marginalizing, and stereotyping, as these read an other as unfit, is neither merely an issue of Nazi and other fascisms nor merely an issue of ex post facto complicity. Perhaps what silently and reticently calls forth is an exigent need to dwell with a way of thought that lets the unsettling essence of *any* collectivity of willed confidence show itself as itself. Silence and reticence are not taken here as mere refusal, but turn on engaged attending, listening, and co-responding. To be at home in this thinking-saying would be to dwell in the notion that "justice," when promulgated as the phantasm of the illusory preserving and increasing power, cries out as ultimately impotent and thereby protean (Babich, 1992, 98-102).

Despite his personal failings, Heidegger contributed a rich body of work as a gift, which let hermeneutic phenomenology show itself as a legitimate alternative to the reductionist paradigm of the day and *thereby changed the face of philosophical thinking.*

The human being of openness is always already face-to-face with, is exposed to, risk. There are risks, which, as strikingly evident, are the dangers of the horrific practices of fascisms and/or the radical effects of climate change on global ecosystems and human habitation. However, there are also nontangible risks not available to the monoculous and myopic gaze of the empirical. This gaze arrogates the reality of all that is real to itself as "the objectness of the real" (*QCT,* 167-170). How do invisible risks show up as risks, disclose and beckon themselves? In the ensuing chapters we will labor to pursue the faint trail of what is in front of us, but never to the exclusion of the play of the always already entanglements of tangible phenomena.

Letting something be sighted as something involves a "way" that participates as a performative interaction, with matters of concern as entities and such, as engaged openness. Questioning obtains as a play of its own casting and recasting, as a procedure of a taking-as of *what is let be,* as something that is listened and responded (called) to.[19] Participatory phenomena show themselves as the indivisible reciprocity of matters of concern that are hearable as calling to, sightable as seeing of, and thereby seen as sighting and listening.

Heidegger rendered the implicitness of the engaged openness of matters of concern as its ability to be of concern for possible human engagement. Engagement as significance, understandability, usability, and explicitness shifts sense as a matter of concern's "'being-out-there' to its 'appearing-as,' that is, its 'intelligibility' in the broadest sense" (*KE,* 6). Engagement as such "listens" to the human being by making itself available. Humans are inexorably claimed by engagement *as* engagement exigently needs humans.

Exposure to the risk of intelligibility in the broad sense finds two kinds of phenomena, ontic and ontological (*ZS,* 187), incipiently offered to practical and prudent involvement as actuality and possibility. Possibility is the impossibility of "metaphysical closure, full self-presence, and perfect self-coincidence" (*PS,* 199).

Possibility is not to be viewed as a metaphysical modality: In the ambit of hermeneutic phenomenology, possibilities always already arrive and depart as involvements for the human being of openness (*ZS,* 159). The temporal particularity of the human being is to be always already what it is not, but can be (*BH,* 212; *GBT,* 504). Can-be qua can-be is care as the engaged openness of being-ahead-of-oneself, of the always already and of the temporal-historical essence of the alongside (*ZS,* 174).

Productions imputed to human beings or a supreme creator are an integral part of the concernful narrative telling that the human being is. First and foremost, humans are always already comporting themselves toward available matters of concern and *are* as a matter of concern. Humans mediately, practically, and prudently discern about themselves not only *that* they are a matter of concern, but also *about* their engaged openness with available matters of concern. They are concerned, one way or another, with themselves and how they are. Engaged openness concerns human beings, whether it is a matter of the entity that they are themselves or those entities they are not and never can be. A human being is always that entity which is concerned with engaged openness, and, as thus concerned and struck, finds in engaged openness what is most true (*BC,* 55 [paraphrased]).

In order to move beyond the situatedness of the modern tradition, in *Zollikon Seminars* Heidegger pointed out that, in *Being and Time,* the matter of thought was no longer entities as entities but the *sense* of engaged openness in general (*ZS,* 119). It is important to note here that the end of this sentence contains an ambiguous genitive that travels in both subjective and objective directions at once.[20] Heidegger is *not* talking of "being" in the traditional sense as such. He later states, "In *Being and Time,* the question of who, what, and how the human being is (which has become necessary) is discussed exclusively and continuously in relation to the question of the meaning [sense] of" engaged openness (*ZS,* 119-120). Our book is engaged herewith as an offering of another place to start.

Chapter 2 Notes

1   See also *QCT,* 173-180.

2   See also *4S,* 55, on the possibilities of a "universal world formula" as a search for an ultimate theory of theories.

3   See also *ZS,* 225-226.

4   See Zarader, 1986, 15-20, for transposition as a leap, a step back, and a step to the side.

5   The following is abstracted and synthesized from the writings of Kisiel, Sheehan, Heidegger, Gadamer, and Nancy. See bibliography.

6   The authors wish to acknowledge Dr. Kenneth Maly's translation of *Streit* as con-tension (usually translated as "strife") as more in tune with Heidegger's thinking (included in conference materials presented at the 2008 Institute for Hermeneutic Phenomenology, Indiana University School of Nursing, Indianapolis, Indiana).

7   See Dallmayr, 1984, 104-132, for a discussion of Heidegger's notion of freedom as "the condition or ground of possibility of" the human being of openness.

8   See also *BW,* 441-449; *CP,* §163, §200; *OWL,* 91-93.

9   See also McNeill, 2001, 136.

10   See also Dreyfus, 1991, 108-127

11   See *BT,* 167-224, for the problematic surrounding the essence of the anyone as a possibility for understanding. The latter is claimed by somnambulant meaning such that there is no acknowledgment of any lack of knowledge except as a mere ontic deficiency.

12   See also *PLT,* 165-182.

13   We are assiduously avoiding the use of the Greek term *logos* in order to bring traditions other than that of formal philosophical thinking into our converging conversation. The reader should be aware that *logos* is a pivotal moment in the historicality of Greco-European thinking. *Logos* is at once gathering (*ID,* 57), saying and being (*OWL,* 155, 80), reading (interpreting) (*HPM,* 299; *DH,* 213), world (*HNA,* 212), preverbal revelation or disclosure (*DH,* 208; *OWL,* 80), and *physis. Logos* is thought here, not as object, but as "the self-presentation of presence" (*BSP,* 17), the temporal opening of sense/meaning (*BSP,* 23), and "the self-showing of what shows itself" (*OWL,* 132; *RHT,* 283). The modern tradition has reduced the word *logos* to a name for mere "rational" thinking.

14　See Wolin, 1991, 31.

15　Cited in Babich, 1992,103.

16　See *CP,* 94-98; *QCT,* 135, 153.

17　See also *ETT,* 30-44.

18　See *ETT* and David, 1995, for opposing viewpoints.

19　See J. Diekelmann, 2005, 52-53, for a discussion of listening and responding.

20　See also *RHT,* 264-265.

Chapter 3

Starting From Another Place

Hermeneutic phenomenology invites starting from another place. This place is not the enforced placement of cognitive processes, but its locale is the understanding of world and being human. Alternative paths to thinking world and humans are those that do not enclose humans as *the* determinable determining conscious subject.

Nearness of the Near as Always Already

> *The "nearby" of the* with, *the simultaneity of distance and close contact, the most proper constitution of the* cum-, *exposes itself as indeterminantness and as a problem.*
>
> BSP, 81

The everyday experience of human beings is so near to them that its proximity can be easily forgotten or overlooked. That which is readily understood is only rarely brought forward into a thinking that meditates on sense as sense. Heidegger describes the problem of thinking the nearness of difference:

> The matter of thinking has been handed down to [is already freed up for] Western thinking under the name being. If we think of this matter just a bit more rigorously, if we take more heed of what is in contest in the matter, we see that *being* means always

and everywhere: the being of *beings.* The genitive in phrase is to be taken as a *genitivus objectivus. Beings* means always and everywhere the beings of *being;* here the genitive is to be taken as a *genitivus subjectivus.* It is, however, with certain reservations that we speak of a genitive in respect to object and subject, because these terms, subject and object, in their turn stem from a particular character of being. Only this much is clear, that when we deal with the being of beings and with the beings of being, we deal in each case with a difference. *(ID,* 61-62)

Any movement toward a richer understanding of difference and the question of the truth of engaged openness must also take time into account. "Ontically, of course, Dasein [the human being of openness] is not only close to us—even that which is closest: we *are* it, each of us, we ourselves. In spite of this or rather for just this reason, it is ontologically that which is farthest" (*BT,* 36). Time as temporality obtains as the nearness of the near, as the flow and flux of the always already.

To be human is to somehow or other come to grips with a self-existence amidst an undifferentiated play of possibility, in an indifferent universe. The way this has been done in the Greco-European tradition turns on the assertorial use of the word is. For the Greeks the "is" was the self-revealing of a nonquantifiable cosmos; for the scholastic tradition, "is" was the exclusive domain of the Christian God. The advent of modernity saw the "is" become the certainty of Descartes' thinking ego. The danger lurking in our own epoch of technicity is such that even the subject-object split will disappear and devolve into nothing but free-floating, disconnected objects (*QCT,* 173).

The question that arises is one that grows out of the specter of relativism: If there are no absolutes, how do humans evaluate given situations? An answer often given is that humans always have values so they just have to make sure that the values they have are the right ones. The question turns back on itself when it self-interrogates on how the "right" values are established. Are they based on theology? On allegedly value-neutral empirical observation? The relativism problematic refuses to go away. Absolute knowing is absent. There is the open clearing as the with of engaged openness.

Engaged openness is a way of letting matters of concern be possible, which must, in their turning, listen to certain historical callings (*QCT,* 36-49). Engaged openness delivers, dispenses, and distributes boundary as that which lets matters of concern be as possibility. Letting things be possible as engaged matters of concern is not the equivalent of creating, or producing, discrete items. Engaged openness is distinct from the productionism that the modern human subject arrogates to itself. If the human being of openness were merely an entity producing matters of concern, it would have the power to arbitrarily determine the sense that lets a matter of concern be meaningful. Sense-*cum*-meaning cannot be forced to occur. Engaged openness must not be taken as "an unrestricted mode of making entities possible." Engaged openness is what *lets* matters of concern be (Tanzer, 1999, 85).[1]

Engaged openness lets matters of concern be by offering matters of concern as the circulating meanings that let them be what they are. Letting be is not the creation of matters of concern; engaged openness discloses and beckons face-to-face with letting (*4S,* 58-60). Letting can act as an "equally active, antagonistic power, giving [matters of concern] an essential insignificance, thereby preventing [a subject] from completely dominating them" (Tanzer, 1999, 1990). The open clearing of disclosing and beckoning precludes the human being of openness from arbitrarily determining historically fixed significance of matters of concern. The self-rendering of disclosing and beckoning, impenetrable to the human subject's power to give significance and as the possibilities that engaged openness offers to the human being of openness, is what shows moments constituted by matters of concern as moments of engaged openness.

Engaged openness cannot obtain as some ultimate or absolute reality. If complete realization self-realized itself it would "attain a position of complete and unconditioned dominance." Entities as entities would have to be devoid of meaning or be completely insignificant (Tanzer, 1999, 94). The human being of openness obtains as the releasement of any imputed power to render matters of concern insignificant. Engaged openness as an offering releases the play of significance, meaning, and sense as temporalized presencing.

Heidegger discusses the temporal play-space as bringing-before-the-eyes[2]—not, however, as a subject's determination of an object, but as the realm of belonging-together. Objectifying concepts attempt to seize and subsume things under formations and abstractions. *Time is not filled by anyone or anything; time rests in itself as the always already between the human being of openness finding itself disposed as singular plural.*

Boundary

> *For the Greeks, limit is not that whereby something discontinues, something negative, but whence it stands, whereby it is determined in its form.*
>
> ZS, 32

> *The boundary is that from which something begins its essential unfolding.*
>
> BW, 356; *PLT,* 154

The work of hermeneutic phenomenology consists of letting limits as such allot themselves to being made thematic, that is, as explicating presuppositions as recurrence of experiences as they show themselves. *Hermeneutic phenomenology is not an approach to thinking that imitates, confirms, or extends scientific results.* Scientific results can never solve philosophical questions where understanding is constantly confronted with its limits. The limits of understanding are not extraneous to understanding, they are part and parcel of what understanding is in the first place. Mindfulness (understanding) is necessarily hermeneutic phenomenological whereby it finds itself as its meaning in the self-understanding of human beings.

Heidegger participated in the uncovering of the hidden assumptions or presuppositions of what has come to be known as "the subject-object paradigm" or "metaphysics." His work was instrumental in calling forth the work of Gadamer in explicating the nature of experience and Jean-Luc Nancy's work on the play of singularities and pluralities. That which these thinkers share is the task of not letting their thinking fall into the ensnarement of fixing esoteric meanings, for example, "being" as a reductionist meta-narrative. They also share working to make thematic the forgotten or overlooked presuppositions of foundationalist positions (*OWL,* 135; *SV,* 248).

The subject-object paradigm is claimed by the necessity of absolutely self-identical parts. The fundament of its thought cannot allow for any contingency. *The mission of this paradigm is held in thrall either to the reducing of mind (consciousness) to matter—realism—or to the reducing of matter to mind (theoretical or correlating constructs)—idealism.* For example, in realism, stress is described as a physiological state in which certain neurohormones are present (reducing mind to matter or mind and soul disappearing into the physiology of brain matter). In idealism, stress is described as a response to situations in which certain needs or desires are blocked (reducing matter to mind or matter consisting in conceptualizations).

Inherent in the subject-object paradigm is the necessity to freeze time into a discrete "now" either as some determinable instant or as an eternal verity. Thus research from a realist perspective freezes or controls for such variables as neurohormonal levels. Idealist research studies control for psychological or personality variables such as codependency or theoretical constructs such as resiliency in order to rectify "deficiencies" and resolve them into some ideal state.

The subject-object paradigm is beset with irresolvable aporias. Therefore humans often see research methodologies justify their realist perspectives via recourse to vague notions of idealized ethical, moral, or intellectual constructs. For example, a particular kind of cancer research shows that two treatments (rounds of chemotherapy) are the most effective in producing an 85% "cure rate." However, even in the absence of other research, four treatments are advocated to remove any cancer cells that "may linger" because in other variants of cancer, research has shown that lingering cancer cells may, in fact, linger. The hidden value of "let's not take a chance" and the economic values that possibly accompany this practice are not supported by available factual or statistical data. In this way, the fact-value divide is only seemingly bridged, but only by acts of will or belief. The ground shifts under itself.

Phenomena as hermeneutically interpreted phenomena do not admit of any enforced closure such that they are placed into binary categories. Such placement in binary relationships is faced with the inability to decide between "nature" and "nurture." Unresolvable tensions obtain within the namings of these oppositions as adversarial debates, which turn on conceptualizations of "immanent and transcendent, psychic and physical, rational and animal, personalistic and naturalistic, consciousness and reality, spirit and nature" (*HWT,* 37).[3] In a seeming paradox, while either side of these dichotomous pairs cannot be rendered unambiguous via either theory or mathematics, their "ands" are given (bestowed/granted/ delivered) as comings-between. Connectives disclose *and* beckon themselves as the offering of assemblings, claims, addressings, and bestowals rather than as absolute linkage.

For Heidegger, a phenomenon "always has the character of an assembling, not of a cutting off." This emerges more in the Greek sense of limit as "that from whence and wherein something commences, emerges as that which it is" (*POR,* 72).[4] The name of the Greek god Hermes is taken from stone monuments that were erected to delineate boundaries. A boundary does not necessarily indicate direction; it merely indicates a boundary. In Greek mythology, Hermes traveled between the levels of gods and mortals and *translated* messages. (The term "hermeneutics" is derived from "Hermes.") Boundaries call out to be interpreted in light of their sense as these concomitantly show themselves; they show as distinct. This distinctiveness is always already preoffered as what counts as a distinction (*ZS*, 75-77). Boundaries as openness and clearing belong together; they are mutually engaged (*ZS*, 282).

What counts as a bounded entity? And for whom? Can any temporal and spatial homogenization obtain? Is a reduction to the normative or ordinary a practice that does away with decisions? Or does the play of decision turn on the notion that "everything decisive is 'despite' the ordinary, for the ordinary and usual recognizes and wants only its own kind"? (*BC*, 35). The issue for interpretive thinking is not the repeatability of a phenomenon via experiment or cause-effect relations (*4S*, 53). These are "correct" within a given attempt to effect a closed system, but it should be noted that "mere success is never a proof of truth" (*BC*, 48) wherein truth in its proper historical-temporal essence obtains here as that which enables questioning. Truth for Heidegger is not a determination but a gathering that can be made thematic (articulated) as difference (*4S*, 41, 48).

The Human Way of Existing: Openness

> Scientist: *The relation between the ego and the object, the often mentioned subject-object relation, which I took to be the most general, is apparently only a historical variation of the relation.*
>
> *DT,* 78

In hermeneutic phenomenology, the human way of existing is rendered as an openness (Da-sein) whereby that which the human being is always already turns on thrownness, understanding, and language (*ZS*, 139, 141; *PS*, 192-195).[5] Modernity's take on engaged openness assertively interprets (reads) truth to be located in a conscious subject, and thereby forgets or overlooks the engaged openness of its isolated subject. The works of Darwin, Marx, and Freud called into question any notion that there could be an *unconditional* cognizing ego-subject. The purely self-knowing conscious individual evades any signification of finality.

In *Four Seminars*, Heidegger discussed the immanence of consciousness as a barrier to the unfolding any question turning on the givenness of entities or matters of concern (*4S*, 70-71). If immanence as *ego cogito* is a self-enclosed location of some sort, the question becomes, How does anything enter or exit, arrive or depart? Is the whole thought of anything's entering or exiting a self-enclosed location inherently contradictory? The play of the subject-object paradigm includes a deferred promise that the ingress-egress problem will someday be qualified and/or quantifiable. Heidegger's solution was to simply begin from another place. There was a need, as he saw it, "to start from something other than the *ego cogito.*" That something was "world" where everything that can be taken as a matter of concern is encounterable as a region which offers the possibility for a matter of concern to manifest itself temporally and historically.

Heidegger's opening up of what it means to belong engagedly in a world circulates around the word "Da-sein." This circulation as such means to be always already involved/engaged in a with-world of relationships. The with-world "is mediated each time beforehand, that is, made possible and granted by the enactment and reenactment of the [takings-as] of being human in the sense of Da-sein" (*ZS,* 223). Da-sein's ownmost openness is the sojourning in the clearing, which gives "the possibility for comportment in the first place amidst things" (*ZS,* 226). Da-sein as "being-in-the-world is never a property of a subjectivity [ego-subject] no matter how it is represented or perceived, but from the beginning it is the human being's way of existing" (*ZS,* 227, 286). The human being of openness (Da-sein) and the open clearing mutually belong together as they co-constitute each other. The human being of openness and the open clearing are to be taken as the nonrepresentable showing of the inaccessible enigma to the giving of the givenness of the given, or put another way, to the engaging of the engagedness of the engaged.

With the disclosure of the self as "governed by a temporal-historical clearing rather than an eternal Mind," Heidegger brought forward the sense of a "concrete situation of action" whose constitution is given as care.[6] This transposition of possibility is offered as a being-in-the-world wherein the human being is sighted as first existing "outside" of an enclosed mental information processor. Released from (freed of) the closure of mentalisms, the human being of openness can let the clearing/letting of engaged openness call human beings into their ownmost openness.[7] Understanding-listening lets the eye sight and be sightable and the ear listen and be listenable in the widest play of sense such that sense, meaning, and significance are always already present as themselves. As the human being listens to tradition that it is, it listens to that call which frees up the human being of openness as present in the sense where matters of concern are present as reciprocal play-space as they become sighted and listened to and thereby "must be present to" human beings (*4S,* 16).

The temporal, historical understanding of the above is designated as "care" by Heidegger (*ZS,* 190). Paradoxically, the inaccessible is what gives accessibility its possibility, not as actuality but as finitude. Care is the response to the question of what is at play as the with of engaged openness (*BSP,* 27). The with of engaged openness "is not a presentable property, since it is presentation itself" (*BSP,* 95). As explicated in *Being and Time,* "*care* is nothing more nor nothing less than the term for the whole essence of Da-sein" (*ZS,* 286). Therefore all everyday, perceivable "ontical relations of those who love and also of those who hate as well as the relations of the objective natural scientist, etc., are thus already founded in *being-in-the-world* as *care*" (*ZS,* 286). Care runs ahead, so to speak, letting the possible open up as closing-down-on or as remembering-retrieval. *Therefore care should not be taken as a moral or solicitous phenomenon, but rather as being-in-the-world.* The play of "wishing, willing, propensity and urge also always refer[s] to modifications of all three structural elements of care, namely of the being-ahead-of-itself, of being-always-already-in-the-world, and being-alongside" (*ZS,* 219, 192).[8] These three structural elements point to the human being of openness as existing-with (*BSP,* 29).

The inaccessible enigma of being human turns on the having of each human being to be the always already *becoming* moment of its mortality. This shared having does not indicate ownership but rather the impossibility of ownership.

> Contrary to an available thing possessive of its properties, ex-sistence [being human] indicates an incessantly expropriated, dispossessed relation not only to death but also to life, from birth. To begin with, my life is not my own, though it is given to me to make our own, albeit temporally. (Kisiel, *HWT,* 184)

The nonidentical singular plural same of the human being of openness is not about a claim to possession, but is about being disclosed and beckoned by nonpossessable temporality. The human being of openness is never in possession of its plural with-world but is always already exposed to the flux of worlding, unworlding, reworlding. In addition, the human being of openness is bound (called to attention) to become its ownmost proper possibilities as the flux of never to be finalized tasks. Proper engagement with the world is to be exposed to its flux (Kisiel, *HWT,* 184).

Tasks, as such, are not performed by some robot or ghostly apparition, but by an embodied me and thou. Bodying forth and its accompanying motives are founded upon co-responding with a with-world. "The body is the necessary condition, but not a sufficient condition" for any co-responding play of nonobjectifiable relationships (*ZS,* 186). Responding must always already be a co-responding. Understanding sees the contextual connection between motives. Motives are understood in a hermeneutic phenomenological sense as something that addresses the human being of openness as a "for what" or as a "reason for" (*ZS,* 22, 186). Hermeneutical insight describes "how something is connected with something else—when [the human being sights] the meaning of something someone is talking about and how something that was said corresponds to the matter intended" (*ZS,* 217). Motives call forth freedom, freedom from the restrictions of narrowly construed cause-effect relationships (*ZS,* 21). The situated motive is not the *cause* of an effect. The situatedness that counts is the situatedness of any matter of concern, be it the most exalted, the everyday, or the most humble.

From the initial words of this book we have attempted to avoid starting from a place of taking entities *as* objects. We have taken our hints from various thinkers (in the formal sense) and from the thoughts of those involved in the encounters that we have named schooling learning teaching. The task of hermeneutic phenomenology is to make accessible the human being of openness as being-in-the-world "which is in each and every case our own" (*OHF,* 11). Access in this sense turns on the always already arriving facticity as a temporal particularity (sojourn/whiling) "articulated with respect to, on the basis of, and with a view to" its ownmost expression (*OHF,* 5). Proper temporal instantiation as relationship to world "is that openness according to which the human being is always already addressed" by entities other than itself (*ZS,* 137). Thus Heidegger asserts, "Only on the basis of the belonging together of thrownness and understanding through language as saying, is the human being able to be addressed" by engaged openness and matters of concern (*ZS,* 139).

Thrownness

What does Heidegger mean by the word "thrownness"? For science, thrownness shows up as thatness—the ontically determined fact that humans exist in a given set of tangible circumstances. Heidegger discusses the self-grounding of science as the securing of what is real for it. When the "real becomes secured in its objectness there result spheres or areas of objects that scientific observation can entrap after its fashion" (*QCT,* 168). Various domains of scientific practice are necessarily directed to the phenomena they must exhibit to effect sensory perception (*QCT,* 173). "Scientific representation, for its part, can never decide whether nature, through its objectness, does not rather withdraw itself than bring to appearance the hidden fullness of its coming to presence. Science cannot even ask this question, for as theory, it has already undertaken to deal with the area circumscribed by objectness" (QCT, 174).

Proximally and for the most part the human being is disposed to do what it does via disposedness as disposedness. That is, the human being is thrown or called to attention as the situation it is. Each human being is fundamentally disposed to do this or that by the situation it is. Disposedness displaces the human being "into such and such a relation to the world, into such and such a resolve or occlusion of one's self, a self which is *essentially* a being-in-the-world" (BQP, 140). Exigent need as finitude compels "by disposing, and this disposing is a displacing in such a fashion" that the human being finds itself "disposed (or not disposed) toward [matters of concern] in a definite way" (BQP, 140). Recall that "way" here resonates with being-on-the-way and should not be thought of as fixed in the manner of a railroad track.

Disposedness refers to "*how* one 'finds oneself disposed,' situated, positioned in and by the world" (HWT, 68). Thereby "being had by one's situation, being-put-upon by the world constantly being moved by the 'happening' of life's contexts into 'be-having' in one way or another" (HWT, 68) is what befalls the human being prior to any internalized sensing. Disposedness is "not simply what is had, but is really the having itself" (ZS, 63) and as such "can only exist in the realm of how" the human being finds itself (ZS, 63). Recall that the human being is "exposed toward [entities] as a whole" in a correlation of thrownness and understanding "whose unity is determined through language" (ZS, 139).

For Gadamer, disposed meanings that occupy the human being are not at its disposal. The on-coming of disposedness enables understanding one way or another and for better or for worse (TM, 295). There is always already a play of hindering and facilitating. Situatedness as the condition of mutual possibilities is what the human being of openness is thrown into (unto) such that it always already finds itself as the with-others of engaged openness. Rather than "a regrettable distortion that affects the purity of understanding," historical-temporal situatedness offers "the condition of its possibility" (TM, 472).

The human being finds itself disposed one way or another. This disposedness of disposedness can be seen as an onus that must be escaped from or dealt with as that which can free comportment. There is a distress that accompanies disposedness: "as disposing the distress," the "not knowing the way out or the way in" (*BQP,* 134). But here there is no compulsion simply "into already determined relations to beings, one's already opened up and interpreted in their beingness" (*BQP,* 134). The point of departure possible as hermeneutic phenomenology is to let the disposedness of a disposedness show itself as a "transformative displacing of [the human being of openness] into [entities and matters of concern] and before them" (*BQP,* 149) as possible belonging together.

The plurality of disposedness shows itself as possibility. Therefore in *Contributions to Philosophy (From Enowning),* startled dismay, reservedness, and awe are articulated as fugal possibilities. Startled dismay obtains as a possibility for thinking the enigma of engaged openness such that everything is reduced to mere orderability. Awe has resonances of reverentiality (respect) such that the temporally particular engaged openness is listened to as its ownmost need to let it occur as historicality. At play as the between is reservedness, as allowing (enduring and sojourning) engaged openness, as a privative situatedness that the human being belongs to (Vallega-Neu, 2003, 36-43).

Restraint (reservedness) shows up as "terror in the face of what is closed and most obtrusive, namely that [matters of concern] are, and awe in the face of what is remotest, namely that in [matters of concern], and before each [matter of concern, engaged openness] holds sway" (*BQP,* 4). Terror is "preserved and conserved through awe" (*BQP,* 4). Boredom or ennui is temporalized anxiety, the "dark emptiness of irrelevance" (*BQP,* 169). Reservedness is the possibility of leaving boredom and anxiety (dread) to themselves.

A basic character of the human being is exposure such that disposedness (ontological situatedness) and attunement (ontic mood) belong to everyday comportment (*ZS,* 165). The "from which and according to which alone everything is able to show itself is always already present" (*ZS,* 165). Attunement as "the way and manner of being able to be addressed" (*ZS*, 211) belongs to the human being. The with of attunement and the drawnness into the engaged openness of entities and matters of concern are the same (*ZS*, 203). The with "stays" the between (*BSP*, 62). Recall that the disposedness of understanding reveals/conceals as discursive saying: "a showing of something" (*ZS*, 211).

The paying of attention to any assertion resides in the question it implicitly poses.

> [To] consider the way in which it speaks, or how it speaks ["Way" or "how" is meant as] something other than manner or mode. "Way" here means melody, the ring and tone, which is not just a matter of how the saying sounds. The way or how of the saying is the tone from which and to which what is said is attuned. (*WCT*, 37)

To be an understanding human is to be attuned as the play of disposedness.

Captivation in all of its senses obtains as dispositions present themselves as both a calling to and a roadblock in how the human being participates, of necessity, in engaged openness. Disposedness is that which both possesses and dispossesses. Via disposedness, the human being of openness is transported *as* the play of sighting's and listening's possibilities to matters of concern as such.

For Heidegger, the issue then turns on thatness or the "that" which holds sway as that which is not to be gotten around (*QCT*, 174-179). For physics, theory can never make its way around already presencing nature, such as the theory of a theory of a theory, *ad infinitum*. Psychiatry cannot get behind the "opene*d*ness" that the human being of openness sustains (*ZS*, 218). For example, the meaning of psychosomatic phenomena (blushing, for example) cannot be fixed in place and thereby predicted. Historiography as a science cannot create history. The historicality of history is its own agentless on-coming such that it "takes its course as it is prepared and disposed in such and such a way, i.e., set in order and sent forth" (*QCT,* 175).

The temporal particularity of the human being of openness is its inability to remain and yet inability to leave its place. As the taking something as something, the human being of openness always already throws the human being into possibilities. As its thrownness, the human being belongs to what is actual about itself. As historically thrown the human being is always already in transit. The history of the human is the human of history. The human being stands-in (whiles/sojourns/abides/dwells) as this transition and therefore is essentially "absent." The fundamental sense of absence is never to be merely not at hand, but is to be removed into alreadiness and becoming. The human being exists in the open possibility of its absence but not as an absence. "*Transposed* into the possible, [the human being] must constantly *be mistaken* concerning what is actual" (*FCM,* 365-366). This need not be taken as a negative occurrence. The human being's ability to take-as, as a mediation, is what enables it to understand finitude finitely. In this way it can be said that temporally particularized thrown openness and opened thrownness belong to each other (*KE,* 12-13).

Thrownness shows up in the with-world of the everyday experiences of teachers and students. Here, Sienna speaks of being a teacher and of being thrown into situations with students.

> *As teachers, we act too much like we know what we are doing, sort of like we're know-it-alls. But when you get down to it, students and teachers come to learning situations together. Quite honestly we have no idea about what will happen and where our discussions will go or what experiences we might run into. Things are always showing up and there are always things we overlook and things we think will happen often don't . . . and we have no control of any of it—not really. Of course you have to know some things about what you are teaching, but we have gone way overboard in acting like we all know*

what is going on and that we've got everything under control. There are no guarantees that things will happen this way or that . . . there are simply no guarantees in life!

Thrownness includes being available as thrown and as the throwing-off of understandings or takings-as. Matters of concern occur such that they must be taken as something. The open clearing where the human being of openness abides is a space-time that obtains as its own way of play. Human beings are proximally and for the most part thrown into the modern epoch as those who assign (sub-ject) objects to a lower place under them (human beings) in order to determine their whatness (essence) and/or their thatness (existence). Engaged openness shows up (discloses and beckons) as domination and provocation. Thrownness serves as a double indicator. *First, matters of concern are here (present) prior to being taken as something,*[9] *and second, what a matter of concern is, is based on absence.*[10]

Any interpretation of the concernful character of a matter of concern is based on its in-order-to, its towards-which, and its for-the-sake-of-which. These characteristics are in turn based on absentiality, that is to say, on the possibility that an entity is other than what the throw of engaged openness already determines for it. This in turn is based on a future that is a possibility for either presence or absence. The human being already understands a matter of concern as a matter of concern is thrown into its own absence as its fundamental finitude. The entity that each human being is, *is of* openness where its past is always already in front of it (*BT,* 41). As never to be completed, the future of the human being is always already on the way as a past that never arrives but can only while as the particularized possibility of one's own death: the instantiated sojourn of the human being.

The thrownness of taking something as something happens *of* openness. The human being of openness becomes instantiated of itself *as* a taking of some matter of concern as a matter of concern (*CP,* 249). Engaged openness discloses and beckons the human being to itself, and indeed in such a way that [disclosing and beckoning] first needs something of its own, proper to itself, a *self,* whose selfhood the human being has to persist and endure in *that* instantiation that lets human being, *standing* in [openness], become *that* [entity] which is first encountered only in the who-question.[11] (*CP,* 173)

Thrownness is the ungraspable emergence/elusion of the who of I, you, we, and they as the always already that calls the human being to attention as it reciprocally belongs to its thrownness.

Understanding

Thrownness lets human beings into the world understandingly. Fundamentally humans comport themselves ontologically. Sheehan puts this in stronger terms: "We are condemned to ontology, which before it is a thematic science, is a matter of relating to entities [matters of concern] mediately through their being [engaged openness]-as, rather than directly by intellectual intuition" (*KE,* 12). For the human being, whether unquestioningly involved in quotidian everydayness or absorbed in the most globally significant problems of the time, there exists a fore-structure of understanding (*BT,* 188-195).

Any beginning must have started somewhere and at some time in order to enable a glimpse of its on-coming emergent/elusive origins. No fore-understanding, especially an enacted phenomenological hermeneutic, can be presuppositionless (von Herrmann, 1996, 178). Interpretive practices *are* the play of thrownness, understanding, and discourse. Enacting interpretation turns on fore-having, fore-sight, and fore-grasping. "Thrownness is carried out in fore-having; projection [understanding] in fore-sight; and *Rede* [discursiveness], in fore-grasping" (von Herrmann, 1996, 177-178). Kisiel translates differently but points to the same: "Pre-having, pre-viewing, and pre-conceiving constitute the 'hermeneutic situation' in which every interpretation has its possibility" (*GBT,* 351).

Whether translated as "fore-" or "pre-," understanding as it circulates is futural as (1) that situatedness wherein past human beings are already apprehended in advance as the showing up of a culture, as an individual and/or as a matter of concern in a causal context; (2) the abiding in which human beings as well as matters of concern thus apprehended are asked after; and (3) the contexts of meaning that while as disclosing and beckoning and *let* understanding abide. The past as alreadiness "is interpreted out of the interpretedness and average comprehensibility—what everyone understands by art, religion, life, death, fate, freedom, guilt—of the particular present to the historian" (*GBT*, 351). As Kisiel (*GBT*, 441) translates *BT*, 193, "Sense is the toward-which already structured by a prepossession, preview, and preconception." Engaged openness obtains as a future that both draws and gives. The human being is claimed by the future, and reciprocally the future needs the open clearing. Of the open clearing, "the human being is already had, and so holds forth, is already sighted in sighting forward, already grasped in its continuing conceiving. The spiraling movement of making sense out of existence in its being" is both claim and possibility (*GBT*, 442). Therefore understanding in its widest sway is understanding as matters of concern (*TM*, 90). Any "pure" stimulus-response relationship is merely a forcefully idealized case. Ideals, values, concepts, and theories can never obtain as absolutes.

The ground of understanding shows itself as grasping the ground of engaged openness. As a whole, engaged openness does not let itself be represented cognitively such that thoughts about it can be concretized. Engaged openness is grasped (understood) when it itself has opened up to human beings. For the most part human beings are always already "transported into what [is] opened up and remain determined by it from now on" (*BC*, 18). Understanding ground as ground means to be embraced by the proper temporal essence of grounded understanding such that this essence lets itself show itself *as* an embrace (engaging).

The embrace-of-understanding speaks to the human beings as they are listening to it. Understanding calls to itself as it can announce itself as that which engagingly embraces any listening of itself. The rejoining of call and listening is a belonging together.

The hold of engaged openness "does not consist exclusively in a knowing, although it has the essential characteristic of a knowing. This knowing, however, can remain concealed from itself for a long time, and can block the way to itself" (*BC,* 18). Despite being concealed, overlooked, or forgotten, knowing as understanding is an unseparatable moment of historicality and temporality and thereby forms an unshakable ground. The human being of openness cannot effect understanding through "mere flashes of insight, nor can they force it through the art of mere cleverness. What [they] can do and constantly do in one way or another, is only to remain within this knowing or forget it, to become aware of it (remembrance) or evade it" (*BC,* 18).

Knowing is knowing only when it is freed from the shackles of epistemology and is allowed to first and foremost offer itself as the immediacy of historically situated (thrown), discursive understanding. The human being of openness is thereby an engaged can-be such that the material conditions of "average intelligibility" as they manifest themselves in language can serve to assist, reveal, or blind it to the significant, the dangerous, or the unfree. On the contrary, the everyday language of an essential understanding often shows itself as inessential (*EHP,* 54-56).

Understanding is the way human beings practically and prudently comport themselves. It can be said that "one has understanding when one has insight into how something is connected with something else" (*ZS,* 233). The human being always already makes its way through its involvements. Understanding as thrownness (*ZS,* 139) and interpretation belong together (*TM,* 388-389). Likewise, understanding, involvement contexts, and language belong together with interpretive practices (*ZS,* 220; *TM,* 259). *Interpretation and understanding circle around each other as the calling play of language.* The human being circulates linguistically in order to be enabled to speak from the saying of language that "understanding is always interpretation, and hence interpretation is the explicit form of understanding" (*TM,* 307). Each human being always already understands, and concomitantly language is the originary sharing of sense as "the circulation of a meaning of the world that has no beginning or end" (*BSP,* 84). To be human is to understand originally and immediately (*TM,* 259).

Language

To what and how is the human being held or related? For Heidegger, the human being is indeed able to speak, but the human being is "had" by (belongs to) its own words (*OEL,* 3). The saying of discursiveness is "always an answering [that] remains forever relational. Relation is thought here always in terms of [disclosing and beckoning], and no longer conceived in the form of a mere reference" (*OWL,* 135). The play of language, according to Kisiel's reading of Heidegger, comes about as the "hold of all holds, relation of all relations" (*HWT,* 199). The human being is called-to and must sight and listen-as the enabling medium where the said and the unsaid come together but never necessarily meet or permanently fuse. There is a thesaurus of the availability of entities and matters of concern enabling them to be thought-said. There also is the possibility of a recalling to thought wherein the circulation of human experience always already discloses and beckons as possibility.

In his dialogue "Conversation on a Country Path about Thinking," Heidegger has the scholar (presumably himself) assert, "One can do hardly anything with a single word" (*DT,* 88). But of course Heidegger himself found in the unobtrusive smallness of the word "is" the revealing/concealing engaged openness of that which calls forth thought (*PM,* 343, 362). Does the 2,500-year-old struggle of Greco-European philosophical thinking speak to a lack of ability or to a never to be satisfied need?

The human being occasions discussion "by responding to language in a twofold way, receiving and replying. The mortal world speaks by co-responding in a multiple sense" (*PLT,* 209). Thereby the rejoining human being comes to see that "the expression 'to correspond' means to answer to the claim, to comport oneself in response to it" (*ZS,* 161). Answering-for is a responding to calls, invitations, and questions and even to a defiance of meaning as the understanding of finitude. When one responds *to,* one answers *for*—for meanings which are held out as available (*FT,* 296). All utterances contain responses as answering, encountering, and the letting of showing. When the human being of openness is disclosed and beckoned for showing-openness it is let into the exigency out of which it is enabled for bringing soundless aphonic showing to discursiveness (*OWL,* 129). Language as discursive saying claims human speaking as it responds. Thereby "responding is a listening-hearing. It hears because it listens to the command of stillness" (*PLT,* 210). Language as saying is a silent command—in this way language needs humans to co-respond with. Human beings are called to listen before they hear mere audible sounds. They can speak only as a response to language as its ownmost discursive saying (*OWL,* 107). They "can have no footing outside of the possibility of discursive meaningfulness" (*DG,* 158). The latter is what holds human beings in their sojourning co-responding and lets them take, use, engage, hold, grasp something as something (or nothing). This mutual hold is world: "something one assumes rather than creates" (*DG,* 158).

For modernity the structure of language is studied as the science of philology. But a structuralist/scientific approach to language cannot take into account language as a saying that unfolds out of an inaccessible silent origin. For Heidegger, human beings "speak of language, but constantly seem to be speaking merely *about* language" (*OWL,* 85). They are already allowing language from within itself to speak to them. Language *itself* is the showing of its unique essence (*OWL,* 85). The everyday use of language as an instrument borrows from a stock of words and has rules for combining them. But this is only a narrow and exterior aspect of language. Language comes to the human being in excess of being a mere tool that is possessed in tandem with a variety of other devices. The widest temporal play-space of language first offers the possibility of sojourning in the open clearing of engaged openness. The historical world is only where there is language. "The constantly changing cycle of decision and work, of action and responsibility, but also of arbitrariness and turmoil, decay and confusion," is where the historicality of world and language holds sway (*EHP,* 56). Language is not without its historically understood world.

Heidegger's project is to listen to and respond to a questioning-call on "whether the physiological perspective of vocal utterance, on the sound character of language, and on the body as [mere biological entity] constitutes the sole means of access to language—or whether this perspective is only *one* possible access, preceded by another access" (von Herrmann, 1989, 31). To listen and respond properly to language, human beings must let themselves "become involved in the questioning of the question" (*WCT,* 122). The human being of openness is immersed in language—there is no guarantee that it can find its way to language and that the way it has found is the right way. Indeed the way to language can never divorce itself from the question of what it means to be historically particular humans.

The course of discourse would include "the silent power of the possible" lying at the ground of the historical conversation of the play of traditions. This is a play that does not forget "the spontaneous self-forgetfulness of ordinary language" (*HWT,* 78). It is a play that in its possibility as possibility recollects "traditions within *living* language which constitute the meaningful context without which we would not understand anything at all" (*HWT,* 196). All tradition allows "its own unsaid in what is already said which it alone is called upon to say" (*HWT,* 197).

The calling-allotment of "what is sayable receives its determination from what is not sayable" (*EP,* 78), that is, the calling-allotment *itself.* Language silently demands that things (matters) be said: *"Language speaks as the peal of stillness"* (*PLT,* 207). In this significant way, language always already presents itself as the lack of linguistic utterance. This lack as the open, asymptotic difference is the unfolding of disclosure and beckoning wherein the human being is held to the offering of language as discursiveness. Humans speak as they are called into the open rift of difference between engaged openness and matters of concern. The open-endedness of ongoing quickening movement precludes any metaphysical closure. "In the absence of unity, one lives and acts in unending plurality" (*DH,* 214) as engaged responding and rejoining. Human speaking must, first and foremost, listen to the saying call of language "which the stillness of the difference calls world [engaged openness] and things [matters of concern] into the rift of its one-fold simplicity" (*PLT,* 209). Each word of human speaking can only speak out of such calling and as such is calling itself. Calling never discloses and beckons as a predetermined cause adhered to a desired effect. Even propaganda as the most tendentious and instrumental use of language cannot be certain that its effect will conform to its intent.

The saying of language and thinking belong to each other. Heidegger writes:

> Thinking is offered the way for thinking this self-suspended heart and core as the gifting of language. Language is the most sensitive and intricate and thus the most precarious resonating, holding each matter of concern within the suspended structure of disclosing and beckoning. The human being of openness dwells (abides/whiles/sojourns) in language inasmuch as its historical-temporal prevailing essence is delivered over to language. (*ID,* 38 [paraphrased])

Dwelling as such finds that "there is no ultimate language, but instead languages, words, voices, an originally sharing of voices without which there would be no voice" (*BSP,* 85).

The field of language as discursiveness is excess to engaged openness and clears and holds open access to matters of concern (*HPM,* 304). Language as discursive saying (showing/letting appear/sighting/listening) is the incipient appearing of matters of concern as "preserved by the human being in different ways" (*ZS,* 140). Language self-establishes and self-articulates when taking a matter of concern *as* a matter of concern arises (*BSP,* 88). The human being who understands is always already drawn into an on-coming through which sense self-presents itself (*TM,* 490). The way of understanding as such is always already prepared as language

(*HW,* 109). Language as field, excess, and clearing is the medium "of the with *as such:* it is the space of its declaration" (*BSP,* 88).

The with as with-world needs the speaking of language to beckon by calling matters of concern and engaged openness into their disclosed difference (*PLT,* 206). Difference is thought here as disclosing-beckoning that offers and holds apart the "between" in which disclosing and beckoning "are held toward one another, are borne away from and toward each other" as the issuance "of the two in *unconcealing keeping in concealment*" (*ID,* 65).

The place where hermeneutic phenomenology emerges/eludes is at the essentially unfolding boundary of words, not at a putatively fixed ego-self or a mathematically determined phenomenon. A word or groups of words unfold in their proper essence such that "a wide range of meaning belongs" to them (*WCT,* 191). To be linguistic is to be claimed by "a swarming multiplicity of meanings" as they nest in "dangerously harmless words" (*EGT,* 69). The indeterminacy of possible juxtapositions allows an olio of assertive statements. Language shows up in the company of human beings as a pathway that lets itself be traversed but does not admit of any final knowable destination. Human beings always already find themselves at the open clearing (locus of sense) wherein "language always speaks according to the mode in which [disclosing and beckoning] as such reveals itself or withdraws" (*OWL,* 131).

Hermeneutic phenomenology finds itself at its own thrown existential a priori as "that which is in each case always already ontologically operative" in the human being of open*e*dness (*DG,* 163). Human dialogical experience and the historical world cannot be separated into fixed information (data) units. The human being of openness as it whiles (sojourns/dwells/abides) in the opened open *is* sense in its meaningful dialogue with others, be they other humans or shared matters of concern. The discursiveness of engaged openness and the human being of openness belongs to disclosing and beckoning as the possibility of saying-showing.

Hermeneutic phenomenology as we read it takes discursiveness as the articulation (in all of its senses) of engaged openness such that engaged openness unfolds in discursiveness. Therefore, engaged openness cannot be looked at as some entity present as some isolatable categorizable other related to a given representing signifying practice. Engaged openness is to be taken as an on-coming that "becomes manifest (or not) *in* words — if they are able to say it." Representational significations restrict engaged openness to some entity present as calculated or theorizable. Words in this restricted (closed) mode cannot articulate engaged openness as a temporal whiling, which in its own unique and proper way withdraws "'behind' these words and remains unsaid" (Vallega-Neu, 2003, 26).

The task of hermeneutic phenomenology is a call to open up (release) saying into its widest play-space. The historical marks that hermeneutic dialogue bears are not those of the absolute certainty of firm conclusions, but are those of hesitating along the way, deliberating, and renunciation-as-forsaking, which, as an accepting (*ZS*, 5-6), enables a possible thinking dialogical experience with the originary (kinetic) temporal-historical essence of language (*OWL*, 64-73; 150-152).

Hermeneutic phenomenology is intimately and necessarily involved with language as are all humans in one way or another. On the surface of the matter at hand, language is taken as a mere instrument of communication, that audible or written demonstration of mental functioning in order to represent phenomena as images or concepts (*PLT*, 192-193).[12] This position, taken as a static union between the expressed and its perception, holds its place by dint of its perfect obviousness. But if thought is given to its fundamental answer, position, and logic, its ideal "disintegrates in the turbulence of a more originary questioning" (*PM*, 92).

A somewhat commonplace occurrence will serve to illustrate the shortcomings of an approach to language that takes as its truth that messages can be a pure sending from one ego-subject to another ego-subject as "context-free code" (Dreyfus, 1991, 221). In many comic strips, words or images are transferred from one balloon to another without any interference from some outside source. The taken for granted assumption is that pure communication and expression can be represented and therefore be made identical for each language participant. There is sharing, but it is the open between of world that is shared, not putatively identical cognitive/mental representations. World is mediately experienced as a "pre-object, pre-theoretical contexture of meaning" (*HWT,* 180).[13]

Language is not independent of context but is the very medium that enables the human being of openness as the experience of the play of world—world thought here as the nontotalizable totality of significance involvements. The way back to the emerging of language lets language show itself as a showing-saying. This showing-saying is not to be taken as an ontic beginning of vocal utterance either as an idealized creation or as a measurement of audibility. It follows then, from the nonclosability of any proper essence of language, that language possesses human beings, holds (calls) them to itself, and thereby cannot be product of human willing.

The opened task of hermeneutic phenomenology is to let the silent (not as silenced) source of language speak as showing-saying. Showing-saying lets itself be thought. All human experience is "already articulated, though not necessarily in words, by a prior understanding and interpretation that guide and determine them and so bring them to fulfillment" (*HWT,* 98).

In order to let world as a phenomenon of preverbal disclosure show and beckon itself, we borrow from Gadamer and reinterpret (slightly) what he has written of learning a foreign language (*PH,* 67-68). If world is taken as (read as) a foreign language, interpreters find themselves already immersed in something they immediately understand as world but do not know in any cognitive sense. Foreign languages call out for interpretation even if the call is ignored. The world as discursiveness (language) discloses and beckons in an analogous way. Each human being comes into a language world as a nonresident resident. Nonresidency calls forth residency and, in a seeming paradox, is necessary for proper residence. Interpreters are claimed by standing-in the call of language, but they cannot merely make a foreign language or world their own by willfully repeating or utilizing names. The infinite play of world as phenomenon is what it says as an offering, which shows—lets appear, sighting and listening (*OWL,* 93, 122). Sighting includes sighting of the invisible and the listening of the silent. Von Herrmann (1989, 40) submits these thoughts for consideration:

> If the sounding of language is experienced from the earth bound emergence and if this emergence is experienced in terms of a sounding as the calling gathering to which earth belongs, then the sound character of language is no longer subordinated to the bodily organs alone, as in the physical determination of language.

The historically particular opening of sense is world. World needs interpretation to respond to the saying-showing that co-responds to what is silently said by world.

Human beings near the essence of discursiveness as they speak by being silent. There is a coming to presence of language "when they are unable to find the correct word for matters of concern as concern carries away, oppresses, or encourages" (*OWL,* 59). *Speaking is not the mere utterance or nonutterance of vocalized sound. The craft of thinking belongs to discursiveness such that the former and the latter bear each other through each other.* The human being speaks insofar as it listens (*PLT,* 209); it is all ears. All speaking of human beings interrupts the silent difference but is held to ultimately return "to whence it was granted" (Fynsk, 1996b, 28-29). Language offers itself as a holding itself back as its possession of "astounding power" of a "mysterious wonder that makes us wonder" (*OWL,* 88).

Language as a speaking and calling out to understandings discloses and beckons as possibility, not as a productive capacity. Speaking "as the speech of mortals, is not self-subsistent. The speech of mortals rests in its relation to [in the hold of] the speaking of language" (*PLT,* 208). Therefore, "language gives itself *as language,* that is, as speaking, only by way of a kind of contrast, or countering, that is, in and through the *difference* between modes of speaking" (Fynsk, 1996b, 20). Language dwells in the rift, the tracing of the between, the open, the boundary "by drawing out, tracing out the differential (asymptotic) articulation as the difference between world" and matter of concern, as the play of the loci of sense "where the speaking of language is gathered and set out" (Fynsk, 1996b, 24-25).

Difference, opening as itself, is reflected in the question: Why is there something rather than nothing? As it persists and subsists, the human being of openness is the possibility to hold what is already said, out of which there is yielded "the unsaid that is yet to be said. Language [as we have cited] thus deserves the title 'hold of all holds; relation of all relations'" (*HWT*, 499)[14] such that world cannot world without it.

As a mutual re-collection of holding and grasping, (1) language presents the sayable of the engaged openness of matters of concern as food for thought and (2) grants the unsayable as the focal point of the sending, temporal particularity of human situatedness as the way that the human being of openness belongs (*BW*, 425). The human being *is* and is thereby claimed by the possibility of opened*ness* such that it cannot practically and prudently comport itself without language as discursiveness (*ZS*, 16). Language is not merely utterance and writing but is being-with. Language is more than manipulable word-things to be used at will. Words show significance as significance. The abiding of language is even more basic than sounds. Human beings can understand the same meanings in different languages without knowing the words. What is properly or uniquely essential to language is its saying. A word says a matter of concern—it does not sound of some entity. It is crucial to see that a word shows a matter of concern and is not the expression of an interior state of consciousness. "Saying = showing. Language is that which shows something" (*ZS*, 185), whether it occurs as highly specialized technical terminology or in the argot of everyday conversing.

A certain attentive belonging to language can be a central focus when teachers introduce students to disciplinary languages and language practices. Ashley, a new teacher, describes her concerns and experiences with language in her attempts to teach student nurses.

We spend way too much time as teachers trying to get students to use an exacting language. One that is precise and clear . . . and in certain contexts of course, this is imperative, and it keeps both patients and nurses safe. Sure, there are places in the curriculum where we have students look at the power of words and the meanings that go along with the languages they use. We have them reflect on terms like "knowledge deficit" and "noncompliance" and what these terms assume about patients and what it means to nurses to use them. Or we discuss how pervasive the language of business is . . . referring to patients as "revenue units" or "consumers" makes healthcare a business. There is much more to language than we think. The more we think about language, the more insight we have about how we are with the folks we are caring for. And yet, it isn't about controlling the language we use either, I mean, we've all had times in our practice when we were talking with a patient or giving a presentation, when something just popped into your head and you said it. And then when you heard what you said it's like, "Wow, that was important!" I guess that's how language speaks.

The human being of openness dwells in the neighborhood of language. This neighborhood is an open region wherein speaking is saying as showing and letting be sighted. Communicating and listening accordingly let the meaning of this open region show up such that the human being of openness can always already belong to and respond to claims that address it. The neighborhood of language is that which the specific individual can only ontically leave only as a result of the direst of human circumstance such as severe brain damage or death. Autistic children, the visually and hearing impaired, and persons with Alzheimer's disease all dwell in the openness of the with-world. Despite the demise or disability of an individual, the neighborhood of language always remains in order for the human being of openness to be engaged as possibility. In its widest sense, the with-world is inclusive such that all temporal-historical discursivity is in play.

The fundament of any saying is sighting something as something. It is always already evident that matters of concern *are.* "Thus the human being has something to say, because saying as letting-see is a letting-be seen of something as such and such a being. The human being, therefore, stands in the [open clearing of engaged openness], in the unconcealedness of what comes to presence" (*ZS,* 90). Language allots the same as prior to any intuition or reflection and thus enables ways of making the identifiable thematic. Therefore, the human is able to see that in naming entities, in addressing matters of concern as this and that, "that is in language, all formation of concepts is already delineated" (*ZS,* 131). Thrownness, understanding, and language are of Heidegger's historical-temporal particularity. Where do these come from? Where do they go? When and how is their place?

Articulation

Articulation, as the play of its significations and senses, offers hints by which whereabouts and wherewithals present themselves as points of access to the play of phenomena. "All understanding-as is an articulation of what is there, in that it looks-away-from, looks-at, sees-together-as" (*TM,* 91). Sightings such as these can occupy the focus of an interpretation or can merely slide along its margins and rest in its surroundings. As an articulating interpretation of the open clearing, sighting can also be a not-sighting. Foresight as a not-sighting is not necessarily negative if it leads *to* a reading of "what is not there at all" (*TM,* 91). Sense directs the way in which what is sighted is interpreted. Sighting means the possible articulation of phenomena other than those dominated by the purely evident. Attempts to posit isolated pure sense perception as what is purely seen in the optical sense "are dogmatic abstractions that artificially reduce phenomena. Perception always includes meaning" (*TM,*

92). Seen in light of the play of articulation, meaning can always be otherwise.[15]

In their translation of *Being and Time,* Macquarrie and Robinson discussed their use of the English word articulation. The German verbs *artikulieren* and *gliedern* "are nearly synonymous, but in the former the emphasis is presumably on the 'joints' at which something gets divided, while in the latter the emphasis is presumably on the 'parts' or 'members.'"[16] *Artikulieren* was thusly translated by Macquarrie and Robinson as "Articulate" and *gliedern* by "articulate." Perhaps this can be best illustrated through reference to the structure of a skeleton wherein discrete parts are joined at joints. Both parts and joinings are necessary for a skeletal structure to be what it is.[17] And, of course, the meaning and significance of any articulated skeletal structure equipped with organs, as biologically determined, go one step farther. More than, but not without, mere biology, articulation is a with-world of being-together, always already, on-coming, articulately exposed as the jointure of conversation and discourse as narrative telling.

The third sense of "articulation" turns on discursiveness. Above we have submitted that humans must attend to the difference between verbal articulation (utterance) and articulation as saying. Utterance "must always be strictly distinguished from saying, since articulation can also occur without verbal articulation" (*ZS,* 97). "Saying is always a letting-be-shown of something" as an occurrence through language (*ZS,* 97). "The intelligibility of something has always been articulated [as parts or members], even before there is any appropriative interpretation of it. Discourse is the Articulation [as joinings] of intelligibility. Therefore it underlies both interpretation and assertion. That which can be articulated in interpretation, and thus even more primordially in discourse, is what" is called sense (*BT,* 203-204). The play of parts (or members) and joinings always bears (issues-forth) and sustains sense as some "totality-of-significations" (*BT,* 204).

Paratactical readings as opposed to the syntactical allow us to take matters of concern as the possibility of reciprocally belonging to each other (*4S,* 2). We attempt to let the words schooling learning teaching articulate paratactically. The disclosing between where there are no words articulates as beckoning "nearness, in the sense of the radiance issuing from unconcealedness into unconcealedness" (*WCT,* 237).

Being singular plural, thrownness understanding language, building dwelling thinking, schooling learning teaching: These series of three apposite words mark an equivalence of apparent and inapparent appearance. The translative, transposing play that belongs to these terms is a co-implication of the sharing of the world, the world as "the coexistence that puts these existences together" (*BSP,* 29). None of the four sets of three terms should be taken as idealized entities that precede or ground the others. They co-translate.

Discourse as the joinings of the intelligibility of the open has the possibility of disclosing the open clearing as the human being of openness. Discoursing or talking is the way in which the human being articulates (members and re-members) the open clearing of the human being of openness. "Being-with belongs to [being]-in-the-world, which in every case maintains itself in some definite way of concernful [being]-with-one-another. Such [being]-with-one-another is discursive" (*BT,* 204) in all its aspects including sighting, listening, and the keeping silent of silence.

Articulation obtains as a joining of regions. In geometry, a line is formed by the joining of two planes. It is significant that a line does not require a given length and has no other dimension. The German word "'*Fuge' means not only a musical fugue but also 'joint,' 'seam,' 'cleft,' or 'fissure.'*"[18] Pathways, lines, articulations, clefts, rifts, and mirror play are terms wherein difference originates as an issuing or playing forth. In this way, articulation shows up as an engaged open belonging together of joinings and regions as these are asymptotically held near each other but are concomitantly held apart as the belonging together of their difference.

The Circle of Participation

> *One's always-already-opened-ness constitutes the*
> *ultimate circularity of human being and is the basis*
> *of all other circularities that characterize thinking*
> *and acting.*
>
> *KE,* 13

The circle of participation (*ZS,* 79; *BT,* 2, 193f; *P,* 135) does not presume to valorize knowledge over action or vice versa. Indeed, prior to any theory-practice distinction is releasement into the circulating circle as a participatory phenomenon (*DT,* 61, 76-77). Participatory matters of concern always already show up out from a historical, particularly disposed engagement with the world in which the human being of openness is sojourning (*ZS,* 166). An exposition of the theory-practice distinction enables the human being of openness to catch a glimpse of hints that are given by the historical movement of human life which is "never absolutely bound to any one standpoint" (*TM,* 304). As we have attempted to illustrate, there is always the possibility of a leap that would enable a transposition to a different standpoint or path. A transposition as jumping into the thick of things is not empathy or a subordinating of one to another but is an attempt at a "higher universality" (*TM,* 305). The latter term resides in the practice of hermeneutic phenomenology in the sense that there is not an ideal something which is outside and desires or demands admission. Noriko, a nursing student, describes a transposition to a different standing point.

> *You never think of your teacher as anything other*
> *than a teacher, an authority figure. We have a new*
> *instructor and she always seems disorganized and*
> *late in returning our assignments. Then one day I*
> *ran into her at the grocery store and she had twins*
> *and they were two years old! I was standing there*
> *thinking about what it was like when I had a two-*
> *year-old, realizing she and I were probably more alike*
> *than we were different. Not identical because she's*

still the teacher and I am the student. She has all the power to give grades and I don't. Some differences cannot be gotten around, but in a lot of ways we are more alike than different. That doesn't mean that we always agree because on a lot of things she thinks and wants us to do, I disagree. It's more that we share a lot of common understandings, like what it means to be overburdened with responsibilities, to be respectful, or to feel safe. My eyes were opened in a lot of ways.

The human being of openness is disclosed and beckoned as matters of concern and precisely in this being underway is opened up for the unique, the surprising, the richness of each time. "Higher" and "universality" in hermeneutic phenomenology are terms that offer possibilities that can overcome narrow particularities in favor of those that let the juxtaposing play of the reciprocal resonate.

Participation by definition is a being-with. But there is more. Participation turns on an open clearing that is already present, always already lies present.[19] The open clearing as locale is what frees or grants the possibility of participation or its privation (*OTB*, 64-67). The call of the with does not define the call or the caller. The call issues forth from the with.

Circling as Dis-Jointure[20]

What is decisive is not to get out of the circle, but to come into it in the right way.[21]

BT, 195

If viewed from the strict position of structural logic, any argument that depends on itself to prove itself is trapped in itself and cannot thus lead to a proper if-then determination.[22] But, for hermeneutic phenomenology as we read it, the presupposing of what needs to be established must initially draw on the always already historical anticipations of understanding. In this perspective, to consider an interpretation as free from any anticipations is both naïve and uncritical. The circle of understanding occurs as a double genitive that turns on the belonging-together as origination and accomplishment (*RHT,* 263-287). Our pathway follows a hinting that calls us away from origin and action as static and quantifiable entities.

Any self-showing of a phenomenon in character as a matter of concern should reveal itself as that character. Heidegger notes, "Anyone can easily see that we are moving in a circle. Ordinary understanding demands that this circle be avoided because it violates logic" (*BW,* 144).[23] Common knowing adheres to the position that what something is, is determined by some examination of similar things. The question that this assertion opens up is, How can we be certain of what, that, and how any given grouping is if there is not prior knowledge of what it is? Can the essence of the grouping be determined by recourse to some higher concept? The latter ensures itself because it is already in view. Can the collection of ontic characteristics match predetermined fundamental principles? Are the practices based on such putative fusions self-deluding? (*OTB,* 2). What do proofs prove?

As we have written earlier, Jean-Luc Nancy's tautological "hard shell" (*BSP,* 35) hints at questions turning on the belonging-to of belonging-with. The sentence "is is" calls as both absurdity and mystery. It can be dismissed as meaningless, or it can be puzzled over in order to come to grips with the play of nonquantifiable moments as these call the human being to be the human being of openness.

The play of the circle of participation *is* one wherein there is no forced stasis. It cannot be taken as "some flaw that can be wished away," but rather obtains as the "constitutive element of understanding" (Grondin, 2002, 50). Heidegger's circling movement cannot be equated to the closed subject-object circle that metaphysical thinking is claimed by. The circle of hermeneutic phenomenological understanding is not static—background as implicit is continually listened to and questioned in order to render otherwise normalized assumptions explicit. But in Heidegger's writing on Anaximander, the explicit is only proximally made explicit as an "apportioning of participation" (*EGT,* 54; *OBT,* 277) in any jointure.

Jointure as the apportioning belonging together of order (as an enjoining surmounting of disorder) and reck (as to let or allow something to be itself) is the presencing between of a twofold absence (*EGT,* 48; *OBT,* 272). Jointure emerges as historicality wherein difference as difference engages possibility as possibility. This engagement "hands out boundaries" (*EGT,* 54; *OBT,* 277) as whiling between emergence and elusion. For Heidegger, thinking collects and re-collects what is sent as a silent address of engaged openness (*EGT,* 56-58; *OBT,* 279-280). Engaged openness as historically sent ability of matters of concern to be of concern for the human being of openness turns on availability and accessibility, as an engagedness that necessarily includes usability, and understandability (*KE,* 6). The essence of the circle rests in the temporal play-space of saying that responds to the sending of the most simple of questions, circling as the issuing forth of engaged openness and matters of concern about each other (*ID,* 69).

Proximity to questioning is taking the temporality of questioning seriously as "the most appropriate manner of access to time" and dealing with "being questionable" (*BH,* 213). Heidegger has noted, "Whenever we come to the place to which we were supposedly first bringing difference along as an alleged contribution made by our representational thinking, we always find that [engaged openness and matters of concern] in their difference are already there" (*ID,* 62). The human being of openness is ultimately called to listen to the circularity of its existence. This can be declared to be neither makeshift nor defect. As human beings engage this being-on-the-way, they are strengthened in thought and enabled to participate in the craft that harks back to hermeneutic phenomenology. Listening to the calling of the call is the step back from entities as objects to things as matters of concern. On the other hand, matters of concern include the onticness of entities and must be paid heed to. Heidegger submits the thought that "every separate step that we attempt circles in this circle" (*BW,* 144).[24]

In this book, we will attempt to think out of our debt to tautologies as they turn as quickening's essential unfoldings. The way to the groundless source gives the human being to think. There is a unique characteristic of hermeneutic phenomenological thinking "in comparison with every scientific orientation that at the moment when [thoughtful] knowledge is to emerge, what is decisive is not so much taking hold of the matter, but appraising the standpoint of the investigation—and this has nothing to do with methodological reflections" (*FCM,* 287). It is possible to see starting as earliness, not as a discrete beginning, but as an always already "counter-play of call and belonging" (*CP,* 219)[25] such that moments must be taken as arrivals and departures that belong to, are engaged with each other. Presence is not presence without circulation, passage, and pathway. The ensuing chapters look at phenomena as we see their showing of themselves. Our practice, as well as our own looking at our practice showing itself, is the enabling that allows us to continue on our way.

Chapter 3 Notes

1   See also *BT,* 117.

2   See *ZS,* 59-75.

3   See also *HCT,* 123, 129.

4   See also *WCT,* 50; *P,* 82; *BW,* 208.

5   See *KPM,* 157-158, for further discussion on *Dasein.*

6   See *BT,* 402.

7   See also *GBT,* 441.

8   See also Sheehan, *HPM,* 306-307, for discussion of care.

9   See "The As-Structure," Chapter 1.

10   See Chapter 2, "Nearness and Temporality as Absence and Presence."

11   Translation used here is by Theodore Kisiel (*RHT,* 266).

12   See also Taylor, 1985, 215-292.

13   See also *BT,* 114-122.

14   See also *OWL,* 120, 127, 135; *BW,* 415, 423, 425.

15   See also *GBT, 265-268, and BT, 56, 195-203.*

16   See *BT,* 195 translators' fn. 1.

17   See also *WCT,* 182-183; *BSP,* 37, 96.

18   In Vallega-Neu, 2003, 32.

19   See *EP,* 26-32.

20   See *EGT,* 42, *OBT,* 267.

21   See also *EGT,* 42; *OBT,* 267; *TM,* 291, 293-294, 298.

22   See also circling as dis-jointure, *EGT,* 42-44; *OBT,* 267-269.

23   See also *OBT,* 2.

24   See also *OBT,* 2.

25   Translation used here is by Kisiel (*RHT,* 264).

Chapter 4

Attending, Listening, and Co-Responding as Phenomena: The To and Fro of Phenomena

> Scientist: *Again this restless to and fro between yes and no.*
>
> Scholar: *We are suspended as it were between the two.*
>
> *DT,* 75

If thinking and questioning are not the securing of certainty, what other ways lead to (and from) phenomena? Calling into question contemporary notions of phenomena and conscious agency, Heidegger proffered that "imperceptible, ontological phenomena always already and necessarily show themselves *prior to* all perceptible [ontic] phenomena" (*ZS,* 6). Imperceptible ontological phenomena refer "to a possibility of [engaged openness] and not merely to the logic of a" proposition (*ZS,* 47). An existing object is seen immediately whereas "existing as such" is not visible (*ZS,* 187). Everyday, ordinary experience *first* gives any matrix of involvement as "the condition for the possibility for the appearance of the ontic, for the appearance of" matters of concern as matters of concern (*ZS,* 187). The play of engagement as such is its own phenomenon in that it self-obtains as possibility.

Our next question becomes deceptively simple: What is a phenomenon? For Kant, as well as most of our current tradition, a phenomenon is something to which real predicates can be ascribed. Attributes such as mass, weight, and temperature are among Kant's real predicates. A rational ego must ascribe these predicates to a thing, as part of a process that synthesizes thing and judgment. For Kant this process transcends historical and other contingencies (*PM,* 337-336).

But for Heidegger, the contingent is the calling of human beings to an asymptotic closeness to the temporalized discovering or uncovering of the historically situated essence of phenomena. Existence is not that something is physically present or cognitively known (ontic), but it is, first and foremost, how something exists[1] or comes to presence as presencing itself. The contingent becomes "more real" than the real of the tradition. For example, the existence of the human being of openness is contingent upon its finitude: the possibility of the future as its permanent absence and the possibility of the future as an incompletable incompleteness. Between the two kinds of phenomena lies a topos made possible by practices of accepting and differentiating. This is the ontological difference: the difference between being as engaged openness and beings as matters of concern. The difference is *not* anything (or any thing) that can be willed or called forth. The difference is

> the distinction within which everything ontological moves and which it presupposes, as it were, for its own possibility. It is the distinction in which being [engaged openness] is distinguished from [matters of concern] which it also determines in the way their [engaged openness] is constituted. The ontological difference is the difference sustaining and guiding such a thing as the ontological in general, and not a particular distinction that can or must be made within the ontological. (*FCM,* 359)

There is no imperative that is delivered to the human being to think this difference as difference. Thinking-saying is "free either to pass over the difference without a thought or to think it specifically as such" (*ID,* 63). Thus "it is nowhere written that there must be such a thing as ontology, nor that the problematic of philosophy is rooted in ontology" (*FCM,* 359). Despite the invisibility of the difference it calls as difference, it gives, offers itself for thought.

In an initial attempt to trace and illuminate what difference as difference *says,* we first "follow the long habituation of a firmly ingrained way of thinking" (*BC,* 58). The way moves with us such that "one cannot settle a two millennia heritage in ten or twenty years" (*4S,* 51). The human being of openness sojourns in the ontological difference (the difference between engaged openness and matters of concern) and can neither be enabled to, nor desire to, overcome this difference via a theologically determined difference between angels and nonhuman animals.[2] The ontological difference marks the open region that Heidegger subjects to exploration in order to get beyond the subject-object schema that claims the modern epoch. The human subject has arrived somewhere between the horizons of theology and biology via the gathering of logos[3] as the saying of language. The human being of openness is free for the possibilities this arrival proffers, as a complex of accepting listening practices or comportments (*4S,* 56-60).

For Heidegger it is human beings who listen and not the ear as a mere auditory organ that hears: Hence we do not have ears in order to hear but rather listen in order to have ears (*POR,* 47). Hearing is a kind of perceiving, as is all sensuous perception. Traditionally, though, this kind of sensibility has been seen to be inferior to and separable from abstract cognitive activity. Theory development and/or dispassionate observation have been looked upon as forms of transcendent truth. In simplest terms these positions obtain as forms of effects. The atom bomb was theorized, then utilized. To be sure, microbes in drinking water were observed and duly removed, enabling the prevention of water-borne diseases. But could it be that the practice of boiling water for tea offered the hint that enabled the discovery of water-borne pathogens via the microscope?

As stunning as the achievements of science are, there is the necessity that one must always already listen to whether one wants to or not. Discursiveness as conversation, reading, and writing obtains as the passage of participatory experience of world, because it *can* be listened to and sighted. There is not a single knowing sense organ or choosing, isolated, exhaustible consciousness. Therefore, what calls forth the hermeneutic phenomenological event proper is not language as grammar, utterance, or lexicon (*TM,* 463). Language itself consists in the coming into speech of what is already a tradition of saying as disclosure and beckoning which lets interpretation occur. The human being is discursively engaged. Language says "the immanent domain of possible experience to the outermost periphery of the unconditioned" (Schalow, 1992, 428) wherein it "speaks for all and of all" (*BSP,* 3).

Being in Attendance

> *The call is precisely something which we ourselves have neither planned nor prepared for nor voluntarily performed, nor have we ever done so. It calls, against our expectations and even against our will.*
>
> *BT,* 320

Humans are of the world. Attending as a phenomenon cannot be thought without world. The reverse also holds, but not as cause to effect or as an if-then relationship. The open clearing is at once the site of the incipience of the listening belonging together that characterizes the human being of openness. Thrown disposedness can be a forgetting of engaged openness but must still attend to the ontological difference which shelters engaged openness. The human being belongs to a listening-co-responding *with* entities other than itself as well as other humans. This is only possible because there is always already understanding as engaged openness (*ZS,* 153). Engaged openness "assigns 'letting-lie-before us,' not the other way around" (*BP,* 181). There is *"there is"* such that "neither anything in the world nor the world itself—an unsummable totality, unassumable by the 'there is'—obeys any other necessity than 'there is.' And this necessity of existence is radically removed from the existence of any necessity" (*CP,* 186).

Human beings essentially belong to and are in attendance with the open clearing of engaged openness. The open clearing of engaged openness exigently needs the human being of openness of its (the clearing's) manifestation *(4S,* 63).[4] Attending in the sense of disposedness obtains as a temporal play-space, waiting, giving heed, staying with, serving, destining, presencing, and comporting.[5] The manifestation of the open is imperceptibly grounded by what is not in attendance as historically particular disposedness. Heidegger has identified wonder *(BQP)*, angst *(BT, IM)*, boredom *(FCM, BH)*, and reservedness *(CP)* as modes of disposedness. The possibility of each mode of disposedness is such that each calls the human being into the open clearing of its never to be a complete and perfect knowing presence. The human being of openness as attendant has a sense of owing which, by virtue of its always already lack of complete presence, can never be finalized as some ideally fulfilled entity *(KE)*.

According to Heidegger, the story holding sway that was necessary to challenge was put in motion at the beginning of modernity's thinking. The task for him turned on retrieving "need" and "distress" from their everyday negative connotations *(BQP,* 131). As we mentioned earlier, the need he was concerned to explore grew out of the angst of neither knowing the way out nor the way in. He wrote of the human being's "inability to remain and yet [inability] to leave" its place *(FCM,* 365). For Heidegger there was a between wherein practical interpretive comportment had not been determined per se, but nevertheless any of the incoherence and indifference to the undifferentiation of engaged openness and lack of matters of concern did not and could not avoid questioning by letting one matter blur into another. "Distress [or concern], as such a not knowing the way out of or into this self-opening 'between,' is a mode of" engaged openness. Thus the human being arrives or perhaps is thrown and for the first time experiences—but does not expressly consider—the call of world as matters of concern *(BQP,* 132). The questionable is disclosed and beckoned as distress or as the necessity to ask "Is there?" The human being of openness is called to thinking-saying the open clearing as the open, not as a lack and not as a deprivation but as the surplus of an offering *(BQP,* 133). The fundamental and ontic finitude of each human being seems less onerous to think than open ontological possibility itself.

Heidegger averred that this distress is a character of the givenness of the given and not a product of human beings. For him human beings "first arise out of this distress, which is more essential than" human beings themselves as they are essentially given as concerned distress (*BQP,* 133). Engaged openness toward death is the engaged openness of the entity that is mortal.[6] World does not arise *for* the human being and thus remains strange. It allows or allots withdrawing of any familiar such that the human being of openness can be called steadily into the question of itself, of its meaning—which it always already "is" as engaged openness. The "is" advenes as on-coming temporality, fated "to be always open." The human being is "likewise fated to be exposed and receptive." As engaged openness, the human being of openness is "thrown into the necessity of being present-unto, into needing the presence of other entities" (*KE,* 12).

In Chapter 3 we discussed Heidegger's notion of starting from a place other than the *ego cogito* as modernity's presupposed foundational inner experience (*ZS,* 54) in order to get at alreadiness (*ZS,* 67-75). The human being of openness does not represent some thing mentally in order to determine an entity-for-itself. Rather, to be-in-the-world is an immediate engaged openness as "being right at," without any prior mediation of a mental representation or picture. The human being is simultaneously "right at" entities that are its world. *For there to be world, the human being must be in attendance.* Hermeneutic phenomenology asks how the belonging to a matter of concern is determined—how the proper essence of a matter of concern is a referent of world (*ZS,* 54).

Mutual Encountering

> *To gain a correct understanding of the phenomenal structure of* availability *in advance, it is important to see that the in-order-to and for-what, make up the originally given "there" which is closest to us and not to explain them as something we come across subsequently in the sense of an external point of view imposed on and affixed to what is already there.*
>
> *OHF,* 75

The world humans are is simply available to know-how. This does not imply some absolute possession. The world allows the human being of openness to become world such that the human being is enabled to enact taking "something as something." That which is a taking-as, in its very taking-as, "*compels* us before what is possibly" (*FCM,* 363) actual in the sense of that which is delivered over to the open but is never possessable (*FCM,* 365). The human being of openness inherits and *is* a world as relationship, and this relationship, as the between of mutual encountering, is offered in any taking something as something.

Recall that for Heidegger the human being of openness is historically and temporally "face to face with what is as such—and no longer with the mediation of a representation" (*4S,* 71). As a result of transposing thought from claims of the centrality of consciousness, hermeneutic phenomenology is claimed by letting the open clearing show itself as the play of possibility and actuality. *Actuality is not the real.* In Heidegger's view the real belongs to science as technoscientism, wherein the objectness of objects as the real is merely disposable in advance to be ordered up by human willing (*QCT,* 158-168).

The issue that science skirts is its "not to be gotten around" tautology that turns on the possibility wherein "presences can appear, but never must appear" (*QCT,* 176). Presencing: presencing itself (*4S,* 80) as the surprise of "inceptual upsurging" (*4S,* 9) is in attendance as constantly changing ways of mutual belonging to engagement-with. These ways show up "according to the place on the way at which a path begins, ever according to the portion of the way that it traverses, ever according to the distant view that opens along the way into that which is worthy of questioning" (*QCT,* 181). Attending is thereby attendant on the disclosing and beckoning of disclosing and beckoning. Namely, the human being of openness cannot be who it is without listening attendance "to the world that determines an attending in which [the human being] at the same time [attends to itself]" (*POR,* 37). The human being of openness is called to attention by the attraction of what withdraws by its very withdrawing from it (*WCT,* 9).

The particular historical and therefore temporalized temporality of each human being always already obtains as an already had and a holding that so holds forth. This temporal play discloses and beckons together as the reciprocating conditions of a not to be possessed existence. To be the "open is only possible when the [open] clearing has already happened to [human beings] so that something can be present or absent" (*ZS,* 145). Engaged openness gives the possibility wherein one is enabled to and for the finding of one's way.[7] This is what Heidegger points to when he takes the always already as "the a priori of all a prioris" (*HWT,* 199).

Engaged openness as the always already "being encountered has its own *temporality*" (*OHF,* 78). *The human being belongs to its concerns and must attend to them.* To be a concerned-about and an attending-to calls the human being of openness in many ways: "as not yet, as to be for the first time, as already, as approaching, as until now, as for the time being, as finally" (*OHF,* 78). In its self-disclosing "the world as such is not encountered, but simply provides the nexus which lets entities be encountered" (*GBT,* 328) as temporal and participatory matters of concern.[8]

The Commanding/Commending of Retinue

> For *"to command"* basically means, not to give commands and orders, but to commend, entrust, give into safe-keeping, keep safely.
>
> *WCT,* 118

The human being is ontically singular in that it is a single entity, but it is ontologically a plural because the human being of openness is its possibilities. The human being of openness is its own retinue. The human being of openness existing as an exposed belonging to singular pluralities is engaged openness as always already "openness for being claimed by the presence of something" (_ZS_, 217). There is, for Jean-Luc Nancy, the passage of sense as "the opening of a spatial world as meaningful or intelligible, but there is also the contact or touch of something concrete or material" (James, 2006, 106). Being-with is, for Jean-Luc Nancy, a thinking-saying of "bodies, of every body, whether they be inanimate, animate, sentient, speaking, thinking, having weight and so on" (_BSP_, 83-84). Thinking-saying turns on making thinkable "the passage of sense as a bodily event, as an opening up of meaningful spaces and a meaningful world in which such distinctions as mind/body, ideality/materiality" are "prior to any cognition per se" (James, 2006, 107).

The human being is commanded by and concomitantly commended to tradition (the passage of sense) in its bodily (ontic) and interpreting (ontological) engaged openness. Hermeneutic phenomenology presupposes that the traditions humans are always already immersed in constantly offer hints concerning their sway. Tradition in its various guises (combinations and permutations) calls attention to itself such that it allows the human being of openness to understand the call of tradition discursively. To _be_ the open clearing is from the clearing's ownmost always already emergence/illusion. The freeholding of oneself _toward_ whatever matters of concern are offered as the open is "_letting oneself be bound_" (_FCM_, 342). The possible binding (calling) of tuning in (being disposed) to entities as relating to them in practically comporting oneself in such and such a way, is characteristic in general of every "can-be" and comportment of the human being of openness (_FCM_, 342).

Modernity's presuppositions of capacity and behavior constrict and command thinking such that a human being never finds any letting itself be commanded by something commended. For modernity the human being is merely a set of a-contextual, ahistorical, instinctual drives that are thought thereby to keep the human being in bondage (*FCM,* 342). Recall that on the contrary, human beings are commanded and commended as calling to their own traditions and their meaningful contexts—otherwise they would not understand anything at all (*HWT,* 196). Any *"pre-predicative manifestness* must itself be constantly already in which a particular *letting oneself be bound* occurs" (*FCM,* 342). The call (commending) of tradition and its calling (commanding) cannot be separated from practical, prudent comportment. As tradition claims the human being, there is the possibility of a moving passage from being bound by one matter to another. The human being of openness is offered a play-space to choose conformity or nonconformity of its practical comportment toward whatever is calling as catching (nabbing, trapping one's gaze) (*FCM,* 342).

A future of open possibility means that practical know-how "must already bring toward itself in advance, and as something that can be binding, whatever is to provide the measure and be binding in one way or another. This holding oneself toward—toward something [binding]—which occurs in all propositional comportment and *grounds* it, is what [is called] a *fundamental comportment: being free* in an originary sense" (*FCM,* 342-343).

Freedom then turns on being free from the domineering abstractions of immanence, theoretical generalizations, and reductionist, material scientisms and above all, the enslaving illusions of immortality. Freedom obtains as freedom for a "letting oneself be [called] in being held toward" the always already, disclosing and beckoning "in such a way that [matters of concern] are manifest as such in advance" (*FCM,* 343). The human being of openness is thereby commanded/commended and claimed as the possibility of attentive engaged openness by its own historically particular time. Such dependency is not submission but is the belonging to the issuing forth of free thought (*EGT,* 55).

The Time of Attending

How is a non-metaphysical thinking of time possible?

4S, 43

Each time taking something as something raises the human being into the possible as a making-possible, the human being, as active in on-coming and instantiated taking, is persistent such that it must endure (*FCM,* 363). The time of tradition and world is such that it emergingly/elusively offers the human being of openness room as a place which allows for a possible sojourn. "'Possibility' so understood, as what enables, means something else and something more than mere opportunity" (*OWL,* 92-93). For example, finitude as finitude is nothing that can be taken advantage of in order to overcome it. Time can only be seen as the messenger, which always already delivers, as "the lightening—concealing—releasing offer of world" (*OWL,* 107). The human being of openness belongs to the call to attention, of saying in all its discursive play: silence, conversation, dialogue, assertion, narrative, interpretation, poesy, and literature. The showing of particular allotments is the appearing of the human being's necessary engagement.

We are pursuing the human being and its being called to attention, not as the rigid standing of an atemporal posture toward intuitive or cognitive knowledge. There is always already practical, prudent know-how that belongs toward and from matters of concern. Engaged openness is the necessary engagement wherein the intending and the intended are not static but a play of temporal exposedness. There is the option of how temporal exposedness is paid attention to. A message as such must have a delivery context. The precursor of hermeneutics resided in the historicality of engaged openness as it self-unfolded for the Greeks as "saying, explaining, and translating" (Palmer, 1969, 12-32).

The carrier of the message of the unconcealment/concealment of existence and the human being, whether thought as entities or idealities (*OWL,* 26), was (as we have mentioned) the wing-footed messenger-god Hermes, the playful, possibly prevaricating bringer of destiny (*OWL,* 29). Today destiny is still delivered as the on-coming always already that lays claim to the human being. The on-coming of what is already, as the gathering of abiding/sojourning/whiling, needs the human being of openness to submit messages of reception. This reciprocating disclosing and beckoning is the granting of abiding/whiling/sojourning. The message engages the delivering of "the distinction between the common generic universal of the all and the proper distributive universal of the each" (*RHT,* 266). Message bearing as the engaging of human beings to the message's sending and receiving comes from the message in order to reciprocally belong to its distribution (*OWL,* 51).

Listening needs both message and message bearing, no matter whether the messaging is one of finitude and historicality in their richest scholarly sense or whether it is in the everyday sense of living a life that calls for being with (as belonging to) others. The teacher in this narrative tells of listening to the call of students. The message in play here resonates back and forth.

Germaine, a nurse teacher, tells her experience of learning to listen to students.

> *I've been really listening to the students and it has changed everything for me! Like I talked with the students about preparing for class and they told me they learn best by listening to the lecture first and then doing the reading and assignments. So now I talk with them at the beginning of the course and make sure they feel free to come "unprepared" to class. They're learning more and that's what matters. And now I listen differently—or maybe I'm just more patient. I'm often asked how I could not not "require" students to come prepared. We teachers are here to school students but how to do it is always changing, including our school, going ahead to who knows where. Like everything else in life. You can never know all the possibilities; there are always more things to know or do as a teacher or student—it's just part of life. We seem to be never at a point where we can finish listening. Or should I say hearing? I don't know.*

Listening

> *Resounding does not resound* into the "ear," *but* in the "soul."
>
> *OEL,* 95

To be called to attention (to be in attendance) is to listen and give heed to the call that exercises a holding (calling) that comes over and upon the human being (*OWL,* 91).[9] Everyday listening both needs and is claimed by something listenable, and thereby "finds itself always and everywhere" (*OWL,* 83). The play of listening's possibilities is indebted to the play of "manifold experiences with language" (*OWL,* 84). Gadamer called attention to this play when he stated that to say "language speaks human being" is literally more correct than to dogmatically assert that the human being controls language via speaking it (*TM,* 463). Language could not speak human being if language-as-saying had not listened for the human being of openness as the open between of listening.

Any given position that represents or signifies "mind" as ground cannot be "in control of what words of tradition reach" a given human being (*TM,* 461). The proper disclosing and beckoning of listening as an interpretive experience is letting as possibility because discursiveness is freed up for the human being as tradition. The tradition to which the human being is callingly called (directed to pay attention) properly encounters the human being of openness as if the tradition is addressed to each human being and is concerned with it (*TM,* 461). Questioners always already become the ones questioned as traditions call for the calling of rejoinings' counterplays (Fynsk, 1996b, 41-42).

Listening as belonging to the call of traditions turns on the unavoidability of belonging to the address of traditions. Thought in the way of historical transmission, listening belongs to the discursive experience of the world (*TM,* 462). For Gadamer, one can look away, but one cannot "hear away" (*TM,* 462). The universal medium of language enables a coming to pass wherein "everything is comprehensible, except the comprehensibility of everything" (*N,* 313). The listener "can listen to the legends, the myths, and the truth of the ancients" as oral or written as other than a mere sensible immediacy (*TM,* 463). Being thrown as tradition is attending to it in one way or another.

The naming word of a tradition as a possibility "should be thought in relation to an injunction, a command, or an order that authorizes" (Fynsk, 1996b, 43). If the human being lets word relations say what they want to say, it listens such that the human being of openness in its very engaged openness "is in demand, is needed" (*OWL,* 32). The human being of openness belongs to the exigency which claims it "with respect to bringing tidings, with respect to preserving a message" (*OWL,* 32). The call callingly whispers: "The veiled relation of message and messenger's course plays everywhere" (*OWL,* 53). Listening presents itself as being "able to follow, that is, going along with and that is, going ahead of" (*OEL,* 94). Calling to the call of human finitude is neither necessary nor sufficient in a modernist-metaphysical sense. But in the hermeneutic phenomenological sense, the call-calling relationship can be made thematic as the phenomenological essence of hermeneutical listening, that is, as co-responding, converging conversation.

Listening "is not law in the sense of a norm which hangs over our heads somewhere, it is not an ordinance which orders and regulates a course of events" (*OWL,* 128). The human being of openness does "not first need to process and shape a tumult and medley of feelings"; it is always already part of the understood (*HCT,* 266). Engaged openness as the human being of openness is initially "always already involved with the world itself, and not with 'sensation' first and then, on the basis of a kind of theatre, finally involved with" the matters of concern (*HCT,* 266).[10] Listening-hearing includes the possibility of mishearing. A human being "can hear wrongly" (*EGT,* 65). The possibility resides in the familiar such that its ownmost knowability can be what is most foreign to it (*EGT,* 122). Each time the human being of openness listens to something it is letting the call of calling be said to it: "All perception and conception is already contained in that act" of listening (*OWL,* 124). Letting as letting obtains only as the human being of openness is already the engaged openness as the open clearing which comes as discursiveness. Letting here must not be seen as the willful activity of a human agent. Discursiveness is the always already as nonaudible "saying" which offers the listening and the call of language "solely to those who belong within it" (*OWL,* 124). Saying transports all presence of matters of concern into their offered presence; temporal particularity delivers and brings what is absent into their absence (*OWL,* 126).

The human being is the one "called on to recall" (*OWL,* 166), that is, to listen-back-to-calling, as the one who is asked by those concerns of its own (to which it belongs) to subject them to questioning. Put another way, there are announcements as calls in the sense of engaged openness's whisperings in one's ear. Calling as the human's belonging to these whispers comes as "the announcement of the other by the other (*SV,* 247). The calling of listening (whispers belonging to hearing; hearing belonging to whispers) is the infinite alteration of the other" (*SV,* 246) such that interpretation arrives as "the announcement of finitude by way of finitude" (*SV,* 247)—renewed calling as recalling the human being of openness to itself.

In order to be an ontological phenomenon, listening must be silent and imperceptible—phenomena are not uttered, but they speak (*PLT,* 208). Phenomena can be brought into nearness by a reciprocal nonsensory sighting and listening (*PLT,* 208). A phenomenon such as absence ("the nothing") demands obedient attention as it calls from absence, on-coming, and the privative (*PLT,* 208). Ontically speaking each human being, one way or another, "sees and hears words in writing and in sound" (*OWL,* 87). Listening shows itself as touching—for example, "Your words touched me" or "I am struck by your words."

The human being does not apprehend in order to speak, it speaks in order to apprehend, but not as a mere acoustical occurrence. Thus "not-hearing, resisting, defying, and turning away as well as following, going along with" obtain as that which let listening become as possibility (*BT,* 207). The human being of openness belongs to sense. Sounds such as words are never first heard as mere tones; even the incomprehensible is heard *as* incomprehensibility (*HCT,* 266). The sighting of listening as well as the listening of sighting discloses and beckons as other moments of imperceptible or ontological phenomena. The human being is enabled to choose to let itself see and hear the invisible and the silent as these appear and speak in their showing.

Listening and sighting are thought here as other than the utilization of an acoustical or optical device. Listening is thought as belonging to sighting, but sighting as a sighting-as—for example, "*Now* I see what you mean." Thereby sense "does not consist in the transmission from a speaker to a receiver," or of a photon to a receptor. It is "the passing back and forth and sharing of the origin at the origin" (*BSP,* 86). Let us recall here that origin is thought as incipience, emergence/elusion or on-coming/departing, and privation as that which is present by being absent. The singular plural as "the place of sharing and crossing through" (*BSP,* 95) is the site of "the counter-play of call and belonging" (*RHT,* 264).

What does listening bring to light (show)? Listening as "phenomenally more original than the mere sensing of tones and perceiving of sounds" (*HCT,* 266) reveals "a showing in the sense of bringing something to light" (*OWL,* 115). Listening in the hermeneutic phenomenological sense must not be thought in the active and mechanistic sense of a computer command whereby any item can be repeated. The "mind," as thought this way, is a mere computer analog. Hearing as listening is constitutive of the basic and proper way in which the human being of openness is as an engaged can-be. The voice of a friend is the carrying-with of listening. *The can-be of listening as the existentially primary is the possibility of listening.* Only where world is, is there the possibility of listening (*BT,* 206-208).[11] Listening is the implicit enactment of the understanding of being as engaged openness (world as engaged matters of concern).

The human being first listens to historically situated situations (is disposed to them) and not auditory events. The human being of openness belongs to "the thunder of the heavens and the noises of the city" and "yet do[es] not belong to them" (*EGT,* 65-66). Listening arises when that which is called to belongs "to the matter addressed" (*EGT,* 66). Belonging to as calling to is both obeying and allowing what is in front of human beings to be together with whatever lies in advance. If everything were merely heard there could be no listening. Its springing forth lies before as a steering that gathers the on-coming (finitude, death); absence gathers itself into presence.

The proper unique essence of hearing is a co-emergence wherein the human being of openness maintains itself in listening disposedness (*EGT,* 67). Hearing as a concerned letting-lie-before is the disposed, immediate concern of everyday concern of matters of concern that are present-to and with each other (*EGT,* 122). Engaged openness concernfully as the human being of openness in-the-world "is always first on the receiving end of existence, ever in need to be receptive and responsive to its demands" (*GBT,* 435).[12] The amplification of "the discovery of the possibilities of self-finding" comes to pass as understanding (*GBT,* 379).

Discovering does not turn on the targeted goal of a predetermined outcome. Readiness for belonging to the possibility of discovery is calling as obeying and is listening as attending to complying wherein response "to the demand exacted by the discovery" (*GBT,* 379) turns on the how of discoveredness. The call of listening offers possibilities for engaged openness to specifically "be its temporally particular" open clearing (*GBT,* 379).[13] The possibilities of the as-structure always already deliver up and address the human being of openness, contributing to the engaged openness of the with-world. The "domain of the inapparent" is a play of hinting such that hinting "is what shows and lets be seen in that it depicts what is to be seen" (*4S,* 79).

To call-to is to obey as calling. Calling to what? Is the human being constrained to merely obey? An answer rests in the modernist metaphysical opposition of mind and body. The human being by calling listens and sees the invisible limits of the rift opened by this opposition. How is the "if one (mind or body) then not the other (mind or body)" heard and seen? Calling as listening-to means to let the place of any assertion or judgment be retrieved *to* its essence as an emergence from interpretation and understanding. Heidegger has written, "Every assertion, whether it affirms or denies, whether it is true or false, is *synthesis* and *diarhiesis* equiprimordially" (*BT,* 201). That is to say, binding and separating are inextricably disclosed, and beckon each other. The human being does not control how the words of tradition reach it. Mentalist conceptions cannot capture the inception of actual experience as it belongs to everyday comportment.

Co-Responding

> *If our human-mortal hearing and viewing doesn't have its genuine element in mere sense reception, then it also can't be completely unheard of that what can be heard can at the same time be brought into view, if thinking views with an ear and hears with an eye.*
>
> *POR,* 48

The belonging together of call, calling, and listening in all of their senses discloses and beckons as an encounter that commends sense as sense. According to Jean-Luc Nancy, "Every act of language, every exchange of signs, consists in the anticipation of sense" (*FT,* 294). The genitives in the foregoing quote offer the hint that sense "moves along again, passing beyond and elsewhere" (*FT,* 295). Sense, as viewed here, belongs to its own temporal particularity, its own excess—sense discloses and beckons as engaging, reengaging, or disengaging. There is no guarantee that sense will make sense, but sense is never senseless.

According to Jean-Luc Nancy, a significant focus of interpretive thinking hearkens to the phenomenon of sense. As he sights sense, he finds that to exist in the everyday is to be asked "to make sense" (*FT,* 11). Sense discloses and beckons as including, but as not necessarily restricted to, the play of the given and the mediated, as well as surprise, sets of signs, signification—that is, as the emergence of significance (*SW,* 147). The temporal-historical sense *of* the world resides in joining, playing, speaking, and sharing as never to be differentiated or separated "from the sense of 'making sense'" (*SW,* 78).

The on-coming of temporality allows sense to be always in excess of itself. Sense is here but it is always already elsewhere. Each time the future becomes present, encountering has taken place, a work or event is instantiated; sense "moves along again, passing beyond and elsewhere" (*FT,* 295). *Sense as sense can never be firmly grasped; it can only be neared.* Heidegger offers this hint:

> *Thinking itself is a way. We respond to the way only by remaining underway. To be underway on the way in order to clear the way—that is one thing. The other thing is to take a position somewhere along the road, and there make conversation about whether, and how, earlier and later stretches of the way may be different, and in their difference might even be compatible—incompatible, that is, for those who never walk the way, nor ever set out on it, but merely take up a position outside it, there forever to formulate ideas and make talk about the way. WCT,* 168-169 [emphasis added]

Therefore, sense, engagement, and response mutually belong to each other as a "guaranteed exchange without any guarantee of making sense" (*FT,* 96). Without sense there could be no co-responding in the sense of promise, not as the fixity of fixedness, but as the anticipation of the on-coming of the always already coming to know. The human being of openness is delivered over to the calculating passage of sense such that it is "absolutely responsible for sense," while sense is that for which the human being is responsible as the entity "that is in a position to answer for it" (*FT,* 294). The human being finds itself, not of its own accord, thrown into sense not as an author, but having to be that author (*GBT,* 434). The can-be of sense "is not in itself independent of responsibility of sense" as a having-to-be (*FT,* 294).[14]

A predictable response to a preordained stimulus can never include just the mere mirroring of what is present. A response as a reply harbors within it a surplus of meaning. It is an understanding of something as something, an articulation of what is there (*TM*, 290, 295, 299-302). The possible suddenness of addressing obtains as a break into the open as a structured question that enables a response (*TM*, 366; *QCT*, 19). Responding does not solely obtain as the activity of a conscious agent. Mortal finitude is the response which engages each human, and all humans together, as questioners.

The human being is called upon to (is called to) ask questions (*TM*, 374), to test possibilities (*TM*, 375). This testing, whether between a text or a self-unfolding text analog ("earth," work of art, individual, or group of persons), requires that a resonant, rejoining, *saying* language must initially be a mutually engaged part of the needed conversation (*TM*, 378-379). The sharing of understandings can always include accepting that there need not be an adherence to any traditional authority based on logical, lexicographical, or grammatical norms. The most primordial sharing of understanding (death) can never be communicated by word-things but can only be experienced as the belonging together of singular plurals and plural singulars (*BSP*, 88-93).

What must be responded to is the whereabouts of a starting. This starting is not just anywhere and it is not a discrete beginning; it is rejoining as an experience of a shared text or text analog[15] that is understood as not understood or is read as unreadable. Gadamer notes that "the apparently thetic beginning of interpretation is, in fact, a response; and the sense of an interpretation is determined, like every response, by the question asked. *Thus the dialectic of question and answer always precedes the dialectic of interpretation. It is what determines understanding as an event*" (*TM*, 472). Rejoining as a sojourn obtains as the on-coming always already perfect circularity wherein "every beginning is an end, and every end is a beginning" (*TM*, 472). This also resonates in T. S. Eliot's "In my end is my beginning" in *East Coker* (Eliot, 1952). The temporal particularity of each human being is always already a disclosing and beckoning calling call (a whispering in the ear, a hinting-at).

Sense does not obtain as some "available or constructible entity" or as an "illusory fulfillment of its pure intention" (*FT*, 298).

Sense offers the voicing of voices as a co-respondence such that the co-responsibility of the human being of openness belong to the enigma of "the one with the others" *(FT,* 299).

The Soul of Dialogue

A human social conversation is that which constitutes ourselves. It is immediately and constantly experienced but is not something objectifiable.

ZS, 268

Dialogue between individuals can "point to the common structure of understanding and playing: risking a word or keeping it to oneself, provoking a word from the other person and receiving an answer or giving an answer oneself" *(PH,* 56). Words always already come into play as definite contexts of speaking and understandings. Gadamer, in no uncertain terms, maintains that "everything we learn takes place in language games" *(PH,* 56). We reiterate here that the "we" in this thought is not that of a plurality of the isolated ego-things of modernity, but is the occurrence of the incompletability of being-with-entities-of-the-world as matters of concern.

According to Gadamer, the salient point of Plato's Socratic dialogues as dialectics turns on their negativity; they confuse one's opinions *(TM,* 464). Confused or not, "while engaged in dialogue, listening to explanations, and while being affectively influenced by others, we do not refrain from bringing into play our knowledge of humanity, information from various quarters and independent observations" *(RMC,* 280). For Gadamer, as we read him, teaching whiles (dwells/abides/sojourns) as a co-responding that is situated or prejudiced according to one's historical particularity. One's opinions as prejudicial prejudgings need not be considered necessarily unjustified or erroneous to the extent that they cover over co-responsive being-with as truth. Prejudices "constitute the initial directedness of our whole ability to dialogically experience the [historicality] of our existence" *(PH,* 9). Proper dialogue does not hold within itself any guarantee that prejudices will not be confused.

Situated prejudgments of the available are understandings which allow human beings to dialogically experience matters of concern. Engaged openness as encounter shows-says something to the human being.[16] Human beings by virtue of their own manner of engaged openness as the human being of openness are always already disclosed and beckoned for their task as the speakers of the possibilities of engaged openness. The human being of openness is present to and in attendance to listening as disclosed and beckoned that is responsive to and responsible for the saying of engaged openness.[17]

The way the human being of openness encounters the saying of language constitutes its answering. The comportment of speakers resides in answering as a saying-after whether as disagreement or rote repetition. In this way humans give voice to the soundless necessity of discursive expression. Language as silence demands that it be resaid as actual showing through either thinking or poetry (Ziarek, 1994, 30). Thinking-saying and poetic art speak because the human being of openness is *of* listening. Listening and conversing on pathways offer sense as "a responding that listens and brings something into view" (*POR,* 55). To bring a phenomenon into view means that it must already be calling, viewable, regardable, listenable. Thus we find that in order for teaching to be seen as co-responding and showing it *must* be *given* (show up) as co-responding which belongs to (is mutually engaged with) showing (*4S,* 66-69).

Co-responding as re-collective thinking dialogue/conversation is a fore-thinking that responds to the on-coming already which is always already. As a sheltering in thought, the always already "is still unthought as that which is to be thought" (*POR,* 94).[18] The task for co-responding hermeneutic phenomenology is to take whatever is said and let it unceasingly be the guide that draws one into thinking — "providing that thinking submits to the call of what must be thought" (*OTB,* 24). All thinking co-respondents are dependent on the calling address of engaged openness (*OBT,* 279). Within the purview of hermeneutic phenomenology, co-responding obtains as a way of speaking and thinking which is in attendance to attending to letting matters of concern show themselves as they are always already on-coming in their historical particularity. Co-responding is not reading as a particular task; it does not articulate the meaning of some truth as engaged openness. Instead it works as it is in attendance in order to draw attention to the way conversation/dialogue speaks: the occurrence of saying, resaying, co-responding at work. Thus the way of hermeneutic phenomenology "unfolds, underlies, and continuously inflects language" (Ziarek, 1994, 9).[19] The human being of openness presences as a step back into what is ahead of it. The step back as such illuminates no particular direction or gives no directives to thought. Its "'whither' cannot be determined. It can only be determined in the taking of the step back, that is, it can only result from corresponding to that which appears in the step back" (*OTB,* 30).

The saying of inflection is the nondefinable moment and/or place wherein the always already self-differing of spoken language engages its speakers. The play of these temporal loci of meaning is called forth by shifts in gender, number, case, person, mood, and voice. The saying of languages as they grow out of their unique dwelling is marked by humor, irony, and sentiments that are obvious to native speakers but that cannot be logically or empirically determined; language herein *must be dialogical experience.*

Nearness to the saying of language needs re-collection and stepping back. Heidegger has written, "To recall means to 'ponder forgotten things'" (*OWT,* 165). In other words, recalling is a responding to the emergence/elusion of disclosing and beckoning.[20] The retrieval of something forgotten in order to foretell (*OWT,* 174) is not the rote repetition of the past. Even if this were possible, the future as the always already on-coming of historicality cannot be subjected to any kind of ultimate determination. To be historical can never be to collect objects in order to timelessly duplicate them. The human being is "always already affected by history" (*TM,* 300) as thrown and disposed to attend to it. The historicality of language shows matters of concern and their involvements. Word-things can remain ontically the same but have meanings that reveal temporalized engagements. Hermeneutic phenomenology turns on co-responding with what is questionable in any given historical situatedness, not in order to finalize it but in order to let one into the nearness of sighting what is questionable.

Discursiveness[21] is an enabled, evanescent comportment, a speaking out of "what is already there and manifest as a whole" (*FCM*, 345). Heidegger called this *"the prevailing* world" (*FCM*, 351, 354). The fluidity of discourse contains in itself a necessary and engaged play of offering and accepting understandable sense. This offering and accepting places human beings in the play of their mutuality as singular plurals, proper to each's own particular temporality. The human being has its own time as a self whose temporal inception (as ensouled) cannot be grasped. However, as the with of engaged openness, the human being of open-being-with (openness) is granted the ability to encounter questions. The work of discourse turns on expressions, queries, desires, requests, and relations among other aspects. It is a give and take of understanding (*FCM*, 306). Discursiveness is not "primarily world forming even though [it belongs] to world formation" (*FCM*, 341).

Discursiveness always already is *the* presupposition for conversation (*ZS*, 268). As the human being of openness is the with of engaged openness, it remains essentially connected to others via speaking, reading, and the demand (calling) of language (*ZS*, 183). Discursiveness presents itself as the crossing of message bearer, message, receptor, and timely receiving such that "the hermeneutical phenomenon proves to be a special case of the general relationship between thinking and speaking [hence thinking-saying], whose enigmatic intimacy conceals the role of language in thought" (*TM*, 389). *Interpretation as conversation is a circulation always already enclosed in a dialogically experienced rejoining dialectic of question and answer.*

The interpretive undergoing of an experience is discursive in its unique essence such that there obtains experience as a dialogical play between traditions and interpreters (*TM*, 461). The play of tradition means that "we simply are unable to think anything that does not correspond to something already found in our own thinking" (*HW*, 150). However, language traditions as allotment permit disparate things "to come together in a comprehensive gesture of meaning with something totally other; questions which bring all into uncertainty" (*AH,* 114). Uncertainty is not thought here as the putative lack of certainty of the binary logic of contradiction. Hermeneutic phenomenology works to discover the origin of covered-over logic inherent in assertions which order contradictions. Ending one's interpretive work at a supposed logical impasse is discovery without the uncovering necessary for interpreting (*GIC,* 98).

The human being of openness is let into world as dialogical experience which as "tradition exists only in constantly becoming other than it is" (*RMC,* 288). This is possible because language is freed up as tradition (*TM,* 461). Human beings are called to listen to what really encounters them as if it is addressed to them and is concerned with them. Human beings are held and allowed (let) to co-respond as a sojourn (whiling/abiding/dwelling).

What does sojourning, co-responding entail? Paradoxically co-responding includes irresponsibility. The notion of independence as promulgated by various technoscientisms is a form of irresponsibility "not in the moral sense of the word but in the sense of its incapacity and its lack of any perceived need to give an account of what it itself means within the totality of human existence, or especially in its application to nature and society" (*RAS,* 161). Thereby irresponsibility allows the concealed to remain concealed in its way.

Experience is the "oscillating ambiguity" of the pathway of rejoining and not a discrete result (Fynsk, 1996b, 47). The movement of dialogical experience must obtain as an absenting such that it can be simply determined "as the unbroken generation of typical universals" (*TM,* 353). This movement occurs such that false "generalizations are continually refuted" and "what was regarded as typical is shown not to be so" (*TM,* 353). Experience, in its dialogical truth, "always implies an orientation toward new experience" (*TM,* 355). The truth of dialogical experience is not the correctness of an assertion; rather it lies in the enigma of revealing/concealing. Heidegger has written:

> To undergo an experience with something means
> that this something, which we reach along the way
> in order to attain it, itself pertains to us, meets and
> makes its appeal to us, in that it transforms us into
> itself.
>
> OWL, 73-74

All dialogical experience recedes into a past and withdraws into a future. As such, dialogical experience maintains itself as an always already that calls for a becoming, which presences as an on-coming. Dialogical experience can never be complete; it is finitude—a journey whose itinerary is given by the sense of limit as the incipience of unfoldings' unfoldings. Even in any denial of it, dialogical experience is transformative. And dialogical experience is exposure "to the improbable, to the unexpected, to the surprise" (*EF,* 94) of the enigmatic singularity of disclosures' disclosings and beckonings' beckoning. Human agency in any sense can never disclose and beckon itself as its own surprise, its own birth, its own death, its own freedom (*EF,* 95).

The dialogical experience of discursive praxis rests in an enacting "that transforms its agent rather than its object or its matter" (*PT,* 47). This is the heart of the always already. Heidegger practiced hermeneutic phenomenological thinking-saying in his writings.[22] In the essays "The Thing" and "Building Dwelling Thinking," he wrote of human thrownness in terms of simple everyday things like a jug and a bridge (*BW; PLT*). Understanding as thrown and historically situated was part of his project to retrieve the unsaid from the epistemology of the Greco-European philosophical tradition. The saying of language was pursued by Heidegger as he worked to bring out the poetical in poetry in his exegeses on Hölderlin and language (*EHP*). The saying of language reveals/conceals the ontological gathering of physical manifestations. In his essay "On the Origin of the Work of Art," language itself lets the manifest contension of "world and earth" in works of art emerge as a silent participatory self-gathering of self-unfolding sense (*PLT, OBT*). Language as discursiveness holds itself in reserve such that there is always already more to saying than what becomes expressed. The possibility of a work of art dwells in letting human agency into the discursive active play (*BSP,* 14-15) of disclosing and beckoning. All works of art, however defined, are the dialogical experiences of narrative tellings, but all dialogical experiences of narrative tellings are not necessarily works of art. But all, as participatory, offer themselves as always already read (interpreted).

Interpretations as dialogues about narrative tellings involve more than restricted and literal isolations of statements. Rather, "the speakers in the dialogue involve each other in that realm and abode about which they are speaking, and lead each other to it. Such involvement is the soul of dialogue" (*WCT,* 178). The unspoken *is* is a surplus over everyday conversing. In narrative tellings and conversations participants do, of course, deal with the other. All narrative tellings and conversations are a variety of dialogue. But to let meaning shine forth, dialogue participants as interpreters must come to grips with the unspoken as the possibility of disappointment that dwells behind the incompleteness of communication. Jean-Luc Nancy proffers, "Speaking comes by surprise, or by chance, as a chance. Therefore, the best 'model' *of* speaking is the conversation, the loose conversation, where" the participants, in all of their guises, do not know what will be said before it is said (*BP,* 314-315).

The ontic enumerates words, dates, empirically derived evidence, and the like and thereby takes the guise of information. But, as the landslide of information cascades down, the ability to distinguish good information from bad eludes systemization. The addiction to or worshipping of information becomes an end in itself. The quantity of data amassed may or may not suffice for a given task at hand. The task of hermeneutic phenomenology as its questionings and rejoinders calls for more but not in a quantitative sense. Interpretive thinking-saying asks after the unspoken calls— calls that have else been silenced, marginalized overlooked, or otherwise ignored. The "call" that shows up can show up as commending and commanding, disclosing and beckoning.

Interpretive thinking-saying is a search for words to present for translation "what is only vaguely grasped within our factical life experience" (Schalow, 1992, 232). It is necessary for interpretation as translation to enter a play wherein translation occurs as a highlighting (*TM,* 386). Highlighting—as shining a light on—grows out of the presencing of the with of apparent push-pull, contension, and traction: the familiar and the strange of a tradition—its emergence/elusion (*BSP,* 62). The play between the strangeness and familiarity to the human being of openness is the between. The texts of a tradition in their widest sense are the meanings of engaged openness as the disclosing and beckoning play of historically situated, estranged objects and their reciprocity in their belonging to tradition (*TM,* 295).

The proper site of the loci of meaning that hermeneutic phenomenology is addressed by and in turn addresses is "the self-opening middle of the counter-play of call and belonging" (*RHT,* 264). First and foremost hermeneutic phenomenology "shares one fundamental condition with the life of tradition; it lets itself be *addressed* by tradition" (*TM,* 282). Phenomena as they show themselves such that they are the contents of a given tradition "can be dialogically experienced only when one is addressed by them" (*TM,* 282). The movement inherent in addressing calls again and again for calling listening to, as the belonging together of sense, meaning, and significance. The locale of phenomenological hermeneutics is not a set of neutral points on an X, Y, Z axis structure or an unending accumulation of bits of information. There is a nearness that prepares any future thinking-saying for "still unheard intimations" (*EGT,* 105). Dialogue as dialogical experience is part and parcel of any nearing of what calls for thought. The resonating call of thinking-saying always already needs sighting and listening to engagingly claim the human being of openness.

Letting thinking-saying show itself as thematic, and thereby questionable, as other than a mere "a manipulation of operational concepts, representational models, and models of thinking" (*ZS,* 107), serves to bring thinking-saying into view as a dialogical experience with language. The asymptote of nearness obtains here as a pathway or sojourn as opposed to a mere theoretical construct, data stream, empirical datum, or physical measurement.

Phenomena, as sighted and thought-said herein are not reducible to discrete presences. Each and every phenomenon co-appears with/as an other as its own continuous – discontinuous mark. A phenomenon is the how of a historically situated belonging-together-with. Whether ontic or ontological, a phenomenon shows itself as a "singular multiplicity of origins" (*BSP*, 9). Origins are not fixity as metaphysical thought would have it, but obtain as the emergence-elusion of their ownmost offering of access to an access. Accessibility turns on the "the indefinite plurality of origins and their coexistence" (*BSP*, 10). A phenomenon is always already the pendency of a threshold of engagement.

In the following chapters we will continue in our attempt to bring into view sighting and listening as dialogical experience. The with-world of engaged openness as practical and prudent involvements and personal encounterings will show itself as we offer our own enactment of hermeneutic phenomenology.

Chapter 4 Notes

1   See *PM,* 239-276, for *exists* as *ek-sists.*

2   See also *GR,* 357- 371.

3   See Chapter 2, fn. 12, for our comments on logos.

4   Translation retranslated by the authors.

5   See Chapter 11 for further discussion of Narrative Pedagogy and the Concernful Practices of Schooling Learning Teaching.

6   See Gadamer, "What Is Practice?" (*RAS,* 75).

7   See discussion of openness and engaged openness in Glossary and Interpretive Commentary.

8   See also *GBT,* "Being in Attendance," 335-337.

9   See also *OWL,* 107, 135; Fynsk, 1996b, 68-69; *HWT,* 199.

10   See also *BSP,* 66.

11   See also *OWL,* 98.

12   See also *OEL,* 96.

13   See also *OEL,* 96

14   See also *GBT,* 435.

15   Strictly speaking, *everything* is a text which is read one way or another.

16   See also *PH,* 9.

17   See also *OWL,* 128-129.

18   See also *POR,* 96-98.

19   See also Ziarek, 1994, 38-40.

20   See also *HWT,* 184-185, on appropriation/expropriation.

21   See Chapter 3, for our introductory remarks on language as discursiveness.

22   See von Herrmann, 1996, 171-190.

Chapter 5

Enacting Hermeneutic Phenomenology

> *All formulas are dangerous. They force whatever is said into the superficiality of the instant opinion and are apt to corrupt our thinking. But they may also be of help, at least as a promoting and a starting point for sustained reflection.*
>
> OWL, 197

A Play of Moments

The enacting of hermeneutic phenomenology calls for a "*point of departure*" to be properly secured as a sojourn, a journey—an "*access to*" phenomena as enabled by "*passage-through*" practices prevalent, yet overlooked (*BT,* 61).[1] Point of departure is not to be taken as an Archimedean or mathematically determined equilibrium point; it is the always already effective history of traditions that are familiar and habitual. Point of departure means, paradoxically, that one can never leave the place where one already is. The human being of openness is always already "right at" (*BSP,* 10; Raffoul, 1997, xvi) its ownmost point of departure as a task never to be completed or fulfilled and as therefore always already "still to be undertaken" (Grondin, 1994, 114).[2]

We have already started from another place (Chapter 3) in order to be enabled to enact access to the locus of sense that offers meaning and significance. *Access-to* turns on the disposed understanding that human beings belong to, and are claimed by, as a historical-social-personal world. *Passage-to* is participatory understanding—understanding as a dialogical experience of the dialectical play of question and answer: the give and take of rejoinder. Point of departure, access-to, and passage-through as co-occurring moments obtain as possibility.

Phenomenological listening, sighting, and the call of the matter for thinking can always be said in the richness of the granting of disclosing and beckoning (*EHP,* 154-155). As we have written, Heidegger transposed phenomenological sighting such that "hermeneutics means not just the interpretation but, even before it, the bearing [as issuing forth] of message and tidings" (*OWL,* 29). As thinking-saying is enacted in a hermeneutic phenomenological way it lets itself be enabled by an implicit historicality that turns on the on-coming of the givenness of the given. The human being of openness is "in each instance in dialogue with [its] forebears, and perhaps even more and in a more hidden manner, with those who come after [it]" (*OWL,* 31).[3] Hermeneutic phenomenology, as we explicate it, is a practice that turns on the resistance to assigning thrownness, understanding, and language into taxonomic units of indexical meaning.

The human being is taken as of openness—finite, historically situated, and thrown. As the human being of openness is interpreted as practical, prudent comportment, it comports itself in taking something as something. What it means to be a human being is always already sighted as its forerunning and as the always already graspedness of its ongoing–on-coming as its issuance forth, generation (birthing!), and being unto mortality. We will attempt to engage thought as an enacting of hermeneutic phenomenology such that it "is the path of a [co-responding] that examines as it listens" (*PLT,* 186).

The moments of hermeneutic phenomenology are neither abstract time points nor the momentousness of historically decisive events. For the most part, moments are calls to human beings in their specific situatedness—their particular sojourn as they act in a historical-temporal manner in the encircling mesh of the disposedness of habits, beliefs, and choices. Moments as the proper each time of every individual are timely and rich.

Hermeneutic phenomenology can be characterized as an explicit retrieval of a play of moments wherein these are always already temporally disposed as *effect, situation,* and *bearing.* In the following we map out these moments as possibility: possibility for a disclosing and beckoning pathway wherein schooling learning teaching can be brought before the eyes. We endeavor to describe these as matters whose nonpossessable temporal moments claim ways of thinking-saying in advance—the self-emergence of everyday concernful dealings whose absent incipience is denied (ontically to epistemologies and ontologically to hermeneutic phenomenology) and whose passage is claimed by the absence inherent in their own on-coming temporal particularity. The absence *of* incipience is the privative presence *of* incipience.

Effect

> *We would like only, for once, to get to just where we are already.*
>
> > *PLT,* 190

The very sense of where human beings find themselves turns on "the efficacy of history at work" (*TM,* 301). Not only does this sense of emergent situatedness call the human being to inquiry and concomitant appearance of its investigation, but also it does not allow for a final completion of associated tasks. The influence of the source is not at the disposal of the human being (*WCT,* 166). Effect as historical is not thought here as "a causal chain of events" or as the opacity of deterministic conceptions of "fate." Effect turns on the human being enabled (called upon) to give heed (pay attention as called) to world: Attending to that which claims it or calls it to attention, claims the human being of openness (*WCT,* 165-166). The work of history as something that "comes to stand and lie in unconcealment" (*QCT,* 160) allows, allots, sends the following:

- World: As a stark opposition to ontic conceptions of world (i.e., planet, physical universe, democracy, and so forth), world is understood here as an always already interpreted, organized play of meaningful relations. Experience (empirical and dialogical) always already steps along world as something retrieved as unthematic, disclosing and beckoning understandings. Topologies precede topographies. The care structure is in place already.

- Historicality: Its effect compels the human being to recognize that any conception of consciousness is self-limiting. Any self-understanding, interpretation, or reading arrives with and as historicality. Individuals have no fixed borders *and are no fixed or fixable point in time* (*BH,* 241-274).

- Questionings: A can-be (*GBT,* 504) obtains wherein the human is enabled to pursue asking after the answers offered to its becoming the moment of the eventual end of the "brief candle" ascribed to consciousness. A mastering of scientific techniques does not release humans from deliberating on and deciding which questions cannot be sidestepped.

- Encountering: The proper meaning of encountering refers to an awareness of being historically given, especially as given by an other. There is issuance (playing-forth) as possibility wherein the human being can be exclusively claimed by mere entities rather than by the nearness of matters of concern. Heidegger's discussion of "the anyone" and Jean-Luc Nancy's commentary on the same[4] explicate the issuance of this matter. Encountering speaks.

- Noticing: Everyday conventions which arrive as dominant phenomena, which can now include the phenomenon of schooling learning teaching, hold themselves as a stubbornness such that they protect the truth of their own listening and sighting. This enables dominant phenomena to be passed over as matters not deserving of being called into questioning.

- A lack: The human being always already lacks an ability to place itself in an externalized relationship to situatedness. The human being of openness is continually exposed to on-coming and disappearing questions that are beyond it (not as transcendence). There is always a surplus something in excess of what one is uniquely capable of—the plurality of the singular, the singularity of the plural.

- Participating: The with-world is not something dreamt up or hypothesized. Participation is the play of understanding. This play is not an imperative that must remain fixed. Hermeneutic phenomenology offers the possibility that enables an attempt to more richly understand the whole of what *can* be understood. Traditions can be freed up in their porosities, con-tensions, and disruptions. There are no "neutral" positions that are independent of anticipation, intimations, and prejudging. The task of hermeneutic phenomenology is to begin with situations as they play temporally and historically.

Situation

> *Relatedness is difficult to grasp, in its peculiarity —*
> *not because it is situated far away, but because it is*
> *by now habitual to us.*
>
> *WCT,* 32

Hermeneutic phenomenology is a characterization of the "unfolding essence of the human being" not as an object but as situated comportment (*ZS,* 110). Encountering encountering must be participatory.

Situated participating shows the following moments:

- Sojourning (whiling/abiding/staying) and encountering as nonreflective, nonintuitive understanding is familiar with and dependent on its particularity. Proper understanding always already understands its play. Participants are understandingly in play as partners to situated exposure, to world. They are concerned about matters of concern.
- Hearing-understanding replies to the call for a response. Understanding, the understandable, and the understanders belong to and need each other. They are mutually engaged as temporality and historicality.
- Taking matters of concern *as* matters of concern via interpretive comportment is a co-occurrence. Disclosing and beckoning can only emerge from phenomena as

thrown, as they deliver themselves (make themselves available) as presencing, as presencing itself (*4S*, 79-80).

- Translating and interpreting always already issue themselves forth. The work of the translation is never an attempt to replicate the self-presented. Translators/interpreters/readers can let everything be spoken by placing themselves in the directedness (meaning) of any utterance in the light of their own utterances.
- Articulating shows itself as a sense of required questionableness; understanding one's self as what one understands; operating in the saying of the not immediately intelligible (the alien, the strange); operating within a risk such that no rule is available in order to effect the application of rules.
- Accepting a pathway obtains as a traversal that cannot be governed by regulations independent of its practice and possible consequences.
- The readiness to hear the new while at the same time being conditioned by what possesses the human being as what it expects is a task of hermeneutic phenomenology. The task is not to settle into everyday knowing how to get along; the task turns on the questions and answers posed by everyday knowing.
- Engaging in the play of narrative tellings is offering as a release from ordinary time, an entry into incomplete understandability, and a claim such that unique answers are required of each encounter. There are sighting and listening encounters in narrative tellings as well as in religion (the sacred) and thinking-saying (discursive rejoining) despite the hegemony that seems to perdure in the merely utile and hegemonic scientisms and ideologies.
- Apprehending is more than mere hearing. Apprehending obtains as detecting conditions for detecting. These in turn can reveal themselves as what is given for questionings, answers, and their rejoinders to pursue as a following after.
- Abiding the unfillable free space that is discursively filled without being filled. Evanescent meaning is an addressing that says "There is much to say." Narrative tellings do not admit of any application of universal

schema. Hermeneutic phenomenology is not brought to a stand with a revealing of putative contradictions, inversions, or negations. There is always already a reference to the incipient truth of the not understood, the still unthought.

- Rejoining as dual-phase to *and* fro hermeneutic phenomenology wherein (1) interpretations are themselves always already made aware by historicality and discursivity and their concomitant temporal "enduring, persisting, prevailing" (*RHT,* 267) and (2) awareness that is open to the possibility of the dangerous persistence of unwarranted conclusions coming forth from narrow and/or self-serving interpretations. The art to be found here is the art of being on the way.

Bearing

By "way" or "how," we mean something other than manner or mode. "Way" here means melody, the ring and tone, which is not just a matter of how the saying sounds. The way or how of the saying is the tone from which and to which what is said is attuned.

WCT, 37

The above introductory quote initiates our work to explicate Heidegger's assertion "All is way" (*OWL,* 92). To be borne on a way is the essence of the issuing-forth of conversation as an enabling releasement such that "dominant conceptions of precision, rigor and progress" are put into question by thinking-saying (Park, 2004, 311). On the other hand, if a conversation is to be genuine it must find itself "already in conversation with the thinking of the past"— the alreadiness of the always already. Meanings discursively show up as sense: the bearing bearer of alterity. They offer (give/grant/gift/extend) an invitation to take and/or leave them as the tension and traction of encounterings' encounterings (*BSP,* 187). The interruption of meanings is exposed as discursiveness that brings with it the possibility that meanings are meanings insofar as they are shared. Meanings turn on the possibility of non-meaning, which can never be sense-less (*BSP,* 88-93). Self-conduct or bearing "can give an account of itself and answer for itself" (*PT,* 8).

Sense, meaning, and significance as a "can-be" is realized as the give and take of play:[5]

- Absenting of isolatable emergence and elusion is not a showing up as producing, but as a retrieving.[6] This passage is an always already circulating intermediate link, presencing presencing as absencing, living, dead, mortals, divinities, histories—all directions, all times. Thinking-saying as the circulation of "wholes" is a thinking that can never be based on a "logic" that dictates freedom from contradiction.
- Rejoining as a back and forth is the saying and resaying of the play of a simultaneity and/or simultaneities. It is a shared crossing through of shared incipience. Solicitude (*BT,* 158-163) is the possibility for sharing *or* dominating the other's proper temporality.
- Recovering of what is said or written is an art that allows itself to recall. Words whose sense is aged, used up, or hidden can be put back into play. Representations that have become "commonplace and empty" are retrieved from their exhaustion. The truth of hermeneutic phenomenology is in its recalling and resaying. *Thinking-saying is brought back to life when the desire to define in fixed propositional statements is given up.* The finding of the saying of any interpretation involves releasing all customary words and modes of expression into their expanse of possibility. A venerable principle of hermeneutics has been that interpretation should proceed from what is taken as clear to an enacting of releasing into the obscure.
- Co-determining the particular and the whole is never without belonging together. The response of hermeneutic phenomenology is an enabling wherein dogmatic rejection of a tradition and considered appropriation of it are not mutually exclusive. Co-determining absorption takes place only slowly even where understanding seems to be present. *Dialogue is claimed by the need to unblock sedimented understandings.*

- Establishing exhaustive meanings cannot be produced by assertive statements. Hermeneutic phenomenology is a giving of an ability to see the questionable. It questions the traditional that *things are prior to how they are revealed in language.* Tradition is the emergent/ elusive on-coming character that conceals/reveals linguistic (dialogical) experience. Any evaluation of the thoughtfulness of thinking, according to the forerunning movement of universalized determining and prescriptive planning, such that technical achievements are justified by economic successes, narrows and blocks access to phenomena.

- Understanding can turn on the infinite dialogue of inner experience. However, spoken language is not located here. Interpretive practices are necessarily written or spoken out loud. These practices, however, do not and cannot reveal the full play of an individual's intended meaning. Private languages cannot speak and thereby forfeit any enabling possibility. *The work of hermeneutics is not to develop an epistemology of understanding, but to bring to light the world in which understanding plays a role.*

- Narrating is exhibited as listening: the speaking of works of art, the unsaid of words, speechlessness—the unsaid. The essence of narrative tellings is the enabling of the possibility to hearken to the other, to oneself, and to things other than the human. Listenings in this sense can never be totally expressed linguistically or conceptually—they can only be made thematic.[7]

- Being together as "historically effected consciousness"[8] shows up as rooted in discursiveness and understanding and offered as an essential locus in any hermeneutic phenomenological dialogic experience. Discursiveness is the site wherein matters of concern advene as the letting of words. The game human beings are engaged in, *the universal medium of understanding, is co-responding.*

- Raising questions always already includes silent matters. No give and take of rejoining is without presuppositions. These play a back-and-forth game between entities, matters of concern, and interpreter-readers. Thereby question and answer are inextricably intertwined. Human beings understand an utterance only when they understand it as a response that becomes a question again. Why is there a saying and what is its play responding to? Questioning, enacted in a thoughtful way, always already hints at the enigmatic such that questioning itself unsettles its own path of questioning.

- Rejoining as dialogue is the hermeneutic phenomenological passage of the dialectic of question and answer. This turns on enabling as a human capacity for true participatory interchange with the singular plurality of others. Dialogues are not necessarily agreement. The silent, the oppositional obdurate, the hesitant can obtain as harking as well as easy exchange and communication. Interpretation turns on the attempt to hear "between the lines" of one's conversation partners whether they be other humans or the play of nonhuman matters of concern.

- Thinking-saying can bring tidings of messages. Giving an account of these must be convincing, exemplary, and successful. Thereby the practice of hermeneutic phenomenology is an art, not the doctrine or "ought" of a technical procedure. Art as thought herein is not part of modernity's art-science binary opposition, but is thought in the sense of a revealing-gathering of the con-tension of "world" and "earth" (*PLT,* 17-87; *OBT,* 1-56; *HW,* 95-109).

- Bearing (issuing forth) of conversation is an endless pathway which can let the meant as articulated become each participant's own. Meanings play as multiplicities and as this movement, as the element of rigorous thinking. Encounters can show the upwelling of the human being of openness out of the restrictedness of mere empirical experiences. Richer neighborhoods are opened up in genuine conversations. Truth does not reside in an existing by oneself. Truth turns on the unavoidable entanglement of co-appearing.

- Carrying/bearing along of the human being such that its sojourn/journey/whiling/dwelling turns on acknowledging and respecting calls for a readiness to let thinking be repeatedly overturned by the unthought.

- Co-responding is a self-finding in discursiveness; incipience is the absolute of prior aheadness. Experience as historical awareness of a past that is always already in front of (in advance of) one mediates the human being of openness in conjunction with never to be complete possibilities of becoming. In order to interpretively retrieve a phenomenon, an attempt must be made to turn (step) back ahead toward its proper historical-temporal forerunning essence.

Dismantling the Obstructions

> *The way we experience one another, the way we experience historical traditions, the way we experience the natural givenness of our existence and our world, constitute a truly hermeneutic universe, in which we are not imprisoned, as if behind insurmountable barriers, but to which we are opened.*
>
> *TM*, xxiv

Hermeneutic phenomenology can come to grips with the barrier established by intellectually determined conceptions of the immanence of consciousness and its self-imposed closure into an inescapable shell. In order to arrive and depart, the human being has to always already be somewhere. What are the constituents of any barriers that block the unfolding of questioning into its taken-for-granted presuppositions (including itself) to itself? The modernity of the subject-object paradigm posits that thinking is prior to sense (meaning and significance) as it speaks. *On the contrary, discursiveness is what enables thinking-saying (WCT,* 16). One of thinking's possibilities is that it can bring dangers forth. Is the most extreme danger that of humankind arrogating the production of everything, including the production of itself, exclusively to itself? Biogenetic research stands at that threshold.

Can the production of "everything" include the absolute production of sense, meaning, and significance? For anything to make sense it must include its relation to the production of sense. Human finitude as it resides in sense and making-sense is what calls forth thinking. Heidegger has asked, "In what does this calling consist? How can it make its claim on us? How does the calling reach us" (*WCT*, 124)?

The way of thinking can bifurcate into two paths: calculative and meditative (*DT*, 46). Meditative thinking is rooted in *"praxis, that is, action that transforms its agent rather than its object or its matter"* (*FT*, 47). Calculative thinking, accomplished and successful in its own right, demands results that serve specific purposes (*DT*, 46). Meditative thinking requires letting thinking practices be "conducted by the experience of a question" (*FT*, 194). Letting a question question needs greater effort to allow the biding of time as its own issuing forth of what calls forth questioning (*DT*, 47). Issuing forth discloses and beckons as its own time. Therefore the human being does not have to set out in order to be always already underway (*WCT*, 169). Meditative thinking *does not* absolve human beings of involvements and participating but calls them into participatory thinking-saying.

Hermeneutic phenomenology in all of its guises and permutations "encourages not objectification but listening to the call of an other— for example, the listening and heeding (belonging with) someone who knows how to tell a story" (*F*, xi). *Conversation, dialogue, and questioning summon (commend/call to) the gathering powers of language as a letting-be-sighted.* The letting be sighted *of* language returns the power of determination to matters of concern such that "they can regulate the expanse of their own unconcealedness" (Schalow, 1992, 89-90). Or to put it in another way, world as a belonging together discloses and beckons—engages human beings such that they are, as this turning, necessarily involved in the world (*PLT*, 179-182).

There is a letting-be that "calls for the network of involvements through which any human activity and the ends endemic to it, even the most inherently speculative, first becomes meaningful" (Schalow, 1992, 101). Significance and meaning are other than and more than mere value posits *or insights* of isolated or pure consciousness. In his preface to *Introduction to Philosophical Hermeneutics,* Grondin describes "the inner word." The inner word is not a hidden meaning, which consists of a "private or psychological inner world existing prior to its verbal expression. Rather it is that which strives to be externalized in spoken language." There "is no 'preverbal' world, only world oriented to language" which obtains as the unique play of hermeneutic phenomenology (Grondin, 1994, xv).

Hermeneutic phenomenological thinking is not entrapped in an "inner/outer world" dichotomy. The outer world of scientific observations and their associated metaphysical assertions and propositions pretends to self-sufficiency and evidence-based clarity as established by some putatively established inner world of "mind" or electrochemical processes. For interpretive thinking, however, mere facts do not admit of finality. There is always already a surplus of sense, which cannot be passed over, ignored, or otherwise forgotten.

Hermeneutic phenomenological interpretive work is always already preparatory. Heidegger called on the human being to listen to the preparatory as a running ahead into the becoming of historicality. "Only the initiating and incipient pertains to [becoming]; what is [present-to] is always already [alreadiness]. The inception knows no haste. Whither should it hasten, since everything incipient is only incipient if it can rest in itself? [Mindfulness of] the inception is thus also an unhurried thinking that never comes too late and at best comes too early" (*BC*, 78).

Modernity's thinking of time as a stasis was called to question by Heidegger as he pressed to free time from the willful agency of calculative thinking into its on-coming immediacy. The issue that turns on how agency obtains is the one on which hermeneutic phenomenological practices must rise or fall. We have followed the saying that ontological phenomena, such as attending, listening, and co-responding, are listenable yet imperceptible. Therefore, in this book, agency does not rest in a conscious subject but is a locale that is a confluence of sense relationships (*PLT,* 158). A locale is a particular temporal occurrence of coincident phenomena. Time is the always already presence-to that draws already participatory becoming as a future that is possibility.

If hermeneutic phenomenological thinking is sustained there are no guaranteed outcomes. However, the question also obtains whether metaphysics, technoscientism, or calculative thinking can ever grant or provide freedom from the unknown. The will to the orderability of everything as orderable can serve to open a pathway and not shut it off (*HOP,* 32). Letting the enigma be as enigma shelters a call wherein thinking-saying and narrative telling can recall the loci of meaning as a listening to the rejoinings of matters of concern. Readiness for the rejoinings of matters of concern is a possibility wherein a way can be open once human beings have let all of what is let, be placed face-to-face with themselves.

Hints: Following the Movement of Showing

> *Hints are enigmatic. They beckon to us. They beckon away. They beckon us toward that from which they unexpectedly bear themselves toward us.*
>
> *OWL,* 26

For all of their density and putative obscurity, the writings of Heidegger often presented hints for consideration. We shall continue the open pathway of our conversation with Heidegger and associated thinkers with one of these. In the essay *On Time and Being,* Heidegger suggests that listening to is not to hear "a series of propositions, but rather to follow the movement of showing" (*OTB,* 2).

Operative terms and their namings are at once simple and obscure. In the writings of Heidegger, words reciprocate and resonate between their everyday and self-revelatory meaning possibilities (*CP,* 58). Thus as a result of the hint the above quote offers, the play of words like "listening," "hearing," "propositions," "movement," and "showing" needs to be allowed, let, released, such that they become enabled to reveal the range of their possibilities. There is no imperative to coin new words, but there are always already possibilities that enable a speaking and listening in response to a hinting's call. Often a thinking-saying response to a hint calls for a step back as a pointing to a realm that as the present is already "skipped over" (*ID,* 49). Steps back belong to goings-from and the retrievings of what is unthought, what is not yet thought, and what calls forth thought (*ID,* 50).[9] Matters of concern as they are thought-said are their own retrieving; they let themselves be shown as they ripen.

Are hints there for the taking, as is so often assumed, or do they present or retrieve themselves of their own accord? Hints, as themselves, are always already engaged in their ownmost "widest sphere" wherein they are enabled to play (*OWL,* 27). Hints obtain as preliminary and preparatory, thereby sheltering within them the possibility of errancy. That possibility calls the human being of openness to dialogue and vigilance (*OHF,* 120, Translators' fn. 62). Hints as the basic character of words are other than the closure inherent in metaphysical significations or indications. The spoken word is always already an answer, co-responding as the ongoing arriving at engagements (*OWL,* 129). Words must not be taken-as fixed relationships; rather words disclose, they open up (*ZS,* 185).[10] The open clearing is a calling that lets itself be followed but never allows humans to be free of the addressing of asking (*WCT,* 168).

Zabdiel, a professor and nurse researcher, tells of organizing a seminar for postdoctoral students.

> *Teaching a required seminar of invited guest speakers for postdoctoral students has taught me a lot about teaching. Postdoc students can be highly critical of guest speakers, and the evaluations of this seminar were not good. Then I started looking very carefully on how guest speakers were listening and responding to students. I began to get a hint at what matters to them. I could see the differences between successful and unsuccessful guest speakers. I now meet with each of them before I invite them to join our seminar. I talk in general about the seminar but then I figure out how to ask, "What would it mean to*

you if you were invited to join our seminar as a guest speaker?" Most say something like "It would be an honor," "a chance for me to share my research," or "a chance for me to influence future researchers." What I am listening for is some hint of attending our seminar as "a chance to learn with the students." The "chance to bring some questions or thinking" to our seminar. The guest lecturers who are the most successful come in and seem to learn right along with everyone else, as we put our heads together and have some great conversations. It's hard to listen for these hints of learning-as-teaching; they're subtle and elusive. But since I have begun inviting more guest speakers who are learners through and through, evaluations of the seminar have soared.

Hints are present but they have no magnitude or location; their presence as such is let out of absence. Hints have no measurements as atoms do depending on the side of the quantum divide from which one prefers to look. As such, hints cannot be observed. Hints, called *Wink* in German, belong to the moment of insight as described by Heidegger *(BT)*, Sheehan *(COF, HPM)*, Kisiel *(GBT)*, and Gadamer *(TM)*. They arrive as a "glance of an eye" (McNeill, 1999). As we mention in Chapter 3, Hermes, the hinting messenger of the gods, was named after stones piled as boundary markers. Boundary markers hint at a boundary but do not indicate any absolute identity of direction. They only sketch undecidable separation or difference. These should always be kept in mind as still belonging to each other, one way or another, especially as they recall one's attention to a limit as that which allows the essential unfolding of a matter of concern.

Ontically, hints can be given to enable the solution of a puzzle; they are part of a rule-governed game. But taken in a hermeneutic phenomenological sense, hints show up on their own as possibilities to whoever is ready and open for them as they show up. The hints Heidegger was open for included the deceptively naïve notions of finitude, enownment, difference, line, rift, cleft, between, limit, furrow, fissure, and the near, as they play as the senses of articulation. His task was to let himself be claimed by the struggle to think the tautological, enigmatic, primordial essence of "presence: presencing itself" (*4S*, 80). Hints, having no magnitude or ideality, cannot be subsumed under the putative metaphysical control of either idealisms or realisms. What emanates from (issues forth out of) disclosing and beckoning of presencing generates a surplus or even a superabundance of sense, meaning, and significance. *When a hint is taken as something present, the taking leaves behind an abundance of absence, which belongs to an excess of presence. Hints abound, resound, and astound.*

The subject-object split is an abyss of difference that cannot be spanned save via an exercise of power: Subjects herein are reduced to mere objects with no meaning or worth, or objects are subsumed under generalities within which no individual can be found or established. The fixity of the absolute as closure must be effected by some exercise of power. As Gadamer reminds us, the world as the play of understandings is the open clearing of discursive human understanding or not understanding and, as such, cannot be subjected to the hypostasized conceptualizations of idealisms or realisms (*PH*, 31).

Jean-Luc Nancy has written of the hinting of hints as they arrive as sense. In Chapters 1 and 4 we discussed the advening of sense as sense "is always a movement to, onto, or a passage and spacing which is irrecoverable and ungraspable, but which nevertheless *is* the space of the world as meaningful, intelligible, and experienceable as such" (James, 2006, 102). Sense and world are the same as they comprise and hint of a ground, locus, or site (locus of meaning). Sense and world offer (let) passages and or movement-to akin to births. "Sense never returns to itself; it opens, spaces, makes intelligible while exceeding any logic of subjectivity or any possibility of fixed and stable signification" (James, 2006, 102). Sense hints of itself as the temporal-spatial movement wherein "the arrival, passage or movement-to" obtains as the coming of presencing (James, 2006, 103).

For Jean-Luc Nancy, the hinting of "sense, in terms of a shared finitude and a shared relation to death [is] that [which] is at once the being-to of sense and the fundamental being-with worldly existence" (James, 2006, 104). Sense is the nearness of the near (*PLT,* 181) where the con-tension of difference shows up (*BSP,* 35). The nearness of matters of concern shows up for Heidegger as the hinting of their own self-sheltering (*PM,* 135, 260; *4S,* 63) and for Gadamer as the hinting dialogical experience of conversation, history, tradition, and dialogue (*TM,* 367-368). In their same but not identical ways, Heidegger, Gadamer, and Jean-Luc Nancy have assumed their respective tasks as letting the conversations of history, tradition, and phenomena show themselves as hints.

The human being of openness is disclosed and beckoned to by hinting finitude. Hinting as hinting is a sharing possibility wherein there is practical and prudent comportment that "already stretches ahead, in advance of all propositional comportment" (*FCM,* 346). The aim of a propositional assertion is a comportment that holds the producer of the assertion toward those entities to which it is bound. To be bound to assertion qua assertion is to be claimed by the dialectic of conformity and nonconformity as the ultimate meaning of metaphysical notions of truth (*FCM,* 346). As thus thrown, certain everyday understandings are unable to listen to world as an excess to the entities that everyday understandings are given to maintain themselves. In order to exclusively focus on the entities *of* everyday understanding, matters of concern (*as* sense) are passed by, overlooked (*FCM,* 347). The movement of sense calls toward and as the future, as this calling sense hints of its own time.

Gadamer writes that it is the game that plays and always already draws the players along with the game as they play along (*TM,* 490). The claim of the game discloses and beckons as sense that asserts itself as historically effected prejudgings. The human being of openness as drawn into presencing can also be called to be in thrall (as heeding to) to unwarranted ontic biases. The task that can obtain is to come to terms with such calling (ordering-up) (*TM,* 490). The concomitant task is for the human being to listen to its own finitude (Richardson, 1974, 164-167; *PM*, 125-135). Each human being as its own, but not possessed, temporal particularity is disclosed and beckoned as a sojourn which offers it "in each case, time for something" (*ZS*, 66). Sojourning is a way before it is a what or a that or even a how. The whiling *of* sojourning is offered as time-space, dwelling of "care," "concern," and "solicitude."

Sojourning-with is the same and at the same time is the with, as letting come to presence of matters of concern. That this "comportment carries itself" and as such is "what is wonderful about it." It is a kind of absorption that is other than a dissolving of a substance into a liquid (sugar in water); it is to be simply engaged-with as alreadiness, presence-to, and becoming as possibilities (*ZS*, 160).

The human being of openness can always already take itself (understand itself) as a matter of concern. As caring-for, the with of engaged openness is the encountering of others but never as a self-contained subject. The human being of openness is understood as a "standing-within the clearing as sojourn with what concerns it and what is encountered" (*ZS*, 150). The ineffability of living a life throws obstacles in the way of finding words that allow the mystery of engaged openness and temporality to speak for themselves "out of a surplus of sense" (*HWT*, 195). Words are hints (*OWL*, 27). Hints open up. Words as hints cannot exist without discursiveness, as it discloses and beckons as conversation and dialogue.

Chapter 5 Notes

1   See also *PM,* 318.

2   See also *TM,* 300-307.

3   See also *HNA,* 220-227.

4   See *BT* and *BSP,* 27-28, 93-99.

5   The following commentary is distilled from the hints given by Gadamer *(TM, RAS, PH)*, Heidegger *(BT, WCT, PM)*, Nancy *(BSP, FT, SW, SV)*, and von Herrmann (1996).

6   See J. Diekelmann, 2005, 3-57.

7   Making thematic is not referring here to the identification of themes or patterns, but rather to dialoguing about or explicating forgotten or overlooked presuppositions.

8   See Glossary and Interpretive Commentary.

9   See also *4S,* 61.

10   See also *4S,* 79.

Chapter 6

È méthodos:
Of Conversation, Narrative Telling, and Dialogue

> *The one thing that matters is whether this dialogue,*
> *be it written or spoken or neither, remains constantly*
> *coming.*
>
> OWL, 52

The perplexing problem of method offers this question: Has stable, uncontestable certainty given way to an oscillating ambiguity that interrupts the ideal of methodological progress? Heidegger, in particular, retrieved the theme of ambiguity in the determination of method. For him, particular subject matters determined the way toward themselves and thus could not be readily "determined in advance for each case" (*ZS,* 102). Any grasp (making thematic) of a subject matter turns on how it shows itself as the regioning regions (neighborhoods) of engaged openness—in the *mediating immediacy* (openness, between) of concerned involvements. Hermeneutic phenomenology offers the seemingly paradoxical claim that any putative absolute certainty can itself obtain only as ambiguity. The only certainty is that of mortal human finitude. The certainty of finitude goes beyond (not in a transcendental sense) calculation and measurement.

The modern sense of method as ultimate controllability cannot avoid the always already underway of engaged openness. Engaged openness lets itself into "method" without an invitation.

For the Greeks, method was a to-be-on-the-way: *È méthodos*— "namely on a way not thought of as a 'method' [that the human being] devises but a way that already exists, arising from the very things themselves as they show themselves through and through" (*P,* 59).

Thrownness, understanding, and language offer each human being its sameness and simultaneously its identity such that the historically situated human way to be of openness is engaged with conversation, narrative telling, and dialogue.[1] There are no *absolutely* discrete conversations, ahistorical narratives, or solitary dialogues. Absolute or isolated signifiers as word-things "can *touch* on neither senses nor sense" (*SW,* 133). Each human being shares "the secret of language as something more remote than language itself—but nowhere else than exposed on the flowering surface of language" (*SW,* 136).

Hermeneutic phenomenology is not ordered and originated by a method wherein "the absolute self-certainty of the human being as the subject asserting itself contains and projects standards for the possible determination of the objectivity of objects" (*ZS,* 107). In order for this form of method to obtain, phenomena must be ordered such that they are atemporal (eternal) and ahistorical (idealized). Objects of all sorts must obtain as calculatable and theorizable, thereby controllable. Therefore in this book the so-called scientific method is not viewed as one that provides absolute certainty as it claims, but as a regional mode of *engagement* wherein certain kinds of *relations* obtain.

Engaging and Relating

> *Belonging-together is precisely what remains genuinely opaque and questionable. This belonging-together must come to light from out of what belongs to the "together," granted that here the "together" means something else and something different than the welding together of two otherwise separate pieces.*
>
> POR, 105

The question arises that asks after engaging and relating. Engaging and relating in the variety of their senses turn on conversings with, concernings about, evidencings of, mentionings of, and bearings on, as well as referrings, pertainings, and addressings to. The matter of concern for all methods pertains to conversing, narrating, and dialogicity as co-respondings, which self-engage as the play of the temporal/historical and as the between of contact-separation. This play obtains neither as encompassing identities nor as mere isolatable exteriorities (Raffoul, 1997, xxv).

Hermeneutic phenomenology must not be confused or conflated with methodologies as they are manifested in algorithms. First and foremost, algorithms, even extremely complex ones, must have preestablished outcomes. Inputs must be correct, controllable, and discrete in order for any algorithm to provide *its* correct answer. The presupposition inherent in algorithmic thinking is to restrict decision making such that the function of the human being is merely to provide inputs to formulas. These formulas are produced to reflect past patterns as these are valorized and selected by those who devise and utilize algorithms in their attempts to establish unalloyed facts.[2]

In hermeneutic phenomenology, facts as facticity show themselves as themselves as they disclose and beckon. We believe this is aptly shown in the circumstances surrounding the life of Philip Farkas, internationally renowned French horn player. His career spanned 65 years, including 13 years as principal French horn player with the Chicago Symphony Orchestra, several under the direction of the famed conductor Fritz Reiner. Philip Farkas presents his own story:

> My tuba playing didn't last long, after the streetcar conductor refused to have an instrument that size inconveniencing the other passengers. I immediately went to Lyon and Healy's and rented something considerably smaller, a French horn. (Farkas, 1990, 3)

Philip Farkas' life was shaped by many events as all are, but significantly telling for our purposes is an event that falls outside of any algorithm. When Farkas was a high school junior he played the tuba. The ungainly instrument needed to accompany him to school on a crowded Chicago streetcar—but not for long. The streetcar conductor observed that the tuba was taking up too much space and thereby presenting difficulties for other passengers. The conductor pointed to a French horn and recommended that Farkas play that more acceptable (to the streetcar conductor at least) instrument (Stewart, 1990, 3; Falso, 1998, 8). The listening here turns on how everyday nonstatistically significant events cannot be predicted vis-à-vis their outcome. An algorithm could never have predicted the historical presence of a respected and talented French horn player and teacher. Farkas himself wondered what would have happened to his life if the conductor had pointed out a flute. The essential play of world does not admit of algorithms no matter how much effort and thought are put into them.

Methods that require immediate, observable, controllable phenomena cannot include those phenomena whose movement turns on a temporal on-coming which is offered by the alreadiness of historicality. First and foremost, historicality and temporality offer themselves as presence and absence; they always already instantiate themselves as their own disappearance. The scientific method, despite the protestations of scientistic practitioners, is an always already *on-coming* such that the past as alreadiness is in front of its possible thematizing that must reside in fixity as an ultimate goal. The future must be identical to the past—right now.

On-coming movement rests in conversation and dialogue—the narraticity of narrative telling. Hermeneutic phenomenology offers a different view of method that turns on a play of engaging such that relationships to what is encountered are seen as a sojourn in the sense of the letting of engaged openness show encounterings themselves in/as their offerings.[3] Method herein is transformed into a way unto openness rather than a way toward or from an autonomous, mainly singular ego-self (*ZS*, 110).

In this approach to method, humans are present to the reader-interpreter (or researcher) not as I-Thou or as an other mind, but as a *"being-with"* (*ZS,* 112). This being-with entails a way of a mutual engagement with others as a being-in-the-world. Being-with means being-with one another as belonging to the matters of concern encountered (*ZS,* 112). Encountering is a temporal presence-to as experience which is undergone or suffered such that any experience is essentially transformative (*OHF,* 5, 78-80) as dialogical. The stance of objectivity in the scientific method obtains where the dispassionate researchers are taken to be disengaged from their predelineated area of study.

Engagement in hermeneutic phenomenology as method is not the disengagement of the putative objectivity of the scientific method. For Gadamer, engagement as interpretive or hermeneutical dialogical experience "is concerned with *tradition*" (*TM,* 358). This is in contrast to the scientific method and its anonymous society of investigators. As Gadamer opens up the word "thou," he uses it to indicate tradition as "a genuine partner in dialogue" (*TM,* 358). The human being is engaged with tradition as an I with a Thou. Engaged understanding is not an attempt at detachment from or abstraction of the other as in the scientific method. It is a letting of something be said—the open clearing as encountering-relationships possibilizing the proper essence of what it means to be human (*TM,* 358-362).

Hermeneutic phenomenology is involved with springing forth. Springing forth is not a physiological or theorized ego subject's leap from firm ground back to the same firm ground. Leaping or springing forth as thought here gives "a free and open possibility of thinking" (*POR,* 93). Agency is hereby shifted (better: shifts itself) to the play of phenomena from the centrality of modernity's ego-subject. For example, this means that "listening" is not the exclusive property of "the rational animal," but neither can it be thought of as a causal factor (agent). "There are phenomena" means that there is always already the possible historical-temporal play of a given phenomenon such that it shows itself for thinking-saying.

Phenomena are possibilities that the human being of openness has but does not and cannot possess.

The each time of engaged openness historically and temporally endures, persists, and prevails as an offering. Of disclosing and beckoning, engaged openness reveals/conceals (emerges/eludes) as the heart (the open clearing) of turning. The heart of turning shows itself as two moments of possibility: (1) Disclosing and beckoning needs the engaging of the human being of openness and as this need places the human being of openness unto its call, and (2) the sojourning of the human being of openness, as the experience of thrownness unto the open clearing, is of belongingness to the call of disclosing and beckoning. For Heidegger, "turning is counter-turning" (CP, 287).[4] Turning calls as (1) the aboutness of the about and (2) the of of aboutness.

Thinking-saying is engaged by the task of making the otherwise habitual nature of the everyday from which one can leap visible, thereby letting the relationship one is sustained by, as an always already forerunning (futural) realm, show itself as itself (POR, 93). In contrast to scientific studies that "report findings or outcomes," hermeneutic phenomenological studies seek to make participants' interpretations visible in order to let possibilities for richer understandings show up. When thought-said, as the call-response of the turning in disclosing and beckoning the inevitability of the future as on-coming becoming, commends itself to listeners, it is not as decisive agency but as participatory possibility.

Understandings are offered as the self-presencing of presence: dialogue, not as outcome by consensus, but as the conjoining of sense—the many-sidedness of springing forth (BSP, 87). The self-presencing of presence (presencing: presencing itself) as "logos never means 'reason,' but rather discourse, conversation" such that the human being "has its world in the mode of something addressed" (OHF, 17).[5] Understandings of the meaning of engaged openness are shared understandings that understandings are shared between understandings (BSP, 99). Understandings are made possible by "the relation of singular origins among themselves" as the relating of sense (BSP, 84).

Language lets plural singularities be exposed as one speaks to or with others as well as to oneself. Therefore the self "is not individuality; it is each time, the punctuality of a 'with' that establishes a certain origin of [sense], and connects it to an infinity of other possible origins" (*BSP*, 85).

The doing of hermeneutic phenomenology is not the performance of an actor playing a role. This scholarship's jumping-off point is not a jumping-off at all; it is a jumping-in to where each and all (world) are always already in the everydayness of their singular plurality. Before and as hermeneutic phenomenology is given a formal name, interpreting always already calls the human being to be involved *as* it (*OHF*, 24-26). The temporal particularity that each one is always already appears (self-shows) as the human being of openness: "'It' calls" (*BT*, 270-271; *4S*, 59-60); "'It' gives, 'It' gives to understand, which means that 'It' of itself discloses" (*GBT*, 433). "Each one's relation *of* openness is the locale of 'being it'" (*HWT*, 53). This is the everydayness of singular plurality as embraced in hermeneutic phenomenology.

Everydayness as conversation, narrative telling, and dialogue is a field (locus of meaning) of hermeneutic phenomenology, which always already obtains prior to theoritized structures of comportment. Everyday tasks are always already involved encounters with matters of concern (*HPM*, 293-294). Hermeneutic phenomenology is offered the task of thematizing conversation, narrative telling, and dialogue; but the historicality of these phenomena never admits or enables them "to be gotten around" (*QCT*, 173-179). They are just here: "nothing preexists; only what exists exists" (*BSP*, 29).

Our task as we get underway will be to let the moments of conversation, narrative telling, and dialogue show themselves as they present themselves. In hermeneutic phenomenology, interpretation is the mutual turning in co-responding and enacting such that the original sense of method as asking after the appeal of matters of concern toward their engaged openness is retrieved (*QCT*, 44-47). The call of method shows itself as an open pathway rather than the constriction of a drainage channel or a railroad track.

Conversation

> *"To speak with" is the conversation (and sustaining) and* conatus *of a being-exposed, which exposes only the secret of its own exposition.*
>
> *BSP,* 92-93

Human beings, as the mortals that they are, are delivered over to, are always already conversant with, "a world already interpreted, already organized in its basic relations, into which experience steps, as something new" (*PH,* 15). In order for them to be conversant, historicality itself must allot its finitude as limit such that humans are permitted to be historical. Historicality announces that humans have "to recognize the *limitation* placed on consciousness by history having its effect" (*RPJ,* 47). Conversation is always already historically situated.

To be in the world is to be involved as conversation with the historicality of what it means to be human. Being engaged with possible matters of concern encounters, claims the human being of openness. As everyday, practical, prudent, and usable interpretations, conversations are more than "mere accommodation" (*TM,* 388). Conversations obtain as narrative understanding, which lets the historical situatedness of the participants disclose itself—they are not exclusively the production of autonomous ego-subjects. Conversations self-conduct such that no one individual or group of individuals can know in advance what will come out of them (*TM,* 383). From myriad casual interactions from therapeutic practices, police interrogations, and courtroom testimony to processes of coming to understandings, conversations let the free play of their speaking be shown (*TM,* 388). Conversations also occur as the saying of poetic or musical interactions in which the participants are other than speaking subjects. In its broadest sense, conversation obtains when a matter of concern (e.g., contract, theory, tool, food, treatment modality, performance) either does or does not "do its job." When matters of concern do their job, conversations are invisible. If there is breakdown, such as a dispute, conversational tensions rise to the surface and require adjustments to be made in the relationships of the participants' practical, purposive (intentional), and prudent comportments. Neither agreement nor disagreement holds back conversation as conversation from its essential disclosing and beckoning.

Conversation, taken in its widest sense, is a self-showing emergence of "the mark of the presence and absence of everything that is present, of every kind and rank. Even when showing is accomplished by human saying, even then this showing, this pointer, is preceded by an indication that it will let itself be shown" (*OWL,* 123). World as emergent/elusive engaged openness becomes unconcealed to humans, not as the product of human willing, but as the self-presencing of presence which shows itself as a "preverbal 'reading' before it is ever spoken out" as vocal utterance (*HPM,* 299). Showing, letting appear, being seen and heard makes its way into and as conversation such that the human being of openness can belong to (be always already betrothed to) engaged openness.

Conversing, narrative telling, relating, and storytelling need partners. These partnerships are not limited to side-by-side ego-subjects, but must include historical situatedness, that is, world. Only through the contextual historicality of being-with is there any issuing-forth (genesis) of the self-understanding and interpretation of each human being. Therefore it must be seen that "the individual has no fixed borders" (*GIC,* 56). Boundaries show themselves as meeting places, which are offered as the play of space and time self-presence as co-presence. Every unique individual exigently needs encounterable partnerships in order to be able to "designate *itself* and *relate itself* to itself" (*BSP,* 40).

Raven, a sophomore nursing student, waits outside his instructor's door. His instructor, Signe, arrives from down the hall.

> Raven: *I was wondering when you will have grades posted?*
>
> Signe: *[Deep sigh] Remember I said I would email you your grade tomorrow? In fact, I mentioned this*

*three times in class just before the exam! Raven, you
really have to learn to listen better.*

Signe opens her office door, enters, and turns her back on Raven.
He leaves.

The with-world is readily forgotten or overlooked as a familiar
"which prevails for a while at the particular time" (*OHF*, 77). It (the
with-world) enables one to find one's way, but concomitantly it can
obtain as a soporific such that the proper essence of the open
clearing is covered up. The proper sense of the finite human being
of openness or its thrownness consists in the fact that it becomes
aware, not only of its being historically conditioned, but especially
of its being each finite time reciprocally conditioned by the other
(*COP*, 28). In *Being and Time,* Heidegger's discussion of "the
anyone" points to this.[6]

Hermeneutic phenomenology is a reciprocating address-
response, enabling and engaging self-opening—the time and
time again self-retrieving of the origination and accomplishment
of the as-structure's sense of the *each's* mediating middle region
in its unique singular-plural exposure: its interpretive, context-
dependent, temporal, historical, non-eternal inception (*RHT*, 264-
266).[7] Hermeneutic phenomenology must obtain as the on-coming
conversation that each human being and matter of concern is and
must be. Gadamer has averred:

> [The] total experience of the world presents a process
> of coming to be at home that never comes to an end
> in a world that appears ever more strange because it
> has been all too changed by ourselves; an unending
> process realized not only [in] the conversation which
> each of us conducts with ourselves in thinking but
> also the conversation in which we are all caught
> up together and never cease to be caught up [by].
> *RAS,* 20

The relating of call, calling, and listening, wherein narrative tellings
are always already related, is such that their belonging-together

is the tellings-of their on-coming co-responding. Conversation as nonpossessable having delivers commands, and commends the human being of openness to the attending being-together of plural singulars. Conversance is the dialogical experience of engaged concerned whiling (dwelling), the exposure to conversation.

Conversation is about enabled relating. It offers "the relations between the spoken, the unspoken, speakers, and what is spoken about: that is, the entire structure of the relation between humankind, word, and thing that makes it possible for humankind to say 'is' of something" (Fynsk, 1996b, 64).[8] Discursiveness engages the speech of humans in order to self-present itself to humans, to make itself hearable. Only insofar as humans hear are they enabled to speak (Fynsk, 1996b, 26). Therefore Heidegger was led to say, "The simultaneousness of speaking and listening has a larger meaning" than conversation considered as mere utterance (OWL, 123).

Conversation as world encounter offers the revelatory place of voice as possibility for the play of the absolute and the authoritative. Silent interweavings of conversation offer narrative loci of meaning— the ground of radical otherness. The ensuing play of disruption and interruption to the above "first brings into view the limitations that would be overcome in the drama of autonomy and marks in advance the privilege [as situatedness] to be enjoyed" (Eisenstein, 1989, 275). The seeming paradox of authority as ground lies in thrownness such that concealed alienation is merely understood as the existence of historical language. On the contrary, what human beings share in language is the "always already as a place of reciprocal being-in-the-world as openness [the open clearing] which emerges out of all experience" (Eisenstein, 1989, 270). This ontological-existential a priori undergirds and thereby undercuts the position of epistemology and its associated scientific method.

What does the subject-object paradigm in its various guises say about conversation? A meaningful conversation for science must be a neutralized, fixed agreement of logically determined utterances. These in turn must be dependent on some universal grammar and syntax. Any ambiguous meaning and conditional context must be expunged. Conversation that adheres to an idealized atemporal context must in all cases be identical to itself. In other words, all consciousness must admit of not being differenced. But what of difference? Does difference become the merely personal, not having any validity outside the subject? Co-responding as attending to, not as an interposing or imposition, is the letting wherein the human being of openness is called on to listen.

Neither some model of subjective consciousness nor transcriptions of speaking and address can ever fully encompass the situatedness as that calls to itself while at the same time offering light to the play of conversation. Dialogical experience is always already each time a plural-singular we. But, "as a linguistic 'shifter,' *we* has no signification" (*GT,* 61); that is to say, it cannot be fully determined via calculative or idealist methods. The "we" of conversation includes speaking *with* entities (*ZS,* 140); the conversation *of* sense cannot be objectified. Noncalculatable "talking with one another means to say, which means to show and to let be seen. It means to communicate and correspondingly, to listen, to submit oneself to a claim addressed to oneself to comply and respond to it" (*ZS,* 214-215). In the "we" that embraces conversation "it is *something* that comes to language, not the persons of one or the other speaker" (*HL,* 122). Therefore, "conversation gets its illumination from out of the conversational situation" (*HL,* 124).

The self-showing phenomenon of conversation needs the human being of openness in order to be disposed (affected). Disposedness "denotes a passivity with respect to the givenness of what is given to it; but as a reception, it implies an 'active' participation in givenness itself" (Raffoul, 1997, xvii).[9] Engaged openness disposes the human being of openness as sense. Dialogical experience as the possibility of (participation in) sense "means to 'suffer' or undergo the event of [sense]" (Raffoul, 1997, xvii). The capacity to receive and be disposed to (be affected by) sense turns on how a given particular time calls for what makes "unsense, unsense and no-longer-sense" (*GTT,* 313). Conversation announces itself, not as vocal utterance, but as the drawing into the dialogical encounterings of human experience such that humans are disposed (attuned) to world as the historicality of significance and meaning.

"The art of having a conversation with oneself and fervently seeking an understanding of oneself is the art of thinking. But this means the art of seriously questioning what one really means when one thinks or says this or that. In doing so, one sets out on a journey, or better, is already on the journey" (*RPJ*, 33). To be underway is to hear the call of questions, which can "open up possibilities and keep them open" (*TM*, 299).

The preverbal exhortation of language needs speakers to listen to language as "it 'says' its coming about" (Fynsk, 1996b, 53). Language offers itself to listening and sighting. In other words, as language is its own way, listening to its *saying* (showing, letting appear, being seen and heard) is prior to any questioning of it. That said, "every statement has to be seen as a response to a question and the only way to understand a statement is to get hold of the question to which the statement is an answer" (*RAS*, 106). Naming statements allow world to appear as emergence/elusion—the intimate belonging together between emergence out of concealment and the elusion of emerging.

Conversation as the always already infinitely finite other of itself, engages (calls) the speaking of humans in its own way such that humans can make their way back to listening. They unfold, not from speakers, but from the call to language by language as it draws/holds/calls the participants unto *its* way (*TM*, 383). Like all constitutive, imperceptible phenomena, conversation is revealed (self-presences) as the moment of its absence. For example, when individuals affected with Alzheimer's disease lose the ability to communicate, their understandings seem to be lost to themselves (or so it might be assumed) and to others. The play of conversation is thus revealed as the lack of the particular participant's ability to participate in the broad sense of the world as it turns on matters of concern. In this example, there is still sense, never to be lost, but as merely reattuned.

The step back into hermeneutic phenomenology entails letting oneself into "the silent course of a conversation that moves us" (*DT,* 69-70) as singular plurals. The question becomes, How does one let everyday conversation as mere lack of involvement transform itself into a phenomenon that always already silently calls for engaged involvement (*WCT,* 178)? One can choose to be in a conversation such that one goes beyond oneself in order to think with an other and thence to come back to oneself as transformed (*DD,* 110). What can take place in a conversation as it sojourns is a temporally particular "give and take of conversations" (*HL,* 125). Historically situated conversations are always already, as questions, pointing in directions for inquiry (*DD,* 111). In hermeneutic phenomenology, conversations are explicated as interpretive readings such that they grow out of coming to understand the alterity of narraticity prior to any formal dialogue that each time reveals, discloses situatedness. The task of Narrative Pedagogy, on the other hand, is to let the narrative tellings as stories of the everyday speak in order that they might reveal otherwise overlooked belongings-to.

The everyday "carries disclosedness along with it, gives disclosedness" as "the place, and the taking-place, of the *each time* according to which existence appropriates its singularity" (*BP,* 89). The thoughts *of* the everyday are the always already "meanings superimposed on the world of everyday experience" (*BP,* 103). Of particular significance here are Jean-Luc Nancy's remarks on *Being and Time*'s references to the everyday in relation to Heidegger's forgetting or overlooking of the "dignity of existence" (*BP,* fn. 45, 405-406). While Heidegger's pivotal contributions, which call into question modernity's subservience to the subject-object paradigm, are of crucial import, his dismissal of everyday conversation and writing as idle talk, hearsay, and scribbling contributes to isolating his thought from the practical and prudent "world" he so assiduously labored to explicate.

The surprise or interruptedness possible as conversation is the play of discursiveness as offered to the human being of openness such that there is available a sense of being claimed by whatever manifests (self-presences) itself as itself. The always already self-presencing of presence can never take leave of the conversation through which openness is claimed by engagement. In order to let conversation claim the play of singular plural for itself, we present herewith a series of possibilities that offer the "each time" (*RHT,* 266) of emergence/illusion. Conversations disclose and beckon by saying-showing that:

- There are questions in excess to the answers posited by science (*RAS,* 149). Putative masteries of technique and control cannot offer relief from deliberation and decision (*RAS,* 92).
- Consciousness as an offering cannot disengage one from the specificity of one's mortal end (*RAS,* 145; *OWL,* 37-40).
- Auras of benign indifference, in which the familiar can harbor and hold a danger, are such that what merits questioning is passed over (*WCT,* 154). Finitude is the exposing of the human being to questions that do not admit of answers (*RAS,* 53).
- Presuppositions and preconceptions hold within themselves their own stubborn truths (*WCT,* 152). Disposedness always already finds one *as* a situation presented by effective history (*GIC,* 46).
- One's cognitive capacity falls short of any perfectible total realization (*GIC,* 46; Hyde, 2008, 15). Temporally particular (ontological) historical situatedness cannot be stepped out of via mere intellection (*GIC,* 46).
- Tradition is not an impervious enclosure but is free for coming and going (*PH,* 211). Conventions advene as letting one read relationships of domination (*RAS,* 82).
- The world as interpreted (read) works, texts, and comportments is not something merely dreamed up (*RPJ,* 44).
- Understanding always already brings along an advance understanding that joins one to the understood (*RAS,* 136).
- Understanding as *offered* to the human being of openness is marked by the lack of fixity and absolutes. There is a call for understanding to understand everything that can be understood (*PH,* 31; *N,* 313-314).

- Thoughtful understanding emerges/eludes as matters of concern call the human being of openness (*TM*, 299).
- Tension- and disruption-filled human beings of openness always already call back to common understandings and existence (*PH*, 42).
- Human beings cannot enter into a conversation isolated from thought, and thought cannot enter into conversations isolated from humans (*QCT*, 176).

Narrative Telling

The veiled relation of message and messenger's course plays everywhere.

OWL, 53

[Sense] does not consist in the transmission from a speaker to a receiver, but in the simultaneity of (at least) two origins of [sense]: that of the saying and that of its resaying.

BSP, 86

Narrative telling is discursiveness as the con-tension between birth and death as an addressing, understanding, and conversing (*BSP*, 90). Narraticity as sense is the commonality of engaged openness such that the noncommonality of each incipience is necessarily and incipiently the common of the "with" (*BSP*, 90). The "with" is not some neutered, leveled off "is" of sameness conceptualized as "pure consciousness apart from the concrete individual" (*HPM*, 296). The sphere of pure consciousness (immanence) cannot allow for the ego-subject to be *nonidentical* "with regard to its potential to every other self" (*HWT*, 53). Narrative telling as abiding, the temporal singularity of singular plurals, "is that in which and out of which I 'while,' circumscribed in its outermost here and now" (*GBT*, 291). Each singular plural (openness) dwells as "my while, my birth, my death," as an "ever unfinished to-be" (*GBT*, 425-426).

Narrative loci as sense as dwelling extend "to various interweavings of voices in tensed equilibrium—particularly to the problematic balancing of authority and openness in speech"

(Eisenstein, 1989, 282). The experience of dwelling (sojourning/whiling/abiding) is prior to "all metaphysical questions of identity and embodiment because its ground is not in the 'substance' of consciousness but in the dramatic, narrative coherence of the day-to-day events with which [the conscious individual] finds itself involved" (Eisenstein, 1989, 279).

Narrative tellings are shaped in the aroundness of thrown disposedness as unique situatedness and reliance on the nonhierarchical privilege of shared worlds of sense. The parlance of a given telling "is not to be viewed as a mere code that could be broken: its privilege is manifest through the necessity of *being in* the story, not of knowing its structure of objectivity" (Eisenstein, 1989, 279). The privilege of shared telling is the dynamic each time. The wholes of narrative telling reveal themselves as their limits, disruptions, interruptions, as the on-coming presence of their absence. Telling lives as facticity, ever in light of the fact that each human being has a possible nonfinalizable narrative dead end.

Hermeneutic phenomenological thinking-saying sees "dead ends" as moments where loci of meaning self-originate as emergence/elusion. These are seen as limits, which are almost imperceptible trails, traces, or tracks that announce possible releasement into the open. They emerge "now dark and perplexing, now again lightning sharp like a sudden insight, which then in turn" elude attempts to say them (*OWL,* 41).[10]

"Tellers, listeners to, and characters in a unique narrative are its privileged interpreters" (Eisenstein, 1989, 278). A single telling's locus of sense belongs to its singularity and concomitantly belongs to the tradition that the narrative and its participants are delivered-over-to, thrown-as. Traditions are transmitted to participants while at the same time the play of matters of concern always already "abruptly trail[s] off into obscurity" (*HWT,* 198).

Telling is sense—there are no narratives that can be absent of it. Meaning needs sense as that which divides tellers and listeners as well as that which joins them. Sense discloses and beckons as "its own communication or its own circulation" (*BSP,* 2). Engaged openness is the on-coming of sense. Narrative tellings always already engage the "from one to the other" as "the syncopated repetition of origins-of-the-world, which are each time one or the other" (*BSP*, 6). *Each other*, so to speak, is the "silhouettes that are both imprecise and singularized, faint outlines of voices, patterns of comportment, sketches of affects" (*BSP*, 7). Narratives are let by engaged openness to be telling—where sharing, as the division *of* joining, resets in the double-genitive structure's belongingness. The sense of belongingness as telling and as connecting-disconnecting "brings active and passive voices together into a simple and intimate unity" (*RHT*, 265). That unity is the open passage of sense as the announcement of a surplus of intelligibility that exceeds the logic of subjectivisms or the possibility of fixed and stable significations.

Telling as telling participates in announcing nondiscrete regions, neighborhoods, areas, or scopes. These play as understanding wherein "the way any given utterance, discourse, context is to be understood depends upon its particular scope. If the truth of narratives is to be understood and safeguarded, one has to understand their scope" (*RAS*, 164-165). The circulating scope of narrative "itself opens up in the structure of understanding" (Raffoul, 1997, xii). Between each narrative articulation as said, read, or written, "there is only an indefinite return to the understanding of understanding" (*SV*, 227). Telling is the site of the issuance of the understandings of understandings, which is always already retrieved as "difference, the asymptosis which issues in, but is not reducible to, all the asymptoses or differences that we call, as a whole, meaningfulness or language" (*DH*, 217).

The incompletability of narrative telling means that every finite present shows itself as its limiting (*TM*, 302). But limit here, we remember, is the regioning where a matter of concern or topic begins its essential unfolding. The pre-given historical movement of the open clearing "consists in the fact that it is never absolutely bound to any one standpoint" (*TM*, 304). There can be no discrete regions or neighborhoods. Narrative telling obtains as bound to the situatedness of "the webs of historical effects" (*TM*, 300).

The polarity of familiarity and strangeness is hermeneutically regarded as the linguistic situatedness of an encountered telling as "the story that it tells us" (*TM*, 295). Tellings are always already available in advance as meaningful contexts as the with-world of singular plurals appears each time (*OHF*, 74-77). In turn, tellings cannot be isolated from the care structure ("becoming what one already essentially is as being-present-to-entities" [*HPM*, 306-307]). The human being of openness as possibility is "concerned about itself and attends to itself and all the while—since care has in each particular case a language—addresses itself in a worldly manner" (*OHF*, 79-80). Narrative telling as understanding is not enclosed in pure consciousness but encounters and participates in tradition as a "process of transmission in which past and present are constantly mediated" (*TM*, 290).

Narrative telling announces, addresses, and calls forth:

- Readiness to hear the putative new as necessarily determined by the old that has already taken possession of us (*PH*, 9).
- Origins as always other, unpossessable, and open, but each and every time present as unique (*BSP*, 19). Participants are absolutely nonreducible to each other as generic universals.
- Paths to scattered origins in their very scatterings as the plural touchings of singular origins as the on-coming of each presence, each time unique (*BSP*, 14-15).
- Translation or interpretation as a task that does not repeat what is said, but as a placing in the aboutness of what is said (its sense) such that saying becomes mutual, reciprocal retrieval (*PH*, 68).
- Understanding as listening to the exigency of questioning; thought and thinking as attempts to sight that which gives thinking's ability for questioning (von Herrmann, 1996, 188).[11]
- Hermeneutic phenomenology as other than a preordained know-how wherein a specific task can be chosen. The human being's proper, ownmost open possibility itself poses tasks as possibilities (*RAS*, 135).
- Hermeneutic phenomenological understanding as other than a mere technique that can be learned independently

of application and interpretive consequences (*PH*, 143).

- Linguistically articulated free space as understandings that are a "filling" of the particular response to the word but do not fill it out completely.
- The possible nonpossibility of universal schema, which could be indifferently adhered to each interpretation (*WCT*, 71). There is an enigmatic paradox where the application of rules exists in the absence of a rule (*RAS*, 49).
- The struggle to allow for *engaged openness-in-common*. Any focused assertions or contradictions forget possibility (*GIC*, 98).
- "There is much to say" as the basic hermeneutical relation. Interpretation can never be a fixing of fleeting meanings (*PH*, 211).
- The saying-relating of a narrative telling, which distinguishes itself in that it never admits of final understandings. Co-responding is claimed by the need for different answers of each encounter.

The narrative path of hermeneutic phenomenology can be seen as two recurring but *not* repeating phases: (1) takings-as that have already occurred where a given language holds sway and (2) takings-as that allow richer interpretations to always already come forth from the initial takings-as. The work of language is narrative telling such that matters of concern as they are offered give thinking-saying that retrieves narrative gathering as disclosure. Narrative telling as language is itself always already on the way to language (*PH*, 228).

Raven's story continues. He is talking with Josh, a fellow security guard employee.

> Josh: *So how did you do on your test? Did you pass the course?*
>
> Raven: *Still waiting. Won't know until I get home tonight. You know waiting is worse than studying for the final itself. I don't know, Josh, if I have what it*

takes. I thought moving closer to my mom so she can help me with the girls would really help me in nursing school. But I just don't have enough time to study. Today I was up at 3:45 a.m. so I could put in a load of laundry, make the kids' lunches, and get them up, fed, and all of us on the subway by 5 a.m. Takes 30 minutes to get to my mom's. Then I have to be on my way to school by 5:45 in order to get to my clinical [practicum] by 6:45. You know I sold my car and getting to this clinical means I have to transfer twice on the bus. Working this job and my weekends delivering pizzas means the only time I can study is here when we are not busy. Josh, I feel like I am always behind and doing a lot worse than I know I can. Sometimes I fall asleep in the morning on the subway with the kids. Becoming a nurse is my dream and my lifeline—a ticket to a decent job and a good future for my kids. But now I'm worried about failing and having to retake this course again in the fall. It costs me more money, slows me down, and if I get one more failure I am out of the nursing program. When I asked my teacher yesterday about when grades would be posted, she seemed angry that I forgot she said three times in class we would get them today by email. It's embarrassing when you forget, but I was so nervous I might fail. When she walked away and turned her back on me, I thought, I'm not going to make it; I'll never become a nurse. Tonight when I get home and look at my email, I'll know. Maybe I wasn't meant to be a nurse?

Josh: *Wish there was something I could do to help. Maybe I could take your second floor rounds for you. That would give you an extra hour to study. Nobody would know and I can use the exercise. You know my wife says we can't afford for me to have any more trouble with my diabetes, so she is always telling me to get more exercise. Don't be hard on yourself, Raven. I'm sure you passed!*

Narrative telling gathers and retrieves but cannot be thought as a self-grounding certainty in the Cartesian sense. Telling cannot be reduced to theoretical sameness or objective isolation, despite quests for certainty that turn on ego-subjects. Narratives infinitely issue-forth as moments of disclosure only as they paradoxically withdraw as limit (James, 2006, 49-63). Narrative tellings are not immanent to an autonomous self. They can only be seen as letting their own self-revealing as disclosing and beckoning self-retrieval. They are *not* exclusive to human production. Narrative telling is co-originary with conversation and presents itself to dialogue.

Dialogue

The sharing (the dialogue) is understood here as a provisional necessity, whether this is fortunate or unfortunate, whether it is an enrichment or an impediment to the community of interlocutors.

SV, 247

We heed the hints of that message whose proper bearers we would want to become.

OWL, 48

Dialogues speak from the enigma of finitude such that the future as its own retrieving (ripening) possibility can be retrieved, but not fixed (or foretold!). Dialogues as they are read (interpreted) are certain paths *from* thinking-saying as well as *in* thinking-saying; they take into account the excess of thoughtful interpretations to which interpretation as itself offers itself. The difference between the singular proprieties of voices, ways, modes, is invited as announcement. It is to an announcement and to an opening of the very dialogue of thinking-saying that *all* are guests—all share in the hospitality/gift/offering of difference. From the temporally particular always already to the on-coming self-presencing of presence—each time the hermeneutical, thinking-saying circle does not cease from breaking off (*SV,* 230). The back-and-forth rejoining reciprocity of dialogue cannot be effected as perfect closure, but can be retrieved as disclosure only as dialogue allows itself to be retrieved in its retrieval of itself.

In Chapter 1 we presented the as-structure. Recall that dialogues are claimed by conversation as the engaged openness of narrative telling such that "the synthesizing 'as' and the differentiating 'as-not' are not disjunctive but mutually inclusive" (*DG,* 158). The *as,* as presence, and the *as-not,* as absence, reciprocally self-presence in dialogues such that the proper essence of self-presencing *is* absence itself. The self-presentation of presence "is *dialogue,* but the end [or purpose] of dialogue is not to overcome itself in 'consensus'; its reason is to offer, and only to offer (giving it tone and intensity), the *with* of [sense], the plurality of its springing forth" (*BSP,* 87). As dialogues are disclosingly and beckoningly let out of sense they disclose and beckon the "as" as such (*BSP,* 88).

The coming to presence (appearing) of dialogue is the open clearing where conversations announce themselves and allow themselves to be announced at the same time. The interpretive task is to let the proclaiming dwelling in a given dialogue be revealed as conversation and narrative telling. The giving, offering "essence of the dialogue is in the infinite alteration of the other, and in that puts an end without end to the end of the dialogue. At each time it is put to an end, the announcement is renewed" (*SV,* 246). Interpretive dialogue is held in advance as "not positing an end, but reckoning with being-on-the-way, giving *it* free play, disclosing it, holding it fast to *being-possible*" (*OHF,* 13).

One must take care not to enter "the paradigm of dialogue as unidirectional questioning and answering" (Eisenstein, 1989, 271). Everything turns on the participants' willingness to listen to the conversations they are claimed by as moments of narrative telling—stories of lives, experiences, and world (Eisenstein, 1989, 277). Thought of hermeneutically, dialogue can shelter within itself the paradoxical position such that it tries to do for everyone "that which each can only do for" him- or herself (Eisenstein, 1989, 277).

That is to say, practical and prudent involvement with engaged openness of matters of concern is the call or calling that claims each human being ahead to, and therefore as, its possible historically situated self (*HPM*, 303-304).

"The essential dialogue or polylogue" of discursiveness "is both the one in which" one speaks to an other and, *"identically,* the one in which "one speaks to oneself as an entire world unto oneself. Engaged openness as discursiveness always already claims the human being of openness simultaneously as the possibility of *"'us' and 'me' and 'me' as 'us,' as well as 'us' as 'me'"* (*BSP,* 85). Engaged openness exigently needs the play of nonidentifiable open clearing for dialogue to play as difference and as between singular plurals. There can be no indifferent subsumption of instances into generic universals (*GBT,* 426).

Any given dialogue is a journey that intersects with itself while other dialogues intersect with it and with themselves as they all cross such that points of intersection punctuate as re-traversals of the same points. Arrivals and departures do not allow any hierarchy; they allow only the possibility of retrieval (Diekelmann, J., 2005). The fore-structure of "understanding is bound to elements that can never be made commensurable with future interpretation" (Eisenstein, 1989, 283).[12] The "binding-together of heterogeneous sense" (Eisenstein, 1989, 280) as "the meaning of the 'with' or the 'with' of meaning, can be evaluated only in and by the 'with' itself, an experience from which—in its plural singularity—nothing can be taken away" (*BSP,* 98).

The play of showing, letting appear, being seen and heard makes its way into dialogue such that the human being of openness can belong to engaged openness. Therefore, "the disparity of intentions and the heterogeneity of linguistic functions" do not admit of absolute closure of the sphere of immanence (Eisenstein, 1989, 276).

The dynamic of the always already retrieving, never-to-be-finished end calls for a viewing of language "not as a homogeneous dialogical space but rather as a heterogeneous narrative one" such that thinking is claimed by factical existence "in a socially productive way" (Eisenstein, 1989, 282). The "way" of production becomes thought herein, not as the imposition of some preestablished form, but as the self-retrieving (ripening) of the proper essence of matters of concern addressed as being lived from out of the world. The proper mode of the latter "is *caring* in the sense of producing, putting in place, directing ourselves to tasks, taking into possession, preventing, protecting against loss" (*OHF*, 79), and so forth such that care is always already the open each time. Care can appear to disappear "in the habits, customs and publicness of everydayness—it does not show itself any longer, it is covered up" (*OHF*, 80). The world as self-evident is encountered as leveled off and putatively care free. But care always already each time reveals itself as the possibility of disruption or interruption as the human being as self-retrieving becomes the proper, unique, and concrete possibility that it already is: to be right at its open moment of finitude.

Finite human beings are exposed to dialogue, narrative telling, and conversation as engaged openness underway as world and care. Dialogue presences as the open clearing prior to any determinations of signifiers. In a world of practical and prudent concerns, sense as the showing of "language offers itself in a co-belonging with presence that sets thought a new task" (*GT*, 56).[13] Sense takes place "between us and not between signifier, signified, and referent." The between us, in its widest sense, is not "exhausted by the codes of 'significance,' by those pragmatics of enunciation, or the psycho-sociology of communication" (*GT*, 57).

Each particular temporal encounter holds practical involvement in itself as countering and countermanding. Personal encounters as differing interpretations of meaningful contexts of what presences in concerned preoccupation are properly seen as a mindfulness of guiding presuppositions and involvements. Hermeneutic phenomenology turns on "the discussion of those presuppositions" (*WCT*, 177). Understandings require some sense, a moving into nearness with dialogue's way. Interpreters always end up having to reinterpret themselves, and are then changed themselves in the light of dialogue. Understanding is not only to grasp meaning; it is to understand the claim meaning has (Bruns, 1997, 77).

Interpretation is not without (apart from) conversations and narrative tellings. Interpreting can show itself only as a dialogue of conversations and narrative tellings. As an involvement of speakers in the region/neighborhood of their speaking and as the heart of their dialogue, interpreting must not confine itself obdurately to what is directly said. The task of interpreting lets a call pose itself which points to origins/inceptions/issuings forth of thoughts and their thinking-saying (*WCT,* 178).

Concomitantly the work of interpretive thinking, in its discipline and its rigor, does not consist in subjugating an infinity of sense to absolute meaning. To be on the way, as interpretation, lies in experiencing the always already excess of sense as "remaining exposed to it" (*GT,* 67).

The open engagement of dialogue lets itself be seen and heard as:

- Awareness that there are non-understandings that cannot be cured by information because they are not caused by a lack of information.
- The attempt to hear between the words of conversation partners just as one must see what is behind matters of concern (*RAS,* 129).
- A dialectic of entangled, rejoining question and answer wherein the always already play of the hermeneutical process co-responds with the basic structure of dialogue (*RPJ,* 39). Assertive statements are only understood as they are understood as responses (*RAS,* 46).
- The danger in speaking of the language of conventionality such that it forfeits possibilities of meaningful address and evocatory power (*PH,* 85-86).
- An inextricable ownmost historical situation wherein whatever is other is read only from its own time and place (Bruns, 1997, 76).
- The discursive locale of hermeneutic phenomenology as it mediates where a blockage advenes, preventing making questioning clear to oneself and to others (*PH,* 92).

- How the matter which hermeneutic phenomenology teaches—to see through the narrow asserting of an opposition and separation between on-coming tradition and interpretive mindfulness of it (*PH*, 28). There is difficulty in letting something be said even if understood right away (*PH*, 101).
- How the illusion that mere entities can precede their manifestation in language can conceal the fundamentally discursive character of the human experience of world (*PH*, 77-78).
- The art of letting what is said or written be brought to speech again and again (*RAS*, 119); letting old, used-up words show themselves in their play.
- Letting the essence of the word lie in not being totally expressed but rather left to what is unsaid, as especially the speech left remaining silent (*PH*, 234).
- The proper essence of the interpretive experience as calling forth the commonality of all understanding as located the linguistic experience (*RAS*, 110) such that matters of concern are allowed to come into words (*TM*, 389). Linguistic experience shows up as the "rhetoric" of "a communal listening" (*HR*, 62).
- The imperative of endless conversation, in all the senses of "end" wherein matters of concern are articulated, and as necessary articulation, becoming something each has but does not possess (*RPJ*, 52).
- A successful convincing that is not a rhetoric claimed by a technical doctrine, an ought, or an untruth (*RAS*, 111). Rhetoric as "a form of discourse that works hand in hand with emotion in order to promote collaborative deliberation" (Hyde, 2005, 96) lets the engagement of dialogue show itself in its richest sense.

The movement and appearance of taking a matter of concern as something can be taken-as a response to a question.

With Talitha, a faculty colleague, Signe shares her frustrations.

Do you think Jill [the department chairperson] is going to nonrenew my contract? Brian [Signe's partner] and I talked last night, and he is sure he is going to be laid off next month. And with a baby coming, I am really worried, especially about losing his insurance. It covered everything. I feel like I have done everything Jill told me to do, but when they didn't work she had no help to offer me, only blame. I was hired a week before classes started, and I was only one lesson ahead of the students all semester. And to give me a required class with 134 students with no TA [teaching assistant] and to tell me everyone teaches three courses regardless of how many students each course has. That's ridiculous.

Talitha: *I see the students line up outside your door when you have office hours. I feel guilty because I teach a required course too but only have 67 students. I don't know how you do it!*

Signe: *I am afraid I am losing it. The students are wanting their final grades instantly and you can't blame them, but just entering and calculating the grades takes time. Not to mention grading the final group projects! I was in the hallway this morning and one of the students wanted to know when I will get the final grades done. I try to use humor, you know, like, "You and 500 other students!" but it feels like I am failing in everything I do!*

Talitha: *Ouch! Humor can be a tricky thing, especially when you start teaching. Maybe just saying, "It must be awful waiting to find out your final grade; I am working as fast as I can," would work. Listening to students and listening to your situation is what we do. We all get "hallway questions" from students this time of the year. I try to just listen and know, in this case, the waiting is hard, plain hard for students, especially when their grades are borderline. Maybe it's your situation speaking too?*

> Signe: *I think you are right. I'm too overwhelmed to listen to the mess I am in!*
>
> Talitha: *Maybe and maybe not.*

Is the only way to understand a statement the grasping of the question to which the statement is an answer (*RAS,* 106)? The task of understanding is restricted to immediate awareness. In the immediacy of the everyday, matters of concern offer resistance, which can be brought to an end only via an always already regaining of meaning as the historical particularity shedding of light on differences of opinion or misunderstandings. The temporal-historical particularity of conversation, narrative telling, and dialogue resists finalization. But there can be a bringing to shared meanings a truth that holds for its time.

Movement and Appearing

> *The radiance of the glancing movement moves the listeners' saying.*
>
> OWL, 191

The unique or proper essence of hermeneutic phenomenology as we explicate it lies in the enigma of disclosure as disclosure. Through the first chapters of this book the difference of hermeneutic phenomenology with the methods prescribed by modern science has been explicitly articulated. Scientism and all of its variants must have, whether they know it or not, the stable presence of objects given to a stable observing of them performed by a stably disclosive human and/or its technology. It is necessary for modern science to provoke or absolutely control or explain its results through either repeatable physical experimentation or via generalizable theories. Phenomena as thusly established are rendered absolutely disposable for human use. Anything less is considered to be a flaw, a danger, or an index of weakness in scientific investigations (*HPM,* 310-313).

The thread that winds its way, as historicality, through humans as interpreting entities or *the* human as absolutely self-positing subject is the questioning which turns on movement and appearing. As we have mentioned, science must ultimately fix movement and appearance such that they can appear as eternally graspable. But the question that silently looms up out of the background is, Does science as scientism founder on its attempt to establish the eternal and the nonpersonal, the human entity as merely consisting of infinitely exchangeable and replaceable parts?

The answer must be yes if the methods of science pretend to *absolute* control of their subject matter. The answer can be yes and no if the place of science is to determine quantity and measure inherent to physical or demographic phenomena while interpretation explicates determination and measurements as their historical and practical involvements. Hermeneutic phenomenology is a response to the nonquantifiable and nonmeasurable all that emanates from absence and silence. There is a disclosing and beckoning con-tension between the anticipating, practical, prudent, meaningful human being and the stasis of a prevalent sense of rationality. Responding to this invisible play of tension is the calling of questioning, answering, and rejoining as such (*RAS,* 107).

How can this response as a call to questioning be present as other than some kind of mysticism or romanticism? Modernity as metaphysics dismisses as mystagogery anything that purports to "sight" the invisible or to "listen" to whatever is silent. But in spite of itself, the metaphysics of modernity catches sight of and listens to the call of human finitude and mortality as it searches for answers to the questions of being and time. Sighting and listening show themselves as phenomena, not as objects.

The fundamental fact of human mortality dwells in each human as its own temporal particularity. Each fated human is called as the human being of openness, never to be complete but to be always already on the way to the moment of its end. As this movement, matters of concern immediately appear to each human as reasonably practical, prudent, and historically situated involvements. Each human is dependent on matters of concern as they show themselves, the interpretive notion of appearances as appearing. Human beings are enabled by the hold of the call to properly take up (retrieve) their own movement in order to unconceal the concealing movement that is engaged openness itself (*OWE*, 163). They are also free for remaining unresponsive and care free. But, if hermeneutic phenomenology is the truth of engaged openness, unresponding is a responding, and to be care free as a denying of care is a constitutive moment of the phenomenon of care.

Showing, letting appear, and being seen and heard make their way into speech such that the human being as called by the human being of openness can belong to engaged openness. For Heidegger, showing meant that matters of concern historically assumed their radiance and in that radiance they still appear, albeit as historically conditioned. Thus he wrote that appearance is "the basic trait of the presence of all present [matters of concern], as they rise into unconcealment" (*OWL*, 38). As the absent source of appearance, matters of concern come toward human beings as sighting and listening such that the self-presencing of presence is disclosed and beckoned and as such is held in and as itself.

The self-presencing of presence has always already offered itself to the human being of openness even though its proper or unique essence remains veiled by the struggle of modern metaphysics to maintain constant the presence of everything (*OWL*, 40). The unique essence of presencing calls forth the source of self-presencing as absence. Absence is not thought here as the non-presence of some entity but as movement qua movement which delivers matters of concern to presence "by remaining itself in relative absence" (*HPM*, 290). Hermeneutic phenomenological movement is present privatively; that is, it is present as an absence which points to the always already lack of completeness. Thus following Heidegger, we can claim that if to be present itself is thought of as appearance then there prevails in being present the emergence into openness in the sense of unconcealedness. This unconcealedness comes about in the unconcealment as a clearing. (*OWL*, 39)

This clearing as disclosure and beckoning must remain unthought if movement and appearance remain dissembled as controlled and fixed atemporal answers. Answers do not emerge as incumbent on humans, nor do they help them, for "what matters is to see appearance as the [disclosure and beckoning] of presence in its essential origin" (*OWL*, 40).

There is a playing back and forth between human beings and that which they encounter. Encounters with alterity let the individual be lifted above the narrow confines of its own knowing. Other neighborhoods can open up what was previously unexperienced. In every genuine dialogue, truth is only neared asymptotically because the human can never exist as an absolutely pure immanence.

Hermeneutical dialectic is "the art of questioning ever further — i.e., the art of thinking. It is called dialectic because it is the art of conducting a real dialogue" (TM, 367). Dialectic is disclosed and beckoned as conversation, narrative telling, and dialogues as synchronous rejoining moments. The proper or unique essence of a dialogue is for it to remain incipiently coming about as disclosed and beckoned to saying as showing: letting appear as being seen and listened to. Dialogue is other than conversation as merely "talk between people." The word "dialogue" can be listened to or seen as a focused calling to the proper essence of discursiveness (OWL, 52), its showing itself as itself.

Conversations, narrative tellings, and dialogues are inextricably intertwined such that the finitude of infinite communicative telling announcements and the silent course that calls, offers the possibility of constant prologues as the self-presencing of presence, concealing/unconcealing. The proper essence of the abiding movement of whiling self-presence (disclosing and beckoning) *is* absence (concealing/closure) itself (*OWL*, 53-54). The locale of dialogue is at the threshold of "the infinite alteration of the other, and in that, puts an end without end to the end of the dialogue. At each time it is put to an end, the announcement is renewed" (*SV,* 246). Hermeneutic phenomenology as showing claims the human being of openness as the jointure of a sharing that cannot be a mere parceling out. Therefore "acknowledgement and respect call for a readiness to let our own attempts at thinking be overturned, again and again, by what is unthought" (*WCT,* 77). "Paths end with a wink at the timelessness" (Eisenstein, 1989, 273) such that "in shared meaning the universally intelligible components may not be what is significant" (Eisenstein, 1989, 279).

Talitha continues talking with Signe.

Talitha: *How do your final grades look?*

Signe: *Last night I sent out emails to the students in my largest class. Then I was up until 2 a.m. getting my next course done. And tonight is my seven-year-old's birthday, but thank goodness it will just be our family over for dinner. Still it will be another late night.*

Talitha: *So how do your grades look?*

Signe: *That's why I think I'll be nonrenewed. I had almost 15% of the students fail. This morning when I ran into Jill and said how disappointed I was so many students failed and told her how many, she got really upset with me. Why didn't I come to her earlier? Well I did, and every time I had a problem and she told me what to do, it got worse. When the students complained there were too many assignments, she said drop some, and I did, but then the students said the remaining ones were each worth too many points. I give up, but I can't, I need this job.*

Raven calls up his email. He stares at the screen. *"See you this fall"* is all it says. Raven bows his head and cries.

Dialogue is understanding that can be said. Conversation discloses and beckons as narrative telling, which can be a dialogue but never as mere argument (Palmer, 1969, 199; *TM*, 367). As thinking dialogues *with* interpretation itself (Palmer, 1969, 149), conversations openly hold themselves in convergence as *converging conversations*. These show the playful gatherings-dispersions of conversation, narrative telling, and dialogue. Matters of concern appear in their own time, as possibilities of conversation, narrative telling, and dialogue. Their on-coming, anticipated movement is abiding/whiling/sojourning/dwelling as disclosing and beckoning; conversation as shared appearance;

narrative telling as historical movement and the saying-telling of language; dialogue as the always already engaged awakening of the self-presencing of presence.

Hermeneutic phenomenology as we have elucidated it does not admit of procedures that must be adhered to as a "decision tree," which dictates each step toward an outcome. The step-by-step pathway of hermeneutic phenomenology is filled with unpredictable meteor strikes, side roads, crossings, and bottomless sinkholes. Meteors as they disclose and beckon as sudden flashes of deafening and blinding light and sinkholes as they disclose and beckon as illuminating silence and darkness are one in their play of revealing/concealing. Truth can be neither total darkness, blinding light, perfect silence, nor deafening roar; truth dwells in disclosing and beckoning such that interpreters are enabled to be always already underway. The proper and unique listening essence of *È méthodos* holds us in its sight.

Let us continue on our way.

Chapter 6 Notes

1   See Chapter 3 for our discussion.

2   See Dreyfus, 1992.

3   Note here the use of the ambiguous double genitive. See *RHT,* 264.

4   See also Vallega-Neu, 2003, 42, 74.

5   See fn. 12 on logos in Chapter 2.

6   See *PH,* 9, and *BSP,* 6-10. Exposure to the other is exposure to a faint call that hints at the nonpossessable engaged openness wherein pretensions to the total ownership of meaning are given up (Raffoul, 1997, xvii). The engaged openness to which the I is exposed always already alters the I itself (Raffoul, 1997, xxvii).

7   See also *BSP.*

8   See also *OWL,* 121-125.

9   See Chapter 3 for our discussion of thrownness and disposedness.

10   See also RHT, 281; *OWE,* 144-145.

11   See also *WCT.*

12   See Chapter 3 for our discussion of the fore-structure of understanding.

13   See also *GT,* 57-64.

Part II

Narrative Turn: Pedagogies of Possibilities

Chapter 7

Schooling as Attending

> I: *To assign the naming word is, after all, what constitutes finding.*
> J: *Then the confusion that has arisen must be endured.*
>
> *OWL,* 20

The human being always already attends school. From its first emergence into world to its last breath, the human being is right at or face-to-face with school. Schooling, thought as *engaged attendance*, is not primarily an institution or a physical or electronic site. The effect of human historical finitude must not be omitted from any explication of schooling as a phenomenon. For hermeneutic phenomenology, schooling is more than the processes inherent in knowledge acquisition and skills training. These occur in relation to theoretically or biologically determined entities, information transfers, and socialization of one form or another. Schooling, as engaged attendance, discloses and beckons as the immediacy of the facticity of the human being of openness.[1]

Attendance, attending, and attentiveness enable the human being of openness to be alert to "itself and its ownmost possibilities" (*HWT,* 145). Possibilities of understanding that the human being of openness belongs to can be awakened and highlighted such that being called to attention as facticity releases the human being of openness from being "an object of an intuition" to being-in-the-world (Kisiel, *HWT,* 145). The human being of openness is disclosed and beckoned as "the intricate relationship between the necessity of facticity and the possibility of" its "has to be" and its "can be" (Kisiel, *HWT,* 147). The human being of openness begins where it is: It is in attendance. Heidegger cited "I'm here already," from Grimm's fairy tale "The Hedge Hog and the Hare" (*ID,* 62-63), as the unnoticed open clearing that calls for thought, but cannot compel thinking (*ID,* 63).[2] The fairy tale can ask for the listening response of responsive listening. Each of the tale's words announces the enigma of the story's situatedness. Thinking is free for the dismissal of children's stories as mere childish fantasies or for listening to the hints they offer. Fairy tales, like myths, stories, and narratives, are peculiar in that they are diffuse and often incoherent and allusive. But they tell (relate) meaningful stories. Narratives as a whole do not unfold (tell of themselves) uninterrupted by regressions, emanations, repetitions, and surprisingly abrupt new starts.[3] The clarity of narratives as disclosing and beckoning opacity will be the matter of ensuing chapters. Open narrative telling harks back to "attentive belonging" (Kisiel, *HWT,* 180) as that which draws *as* withdrawal.

The human being's lack-in-being, its fated to never be complete (*HWT,* 184), is the presentation wherein the human being is called to be who it is as the human being of openness. Only that entity that "can-be" (*HWT,* 183) called to attention *is* called to attention. A stone cannot attend schooling. Only that entity that can-be called to attention can be called to attention in such a way that it belongs to listening and co-responding. *Schooling as we are taking it in this work is an excess over the traditional modes of training and socialization into established norms of skill acquisition and conduct.* It is given as the exigent need to listen-to and co-respond with the overwhelmingness of thrownness (*PT,* 145).

The expressiveness of schooling is the whereunto and wherefore wherein the overwhelmingness and coming-over of the ontological difference of engaged openness and matters of concern are played out (*ID,* 64-70).[4] Seen this way, schooling discloses and beckons as thrown-attending-to what must be received and retained. Reception and retention is other than the rote repetition of an ego-subject. Schooling includes attentive belonging (*HWT,* 180) in the play of existence and facticity. Existence is the measuredness of practical, prudent comportment of everything that comes to presence. Facticity is that cavity of the prior measure (finitude) out of which *all* measure derives. Possibility obtains as a mutual magnetism (*HWT,* 180),[5] which gives play to emergence/elusion as the emergence of elusion, as "the preservation of the truth of presencing as distinct from what is present" (*PT,* 166). Thereby schooling as a reciprocating retrieval of "the full sense of the worlding of world" always already obtains (*PT,* 166).

Schooling as a phenomenon never ontically begins with "educational toys," "preschool day care," or kindergarten. Reading or playing music to a fetus in utero in the hopes of ensuring that one will give birth to an intellectually literate or musically sensitive child may or may not effect the desired result; there is no way to separate association from cause and effect. The inculcation of normative values as the above practice shows, turns on how schooling is claimed by world. For a modernity claimed by Cartesianism, *each* thinking child is thought to enter the world as measurably above a targeted status (e.g., in its IQ). Schooling as attendance both holds and offers what can or cannot be taken as schooling—whether as the ontically determined efficacy of certain practices or as ontologically interpreted situatedness. Schooling obtains as what the human being of openness can attend to: the enigmatic temporal play-space of a never to be possessed, finite engaged open clearing and an ability to take sense *as* sense. These go into letting the human being's "exposure" be such that it is both able to and exigently needs to be affected by, and to effect (as a letting, not as a production), the play of otherness (*PS,* 199).[6] The already is "the always-already-operative openness opened up by our essential finitude" (*PS,* 200). For Heidegger, "being-in-the-world [the human being of openness] was never a property of a subjectivity no matter how it was represented, but from its incipience it is the human being's way of existing" (*ZS,* 227). As this way, the human being of openness "is always already dependent on something showing itself to it, insofar as it is always absorbed from the start in whatever specific relationship to [what shows itself]" (*ZS,* 227). The mental human agent thought as immanence does not and cannot dictate the offering of engaged openness. This play presents itself as possibility only when the open "has already happened to [it] so that something can be present or absent. The being open 'to' lies in the manifestness of presence. There would be no relationship without it" (*ZS,* 145). Relationships here are not thought as mental constructs but as the possibility of belonging-to. Belonging turns on the finitude of time's superabundance: "The Many, the unlimited Two, sustains (and restricts) both the order of the world and, equally, the possibilities of human knowing" (*D&D,* 121). Surprise and on-coming reciprocally appear as presencing and engagement "circling around each other" (*ID,* 69).[7]

Schooling is an involvement always already joined (attended to) in progress as the open clearing of on-coming immediate mediate belonging-to. To be human is to be born into perplexity as this is accompanied by the enabling of the human to be claimed by possibility. Possibilities manifest themselves historically as "the real preconditions and necessities of the human political and social task" (*D&D,* 193). The historically situated human being of openness comes about as its own persistent hold such that the real precondition of the with of engaged openness is in its never to be perfected thrownness. There necessarily belongs to the alreadiness of the human being of openness the assumption (as the possible can-be of taking-up) of attendance-with-by-attending-to (*GBT,* 439-444). The open clearing itself that "first gives the region for all belonging-to and -with each other does not arise from any mediation. The open [clearing] itself is the immediate" (*EHP,* 83).

The Situation of Schooling

> *The immediate is itself near something mediate; on the other hand, the immediate, strictly speaking, is the mediation, that is, the mediatedness of the mediated, because it renders the mediated possible in its essence.*
>
> *EHP,* 84

For realisms, schooling is the transfer of putatively neutral information via an accepted technology or from a place, facility, or mode designated for this transfer. Information and/or its transfer is effective only when considered to be new or more advanced. Schooling (for realisms) is considered to be independent of history and culture wherein all "outputs" (outcomes) are expected to end up at identical skill levels. Level-skill interfaces are established as a result of the production of objective categories. Differences in skill acquisition are considered to be manifested via neutral evaluations in the guise of objective examinations and other grading procedures. When skill level evaluations reach a predetermined point considered acceptable, "outputs" are permitted entry into institutionalized functioning apparati such as work roles or advanced studies. Steps forward (progress) are stipulated by absolute degree requirements for graduation.

Matters of concern that obtain exterior to the above functioning are considered merely personal matters and are of only tangential significance to that which is to be taken-as the efficacious. "Outputs" must be considered to be identical and therefore need to be infinitely interchangeable in relation to predetermined skill categories. The individual becomes anonymous and disconnected as a neutral "one" and the partitioned infinity of the merely personal. Those personal traits that preclude skills acquisition (e.g., attention deficit disorder, ADD) are to be remedied (corrected) such that the desired result can be effected. The individual is to be made into a predetermined whole.

Idealisms attach themselves to varied notions of transcendent reality. The ideal real is taken-as what essentially conforms to absolute standards. The identity of the ideal is led by itself to an ahistorical truth wherein it resides in determinations produced by either a rational, logical ego-subject or some entity or theory accepted as supreme. All cognitive functioning is directed toward conforming to preexisting notions of the ideal. Schooling obtains as training wherein subjects are expected to adhere to standards established by pure reason or belief structures independent of direct empirical experience. The appeal of an atemporal normative self-identical order is what calls individuals to be subservient to the goal of the transcendent norm. All must be seen as working toward this goal in all facets of their existing.

The mutual dependence of realisms and idealisms on each other for their ground is simply overlooked. The modernist self has no origin other than itself; therefore it only needs training and/or forming. Modernist educational structures focus on the implantation of rules of judgment into the mind as it is determined (was invented) by the Cartesian analytic tradition.[8] The absolute self-certain mind is absolutely self-receptive to rational certainty! Learning and knowing in the abstract are assumed to have already occurred as the certainty of the self, but then always face the need to be subsumed under some rationalized universal. However, the universal itself is determined as the already occurring self. Modernity is claimed by nothing other than the lacuna of its own forgotten or overlooked presuppositions. But the fly in the ointment, to repeat Sheehan's apt phrase, is that the human being is "condemned to ontology" (*KE,* 12).

It seems to be very difficult to think "schooling" as a phenomenon other than the activity of a variety of interactions that are based on or grounded in a given framework that necessarily turns on the actions of a conscious subject or subjects. In thinking schooling as a call to attention, interpretation must be the prudent *practice-of* as releasement. The genitive at play here allows interpretation as releasement and releasement as interpretation. Releasement as interpretation entails a from-to. But as both Gadamer and Heidegger have shown, *the from is from where one is to where one is.* In other words, all are in attendance; all are called to attention.

The human being of openness understandingly exists as a call to attention. The attention to which each human being is called as is the thrownness described in Chapter 3. The reciprocating play of "calling attention to cannot ever be calculated and worked out in advance" (*OHF,* 14). Thrownness is a calling or command, which commends the human being to where it is already (*WCT,* 117-119). The human being cannot escape from its nonpossessed already to some imagined ultimate position of knowledge. Schooling is claimed by the finitude of thrownness. Infinite knowledge or absolute ignorance or knowledge would render schooling unnecessary and impossible. Thrownness as discursive and temporal particularities enables schooling such that the human being must be called to attention (*TM,* 358).

Schooling as a tradition's linguistic call to attention is akin to an order that is followed in its general sense, not in the sense of any literal meaning (*TI,* 35). The ordering call of a tradition is hidden but can be thematically disclosed only as a matter of mediate thinking-saying. Tradition is the expression of an ordering call (*TM,* 333-336). Being called to attention is not a robotic obeisance to the everyday but includes belonging to the necessary possibility of countering and countermanding inherent in learning as listening and teaching as co-responding.[9] Tradition discloses and beckons as a "genuine partner in dialogue, and [humans] belong to it, as does the I with a Thou" (*TM,* 358).

The human being of openness is always already present-to (opened to) matters of concern by virtue of temporality, which is the exposure of openedness to the offering of sense as such. Matters of concern call forth entities in order to be deployed in involved dialogical experience (*HWT,* 56, 187). To be open is to be exposed to a world, that, of necessity, must be dealt with. World obtains as open, contextual, and temporal *immediacy.* "The standing open as which the human being exists, must not be misunderstood as something present-at-hand, as a kind of empty, mental sack into which something could fall on occasion" (*ZS,* 216). Human beings always already find themselves dialogically "experiencing experience" (*HWT,* 177). Human beings do not just stand around like a utility pole no matter what state they find themselves in.

Schooling as a regioning of its historicality shows itself as a *schole,*[10] an untroubled pure apprehending detached from everyday concerns. This comes to the present as modernity's notion of theory as an abstract conceptual construct. Heidegger's reading of Aristotle drew attention to schooling as an attempt to ontically separate the moment of care as concerned involvement from pure atemporal seeing (McNeill, 1999, 2, 127-131). Schooling when

claimed by modernist thinking discloses and beckons as a separate entity removed from the everyday of community life. *Theōria*
concomitantly becomes separated from being a participatory (co-
responding) experience to being a construct, divorced from everyday states of affairs (matters of concern). There arrives for modernity only the theoretical as validity, the permanence of the closed
system of that which is explicitly determined (*HWT,* 188-191). Does
a paradox lurk in the putative imposition of categories that isolate
phenomena from their origin? *Schooling is the human being's belonging, as being in attendance, to historical sending* (*4S,* 61-62).

Schooling lets the human being belong to the pathway of
belonging-with. Such letting is an offering and not a permission
granting. Inherent in schooling is the always already, not to be
forgotten, possibility of not listening-to or seeing the offering as
offering. Indeed offering can be taken as authority to cover over the
offering as an offering that the human being of openness can belong
to. Presencing, as such, offers itself as the free possibility for leaving
presencing open as it shows itself. Or presence, as calculative
thinking, can be willed to establish mere physical appearance as the
desirability of calculability. Questionings are their own circulation as
one asks, How is attending-to attended to?

Heidegger asked, "Where does the encounter take place
between that which presences and the [the human being of
openness], whose mode of presence is a self-opening for the
welcoming of this presence?" (*4S,* 16). The response to this question
resides in the movement of revealing/concealing. Welcoming
relationships can obtain as comportment "in correspondence with
exploitation and consumption" as that which "requires the human
to *be* in relationship" (*4S,* 63). The human being is compelled and
enabled by sense to make sense of sense. This obtains as the
particularized historical-temporal pathway of tradition, and as that,
is the always already possibility for retrieving what "one already is"
(*GT,* 312).

Retrieval shows itself not as the "rote repetition" of "the common
generic universal of the All," but as "the proper distributive universal
of the Each" (*RHT,* 265-266). In each instantiation, "the Each" is not

to be understood as the isolated ego-subject of modernity, but as the human being of openness wherein it can "persist and endure in that instantiation" such that it can be "first encountered only in the who-question" (*CP,* 173, as translated in *RHT,* 266). The "who-question" is the exigent need of always already repeated retrievals in order to grasp the never ontically repeatable or graspable pasts and futures. The proper and plurally singular is of the interpretive, the situation and time. Each human being can never be the source of itself, but as belonging to the retrieving of itself it can be the human being of openness.

The Schooling of Place

> *What we are concerned about and attend to, shows*
> *itself as that* where from *out* of which, *and* on
> the basis of which *factical life is lived.*
>
> *OHF,* 65

Schooling must always be the attendance of a sighting, listening, co-responding historically situated, temporal particularity. Schooling must have (exigently needs) its observer-speakers, as observer-speakers must belong to (must be claimed by) schooling. Heidegger has written:

> Everything spoken stems in a variety of ways from
> the unspoken, whether this be something not yet
> spoken, or whether it be what must remain unspoken
> in the sense that it is beyond the reach of speaking.
> Thus, that which is spoken in various ways begins
> to appear as if it were cut off from speaking and
> the speakers, and did not belong to them, while in
> fact it alone offers to speaking and to the speakers
> whatever it is they attend to, no matter what way
> they stay within what is spoken of the unspoken.
> (*OWL,* 120)

Schooling speaks but not exclusively as a vocal utterance, a skill, or a mathematical procedure. Schooling calls into presence those who listen, not as mere listeners, but as *participants*. Schooling needs a participating way as well as participants who belong to schooling, those who are always already underway to schooling.

We submit that attended schooling as disclosing and beckoning is trenchantly brought to presence by a publication from New Zealand (Aotearoa)[11] titled *Ako* (Pere, 1994). What is most interesting is that the title word is never defined as such or even mentioned in the body of the text. Therefore, it becomes necessary to dialogically experience the text by reading it in its entirety. As a significant aspect of the text, it is brought to the reader's attention that the Aotearoa Maori should not be seen as a uniform category imposed on them via external viewpoints. The reader is thereby enabled by the text to move into nearness with tribal groups' ways of being-in-the-world but never enabled to be an integral member of their historicality and temporal particularity.

Reading the text of *Ako* reveals a complex web of being-with. Tribal ways "do not stand in isolation but actually merge into each other, and therefore need to be understood [as they belong] to each other and within the context of the whole because there are no clear cut boundaries" (Pere, 1994, 5). Recall our earlier references to boundaries as the place of unfolding incipience rather than the delineation of a terminus. The silent saying of language as tribal tradition is brought to the fore:

> One word or one simple phrase can convey a host of meanings depending on the context in which something is said, including the intonation and tone of voice that is used. (Pere, 1994, 18)

Matters of special significance to a tribal group are guarded such that a meaning in a given nontribal context only belongs to the external aspects of that context. Meanings always already belong to situations as they are historically given and encountered. The absence of the said offers possibilities for conversation if one realizes the unattainability of issuings forth as they always already emerge out of and return to absence. The visibility of language lies in what is not and cannot be seen. The *melos* (melodiousness) of language lies in what is not and cannot be heard.

The human being of openness can be in attendance with listening and co-respondence. Dialogue, conversation, and narrative telling show themselves from such attendance. Hermeneutic phenomenology is a pathway that takes dialogue as other than idealized empathy and takes narrative telling as other than the pursuit of mere curiosity (intellectual or otherwise). Conversation is not exclusively a structured taking place between speakers utilizing preestablished syntax. Jones (1999) wrote of a classroom experience wherein the modernist/enlightenment/critical conception of free and open dialogue broke down because it could not take into account the silence of those who did not wish to speak in the manner of dialogue dictated by European traditions. In this specific occurrence Maori and Pacific Islands class participants favored talking among themselves to the exclusion of talking with those who were part of the European tradition. Ontically dialogue did not occur; ontologically this dialogical experience offered meaningful hints for those who could be open to the openness that silence offered.

Practices often separated by thousands of miles and thousands of years can offer hints to both the roots and the possibility of schooling. The grounding play offered to the human being of openness lets the always already into nearness. Each human being finds itself delivered over to phenomena out of an ineffable groundless incipience which requires (calls for) becoming-aware-of phenomena and concomitantly apprehending them in essential ways (*ZS*, 28). Human beings have to take something as something if it (the something), in turn, is offered or is available. Hermeneutic phenomenology works to reveal schooling as thrown attending as that which can be offered as "that which is always already *holding sway*" (*ZS*, 41). From Heidegger, we can come to understand the open clearing as that which "happens continuously and necessarily in a strange and even wondrous way" (*ZS*, 72-73). To be the human of openness is to be enabled to be with entities that it itself is not.

> "Being-at" is usually characterized by the bodily perception of things physically present. But our being here can also engage itself in being with things not present physically. If this possibility did not exist and could not be performed, then, for instance, [one] could never arrive at home this evening. (*ZS*, 72-73)

The human being is placed into the place of attendance prior to its being made a theme for biology or psychology.

Attending Attendants

> *We are exposed to one another and together to the world, to the world that is nothing other than this exposition itself.*
>
> *FT,* 296

The necessity of the calling of mutual involvement is such that the human being is "so related and drawn to what withdraws" that it thus finds itself disposedly "drawing into the enigmatic and therefore mutable nearness of" the withdrawal's summoning to attention (*WCT,* 16). The unsettling as calling distress is an open rift (between, difference), which simultaneously divides and joins (Taylor, 1987, 48). The rift as difference attracts, sketches out, outlines, binds, cleaves, differentiates, sets free, releases (*CP,* 340).[12] This tension to be set out, to be set free, can be concernful, unsettling, frightening (Vallega-Neu, 2003, 13, 38). Schooling is sojourning (whiling/ dwelling/abiding) *as* a dialogical experience, which calls one to attention *as* one calls attention to it. The human being as such is overwhelmed by the possibility of there being no possibility at all. The possible lack of unsettling strangeness in a seeming paradox is what calls the human being of openness to itself.

The human being of openness can be called to attention such that the total enigma of engaged openness can show up as disposedness.[13] The manifestness of enigma as enigma, that is, boredom, wonder, or angst, lets any "why" be present-to the human being. "Only because the 'why' is possible as such can [the human being], in a definite way" (*PM,* 95), attend to matters of concern as their letting. The letting *of* matters of concern enables entities and involvement as such in order for the latter pair to belong to each other.

The play of entities and humans must mutually belong to each other in order for there to be schooling at all. Thrownness and disposedness place entities and humans together prior to formal determinations. For Heidegger, the human being, called upon by the voice of engaged openness, "experiences the wonder of all wonders: *that* [entities] *are,* The [matter of concern] that is thus called in its essence into the truth of [engaged openness] is for this reason always [disposed] in an essential manner" (*PM,* 95). The human being of openness is called such that "pure dispassion of thought is at the bottom only the most rigorous maintenance of the highest disposition, the one open to the uniquely uncanny fact: that there *are* [entities], rather than not" (*BQP,* 3).

Temporality calls understanding as engaged openness. The human being must understandingly "live in a neighborhood, and yet [it] would be baffled if [it] had to say in what that neighborhood consists" (*OWL,* 83). This does not mean that a lack of structure, a chaos and randomness, reigns supreme, only waiting for a scientist or philosopher to sort it out for everyone. After all, life is perfectly obvious in its contents and direction. Or is it?

The somnambulance of the everyday can obtain as "consolation of the obvious" (*BQP,* 170). Does the relaxation tendered herewith offer "the most uncanny—namely the semblance of obviousness" (*BQP,* 171)? Is the obvious a fact that needs revealing? Does the play of entities and matters of concern allow them simply to be accepted as they arrive? If everything is obvious, why is there a need for schooling? Does there dwell a hidden need to ask after the emergence of engaged openness as entities "come into the open and what this opening might be, and how it takes place" (*BQP,* 170)? Has modern physics ended the necessity of questioning? Or is there an enigmatic exigent need "arising from the lack of need" (*BQP,* 176)?

The human being of openness can be called by the suggestion that hermeneutic phenomenology offers the human being. That is to let oneself be "compelled by the most hidden and consequently the deepest need of the age, and by that alone" as a task which does not admit of conceptualizations of completability (*BQP*, 170). Theoretical physics has finished its project, but questions remain. These questions can be reduced to the merely comical ("Monty Pythonesque," if you will) search for "the meaning of life." Life (clearing or openness) is not asked about as a natural or a rational object, which are the same. What is asked about is dwelling (*BC*, 71-72). A question that can arise turns on asking after the comical *as* it obtains as an appearing that abdicates a responsibility to question. The face of enigma even here shows itself. The comical shows itself, not as a revealing of some mystery of the subconscious, but as an avoidance practice wherein pivotal matters of concern belonging to the open clearing can be overlooked. On the other hand, the comical can be attended to as revealing the enigmas surrounding the play of the obvious. Satirical films like Terry Gilliam's *Brazil* and Stanley Kubrick's *Dr. Strangelove* call forth thinking of the obvious such that the everyday is not as clear as it might seem. Questions must always already be asked from answers answered as rejoinders rather than asked with an answer in view.

The open clearing obtains as a surplus over life as determined as biochemical processes, stimulus-response reductionist zoology, and the pure apprehending of cognitive idealism. Heidegger's pathway demonstrated his struggle as he thought life as a not-yet, thence as an open clearing never to be finalized as the direct stimulus-response necessity or as pure cognitive functioning. There is a surplus over these modernist-metaphysical attempts, an open clearing wherein the "not yet differentiated and not yet worldly is the 'index for the highest potentiality of life'" (*GBT*, 51). Living is an exposure to the thrownness of taking some matter of concern as a matter of concern which takes it (living) out of "the leveling 'not' of indifference to the 'not yet' of potentiality" (*GBT*, 52).[14] The on-coming "incipient moment of life" (*GBT*, 55) obtains as "motivated tendency and tending motivation" (*GBT*, 53).[15] The toward which of sense is always already a reaching forward touched by a withdrawing, retrieving reaching back.

The human being is faced with the enigma of life as the historical with "no dissection into essential elements," but obtaining as connectivities and contexts (*TDP,* 99). There is movement as "spontaneous experience of experience streaming return of experiencing life upon already experienced life, as the immanent historicity of life" (*GBT,* 48). The human being finds itself belonging to the "temporal intentional movement of finding oneself experiencing experience" (*GBT,* 49). This movement is not a robotic repetition but is claimed by intentionality as a practical and prudent comportment relating itself to matters of concern as involved, dialogical experience (*GBT,* 50). Comportments do not obtain as measurable magnitudes or mathematically determined vectors. Life experiences reciprocally disclose and beckon as "expressive formations of the tendencies of concrete life situations" (*GBT,* 120). The engaged openness of the human being of openness as "the self-world in factic life is not a thing nor even an I in the epistemological sense, but rather a significance to be understood" (*GBT,* 121). There is no enclosure to be measured or theorized or indeed *that is* measurable or idealizable. The "'I myself' is really a meaningful context in which I live" (*GBT,* 121).

How does the human being dialogically experience being called toward? Not only as mere lived experience, but also as not forgetting that there is experience undergone as disposedness.

Herein is where *schooling schools* the dialogical belonging together of words and engaged openness belong together "in a veiled way, a way which has hardly been thought and is not to be thought out to the end" (*OWL,* 155). After all, as we have mentioned, it is perfectly obvious what a word is and what a school is. The dialogical play of words schools because it asks enabled, receiving-perceiving, apprehending human beings about their belonging to each other. *Words school, not schools.*

One can undergo a participatory experience with the is of schooling learning teaching in many ways. The word "is" generated more than 100 volumes within Heidegger's collected works.

Gadamer and Jean-Luc Nancy, along with numerous other writers, have contributed their thoughts on the matter. These writings in their on-coming totality let the human being sight and listen or turn a blind eye to what is enigmatic in the enigma that the human being of openness is.

The matter to be listened to as we see it in this book is to let that which evanesces into obscurity (*HWT,* 198) come into its own light. How can this be done? Of what use would this be? Perhaps, none, perhaps as errancy—but perhaps this is less dangerous than to be claimed by a will to will that attempts to effect the permanent closure of the future as the enclosure of all that is into the narrowness of the immediately useful. The useful is a standard that cannot be applied to schooling as a phenomenon issued-forth via the disclosing and beckoning of sense. Without sense as sense, schooling would be bereft of the possibilities of practical and prudent involvement (*TL,* 130-131).

Schooling grows out of the excess and overwhelmingness of what the human being is struck with. The human being of openness can be addressed by schooling such that "thoughtful questioning is not the intrusive and rash curiosity of the search for explanations; it is the tolerating and sustaining of the unexplainable as such, despite being overwhelmed by the pressure of what reveals itself" (*BQP,* 148-149). Recall that the engaged openness of entities as well as matters of concern as thought-said always already obtains as an offering for possible human engagement (*KE,* 5-7; *PS,* 187-192; *N,* 282-283, 301-303). Disclosing and beckoning calls forth engaged openness as a pathway that traverses life, world, and the open clearing: It is a pathway that calls for the attendance of matters of concern as always already disclosed and beckoned.

The Place *of* Schooling

> *In going through spaces we do not give up our standing in them. Rather, we always go through spaces in such a way that we already experience them by staying constantly with near and remote locations and things.*
>
> *PLT,* 157

Schooling is the immediacy of the open clearing. Schooling, in its own way, obtains as the "mutual engagement (custom, tradition) reciprocating" of engaged openness as offering to the human being of openness (*HWT*, 180). One must always keep in mind that offering is not the making present of something in terms of a mental representation. Offering is a proffering as a letting something presence while the letting itself "holds itself back and withdraws" (*4S*, 59).[16]

We are taking the place of schooling as a way in which the gathering of disclosing and beckoning lets sense as sense presence. Schooling is first seen here as a place where a matter of concern is temporally allowed to appear as the locales thrown open (*OWL*, 106) such that the human being's comings and goings are enabled. The human being is "right at" these loci of meaning (*PLT*, 156; *BW*, 358; *BSP*, 10-11, 17; *GT*, 70; *ZS*, 67-74) but not as an isolated representation. Schooling is the coming of and the undergoing of dialogical experience, not the representation of a controllable, orderable image.

In our discussion of boundary, the essential unfolding of schooling begins as something made room for: "that which is let into its bounds" (*PLT*, 154; *BW*, 356). Schooling receives its essential engaged openness from loci of meaning and not from some pure manifold or spatially locatable distribution system. Therefore limit, thought in this sense, calls the human being of openness to "always let the limit present itself anew" and as such "it always presents itself as new" (*GT*, 67). It is our interpretive pathway that calls into question schooling as the practices and dialogical experiences of teaching and learning that occur within schools or any positing which asserts that schooling is merely an educative practice that places undifferentiated phenomena into some notion of a container in order to be encapsulated therein.

The place of schooling is where the human being is let be right at already. In order to be openly engaged in/with, at a place, one cannot merely conceive of it as a mental representation. Recall that to be the place of the opened open, the human being as the human being of openness "is already had and so holds forth" (*GBT*, 442) as where-to-be, can-be, and having-to-be as the unity of its temporal particularity (*GBT,* 442). The human being of openness can be possible, not as an "empty logical possibility" of the merely not yet actual and necessary (*GBT,* 440) but as a temporally instantiated open clearing. The biological-theoretical human is not lost but is hereby shown as its proper locale. The temporal play-space of engaged openness is "the exposition of meaning, investing human being with the manifold sense of direction which carries it forward in all that it does; both forward toward the world and toward itself" (*GBT,* 441). A hermeneutic phenomenological investigation of schooling works to free schooling from the conceptualizations of validity, standards, and norms as these show themselves as repressive holding powers (*GBT,* 443).

Again, the human being in its ownmost appropriate having is claimed by disclosing and beckoning as an already belonging to and as a holding forth. The suitability of its can-be belongs to fittingly ordered engaged openness where "'things hang together, fall into place, and so make sense,' providing a 'work*ing* context' like the world" (*GBT,* 443). Human beings as themselves find themselves in the opened midst of what is temporally proffered. At the same time they are proffered as the temporal clearing of engaged openness as an on-coming. The human being of openness is concomitantly touched by the refusal and withdrawal of its own essential provenance. Touching discloses and beckons the human being of openness as "the ones engaged in and for" a temporal play-space. The source of engaged openness is in the coming upon, the discovery of things and matters of concern that need to be taken as something (*POR,* 86). Concrete situations of action let "the truth of the disclosure of the self" (*GBT,* 441) be seen in their disclosing/hiding movement such that they always already disclose and beckon as hints.

Ontologically considered, schooling is the open clearing wherein world shows up as historical sending, surplus of presence, a delivering-over-to, placedness, time-space, and presencing itself (*4S,* 63, 70) and as such is the immediate and possible engaging that the human being of openness *is.* Ontically speaking, schooling is of the finitude which pulls the human being along as its withdrawing. There is no guarantee of any immediate awareness.

Schooling must be inclusive of wonder, not as curiosity but as the surplus of the between. According to Heidegger, the play of the between, as the whole of undifferentiated matters of concern, does not admit of a theoretical outside to which an exit would be desired. But also, because the between is this undifferentiated whole, fixed standpoints inside do not admit of a pathway to some absolute determination of an inside.

Schooling must dwell in the exigency of absence as absence in order to be borne into the future-as-becoming. This becoming is not to be taken as some unfinished product but is the essence of possibility as it always already becomes possibility.

Commending: Attending to the Call

Calling offers an abode.
WCT, 124

The pointing which calls the human being to think, gives it directions as mode in such a way that it always already becomes enabled to think. The human being of openness is as thinker-sayer only by virtue of the pointing's pointing (*WCT,* 115). At first glance, this statement comes to us as a tautology or a begging of the question. But if we recall, for Heidegger, call and thinking co-occur but are not identical. The particular always already presence-to of the human being calls out to its ownmost engaged openness. The calling of questions has already pulled the human being "into the substance of the inquiry" (*WCT,* 116). That there is "the 'call' does not necessarily imply demand, still less command; it rather implies an anticipatory reaching out for something that is reached" by the human being's call, via its calling (*WCT,* 117). The calling, the call, and the caller "share out" (Raffoul, 1997, xxiii) the phenomenon as one of sense.[17] Here the sense of "to call" "means to set in motion, to get something underway—which may be done in a gentle and therefore unobtrusive manner, and in fact is most readily done in that way" (*WCT,* 117).

Schooling as a call to attention "means not so much a command as a letting reach, that therefore the 'call' has an assonance of helpfulness and complaisance" (*WCT,* 117) such that "the sense of 'instruct, demand, allow to reach, get on the way, convey, provide with a way'" in its turn allots/allows schooling (*WCT,* 117). A call to attention "basically means, not to give commands and orders, but to commend, entrust, give into safe-keeping, keep safely.[18] To call means: to call into arrival and presencing; to address commendingly" (*WCT,* 118).

Schooling is necessarily populated with temporally contextualized, intentional mortals. The "situated and exposed existence" (*HWT,* 186) as "the historical and linguistic situation in which [they find themselves] is not that of a soul to eternal Ideas of rational faculties to universal and necessary categories but of a 'Being-in-the-world' structured by the concrete universals of language and tradition" (*HWT,* 196-197). These concrete universals are the reciprocating origin of dialogical experience. The play of their circulation as "an originary or transcendental 'with' calls with a palpable urgency, to be disentangled and articulated for itself" (*BSP,* 41). There exists no imperative that the "call" be paid attention to and there exists no ultimate "for itself." *There can be no once and for all getting back to any originary or transcendental with.* "The with is strictly contemporaneous with all existence" (*BSP,* 41).

There is attendance with and attending to such that there are always comporting entities—"actual, possible and necessary" (*BQP,* 177). The human being as an entity belongs "in this circuit of [entities. Entities] as a whole are known and familiar in a definite way" (*BQP,* 177). Even where human beings are not turned to explicitly, they are manifest as an accessible manifold (*BQP,* 177). The accessible calls the human being of openness to possibility— possibility not in the metaphysical sense, but possibility as that which is given by time. There is no ownership here in the entrepreneurial or any other sense; there is the wherein in which the human being, always already in the thick of entities, is the open clearing. That is, of entities, such an open clearing "holds sway" (*BQP,* 177). The temporality of the human being of openness is such that entities placed differently as temporally different ways via engaged openness are never to be accessed. Disclosing and beckoning can never be found, founded, or even lost, but can be submitted to, not as obedience but as belonging-to (*BQP,* 178). The dialogical experience of schooling (objective and subjective genitive) grows out of the possibility of thrown calling to attention. *One can choose listening as a call to attention or continue to reduce schooling to the indifference of information transfer and/or socialization.*

Attendance Taking, Inhabiting, Being Drawn

> *What withdraws from us, draws us along by its very withdrawal, whether or not we become aware of it immediately, or at all.*
>
> *WCT,* 9

The world in its emergence/elusion as "a locality, being the essential locale of the homely [the unsettling in the settling], is a journeying into that which is not directly bestowed upon one's own essence but must be learned in [sojourn]" (*HHI,* 142). *Sojourning is essentially hearkening to pathways that call.* If one accepts, along with Heidegger, that "there is" a call or an unsettledness in the settledness, then ways are opened up as they open up. The ambiguous "as" circles as a call. The movement of sense, unsettling as it unsettles, undoes fixed positions such that one's true abode is shaken up. To be unsettled is to be settled in the abode of a sojourn, a sojourn in which one must think and act anew, which one always already does in any case.

The matters that befall the human being of openness as it sojourns are dialogical experiences. Dialogical experience is a sojourn that

> in the eminent sense is one that is made for the very first time. Although there is a destination, it is at the start nothing but an unreal sketch for guiding the traveler. Although there is a route set up in

> advance, most of it is utterly unknown ahead of
> time, and the [matters of concern] and the [dialogical
> experiences] that will make their appearance along
> the route cannot be anticipated. It cannot be known
> in advance whether [dialogical] experiences to be
> had enroute may outweigh the journey's end in
> their eventual importance and impressiveness. Nor
> can one know in advance whether the journey may
> change one utterly, in body or in mind. (Misgeld &
> Nicholson, 1992, ix)

For Heidegger, Gadamer, and Jean-Luc Nancy the self does not persist outside of the temporally particular moment wherein it is exposed as a singular-plural involvement with disclosing and beckoning as an adventure; as a dialogical experience it needs a with-world as a plying of wind and waves. "It cannot constitute itself in advance of its application upon another; it constitutes itself only through application. Our modern English-language empiricism and behaviorism, on the other hand, have processed experience through a preconstituted atomist matrix" (Misgeld & Nicholson, 1992, ix).

Dialogical experience is first and foremost to be in the thick of things wherein the human being has its everyday sense and language that tradition has delivered over to it. The belonging together of call and "being called" is not an unconditioned relationship. It is particular and shared as a "same" that *is not* reductively identical with one's own self or with all other selves. The calling of time is other than "an indifferent relationship to time as an object. Rather, it is time insofar as the human being's *sojourn* temporalizes itself in it" (*ZS*, 66). Time heterogeneously gives matters of concern as present-to and passage as always already. We remind the reader that sojourning for Heidegger presences as a threefold presencing-temporalizing of past (alreadiness), present (presence-to), and future (on-coming becoming) and, as an offering, is "in each case, time for something" (*ZS*, 66). Sojourning is a way before it is a what, a that, or even a how. The whiling of sojourning is given as a time-space as the dwelling of "care."

The human being of openness must always be a sighting "as being-in-the-world, as concern for [matters of concern], and as caring for [the] other, as the being-with the human beings it encounters, and never as a self-contained subject" (*ZS,* 159). Thus the human being of openness is understood as possibility, abiding in "the clearing as sojourn with what concerns it and what is encountered" (*ZS,* 159).

Real thinking, Heidegger averred, "cannot be learned from books. It also cannot be taught unless the teacher remains a learner well into old age. Therefore, let us hope for a dialogue" (*ZS,* 239). For Heidegger, comportment as sojourning-with turned on "the interconnected ways of relating to [matters of concern] as a whole"; these ways of relating (as belonging) are mostly not expressly even noticed, they are merely "let" come into presence as their ownmost self-carrying (*ZS,* 160). The emerging play of transposing, transporting, and practical-prudent comportment in its elusion does not allow of any questioning; the play carries itself.[19] Heidegger averred that the "toward-which of the being-toward, which is care, is however nothing other than the [engaged openness] of [the human being of openness], namely, in each instance the [matter of concern] which is not yet but can be; implicit in the 'it goes about' there is accordingly, a *being-out-for* its own [engaged openness] *qua* can-be" (Heidegger, *Logik: Die Frage nach der Wahrheit,* 234).[20] This is the genesis of the practical, the self, the worlding of the world (*HWT,* 186).

Schooling as Dialogical Experience

> *In so far as we are at all, we are already in a relatedness to what gives food for thought.*
>
> WCT, 36

The human being of openness is called to thinking-saying by that which calls it to thought. This circular statement recalls Heidegger's thought on thoughts: "We never come to thoughts. They come to us" (*PLT,* 6).

Schooling as a thrown calling to attention is a path "forward to somewhere else, underway toward, onward to the encounter with what is kept in store for it" (*OWL,* 163). The familiar obtains as the unfamiliar or the strange. Being forwarded into the future as unknown know-how, "the 'strange' is already following the call that calls it on the way into its own" (*OWL,* 163), the "way into the 'underway'" (*OWL,* 167) where the human being of openness always already is. Hermeneutic phenomenology is claimed by a focus on dialogical experience. Heidegger explicated experience as dialogical, stating, "To experience is to go along a way. The way leads through the wonders that enthrall and the dreams that enrapture" as one is open to understanding (*OWL,* 67). The mystery of understanding as "something age-old has struck thinking long ago and ever since has held it captive, though in a manner that has become both commonplace and indiscernible" (*OWL,* 80). Gadamer has added that an "ought" is delivered over to [one] such that [one] can "entertain whether the movement of human existence does not issue in a relentless inner tension between illumination and concealment" (*RAS,* 104).

The human being is of openness such that it is receptively open to itself, entities, and matters of concern other than itself. Its own finitude leads it to an exigent need to continually come back to and retrieve itself as being-in-the-world. As we have shown, hermeneutic phenomenology's point of departure involves letting the world proffer itself as something other than theoretical conceptualizing. As this proffering the human being of openness is always already thrown in attendance to enabled listening as the call of its always already exigently needing to be the temporal movement of engaged openness.

Chapter 7 Notes

1   See Chapter 3 for our discussion of the human being of facticity and openness.

2   See also *HWT,* 52.

3   Richard Wagner's tetralogy of music dramas *Der Ring des Nibelungen (The Ring)* is a significant example of the narrative structure of myth.

4   Note that Heidegger's term *Austrag,* translated as "perdurance," is more aptly taken as on-coming, carrying out, bearing, birthing, or issuance (Taylor, 1987, 43, fn. 12).

5   See also *BSP,* 62.

6   See also *BS* and *KE.*

7   See also *KE,* 6.

8   See Rorty, 1980, 17-69, and Taylor, 1989, for the sources of "mind."

9   See Kisiel, *HWT,* 197; *BT,* 438, and *POR,* 112.

10   See McNeill, 1999, 62, 128, on the tradition of school as *schole* in ancient Egypt and Greece.

11   Aotearoa is the Maori word most commonly translated as "long white cloud" (King, 2003, 39-43).

12   See also *CP,* 75, 340, 331.

13   See Chapter 3 for our discussion of boredom, wonder, and angst as disposedness.

14   See also *TDP,* 97.

15   See *ZS,* 21-24, 186, 200, 209-210, on motive-motivation.

16   See also *OTB,* 37.

17   Sharing out "indicates *at once* a separation and a sharing." The common lot of each human being is to share what cannot be divided—the division itself—the co-appearing (presencing) of singular, plural human beings (Raffoul, 1993, xxiii).

18   See *BW,* 387-388, for sentence missing from *WCT.*

19   See also *4S,* 59-63 and 72.

20   Translator, Kisiel, *HWT,* 183.

Chapter 8

Learning as Listening

> *To learn means: to become knowing.*
> *OWL,* 143

> *To know means to* be able to learn.
> *IM,* 23

Coming into learning is presupposed by the experience of listening and understanding, not as a causal chain of events, but as a practical and prudent historically situated belonging-together. Listening offers itself as an always already modification of "the counter-play of call and belonging" (*RHT,* 264) where the always already issuing-forth of sense as conversation/dialogue and reading/writing shows up. Listening is the place where matters of concern call forth thought and where thought as thinking-saying engages matters of concern as the core of dialogical experience.

Listening here should not be taken as the remembering of what one says aloud to oneself—the hearing of oneself talking. Listening is neither a rote repetition nor a mere exercise of the ear as a biologically determined bodily organ. Rather, learning as listening risks a lack of listening such that what is listened to/for always already exigently needs to be a listening to/for again and again. According to Richardson, the experience of learning is not a discrete doctrine, but a practical and prudent risk to be taken "inexorably and without respite" (Richardson, 1974, 551). Danger and risk,[1] as well as the somnambulant, resonate in learning's possibilities as each human being is always already underway as the listening of the call of the heart dialogical experience. But as Jean-Luc Nancy writes, "The heart of things resembles nothing, because it does not resemble anything. It does not resemble anything known, but that doesn't mean that it never stops coming to presence, and putting [the human being] in its presence" (*BP,* 188). The heart and core of matters of concern *take* and *let* as the back-and-forth play of offering. Learning cannot help but precipitate itself out of listening in one way or another (*BP,* 169, 186).

The way of learning is today separated from schooling and teaching such that it is thought as a discrete category. Today learning as cognitive gain is claimed by computer jargon as the schooled down or uploading of information. Teaching as a phenomenon is leveled off as mere facilitation of data transfer. Learning as letting knowledge occur, narrative telling of something, the affective self-finding of disposedness, or discovering is declared by modernist thinking to be tangential to its *(the)* real purpose. It is exactly these less familiar, overlooked encounters of learning that reveal learning as the way and whiling of listening. In this chapter we will look at how the heart of learning lets learning take its way as listening to the call as paying heed and attending to matters of concern.

Listening as way is a participatory and historically particular experiencing. As the non-beating heart of the "proper instantiation of the distributive universal of the Each" (*RHT,* 266), there is an on-coming offering, a letting-lie-before as a taking-to-heart of issuing-forth as the always already play of originating and accomplishing. The soul as beating heart of an enowned, persisting, enduring lets the human being, as a sojourning of openness, become that matter of concern, which as a nonrepeatable each time, be encountered uniquely in its who question (*PM,* 283-285). When let be in this way, listening can show itself as the heart and core of the play of relationships which turn on possibility's self-disclosing and beckoning of itself as the always already on-coming of world.

Unobtrusive Prevailings

We had the experience but missed the meaning. . . .

T. S. Eliot, *The Dry Salvages*

In the subject-object paradigm, learning is reduced to the determinable transfer of neutral (as neutralized) information. What this position forgets to do is to listen back to what is seen in advance and to listen to that which can be heeded. The listenable exigently needs listening, and listening necessarily belongs to the listenable. Listenings as engaged to and with world are in excess of mere biologically, psychologically, or philosophically determined discrete or idealized entities.

Realisms are claimed by the necessity to quantify the uptake and retention of information as reflected in the quantifications of institutionally determined outputs. If quantifiable information uptake cannot be demonstrated by a given number of acceptable outputs, learning simply cannot be considered to have occurred. Observable evidence must be observed in order to be observable! Evidence must be held to a stable standard in order that facts can be accepted as valid. Students/learners are herein reduced or restricted to information processing entities. They are taken, in Jean-Luc Nancy's words (*BSP,* 60), as "the 'together' of juxtaposition *partes extra partes,* isolated and unrelated parts," or they are taken-as "an indistinct 'we' that is like a diffuse generality" (*BSP,* 65). For example, students are taken as interchangeable and anonymous functionaries in the sense of Kafka or Chaplin.[2]

A pair of faculty members tell of their experiences as they listen to unforeseen disconnects between intent and outcome.

> Minna: *I think it is really hard to get to the heart of the matter when you are teaching in a practice setting, or maybe just teaching a practice. I mean we have all these regulations and "standards" by which our program is judged. You simply can't turn out nurses who can't pass the board exam—that seems to be the sole measure of accountability in*

nursing, teaching and safety in practice. So as a result we [the faculty] spend an inordinate amount of time mapping the content in our courses and testing students' knowledge and ability to apply that knowledge. We've even instituted several high-stakes tests at the end of the program to better our chances of achieving a high board pass rate. Yet clinically you see that these measures are far from the whole story. I often have students, the straight A students, who really struggle clinically. They get so frustrated when a particular patient's condition doesn't present like they anticipate from class—from the knowledge they are trying to apply. Similarly, I often have students whose practice is exquisite; they readily see the big picture, respond to the patient's situation, and so forth, but they are barely hanging on in the classroom. So if we are so good at measuring who has learned the most, who knows the most, and who will be safe, why does this difference persist? There seems to be something important we are missing in our rush to document exactly what students have learned.

Trevor: *What about the teachers who exhort, "THOSE STUDENTS!" with an exasperated sigh every time they struggle or make a mistake? Any hiccup in data transfer is the "students' fault"—there are even teachers who basically contend "My job would be a lot more enjoyable if it weren't for students!" They treat students as only resources that make their jobs as teachers possible. My question is this: Wouldn't we all be better off if we treated students' coming into nursing as a learning experience that we are all privileged to undergo?*

Listening needs listeners—listening is presented to listeners as available and possible. Listening as a phenomenon cannot guarantee anything other than itself.

Idealisms are claimed by the necessity to theorize understanding as a function of mind. Mind is, as an albeit ambiguous entity, to be equated with consciousness which in turn is held to be connected to sensory perception. Sensory perceptions thought as data inputs are the assigned values given by the cognizing acts of a unitized (collective "we" as a) functioning consciousness. These cognizing acts must conform to predetermined social or epistemological structures in order to be considered learning in any positive sense. Cognizing acts that do not conform to cultural or knowledge ideals are considered to be antisocial at worst and incoherent at best. Knowledge as domination is what must be conformed to by the learner, who must be trained (or formed) to see with the correct vision. The Greek term *paideia* is rooted in an outgrowth of Platonisms (*HPM,* 311) wherein the ideal is considered the objectifiable culmination of education as the process of proper formation (*TM,* 450-451). Shulman[3] advocates that the proper formation of learners is the central issue of schooling, especially in the professions.

For idealisms such as the above, "the 'psyche' is conceived as an independently existing and therefore malleable inner realm" (*ZS,* 172). What is to be processed by this realm is considered adequate knowledge. In the Kantian sense, "all knowledge in the sense of scientific experience is not only sensory perception, but is also always perception or observation determined by *thought*… as a mathematically founded knowledge of nature" (*ZS,* 114-115). Pure consciousness, unadulterated even by language and history, is the absolute ground of the enclosed sphere of immanence. This is seen as "knowledge, not only relating to what is perceivable in a sensory way, but also relating to what makes possible the experience of objects, namely their objectivity, possible as well" (*ZS,* 146). Again, Jean-Luc Nancy (*BSP,* 60) has gone to the heart of the matter as he describes the ideal together as *"totum intra totum,* a unified totality where the relation surpasses itself in being pure." Ego-subjects are valorized only as they can be taken as a standardized element in repeatable productive processes (*BSP*, 73). It is here that the questions swirling around the possibilities of cloning human beings can be found.

The Offering of Possibilities

> *It is a question of what makes the gift as such: an offering that may not be returned to anyone, since it remains in itself the free offering that it is.*
>
> *EF,* 146

Let us start to converse with learning as listening in terms of something other than a mere biological mechanism or an ambiguous *ego cogito.* Listening-back is a possibility of letting world encounterings as the offering of care show themselves. Origin and incipience come as the gift of a past, which is still (always already) an in-front-of on-coming. Listening can tell the human being that it must give ear to (listen to) the listenable, not as cognitive gain or other such quantifiable magnitude, but as immediate, practical, and prudent understanding. In a crowded, noisy setting, mothers often report being able to hear their infant's cry when the child wakes up upstairs or across the room. This can't be attributed to mere cognition or to the measurable pitch or frequency of the sound emitted by the baby. It is the "giving ear to" and "giving to the ear" that is immediate, practical, and prudent understanding engagement.

Historically situated understandings enable the listenable to be taken-as something. The listenable is attuned (called) listening such that listening gives ear to (harks to) solicitous heed in its ownmost possibility. The reciprocal play of listening-back and listening forward is what enables hermeneutic phenomenology to be "precisely what it brings forth, i.e., [taking-as] and interpretations" (von Herrmann, 1996, 176). The myth of the absolute immanent agent (ego-subject) must be left to itself in order for the possibility of the temporally situated the human being of openness to be in the world as the appearance of finitude, a thereby never to be completed (open) involvement with an on-coming future of engaged possibility (*HPM,* 306-307).

The human being is always already doing (is involved with) matters of concern, taking something as something. Taking is not to be thought as the mere possessing of an object by a subject or vice versa. The human being of openness is called to belong to "a self-opening middle" wherein the instantiation of particularized historicality can be retrieved (*RHT,* 264-266). Retrieval is not the act of a willful subject but is a calling forth into the future as the becoming of what a matter of concern always already is, for example, the participatory human being as finite, historical, and temporally particular.

Heidegger posed the question, "What kind of taking is learning?" (*WIT,* 71). A response dwells with matters of concern insofar as they are listened to. But a context-free entity cannot be listened to in the strictest sense. Only its engagedness as the exposure of an offering can be listened to. Listening is therefore the underway of takings-as which disclosing and beckoning lets show up such that engagedness always already discloses and beckons. Disclosing and beckoning reveals itself through the engagement itself (*WIT,* 71). The circularity inhering in these necessary relationships cannot be sundered or broken into via the formal structures of scientistic (structural) logic.

Learning in its richest sense can never obtain as a presuppositionless science wherein its putative self-consistency is "free from contradiction, self-evident and therefore absolutely certain, and self-founded" (*HWT,* 189). Self-certainty and self-founding of all knowledge can only obtain as some asserted point of pure reason absolutely independent of historical experience. The stabilized workings of technicity (*HPM,* 312) and the correct seeing of science (*HPM,* 311) alone attempt to decide in advance what a matter of concern is without any concomitant consideration to how all of these phenomena are "encountered in the confusion of experience" (*HWT,* 189).

Confused experience and experienced confusion dialogically play as the groundless ground of the con-tension between listening and the listenable, world and earth.[4] It is the thesis of this book that learning is not the more or less continuous shoveling or force-feeding of fact particles into a bottomless self-enclosed, infinite ego-thing. On the other hand, it is the very play of confusion that discloses and beckons as an allotment, the offering of listening and the listenable.

Marisa, an experienced teacher, offers her experience.

> *When using Narrative Pedagogy I always begin with the experiences students are having as they learn nursing. But this isn't like just sharing stories or recounting the procedures they did in clinical or the list of signs/symptoms they observed. As these experiences are shared, I try to follow what catches the students' gaze, and that is always interesting and compelling and challenging and confusing all at the same time. It took me a long time to get over trying to control where the discussions would take us or to direct the discussion into a particular topic. What I found helped is to pay attention to what calls the student in the narrative—what fascinates them or confuses them. What insights does the student offer that raise new questions for me as a learner?*

The everyday go-around of living a life can show itself as the absorption in matters of concern which obtain as mere material entities or as adherence to given idealized or ideological fixed states. The movement and appearance of disposedness as disclosing and beckoning in terms of what lets disclosing be (the presence of absence) is overlooked (covered over, forgotten) in favor of the risk-free familiar (*HPM,* 309-311). Dakota, an experienced teacher, describes this situation in the following way:

> *My courses are a mess, and if you can show me what to do to fix them for sure, I would do it. But I am not about to take a risk that the course will get even worse, even though I hate the way things*

currently are! I know this squeezes any sense of excitement, inquiry, and questioning right out of the students. But what can you do! The risks are simply too great.

For learning to properly disclose (offer) and beckon (call) as its hinting self, it must arrive in advance as heeding (belonging-to as the necessity of attending-to) the call of possibility as risk. Disposing and beckoning opens up ways. Surprises, subtle shifts, and the unexpected reshape tacit assumptions belonging to the gesture and bearing of practical and prudent involvement (*HWT,* 197).

Thrownness and disposedness presuppose each other such that they are always already a plural singular that has priority over any dialogically taking something as something. The human being of openness is the possibility of thrownness and disposedness as a "being opened up" (*KE,* 15). The human being of openness originally (incipiently) finds itself comported to matters of concern as it stands face-to-face with them. These matters of concern need the human being of openness in order to be themselves. They require it to receive/perceive/apprehend/take-to-heart their offering in a fitting way (*ZS,* 28). Experience is immediate and dialogical.[5]

Sustainings

That which calls on us to think and appeals to us to think, claims thought for itself and as its own because in and by itself it gives food for thought— not just occasionally but now and always.

WCT, 125

The human being of openness as a listening attendant in the open clearing is always already ahead of itself as possibility. It is *not* a fixed entity, soul, psyche, ego, substance, subject, or person. The human being of openness and engaged openness belong to and presuppose each other, not as object, or as cause to effect, but as disclosing and beckoning, each to the other. Engaged openness discloses and beckons the human being of openness as itself in such a way that disclosure and beckoning "first needs something of its own, proper to itself, a *self* whose selfhood that human being has to persist and endure in *that* instantiation that lets the human being, *standing in* [openness], become *that* being which is first encountered only in the who-question" (*CP,* 173, trans. Kisiel; *RHT,* 266). The listening human being is sustained and nourished by its very openness.

The definition of the human being as rational animal is correct as far as it goes. But the question remains as to how the faculty of reason belongs to the truth of engaged openness (*PM,* 246). Can the essence of the human being be sustained merely by being outfitted "with an immortal soul, the power of reason, or the character of person" (*PM,* 247)? The temporal particularity of the human being of openness as a can-be "is intensified as [can-be] in its enactment and in its being enacted" (*ZS,* 164). Can-be is the proper "phenomenon by which [*of* openness] shows itself" (*ZS,* 164). Matters of concern show themselves as engagement as the human being is exigently involved with, sustained by them (*ZS,* 5, 8).

What is fitting and proper to the human being of openness is the skilled can-be that enables it to bring to language matters of concern in their engaged openness (*POR,* 87). The human being of openness is sustained *as* the understanding of engaged openness (*ZS,* 191-193). Of openness it *stands in* a situation, *is* a situation, and thereby is a situatedness always already marked by each historically situated temporal particularity. The human being as such is enabled to hear the call of the open clearing wherein unique questions show themselves: What gives, offers learning its imperative? What necessitates learning? Does the can-be of the human being of openness suggest other possibilities? The putative power of rationality, thought as the possession of the human as rational animal, has today devolved into, entrusted itself to, its own empowering context. Heidegger's leaving the subject-object paradigm to itself was an attempt to show that the open clearing of engaged openness as such can be seen as the "which and by which the human being [of openness] is 'out for' its [engaged openness], in order to be" (*GBT,* 441). The human being of openness is letting the finite possibility of sense as meaningful or meaninglessness lie before it (*BT,* 193).[6] There can be no absence of sense.

In Chapter 3, we discussed the nonseparatable reciprocating back-and-forthness between the human being's thrown-open unique essence and "the possibility-of-sense-making" (*PS,* 13). This "a priori interface constitutes the dynamic structure" of what it means to be human as other than the position that is grounded in the Cartesian *cogito* (*PS,* 13). Therefore, on the one hand the human being must pay heed to its thrown-openness, while on the other hand it must make sense of it. In this way listening is first and foremost a face-to-face engagement with the ultimate incompletability of any "metaphysical closure, full self-presence, and perfect self-coincidence" (*PS,* 17). At this same time, learning listens to the call of the attendant necessity of the *with* of engaged openness.

Gathered Sendings:
A Different Kind of Magnetic Resonance

> *The greeting has kept the greeted one well in mind and in memory. The greeted one was never forgotten. Nor can it ever be forgotten. For the greeted one has conveyed itself in thought to the one who greets. Thus the greeting is not simply the work of the one who greets.*
>
> *EHP,* 122

Something other than the centrality of modernity's conscious subject has to open up learning. The possible emergence of learning as listening is enabled by the magnetic call of the present absence of presence (finitude). Presence, any presence as a greeted greeting, is always partial and imperfect. The otherness of not knowing means that while the human being always already understands, its understandings are always conditioned by the magnetic draw (call) of absence—its own. Thus "the otherness to which the I is exposed alters the I itself" (Raffoul, 1997, xxvii). This alteration occurs as the dialogical experience of the human being of openness which belongs to the region of engaged openness.

Somewhere between the hustle and bustle of activity and the somnambulance of passivity, enigmas thrust their silent voices toward attuned ears (*OWL,* 149). Listening as "a sudden experience" (*OWL,* 148) arrives in an instant. It is a "wholly different rule" wherein it discloses and beckons as a disturbance that disrupts earlier dialogical experience. Listening can be undreamed of, terrifying, anxious, surprising, dreadful, painful, pleasurable, wonderful, strange, astounding, or boring. It is unpredictably and occasionally "abruptly caught sight of" (*OWL,* 154).

Alana is a dean who has taught for 20 years.

I'm surprised at the long slide downward of so many teachers. I've seen faculty who start out with above-average student evaluations end up teaching only required courses because students refuse to take their elective ones. Sometimes these teachers end up teaching a course no one wants to teach, like the beginning nursing course. The change in some teachers can be overnight and permanent. Word gets around they have a teaching problem. They become difficult to deal with, closed minded, and rationalize away every problem they have. They say things like "The students have trouble in my courses because they are less academically prepared." When we point out these same students do fine in other courses, they say, "It's because I have high standards for student performance in my classes, not like my other faculty colleagues!" I can never get anywhere with these kinds of teachers.

I used to think if a teacher was open-minded and wanted to develop better teaching skills, they could improve with the right kind of help. But I am amazed at what just happened to me today. There is a teacher who is a quiet person, very reserved, who continues on the slide downward, who is making bad pedagogical decisions. After a semester of a colleague going over with her every week a videotape of her lectures, after attending a national week-long Institute on Teaching at her own expense, after she attended and followed through on our department of education teaching assessment program—after all this, when she was teaching on her own, she decided to change the grading scale in the middle of the semester because the students were getting too many A's! I'm beginning to change my mind. If you are closed minded and on a downward slide, no one can help. But even if you're open-minded, for some people, "having a teaching problem" is terminal. Today I was not looking forward to meeting with this teacher because her evaluations are the worst they have ever been. My only recourse, since we are unionized, was to begin a series of performance reviews, hoping that over the long period of time it takes to non-renew her she would leave. When I saw her she was upset and tearful. I commended her for trying to improve her teaching. This semester she is using Ipods of her lectures to free class time for discussions. Then I blurted out, "Maybe at this time in your life, you weren't meant to be a teacher." The silence that followed shocked both of us. Then she said, "I agree."

Where does the understanding that lets listening and questioning a can-be-possible phenomenon come from? Understanding, if taken as complete or perfect knowledge or total ignorance, would obviate the need for listening or questioning. The ideal, totally knowledgeable human being could not know if total knowledge is so, paradoxically rendering total knowledge impossible. Total ignorance speaks for (or is dumb to) itself. Listening belongs to disclosing and beckoning as the human being of openness is always already exposed as "unfinished and always on-the-way" (*PS*, 199). The conundrum arises here (shows itself) as to whether immediate knowledge per se is anything that can be cogently discussed or established. As exposed, the human being both is enabled and needs "to be affected by others: approached, touched, engaged" (*PS,* 200). Any conceptualization of knowledge is itself presupposed by the situatedness that each human being finds itself engaged with.

Sharing and Encountering

> *We are our identity—in the simultaneous and Undecidable reference to our "singularities" and our "community"—an identity that is necessarily shared out, in us and between us.*
>
> GT, 64

Participation in world of the human being of openness (being-in-the-world) turns on invisible, silent, nonmeasurable capabilities for apprehending the encounterable and its call to attention. The reciprocity of engaged openness and the human being of openness as sense holds open time-space as a can-be (not as a guaranteed steering mechanism) which apprehends matters of concern as sense that are offered and that call by virtue of the at-*the*-time of a historically particular "open" (*ZS,* 4). Each human being is are always already face-to-face with brushing up against whatever it comes across (*BSP,* 98). Note that the "we" in the above epigraph is thought as a shifting common lot such that *the ipseity of anything* is entirely consumed "in the relation-to-another and in the 'with' of" engaged openness (Raffoul, 1997, xxiii-xxv).

The human being of openness is a *circulating with,* possessing no locale of its own and being available and hence engaged for every locus of meaning. *With,* as the proper essence of engaged openness, is not an other adding itself to some modality of existence or another. *With* constitutes "the drawing apart and drawing together" of never to be perfectible self-presencing. It is a letting that "constitutes the traction and tension, repulsion/attraction" (*BSP,* 62), of the "between" of human beings, as themselves, with matters of concern. The sojourn between is each time a temporally particular moment with *with* "as the interval between" (*BSP,* 62). As such, a nonperceptible trace is offered as "drawn out over" always already imperfect self-presence, crossing over it and underlining it at the same time (*BSP,* 62). The human being has to participate in back-and-forth listening and attend to presence as possible co-presence, co-appearing as the movement of compearance. Human beings necessarily abide/while/sojourn/dwell with the aboutness of what concerns them (*ZS,* 218) in order to find their way.

Finding one's way—openness as each human being's sojourning (whiling, abiding, dwelling) in the open—"provides the possibility for comportment in the first place" (*ZS,* 226). Each particular practical and prudent comportment's moment is dialogical experience, which "in its own way opens and plies itself to that toward which it comports itself" (*PM,* 146). The reservedness of letting-be as freedom must have already granted comportment its endowment as the call for the co-responding presentation to the human being each time (*PM,* 146). Freedom is not possessed by the human being; the human being is disclosed and beckoned over to the call of free openness.[7] The human being of openness is enabled to always already listen-to phenomena, which show themselves as simple apprehension and thus do not need to be proved. They show themselves and are accepted as such. Practical, prudent involvements as "imperceptible, ontological phenomena always already and necessarily show themselves *prior to* all perceptible phenomena" (*ZS,* 6). In this way phenomena as matters of concern are conjoined with humans in listening. Attending to the call of engaged openness exceeds mere sensuous perception but is not without it. Listening concomitantly always already fills in, exigently needs to fill in, what is absent in mere sensory perception (*HPM,* 290-292). Human beings always already listen to the call of the essential as it is seen (*ZS,* 35). The call as itself always already listens to humans in their disposedness as "already being co-disposed in mutual concern" (*GTB,* 546, fn. 11; see also *BQP,* 133-134).

Sue, a nursing professor, tells of her experience with graduate students.

Some students enter the doctoral program and they know exactly what they want to study. Many others look around or change their minds often. Renata, a doctoral student, asked me to be on her committee recently. She is a highly motivated future nurse researcher. When I asked her to describe her study, she recounted studying palmar sweating as an indication of hopelessness. She was very excited about this study, as was her advisor, a nurse physiologist. Later, I did a lot of thinking how as nurses we want to figure how to measure or quantify everything, even things like hopelessness. Rather than listening to hopelessness as inexplicable, submitting our dialogue to the inexplicable, we close down on this possibility in a rush to make everything explicit.

The listening *of* what is proper and unique, historical, and temporal in the essential can be taken as that which is merely the necessary givens of the everyday. If the human being listens to anything from history, it can be enabled to see that sheltered there is the message that "everyday understanding believes that one has knowledge when one needs to learn nothing more, because one has finished learning" (*IM*, 23). In its own way historicality is enabled as listening, not as an audible phenomenon, but as a temporally situated particularity. When seen in the purview of hermeneutic phenomenology, listening becomes retrieved from the enclosure of modernity's ego-subject.

With whom or where is the guarantee that the customary conceptualizations of learning, merely because they are so common, touch the proper essence of learning (*PLT*, 224)? Our questioning in this book turns not on answers but on how the proper or unique essence of learning as listening endures, sustains, persists, and prevails as a particular "historical temporal duration rather than the 'eternal duration of constant presence'" (*RHT*, 267-268).

Is learning to be understood only in the meanings current to it? For the beginnings of Greek philosophical thinking as read by

Heidegger, the heart of something (as *hypokeimenon*) "was its ground and was always there" (*OBT,* 5). It can be said that the heart of something was what was cared about as what was closest to the heart (van Buren, 1999, 116, fn. 35; 122-125, fn. 75). For something to be taken-to-heart it has to be reliably available in advance of concerned involvement (*OHF,* 71-74). The free lets matters of concern lie before the human being as reliable (*OBT,* 15). But in its own turn, the emergence of the free is taken into itself such that the free assures itself to itself as its mystery. The self-presencing of presence as "that which frees—the mystery—is concealed and always concealing itself" (*QCT,* 25). As we have written, the project of modernity overlooks or forgets the movement of matters of concern into appearance as emergence/elusion out of privative absence. Learning as mere ontic presence forgets that the human being of openness is always already permitted or let to listen to sense *as* sense.

Letting

> *Letting means: to let go, let go away, put away, let depart, that is, to set free into the open . . . to admit, give, extend, send, to let-belong.*
>
> *OTB, 37*

Letting takes hold of the listening human being such that non-listening must always already be present as the possible absence of the listenable. In this way engaged openness releases itself *as* itself as the emergence/elusion of the offering of disclosing and beckoning (*4S,* 59-60). Only when letting is released from the intentional action of an ego-subject can it be retrieved as listening.

The temporally-historically situated particularity of listening's each time turns on the attending-to the call of listening's hold as sojourn/whiling/dwelling. Learning as the listening-to of the self-presence of presence is held by the disclosing and beckoning call of non-listening as the possible absence of meaningful presence. Listening is held in the circulating bivalence of the movement and appearing of presence and absence such that "*Only because there is letting of presence, is the letting-presence of what is present possible"* (*OTB,* 37). Engagement let as the play of disclosing and beckoning emerges/eludes as the telling relation of all relations, the belongings-to of all belongings-to.

The primary task of this chapter is to belong to letting the words "learning as listening" speak in the widest swing of their retrievability. In terms of the binary oppositions that claim the subject-object paradigm, learning-of presents learning-to with an aporia. Human circulation is always already a listening-to learn and a listening-of learning. Being held by the thrown attendance of modernity's underway-to its self-inflicted fact-value conundrum does not effect admittance to the final closure of genus-species structures, nor can it admit of a resolution to dualisms such as mind-body, accurate-inaccurate, profit-loss, true-untrue, right-wrong, and correct-incorrect.

Learning as the phenomenon of listening is the pivotal point wherein this book stands or falls. Therefore the reader is urged to be mindful that listening is presupposed by and belongs to the play of thrownness, care, alreadiness, attendance, understanding, presence-to, language, becoming/on-coming, and co-responding, as these phenomena issue forth from disclosing and beckoning.

Listening as a noun indicates, designates, that a matter of concern is as a meaningful appearance, while listening as a verb indicates, designates, the engaged openness of learning as resting in movement. Listening is experiencing as an always already undergoing the play of matters of concern as they disclose and beckon themselves. Therefore our reading of call to attention, calling, and listening leads to the questioning of whether learning can be taught. Calling as the hold of dialogical experience cannot be reduced to a rationalized step-by-step procedure external to a given listener. Paradoxically, or so it seems, listening *is* a step-by-step dialogical experience, at times thrust forward into the known, at times back into forerunning unthought and its exigent need to be rethought. The possibility of dialogical experience takes place in a "world that 'worlds'" and is "structured dynamically by time" (*HWT,* 193).

Engaging as a holding itself, and attending to, is the human phenomenon of comportment. Listening holds out as itself—withdraws or conceals itself as it offers the possibility of truth as untruth. It is modification of understanding that shows itself as the back-and-forth play of practical and prudent comportment. Listening can only offer itself as available—it cannot be taken-up. Learning as listening only offers itself as a can-be of the human being of openness and engaged openness insofar as learning as listening responds to the call of engaged openness. Listening is held by engaged openness taken as a "letting-lie-present that assembles" (*POR,* 110).

In order for there to be listening, there must be a lack of complete or immediate attendance as matters of concern are listened-to as listenable. Listening-to and understanding are the same but not identical. The former is a possibility that, as historically determined and intrinsically restricted, is in each case the unfolding expansiveness that can be dialogically experienced as a whole out of which human comportment can comport itself. Understanding as a can-be is always already actualized as a being-held-to such that making-possible is held open (*FCM,* 363-364). Listening exigently needs (or turns on) immediate and nondeliberative understanding as "first a moment of existing before it is a mode of cognition, therefore more an understanding that we *are* rather than have" (*HWT,* 194).

Human beings may or may not dialogically experience their sojourn; they may or may not pay particular attention to what they know, but their stay in this world, their "sojourn on earth, is constantly under way to grounds and reason" (*POR,* 11). Everyday dialogical experience is held to a foundation of one sort or another (*WT,* 14). The Greek word *paideia* is met again here as superficially translated as "education." But its historically situated meaning is "the circumspect and vigilant sense for what at any time is appropriate and inappropriate" (*POR,* 13). This reciprocating play obtains as questioning back and forth (*WT,* 31) such that entities as matters of concern "affect each other and resist one another" (*WT,* 33). The unknown or unknowable as the dark allows non-forced holding-to as concentration (*DT,* 60). A possibility obtains wherein "the world becomes mere representedness." Matters of concern "as a whole set are in place as that for which" the human being is readied (*OBT,* 67). Readiness whiles/sojourns/abides as the simultaneity of withdrawing and showing forth such that matters of concern "as such appear in a new manner according to which they intrude and *impose* themselves on cognition" (*POR,* 55). Therefore it can be seen that the self-presencing of presence as that which is said at the same time shows itself as that which is already said. Sense plays as what is always already "shown, which means, what-lies-present as such—what comes to presence in its presencing" (*POR,* 107).

Listening shows up as a sojourn of attending to that which the human being of openness is already let into as involvement in the prior knowledge of matters of concern in their hold on the human being (*HWT,* 187).[8] Matters of concern listen to the call of the human being of openness by being available to the human being. Prior acquaintance shows up as intentionality, which is "primarily operative in the realm of ordinary habitual experience" (*HPM,* 293). Learning as listening (attending-to calling) hides itself in the everyday, right out in plain sight!

Taking-to-Heart

> *To learn means to make everything we do answer to whatever essentials address themselves to us at a given time. Depending on the kind of essentials, depending on the realm from which they address us, the answer and with it the kind of learning, differs.*
>
> *WCT,* 14[9]

The coming-to the basic can-be of the human being of openness is coming-to "as the claim and appeal of the measure to the heart in such a way that the heart turns to give heed to the measure" (*PLT,* 228). Learning as ongoing pathway of the play of listening, attending, and call shows itself as the can-be of taking-to-heart and waiting in their reciprocating, resonating belonging-to each other. Waiting as outlined in *Discourse on Thinking* is neither a passive standing in place nor a systematic anticipation of a predetermined result (*DT,* 68-69). The word "waiting" names (lets show) comportments that include caring, attending-to respectful accompaniment, and expecting and readiness to receive. Waiting reveals/conceals a sojourn that stays (whiles/abides/dwells) in place: the temporal particularity of the human being. Taking-to-heart and waiting belong to *world* wherein the relation of the human being of openness as knowing subject to entities and matters of concern always already changes along the way (*POR,* 7).[10]

It is important to see waiting and taking-to-heart as a movement and not the stasis of a putative representing subject (*DT,* 68, 69). The world is not represented as a picture (*OBT,* 57-85) but can be allowed (not as an act of subjugating will) to abide into the range of its possibilities (*DT,* 69). Thereby one can let oneself into the already open of waiting and taking-to-heart as course (ebb and flow) of conversation.

The human being as historical is disclosed and beckoned to presencing, which always already waits on (tends to) encounter (*POR,* 33). Presencing as engaged openness "manifests the character of holding itself back" (*POR,* 63). It shows itself as "the inconspicuous guide who takes" human beings by hand and word (*DT,* 60). *It lets* human beings, as finite possibility, be "constantly addressed by, summoned to attend to, grounds and reason" (*POR,* 3). Finitude holds and watches over (*OBT,* 32), as well as in its own way looks upon, the human being as "the one who is gathered by self-opening [matters of concern] in to presencing with them" (*OBT,* 68). The human being is held to (disclosed and beckoned to) watching over being exposed to being included, maintained, and supported by matters of concern in their "divisive confusion" (*OBT,* 68). The play of listening and listening-to listenables always already advenes as a mutual letting and taking into view of "the openness that surrounds" but does not enclose all (*DT,* 66). In its own way disclosing and beckoning sights the listening of the human being of openness in order to disclose and beckon, but not as cause to effect. In its own way the human being of openness is enabled to sight the listening of disclosing and beckoning; the human being of openness is claimed by disclosing and beckoning in order to understand matters of concern—to take them to heart.

Taking-to-heart (1) emerges out of letting-lie-before (*WCT,* 211) and (2) self-conceals as held within letting-lie-before. Letting as belonging-to is not undertaken as a reduction to consciousness, but as a taking-into-view the heart of matters. This points to the seeing of physical phenomena as extended and to the paying attention to sound as extended in time (*4S,* 22).[11] Historicality reveals differing experiences of measurability. The representational hold onto an object by an autonomous subject as a "reality" is freed up to the human being as that which foreruns and lies behind the human being of openness. Tradition comes toward the human being because tradition is the human's claimant as tradition comes on (*WCT,* 76).

The holding back of taking-to-heart "does not turn on a clutching or any other kind of grasping, but rather in a letting come of what [is already] dealt out" (*PLT,* 224). Taking-to-heart does not name a subject or object; it listens as a suspension and an escort. As a deference it sets the human being "the task of learning from it while questioning it, that is, of letting it say something" (*OTB,* 66). Listening whiles/sojourns as a holding in place of its own saying. Listening as listening says the learning of learning.

Saying-attending shows listening such that "its own deepest core is left unspoken" (*WCT,* 232). Listening to attending cannot be other than the hold of sense. *Sense issues forth in unique moments when attending and co-responding let each other happen.* Engaged openness as the self-presencing of presence manifests matters of concern such that the human being in its taking-to-heart can let itself be reached (*OTB,* 23). The rising up and self-opening of matters of concern apprehend the enacting human being of openness as involved tasks.

Listening as listening can be the acceptance or refusal of a claim (*OWL,* 150). Can one unlisten? Or does listening as listening always already dwell as one possibility of disposedness or another? Yes and no play into each other. "The play itself which attunes the two by letting the remote be near and the near be remote is pain" (*OWL*, 153). Pain here is not to be thought the empirical experience of bodily sensation but as an exposure to "divisive confusion" (*OBT*, 68), "the gatheredness of conflicting unrest" (*IM*, 142): engaged openness. Thereby listeners belong to the listenable as the listenable holds listeners painstakingly attending-to. Again, there is always already a give-and-take reciprocity, movement, which by its very absence enables the human being to relate to entities and matters of concern mediately, not via intellectual intuition (*KE*, 9-12). The phenomenological essence of listening can be glimpsed as moments of insight.

The Sighting of Insight

> When insight [discloses and beckons], then [human beings] are the ones who are stuck in their essence by the flashing of [engaged openness]. In insight, [human beings] are the ones who are caught sight of.
>
> *QCT*, 47

Perhaps it is just an accident of language that taking-to-heart and gaining insight both point toward listening and sighting as enigmatic groundlessness rather than absolute empirically controlled perception as certainty. If certainty is taken to heart and gained insight into, the extraordinary becomes revealed. This certainly can be all to the good. But a question shows itself: How does the extraordinary belong to the ordinary? Can the ordinary be gripped by the extraordinary?[12] The ordinary and the extraordinary belong together as the attending-to of calling, the calling of attending-to. To attend-to is to compellingly respond to the demand exacted by the belonging which in its own turn "points to the fundamental harmony of togetherness" (*GBT*, 379). As a receiving and taking up "into the relation of" (*P*, 108) engaged openness as thrown, attending-to is the excess over the attempting to neutrally sense isolated tones and sounds. Listening attendance as listening is an "understanding hearing" (*HCT*, 266). The human being is initially "always already involved with the world itself, and not with 'sensations' first and then, on the basis of a kind of theater, finally involved with" matters of concern (*HCT,* 266). "The from-which and the toward-which" (*GBT,* 306) meet each other, cross each other, encounter each other as the same, which, as we have written, is not the merely identical of modernism's subject-object paradigm. The human being must attend to be in attendance with its listening.

As we have noted, the human being sights what it says rather than says what it sees. "Even the simplest perception is already expressed and interpreted" by prior understandings that determine the how of perception (*HWT,* 99). Discrete categories can be found only if they first reveal themselves as involved, practical, and prudent; the categorial (*HWT,* 96). Seeing is always already primarily involved doing. Seeing and conversant conversations hold each other in their sighting of each other. They are not "talked over" first. Conversational gestures obtain as sighting-listening gatherings of the hold of an issuing-forth (*OWL,* 18). Sighting-listening cannot ask about epistemic knowing (*P,* 162) because sighting-listening is here not thought as an all-encompassing that gathers everything into a fixed union (*OWL,* 19). Gathering is here thought as an offering of bearing (emergence) and counterbearing (elusion), "a beholding that is itself invisible" (*OWL,* 19).

To participate with hermeneutic phenomenology is the sighting of a listening for and to respond to the call of questions from the open, often listening to how certain questions risk, upset, or interrupt perfectly obvious pre-held holdings. Listening is not sighted without non-listening. Listening's possibility cannot be forced or otherwise coerced by arbitrarily imposed external imperatives to hear in the manner of analytical or mathematical language or see in the sense of the mere observation of a discrete physical phenomenon. Listening's possibility glimpses the human being of openness as the latter invisibly and silently manifests itself.

Glimpsing Listening

> *Can we see something that is told? We can, provided what is told is more than just the sound of words, provided the seeing is more than just the seeing with the eyes of the body.*
>
> *WCT,* 232

In *Being and Time,* Heidegger pursued sighting and hearing not as physiological attributes, but as these manifest themselves in the human being of openness as the possibility of understanding. The human being of openness lets the engaged openness of matters of concern as possibility (*BT,* 138). All sighting can only be grounded in understanding (*BT,* 187). Understanding gives the sighting of the available, and sighting is concomitantly always already understanding and interpretation (*BT,* 189). Understanding as thought herein is such that both discursivity and listening are based upon it (*BT,* 208). It follows that listening first and foremost "has the kind of [engaged openness] of the hearing which understands" (*BT,* 207). Eyes and ears come to the human being of openness as the possibility of understanding-listening. Heidegger wrote of interpretation grounded in matters of concern sighted in advance (*BT,* 191). He did away with the ontic distinction between hearing and seeing by interpreting the human being of openness as the one who immediately understands and is thereby enabled to see and listen (*BT,* 208). A tautological abstraction discloses and beckons as sighting and listening self-reveal/conceal as sighting and listening. The task of hermeneutic phenomenology is claimed by the circulation of seeming tautologies when it is called to deal with belonging-to as opposed to cause-effect relations.

The offering/granting of letting-lie-before and taking-to-heart as the understanding of the significance of matters of concern turns on their self-emergence as available to human involvement (*ZS,* 185).[13] Listening can mean to be right at sighting wherein what is caught sight of is never again lost sight of. Listening belongs to reaching, as always already being on a journey. Sighting and listening as putting oneself on a journey is the dialogical experience of learning (*OWL,* 143). Dialogical experience in the sense of calling means undergoing an experience with something. As such experience, the human being stretches along its sojourn. In order for it to engage the experience, the experience reciprocally must engage the human being. The human being is greeted and appealed to such that *the human being is itself of openness* (*OWL,* 73-74). Experience in its richest dialogical sense means becoming aware of, apprehending, and listening, learning, and understanding[14] in the sense of discovery while traversing. Therefore "to undergo a dialogical experience means that in submitting to it one endures it, suffers it, receives it, as it strikes one as not of ones own making" (*OWL,* 57). One lets oneself be properly concerned by and belong to its claim by "entering into and submitting to it" (*OWL,* 57). Call, calling, and listening are at play wherein each belongs to (is engaged by, is related to) the other.

The human being is enabled to catch a glimpse of engaged openness as a unique being held in readiness for taking-to-heart. To let oneself be held by (belong to) taking-to-heart "is a distinctive act of the human being" (*ZS,* 18). Human beings are always already disposed and attuned to the call of their birth *and* their mortality. These limits show themselves such that humans cannot give birth to themselves or possess "death as an object of knowledge" (Fynsk, 1996a, xiv). Learning as listening turns on limit, which is the same for each but is not identical to that of another. The call enjoins each human being and matters of concern as open to and exposed to other and as the same-as. The human being can listen-to the play of other and the same "each time, and each time differently—but always in relation" (Fynsk, 1996a, xxiii). The showing of sense as an emerging out of the historical world, out of immediate understandability, enables interpretation, knowing, and acting as possibility. The self-presencing of present humankind as a process of disruption obtains as the way in which engaged openness is gathered in its ownmost gatheredness.

To take something as something is to let sense show itself as sense; it is to take meaning as a temporal particularity out of a range of temporally particular possibilities (the current meaning/

presence of something as for something). Engaged openness obtains only in the "discursive, synthetic-differential activities" of human beings (*PS,* 190-191). The temporally particular engaged open clearing of a matter of concern is what and how, the human being happens to take this matter of concern as/for at each present moment (*PS,* 190). The availability and understandability of matters of concern are infinitely finite. There is no entity that can become fully self-coincident (as fated or enabled) as an all-at-once in its presence. Therefore the absence of perfect self-presence opens up the human being (*KE,* 15) and enables it to listen-to the calling of its own finitude. The human being of openness listens when it disposes everything it is practically and prudently involved with such that its comportment is a paying heed to whatever historical particularity is addressed as listening to it at a given moment. The human being of openness listens to thinking's call by paying heed "to what there is to think about" (*WCT,* 4).

Listening Ahead

> *The human being is already sighted in sighting forward.*
>
> *GBT,* 442

Listening is not a looking back into, a reading of, some conceptualization of, pure or conditioned consciousness. It obtains as a thematic "looking ahead" into a region of possibilities wherein the practical and prudent involvement of human beings reveals their *way* as the self-presence of engaged openness (*HPM,* 296-297). The future as a self-presenting, on-coming phenomenon is a call that never allows itself to be grasped as the same, but only as a possibility to be retrieved each time it is read as a past which is already in front of the interpreting human being (which is each human being each time). Listening is to-be-on-a-way, not toward "a mere wanting to know" (*QCT,* 42) or as an "entrapping" (*QCT,* 43), but as a scenting, trailing, or tracking of a matter of concern that has already come before to go ahead.

Listening, as a practical and prudent way of taking into view the loci of meanings, lets itself be seen. Listening is a sighting wherein "'looking over' the whole 'with a glance' and 'listening to every thing at once' are one and the same" (*POR,* 67). The unified sameness of the self-presencing of presence as "bringing-into-view and listening determines the essence of the [thinking-saying] that is entrusted to" human beings who are interpreting (thinking) as their ownmost, unique, proper essence (*POR,* 67). The human being is always already held in advance (listened-to) as a hermeneutic phenomenological entity, held to the nonpossessable but bearable and viewable address of the human being of openness. Of openness, the human being is itself engaged as a matter of concern.

Human beings are addressed by matters of concern, which *do not* cause something in them. What humans sight and listen to leads to determinations of their acting. What is sighted "in this or that way is the determining ground [motive]—that by which comportment is determined in this way or that" (*ZS,* 209). Hermeneutic phenomenology is held by the movement of reading the implicit as the exposing of sense wherein the human being is invested with itself as being drawn into its absence—a listening, which cannot be heard as mere sound waves. The human being holds and is held in advance both toward its proper essence as the human being of openness and toward the world. Sense can be seen as clarity (openness) such that the human being of openness encounters the matter of concern which it is itself. To sight something is to attend to it such that it is preserved, safeguarded, in the sense of letting what is sighted come to the temporally particular human being (*4S,* 68). Care-taking in this sense announces itself "and maintains itself in many intrinsically related ways" (*CP,* 49f, translation by Kisiel, *RHT,* 268).

In Attendance of Questioning

> *Only one who is truly climbing can fall down.*
>
> BQP, 21

> *In the unfolding of the question, everything depends on the course of our procedure.*
>
> BQP, 126

Is learning a knowing or a known? How can it be measured, if at all? If learning, here taken-as a listening to a calling listening, cannot be knowing or known, "How can that which by its very nature remains unknown ever become a measure?" (*PLT,* 222). Has thinking arrived at a roadblock, or are there measures whose ways allow human beings to handle the obstruction? Handling as tending-to is possible when "hands do not abruptly grasp, but are guided by gestures befitting the measure here to be taken. This is done by a taking which at no time clutches at the standard but rather takes it in a concentrated [apprehension], a gathered taking-in, that remains a listening" (*PLT,* 223). Practical and prudent encountering (use/handling/involvement/connection) "implies fitting response" (*WCT,* 187). To be already engaged (in use) does not admit of actual measurement in the ontic sense. The to-be-already-engaged calls forth what is to endure in the encounter (*WCT,* 234). Enduring here is understood as being disposed and beckoned to, being inclined to (active *and* passive sense) letting. Learning as listening is letting oneself answer and respond to the on-coming dwelling of gesture and bearing relatedness-to.[15] The human being is *free for the* calling call of listening.

Relatedness-to gesture and issuing-forth as they belong together can appear as a "slumbering" (*WCT,* 14), a fading (*OWL,* 36), or an abrupt trailing "off into obscurity" (*HWT,* 198). There is nothing to guarantee that a given play of phenomena will remain other than the unnoticed, obscure, shadowy, concealed, invisible, silent, or numb. Science can cause or provoke certain kinds of ontic phenomena to become visible or conceptualized, but it cannot sight itself *as* its own revealing. The human being is called by modern science to learn to conduct a scientific experiment, but the human of modern science cannot listen to the results of the experiment without being disposed and attuned to its meaning.

Learning in its traditional sense becomes modified when enigmatic hints beckon toward or away as they surprisedly show themselves as their belongingness (*OWL,* 26). The exigent need of hints shows itself as "the widest sphere in which to swing" (*OWL,* 27). Listening calls to the "step back" which retreats from metaphysics as "the sole meaning of enabling in the gathering of thinking upon itself" and reveals itself as "a glance ahead to what comes" (*4S,* 61). The question that arises turns on asking after the whereunto of the wherein and wherefore that lets the human being claim to arrive at the "enduring, persisting, prevailing" essence of matters of concern (*RHT,* 267). The human being can make such a claim only where it "receives it from the telling [saying] of language" (*PLT,* 215). Listening cannot be a nondiscursive empirical experience (*OWL,* 147). Dialogical experience always already announces "a different articulation, a different *melos,* a different tone" (*OWL,* 147). Transpositions become transposed as historically particular moments. Hintings in their enigmatic on-coming as the listened to "on the whole belong to language" (*ZS,* 96).

Participating-In

> *Any individual actuality in all its connections is possible only if before all else nature grants the open, within which immortals and mortals and all things are able to encounter each other. The open mediates the connections between actual things.*
>
> *EHP,* 83

Listening as a participle takes part (participates in) both the nominal and verbal meaning of "to learn." As a matter of concern, attendance has its mediate howness, thatness, whatness in engaged openness, and its essential way of engaged openness persists as the engaged openness of a matter of concern (*WCT,* 221). Paying heed self-presences as the retrieval of its presencing.

The above may be perfectly appropriate as a phenomenological description, but listening needs an agent, at least as some kind of dative, for it to show up at all. That dative, or agent, must always show up as engaged agency wherein the human being pays attention, heeds the call, and plays itself out as difference. Difference is not thought here as the unbridgeable difference between the subject and object of the modernist tradition, but as difference which shows itself as the mutual belonging together of an ambiguously double genitive as expressed by the reciprocity of enabling and enacting as an issuing forth. In the next chapter we will attempt to let teaching show itself as co-responding. Therefore learning as listening cannot stand alone without being in attendance with and to co-responding. The privative presence *of* absence's callings to attendance is the possibility of the listening *of* co-responding and the co-responding *of* listening.

The words "listening" and "co-responding" in the above phrases shift from noun to verb such that they belong, disclose, and beckon to each other as hints which suggest that their on-coming is here to be questioned (*OWL*, 94-96). The proper or unique essence of the namings "listening" and "co-responding" is their verbal essence as the "historical temporal duration" of their "enduring, persisting, prevailing" (*RHT*, 267).

In order to bring our thinking-saying into sharper relief, we call upon a thought of Aristotle. The question of whether attending schooling as learning (listening) and teaching (co-responding) can ever be sundered is one that has prevailed as enduring and persisting for over two millennia. Kisiel (*GBT*, 301) calls the reader's attention to Aristotle's offering of "the example of the indivisibility of teaching and learning to demonstrate passionate action." Teaching means to speak to an other, to *get to* the other by way of communicating, so that the other in hearing *goes with* the teaching. This play discloses and beckons in the presence of schooling, not as a leisure activity but as involved necessary attending.

Thus one can be enabled to present the claim that listening in its own turn enables responding.[16] Listening enables the human being of openness to carry what it does and does not do into co-respondence with the time-space of each moment. Listening offers itself to the human being of openness as what is unique and proper to co-responding as co-respondence-with (*TL*, 30). Being enabled to listen (learn) always already presupposes being enabled to co-respond as questioning-teaching-rejoining (*IM*, 23). Being enabled to listen and co-respond as questioning, answering, and rejoining "means being able to wait, even for a lifetime" (*IM*, 221).

Does the human being of openness, "which is the sojourning in the open, [provide] the possibility for a relation to the human being's finding its way in the first place" (*ZS*, 145)? The individual human being cannot pass beyond itself; brain scans do not reveal the other *as* the other. Questions arise out of answers and rejoinders. What is needed such that learning can always already listen as a can-be? Even if various matters of concern belong to proper thinking-saying, what is decisive? Everything that belongs to thinking does indeed belong to the human being of openness because it can always already belong to listening as its nonpossessable belonging-to (*WCT*, 158). Listening-to turns on not disposing of questions and questioning via recourse to quick and final answers (*WCT*, 159). Listening and attending belong to each other; they co-respond with each other.

In this chapter we have looked at the possibilities dwelling with listening as a surplus over modernity's enclosed, representing, conscious subject as a taking in or up of unconditioned or neutral data. There never exists a "blank slate"; the human being is of the open clearing of always already listening and sighting, of listening and encountering the call as participatory, historical matters of concern. Participation does not depend, as we have written, on the possession of physiologically articulated sensory organs. Those without eyes are capable of penetrating vision; those whose ears do not receive sound are present to the resonance of tellings that call forth "persistent, courageous thinking" (*DT*, 56).

Learning as listening is the telling which calls the human being to itself, not as a dictate, but as a commending. Commending, we remind, is a possibility that comes as the invitation which discloses and beckons the human being of openness to become involved, here in the listening of questioning as questioning. Teaching attentively waits on (attends to) the call of attendance with its disclosing and beckoning co-responding.

Chapter 8 Notes

1   See Chapter 2 for discussion of danger and risk.

2   See Franz Kafka's novel, *The Trial,* and the film *Modern Times* by Charlie Chaplin for their instantiations of isolatable, anonymous person-things.

3   See L. S. Shulman, 2005, Signature pedagogies, *Daedalus,* 134(3), 52-59.

4   See *OBT,* 1-56, and *HW,* 95-109.

5   See Chapter 3 for our discussion of thrownness as well as disclosing and beckoning.

6   See also *SW,* 29-33, 157.

7   See Chapter 2 for our discussion of freedom.

8   See also *WT,* 73.

9   See also *WCT,* 5, 8.

10   See also *DT,* 76-79.

11   See also *ZS,* 98, on measurability as "the possibility of the measuring comportment toward" entities and matters of concern.

12   See *P,* 101-111.

13   See also *ZS,* 216-217.

14   See *IM,* 106.

15   See *WCT,* 14; *OWL,* 16-19, 26; *RHT,* 268.

16   See also *OWL,* 8.

Chapter 9

Teaching as Co-Responding

> *Thank you for your letter. Your questions are important*
> *and your argumentation is correct. Nevertheless it*
> *remains to consider whether they touch on what is*
> *decisive.*
>
> *PLT,* 183

In his letter to a young student, Heidegger presented an example of his teaching. It shows a way station as the play of responding, wherein there was a response to a respondent that in its own turn retrieved itself out of a particular historical situatedness. Not only was Heidegger responding to the student, but his was a responding to his own question pertaining to the meaning and truth of being (our "engaged openness"). The student was responding to his reading of Heidegger as well as to the then prevalent understandings of historical phenomena. Both were, as co-respondents, responding to the call offered as the play of sense. For hermeneutic phenomenology, sense is sighted as a self-obtained "element in which there can be meanings, significations, interpretations, representations" (*GT,* 59). The play of sense is the call of possibility and therein teaching as co-responding can be listened to.

Heidegger ended his letter with words of encouragement:

> Everything here is a path of a [co-responding] that
> examines as it listens. Any path always risks going
> astray, leading astray. To follow such paths takes
> practice in going. Practice needs craft. Stay on the

path, in genuine need, and learn the craft of thinking, unswerving, yet erring.

Yours in friendship . . .
PLT, 186

Heidegger, according to Gadamer, during the early years of the growth of his thought, prior to *Being and Time,* "was truly amazing, even fantastic, in his interaction with students. It was amazing how he took hold of every question that was asked and saw something in it that was positive" (*AH,* 6).

Terrance encourages students to participate.

> *As a teacher I try listening so that I can find something positive in what every student says and that's not easy. If they've given a wrong answer, sometimes it is connecting with the student and trying to understand more. Saying something like, "I'd appreciate hearing more about your thinking that led to that answer." Inviting students to share their thinking sometimes helps them to see it's a wrong answer and me to learn where they're coming from. But there are other times when the student continues down the wrong path, and you have to respond with "A thoughtful answer but regretfully it is incorrect because. . . ." I learn more when students share their thinking rather than their answers, whether it's correct or incorrect. I've had students come up with the right answer but for the wrong reason and vice versa. It's taking hold of questions and listening that matters and then back and forth in conversation as much as we can.*

Teachers both shape and are shaped by the questions they ask and the rejoining that co-responding with students that questioning holds. As authors, we respond to the teachings of those authors we cite as part of this work, who in turn have responded to their situatedness and to the questions presented to them. In the formal, or institutional, sense we respond to learners as they respond to us. In the originary sense, teaching co-responds with listening as co-responding-with. In the widest sense, the human being co-responds as, and with, the world. World in its ownmost proper or unique essence co-responds as being-the-open clearing wherein human beings are allowed to participate. Can there be no isolated or isolatable responses?

Teaching is claimed by sense. In order to be itself, sense needs teaching. Teaching does indeed include the putative neutral transfer of information and/or socialization into normative modes of conduct. These are always already first claimed by a surplus which accompanies sense. Teaching cannot be restricted to the classification of mere objects, to object transmission, or be aimed at an ambiguous location assumed to be in the interior of a subject. Therefore teaching must be considered other than "the imposing of categorical forms upon" a predetermined pure schema of mathematical application and empirical experience (*HWT,* 192). There is always a categorial surplus to the categorical.

If the imposition of conceptually determined characteristics onto a given human being does not get at the phenomenon of teaching, where might teachings for a teaching be sighted, read, and listened-to? Gadamer submits that practical and prudent wisdom offers a possible ground by which the abstractions of science may be employed as a practice that is more open to its contexts. Since prudent and practical comportment first turns on engagement, it must be the basis of any theory. Practical and prudent comportment discloses the loci of meaning for "each scientifically grounded capacity to do things" (*RPJ,* 56-57). As Gadamer and Heidegger read Aristotle, practical and political modes of disclosure obtain as a fundamentally different mode of disclosure and comportment "than all the teachable forms of knowledge and their 'practical' applications" (*RPJ,* 56-57).[1] The abstract applying of "natural scientific methods do[es] not show us how to apply the results of natural scientific work to the practice of living life in a rational way" (*GIC,* 42). As we have emphasized, the rational here is meant as prudent and practical comportment, *not as a self-enclosed logical system.*

From a realist perspective, teachers are self-contained neutral conduits whereby associated self-contained putatively neutral transmission of facts is conducted. One becomes educated when one demonstrates to the satisfaction of an authority that these facts are retained and utile. From an idealist perspective, teachers are an initiated elite wherein authoritative ideals provide the impetus to train acolytes who must adhere to the overarching tenets of the manifestness of the outward appearance of the given and binding doctrine.

As we listen for the unthought in the above, we listen to the overlooking of the historical and the between. The historical, as we have written, is that which is not past, but is on-coming and present-to as alreadiness. The between is not some calculable magnitude between objects and ego-subjects but is the essential spacing and nearness of humans as singular plurals *(BSP)*.

Engaged Giving Due:
Teaching and Learning Belong Together

> *The gift gathers what belongs to giving.*
> *PLT,* 173

We have explicated schooling as attending and learning as listening such that these are *nonseparatable* moments of the human being of openness that are in turn nonseparatable moments of thrownness and understanding. The third equiprimordial moment of the human being of openness, as articulated by Heidegger, turns on discursiveness as the possibility of nonobjectifiable play of "talking with one another" *(ZS,* 214). For Heidegger, "to speak means to say, which means to show and let [matters of concern] be seen. It means to communicate and, correspondingly, to listen; to submit oneself to a claim addressed to oneself and to comply and respond to it" *(ZS,* 215). Co-responding as such is the fundamental give-and-take moment of what we shall articulate as teaching.

Human co-responding is claimed by the worldly as historically particular motives *(ZS,* 217). The human being "cannot exist at all without constantly responding to this or that address in a thematic or unthematic way" (*ZS,* 217). A single step, glance, or thought could not be possible without the co-responding of available matters of concern. We repeat in the strongest terms that our sense of responding is not to be taken as part of behavioral psychology! Respondings are not responses in the sense that they can be correlated with isolatable stimuli. Respondings in our sense are always already claimed by an excess of sense which calls for responses. By themselves these responses do not dictate respondings as necessitated by the closed circuit of psychologistic theories. We take the position that responding is more originary than a determinable outcome of an if-then methodological bias. Responding must be a co-responding which as teaching turns on the play of language as saying.

In earlier chapters we have followed Heidegger, Gadamer, and Jean-Luc Nancy as they have interpreted the phenomenon of the truth of language. As Jean-Luc Nancy, for example, proffered, "The modern world asks that this truth be thought : that [sense] is right at. It is the indefinite plurality of origins and their coexistence" (*BSP,* 10). That is, presence presences itself "right 'at' and in unconcealment" (*4S,* 96) as disclosing and beckoning. Language is taken-as a play of conversation whereby "what I say is not simply 'said,' for [sense] must return to me resaid in order to be said. But in returning to me in this way, that is, from the other, what comes back also becomes another origin of [sense]" (*BSP,* 86). *Among its range of possibilities co-responding advenes (emerges/eludes) as conversation, dialogue, argument, and dispute; it can never be finalized as agreement.* Co-responding is always already exposed as speaking-with wherein the with of engaged openness includes but is not restricted to "the effort and desire to maintain oneself as 'with' and as a consequence" (*BSP,* 87). The maintenance of some matter of concern as a nonstable substance must include sharing, crossing, and passing along. In teaching as a practice, "one must discern how language, at each moment, with each signification exposes itself as the with" (*BSP,* 87).

As mentioned earlier, thinking teaching is called forth as matters of concern play "back and forth between the human being and that which he or she encounters in the world" (*GIC*, 49). This back-and-forth play is not an attribution of "false action predicates" because "in understanding a 'subject' does not stand over against an 'object' or a world of objects."[2] A response is necessitated by the question: How is the meeting with what is freed up for the human being and in which something is said concomitantly a conversation? (*GIC*, 49). Gadamer has offered this response. "It is a conversation because what comes to meet us from a tradition poses a question to us that we have to answer" (*GIC*, 49). In any thinking that turns on what it means to be the human being of openness, the phenomenon about which one wants to know "has first to be *said* to us that we respond by saying, 'I understand'" (*GIC*, 50). That said, we concur with Gadamer when he offers that in the proper essence of a genuine conversation, "each remark calls for another" (*GIC*, 59). Co-respondings do not realize answers, for initially and for the most part they can only be read as themselves.

Questions come from Terrance as he participates in co-responding.

> *I ask the students, "How are we to think AIDS?" Questions like this are good as they call for a response, but the question doesn't close down on only making the response, a possible answer. Even as students search for an answer, they are engaged in thinking. Some even think about the meaning of the question and all the ways they could respond. These responses are not necessarily answers. It gets them thinking and we let the conversation go from there. I think we addict students to question and answers. What we want is for them to practice wide-ranging thinking. But we ask questions like "What is the major side effect for patients with AIDS in taking drugs X and Y?" These kinds of questions call out causal, analytic, and reductive thinking. Not that this kind of thinking isn't important. But questions that have no answer call out conversations and*

dialogues. The question "What did it mean to you as a nursing student to read this study on patient safety?" doesn't have an answer, but it is a call to thinking and conversation.

Conversation and dialogue harbor within themselves accident and favor offering and surprise as that which bears as suspension and buoyancy. There is a flotation present, which belongs to the proper essence of what is at play (*PH*, 57). Teaching sighted in a hermeneutic phenomenological way "is a path that leads away to come before and it lets that before which it is led show itself" (*4S*, 80). Therefore the offerings of surprises are not looked on as imperfections or as theoretical limitations but are taken as unpredictable favors offered by and as the never to be perfected phenomenon that each human being in conversation always already is.

Temporally particular finite humans must "follow after the 'something strange,' that is to say, after the stranger who is called to go under" (*OWL*, 170). Human beings as imperfect and mortal always already enter strangeness from strangeness, always already are strangers and concrete individuals. The play of possibility, being claimed by the striving to escape from the discord that is strangeness and isolation, includes a co-response which leaves the discordant as determined by metaphysical thinking to its own. In other words, metaphysics and metaphysical thinking as their own turmoil are to be left to themselves *as their own narrowly described turmoil.*

In Chapter 8, we indicated how learning was called away from its closeness to teaching. Whereas teaching was once integral to learning, the pathway of etymology traces how the separation of teaching from learning took place as modernity's on-coming course of isolated, enforced neutralization (categories). *Teach* in its varying grammatical forms stems from the Old English *taecan,* related to "token" as a pointing out of something. In turn, the verb "teach" is from the Indo-Germanic base *deik,* meaning to show. These all can be included in the complex of sense that includes signals, signs, gestures, saying, showing, indicating, and imparting a view of something (*OWL,* 123).

What is teaching as teaching? Teaching is a showing in the tradition of Old English, Germanic, and Greek usage. As a showing that shows itself, our task in this book is to let teaching show itself as a co-responding that shows itself as a play of responsibility and responsiveness. To be responsible (*obs.* "response-able") is to be indebted to, as akin to being thankful for being gifted.[3] Giving thanks is a responsiveness that is possible as part of the reception of a giving. It is not necessarily a quid pro quo, but can be a mirror play[4] wherein giving (or offering) and acceptance disclose and beckon each other.

The sense of hermeneutic phenomenology as a pointed response is not the orienting of a self-conscious, representing subject, such that everything that is determined "to be" is placed into orderable storehouses to be called forth as required. Hermeneutic phenomenology designates practical and prudent comportment as interpreting (*BT,* 62). There is an open possible letting such that that which shows itself can "be seen from itself in the very way in which it shows itself from itself" (*BT,* 58).

Let us take an example from disparate, situated comportments using the hypodermic needle as context. In a therapeutic milieu, a sterile hypodermic needle can be utilized to deliver lifesaving medications. If not sterile or not properly used to ensure sterile technique, a hypodermic needle can be a serious, if not fatal, threat to well-being. The world of addiction to drugs presents another milieu. Reused needles pose a danger to addicts in the threats of AIDS and hepatitis. One option is to provide drug users free needles in order to prevent disease. A controversy swirls around this practice, a complex debate that is beyond the scope of this book. What our needle example initially takes to heart (co-responds with) is the evident fact that a hypodermic needle is not a merely isolated, neutral tool; it is a historically particular context; it shows up as a matter of concern.

The hermeneutic phenomenological pathway is free for either recollecting or forgetting that any showing accomplished by discursive practices is a pointer "preceded by an indication that will let-itself be shown" (*OWL,* 123). Teaching is called upon, as possibility, "not to reactivate the signs and significations that are in the process of being consumed in a spellbound exposure to the compass of a meaning; it is rather to think the exposure itself" (*GT,* 51-52). The hypodermic needle as an example works to show this as a possibility.

The movement of disclosing and beckoning lets sense as the open clearing that offers the human being of openness the possibility of saying "we" or "I." Jean-Luc Nancy, as we interpret him, has written of sense taking place as the open clearing. Sense is not the between of significations but is of the practical and prudent practices that do or do not engage human beings in the discursive sharing of that which divides them (*GT,* 57). Sense calls the human being of openness to the questioning of that between.

Teaching can arise when the human being of openness lets itself belong to that which calls forth thought, never to be guaranteed and never to be "thought out to the end" (*OWL,* 155). Signifying needs a receptive listening which "is at the same time a recognition that makes due acknowledgement" (*PLT,* 209). Who *has* the signifier at their disposal? Where is the control of the treatment modality in our needle example? What is the locale of the "inertia of signification" (*GT,* 44)? How does the locus of meaning obtain which gives the understanding of the possibility for a needle to be an avoidance of a problem or to be a life saver? Signifying belongs to connotative contexts but always already is a surplus over identifications of intent, measurable/observable activity, and instrumental representation. The possible ways in which a hypodermic needle can be connoted are not necessarily finite.

Receiving and replaying (retrieving) is the heart of co-responding as an open clearing where one is in attendance with listening-to the unsaid. Is there a complete answer to the questions that the encounter with the context of the needle poses? Co-responding as conversation, narrative telling, and dialogue, and the acknowledgment that there is always already some unsaid, does not guarantee answers but only calls forth rejoinders. There is the possibility for the releasement of the heretofore unthought and unsaid.

Proper listening must include as listening-to a recognition of possible holding back and never to be known in any cognitive sense.[5] An example from the past is the use of double meanings by African American slaves wherein they were enabled by the play of language to present themselves in a twofold way in order to effect their liberation. For example, the words "follow the drinking gourd" meant that an escaped slave was to follow the Big Dipper constellation north to freedom. Responding inhering in the various holdings-back of language's saying-possibility enables attuned speaking and listening. Co-respondence does not found teaching; rather, teaching is grounded in the incipience of (emergence/ elusion of) co-responding. Co-responding discloses and beckons as opening-to-alterity and possibility.

Responding responses are not merely answers; they are engaged-openness-with *as* with-engaged-openness. The with of engaged openness is calling-attention-to as thrownness wherein listening is as possibility and understanding. At play here are offerings of offerings.[6] Do we belabor the obvious when we think the common and everyday with Heidegger, Gadamer, and Jean-Luc Nancy as they in turn have thought-said the play of a world of mortals? Heidegger risked submitting the obvious for consideration: "Speaking must have speakers in the way of speaking, they are present together with those with whom they speak, in whose neighborhood they dwell because it is what happens to concern them at the moment" (*OWL,* 120).

The Co-Responding Ways of Origin and Neighborhood

An origin shows itself by its giving forth.

EHP, 116

Nearness to the origin is a nearness which still holds something back in reserve.

EHP, 43

Encountering origins as origins means that the human being of openness is other than entities (beings, things) that make (produce) themselves (*4S,* 56). The human being of openness participates in "the consciousness in which history is ever at work" (*PH,* 19-20). To *be* an origin is to be caught in an age that possesses each one without itself being possessable. Caught in the conflict between education in the humanities and scientific forms of planning, every reflection on this conflict is itself caught in the conflict as disposed to it, necessarily responding to the historicality which delivered, sent, brought it (Misgeld & Nicholson, 1992, x). For Heidegger, truth "is of the origin, i.e., it is essentially not a characteristic of human knowing and asserting, and still less is it a mere value of an 'idea' that human beings (although they really do not know why) are supposed to strive to realize" (*PM,* 230). Truth as the movement of concealed self-unconcealing belongs to engaged openness itself.

For Gadamer, "The consciousness that is effected by history has its fulfillment in" language (*PH,* 13). Therefore, thinking finds itself responding to historicality's call to attention (summons) as a compelling which draws the human being of openness along with it. Co-respondings always already include failure to hear, expectations of meaning, reliance on one's accidental fore-meanings, being-prepared-for, fore-groundedness, any reading of what is there, belonging to history as historicality, letting oneself be addressed, and participation and sharing (*TM,* 269, 282, 290, 292, 295, 298). Responding itself as instruction about what is necessary means an irrefutable exposure *to* disclosure and beckoning: an exposure *of* disclosing and beckoning. Respondings cannot get around their own co-respondings (*BSP,* 17-19, 27). Respondings *as* co-respondings disclose and beckon world.

When teaching is read as co-responding, the division between teacher and student becomes open, serving to lead into uncharted territory. The primary phenomenon that shows itself is teaching-as-co-responding wherein teachers and students as discrete, separatable entities are allowed to disappear. Our starting point comes from co-responding itself. The human being of openness can respond by letting matters of concern show themselves as themselves. Matters of concern themselves show themselves as issues and entities engaged by the human being of openness (*PLT,*

165-186). Human beings are always already called to attention as learners by schooling, but they also exigently need teaching in order to belong-to as engaged with/by learning as a listening context which they are delivered over to (thrown as).

We have seen how the learning play of teachers and learners is given as listening.[7] Teaching now shows itself as that which enables learning to be itself. Our first steps must pursue the matter of teaching without grounding its relatedness in any subject-object teacher-student dichotomous paradigm. Only co-responding "itself is truly present"—it "is everywhere as the same in its own center" (*PLT,* 123). Co-responding as the movement of back-and-forth play cannot offer absolute status or privilege; it can only offer itself.

How can matters of concern, other than humans, teach? Sayings such as "Experience is the best teacher," among others, are available for thought if they are allowed as hints rather than dismissed as clichés. The subject-object schema is claimed by the position that teaching is only ultimately effected by the human agent who participates in representing objects as quantified or theorizable. Heidegger implicitly dealt with such teaching as a closing off of learning in his discussion of a solicitude "which leaps in and dominates" as related to "that which leaps forth and liberates" (*BT,* 158-163). But here leaping forth and liberation should not be confused with an infinite self-consciousness putatively transparent to itself (*RAS,* 16). Domination, on the other hand, is itself paradoxically dominated by the claim to understand an other in advance such that the other is "kept at a distance" (*TM,* 360).

Many conceptions of teaching turn on the assumed grounding of all putative reality in the logical and rational and absolutely self-conscious human subject. For example, course content on patient safety is saddled with a language that implies that any deviation from the prevailing logical-rational approach equates to disregard and compromising the health and well-being of the patient. The overlooked presuppositions are, among many, that nurses who will and will not be safe can be determined in advance, that the cause of the unsafe incident can be eliminated with a course on patient safety, and that teaching a course in patient safety will translate into safer patient care. Hermeneutic phenomenology calls into question the play of "conscious humans," the teacher, the taught, and teaching as a matter for thinking-saying. Teaching, when thought as co-responding attending with listening, cannot be reduced to a mere transfer of information or indoctrination.

Matters of concern in their richest sense call forth thinking-saying as they become available in relation to practical and prudent comportment. Finite openness is to be "bethinged"[8] (*OWL,* 151). Teachers and students "be-thing" (*PLT,* 181) (belong to and affect) each other as matters of concern rather than as mere constructs. Moments of responding found in teachers and students as matters of concern are the showing of all of these moments as being engaged by openness, namely, in having something to do with them as matters of concern (*ZS,* 8). Having to do with matters of concern is the authority, which obtains as *the retrievable possibilities of retrieving* allotted to the human being of openness (*BT,* 443). The human being of openness is herewith allotted "understanding as the interplay of movement of tradition and the movement of the interpreter" (*TM,* 293).

It is important here to recall that for Heidegger, Gadamer, and Jean-Luc Nancy, the human being was not to be restricted or reduced to some biologically or theoretically determined static phenomenon. For these thinkers the meaning of the human being as the human being of openness is given in part as conversation. Conversation can show itself as a presence-to as the co-originality of being enabled to talk and to listen.

Hermeneutic phenomenology explicates the "being of beings" (our engaged openness of matters of concern) as other than the correspondence of the presence of entities "in the form of substantiality and subjectivity" (*BW,* 438). The existence of what is discloses and beckons as engaged openness as the always already play of saying-showing-speaking. Sense as thought this way shows and lets itself be sighted. Showing and letting be sighted means to be available as communication and "correspondingly, to listen; to submit oneself to a claim addressed to oneself and to comply and respond to it" (*ZS,* 215). Showing cannot be attributed to exclusive and/or definitive human doing-willing. Even where showing lets itself be read via human saying (assertion), such showing is preceded by a matter of concern's allotting itself in its ownmost showing (*BW,* 410). The several senses in which engaged openness may be said are disclosed and beckoned as the dispensing which allots and allows anything "to come into its own" (*BW,* 415).

In a play of thinking that resonates for our themes, we listen to a tale of two translations of a sentence. The first is from the translation of Heidegger's *Kant and the Problem of Metaphysics,* fifth edition (*KPM,* xx). In this work Heidegger is responding to critics who call into question his reading of Kant. Part of his response is to deliver to himself a message on how to move forward on his path of thinking. His statement is translated thus: "Thinkers learn from their shortcomings to be more persevering." An alternate translation of this sentence, presented by Joanna Hodge, reads, "Thoughtful people learn more enduringly from what is lacking" (Hodge, 1994, 294-295). Thinking either "lack" or "shortcoming" shows itself as a call to teaching as co-responding with the presence of absence.

Teaching carries with it the possibility of error in a disruptive letting a lack, absence, or shortcoming show itself. Heidegger's four prefaces to his "Kant book" participate, in their own way, in a dialogue wherein identity, meaning, and subject are in transit (Hodge, 1994, 299-300). *Every* reading or translation is an interpretation, and *every* reading or interpretation is a translation. To be in listening-attendance, the human being must read and read again in order for co-respondings to show themselves as themselves. Even a denial of co-responding comportments obtains as a co-responding comportment. To let oneself into denial as the closure of the play of phenomena as letting is to let oneself be taught. The circulation of letting offers itself, calls forth thought and co-responding.

Questions of Teaching

Every posing of every question takes place within the very grant of what is put in question.

OWL, 71

The presencing of teaching and the taught turns on the offering of a complex play of questioning answering and rejoinders. These can include but are not necessarily restricted to the following:

1. Do teachers compel the production of learning?
2. Do teachers efficiently and effectively cause learning to occur?
3. What does surprise offer teaching? Learning? Schooling?
4. Can learning be facilitated without teachers? Without schooling?
5. How does teaching belong to the very character of learning and schooling?
6. Does teaching need teachers? Schooling? Students?
7. How does teaching engage teachers? The taught?
8. Does a teacher or the taught effect constancy or permanence (the purely "real")?

Questioning is more originary than the question because questioning turns on rejoinders. The practical and prudent practice of questioning is itself a rejoining response to the call that tradition and sense ask of humans. This call asks: Is "the sense of the question the only direction from which the answer can be given if it is to make sense"? (*TM,* 362).[9] Matters of concern "always presuppose an orientation toward an area of openness from which" something can disclose and beckon. Questions can emerge as the open wherein answers are made (allowed to be, let be) possible (*TM,* 366). Answers to questions are "only the final results of the last step of a long sequence of questioning steps. Each answer remains in force as an answer only as long as it is rooted in questioning" (*OBT,* 44). Questioning always already obtains as the open finite lack of completability. Therefore "to answer means to respond, in the sense of co-respond, to the essence of what is being asked about" (*QCT,* 23). Co-responding as a phenomenon is not without rejoinders.

The finitude of the human being, whether thought in terms of the facticity, mortality, or the ultimate unknowability of anything, asks about itself; the ambiguity which dwells as openness in this questioning cannot be gotten around. Phenomena ask questions of themselves: What are they? The human being asks: What are they? These same but not identical questions originate/unfold in the temporal play of the human being of openness as it is part of a tradition. The temporal play-space of "tradition can be understood only as something always in the process of being defined by the course of events" (*TM*, 373). Tradition is a game "that plays, for it draws the players into itself," (*TM*, 490) such that "the voice that speaks from the past—whether text, work, trace—itself poses a question and places meaning in openness" (*TM*, 374). Therefore, "every word, as the event of a moment, carries with it the unsaid, to which it is related by responding and summoning" (*TM*, 458).

A thread that weaves its way through this book is how modernity's claim on science is that of a "technoscientism" wherein the method is one that necessarily must provoke its results. The physical world is called on to be constantly on hand for forceful practices that demand certainty of outcome. Any teaching that falls within the purview of this claim must be assured of its response. In this sense of teaching, teaching needs a phenomenon not only to be docile but to be cognitively graspable in order to concretize its effectuation.

The responding that we are taking as possibility turns on letting the phenomenon of teaching show itself as an answering (as rejoining) such that it is not detached from questioning, but belongs to its self-issuing emergings/elusions (*BQP*, 114). The practice of a woodworker can serve as an introductory example. There are woodworkers who take great pride in responding "to different kinds of wood and to the shapes slumbering within wood—to wood as it enters into [human] dwelling" (*WCT*, 14). Wood, as it presences, responds by allowing itself to be engaged, made available, for human dwelling. The woodworker, in turn, is teacher as enabler, allowing the worked wood to enter the play of world as a co-responding of move-countermove (*TM*, 105).

Perhaps more appropriate for our purposes is to think the practice of midwifery. The midwife is present-at the presencing of a shining forth which allows a co-responding involvement that simultaneously demands attention and calls out to be left alone as a letting be. Raewynn, a midwife attends, listens, and co-responds.

> *I could sense and hear in the mother's voice . . . and see in her actions that labor was progressing well. As I look after her, all the while never forgetting the monitoring technology, I begin to appeal to her to prepare for the birth of her child. Timing is important. Technology has something to say too. Beginning mobilizing her too early can result in exhaustion when energy and strength is needed. To delay in preparing her is to catch her off guard and unprepared for a stage of labor where her participation is crucial. The mother, sensing the birth is imminent, looks for guidance and assurance. Caught between managing an embodied response and a vulnerability that threatens, she reads the situation and joins with me to find a safe place and way for her baby to be born. Together in the company of others, we both shape and are shaped by co-responding. It is a never to be fully anticipated experience, no matter the circumstances. Surprise reigns and hints prevail while danger and safety are but moments from each other, even arriving together.*

The temporal play-space of the midwife offers the possibility of discursively encountering the other as the mystery by which the human being is touched. In the maieutic practices of nurses and midwives, birthing does not allow for absolute control over the outcome but calls forth care, concern, and solicitude (Fiumara, 1990, 146-168). Because birthing is also a linguistic experience, mothers, newborns, and their extended family and community are of the world, which for its part exposes itself as instruction and origin. The otherness at play allows the human being to touch the mysterious, the curious, and the surprise of the concealed (*BSP*, 19-21).

We are asking about teaching as co-responding. We also have committed ourselves to following the path of hermeneutic phenomenology wherein we do not initiate our questioning from the putative enclosure of a conscious subject or initiate questioning about the efficacy of calculatable magnitudes or extents. If teaching is not grounded in willful human agency, what could it possibly be? A cause? An effect?

The Bounds of Teachings: The Teachings of Bounds

> *Why is it that the parametrical character of space and time prevents neighboring nearness?*
>
> OWL, 103

> *Cause and purpose are getting mixed up.*
>
> ZS, 21

We have already asserted that responding is not a cause-effect relationship that is empirically or mathematically verifiable in parametrical terms. Heidegger showed a different take on the phenomena that causality turns on. In *Being and Time* he explicated "lack-in-being" and "openedness" (*COF, PS*) as a-causal phenomena. As a "never arriving," one is possessed and defined (disclosed and beckoned) as an always already possible absence in excess to some conceptualized perfect self-presence. One is face-to-face with one's possible absence. Responding can be viewed as the mutual interdependence of that which gives bounds and one's being allotted/enabled as a letting which grants bounding as "the absence that opens the open" (*PS*, 199).[10] Finitude *is* as a thrownness which "not only specifies the limits of sovereign self-possession but also opens up and determines the positive possibilities that" (*PH*, 49) the human being of openness is.

We have, in a way, come full circle. Sheehan has written, after Heidegger, "That which is intrinsically withdrawn has always already drawn us out and opened us up . . . : the—intrinsically—withdrawn has apriori opened the open" (*PS*, 198). The opened open is the site of an always already disclosing-beckoning wherein revealed/concealed incipient finitude "engages human responsiveness and responsibility" (Mc Neill, 1999, 214).[11]

The reciprocity of "call-response and mutual need and usage" of engaged openness in its historicality lets the "counter-play of call and belonging" come into their own (*RHT,* 264).[12] We can only reiterate that "the very heart and core of the dialogical experience of" the human being of openness belongs to "a mediating middle region" proper to each as the same but not identical (*RHT,* 265-266). The word co-respond shows up as an answering to a claim and to an exhortation to prudently and practically comport oneself in responding. Taken in this sense, responding is taken as answering to as a rejoinder (*ZS,* 161). This heart and core of the middle region is not thought here as an ethereal one populated by ghostly apparitions or nothingness. Human beings, as we have mentioned, could not *be* "if there were not 'dogs' and 'stones'" (*BSP,* 18). Therefore corporeal existence "is founded upon responding [to a world]. The [biologically defined] body is the necessary condition, but not an all-inclusive condition, for one's being concerned and letting oneself be concerned. [It is] a responding, a claim, an answering for, a being responsive on the grounds of the clearedness of the relationship" (*ZS,* 185-186). The world, as its turn, responds to the corporeality of human beings by being available *to* (not necessarily *for*) the bodily.

The human being of openness is free for a finitude that calls for a response. Concomitantly "responding can only exist when one is able to say yes or no" (*ZS,* 219) as "being-free for a claim" (*ZS,* 218). One has the choice of succumbing to objectified, grasping urges such that the dialogical experience of a matter of concern *as* matter of concern is covered over (*ZS,* 219). Responding to the addressing of the offering-open clearing frees the human being of openness in letting the open clearing take the other as the other as all are drawn to co-respond to their ownmost engaged openness. The human being is free to respond; the human being of openness is free for the address of its finitude as the always already claim of the other.

The givenness of entities as matters of concern "as the responsive, clearing-furnishing of the temporal play-space for whatever appears in whatever way" calls forth to be clearly thought-said as that which is "never first posited by human cognition" (*POR,* 75). Hermeneutic phenomenology is the thinking "answer of a humanity that has been struck by the excess of presence" (*4S,* 38). The human being of openness is free for a decision as to whether the world as the text it reads is not an entity it dreams up (*RJP,* 44) or whether the world is to be determined solely as the human will to will.[13]

As we accept Heidegger's position on the need to displace thinking from the will to will of modernist conceptions of immanence to world, we also accept that *we must first think teaching without teachers.* How can this be done? Our project is to render the hidden or forgotten presuppositions of modernity questionable. In order to perform this task we start here with the notion of what a cause is. Generally speaking, for modernity a cause is something establishable which is certain of its resultant effect. It is, in this way, self-certain. For contemporary science, the certainty of an ensuing effect is a result of its (science's) manner of provoking its results (*QCT,* 15-27). In order to retrieve a non-subject-centered notion of cause, we again turn to Heidegger and Gadamer.

Gadamer (*HW,* 150) traced the historically situated movement of the word "cause" as it was wedded to thing, matter, or affair and thus called into question this word's reduction to mere causality, which in turn is instrumentalized in order to exclude other meanings. Temporally particular historical situatedness as consequential calls out pre-understandings as co-respondings. Therefore in a historically particular "conversation one does not know beforehand what will come out of it" (*GIC,* 59).

For the cause-effect practices of modernity's science, cause and effect must be pure and isolatable, if-then relationships. This position turns on the necessary freezing of time and space into eternal abstractions. According to the tenets of hermeneutic phenomenology as we understand them, the historically situated human being does not admit of this hypostasizing. For Gadamer, "pure perception conceived as the adequacy of response to stimulus, is merely an ideal limiting case" (*TM,* 90). His question turned on the possibility or nonpossibility of locating the ideal.

The co-responsibility of the play of phenomena is indebted to the movement of self-showing. Even if consciousness could be isolated in terms of pure perception as a necessary response to a stimulus, it "would never be a mere mirroring of what is there. For it would always remain an understanding of something as something. All understanding-as is an articulation of what is there, in that it looks-away-from, looks-at, sees-together-as" (*TM*, 90-91). As we have written, the historical world does not admit of controlling the always already on-coming. The "real" plays as the visible (as presence) and invisible (as absence) claim made on each human being. It is self-emergence "which brings hither and brings forth into presencing, and that which [is already] brought hither and brought forth." The proper historical essence of the real "does not lie in *efficere* and *effectus,* but lies rather in this: something comes to stand and to lie in unconcealment" (*QCT,* 160). There is surprise.

Teaching turns on the richer notion of belonging-to wherein co-responding is the primary groundless ground. Hermeneutic phenomenology leaves effect to itself if effect means only "(1) the results of that which is 'previously posited' in a theory and (2) the objective establishment of reality upon the basis of the arbitrary repeatability of an experiment" (*4S,* 54). For the thinking-saying of hermeneutic phenomenology, entities as matters of concern mutually emerge from and thereby belong to each other as the human being of openness belongs to the disclosing and beckoning of engaged openness.

The teaching teacher is not an ultimate agency or the activity of a subject. Teaching shows itself as respondings to listenings as disclosed and beckoned possibilities. Teaching itself lets possibilities show themselves as possibilities, especially that of human finitude as the possibility of absence. Teaching leaves an invisible trace as schooling learning, learning schooling, and co-responding showing. As this play, teaching is participatory. It turns on the discursiveness that each human being is claimed by.

There can be no private or universal discourses. Speech never means abstract or believed-in reason but rather shows itself as fluid discourse or conversation. The can be of the human being of openness is a matter of concern "which has its world in the mode of something addressed" (*OHF,* 17). Individuals who practice as teachers, who are necessarily learners, are those "who can freely question their own prejudgments, and who have the capacity to imagine the possible" (Misgeld & Nicholson, 1992, 58). Teachers, as such, can show (enact) pathways of questioning wherein all participants are always already open to the surprising ways that lead back to the on-coming incipience of the questions themselves.

What is "at play" in teaching? Teaching in its richest interpretive sense always already discloses and beckons as an engaged belonging together of co-responding as responsiveness and responsibility. Teaching calls forth a sighting and listening which lets teaching be disclosed in its invisibility and silence. We have followed an interpretive pathway whereby sensory visibleness and the aural sounding of phenomena in the mere psychosomatic modernist sense are seen as artificially isolated from the offerings which are released as practical and prudent comportment.

Practical and prudent comportment shows itself in many guises. An example that speaks to a significant issue of the day turns on responses to racism. There are African Americans who choose to let racists be: as the racists that racists are. This does not preclude the necessary overcoming of racism, but includes richer notions of dealing with it wherein the roots of racism become revealed, discovered, and disclosed—not to valorize them, but in order to bypass their inherent flaws. In this way the dialogue on racism is one of buoyancy such that racists are marginalized or suspended *as* their racism rather than confronted in ways which could serve to give them credence.

The game of dialogue, played in this way, includes not only players but matters of concern around which the players play and the game which co-responds as move-countermove (rejoinders) (*TM,* 105). Matters of concern do not express countermoves as some kind of conscious volition but as an availability for human apprehension/understanding (*KE,* 6).[14] One can only participate in the play of possible availability and understandability as a partner (*GIC,* 113). The discursive practices of humans show and let appear, not as a mere faculty, but as a self-reserved phenomenon, which holds its unique essence back as it offers itself. Human beings belong to discursive saying and can speak only as they respond to the hold of language (*OWL,* 107). The co-responding of question and answer as "the play of language itself addresses [human beings], proposes and withdraws, asks and fulfills itself in the answer" (*TM,* 490).

The movement of co-responding as the play of discursivity, availability, and understanding "has no goal that brings it to an end; rather, it renews itself in constant repetition" such that "it makes no difference who or what performs this movement." Therefore the game is not dependent on specific ego-subjects; "play is the occurrence of the movement as such" (*TM,* 103). Co-responding discloses and beckons as the game which lets itself be played. Said in another way, "when one plays a *game,* the game itself is never a mere object; rather, it exists in and for those who play it, even if one is only participating as 'spectator'" (*RPJ,* 27). The significance of hermeneutic phenomenology resides with interpretation as discursive co-responding such that participation is claimed by respondings, searchings for words and understandings. It is through the play (whiling, temporal-historical particularity) of these that responsive understandings can be applied to "the interpreter's present situation" (*TM,* 308). Co-responding as interpretive practice is claimed by the call of engaged openness and matters of concern. Co-respondents are enabled to listen to what they are silently in attendance with, such that they can respond with offerings of their own speech.

A question arises that turns on silence, on the invisible. What does the silent unsaid, the empirically unseen have to teach? How can there be teaching without the presence of teachers? Ontically we will, in subsequent chapters, articulate the unsaid and unseen as practices that are ignored or overlooked by theory-based or information transfer pedagogies, such as outcomes or competency-based education. Uncoverings as they obtain in this order of things certainly are not without merit. But for hermeneutic phenomenology, as we are attempting to present it, the question must remain: What is not showing itself or not letting itself be sighted? How does one keep before one's eyes as face-to-face that which does not give an answer but lets tentative responses be sighted? The human being is summoned as a mutual bearing that must submit to the silent summoning of its own particular mortality. The silence of the aphonic, the invisibility of the empirically unseeable, calls forth efforts to repeatedly retrieve sense, meaning, and significance (*HWT,* 195-196).

When thought-said in a hermeneutic phenomenological way the human being of openness does not have ears to hear and eyes to see. The human being of openness hears in order to have ears and sees in order to have eyes. There is a listening and sighting that always already issues-forth as a phenomenon.

Dara, a preceptor, describes her experiences with Wyston, a nursing student.

> *I was precepting Wyston on her first evening shift on the unit. I told her that one of her patients, who was comatose, might expire. This was a first experience for her. I went into the room with her. The husband was sitting at his wife's bedside stroking her hand. He looked pale and red-eyed. I asked, "How is she doing?" He said, "The time is near maybe . . . the time is, I don't know." "We never know for sure," I said, "but it will probably be soon. Have you had dinner yet?" "No," he said, "But I would like to go home and feed our dog." I talked to Wyston about this man's wife and their 55-year marriage. Without children or close family, their little dog, which was so attached to his wife, meant a lot to them. I told her to assure him he could go home. We would both check on his wife frequently and call him immediately if anything changed. Not long after he left, I entered her room and I knew. I could just feel it. She was dying.*
>
> *I went and found Wyston. We entered together, and as I held the woman's hand I helped Wyston learn*

how to comfort a dying patient. Then she left to call the husband. There was a lot of commotion on the unit that evening. Our nurse manager was angry and seemed like she was looking for a fight. The nurses were avoiding her as new admissions arrived.

On my way out to get some medication for this dying woman, I saw the elevator doors open, the husband arrive, and Wyston rush to meet him. She took a large cloth bag from him and escorted him past the nurse manager to his wife's room. When I returned later to the room, the husband was weeping silently and Wyston was sitting next to him, with her hand on his arm. And lying next to the patient partly under the covers was their dog. I was so proud of this student. She has what it takes. In just a few moments with this couple, she had understood the meaning of the dog to them and figured out a way for the husband to bring the dog to his dying wife's bedside. I will never forget seeing Wyston as she walked next to the husband and by our nurse manager. It was in a manner that few would challenge. This husband will spend the rest of his life reliving his last good-bye with his wife, made possible by a student nurse. This kind of caring is always surprising. It can never be taught, predicted, or anticipated, only freely given. But when you see it though, it remains indelibly in memory.

Possibility includes letting responses respond, giving them due acknowledgment and letting oneself be engaged by their invitations. These are obstacles, not to be overcome, but in the sense that they belong to possibility as the releasement of sense, meaning, and significance to understandings if only for an evanescent moment. The surprise of releasement is the breaking of stillness (*PLT,* 208). The co-responding of hermeneutic phenomenology as it teaches is located in the disclosing and beckoning surprises offered in "anticipating while holding back" (*PTL,* 209). There are anticipations which can never overcome the possibility of surprise; there is holding back which always already shelters itself as the possibility of surplus of sense.

Path Begets Path

> *Ever more openly I am coming to trust in the inconspicuous guide who takes us by the hand—or better said, by the word—in this conversation.*
>
> *DT,* 60

The human being of openness is to be always already on a possible way to a possible way. The way offers "a search that does nothing so much as cultivate the search" (*OWE,* 163). The matter of the search lets its source remain hidden, thereby allowing no completion, but showing an end. The truth of the searching pathway lets possibility remain possibility (*OWE,* 133, 151) and lets appearance appear by not directly appearing as a result of some preordained facet of human willing. The moment something is willed to appear-as, appearing as such is lost to presentness as such (*OWE,* 143). One can only arrive at matters of concern as hearkening to possibility as "the retrieving (refinding) of possibility *as* possibility, as hidden-revealed source for the incomplete appearance of" the fluidity of matters of concern (*OWE,* 152).

To be on the way is to be involved with the never to be completed origin and ordering of the on-coming of one's historical tradition. One is always already called into "the analogically unified meaning" of engaged openness as the very meaning of one's involved engaged openness (*OWE,* 156). Thus one's ownmost being possible is receptive to an understanding of the opening up of world. Possibility co-responds with self-aware possibility, not as final or ultimate knowing but as reading the unknowable—"as inconspicuous as the silent course of a conversation that moves us" (*DT,* 70). We take co-responding to mean the risk in trusting the not knowable.

Gadamer has written, "Every word as the event of a moment, carries with it the unsaid to which it is related by responding and summoning" (*TM,* 458). Words offer hints and are not only signs in the sense of a mere signifying. The word "teaching" offers a hint on how its loci of meaning can be thought. Teaching needs teaching in order to be taught in its widest sense, but teaching does not necessarily need a human being as *the* teacher per se. Proper teaching *is the letting* of learning. One does not have (possess) learning teaching schooling, one *is* (belongs to) learning teaching schooling. One is offered these to make one's own, one way or another (*HWT,* 184). Teaching is not without the human being either as ontically determined or as ontologically read as openness. The always already is a wherein such that teaching and the human being of openness are engaged with each other.[15]

Sense always already announces itself as attending-listening, never to be at the ultimate discretion of the human being. Announcing as the same but not identical is always already responded to as a co-responding but not as a fixed correspondence of one thing to another. Hermeneutic phenomenological belongings-to "can only be *announced;* [they do] not allow [themselves] to be revealed or exposed as such" (Ormiston & Schrift, 1990, 32). Announcing, then, is neither interpreting nor anticipating; it is a bringing to speech as a making known (*SV,* 220). Responding is itself as it offers itself (co-responds) as interpretation (*SV,* 227), or "all that is allowed to be understood—the hermeneutic announcement of speech" (*SV,* 226). Dialogue as giving itself from itself is "in this way to be interpreted and comprehended" (*SV,* 228).

Teaching as co-responding is not the province or possession of subject matters, teachers, or students. Co-responding is always already a "partial transcription" wherein it is "unreadable, inaudible, missing in the errance of contingency" (*SV,* 229). In the absence of abstract particulars we find sharing as a primary offering or presentation. Co-responding can, of course, be guided by an idealized goal or outcome either inculcated or acquired through empirical experience (*TM,* 315). But co-responding calls for the regarding of one's own interpretive, historical situation as well as that of possible universals and their play of sense, meaning, and significance (*TM,* 324). Herein we find partnership and dialogical experience in the intimacy of language (*TM,* 358).

Words are immediate, prior to their use as symbols or instruments. Heidegger worked to show this in the teacher's part of a conversation on a country path. The reader should note that later in the ontic sense shows itself as earlier (more primordial) in the hermeneutic phenomenological sense.

> *Teacher:* A word does not and can never re-present anything; but signifies something, that is shows something as abiding [whiling] into the range of its expressibility (*DT,* 69).

> Later on the way (of the earlier of the way):

> *Teacher:* Names are not the result of designation. They are owed to a naming in which the namable, the name and the named occur altogether (*DT,* 71).

> Still later on the way (of the nearing of the way):

> *Teacher:* The regioning of that-which-regions does not cause and effect things as little indeed as that-which-regions effects releasement (*DT,* 76).

> At the end of the way (of the incipience of the way):

> *Teacher:* Ever to the child in [humankind], night neighbors the stars (*DT,* 89).

The vastness of the ultimately unknowable is present in its absentiality as those moments of insight which become enabled as appearances shine forth as incipience. Presence and absence are neighbors and belong to each other in co-respondence. Understandings shine forth as the emergence into language. Always already finite and incomplete human beings are held in their presence by their absence as an always already co-responding.

Co-responding understandings always already self-present whether as in a text or a dialogue or with others who raise issues as matters of concern.[16] Matters of concern as themselves turn on ways of reading how, in disclosure and beckoning, one's ownmostness as "the continual returning to or staying with or repeating-retrieving of absence as the source for presence" becomes disclosed and beckoned into the heart of meaning as the finite emergence into presence itself (*OWE,* 152). The unique essence of human temporality as not being at human disposal needs co-respondent discursivity such that any disclosure of disclosive processes as not-yet-ness remains a possibility. There is a play of letting, allowing, and enduring that one can resolve to let oneself into as a going along with it.[17] It should be emphasized that this going along with is not the acceptance of any previously inculcated ontic phenomenon whatsoever. Enduring as understanding/listening and going along with as discursivity, agreement, and co-responding is "not primarily a way of behaving towards a text acquired through methodical training" (*RMC,* 277). Coming to grips with the issuing forth of what it means to be the human being of openness leaves *nothing* out of the dialogical experience of "social life, which in its final formalization is a speech community" (*RMC,* 277).

As we have written, sense as the shifting of meanings is always already on the way to never to be predetermined loci. Co-responding is claimed by the surprise of the on-coming as possibility. The human being can be properly open to what it is such that in the historicality of thinking its emergence into appearance eludes it as a scientistic monologue. Sojourning/whiling/abiding/dwelling in open matters of concern is to co-respond with the call of engaged openness and as this response to participate in (belong to) matters of concern in their engaged openness (*POR,* 86).

Dialogue, historically speaking, has led or developed into restricted notions of dialectics as one of its possibilities. This reduces dialectic dialogue to a process which is to be reproduced artificially only as empty abstraction (*TM,* 373, 376). A dialectic of this sort, presupposed from the point of view of its completion (consciousness), cannot be deduced from its emerging/eluding issuing forth (*RMC,* 290). Sense as the always already on-coming of conversation, dialogue, and the speaking-saying of language binds the participants to shared meanings. Meanings, however they occur, show themselves in practical and prudent comportment as interpretation (*TM,* 397, 458). For Heidegger, Gadamer, and Jean-Luc Nancy there are no automatic finalizable accords between texts, text analogs, and interpreters; there is only the open dialectic of question and answer as the place of co-responding which situatedness calls for.

Shakor, a nursing student, tells how after failing a course, he passed it the second time.

> *I knew if I didn't pass my pediatrics course this time, I would be dropped from the nursing program. I got two books on how to study, but they were no help at all. I was discouraged and ready to give up when my wife found a woman in our building who tutors high schoolers on how to study. She met with me and I showed her my notes and the course I would be retaking, and she said, "You are writing too much and not listening enough." Then she had me try going to class and taping but not making any notes. She would ask me to see if I could tell her the three most important points in the lecture. On the first day I got to class early with my little tape recorder and sat right in the front where I could see and hear well. And for three weeks, I did not take a note. It was hard at first, but the more I learned to listen to the teacher, the more I found myself learning. It was a different instructor so I also had to take notes while re-listening to the taped lecture, but it was easier as I knew where she was going and what was important.*

> *Then in week 4, the instructor asked me to come and see her. I was feeling upbeat as I knew I was learning the content she wanted us to learn. After she closed the door, she said, "I am worried about you passing the course this time." And she went on to talk about that if I failed again I would be out of the school and why. She reiterated how important it was to keep up with the readings and the assignments. I*

thought what is she talking about, we just turned in our first assignment and I have done all the readings. Then she said, "And you are going to have to be more responsible and come to class prepared to learn. You'll need pencil and paper so you can take notes." Then I realized what was going on and told her what I was doing. She apologized. She seemed embarrassed that she thought I was irresponsible and just coming to class and not paying attention.

This teacher had misinterpreted Shakor's behavior as irresponsible—not listening, paying attention, or learning. Without the dialogue and co-responding that occurred, the meaning of Shakor's comportment would not have been understood by the teacher as attentive. His knowing and connecting with the course lectures through listening in new ways retrieved places for him to keep open a future of possibilities of continuing in the nursing program. This experience helped the teacher to understand the ways in which predominant interpretations of comportment are challenged and made visible to both the student and teacher.

The fluidity and ambiguity of the term "expert" has been subjected to interpretive thinking. For Gadamer, "Experts have become indispensable in the most varied realms, in order to assure the requisite management and control of complex theoretical and technical processes" (*GIC*, 83). The expert in this sense is a replaceable part of a technical mechanism. A warning calls forth when interpretive thought shows that "a fixed structure of tasks is not the whole of a societal existence" (*GIC*, 83). The prudent and the practical does not necessarily reside in conforming to pregiven functions. The thinking that requires only the means for achieving pregiven purposes is technology. Gadamer has asserted that human practices must "consist in prudent choices we arrive at together" via thoughtful consideration (*GIC*, 83-84). One can easily counter-assert that this is readily said. But "what already stands in view is seen with the greatest difficulty, is grasped very seldomly, is almost always falsified into a mere addendum, and for these reasons simply overlooked" (*PM*, 201).

Kate, an experienced nursing instructor, describes her teaching experiences.

> *I teach anatomy and physiology and the students call my course "the killer course." To teach an overview of these two disciplines is impossible, even in two semesters. Knowledge is proliferating quickly, and the textbooks are huge. The online materials are excellent but also very difficult in their detail. I teach this course as a nurse and show students how understanding anatomy and physiology will influence their experiences as nursing students and nurses. Mostly it is about what does this concept, knowledge, or information mean. Still there is a lot of me going over facts and being sure that students understand. Our human sciences become more complex each day. The students have to be able to remember and recall a lot of information and make sense out of it. Not an easy course for any of us.*

Teachers do not exist as teachers without students. It is also obvious that teacher-student exchanges must take place at or in some temporal/historical place, whether that temporalized place be a physical setting or an electronic nexus (locus). We have noted that teacher-centered and scientistic curricula presuppose that teachers are conduits which merely disseminate neutral information. Student uptake is simply the effect (cognized data) of a causal agent (the teacher). However, this "subset" of the subject-object paradigm leaves many presuppositions overlooked. The roots of any causal phenomenon are not explored, nor are any of the necessary relationships to their effects, in this case trained or educated students. Co-responding to the mutual pervading of world and entities and matters of concern is offering and issuance such that all belongs to all as engaged openness (*PLT*, 201-205).

Teaching of students again reveals the ambiguous genitive that calls for the subject-object split to be opened up for thinking-saying. What is a mere ambiguity for modernist thinking is a call for a listening, which hearkens to the grant of possible dialogical experiences. There could be no inquiries and investigations without the necessary granting (offering) of whatever is approached and pursued. Offering as the prior incipience of what is investigated needs thinking-saying as a listening-to as opposed to the putting of predetermined inquiries into a concrete surrounding. Offering shows itself as "the promise of what is to be put into question" (*OWL,* 71).

Co-responding is claimed by what is ownmost to concealment. Humans always already find themselves in the unconcealed open. The unconcealed open is concealment itself as the on-coming as it calls humans "forth into the modes of revealing allotted" to them (*QCT,* 18-19). Humans, in their own way, are offered unconcealment in order to reveal the presencing of what is present. They co-respond with the call of unconcealment even when they attempt to contradict it in some way or another (*QCT,* 19). The modern tradition requires that teaching in the realist sense be an ultimately fixed and repeatable phenomenon. Idealist teaching methods require predetermined ideals or goals that are to be adhered to. However, when teaching is taken as co-responding, non-visible, non-calculatable phenomena let themselves presence as possibilities.

Co-Responding and Doing: Letting Possibility Show

Anticipating an answer itself presupposes that the questioner is part of the tradition.

TM, 377

Response stems from the appeal and releases itself toward that appeal. The responding is a giving way before the appeal and in this way an entering into its speech.

PLT, 184

To be part of a tradition one has to be addressed by (called to) it as sense. The sense *of* a tradition is the presencing of practical and prudent comportment. Responsive engagement with the emergence of sense through "language offers itself in a co-belonging with presence that sets thought a new task" (*GT,* 56). The relation between tradition, speakers, "and what is spoken points to a dynamic process that does not have firm basis in either member of the relation, so the relation between understanding and what is understood has a priority over its relational terms" (*PH,* 50). Essential showing of matters of concern hearkens back to the concealed and absent mutual belonging of showing and engaged openness as they disclose as tradition, word, and entities as matters of concern (*OWL,* 155).

When Heidegger writes, "Gesture is the gathering of a bearing" (*OWT,* 18), he is listening to the call of responding as an always already co-responding. Teaching as co-responding can work to sight the possibility inherent in listening to the neighborhood of the open region where a lack of proper solidarity constricts and flattens phenomena and thus prevents discovering/uncovering of the possibilities of a community that gathers rather than excludes (*AH,* 57-59). Jean-Luc Nancy sought to uncover/discover the meaning of community when he wrote of dialogue as no longer the manifestation of an idea in consciousness. Dialogue as possibility is the limit where the emerging/eluding sharing of voices touch each other without fusing: Limit is the play of the between. Community here is one of articulations (joinings and parts), not one of organization. Communities are not the coalescing of essences, but are exposures to the shared advent of limits (*IC,* 76-78).

The privation of presence obtains as a never to be completed presencing of absencing. Limits wherever and whenever they play are always already the presence of absence. Teaching as co-responding attempts to prepare participants for a dialogical experience of matters of concern "which cannot be openly brought to light. It is thus the attempt to speak of something that cannot be mediated cognitively, not even in terms of questions, but must be [dialogically] experienced" (*OTB,* 26).

Throughout this work we have been discussing and will continue to discuss humans as belonging to engaged openness wherein each and every one of us is always already becoming the moment of our own, not to be possessed, on-coming moment of mortality. When teaching is seen in this light, it is grounded in co-responding. Mortality's call to discursive response in humans is merely to be what it is. Mortality co-responds with humans along with the saying of language such that they are compelled to be in attendance with their possibility. Humans co-respond with mortality by describing it as a biological event, a theological promise, or the mystery of the "nothing." Mortality itself, in its concreteness, offers its teaching in order that it be co-responded with. Human beings are claimed by mortality such that they must respond to its unteachability, its unlearnability, and the always already open possibility of not being able to be in attendance at the moment which is mortality's ownmost attendance. The human being of openness can be this possibility.

Human mortality offers a hint that enables another look into what is peculiar and unique to teaching: its proper essence (*RHT,* 268). Can teaching be understood out of itself (*PM,* 223-224)? Does the self-placing into appearance of the presencing of the absencing that is human morality call for respondings? Can teaching occur where there is no producible repetitiveness or ideal?

Allowing the allowing (or the allotted) is letting "ourselves be told" (*OWL,* 155) such that in listening, "the concrete bonds of custom and tradition and the corresponding possibilities of one's own future become effective in understanding itself" (*TM,* 264). Co-responding as the differing of call and listening acknowledges that the possibility of fore-meanings as determinants of one's understandings "can go entirely unnoticed" (*TM,* 268). Teaching lets learning occur as it co-responds with the call to attendance. Heidegger averred, "Teaching is more difficult than learning because what teaching calls for is this: to let learn. The real [proper, genuine, authentic] teacher in fact lets nothing else be learned than—learning" (*WCT,* 15). In making this assertion he was attempting to think teaching as co-responding through to its origin. Recall that origin here is an incipient, upwelling presencing as the presence of its absence. Origin is not present as a datable beginning. Therefore, teaching is (1) prior to human cognition, (2) necessarily discursive, (3) the mediator of difference between engaged openness and matters of concern as co-responding play, and (4) infinitely finite and never to be possessed as a real quantity or an eternal ideal.

The above gather (respond to) thoughts that arrive via Heidegger's writings. These play as a past which is in front of each human all as an on-coming. Temporal-historical particularity is "shaped by the past in an infinity of unexamined ways, the present situation is the 'given' in which understanding is rooted, and which reflection can never entirely hold at a critical distance and objectify" (*PH,* xv). Human beings are drawn into the future as becoming that teaches them unteachability.

The proper essence of what it means to be a finite, mortal human resides in co-responding with the encircling claim of elusive emerging emergence presencing as a groundless ground that simply manifests itself.[18] Humans are called into attendance as thrown as they listen to this claim by co-responding with the message announcing matters of concern. The presencing via announcing the announcement of the message that they listen to is the bringing tidings of it. Announcing, messaging, and bringing tidings circulate as each other such that co-responding is their unique and proper essence. The circulation that discloses and beckons is what is attended. Hermeneutic phenomenology allows for non-spellbound serving such that interpretation no longer means making manifest.

Methods which attempt to dominate engaged openness are assiduously avoided herein. The human being is claimed by engaged openness and cannot step out of it to find any fixed reference point. The response of engaged openness vis-à-vis humans is to lay claim to them as finite and mortal. Phenomenologically speaking, engaged openness exigently needs humans to be engaged with it in order that it may lay claim to them. The reciprocating co-responding of engaged openness is to be available for the claim made on humans by their finitude and mortality.

Teaching as co-responding is claimed by attempts to speak of the dialogical experience of thinking as a pathway or journey. This is in contrast to the systematized neutralizations inherent in the various forms of empiricism, wherein all meanings and all truths are reduced to more "sensory intuitions and stipulated systems of particular types" (Dahlstrom, 2001, 77-78). Therefore we remind the reader of Gadamer's thought that a text or text analog itself, and not a system or type, calls for interpretation to take place only in the way the text calls for it such that "the apparently thetic beginning of interpretations is, in fact, a response, and the sense of an interpretation is determined, like every response by the question asked" (*TM,* 472). The encountering, saying, discursivity of human beings is always already found as answers and rejoinders. It should be kept in mind that responding does not necessarily show up as a response to a question. Responding can show itself as "the breadth of vision, the depth of thought, and the simplicity of saying" which shines, intimates, and ineffably abides (*OWL,* 184). Thus discursivity in its broadest sense is "always an answering— [that] remains forever relational. Relation is thought of here always in terms of [disclosure and beckoning] and no longer conceived in the form of a mere reference" (*OWL,* 135).

The human being is engaged-as-language in its always already on-coming temporal and earth-bound inceptual melos (*OWL,* 98-101, 147). The reader is called on here to recall *Ako* as an exemplification of the richness of earth-bound calling-saying. The melos of earth-boundedness holds sense *as* sense which co-responds with matters of concern as "the interjoined modes of giving: sending and extending as the extending and sending which opens and preserves" (*OTB,* 20). The human being of openness is allowed by the call of sense to think co-responding. Thinking and teaching are marked by their belonging together with language; teaching thought in this light is never at a distance from the saying of language. If it is allowed that "thinking, as co-responding, is in the service of language" (*WIP,* 93) teaching is served by language on the pathways of question, answer, and rejoinder. Paths extend themselves as they "allow the posing and answering of questions"

(*WIP,* 21). Paths send places as the sites "from where one questions" such that "both the point of departure and the scope of questioning" are given as ground (*4S,* 22). Temporally particular grounds call forth thinking and teaching in their co-responding, saying essence.

Cecelia tells of her experience with storytelling.

> *I'm a new teacher and wanted to use a lot of stories from my practice in the community nursing course I was hired to teach. I am very into calling out stories in my clients as a way of knowing and connecting with them. So I looked at what they call case studies in the book I was supposed to use. But as I read them, I thought, these are not stories! In fact, I found them boring. They were obviously crafted to make certain points about what students were supposed to look for or pay attention to in their clients. The people in these case studies were objects with names like Mr. L. Missing was the heart and soul of the experience, people with real names and faces who we remember and recall not as case studies, but as stories in our lives along a path.*

The circulation of teaching is served by letting the always already possibility of finite knowing and existence be called forth. It is in the play of calling and re-calling that the human being of openness is called upon to always already "become the author of an existence over which" it never has "absolute authority" (*GBT,* 435). The human being *of* openness as the non-objectifiable human situation is not a person. Rather, "'It' calls" (*BT,* 320); "It gives, It gives to understand, which means that It of itself discloses" (*GBT,* 433). The "it" is not some otherworldly agent but is (shows as) a letting wherein the self-presencing of presence is allowed that can be understood as disclosing and beckoning. The giving as an offering is a letting that calls as it holds itself back and withdraws (*4S,* 59-60). Disclosing and beckoning is a letting, not a production.

Questionings allow rejoinders. Rejoinders to a question are "not exhausted in an affirmation which answers to the question by determining what [one is] to understand by the [word teaching]. The answer is not a reply, the answer is rather the co-responding which responds to [engaged openness]" (*WIP,* 60). This latter play is not the affirmable or decidable but is the differentiating movement of proper openness—disclosing and beckoning "which is the undecidable itself, neither presence nor absence, neither inside nor outside" (*DH,* 216). There are not binary oppositions here but the issuing-forth of difference, which is interpreted as "meaningfulness or language" (*DH,* 217), sense or discursivity. Therefore it can be said that there is rejoining as "an answering prepared by questions, an answering which attempts to adapt itself to the matter with which it is concerned" (*OTB,* 25).

Responsive comportment (*PLT,* 209-210) is responding as the responsibility of responsiveness. The responsiveness of responsibility is "the precondition for sufficiently characterizing the 'step back' and for being able to risk it with the required clarity; not as a doing of one's own, but rather from the compliance towards a [belonging to] call that is still held concealed in [revealing/concealing] itself and thus still remains reserved for thinking" (*4S,* 93). It can be read (sighted, listened-to) as what evokes thinking-saying; what "calls for (invites, urges, exacts, demands, provokes) thought" is a "condition of possibility backed by necessity, a harsh reality that 'obliges' thought, a brute facticity that 'voices' its demands louder than words" (*GBT,* 433).

Co-responding lets the unsayable speak "in the service of language" such that the narrative telling possibilities that gather themselves as language "intercede on behalf of language" and thereby give generously "of themselves" (*WIP,* 95). Answers to questions show themselves as the presuppositions they are such that the way in which one asks and answers questions reveals itself as the rejoining way proper to the questions.

Co-Responsiveness and Co-Responsibility

> In . . . co-respondence—which defines our co-responsibility—there must be something that does not close the exchange but, on the contrary, institutes and relaunches it.
>
> FT, 299

What has been unspoken up until now is teaching as co-responding wherein it is taken as the play of co-responsiveness and co-responsibility. Kisiel has written of the ineffable play of retrieval whereby a text is always already instituted and reborn in "different contexts and at different times" (*HWT*, 195). Teaching is the co-responsive self-presentation of world. It is not the formation of absolute, quantifiable knowledge but is the address of finite possibility as infinite possibility. Teaching, taken-as a text, is a nearness which speaks poetically, not as a series of linguistic tropes but as a gathering of meanings that speak as the difference of temporal and historical sense in new ways at different times.

The mutual intra-play of schooling as attending, learning as listening, and teaching as co-responding is akin to a melos: a melodic line wherein these phenomena are never without each other and are always already moving along as difference. We have attempted to explicate teaching in its phenomenal ground as an offering that has givenness but no realized or idealized giver, neither as an objective or as a theoretical determination. Offering obtains as an essence—not as the materialized typification of a fundamental building block or the abstraction that obtains as a theory of everything (these *all* amount to the same)—but more like an "essence" that wafts on a breath of air as an on-coming that goes and a playing forth that comes.[19]

Teaching is first and foremost a dialogue. If we are to let learning occur, we must advert to the mutual interplay that we have uncovered. Teaching as a co-responding dialogue needs the speaking of humans. The human being is claimed by the play of matters of concern in order to be who it is. Circling around, the human being catches sight of the calling play of language in its naming power. The facticity of the human being obtains as dialogue. Each and every reading is a dialogue with sense and of co-responding. Each dialogical human being is responsible for sense in that sense is not the product of a fixed signification. A fixed, signifying response would saturate the offering of sense, thereby precluding the possibility of responsibility as co-responsibility (*FT,* 297). This is not to say that each co-responding dialogue bears fruit.

Co-responding calls forth teaching wherein co-thinking-saying as proper "thought remains open to more than one interpretation" (*WCT,* 71). The open clearing of co-thinking-saying is "movement beyond the self toward the other" such that "this excess of the other in the self, is both sense and responsibility." Called-thinking-saying is "the sense of the responsible *praxis* of sense" inclusive of "each in the other and each for the other" (*FT,* 297). Co-responding and co-responsibility are not seen by hermeneutic phenomenology as mere exchanges of information or as some collective indebtedness; rather they are the offering (disclosing and beckoning) of sense and responsibility that are not a possession but are what each one has but does not possess. Dialogue is sense that may be written, spoken, or neither of these in its privative absence. What matters is the self-presencing of dialogue as a prologue to the proper dialogical essence of discursivity (*OWL,* 52-53)—the enabling possibility of the belonging-to-sense of the human being of openness as exposed, disposed, and attuned. Belonging-to shows itself as the finitude of the sharing of sense. Sense takes place as the temporal-historical particularity of the unique each time singular plurals as their response-responsibility. Jean-Luc Nancy avers that "sense is the lot, the share of existence, and that this share [as sharing out[20]] is divided between all the singularities of existence" (*FT,* 13).

For Narrative Pedagogy, teaching gathers as a play of co-responding, responding to the temporally particular abiding/whiling/sojourning of schooling and learning. In their turn, schooling and learning respond to teaching by being sense as a surplus of sense. Schooling as a call to attention and teaching as co-responding can be without formal schools and teachers. Learning, however, cannot exist in the absence of the singular plurality of learners. As listening, learning is drawn along by the absence of the listenable. Schooling and teaching exigently need learning and can only let it occur.

The way to schooling learning teaching is to let this intra-related phenomenon be held open and "useless." In and of this way, this phenomenon cannot be made into anything but is thought as it offers possible insight of itself. In our thinking-saying in the ensuing chapters we will give thought to how possibility can always be grasped in a rich and timely way. Heidegger has written that the issuing-forth of questions always already sojourns as the call of that matter of concern to which the questions are presented (*OWL*, 71). Let us abide with a way wherein there can be an enabling to sight and listen to *the encircling call* that temporally and historically allows and demands (is concomitantly available for/as) sighting and listening. The reader can thereby decide if teaching occurs here.

Chapter 9 Notes

1   See also *HPM,* 299.

2   See Chapter 3 for the exploration of the fundamental presencing of understanding as phenomenon.

3   See Heidegger *WCT,* 138-147, and Richardson, 1974, 480, 601-602, 604, for thought as thanks-giving.

4   See also *PLT,* 165-186.

5   We have touched on this essence of language in our discussion of *Ako* in Chapter 7.

6   See *GT,* 55-56.

7   See Chapter 8 for our discussion of learning as listening.

8   For further discussion on thingness and being "bethinged," consult *ZS,* 137, 143, 231; *DT; PLT.*

9   See also Sheehan, *GT,* 303-313.

10   See also *QCT,* 7-10.

11   See also *QCT,* 41.

12   See also *KE,* 9-11.

13   See also *EP,* 95-110, on the will to will.

14   See also *BT,* 114-122.

15   See also *KE,* 9-10.

16   See especially *TM,* 362-379.

17   See also *OWE.*

18   See also *4S,* 80.

19   The authors wish to thank Fred Kersten for this important insight.

20   See Raffoul, 1993, xx-xxvii, for "sharing what cannot be shared" as the very between of co-appearing.

Chapter 10

Enabling Narrative Pedagogy

> *Richness is never mere possession; still less is it the consequence of possession—for it is always the very ground thereof. Richness is the abundance of what grants the possession of one's own [engaged openness],in that it opens the way to its [disclosing and beckoning]and has an inexhaustible command to become ripe for what is one's own.*
>
> *EHP,* 154

Hermeneutic Phenomenology and Narrative Pedagogy Belong to Each Other

The enacting of hermeneutic phenomenology calls forth Narrative Pedagogy, a research-based nursing pedagogy.[1] The method of Narrative Pedagogy studies and Narrative Pedagogy *belong to each other* such that their concomitant enabling and enacting can be made thematic.[2] The enacting of hermeneutic phenomenology lets schooling learning teaching as a co-occurring phenomenon show itself such that it can be called forth as a unitary theme.[3]

Narrative Pedagogy becomes enabled by teachers and students in the same interactive way as it is elucidated by hermeneutic phenomenological scholars. *Inseparable from its method, Narrative Pedagogy can only show itself as enabled when it is enacted as hermeneutic phenomenology.* The pathway of this method, often referred to as philosophical or phenomenological hermeneutics, should not be conflated with the restrictive scientific sense of method as mere research design and data analysis. Rather, in hermeneutic phenomenological studies, method obtains as a pathway of scholarship that is undertaken by all participants as a co-relating (give and take) experience.[4]

Enacting pathways of interpretive scholarship does not preclude descriptions of specific pathways. In hermeneutic phenomenological studies, terms from scientific scholarship are often used in a different sense in order to describe the ways in which the tellings of narrative data are analyzed. Findings, which show themselves as narrative tellings, are identified and presented.[5] The difficulty with this approach is that the mere use of terms is not sufficient to capture what the method is about. Hermeneutic phenomenology is a play of moments, and as such, findings that call out thinking resist capture. For example, findings in a particular interpretation of a theme, pattern, or converging conversation will often present, evoke, or invite richer ways of thinking in the interpreter-reader—indeed the evocation of rich understandings is the meant of hermeneutic phenomenology.

In hermeneutic phenomenological studies, readers are engaged and participate in the interpretations which show up in the findings. In order for the interpreter-reader to show the reader-interpreter where the interpretation arose in the text, welded quotes and exemplars are presented in the findings. The reader-interpreter can either accept or reject the interpretations proffered. The text, or in this case the narrative telling, shows itself as an issuing forth wherein reading and interpreting are the same but not identical. Agency is rendered as play rather than as a discrete fact.

Likewise, questionings that have arisen during the interpretations show up as findings that present, evoke, or invite thinking in the reader. Particular thoughts that occur to the reader can never be predicted or controlled. Terms like "findings" in hermeneutic phenomenological studies cannot be used to imply a-causal, if-then applications such as those that occur in scientific studies. Descriptions of method as pathways of scholarship (*È méthodos* —to-be-on-the-way) present narrative tellings as converging conversations in order to make thematic schooling learning teaching, that is, interpreting stories of schooling learning teaching and *dialoguing about* the play of presuppositions' possibilities. Presuppositions as an always already surplus of meanings show the possibility of the nonpossessability of their origin (incipience).

Narrative Pedagogy and Phenomenological Hermeneutics: Enacting È méthodos

How is one to think enacting of hermeneutic phenomenology as methods-on-the way or pathways of scholarship that enable the converging conversations of Narrative Pedagogy? Disclosing and beckoning discloses and beckons the engaged openness of matters of concern. Hermeneutic phenomenology as enacting the engaged openness of matters of concern in its turning enables Narrative Pedagogy. The turning of Narrative Pedagogy can become a reciprocating enabling as an enacting of hermeneutic phenomenology. What can this turning-reciprocating mean?

Converging conversations, as they participate in Narrative Pedagogy, let presuppositions become themes through dialoguing about or explicating forgotten or overlooked assumptions.[6] The interpretations of teacher and student stories from transcribed interviews (narrative data) have revealed recurring threads or *themes.* As those threads proliferated, patterns showed up. In hermeneutic phenomenological studies, themes and patterns as phenomena are taken-as foci in order to organize the belonging together of thematic showing-up. Converging conversations enable themes as patterns to be presented as findings (in our case, as concernful practices) for preparatory consideration cum publication.[7]

We have found a series of converging threads that brought to conversation the *Concernful Practices of Schooling Learning Teaching* (we will describe these in Chapter 11). These were revealed in themes and patterns identified in our narrative data and extant research. These patterns and their attending concernful practices are tentatively identified below for readers to consider as they let our converging conversations be sighted and listened to.[8] The reader should always be cognizant of the fact that our concernful practices are findings that showed up in our research and should only be taken as their possibilities. Other studies are possible that would let a panoply of additional (or lesser) numbers of concernful practices show themselves. Concernful practices belong to the each time of their showing they are not generic.

Concernful Practices of Schooling Learning Teaching

Presencing: Attending and Being Open

Assembling: Constructing and Cultivating

Gathering: Welcoming and Calling Forth

Caring: Engendering of Community

Listening: Knowing and Connecting

Interpreting: Unlearning and Becoming

Inviting: Waiting and Letting Be

Questioning: Sense and Making Meanings Visible

Retrieving Places: Keeping Open a Future of Possibilities

Preserving: Reading, Writing, Thinking-Saying, and Dialogue

Converging Conversations

Converging conversations offer themselves as the heart and soul of phenomenological interpretations. In bringing to conversation these Concernful Practices, we invite readers to participate in the play of our narrative tellings as sighting and listening. Practices and understandings, otherwise covered over, are unconcealed as refocused and articulated loci of meaning. Thoughts come to reader-interpreters out of traditions and practices. Thoughts as such are other than willed, dictated, or predicted. A way for the reader-interpreter to participate in a converging conversation is to follow the movement of showing, or to follow what is let show up. In order to let showing reveal itself as showing, scholars participate in making visible, cycles of their interpretation's presuppositions, which in turn are always already on-coming.[9] Thinking-saying as itself calls forth and lets the free become the possibility for something to reveal itself, always with the caveat that there is always already the possibility of concealing or error. In contrast, the purview of mere calculating processes restricts the concept of freedom such that it is the property of the "rational" subject. Interpreters seek to enact hermeneutic phenomenological thinking-saying as they are free for recognizing what cannot be willed to appearance.

Thinking as such is a language experience, which includes thinking-saying and is thus an offering that can only be received as tradition and historicality.[10] *Converging conversations are never presuppositionless.* They work to demonstrate a way of enacting hermeneutic phenomenology through making thematic or explicating (questioning, answering, rejoining, and interpreting) presuppositions in order to enable the circulation of Narrative Pedagogy to show up. The making thematic of schooling learning teaching, through cycles of interpretation, dialogue, and critique, focuses on converging conversations and is thereby not meant to argue one position or another down, but is meant to lead to richer understandings of the givens of positions and to work in bringing out their strengths.

Hermeneutic phenomenology as it manifests itself in Narrative Pedagogy and converging conversations is not about abandoning one strategy or approach to teaching or learning for another, though this may happen of its own accord. More importantly, converging conversations attempt to keep everything open and problematic— freeing up sense as the unique, proper essence of boundary as unfolding such that richer understandings can come along. To posit that converging conversations can be willed belongs to the danger of being claimed by the thinking that absolute power over everything is the ultimate destiny of the human subject.

Sojourning face-to-face with the finitude of the human being is the phenomenon of schooling as attendance. Not to be gotten around is the self-presence of the presence of schooling as the attendant necessity of being-with. Schooling is more than curricula, physical or electronic sites, and participants. Schooling is necessary for the human being to be in the world at all. Matters of concern school the human being by their available presence; human beings school matters of concern via involvement with the availability of matters of concern. This interaction could not disclose and beckon itself if there were not the sameness of intratwined involvements.

Narrative Pedagogy is revealed in the hermeneutic phenomenological analyses of the experiences of students and teachers.[11] The preserving of thinking and interpreting is central to the enabling of Narrative Pedagogy.[12] Explicating themes and patterns through cycles of interpretations both enables Narrative Pedagogy and extends Narrative Pedagogy research. These cycles transform understanding of schooling learning teaching as an ontological co-occurring phenomenon. Both explicating themes and patterns *and* presuppositions are ways to enact hermeneutic phenomenology in order to enable Narrative Pedagogy.[13] The interpretation of narrative telling as sense enables Narrative Pedagogy and lets presuppositions show up.

Nursing calls for nurses. The schooling *of* nurses belongs to the nurses *of* schooling as a reciprocal belongingness. Nurses need to be schooled and schoolable. Kari, a nursing instructor, describes her experiences on the Admissions Committee.

> *Being on the Admissions Committee for a long time, I have talked with a lot of entering students and have then seen how they do in nursing school. But if you were to ask me if we know what the admission requirements should be for students so we could be sure that those we accepted would be successful and those we turned down would not have been successful, I would have to say, yes and no. There are all kinds of admission tests to ensure that students meet certain levels of competency in math and science. Yet we still have students who pass them and have trouble calculating drug dosages. With reading skills, writing skills, and the ability to communicate, the problem is how to measure them. And for faculty to agree on what level of achievement or score students have to have on these tests to be admitted is nearly impossible and is an area where we often change our minds. Identifying what students absolutely need in order to succeed is impossible*

to predict. We do our best identifying competencies to protect both students and patients. Likewise it seems like we want to get admission requirements down once and for all. Yet admission requirements change, too often sometimes. Like the admission GPA depends a lot on the pool of students who apply. Maybe admission requirements are necessary but they are never enough.

In my experience what really matters is a nonmeasurable kind of openness, ability to listen, curiosity, or paying attention to things. Some students are cognitively gifted, but they suffer in complex situations where answers are not clear. Or they have trouble organizing their days and attending to unexpected situations that occur. Some may be easily distracted by concerns for things like socializing. Or they may be very opinionated and intolerant of any ambiguity and not open to anything other than their view of the world and the ways they think things should be. Relating to others can be challenging for them. These kinds of things are a gray area, full of uncertainty. I have no ideas about how to measure being respectful or being a good listener. I do know we as teachers don't talk enough, and with the students too, about trying to decide who gets in and who does not get into nursing schools! Admission requirements have to be certain and clear, and this really necessitates that we all put our heads together. The students may have some great ideas or they may not. Talking amongst each other about admission requirements and who gets in and who doesn't is what matters. Not to have this important conversation in my view has a negative impact on our profession.

Olivia, a nursing student, relates her thoughts and reveals a contemporary theme of schooling of nurses and concomitantly the nurses of schooling. She reveals her admission experiences as she relates how she both attends to and is attentive of schooling.

I am not a strong student. I am a single parent with three pre-schoolers and I work two jobs to make ends meet. The sciences are especially hard for me because I don't usually have time to figure out what I need to know and then memorize it. I do OK in psychology and growth and development courses where I know the field better just from living. When I finished the nursing prerequisite courses, I only had a 2.1 GPA and all the nursing schools in my area had long waiting lists, some five years long. The baccalaureate programs rank order GPA, and some schools were only admitting students at 3.4 GPA or above! So my only hope for admission was a two-year program, which had lower admission GPAs. Then later I can enroll in a completion program to get my bachelor's degree in nursing. Would I pick another career if I had known this in advance? Probably. I need a job and a good job with security. I was told by my academic advisor several years ago that this was a good career for me because the starting salary is good and they always need nurses. It's taken me a long time to finish my prerequisite courses.

In my heart I've always wanted to be a nurse. Then a nursing shortage came along and caused a lot of students to enter nursing programs. Schools have a shortage of nursing instructors and only so many clinical placement sites. What this all means is there will be no place for me in nursing until the shortage is over and average students can join the profession again. I understand that schools must require a certain level of GPA, but my cousin went into nursing

> *eight years ago before the shortage with a 2.0 GPA*
> *and was accepted, no problem, and did just fine.*
> *Now that very same school has a waiting list of three*
> *years and an admitting GPA last semester of 3.0.*

Schooling as a pathway lets teachers and students reach what reaches out for them by touching them (*OWL*, 91). In their own way, the above two narrative tellings show a converging conversation. It is not necessary that participants talk directly to each other in order for there to be a converging conversation. Through cycles of questioning and interpreting across narrative tellings, meanings emerge (present themselves). The significance of other meanings recedes but they are always present in their absence. The meaning of admission criteria for Kari and Olivia is their situatedness. When admission requirements are published, students assume that they are or are not eligible for admission. Hidden from view is the assumption about how the pool of applicants influences what ends up being the admitting criterion, in this case the exclusive focusing on the reasons for a given GPA.

Kari, aware of the problems with this assumption, says, "*Yet admission requirements change, too often sometimes. Like the admission GPA depends on a lot on the pool of students who apply. Maybe admission requirements are necessary but they are never enough.*" Her concern as a teacher is that admitting GPA is "necessary" but "never enough." Focusing on the constitutive impossibility of predicting which students will and won't succeed in the nursing curriculum, she nonetheless assumes that all students "*need to be open-minded, good listeners who are attentive and relate to others in safe, fair, and respectful ways.*" Her concern about how to measure or ensure this in students, though recognized, is held by the restricted enclosure of measurement.

For Olivia, GPA is linked with long waiting lists that through competition have raised the bar, making her ineligible. Her assumption is that the only way she will gain admittance to a profession she values is to wait out the shortage. She thinks that only an oversupply and a decreasing pool of applicants will bring down the minimum GPA. Unexplicated is the possibility that even with a smaller pool of applicants, if they were increasingly talented the admitting GPA would be still high. The opening of a new school of nursing in the area could decrease the waiting lists, and an increase in the numbers of instructors in the local schools of nursing could cause admitting GPAs to go down because more students might be able to be admitted. The bringing of these voices into a converging conversation reveals how professional membership and diversity are influenced by supply and demand. The economics of the workplace resonates into educational preparation programs. As well, the ineffability of establishing admission criteria that are valid and reliable for all students is presented as a matter of concern.

A theme embraced in both these narrative tellings is the modernist *quest for certainty.* Kari's concern to have more certain admission criteria and Olivia's concern to be certain that the criteria identified are in reality the ones that will determine her admission reflect the theme Admission Requirements: A Quest for Certainty. Kari hints that the possibility of living in the uncertainty of admission requirements is in play:

> Admission requirements really have to be certain and clear, and this necessitates we all put our heads together. The students may have some great ideas or they may not. It's always talking about admission requirements and who get in and who doesn't that maybe matters. Surely to not to have this important conversation is dangerous!

The assumption that schools of nursing should or can or do respond to the call for more nurses during a shortage lies unexplicated. Assumptions as the play of this thrownness and disposedness call forth the possibility for converging conversations with other participants. A group of nursing students converse about the school's dress code and the uncertainty they experience when it is enforced.

Cindi: *I hate the way the personal appearance code is enforced. It's like up to each teacher to either enforce it or say nothing.*

Aiden: *Thank goodness most of them say nothing. I have a lot of body art.*

Sharmiel: *There is a woman who is a transfer student and she told me that in the school of nursing she came from, the dress code required that all body art that was visible be covered with tape. She had a small rose on her ankle that she covered.*

Aiden: *I had a clinical instructor once who looked at my bracelet body art that has my family shield and told me that I should have thought about my patients before I got my "tattoo."*

Cindi: *That's outrageous. Did she make you do anything?*

Aiden: *No, but I knew she did not approve. It is hard when your teacher is discriminatory without expanding on her reasons.*

Sharmiel: *Would it have made a difference if your patient said something like you should have thought about others before you got a tattoo?*

Aiden: *I would have accepted her feelings and then talked to her about my family shield and what it means to me. I would tell her our family shield was designed by my uncle and contains embedded in the pattern the numbers my great-grandmother wore as a concentration camp survivor. I honor her—this amazing courageous woman—every day of my life when I look at my wrist and see our family shield.*

Cindi: *But what if it was a neo-Nazi emblem?*

Sharmiel: *Did you tell the clinical instructor your story?*

Aiden: *She made it clear she was not listening, but rather telling. She came across very closed minded.*

Sharmiel: *That was an assumption you made. But what if your patient was closed minded? They often are, but we still try to connect with them and have a conversation. You only know if your assumption is wrong if you try to connect.*

Cindi: *There should be specific guidelines about dress code that would prevent teachers from making these kinds of statements.*

Aiden: *I don't agree. Actually I think Sharmiel is correct. We need to talk about body art and more than that, about a personal appearance code and its place in the school. Let's look at how appearance is part of learning and caring. Because it can or cannot influence both of these. Guidelines aren't the answer, but talking and listening to each other is. We should have this conversation with our teachers and each other. How does wearing body art, or a head scarf, or a mini skirt uniform affect learning or caring?*

Cindi: *But there should be a dress code to tell students they have to be clean.*

Sharmiel: *Why? Have you ever known a student to be dirty? And if so, would a code help? I mean what would you do if you saw someone appear dirty and disheveled? You'd talk to them, right? You would say, "How are you doing?" but your question is a good one. Should we have an appearance code at all? What function would it serve and how would faculty and students experience it?*

In this converging conversation, three nursing students have explicated the presupposition that a code provides students with certainty on acceptable and unacceptable appearance. They have participated in cycles of interpretation, exploring the meanings of a code. For example, how can any code address body art? Aiden tells of the meaning of his family shield as body art. Simple rules, like "Cover all visible body art," in their simplicity gather in ways that lend themselves to multiple interpretations. They can be profound and complex in their simplicity. Small acts speak. To require that a student cover the family shield on his wrist resonates with multiple questions that call out thinking-saying.

Conversations like these begin to enact hermeneutic phenomenology enabling Narrative Pedagogy. In this enacting of hermeneutic phenomenology, the shift is from interpretations of the body as a physiological entity toward the bodily as a speaking, in this case through bearing the family shield. An embodied world speaks. Often nurses fail to bring a more inclusive wisdom into their practices as teachers. The conversation about what the body art means lies silent as we hear of the pejorative response of the clinical instructor, who refers to the family shield as merely a "tattoo."

Thinking-Saying as È méthodos

Questionings arise: How is hermeneutic phenomenological thinking different from "reflective thinking"? Is a limitation of reflective-calculative thinking its focus on merely recording past events? Hermeneutic phenomenological thinking-saying works to sight/listen to the past as forerunning the human being of openness. Does hermeneutic phenomenological thinking-saying offer a path of scholarship in which interpreting is in the present, along with the already of past experiences and the becoming of future as a showing up of possibilities? Not to be conflated with reflective-calculative thinking, hermeneutic phenomenological thinking-saying describes "what is" but does so in a way that lets the open clearing of a matter of concern come along.[14] The enacting of hermeneutic phenomenological thinking is an *assembling of moments of insight which advene on a given pathway.* To be underway, one can choose to undertake the risk of a leap onto a path that guarantees no outcome, but lets possibility *as* possibility arrive.[15] This kind of thinking includes identifying and describing the presuppositions— assumptions, prejudgments, and background understanding— within the telling of narratives as storied experiences. Human finitude is the open "it" which calls the human being of openness into the possibility of fairness and respect.

In the following exemplar, Maye, a teacher, rethinks her presuppositions. In order to acknowledge her own experiences she turns to a thinking that belongs to their play.

> *Listening more to student and teacher stories I found myself drawn into thinking about what I do. I began to reflect on and realize all the assumptions I make when I teach and I got caught up in this kind of different thinking. I found myself learning again. If you're a good teacher you're always learning something from your students, the clinicians, and keeping up with the literature. But this kind of learning is different, it is addicting—it is deep and profound and compelling, yet easy to do, exciting, and a lot of fun. The rest of that semester I found myself thinking more and all the time.*

When Maye describes as "different" the kind of thinking that is called out for her when listening to and interpreting stories, she struggles to find words for her experience.[16] Is this "different thinking," thinking that is "deep and profound and compelling, yet easy to do," hermeneutic phenomenological thinking as experienced? What does it mean that Maye is becoming aware of "all the assumptions I make when I teach"? Narrative Pedagogy shows itself as it enables a richer sense of thinking to be revealed. Is there anything that can be shown to be missing from this narrative? In this context, Narrative Pedagogy is showing up as a way that embraces explicating the presuppositions embedded in the undergoing of hermeneutic (transformative) experiences.[17] Do Narrative Pedagogy and hermeneutic phenomenological thinking-saying sojourn in a region richer in matters of concern and thereby abide beyond reflective and calculative thinking and writing. In order to illuminate thinking-saying as the prudent and practical experience of the saying of language. Narrative Pedagogy must dwell in the open neighborhood of the telling of one's stories: the relating of relating.

Making Thematic Schooling Learning Teaching

Cycles of interpreting themes often begin with explicating the familiar and at-hand. The familiar and at-hand are the presuppositions of the most common approaches to schooling learning teaching. The conventional pedagogies of modernism, outcome or competency based, are often bypassed without being named as such. In higher and nursing education literature, student-centered strategies, no matter what pedagogy is embraced, are assumed to be desirable and to reflect what good teachers are expected to do. The theme hidden in these pedagogies is the assumption that the teacher must not interfere with information transfer. Indeed the role of the student is based on the presupposition that learning turns on the mere transfer of "neutral" information.

Explications of specific pedagogies can explore how including the students as partners in learning is enacted (experienced) and can advocate for specific changes. For example, in competency-based, student-centered approaches, teachers and students are to collaborate and negotiate in identifying competencies to be learned. Critical and feminist pedagogies critique conventional pedagogies and point to a difference between the dogma espoused in the literature of students as learning partners and the ways teachers enact this commitment. In common practice, most teachers, though they try to include students and often appear to do so, continue to control the identification of student competencies, particularly when disagreements occur as to the right and responsibility of the teacher. In this way, conventional pedagogies remain teacher centered. While students may be actively involved in how these learning competencies are met, students rarely experience significant involvement in establishing what these competencies are.

Critical and feminist collaborative pedagogies or strategies, reflecting themes of co-equal or egalitarian student and teacher decision making regarding competencies, are offered as alternatives. On the other hand, is there the same danger in either teacher- or student-centered pedagogies—that one group or the other has more control over decisions and is more powerful than the other? Can ends be established prior to means? Can absolute ends be known absolutely? Even in collaborative pedagogies, *who* decides what is collaborative?

The issue that presents itself in Narrative Pedagogy is not whether students should be involved and how, but how schooling learning teaching as a co-occurring, intra-related phenomenon is *always already a singular plural.* Articulating particular traditions, institutions, and individuals in the community of singular plurals, namely the school system and its students and teachers, shifts toward the inescapable *attending with the temporal play-space* of how students and teachers *sight and listen as a co-responding* to one another. This shift embraces the centrality of conversation and dialogue. It is not who is in the center of the community—institutions, students, or teachers—but rather it is the tradition which enables how they come together such that learning and only learning can be effected. The proper essence of learning is thought here as a non-subject-centered sighting and listening that always already discloses and beckons. This is the first step back to that which draws schooling learning teaching into itself.

Sedimented Traditions

In enacting cycles of interpretation, teachers and students show how they explicate presuppositions *(assumptions, prejudgments, or background understandings)* in their experiences of sedimented traditions. For example, Maye questioned her presupposition of the traditional role of teachers or what teachers do, that is, how teachers relate to students as defined by conventional pedagogies (outcomes- or competency-based education). She described how this explication of her *assumption* created new partnerships with students. Students became her pedagogical partners. Maye explicates the presupposition of sedimented traditions that define the role of the teacher and the student in conventional pedagogies.

> *I asked the students the week before I taught the class, how I should teach caring for patients suffering with poly-drug abuse. The content in this area is vast, and it is so hard to define the competencies. I told them exactly what concerns I had as a public health nurse and I shared my thinking. What I found was that students knew a lot about the issues. They also had questions about why we don't have more funding to find better or more effective treatments and why is the payment for such services so short in most cases, when the treatment needed by these patients is so long-term and intensive. We got into such amazing discussions that the time flew by and students were not ready to leave the class. I also noticed that the more captivated they became by these discussions, the more they read (AND the more widely they read), the more they participated in class, and the more passionate about the importance of access to expert nursing care they became.*

> *This experience with these students opened my eyes to a different way of working with students and to all the assumptions I make about them and their participation in planning our times together. I had gotten so used to thinking my role was to plan classroom activities and what the students were supposed to do. You assume students either do not know anything about the subject area or about teaching or don't care to get involved in the pedagogical part of the course. Some don't; but many do and relish it! I find I am becoming amazingly more open with students about what I am thinking and experiencing as a teacher in the courses I teach!*

Another presupposition about sedimented traditions is revealed when Maye shows the *prejudgments* she commonly makes about designing learning activities and identifying course materials.

> *Instead of having the assignment all thought out in advance, I talked with the students and we now design every assignment together. And when it comes to identifying course materials, students are very tech savvy about what they like as online materials. When we worked together they found great sites to link that I had missed or never thought about. The students use streaming and download the information to their iPods so they can listen to them in between classes or on the bus. On the other hand, I was attentive to the possibility that some important information or context might be overlooked. There were times I totally disagreed with the students and even when they didn't want to do certain assignments, I insisted. The students did not want to write papers; they said writing papers was busy work. I thought they needed experience in being able to argue a position cogently. I found that most students thought they could, but after seeing their writing on their projects, I realized they could not. So we talked about this together and kept in the writing assignment.*

> *Their opposition to the assignment helped me to clarify what it was that I thought they needed to learn. And though they did not like writing the paper, I found that several said it was meaningful as it helped them express themselves clearly. And the papers seemed to improve greatly. Sometimes we disagreed, sometimes we both compromised, and sometimes we did it the students' way. Their ideas are often better than mine about what works for them. I think it is amazing what teachers can learn if they*

ask students and give them time to think about what is missing in the course or how to make it better. But teachers need to do a lot of thinking about learning. What do we want students to learn and what is the best way for them to learn? Learning is so elusive that we never talk about it. When I started having pedagogical partnerships with the students, in just one semester the entire course changed. It actually was scary to me, but it turned out to be one of the most exciting experiences I've had as a teacher. And I still don't know what learning is!

Maye's prejudgment of how students learn and the intellectual and pedagogical capabilities of students are rethought. She discovers that given the opportunity, students can cooperatively engage in identifying content for the course and participate in (listen to) learning experiences that far exceed her expectations. She learns that students, as they collaborate with her, are capable of a rich play of listening as they sight course content and develop learning activities as these show up as the play of matters of concern. Listening takes place as Maye is called to think through what she wants students to learn. She finds new insight into student capabilities "scary," yet exciting. The theme Rethinking Sedimented Traditions: Students as Pedagogical Partners resonates in Maye's narrative tellings. Narrative Pedagogy calls out overlooked presuppositions, bringing up questions such as these: (1) Has conventional pedagogy reached it culmination? (2) Do the sedimented traditions of conventional pedagogies constitutively close down on the participation of students as pedagogical partners?

The possibilities for richer student-teacher partnerships show up in narrative tellings and converging conversations.

The Unfolding of Information as a Theme

Explicating presuppositions often examines *background understandings.* Benjamin explores another presupposition when he examines his *background understanding* of how students learn.

Although he does not call into question modernity's concept of information as neutral, the unending accumulation of quanta, he hears information as a theme rather than as some absolute given.

I realized one day that students use information differently and expect it to be accessible quickly in easily "digestible" formats. There are problems with that approach, but it is not all bad either. As teachers, we can't think about this very easily because we still often read a textbook chapter or a journal article from beginning to end—boring or not, well written or not. We expect students to do the same, and that means learn like I do!

Benjamin dialogues with students about how they use information and their expectations for accessibility of information, and compares this new understanding with how the course is designed. He realizes that the course is more consistent with how he as a teacher uses information than with how the students do. He continues:

Many of us still print things out and underline, making notes as we go along. We can't imagine learning without these kinds of activities! It is not that these don't sometimes work, but rather that we rarely even stop to consider how learning actually occurs! But that doesn't stop us from requiring particular kinds of activities because we assume they relate somehow to learning. The problem is, we really don't know.

Continuing in his cycles of interpretation, Benjamin questions the meaning of reading assignments. He compares student approaches to learning content with his and calls into *question how rarely we challenge our assumptions about the relationship between these activities and learning.*

We assume, as teachers, we are good learners, the students need help, and so we dump our way of learning on them. I guess we never really look at learning closely. Everything is always about prespecified competencies, content, objectives, and learning problems. Once I got started thinking differently, I began to pay attention to how the students were learning to find information. It is hard to talk about learning because it is so invisible. I would say to the students, tell me what you were thinking when this or that happened. They showed me how when they did not understand something, they immediately went online to find the information rather than using the Internet as a last resort as I do. They shared what they were thinking about when they went into this kind of search. They talked about how they learned to judge what is credible and what was not. I learned so much about how they learned when I finally slowed down and listened and started to ask them about their learning—for me it was a shift away from what they know and don't know to how they are learning. It is watching learning show up!

An epiphany that turns on rethinking background understandings brings about hermeneutic phenomenological thinking-saying for this teacher and the students—one that pays close attention to learning. Understanding that learning is invisible, Benjamin shares how he co-responds with "information" as an answer rather than as a given. Without expressing engaged attendance per se, he sights his and the students' engagement in the course and listens to the thinking-saying revealed. This kind of teaching as co-responding for Benjamin is "a shift away from what they [the students] know and don't know to *how they are learning.*" Benjamin is following the movement of showing as learning reveals itself as listening. Even though he did not explicitly identify learning as listening, he was in attendance with listening.

Thinking-Saying as Dialogical Partnership

Converging conversations are never presuppositionless. In this converging conversation, Viktor's experience as a teacher is on a background of presuppositions that reflect the pedagogical worthfulness of partnerships with students. Similarly the worthfulness of including students as partners in evaluating course activities shows up in the stories of students and teachers. Presupposing students as partners in learning is assumed by some to be constitutive of good teaching, therefore pervasive as something desirable.

> *We really emphasize end-of-course evaluations in our school and it's crazy in a way. Not that feedback isn't good, but when you wait until so late to get student feedback to make changes, you are always designing a course for the students that just left you! I had this final paper as a course requirement, so last semester I started early in the course to take time to talk with the students about why I had it and what it meant to me and got them thinking about it too. I was surprised how seriously they took this conversation. They really got me thinking. I could change the assignment. On the other hand, the more I thought about the assignment, the more I questioned writing an 8- to 10-page paper at all!*

A pedagogical commitment to challenge end-of-course evaluations shows itself wherein students as partners in learning is initially explicated for Viktor. End-of-course evaluations of one kind or another reflect students' involvement as partners in learning. Viktor moves beyond his challenging of including the students in the evaluation of the assignment to begin to make thematic or question the meaning of the assignment itself.

Viktor asks the students for their comments on an assignment. A familiar strategy in end-of-course evaluation in conventional pedagogies is to include students as partners in evaluating the course, with a view toward redesigning learning activities and strategies. Even though the comments and suggestions received are too late to be implemented for the group offering the evaluation, teachers nonetheless do attend to them and often make changes that unfortunately are often incompatible with the next group of students. As Viktor describes his thinking, he moves away from student comments and suggestions on making changes to rethinking the entire nature and meaning of the assignment: *"I could change the assignment. On the other hand, the more I thought about the assignment the more I questioned the whole idea of writing an 8- to 10-page paper at all!"* Viktor reveals how the evaluations can become a pedagogical conversation with students that mutually touches their experiences together. Asking students for evaluations often leads to unanticipated insights.

Another presupposition of teacher-centered conventional pedagogies, frequently listened to in making schooling learning teaching thematic, is identifying themes of preserving reading, writing, thinking-speaking, and dialogue. The theme Writing Papers: The Teacher as Audience shows up when teachers require a paper as an evaluation modality in which students demonstrate their understanding of course content. Teachers often describe papers as a "chance to pull everything together" at the end of a course. These assignments reflect teacher centeredness. Even as teachers allow students to select a topic of interest to them, the objectives of the assignment are commonly teacher designed and prespecified. Based on a linear, causal view of learning, the paper is designed to provide students with an experience of "synthesizing content" (information) learned and "evidence of thinking" as application of that content.

Questionings arise: Is the synthesis of information any evidence of proper thinking? If information is neutral, why does it need to be synthesized? Can neutral information be synthesized without compromise to its neutrality? How is the application of content best evaluated? Is it through a single written paper? Why do students need to learn how to write papers? How many papers need to be written this way in order for students to demonstrate their ability to write? What do students learn from writing papers that teachers do not even intend? Is learning to write and think best taught through writing papers on topics, assigned by teachers, to be read by teachers? What audiences do nurses most likely write for in their practice of nursing?

The practices of reading, writing, and thinking are purported to be paramount concerns in all current pedagogies. Higher education devotes a great amount of time, money, and energy to developing specific approaches in order to teach students various versions of these practices. The teaching that aims at producing students who write clearly and concisely as a direct reflection of cognitive capabilities is an important matter of concern in higher education. This concern includes learning to demonstrate the ability to synthesize ideas from multiple sources; articulate an argument in writing; and use proper grammar, punctuation, and bibliographic annotation. Writing assignments are common evaluation activities for students in many courses.

Conventional pedagogies often include final papers along with a final examination to evaluate student progress in the course and determine grades. But conventional pedagogies do not take into account the issues turning on information and synthesis as a matter of concern. As we have mentioned, the vast array of neutral information cannot contribute to what information gets left out of a synthesis. The process of synthesizing is shadowed by this specter—What is it that is forcibly expelled from any synthetic fusion? And why?

Concomitantly there are various pedagogies that critique teacher-centered writing assignments and offer alternative writing strategies. Viktor rethinks what he assumed about the objectives of his writing assignment and begins to explore the meaning of the experience for him and the students.

> Mostly it got me thinking more and more about writing papers and requiring APA [style guidelines published by the American Psychological Association] and what this assignment means to students and to me. The

next semester I did something different. I thought, Is the learning occurring here other than what I want them to write for me? It seems like all of our courses require papers, and yet as faculty we rarely question the worthfulness of this! I really started to question. What are students actually learning? Are they learning how to follow orders, rules, or directions? I asked, What does the assignment mean to junior level students on their way to becoming nurses? I went to the students again and asked about the paper assignment and what it meant to them. It was hard for them to respond, but when I gave them time to think about meanings, they came up with amazing comments that really helped me learn about this experience and it changed my thinking about writing, and what we came up with was totally different.

The students wanted to have no paper assignment, but too many of them have poor grammar and writing skills. I started having them write short essays of three paragraphs after reading an article. What were the main three points, what did reading this article mean to them as a nursing student, and what three questions do they have after reading this article? I got a chance to see their thinking. They liked the assignment and the feedback they got and because I took all the articles and asked a student to "do our reading for us" and read the assignment aloud in class before we started discussing it. They were pleased because it meant they only had to read three articles during the entire class. They really did a good job writing the short essays; some even went to our school's writing lab. I noticed that more students than ever read the articles when they knew they didn't have to! I also discovered that students who use poor grammar often don't see their peers' writing and know that they have a long way to go. Why I never thought of this approach before, I have no idea! It was a simple doable change. It was easier on me to grade short papers than long final papers and the students found it freeing too. Sort of a win-win.

Viktor questions, *"What does the assignment mean to junior level students on their way to becoming nurses?"* Narrative Pedagogy can show up as teachers explore their assumptions in making the assignment (objectives) and the presuppositions they are held by as they make the link among their intent, the objectives, and student learning. Viktor begins to question how students are learning rather than what are they showing that they have learned via writing.

Questionings arrive: Does explicating the assumed worthfulness of papers, that is, the meaning of learning assumed to occur, begin to reveal alternatives to conventional pedagogies? Can listening to the students, even when the teacher disagrees, result in new possibilities for learning that otherwise would have gone unexplicated or overlooked?

Reading, writing, and thinking show up in different ways. Although Viktor *invited* the students to affirm, extend, critique, or rethink the assignment in order to show other perspectives on its meaning, not all students agreed with him.[18] Some students were adamant that there should be no writing assignment. Viktor as the teacher stood firm. He heard the students' opinion that there were too many readings in the course, so he designed short writing assignments that helped them become better writers. The assignments freed the students from the responsibility of reading all the articles.

Viktor, in enacting hermeneutic phenomenology, shows how things that stand in front of one are the hardest to see and understand. A new kind of partnership emerged here—a pedagogical partnership. Students are often asked in conventional pedagogies to evaluate assignments. In this way Narrative Pedagogy is familiar and at hand. But in conventional pedagogies, teachers match the evaluations with their intended outcomes and thereby decide whether to alter or retain the assignment. Perhaps the difference here lies in the way Viktor and the students co-respond. The evaluation of this experience is communal and dialogical; that is, it is more like a back-and-forth mirror play.[19] Viktor listens anew when he asks students to discuss the *meaning* the assignment had for them, rather than if they "liked or disliked" it. He asks them to describe their experiences of participating in the assignment and what this assignment meant to them in learning to become nurses. He learns more about his assumptions when he discovers that he has assumed that the best way to prepare students is indeed not necessarily the case.

In this narrative telling, Narrative Pedagogy frees thinking for showing otherwise hidden possibilities for re-forming an assignment. The participatory holding open of presuppositions lets meanings and dialogical partnerships show up. In this dialogical partnership Viktor listens to listening as something richer than just the group of individuals as the sum of the people involved. *Dialogical partnerships call out co-responding as thinking.* Narrative Pedagogy enables other possible meanings for partnerships that emerge as the play of the back and forth, the middle, between and among teachers and students in shifting roles and power relationships. Dialogical playing as attending to[20] temporal play-space is a back and forth of listening[21] to the call of learning and teaching as co-responding. The human being in its ontic sense of teachers and students shows up in its ontological, of openness, sense as the mutual encountering of possibility.

De-Centering the Center

The hold of conventional pedagogies is a familiar and strong one. Teachers often describe their journeys away from teacher-centered conventional pedagogies toward including students in more meaningful ways.

Nina tells of her teaching experiences in developing pedagogical partnerships with her students. In this narrative telling, note how student-centered pedagogies do not replace teacher-centered ones. With one or the other (students or teachers) in the center as a focus, there still remain issues of centeredness and marginalization, equality, and power. Rather in pedagogical partnerships Nina describes the difficulty in the identifying who is the learner and who is the teacher. New possibilities are illuminated when these roles are made thematic; partnerships become porous, fluid, contextually co-present and kept in play. Here Nina remains the teacher with the power and control over awarding grades. This ambiguity turns on the making thematic of centeredness itself. The students and Nina experience a partnership that is more than just a sharing in the design, identification, and evaluation of content. They attend to the listening call of learning, and together they co-respond, increasing their understandings of schooling learning teaching as a phenomenon. This kind of pedagogical partnership is dialogical and engenders community in transformative ways.

Nina describes schooling as the historically situated enduring, persisting, prevailing nature of this generation:

> *Students are my pedagogical partners. They are included in conversations with me at every stage, from deciding what we'll do to how it is going and what it means to everyone. It is not just sharing decision making or problem solving together. The most important thing we do together is interpret our thinking experiences for meanings from as many perspectives as we can! In my classes we are always reflecting and interpreting our experiences and sharing them online or in class. As a teacher, I share my thinking with students publicly too. You have to invite them to think along with you and give them time to consider what you are asking. This kind of thinking takes time. I think I used to keep the students so busy with assignments they had no time to think, and neither did I because I was always grading something!*

Is it possible or even desirable for Nina to coequally share all pedagogical decisions, including the final awarding of grades, or would this violate academic conduct expectations? Is it more to the point to listen to the presencing of those present as they are present to each other as plural singularities?

Once teachers are free for the sighting of the narrow conventional pedagogical roles of identifying course objectives, designing learning activities, and selecting, sequencing, and evaluating content, the students are also freed. All are freed for rethinking the above categories as ends in view. Their roles become open for joining in making schooling learning teaching thematic in order to rethink competing teacher-centered assignments vis-à-vis class participation.

Teaching as co-responding shifts an experience of content learning toward one of attending to schooling learning teaching as a co-occurring phenomenon. Hermeneutic phenomenology allows for a return to everyday activities by sighting them in a different light. Nina continues:

> *I now realize that many of the instructional and curricular problems we all just accept as given—familiar problems like too much content, not enough time in clinical courses, or students coming unprepared to class—belong to conventional pedagogies. We need new pedagogies to overcome these time-consuming challenges. I now know there are research-based alternative ways of teaching and learning and that the interpretive pedagogies [critical, feminist, phenomenological, and postmodern] give me new ways to think about these familiar "problems" that many of us have begun to take for granted as just "a given." When I started finding my assumptions, I was free to then continue with them or change them. There are now other ways or pedagogies we can use in our schools of nursing, and some of them are nursing pedagogies!*

This is an understanding of teaching that does not turn on teachers or students as absolute authorities. As Nina explicates her presuppositions, she is rethinking the familiar, what she has traditionally done as a teacher. She explores new pedagogies such that her course and relationships with students are always already transformed.

Certainty's Lack: The Always Already

Enacting hermeneutic phenomenology as an always already ongoing may not lead teachers and students to interpretations they like or support.[22] Partnerships in which teachers retain power or the "power to empower" through putative egalitarian partnerships are neither necessary nor sufficient.[23] Bringing presuppositions to conversation does not ensure that changes will follow or that the possible changes revealed will necessarily be embraced. On-coming rethinking and reinterpretation, in the presence of others, on the background of richer understandings (viewing schooling learning teaching as a co-occurring, invisible phenomenon) reveal new possibilities. There is no guarantee that transforming student and teacher partnerships from the status quo will be in a direction that is taken as positive or desirable. Certainty's lack is an always already occurring possibility.

Along with the students, in cycles of interpretations Karlee, an experienced teacher, shows how partnerships—though intended by teachers to be collaborative—are not necessarily experienced as such by students.[24] However, Karlee remains open and relates her presuppositions as a pointing to further exegeses of intentionality.

> *I began to realize that even when I thought my intentions were really in the students' best interest, when you start inviting students to thinking about the meaning of what I was asking them to do, you get a very different understanding. I learned a lot. Given the chance, if you offer students choices, they don't necessarily pick all the easy ones. Sure, a few will, but a few do the least amount possible now!*

Cycles of interpreting reveal how, when Narrative Pedagogy is enabled, the teacher's intentions are not the issue. Rather the issue is how teachers and students co-respond or comport themselves with one another. Karlee continues,

When I honestly shared my thinking—not feelings, but thinking—as a teacher and worked with the students, focusing on listening to them and being open and engaged in new ways, paying lots of attention to learning and not so much to what I thought or what I had always done that worked, I began to see similar changes in the students. I think they behaved differently because I was different, and because they were different, I was different. Sort of back and forth. I wasn't giving up my power as I was a part of the conversation, and it was more we are all in this together and they showed me they wouldn't let me down.

The students and Karlee experienced a shift to exploring what, and in what ways, they must inevitably attend to the always already on-coming concerns of one another (schooling as attending), to what they sight and how they listen with one another (learning as listening), and how they comport themselves with one another (teaching as co-responding). This shift also reveals increased attention to experiences in which learning and only learning occurs for both the students and the teacher.[25] Listening to the saying of what is said hints of learning.

It is certain that there is no lack of hints, only that hints lack certainty.

Enabling Narrative Pedagogy

The centrality of human agency for contemporary conventional pedagogies, and even within the alternative critical, feminist, and postmodern pedagogies, is a strong one whose persistence cannot be erased in an epoch in which the human being talks only to itself. To critique human agency-centered pedagogies, even to argue for student-centered ones as a way of de-centering teacher-centered pedagogies, is still to embrace the issue of human agency. Likewise, to claim coequal, collaborative pedagogies to overcome teacher-centered ones still leaves the issue of agency intact; that is, whether a pedagogy is teacher or student centered or collaborative, there remains the concomitant concern for roles. In conventional, critical, feminist, and postmodern pedagogies, the agent-subject is either deconstructed, moved to the idealized center, or displaced to some margin. All view human agency and power as central issues. That is, in these pedagogies, teachers and students are viewed as individuals—individual agents—or learners, and groups are composed of several individual agents. In contrast, Narrative Pedagogy challenges agency itself.[26] We submit these questions:

- Is depersonalization *or* individualization of learning a central concern in conventional pedagogies?
- Do teachers use "individualized" teaching and learning strategies such as negotiating objectives and developing learning contracts to overcome depersonalization and thereby strengthen agency-centered pedagogies?
- How do critical, feminist, and postmodern pedagogies critique and call attention to the inequities in agency- and teacher-centered pedagogy?
- Can human agency centeredness and teacher-centered or student-centered pedagogies of one kind or another be avoided?
- How are notions of agency rethought when schooling learning teaching is viewed as a phenomenon that is constitutive and imperceptible?

In Narrative Pedagogy, schooling issues forth as the temporal play-space of teaching and learning. This is a calling into question the hold of traditional boundaries. There is a path to thinking-saying that does not separate teaching from learning. Is one of the issues with agency this separation?—that is, once teaching is separated from learning, must one have teachers and learners as independent objects? As Narrative Pedagogy is enacted, schooling learning teaching as a co-occurring phenomenon enables learning to arrive with and be inseparable from the learnable and learners. Schooling is the genesis of the schooling play-space that gathers teaching and learning such that every teaching is a learning and every learning is a teaching.

Narrative Pedagogy belongs to the co-occurring phenomenon of schooling learning teaching. All pedagogies always already enable schooling learning teaching in their own way. As attendance with schooling learning teaching as an intra-related co-occurring phenomenon, hermeneutic phenomenology is necessarily enacted. Explicating the presuppositions of or making thematic schooling learning teaching lets this phenomenon show itself as the incipience of a ground that can never be cognitively or mathematically known.

On the Trail of Reticent Arrivals

Narrative Pedagogy is at once a whiling with possibility and a trailing after nontangible and evanescent withdrawing. Both are always already offered as the engaged openness of arrivals. Emergence/ elusion awakens not as some object but as a journey.

In this converging conversation, Erica, an experienced teacher, describes her journey to awaken from the way she teaches as she listens for richer pedagogical possibilities. She enacts hermeneutic phenomenology and enables Narrative Pedagogy by explicating her presuppositions. Reflecting on a variety of narrative tellings, she identifies, through hermeneutic phenomenological thinking, the presuppositions embedded in her current approaches to schooling learning teaching. In a self-cycling, reciprocating-rejoining of questionings and interpreting, Erica works to explicate their play of meaning. These cycles enable the circulation of Narrative Pedagogy and work to transform Erica's understanding of schooling learning teaching. There is a nourishing change in how she and the students, as well as her colleagues, attend, listen, and co-respond with one another.

I've always been hesitant about change. But you know, I've been doing a lot of thinking about Narrative Pedagogy and reforming nursing education. The more I read about pedagogies and the more I talked with students, and tried stuff out and worked together on my course, the more I found myself becoming more tolerant of everyone, students and colleagues. You always want to be student centered, but I really think I started being more open. Not that I was not open before, but more a pedagogical openness. You stop being the expert on teaching and learning, you know, the one who is in control of everything. Despite my hesitation I started listening and thinking more, slowing down and stepping back. I found myself focusing more on learning, how the students were learning and how I was learning. I realized I had a lot to learn about learning and teaching for that matter too! You really can't separate teaching and learning. More like when something happens and you say, "That will learn you!" That's teaching really. I have started looking at the world differently and it's changed how I relate to everyone, students and colleagues. Even my kids tell me I'm listening to them better! Isn't that amazing?

How is the hold of presuppositions of conventional pedagogies showing up in Erica's reticent thoughts as she explores how she and the students belong to each other (are delivered over to each other)? Mindful of her experience of learning about new pedagogies and "trying stuff out" with students, Erica describes how she has begun to *"stop being the expert on teaching and learning"* and *"start listening and thinking more, slowing down and stepping back."* The meaning of this experience for Erica is both to risk a shift to *"focusing on learning, how the students were learning and how I was learning,"* and an awareness of the co-occurring of teaching and learning. She comments, *"You really can't separate teaching and learning. More like when something happens and you say, 'That will learn you!' That's teaching really."*

Her thinking is transformed in the circulating cycles of questionings and interpreting. Multiple meanings emerge. Interpreting for meanings grants new possibilities for thinking, understanding, and acting. The possibility of meanings always already dwells as the excess of the self-opening of sense; there is no single discrete meaning.[27] As meanings show up, hermeneutic phenomenology lets there be a movement away from seeking explanations, causality, and categorical thinking. Narrative Pedagogy advenes as a way of thinking and as an enactment of hermeneutic phenomenology. Students and teachers alike are enabled to resist thinking that describes *"why* things are" or "how things *should* be" by following the withdrawing trails of their own thinking-saying and following what then shows up.[28] Erica's listening follows after the withdrawing of sense as it shows itself as reticent arrival.

The Retrieval of Boundary

Erica's narrative telling reveals how when students and teachers participate in cycles of interpreting pedagogical presuppositions, the roles of students and teacher blur and are kept in play. Boundaries open themselves as reticent issuing-forth rather than the secure closure of a termination. The theme Writing Papers: The Teacher as Audience and the theme Rethinking Sedimented Traditions: Students as Pedagogical Partners are in converging conversation as Erica describes how through rethinking evaluation in her course, her role as the one who "awards" grades is changed through a journey paper. Learning takes center stage as students are actively involved in learning partnerships in new ways.

> *I am still the teacher and unfortunately we can't have an ungraded curriculum in our school, so there is always the issue of grading. But when you talk with students and get them working with you, we can come up with all kinds of ways that make issues of*

grading easier to live with, in awarding grades that are somehow equitable. In a small class, I had only 50, I could get to know everyone. At the end they wrote journey papers and conversed around what they had learned and what the course meant to them and then graded themselves. I graded them too and we met only if we disagreed. The first time I did it, out of 50 students there were only two grades I disagreed on, and they were students who gave themselves a lower grade! In another large class of 150 students, we went with take-home exams where they could work together. Everyone did not get an A, though grades were higher. When students also did a journey paper on the meaning of this take-home exam experience, I discovered that some of this inflation was actually learning in their groups as a result of trying to select the correct answers! We want all students to get A's if that reflects their learning. In another class, they took an old exam and critiqued it for what was missing or for questions that were debatable in the literature. They wrote journey papers and I wrote one too! I discovered amazing thinking about the content of this course that I had never seen before. This was an online course. When you look for learning, the issue of "I am the teacher and I'm supposed to award grades" is still there, but it moves more to the back burner for both me and the students. These have been moving experiences for me.

Narrative Pedagogy as an inconspicuous, still pathway of a conversation that moves and motions to is an abiding experience, a way of attending, listening, and co-responding with schooling learning teaching.

The work of Narrative Pedagogy is a shift away from looking at individuals as individual agents or roles toward looking at how the phenomenon of schooling learning teaching shows up. It is not that the individual teacher or student does not matter, for they do. But in the hermeneutic phenomenological world, individuals are thrown into attendance with plurals, and plurals could not be plural without the presence of singulars. There is a need for conventional pedagogical research to include better understandings of individual learning needs, as well as their connections to group learning approaches. The contribution of Narrative Pedagogy is to offer an approach to the consideration of what *enables* (lets) schooling learning teaching show up as a *co-occurring phenomenon.*

Pedagogical Wayfaring: The Experience of Schooling Learning Teaching

Pedagogies as specific approaches to schooling, teaching, and learning help describe the philosophical and epistemological presuppositions that ground both research and practice in education. However, pedagogies are categories and are reductive in that they function as enclosures. They develop their own languages, bodies of knowledge, and specific research protocols. As categories, pedagogies compete with and critique each other in an attempt to argue for ultimate superiority or worthfulness. Interpretive pedagogies such as critical, feminist, phenomenological, and postmodern are alternatives to the conventional pedagogies of outcome- or competency-based education. As such they often describe their contributions through critiquing or devaluing the contributions of conventional pedagogies.

Identifying pedagogies is an important aspect in educational research. Researchers traditionally ground their research in theory, conceptual constructs, or philosophical frameworks. Attention to the origins of pedagogies adds complexity to research. For example, studying a particular strategy such as simulations or lecturing varies considerably according to the approach; for example, one study may have been conducted using outcomes education and another, critical or feminist pedagogy. In order to extend knowledge through research and scholarship, both identification and explication of the theoretical and philosophical underpinnings and their connection to the pedagogies embraced must be clear if duplication and/or extension of the research can obtain.

The practice of matching a pedagogy to a particular and predetermined set of learning objectives or merely adding pedagogies to one's repertoire is as reductionist as eliminating a given pedagogy from consideration merely because it is outside of a particular belief system. The concern of Narrative Pedagogy is to keep all pedagogies in play. Something of what is at play in teaching is revealed as Letena, a new teacher, shares her thinking.

> I don't think it matters what pedagogies you use and even when and how much. It is more that reading about them and bringing research to your thinking about what is going on, that's what is important for me. They help me interpret what is going on as they bring very different assumptions with them, and that is helpful as a reminder.

Narrative Pedagogy can be described as "multipedagogical" in that it is a letting of the alreadiness presence as an always already oncoming. Narrative Pedagogy works to be temporal and historical. While this description is accurate, it is not sufficient because it reduces Narrative Pedagogy to a category of pedagogies. And to argue, as postmodern pedagogies do, that the problem lies with labeling teaching and learning as one pedagogy or another does not sufficiently address the issue. A label or naming can be interpreted in either a closed or open way. In a closed interpretation, a label is reified and claimed by power granted through identification with the label. In an open interpretation there is a belonging to a matter of concern's temporal and historical particularity, allowing the matter of concern to speak about what its engaged openness discloses and beckons. As we have mentioned, "Names are not the result of designation. They are owed to a naming in which the nameable, the name and the named occur altogether" (*DT,* 71).

Schooling learning teaching does not lend itself to categorization. It is difficult to think schooling as a phenomenon other than various types of human teaching interactions that are in turn grounded in a given learning framework. In thinking schooling learning teaching as a phenomenon—*a call to attention*—there is first practicing the thinking-saying of releasement in order to free the human being for the richer understandings that can come along. This play shows that interpreting belongs to releasement and that releasement needs interpreting. Releasement as engaged interpreting always already entails a from-to as ebb and flow.[29] Narrative ebb and flow is the unsettling ambiguity of narrative tellings that follow the ebbing and flowing ways of thinking-saying, questioning, answering, and rejoining as the narrative telling *of* the human being of openness shows up.

To say, as we do, that teaching necessarily always already advenes as engaged play of co-responding, responsiveness, and responsibility, means to say that it needs the invisible phenomenon of sighting and the silent phenomenon of listening. Narrative Pedagogy as enacted in practice and research sojourns on an interpretive journey whereby sighting and listening manifest themselves as the phenomena that they always already are. Narrative Pedagogy scholarship as it explicates the schooling experiences of teachers and students works to show that teaching and learning are *porous* and that the preestablished enclosures and presence of one pedagogy to another cannot be discrete. The ontological moment of Narrative Pedagogy lets matters of concern shift *from specific pedagogies toward the belongingness of schooling learning teaching as an intra-relating phenomenon.* Narrative Pedagogy as a gathering of pedagogies is multipedagogical in that what is common to *all* pedagogies—namely, explicating schooling, learning, and teaching as phenomenon—is the heart of the matter.

Chapter 10 Notes

1   See N. Diekelmann, 1995, 2001, for a description of Narrative Pedagogy.

2   See J. Diekelmann, 2005, 45-47, for the questioning of method.

3   Note that making thematic is not just identifying and explicating themes. It also includes dialoguing about or explicating presuppositions, such as making thematic the forgotten or overlooked presuppositions of the subject-object paradigm.

4   See J. Diekelmann, 2005, 3-57, for descriptions of method as pathways in making method thematic.

5   See Diekelmann & Ironside, 1998a.

6   See Chapter 1 for discussion on making thematic and the as-structure; also Chapter 2 for explication of transpositions and the subject-object paradigm.

7   See Diekelmann & Ironside, 1998b; Ironside 2003a & b, 2004, 2005a & b, 2006b; Ironside et al., 2003.

8   See Chapter 11 for a discussion of the Concernful Practices of Schooling Learning Teaching.

9   See Chapter 3 on the circle of participating and the nearness of the near as always already.

10   See Chapter 3 for explication on language and hermeneutic phenomenological thinking.

11   See Chapter 11 for explication of the Concernful Practices of Schooling Learning Teaching.

12   See Ironside (2003a, 2004, 2005a) and Chapter 5 for more discussion on hints as following the movement of showing.

13   See Chapter 5 for explication of enacting hermeneutic phenomenology and Chapter 6 for discussion of method and Narrative Pedagogy.

14   See *BP,* 174, 185-188.

15   See Chapter 1 for converging conversations as crossings.

16   Refer to discussions of thinking-saying in Chapter 3.

17   Perhaps a better term for the kind of thinking of enacting hermeneutic phenomenology is mindfulness. *QCT (Science and Reflection), M.*

18   Recall that the concernful practices are always present and are neither good nor bad; that is, teachers can create places for

students to evaluate their experiences in ways that are open and encourage thinking, or in ways that discourage further thinking and close down.

19 See Chapter 2 for discussion of conversation and from monologue to dialogue as mirror play.

20 See Chapter 4 for discussion of the temporal participatory world: retinue commending-commanding.

21 See Chapter 4 for responding as co-responding and the soul of dialogue.

22 See Chapter 3 for discussion of nearness of the near as always already.

23 See Ellsworth, 1992.

24 Refer to *TM,* 373.

25 See Chapter 9 for exegeses of learning as listening.

26 See Chapter 9 for discussion of agency in the context of learning.

27 See Chapter 5 for co-responding as harboring a surplus of meaning.

28 See Chapter 3 for transpositions and discussion on thinking, realism, and idealism.

29 See "Conversation on a Country Path about Thinking" in *DT.*

Chapter 11

Narrative Pedagogy:
Concernful Practices of Schooling Learning Teaching

Any matter of concern that offers room and allows
the enacting of something gives a possibility, that is, it
offers what enables. "Possibility," so understood, as
what enables, means something else and something
more than mere opportunity.

WCT, 92-93 (Translation slightly modified)

Of Concernful Practices as Possibilities

A first step on the way to a discussion of practices as concernful is a step back to the possibility shown by the historical (in this case, Greek) thought of something "already lying before and from itself" (*4S*, 76). Heidegger has written of the call to distinguish "bringing-forth into the open" from "the modern notion of production, which means: to set into availability" (*4S*, 76). Concernful practices are not entities set forth as objects opposite a subject; concernful practices let themselves be available as possibility. They offer themselves as possibility. In their widest sense, all practices are concernful. We submit that practitioners in the health and human sciences dialogically experience their practices as concern (care).[1]

Care/concern as it unfolded in Heidegger's pathway showed itself as three intertwined moments: "of the being-ahead-of-oneself, of always-already-[engaged openness] and of being-alongside." These moments also presence "in the modes of unconcern, of indifference, or even of resistance" (*ZS*, 174). Care/concern, in its movement, is thought as an open clearing: "It is the scene of [disclosing and beckoning] and not primarily the site of an activity by [the human being]" (HW, 130). The temporal-historical essence of the human being of openness consists in sustaining (as enduring and facing) the on-coming, gathered sending of the unconcealing of engaged openness as the open clearing. "The clearing itself is" engaged openness (PM, 253).

Care/concern shows itself as temporally-historically conditioned concernfulness. To be concerned with and about is abiding as an open, cleared possibility amidst matters of concern. Abiding is a complex play of waiting, expecting, standing ready, accepting, and tarrying as moments (instances) of instantiation and insistence as persevering. Concern is thereby taken as the sustaining (persisting/persevering/enduring) as the sojourning of the human being of openness of the open clearing as engaged openness (PM, 284).

Concern as we are articulating it means both abiding in practices readily applied to active, involved, practical life (PM, 272) and yet not succumbing to being inextricably entangled in these. Concern as concern allows that everyday prudent and practical concerns are determined as disclosed and beckoned by the temporally-historically engaged human being of openness. There is care not only of entities and matters of concern in their questionableness but also of engaged openness in its twofold emerging and eluding unconcealedness.[2] Concern as abiding "care-taking is conceived not from everydayness but from the selfhood of [the human being of openness] and maintains itself in many intrinsically related ways" (CP, 49f: trans. Kisiel, RHT, 268). There is a play of ways, which include the most relentlessly quotidian to the most noble, thoughtful self-sacrifice. These ways are infinite and always already call out to be read (interpreted) as temporal and historical.

Concern issues forth as the unconcealing of engaged openness in entities and matters of concern as "found in historical time-space" (RHT, 268). Concerns as matters of concern are not grounded in any theoretical volitional comportment of human beings but are sheltered in the temporal-historical essence of the human being of openness.

The play of hinting and how to take the genitive "of" in the concernful practices of schooling learning teaching circulates as the "originarily proper" (RHT, 286, fn. 2) rather than in the genitive's grammatically prescribed sense (*CP,* 302) as a fixed or exclusive relation between subjects and objects. Insofar as the genitive is freed from the inveteracy of the modernist tradition, the genitive can show up as the hinting of attendant circumstances. The "of" is a saying-showing of issuing forth or birthing as the generation (issuing-forth) of incipience. As we have written, the emergence/elusion of incipience discloses and beckons as a mediating middle region of origination (enabling) and accomplishment (enacting). This "double genitive structure" lets (enables) thinking the engaged openness of the enacting concernful practices show up as precipitating out of engaged openness itself.

What is the proper or unique essence of concernful practices in their historical-temporal abiding? Concernful practices *as* concernful practices show themselves as they are sighted and listened to.

Concernful practices:

- Disclose and beckon as the way (fundamental dialogical experience) in which matters of concern are dialogically experienced-as.

- Are always already found presencing (showing themselves) in the open clearing and are thereby not absolute central points but show up as a "summoning and preparing the possibility of new originations" (*MFL,* 155).

- Are neither mere objects of erudition (*4S,* 26) nor normative standards (*4S,* 27).

- Do not posit oppositions as fixed and do not presuppose absolute and nondichotomous identities.

- Are preceded by the aheadness (forerunning) of disclosing and beckoning. They can be sighted, if they are listened to, as a taking into view of their own letting appear.

- Do not determine their matters of concern as fixed entities, but give and call attention to the self-presencing of presence and thereby inquire into (ask after) engaged openness *as* engaged openness.

- Do not start from opposing matters of concern, elevate themselves to engaged openness as objects, and thence return to matters of concern as the product of subjects.

- Are not the ultimate knowing of some perfect correspondence of consciousness and its object, but always already open into ever new experiences though their on-coming questioning (*HGH,* 24-25).

The unconcealedness of the above as sheltered in, and as their proper, unique temporal-historical essence, lets itself be listened to. Concernful practices sighted as openness are claimed by attendant exposure to historical and temporal disposedness.

We now turn to concernful practices as they have shown themselves to us as we, the authors, dialogically experienced our own temporal particularity. Concernful practices in their always alreadiness need names. But "these names are not the result of designation. They are indebted to [claimed by] a naming in which the nameable, the name and the named" are beckoned and disclosed together (*DT,* 71). Naming as naming lets self-opening matters of concern be sighted out of their immediate overwhelming play of on-coming involvements, as they rest in their engaged openness. Naming is not the aftermath of a willful intentional consciousness. Names preserve matters of concern as their revealed engaged openness. They hold, without possessing, the engaged openness of matters of concern as historically and temporally particular (Richardson, 1974, 292; *IM,* 183).

In over 20 years of listening as a play of listening-to, listening-for, and being listened-to we have caught sight of connections which, when dialogically experienced, reveal practical comportments-in-common (the commonalities *of* comportments). It is here that we wish to remind the reader of our discussion in Chapter 1 as loci of meaning wherein sharing and crossing through disclose and beckon. Our naming of concernful practices of schooling learning teaching is not meant to be, and should not be taken to be, the final word on the aforementioned matters of concern. To claim this for ourselves would entail the hubris of closed mindedness. Even our admonishment vis-à-vis any attempt to hypostasize these practices runs the risk of seeming untenably egocentric and authoritarian. Concernful practices are not meant to be categories in the sense of prescriptions but are meant to show the *possibilities* that abide (dwell) in encountering as it takes place as "a never-ending reading between the lines" (*HWT,* 195).

Let us now look at concernful practices of schooling learning teaching as they have let themselves into our sight in order to be listened to. These practices are the following:

Presencing: Attending and Being Open
Assembling: Constructing and Cultivating
Gathering: Welcoming and Calling Forth
Caring: Engendering of Community
Listening: Knowing and Connecting
Interpreting: Unlearning and Becoming
Inviting: Waiting and Letting Be
Questioning: Sense and Making Meanings Visible
Retrieving Places: Keeping Open a Future of Possibilities
Preserving: Reading, Writing, Thinking-Saying, and Dialogue

As phenomena these named and identified practices have ontic as well as ontological dimensions and moments. We will discuss these as we map the first three (presencing, assembling, and gathering) onto schooling as attending; the second three (caring, listening, and interpreting) onto learning as listening; and the remaining four (inviting, questioning, retrieving places, and preserving) onto teaching as co-responding.

Schooling as Attending:
Presencing, Assembling, and Gathering

> *Being-many-together is the originary situation; an originary or transcendental "with" demands with a palpable urgency to be disentangled and articulated for itself.*
>
> *BSP,* 41

The presencing in the concernful practice of *Presencing: Attending and Being Open* turns on the presence of attendant being open. What does this mean? The being open of attendance needs encounterable presence, not as the physical presence of some discrete entity, but as a free open clearing wherein matters of concern can be encountered. Presence enables the open clearing such that the play of being-with as the with-world of engaged openness shows itself. Barbara, a teacher, reflects on how the presencing practices of Attending and Being Open shape her teaching.

> I've learned that being open is a receptivity that happens and is fundamentally not something I can will at the drop of a hat. A student reminded me of this recently. I had her mother as a student several years earlier. She said, "You are exactly as my mother said you would be. But things have changed with me." She didn't say, I am "different than my mother," which of course she is. She said, "things have changed with me." I thought, she is right; the whole world is always changing, including me and with me, we're always becoming. I realized it is not my intentions, like to be open, treat each student as an individual, that matters, but rather how I attend to being with students, that is . . . how I come together with them. Presencing yourself with students isn't just some interpersonal skill or personal attribute, though it is those too . . . it's more like, I brought up in faculty meeting that we need to think about students playing games on their computers, or surfing the Internet during class, and how this influences their attending to learning. Looking together at how this influences attending to learning and presencing among students and teachers—how we come together.

Concernful practices co-occur. For example, in this teacher's concern for how she comes together with students, listening as knowing and connecting resonates in this narrative telling. A variety of ways in which students and teachers can presence themselves to one another are revealed in this story. The very activities of the classroom shape how students attend and are open to learning in the situations in which they come together with teachers. Shifting the focus to attending practices, all the things and ways students and teachers attend to being together, cannot be reduced to a pedagogical problem to be solved (e.g., a rule regarding use of the Internet during class time). Presencing cannot be reduced to interpersonal skills and personal attributes. As attending and being open, presencing is being with one another.

The with-world of engaged openness shows itself as the with of the alongside-of as well as the abandoning of participants to learning situations. The thrownness of temporality plays its role in the letting of involvements show as a play of taking cognizance wherein when and how connections among learners as listeners (teachers, students, and clinicians) show themselves. Showing as the open clearing paradoxically must include closure such that co-responding is blocked off. Closure as either an ontic or ontological phenomenon cannot be forced open coercively, but shows itself as listening.

Assembling: Constructing and Cultivating must not be sighted as the putting together of preformed pieces as in the solving of a jigsaw puzzle. Not only are the parts not preformed; also they are not apprehendable as discrete parts. This problem notwithstanding, the whole is always already understood. Indeed the whole is understood as constructed and cultivated, but the construction methods and cultivation practices do not lend themselves to effortless thinking-saying. Dialogical experiences can contribute to being-many-together, but they cannot guarantee the disentanglement of the Gordian knot.[3] Listening attends to and is in attendance with an open clearing as a mediating between where the human being finds itself (is thrown) as disposed and exposed sojourning (abiding/whiling/dwelling) with others.

Suzanne, a nursing student, tells of her experiences in a nursing course.

> *I got a B in med-surg [medical-surgical nursing] because I got patients, almost every time, that we had not had the lecture on yet. Trying to read ahead and look at the online stuff just to prepare for clinical is really a lot. And my patients were all very sick.*

When I sort of mentioned this to my instructor she said, "I had to make assignments based on who is on the unit." But so where does that leave me, I thought. At an SNA [Student Nurses Association] convention, I talked to some students from other schools and some have clinical courses and theory courses separated, but if you haven't had the theory course yet you still have more preparation than someone who has. Seems like when you take care of patients, you need everything in the curriculum all at once. Getting the whole picture, with all the lectures online, the class materials, links, everything we need—wouldn't that be great! It would probably send the teachers over the edge because they'd have to know the entire curriculum too. That would be what I would do if I were dean of the school. Then we would really be prepared and our teachers wouldn't have to do so much teaching, but more could spend their time thinking with us. Getting to know exactly what is going on with the patient, me, the staff, and all the learning going on everywhere.

Suzanne hints at a solution—providing the entire content of the curriculum at once to allow students and teachers to assemble with one another in ways that construct and cultivate new possibilities for learning and teaching. Presencing, assembling, and gathering practices all reflect attention to schooling in which teachers and students attend to the dialogical experiences of being-many-together.

Three teachers discuss separating theory classroom courses from clinical courses.

Leslie: *You separated theory from clinical? Separated the classroom part of peds [pediatrics] from a peds clinical?*

Trasel: *Right! A lot of schools had done this and we just copied them.*[4] *We have theory taught in the classroom. The clinical courses build on each other and the competencies can be met in any clinical area. It was a great change for me. Before we separated theory from clinical, I would want the students to learn certain things in class and then apply them in clinical. Now we all know how often that happens!* [Laughter] *Usually students have to be given patient assignments they have either not had the content for or they have forgotten that they had it! So we started saying, why don't we make the whole course available at once . . . and then you ask, why not make the entire curriculum available at once! It just seemed to make sense.*

Kip: *So you don't require, for example, a peds clinical of every student?*

Trasel: *Correct!*

Leslie: *Your students are given a lot of freedom for learning! Given students' demanding lives, I think this is a good student-centered pedagogy.*[5] *But I think our State Board of Nursing would not allow this.*[6] *How did the students do on NCLEX*[7] *[State Board examinations]?*

Trasel: *Actually the student satisfaction with the new curriculum is soaring and every year our NCLEX, which was always OK or above the average, gets better and better. But you know, we decided, who knows why NCLEX goes up and down with each class. There sure is very little causal research in that area! What we did notice is that now because students have access to the information they need when they need it AND put online by teachers with the expertise in a particular field, the students are doing much better in their clinical courses. They seem to be getting the whole picture more. The feedback from our clinical preceptors is that they are performing much better! Students receive an updated DVD each year and they can always access the school's curriculum site with their password whenever they want. When they are preparing for clinical and have a surgical patient with depression they can consult the online course content materials related to the surgery from our med-surg courses as well as content on depression from the psych course. They download what they need into their PDAs, and make e-books in preparing for their clinicals. We have them buy certain software for their PDAs, and certain skills and drugs software. And they actually save money now compared with the books that they used to buy . . . not read, and that got out-of-date quickly!*

Assembling as constructing and cultivating is not just about constructing curriculum frameworks and assembling courses. Rather it is the assembling of students and teachers; it is the how of bringing them together in the curriculum. The former is a familiar concern in schools of nursing; the latter is not. In conventional pedagogies, curriculum organization and the relationship of theory and practice in classroom and clinical courses are familiar topics of conversation among teachers.

The overt organization of the curriculum and the rules that govern how students experience the curriculum, such as taking courses in a particular sequence, are common concerns. These common concerns often result in an exploration of some kind of innovation, but always on the background of the conventional pedagogical concern about the influence of innovation on student NCLEX scores. The influence of licensing examinations, certification, accreditation, and State Boards of Nursing on innovation can be significant.[8] Note that in this converging conversation, the return to conventional pedagogical concerns (e.g., tests and testing) is expressed even in the face of significant successful innovation.

The above narrative telling is ripe for making schooling as attending thematic and for the associated explication of the narrative telling's presuppositions. Notice that curriculum design and revisions are framed in terms of accreditation and passing NCLEX. The assumption is that any innovative change reduces NCLEX scores. The implication of this unchallenged assumption is that it discourages exploration of the practices of presencing as constructing and cultivating that influence students' performance on NCLEX. Innovation with pedagogies that have different commitments to epistemology and cognitive gain are assumed to likewise pose a threat to student performance. Left unchallenged is evidence of the causality of curriculum revisions with declining NCLEX scores. What evidence is there that the use of particular pedagogies positively or negatively influences NCLEX scores? According to research, what curricular and instructional factors influence students' performance on NCLEX?

How are we to sight assembling practices in this converging conversation? We can do this by attending to how students and teachers are called on to assemble together. Does the teacher make a patient assignment with a diagnosis familiar to one student and unfamiliar to another, with the class lecture schedule favoring one student over another? Is this situation so often the case that it is overlooked? How often is there a relationship between the theory presented in class and the patient assignment a student receives? A particular assumption of conventional pedagogy, namely that theory is introduced in the classroom and then applied in clinical setting, influences organization of course content in a way that appears to be logical but is *not* in fact experienced that way by students.

To be the human being of openness is to be gathered (assembled) into the open clearing as the play of welcoming and abiding (*WCT*, 190-196). Welcoming and abiding are not thought here as the utopianism of a return to the idealized state of a prelapsarian Eden, inherent in the various desires of dualistic (subject-object) thinking. The constant incompleteness of welcoming/unwelcoming engaged openness can be attributed neither to the resplendence of a pure theoretical state nor to the self-established power of the complete. The thinking-saying of welcoming can be only as an admitting of the incomplete close to its ownmost nature and thereby holding it there. This does not affirm the incomplete, for the incomplete exists because it is engaged openness, so engaged with its proper and unique temporal-historical essence (*WCT,* 195).

Gathering: Welcoming and Calling Forth is mindful that the engaged openness that the human being is let (thrown) into may or may not welcome it and may or may not call forth the richest, most noble of its possibilities. One thing is certain as gathering gathers: Attendance is mandatory for the human being. What is called forth is possibility. Laura, a nursing student, talks about how after seeing the syllabus she was looking forward to the first day of class.

> *I knew the class was going to be a good one. Instead of the first sentence in the syllabus being the objectives, the teacher wrote, "Welcome to the class! It will be a privilege studying with you this semester." Right there you feel more at home. And for a teacher to sound like they were looking forward to teaching you. . . . Words matter and so do all the little things that make people feel at home with each other. It's more than getting off on the right foot; it's getting involved with the course and finding it exciting or meaningful.*

Adrian, a teacher, describes how he attends to welcoming the students by exciting them with some challenging questioning. He tells of the small things he does to make students feel at home in his courses. But he also explicates the presupposition that teachers who see each other every day do not feel isolated.

> *Especially in large lecture or online courses, it is hard to welcome everyone, get them engaged in the course and on the same page together. Some students are very advanced and get bored and other students feel the course is over their heads. I*

used to try and aim for the middle in my beginning lectures, but now I put all my lectures online and they are complete, complex, and full of content. Then in the online classes I post a story, or in class discussions I bring in a story. Sure, it will have all the competencies they need to address in the disease we are studying, but I will ask questions like, "How are we to decide when a treatment has become too painful for this child?" or "For a nurse, when does an invasive procedure become torture?" More than just getting the students thinking, it is a way of bringing them into the course, showing them the important issues we face in pediatrics, such as when high-risk neonatal nurses, for example, administer drugs that cause the skin of the neonate to exfoliate.

To engage the students and to get their interest going in the course is something I have learned to pay special attention to. It's about engaging them so all of us can put our heads together. We worry too much about what we should and should not do in our courses and not enough about getting together with each other. We are always gathering even as a school. Students see the faculty meetings as "off limits" even though they are open meetings. And faculty rarely have coffee in the student lounge and vice versa. It's not just class where we get together. I looked down the hallway of our wing in the school of nursing the other day, and I happened to realize that I knew for a fact that every one of the offices had a teacher in it, but each door was closed so you would never know. I think we are actually pretty isolated from one another. Our isolation is of the worst kind. We think we are not isolated because we "see" each other all the time. But that seeing might only be watching a colleague ahead of you going into the building from the parking lot!

Gathering as welcoming and calling forth is more than creating welcoming, safe, fair, and respectful learning environments for students and teachers, though that is an important matter of concern. Gathering here is the dialogical experiences that result when students and teacher are in attendance as situations that call forth thinking-saying and learning. Dialogical experiences that bring in, connect with, or bring to bear situations that catch the gaze of all gather, welcome, and engage participants in the thinkable or that which is asking to be thought. Gathering is thoughtful and gently compelling in relation to how situations are brought to bear and are borne as both carried and issued forth.

Each human being is brought forth as a generation given by temporality and historicality such that it has to be in attendance with and as what it already is.

Learning as Listening:
Caring, Listening, and Interpreting

> *The subject of listening is always still yet to come, spaced, traversed, and called by itself, sounded by itself . . . is perhaps no subject at all, except as the place of resonance, of its infinite tension and rebound. . . .*
>
> *L, 21-22*

The possibility of listening, as listening-thinking-saying ahead, can enable the human being of openness to ask after who it may be rather than arrogating the absolute representing of itself to itself to itself (*QCT,* 131-153). The world is not encountered as representations, as sense data, or as objects existing for and in themselves. The world is encountered as abiding in the realm of the open clearing openness wherein the human being of openness sustains thrown openness in that it takes the open, the clearing of engaged openness in care (*PM,* 249). Care as "listening to one another, in which being-with cultivates itself, is more accurately a compliance in being-with-one-another, a co-enactment in concern" (*HCT,* 266).

Caring: Engendering of Community as a concernful practice is not the achievement of putative willful subjectivity or idealized subjectivities-in-common. The possibility of engendering is a call, which is listened to even if unheard. The human being of openness *is* engendering such that engaged openness "means: having to do with the world, sojourning within it in the routines of working, of managing and taking care of [matters of concern], but also of examining, interrogating, and determining them by way of examination and comparison. [The human being of openness] is characterized as *concern*" (*BH,* 204).

Leticia, a nursing student, has two small babies and is a single parent. Dealing with all her life challenges, she is left with little energy to tend to patients who have life-threatening illnesses.

> *I remember a class where we were talking about death and dying . . . and I was thinking you can die and live at the same time—I cannot meet my basic needs . . . I have no health insurance, no money, the food is running low—death and dying doesn't mean leaving this earth.*

One day Leticia makes a minor medication error. Knowing what has happened, a nurse, one not even assigned to her, takes her aside and reassures her that she is going to be all right. The nurse offers to tell Leticia's instructor. She reminds Leticia that everyone makes mistakes. She tells Leticia that after she finishes her care of her patient, she could use some coffee, and then suggests that they go on a break together. In the cafeteria line the staff nurse encourages Leticia to also get an apple, as she needs food too. When they sit down, she says, "You have what it takes, how can I help you?" Leticia knows that she cannot tell this nurse, who is almost a stranger, all that is going on in her life, but she is amazed at the generosity of this caring nurse.

> *All I remember about our break together—short as it was—was that there was one nurse who cared about me making it through school and becoming a nurse. . . . We all know we will never be teachers, but every student wants to be a staff nurse! I didn't say*

much of anything to her, but I felt she really listened to me . . . I even remember laughing with her, and it had been a long time![9]

In this narrative telling it is not the teacher but a staff nurse, a stranger, who provides comfort and hope to a nursing student. Finding herself in a world of extreme competing demands, the student is ready to give up. A stranger in the community reaches out to her with a lifeline. Always in community, it is the how of engendering, the being-with and toward others, that matters and makes all the difference.

Banjit, a teacher, tells of her teaching community.

Our dean values our community together.[10] *We've had a Voices Day*[11] *for several years now. She really insists that we don't have to like each other but we do have to be fair and respectful to one another. And she's tough on petty, untruthful gossiping. She's a good teacher and researcher too and can walk the talk. And we've learned that not everyone has to be onboard for there to be substantive change. This experience of trying to revise the curriculum differently*[12] *really got us working together in spite of whether we were personal friends or not. A woman who really does not like me, and that I find hard to get along with, saved my life recently during a teleconference when she stepped in and took over the technology and got the situation settled. My view of her is still the same, but I respect her for helping me out and would do the same for her. Actually I would say our community is stronger now that we are all committed to learning to live together. You know, trying to all get along and making the best learning community we can. There are a couple faculty who just won't, can't join us, but even they are better when the rest of us work on getting along. It's always a community thing, isn't it?*

Learning communities can either be engendered as supportive and fair, with participants feeling safe and respected, or be engendered as so poisoned with personal enmity that they can be defined as toxic and unsafe. There is no imperative for concernful practices to be either good or bad, supportive or toxic. The engendering of learning communities calls attention to practices like rumor mongering such that gossiping, instead of being a means of communication, feeds an insalubrious, disaffected community life. How do the dialogical experiences of revising the curriculum encourage or discourage engendering community? In what ways does revising the curriculum call out or discourage safe, fair, and respectful learning communities?

Caitlin, a new teacher, describes how during her first semester she tries to make her lectures interesting. But she has been spending all her time "getting ready to teach," so she has abandoned this approach.

> *I just straight lectured from the book . . . told the students what they need to know and said the heck with it. My evals [evaluations] were average and a little low on a couple of items. . . . Some of the students who really marked me down were I knew [sic] the students who were getting Cs and Ds. So second semester . . . I still straight lectured, but I made sure the tests were simple and the students were happy. . . . At the end, my department chair told me that I was doing a much better job and improving my teaching, and she was really happy with how I was doing. It's all in how you play the game of getting tenure. I want to do research and get a big grant, and there will never be time for me to spend on teaching. Learning how to teach is too time-consuming to do while you are learning how to become a researcher . . . and everyone knows this is true . . . otherwise why would there be so many lousy researcher teachers? If being a good teacher*

was so important, why didn't my doctoral program insist I learn how to teach?[13]

As a phenomenon, schooling learning teaching is experienced communally. A disaffected community is communal in its very disaffection. Caitlin feels compelled to not spend time on teaching in order to *"do research and get a big grant."* Knowing and connecting and calling out or engendering of community life can be experienced either as safe, fair, and respectful or as competitive, threatening, unsafe, unfair, and disrespectful. What matters is how concernful practices show up in particular situations. Learning communities are always already occurring; they disclose and beckon. Engendering is a reciprocal calling; it has no control over what it calls out. The malevolent rage of fear and solicitous self-transcendence both belong to engendering's possibilities. Engendering as sighting and listening practices can be listened to and for.

Listening: Knowing and Connecting as a concernful practice immediately calls into question the method of science wherein some entity or another is merely stared at so that one can pretend to the position of being dispassionately uninvolved with it. Knowing in the hermeneutic phenomenological sense calls listening and connecting to itself as care. Knowing, thought in this way, is knowing-how. The human being of openness is a can-be, "a being capable of" *for* some possibility (matter of concern) of care. According to Heidegger, the human being of openness "itself, insofar as it is, is nothing but *being-possible.*" To be possible is to be enabled to say, *"I am, that is, I can."* Only because the human being of openness "is defined by the 'I can' can it procure possibilities in the sense of opportunities, means, and the like, and be concerned about them" (*HCT,* 298). Care as the aheadness of the always already of involvement characterizes the human being of openness as understanding which knows how.

Concernful praxis as a can-enact admits of enacting either one practice or another, enacting one practice as well as another, or enacting/not enacting either one practice or the other. "It is only possible because there is an 'either-or' that there is an 'as well as' and an 'and' of concern" (*HCT,* 298). Only "what can be of concern as something understandable is what can be pursued in care and in concern" (*HCT,* 299). That which lets itself be listened to can be connected to as the discovery and rediscovery of the always already connectedness of possibility for some matter of concern.

Teachers often tell stories of learning to know and connect with students. Tamra, an experienced teacher, describes to a colleague how she lectures as a listening to varying groups of students. The either-or of connecting's possibilities is what enables Tamra to enact knowing and connecting as listening.

> *With each group you have to develop a sense of what they like and how they listen . . . but this is real hard because it isn't like they can tell you. In fact, sometimes when you ask students what they like, they give you the wrong answer because it isn't quite an answer to a question you're after. It's not like, do you like PowerPoint, yes or no? It's more like, what does learning look like in you? Trying to learn this for groups is what you have to do, and my classes range from 6 to 120 students. . . . Starting courses is extra hard, so in the beginning I am always overprepared and I make sure and try a lot of different learning strategies to get to know students. Do they like being read a story, or should I walk around and be the person in the story and sort of act it out? Or do they want lots of structure and road maps for the class, such as the three major points in the lecture, with me going back a lot so everyone knows where I was and where I am going . . . sort of a journey.*[14]

The concernful practices of schooling learning teaching co-occur. For example, this narrative telling reveals Tamra's preserving thinking as an important practice in her life as a teacher. She attends to how she gathers students and brings them in and calls forth thinking as she describes using various learning strategies "to get to know" them. Tamra continues by describing her thinking as she tells how she knows and connects with her class through listening while preparing to lecture.

> *You then try to take all of this in and each week work on fine-tuning what you had prepared from the book and articles or what you had taught the last time and sort of "pitch the lecture" for this specific group. You know, [like] what they often miss or get wrong . . . but you want to be on target and in the zone with each group of students no matter how big or small. Of course, you never really know where the zone is going to be. It can even change from week to week, so you always have to have back-up plans too. . . . Lecturing is always living with moving zones, and that is just the way it is. There aren't any assurances when I go in that what I have prepared will work. But I don't mean you shouldn't prepare, because that is bad and a trap, and some faculty colleagues fall into that. . . . They get so used to giving these lectures that they think they don't need to prepare or they can do all this stuff on their feet. . . . Well, you can a little, but it takes thinking time and careful thought to fine-tune lectures. . . .[15]*

Knowing and connecting is always already becoming. For Tamra, it is through listening that she knows and connects with the students and is able to "fine-tune" her lectures. She calls this "pitching her lecture." She assembles, constructs, and cultivates a place where she and the group learningly dwell, known as "the zone." Knowing and connecting is historical and temporal and changes from week to week. Listening as knowing and connecting can never be certain. Tamra says, *"There aren't any assurances when I go in that what I have prepared will work."* With certainty lacking, Tamra advocates always having a plan B and always preparing even familiar lectures *"because it takes thinking time and careful thought to fine-tune lectures."* Tamra listens to listening as it plays forth in the midst of its to and fro.

In this narrative telling, Tamra retrieves places in her day-to-day experiences for being mindful of thinking about thinking. She shares her thinking in her saying of how she listens to the students' listenings, reading them, in order to know and connect as she offers a new teacher her practical wisdom and expertise in the skills of lecturing.

Questions emerge—for example, How can nursing education courses prepare new teachers to listen to listening as knowing and connecting?

Connectedness, which can be listened to, shows up in Gadamer's notion of "fusing of horizons" (*TM,* 306-307). Horizon in his sense is not to be thought as a transcendental horizon that delivers a unified or ideal meaning to all, but as disclosing and beckoning as the effect of the historicality of traditions at work. Participants herein are not reduced to a transcendental sameness (empathy or psychological conceptions of identity) but are connected and listened to from their own particular, situated horizons (neighborhoods, regions). Another way to read connectedness can be found in Jean-Luc Nancy's discussion of being exposed to limit in its Greek sense of unfolding. To be exposed to limit in this sense is to be "right at." Matters of concern, openness, and engaged openness take place *right at* disclosing and beckoning—"not before, beneath, or beyond"—but as the always already exposure to sense (Raffoul, 1997, xv-xvii).

Reading (sighting) a situation is *listening* to experience speak. Teachers and students are always already listening. What matters is how they are listening. Are they listening to each other and the situations they inhabit in ways that know and connect, in ways that sustain, or in ways that serve to alienate one from another? Kaylee, a nursing instructor teaching a distance online course, receives an email from Penny, who is worried about the quiz she just took. The grade is lower than her other grades. She wants to know how much this will affect her overall grade. She tells Kaylee,

> *I should have sent the family out when I took my quiz, but my children wanted my attention at the end*

*of a long day and you know how that goes . . . this
will not put me at failing, will it? I am just so upset!*

Penny responds.

*Hi, Penny. Thanks for your note. It isn't easy to
manage school and family priorities, and my hat is
off to you for trying. To answer your question. . . .*

She ends her email with an offer of continuing help to the student.

*Please let me know if you have questions and how I
can help. Take care and have a good evening.*[16]

Listening as knowing and connecting is often reflected in the small
acts of conversation. Distance online teachers find their time at a
premium, and the struggle is to keep up with student emails. It is
easy to stop greeting students, offering help, and responding to
their outside-of-school situations that are the background of their
emails. Gayle, another teacher, says,

*I can't answer every email, but there are ways you
can personalize your course so students feel you are
connecting with them. And I make sure that we have
times when I am online with the class so that I do get
to know them and they can connect with me as the
teacher and with each other.*

Responding with a frustrated look, her colleague Indu says, "I find
online courses to be so totally time-consuming that I have learned
to just respond and 'cut to the chase.' Sometimes it gets me in
trouble because a student misinterprets what I have written, but it's
the only way I can keep up and respond to every student email I
receive." The challenge in online education is how to safeguard the
silent listening skills of knowing and connecting practices so that
they do not become, over time, forgotten.

The experience of learning is dialogical. For learning to disclose
and beckon as itself there must be a possibility for unlearning to
occur; otherwise learning could not occur. The always already of

listening always already becomes itself—there is no choice here. An exit from the always already via an eternal idea obtains as the becoming of the unattainable goal of the self-identity of the generic all. The forcible entry to the always already via the establishment of a stable norm is entrapped into forgetting the already of the past and doing away with the future, especially as it shows itself as the surprise of the on-coming.

The temporality of interpreting shows itself in the concernful practice *Interpreting: Unlearning and Becoming.* The practicing of interpreting needs unlearning and becoming in order that the enactment of thinking-saying can be kept in play. Interpretation is not pedagogical in the ontic sense of training and formation.

Aracely, an experienced teacher, describes how rigidly interpreting her role as a teacher could have closed down on a student's becoming a skilled practitioner. She co-responds to Tessa, a student in her psychiatric nursing course, who is experiencing the debilitating influence of severe anxiety. Aracely unlearns thinking of what she experiences as a teacher with students in terms of "a role."

> *As a psych instructor I am always reading situations I find myself in with students. Basically in psych, all you have to offer patients suffering with mental illness is a few drugs and yourself. It can be a threatening area of practice for many. I am always on the lookout, interpreting how things are going and what students are experiencing. It's how I teach. I remember a student, Tessa, who was super anxious, as many students are for one reason or another. We talked, but nothing seemed to help her. As the course goes on, it's like that in psych. Some students lose their anxiety; others have theirs get worse. I see my role as a teacher to be a guide, supporting, giving feedback, and accompanying students who may or may not decide to do something about their own anxious behavior. My willingness to help them change their*

behavior is only an invitation. It is always up to the students to decide what they want to do. That is, of course, so long as their behavior is not unsafe to themselves or others.

Tessa was very talented, but feedback about her anxious behavior seemed to go unheeded. Her anxiety continued to force her to always check things out, sometimes many times, before she did them, even small, safe, and inconsequential things. One day she came running to me breathlessly to again check out a drug dosage. Somehow I knew she knew the answer already, but that this was an important moment. I could help Tessa. I smiled and said, "I can't remember. Is that dosage high or low?" She froze, and I thought she was almost going to faint. Then she realized, her color returned, and she said, "It's low." She turned around and left. Later that day she came to me with teary eyes and said "Thank you." That's all we ever spoke about this situation, but the rest of the semester she was a different nursing student, confident, and able to use her talents. Now eight years later she's an excellent nurse manager on our psych unit.

I will never forget her, because she reminds me that my usual role as a teacher to offer feedback but not intervene until the student asks for help, can close down on them becoming themselves, so to speak. I CAN help students with some of their barriers or problems, sometimes. What I did was risky. This response could have been interpreted by Tessa as ridiculing. Or as abandoning her when she needed help. Somehow though, when I responded to her, I knew in my heart it was time for her to move away from her anxious behavior and become herself and, in that moment together, I knew I could help her do it.

I still believe, as a teacher, that it's the student's right and responsibility to deal with their own behavior, in their own time, and in their own way. My role is more a guide, someone who gives feedback and invites change but mostly waits until the student wants/decides to do something about how they behave. What I am learning is to keep my interpretation of my role more open. Tessa showed me that intervening in a way I thought outside of the boundaries of being a teacher, could make all the difference to a student. And I realized that not intervening can sometimes shut down on student's changing . . . becoming what they already are. I haven't a clue what was going on with Tessa. Neither do I know what I really did nor why I did it that day. To me it was more like "being there" in a moment with a student. A teachable moment, I guess.

I still see my role as a teacher in the same way, sort of. I'm just more willing to keep how I am interpreting my role as a teacher more open now. I find now I have a hard time describing what my role is with the students. It would be something like, I am there with them and together we do what we do, sometimes together, sometimes the students lead, and sometimes I do. Talking about my role as a teacher doesn't work so much for me any more.

This is a narrative telling of unlearning and becoming. A student, in a moment of insight, unlearns the anxious behavior that could have prevented her from becoming a more talented nurse. And a teacher learns to unlearn a hard-and-fast rule about her role as teacher. Listening is inclusive of learning and unlearning. The hard-and-fast rule does not go away but belongs to listening as a different way. Viewing her role as a guide, someone who supports and provides feedback, this teacher believes it is *"up to the students to decide whether to do anything"* about changing their behavior so long as it is not unsafe. In this experience she sights and then reinterprets her role and the possibilities her experiences with students proffer. She learns to keep her role more open for interpretation and arrives at thinking that *"Talking about my role with students as a teacher doesn't work so much for me any more."* Interpreting occurs in never-ending cycles or reinterpreting interpretations. It is enacted understanding such that participants and nonparticipants are bound together as right at prior to any adaptation to a given pedagogical situation (*TM*, 397).

Teaching as Co-Responding: Inviting, Questioning, Retrieving Places, and Preserving

> *"Saying" means "showing," keeping and communicating, but only for those who look around themselves.*
>
> HW, 137

The invitation to look around (to listen and sight) is issued as (gives birth to) disclosing and beckoning. The human being can provoke a disclosure but only at the cost of forgetting disclosing in its open beckoning and disclosing as an inviting. The matter of concern that needs to be thought-said is the proper essence of inviting. Inviting in the hermeneutic phenomenological sense cannot be solicited or effected; it must be waited on (tended to) as a presencing of engaged openness.

Heidegger devoted a significant portion of his "Conversation on a Country Path about Thinking" to waiting (*DT*, 62-90). In this conversation, waiting[17] is not meant to be a passive receiving of whatever comes one's way, whether detrimental or beneficial. The sense of waiting abides in attending to the unconcealedness of engaged openness (*DT*, 68, 72-74). One dialogically experiences waiting as the clearing of the open between as an abiding expanse (*DT*, 75). This essentially means that the human being of openness is offered the opportunity (as possibility) to first and foremost exist as a never to be complete mortal entity, always already conditioned by its temporal-historical regioning as presence-to (open clearing). Waiting is abiding with a sense of open but steadfast readiness (*DT*, 81-82).

The concernful practice of *Inviting: Waiting and Letting Be* does not reduce teaching to, but is a surplus over, the mere communication of neutral messages and unconditioned data transfer.

The silence of the unsaid, especially as articulated by Jones (1999), that we cited earlier can show up as a saying which shows. Teaching-learning-co-responding in the midst of an absence of uttered words shows the unique essence of language as discursiveness. One can be enabled to follow the enactment of listening-saying as one is engaged by one's own temporal-historical openness. *Language says itself in its most pronounced way in its holding back.* The letting-be of silence is its own teacher and teaching.

Khalad, a nursing professor, tells how he waits and lets doctoral students be as they near completion of their dissertations.

There is a point in most doctoral students' research where the teacher sees something that the student does not see. Often it is something that stands in front and is clearly visible, yet out of the student's sight. I know some faculty think it is their role to tell or show it to the student. I always wait. And wait and wait, inviting the student to return to the data one more time. Accompanying the student in summarizing the study for implications, I let the student come to the study. And always the student sees it eventually. We, as teachers, are so used to jumping in and helping students that it is hard for us to wait and let learning be. If the advisor jumps in, the student will forever question whether conducting independent research will ever be a possibility. But it is hard to wait in the shadows. It must be done in a way that the student does not feel abandoned or feel that the teacher is testing or withholding information. This is the most difficult kind of teaching I ever experience.

Doing nothing is doing something. Waiting/tending/inviting/letting be do not speak of a quiescence. Rather they speak of a deep engagement that holds open possibility as possibility. This kind of silent engagement does not come easily. As Khalad says, it is *"hard to wait in the shadows."* The boundary between teaching and learning is blurred; learning to teach becomes teaching to learn.

Heidegger wrote that inviting and letting be as teaching is more difficult than learning:

> Teaching is even more difficult than learning. We know that, but we rarely think about it. And why is teaching more difficult than learning? Not because [teachers] must have a larger store of information, and have it always ready. Teaching is more difficult than learning because what teaching calls for is this: to let learn. [Real teachers], in fact, [let] nothing else be learned than—learning. [Their] conduct, therefore, often produces the impression that we properly learn nothing from [them], if by learning we now suddenly understand merely the procurement of useful information. [Teachers are] ahead of [their] apprentices in this alone, that [they have] still far more to learn than they—[teachers have] to learn to let them learn. [Teachers] must be capable of being more teachable than the apprentices. [Teachers are] far less assured of [their] ground than those who learn are of theirs. If the relation between [teachers] and the taught is genuine, therefore, there is never a place in it for the authority of the know-it-all of the authoritative sway of the official (*WCT,* 15).

Silence is evocatory of questioning. This is especially true of the ways the silent nothing of death evokes the questionings of human beings. The very presencing of questions questioning and the questionable makes (lets be) visible the fleeting evanescence of answers and rejoinders. If all were the silent nothing of *the* ultimate answer, there would be no need for questions, answers, or rejoinders. There is a tension between the communicable and the ineffable (Nelson, 2000, 153).

Making visible in the narrow sense of a transcendental phenomenological reduction is a committal "to particular ideas about consciousness, the subject and knowledge" (Nelson, 2000, 155). These are idealized structures, which overlook sense as related to historical self and temporal world. Therefore making visible as letting can never be decoupled from the temporality and historicality of sense and questioning as these make themselves visible not *to* a putative conscious subject but *as* the open clearing.

Questioning: Sense and Making Meanings Visible is a co-occurring concernful practice that also cannot be divided into separate constituent parts. Making visible is claimed by thrownness. Sense as the always already immediacy of understanding shows itself as "opening a direction, a possibility of value—a possibility of 'meaning' but not [as] a meaning" (Smith, 2008, x). Meaningful questioning, answering, and rejoining could not speak the human being if language did not permit hermeneutic phenomenological listening, sighting, and thinking-saying as sense. We have cited the position that meanings can issue forth as the forerunning ever-circulating inclusive play of sense even as sense withholds itself.

Questioning as the opening of sense and meaning making is revealed in the following narrative telling. Linnea, a teacher trying to enact some alternate pedagogies, describes her experiences in a medical-surgical class. She transforms asking questions into a questioning that calls students to sense and the associated letting of meaning-making become visible.

> *I resisted asking questions and answering questions. I more asked these open-ended questions that kept the thinking going. At one point, a student asked about treating diabetic neuropathy, and I said to them, this is content I was going to present today, but in nursing, there will always be situations where you don't have the information you need . . . so let's imagine we need to get this information, and a teacher or book is not handy, so "How are we to think treating diabetic neuropathy?" I am learning*

*. . . that when you use the new pedagogies, you
spend your time preparing for class by coming up
with questions like this one!*[18]

In wanting students to practice thinking, Linnea learns how to take
the questions that call only for a calculative thinking that answers
a question and transform them into questionings that have no
answer. She attempts to call students to think from the sense of
their questions in order to make their possible meanings visible.
"How are we to think diabetic neuropathy?" can be experienced by
students as a vacuous question or as one that has no meaning for
them as nursing students.

But given time to think about it, there are many possible ways
they can sight what this questioning reveals. What this questioning
does not say is, How are we to think *about* diabetic neuropathy?
That would be a question, which although broad, would have
already defined a limited number of ways to respond. "Thinking
diabetic neuropathy" emerges in a student who responds, "One
way to think diabetic neuropathy is in the patient response, 'I don't
have diabetic neuropathy, I *am* diabetic neuropathy.'" The ensuing
conversation reveals how patients are often separated by healthcare
professionals from the meanings of their ongoing experiences
with their symptoms when these become labeled and objectified.
Similarly, a question for the patient becomes not "Describe what is
it like for you to experience diabetic neuropathy," but "What does
it *mean* to you to experience diabetic neuropathy?"

Sense as sense calls for questions as making sense of the
question as sense as the circulation of letting meaning show itself.

Retrieving Places: Keeping Open a Future of Possibilities as a
concernful practice is a co-responding that sustains the openness
(clearedness) of places as it retrieves them. Places are not discrete
neutral locations on a spatially neutral X, Y, Z axis. Places are
loci of meaning wherein understanding is available. Only through
letting places back into the forerunning of their historical-temporal
situatedness can their creative character disclose and beckon. The
sustaining openness of a place does not depend on a conscious

subject's willfully drawing a locus of meaning out of an ahistorical or indifferent void. Retrieving a place is more akin to participation in a birthing or to the surprise of incipience than to an establishment or production of a fenced or walled-in enclosure. Hermeneutic phenomenology is the attempt to trace the open sustaining/ retrieving of a place back to its emergent/elusive birth and forward to its possible emergence/elusion in order to give witness to place as a play of future becoming.

Retrieving is letting the self-gathering retrieving of matters of concern assemble and sustain themselves in ways that are temporally and historically available as meaningful. Therefore retrieving places as a dyadic term must be thought-said in both nominal and verbal senses. These concurring ways belong to an open clearing in which the alreadiness of presence-to and the forerunning of becoming are always already being mediated (*HGH*, 6-7). Glenna challenges a presupposition of conventional pedagogies that teachers can and should preselect content and establish competencies for students. She asks the students what content they are "interested in." She discovers new possibilities for the sighting of learning in her course.

> *I just plain decided to not worry about content this one day and just talk about what the students were interested in, plain and simple. They wanted to look at some actual cases and experiences they had had with CVA [cardiovascular accident] patients and their families. What I discovered was [that] this class was really about learning to listen to one another. I listened as the students helped one another and contradicted one another, exploring and challenging various ideas about providing nursing care to patients suffering the effects of CVA. I didn't direct the conversation, but I was a part of the conversation, too. The class was the best I had had in a long time!*[19]

Retrieving as a practice issued-forth out of disclosing and beckoning finds itself necessary when situations call out (self-retrieve) in their problematicity. It is at that moment that their clearing demands a rethinking-resaying of a matter of concern.

The problem of selecting and then presenting content during a class is a familiar one. Conventional pedagogies are teacher centered in that they embrace the selection and sequencing of content as an ostensible co-participative experience with student input, but they are ultimately under the guardianship of the teacher. How to select, sequence, and present particular information from a vast field of knowledge is an ever-present problem albeit silently (but nevertheless present) crying out for and as retrieval.

Glenna discovers new possibilities for learning when she turns over the class to the students one day. As students become engaged in conversations about the content, she realizes that they are sighting learning as not just content but more: *"What I discovered was [that] this class was really about learning to listen to one another. I listened as the students helped one another and contradicted one another, exploring and challenging various ideas about providing nursing care to patients suffering the effects of CVA."*

Glenna also discovers that her conventional pedagogical role of directing class discussions is transformed into a converging conversation. *"I didn't direct the conversation, but I was a part of the conversation, too."* The retrieval of places (loci of meaning) as an open, self-retrieving future of possibilities resonates as a teacher lets places retrieve themselves in her teaching for students to identify, select, and sequence content. She keeps open the self-retrieving future of new possibilities as they advene for (present themselves for) student learning. She discovers for herself that she can become a coequal participant in class conversations. To be retrieved as such is to be released to the superfluity of the give and take of open luxurious moments of releasing. There can be no such thing as redundance here. In every retrieving experience, the play of possibility is infinite.

The concernful practice of *Preserving: Reading, Writing, Thinking-Saying, and Dialogue* works to reveal how words as matters of concern shelter and preserve the emergence/elusion of available matters of concern. Thinking-saying as dialogical experience (*not,* it should be stressed, causes) discloses and beckons matters of concern in any reading, writing, thinking. Each word discloses and beckons as "something familiar and consequently may be understood only according to these familiar ways" (Vallega-Neu, 2003, 94). No word is or can be free of the possibility that it will be misinterpreted. In order for words to unconceal their essential (unique and proper) unconcealing, an appropriate thinking-saying which shelters unconcealedness as transitory (temporal-historical) is needed as listening. This listening must be engaged with and belong to the unconcealing of engaged openness.[20] Listening as listening[21] obtains in its widest play, from the indifference possible in the everyday to the unsettledness of emergence/elusion as the unconcealing of engaged openness.

Preservation of reading, writing, thinking-saying, and dialogue must allow for a doubling of sense as a conflict of meanings. The first moment calls out not to question the status quo or for that matter not to question any assertion about the state of the status quo. The second moment calls out to think preserving as sheltering the unconcealedness of engaged openness in the matter of concern "found in historical time-space" (*RHT*, 268). The preservation/sheltering of sense as sense lets meanings show themselves as their own play.

Bell, a master's degree nursing student, describes her experiences in a class in which the teacher enacts new pedagogies. Bell describes this course as "mind opening," "freeing," and "thought provoking." Hermeneutic phenomenological understanding is here even though it is never formally mentioned.

Preserving the practices of reading, writing, thinking-saying, and dialogue is a part of every pedagogy. What matters is the *how* of the preserving; that is, how is it that teachers and students experience coming together in reading, writing, thinking-saying, and dialogue situations. Bell describes how her teacher presents a question that is complex and that has caused Bell to do a lot of thinking.

> *A lot of the times when teachers pose a question,*
> *they also have an answer to it right away. And*

so you don't have to really think about it. And I suppose, if I don't have to think about it, I [haven't] really learned it.[22]

Bell appreciates the new pedagogies, but not without a certain amount of confusion or doubt.

I think the hardest thing is giving yourself permission to not feel . . . limited by your learning [and] . . . making sure I have enough time to learn all the things that I want to read or do, or look up. . . . I still don't feel like I know enough solid . . . I don't know something . . . I'm searching for more. And . . . I know that's good.[23]

Bell finds that she can retrieve retrievable possibilities for her own learning that free her from determining reading, writing, thinking, and dialogue as discrete and distinct experiences. Hermeneutic phenomenological understanding reveals for Bell the nature of her searching quest as more of a journey than the effectuation of a discovery.

The modernist metaphysical sense of reading, writing, thinking, and dialogue is housed in literacy as the ability to read advertisements; writing as the production of tendentious and/ or titillating, entertaining news articles; thinking as the cognition of how best to enhance (aggrandize) one's status; and assertive utterances in the service of one's vanquishing of one's opponents. Sense encloses itself in the ego-subject. All of these possibilities rest in conceptions that take the modern subject as the ultimate agent of its own self-produced manifestness.

Preserving is other than the practice of freezing an entity in order to maintain it in a state of permanent suspended animation. Preserving in the hermeneutic phenomenological sense involves the renunciation of the claim to permanence in order to commit oneself to the temporal-historical play of engaged openness. Preserving as a sojourn allows the human being of openness to experience renunciation as the open clearing of the saying word of language. "Renunciation gets the word underway toward that which concerns every Saying as Saying" (*OWL,* 150).[24] As such preserving, learning as listening turns on bodying forth in the world and not on an exclusive focus on listeners.

Human beings as they body forth are always already reading and, of reading, "every reading must come back to 'not knowing' where it is going" (*BP,* 337). The incipience of engaged openness reveals/conceals, presences/absences, emerges/eludes such that there is always already a self-withdrawing from every word.

Bodying forth is the "site of touch that makes sense" but "as materiality is at the same time outside of all sense" (James, 2006, 149). Touch is the limit unfolding of open separation wherein the human being undergoes the on-coming of sense. Sense (1) is a surplus over "any relation of signifier to signified," (2) is "extralinquistic yet finite and embodied," and (3) exists or lets "exists only in the separation-touch of sense and impenetrable matter" (James, 2006, 149). The site of the human being of modernity lets it have, gives it access to, the sharing of reading and writing. The belongingness of reading-writing is claimed by the disclosing and beckoning of opening-reopening (retrieval) (*BP,* 94). Bodying forth as reading and writing "is to be exposed to, to expose oneself to" the offering of sense that has no sense of itself (*BP,* 338).

As has been evident throughout this book, the sheltering-preserving of the truth of engaged openness in historical time-space as a letting-issuing-forth of matters of concern needs the instantiation of the human being of openness (*RHT,* 268-269). There is a letting appear that can be of attuned listening. The truth of engaged openness is sheltered-preserved in matters of concern. But engaged openness must not be thought from out of matters of concern but must be thought out of disclosing and beckoning (*CP,* 5-7). Thinking-saying thought out of its own limit and as its own abolition of the transcendental signifier shows itself as freedom for "the yet-to-be-made, of the need-to-make (something with) one's possibilities" (*BP,* 106, 198-109).

All matters of concern available to the human being of openness are "texts" (*DH,* 213). Texts as "read or readable" (*DH,* 216) are the exscription of embodied human beings of openness (James, 2006, 151). Jean-Luc Nancy writes of exscription as his "clumsy gesture to indicate what can only be written, in the always uncertain thought of language" (*BP,* 339) as the infinite issuing forth of sense. He prefaces this thought with these comments:

> The word "exscription" exscribes nothing and writes nothing—it shows what matters—the [matter of concern] itself. Writing exscribes [sense] every bit as it inscribes significations.

BP, 338-339

Exscription shows itself as the issuing forth of the belonging together of the "separation which is maintained between impenetrable matter and bodily sense, and between bodily sense and linguistic signification" (James, 2006, 149). The turning "point where writing situates itself outside of the sense it inscribes in and as writing" (James, 2006, 150) offers itself as exscribing. Writing as the textuality of texts "simultaneously inscribes and exscribes" (*BP,* 334). As the between of turning, writing shows itself as the always already becoming that obtains as a surplus over "clear and distinct signifiers or fixed moments of meaning" (James, 2006, 150). When thought-said as belonging to "the limit of signification or as signification at its limit" (James, 2006, 150), writing shows texts as the exscribing of their temporal-historical possibility.

The exscribing of a text is the simple fact of its engaged openness right at world and community. The factuality of that simple fact calls the human being of openness as the open clearing. It is as engaged openness and only as engaged openness that the text shows its freedom for its yet-to-be and its exigent need-to-be brought unto language. Thinking-saying[25] is sustained "of the text itself, in the anxiety and the joy of its work of thought, its play of writing, its offer of reading" (*BP,* 107). Hermeneutic phenomenological thinking-saying "as well as thought in general thinks only while being at once and as such caught up" in the possibilities of the simple fact of existence as writing, reading, and understanding (*BP,* 99).

Hidden in every dialogue is "understanding as the disclosedness of [engaged openness unto the human being of openness that] both gives and withdraws itself, opens itself up, and closes itself off, already" (*BP,* 90). Closings-off belong to openings-up, and as such "each takes place just at the other" (*BP,* 91). The on-coming forerunning of taking place is dialogue resting in the differing sameness of engaged openness (*BP,* 102).

Reading, writing, thinking-saying, and dialogue co-occur such that reading is always already the making sense of something written—writing is not without thinking-saying. We risk belaboring the obvious when we assert that all of the above could not be present without dialogue of one sort or another.

Preserving as care's enabling lets Jonna, an experienced teacher, describe how she preserves reading, writing, thinking-saying, and dialogue in her class. At one time in her career she assigned readings with the expectation that individual students would simply read them and that would be that. After all, the educational theory classes she had taken posited that reading was cognitive uptake and that there was no place for the "subjective" in "objectively presented" reading assignments. But to her surprise, she was drawn to rethink the meaning of pedagogies when she used narrative tellings in her reading assignments.

> *I noticed more and more students worked together on reading each other's papers. They also found books and articles for each other. And I found that the papers . . . were reduced significantly [in length] as students did more thinking and rewriting. . . . Class discussions were definitely better.*[26]

Another teacher Sheila, describing a similar experience recounts howto ask for narrative tellings that the students are to write in addition to the case histories for discussion in order to help students think through the points that are important.

> *I think that the stories need to hit home the points that you're trying to make with the dry lecture. . . . I think that if you give them just very specific basic facts, that's helpful. Not always belabor everything,*

but just try to give them periodic, basic facts that they can . . . actually [write] down and highlight and focus specifically on that.[27]

Embedded in these narrative tellings are the presuppositions of conventional pedagogies, specifically that learning begins with mere knowledge acquisition or cognitive gain. Thinking is reduced to memorization and recall of what the teacher has identified as worthy of thinking.[28] Beverly, a teacher, tells of how she transforms a 15-page paper and learns new understandings about reading, writing, thinking, and dialogue as preserving practices.

I wanted to do something different with my 15-page course paper so I asked the students to write a five-page paper about what it means to them as a nurse to care for a patient diagnosed with Parkinson's disease [PD]. I suggested we ask for volunteers to read their papers in class on the date the paper was due. I told them I would write one too. I thought putting my thoughts down on paper would help my thinking about this question and the assignment before I had to grade them. The students liked the idea of a shorter paper, that was until they started writing—then they wanted more pages! But they were confused over what I meant by "what it means to them as a nurse." "Think about it and tell me," I said. They had done a lot of reading about PD, and we spent time in class discussing the nursing care of these patients.

The students were doing well but somehow something was missing. The day they read their papers, I knew what it was. More than pulling together what they had read and talked about in class, what they wrote showed their thinking in ways that I knew they understood. And the class discussions after each reading were amazing. It was clear the students had done an amazing amount of reading, especially the research literature, and done a lot of thinking about treating PD. One student wrote a five-page narrative poem about a writer with PD and about how the nurses help him finish his last novel even though he can no longer write or type. Another student said she interviewed two patients with PD and learned how important advocating for patients with PD was for her as a nurse. She wrote an excellent position paper on restoring state funding for long-term home nursing care. It was a synthetic paper that brought together research and the stories of these patients with PD.

Our discussions were wide ranging and totally engaging. Every student wanted to read their paper but we ran out of time. The students decided to post all the papers, including mine, online so everyone could read them. I was amazed at how their thinking, which was not always visible to me in class, came through as they wrote this paper. One student who is working hard on her writing skills said it helped her most to read the other students' papers and compare her paper with theirs.

Beverly preserves reading, writing, thinking-saying, and dialogue as important practices for nurses by recasting an assignment with a question that called forth thinking. Reading the papers to one another was a compelling dialogical experience for the group. Students gained insights into each other's talents as well. Beverly was enabled to sight the thinking of her students in ways that were not evident to her before. The co-occurring of reading, writing, thinking-saying, and dialogue shows itself in this narrative telling. Although the historical-temporal unconcealing of engaged openness is sheltered/preserved in matters of concern, engaged openness cannot be thought-said out of matters of concern. *Engaged openness exigently needs to be thought-said out of engaged openness.*[29] Preserving as reading, writing, thinking-saying, and dialogue is a co-responding that shelters the human being of openness.

Concernful Practices of Schooling Learning Teaching

Listening to one another, in which being-with cultivates itself, is more accurately a compliance in being-with-one-another, as co-enactment in concern.

HCT, 266

If we have remained faithful to the pathway which has claimed us, we have followed hints as they have beckoned us to their disclosings. Our step back to following after harbors within itself the possibility that we have overlooked other hints. Hermeneutic phenomenology as we are practicing it here is our attempt to both call out and listen to calls to thinking-saying. Thereby being-with-another is dialogical experience as it shows itself as the required attendance that the human being must comply with.

The fundamental presupposition implicit vis-à-vis concernful practices is made explicit when these practices are listened to as only disclosed as conversation (dialogue). Whenever texts are, in the widest sense of the word presence, they are claimed by the need to be understood (*RJD, 55*). This need to be understood is not merely a psychological state or the methodological imperative of the sciences. Matters of concern in their temporal-historical abiding instantiate themselves in the sense of an open clearing (in its verbal and nominal senses) where disclosing and beckoning takes place in and as the mediated showing-saying of language. Direct conversation as well as its lack lets understanding be as possibility.

The convergence of conversations presences as their limit. The task of hermeneutic phenomenology is to trace understandings as the limit of converging (abiding) conversations back to their incipience (their limit) and forward to their possibility, not as givens but as on-coming. The dialogical experience of the "hermeneutic is precisely the phenomenology of the event of understanding traced back to its very incipience, which ultimately means back to the level of the eluding non-understood, to that which can never be understood, the mysterious, the concealment of unconcealment. It is here that the hermeneutical, the process of the exposure of hidden meanings, finds its most radical problems" (*HGH,* 4). The converging conversations of concernful practices are neither agreements nor disagreements; they let their historical-temporal abiding, sighting, and listening be sighted and listened to as the singular plurality of their lettings and offerings

Chapter 11 Notes

1   See our discussion of care/concern in Chapter 3.

2   See Schoenbohm, 2001, 15-31, especially 20.

3   The Gordian knot: an intricate knot tied by Gordius, king of Phrygia, and cut through by Alexander the Great in response to the prophecy that only the future ruler of Asia could loosen it. Cutting a Gordian knot involves solving a problem by "force or by evading its conditions" (*Shorter Oxford English Dictionary,* 5th ed., 2002).

4   Diekelmann & Scheckel, 2004, 2003.

5   Diekelmann & Mikol, 2003.

6   See Diekelmann, Allen, & Tanner, 1989, and McEwen & Brown, 2002, for how NCLEX, accreditation, and State Boards of Nursing can discourage innovation.

7   Refers to State Board licensing examinations, National Council Licensing Exam (NCLEX) that all students must pass in order to obtain licenses to practice.

8   Diekelmann, Allen, & Tanner, 1989.

9   Diekelmann, 2001, 60.

10   See Diekelmann, 2003b, for experiences of students and teachers attending to engendering learning communities.

11   School-wide day of public storytelling in Narrative Pedagogy pilot schools.

12   This school eliminated the curriculum committee and revised the curriculum in a series of student-faculty workshops.

13   Young & Diekelmann, 2002, 408.

14   Diekelmann, 2002a, 241.

15   Diekelmann, 2002a, 241.

16   Diekelmann & Mendias, 2005, 341.

17   See the discussion of waiting and truth in Lilly, 1991, xviii.

18   Diekelmann & Smythe, 2004, 343.

19   Diekelmann, 2004a, 438.

20   See also Vallega-Neu, 2003, 92-96.

21   See our discussion of listening in Chapter 8.

22   Ironside, 2003a, 512.

23 Ironside, 2003a, 515.

24 See also *OWL,* 142-156.

25 See Vallega-Neu, 2003, 14 fn. 9.

26 Diekelmann & Ironside, 1998b, 1352.

27 Ironside, 2005a, 446.

28 Ironside, 2005a, 446.

29 See Schoenbohm, 2001, 24-26.

Part III

Converging Conversations of Schooling Learning Teaching

Chapter 12

Schooling as Attending:
"Oh, no! Not another curriculum revision!"

Converging conversations offer themselves as the heart of hermeneutic phenomenological interpretations.[1] In this exemplar, findings from the Narrative Pedagogy study show up as enacted by four teachers from Narrative Pedagogy pilot schools who converse about their experiences in revising the curriculum. Converging conversations work to reveal ways of enacting hermeneutic phenomenology through making thematic[2] or explicating (questioning and interpreting) presuppositions in order to enable Narrative Pedagogy to show up. They bring to conversation the Concernful Practices of Schooling Learning Teaching (CP)[3] as revealed in themes and patterns.

CONCERNFUL PRACTICES OF SCHOOLING LEARNING TEACHING (CP)

- Presencing: Attending and Being Open
- Assembling: Constructing and Cultivating
- Gathering: Welcoming and Calling Forth
- Caring: Engendering of Community
- Listening: Knowing and Connecting
- Interpreting: Unlearning and Becoming
- Inviting: Waiting and Letting Be
- Questioning: Sense and Making Meanings Visible
- Retrieving Places: Keeping Open a Future of Possibilities
- Preserving: Reading, Writing, Thinking-Saying, and Dialogue

---

[1] For an exegesis of converging conversations as crossing, see Chapter 1.

[2] Making thematic is dialoguing about or explicating presuppositions, such as making thematic the forgotten or overlooked presuppositions of conventional pedagogies or of the subject-object paradigm. It is *not* identifying themes in a text. For further discussion of making schooling learning and teaching thematic, see Chapter 10.

[3] For hermeneutic phenomenological (ontological) descriptions of each Concernful Practice, see Chapter 11.

385

In the following converging conversation, cycles of interpretations[4] bring narrative themes and patterns (Concernful Practices) into dialogue and conversation with one another. The hermeneutic circle as the circle of participating, or cycles of interpretations, is never complete and never-ending.[5] Interpretations reveal the wider play of multiple understandings. There is no one correct interpretation.[6] Correctness is not implicit in interpretations; however, truths can self-disclose. Similarly, there is not one way to present interpretations.

The Concernful Practices of Schooling Learning Teaching were identified in the "data set"[7] of the 20-year longitudinal study of Narrative Pedagogy as reflected in extant research publications and other Narrative Pedagogy studies. In these studies, findings are typically published in a scientific research format, presenting one theme or pattern with accompanying narrative tellings. The difficulty in presenting findings this way is that as experienced, they do not show up as such. Themes and patterns co-found one another and as such arrive together; they do not occur in isolation. They are always narratives, historical and temporally situated.

---

[4] Narrative tellings announce, address, and call forth the saying-relating of a narrative gathering, which distinguishes itself in that it never admits of final understandings. Co-responding asks for the possibility to be allowed such that there may be different answers of each encounter.

[5] See Chapter 3 for discussion of hermeneutic circle as the circle of participating. Interpretations are always already of a background of pre-understandings. In these interpretations, pre-understanding presupposes hermeneutic phenomenology. For example, in hermeneutic phenomenology, dialogues as they are read (interpreted) are certain paths from thinking-saying as well as of thinking-saying—they take into account the excess of thoughtful interpretation to which interpretation as itself offers itself. The difference between the singular proprieties of voices, ways, modes, is invited as announcement. It is to an announcement and to an opening of the very dialogue of thinking that all are guests—all share in the hospitality/gift/offering of difference. From the temporally particular always already to the oncoming self-presencing of presence—each time the hermeneutical thinking circle does not cease from breaking off.

[6] Refer to Chapter 6, for discussion of how narratives announce, address, and call forth: "There is much to say" as the basic hermeneutical relation. Interpretation can never be a fixing of fleeting meanings (*PH,* 211).

[7] The "data set" of this study (approved by the Institutional Review Board at the University of Wisconsin-Madison) is narrative tellings gathered through group and individual interviews as well as written submissions by students, teachers, and clinicians in nursing education.

It is important in hermeneutic phenomenological interpretations to bring the reader into conversation with the text and to make the thinking of the researcher visible. The intent is to engage in conversational thinking between the reader and the text, not the advocacy of one interpretation over another. The purpose is to free thinking and to reveal otherwise overlooked interpretations.

> This commentary extends the explication of presuppositions and the Concernful Practices; all the while recurring themes, patterns,[8] and narratives tellings[9] are made thematic, kept in motion, held open and problematic. Footnotes link the reader to literature and exegeses in previous chapters to extend interpretations of schooling learning teaching as a co-occurring, intra-related, invisible phenomenon. Sidebar comments address the themes and patterns[10] (Concernful Practices)[11] and reflect questionings[12] that point to the exploration of presuppositions. Boxed commentary, reflecting cycles of interpretations, is given as it arises and occurs within the conversation. In the Narrative Pedagogy study, many stories of "Oh, no! Not another curriculum revision" were gathered.

Themes and patterns always show up in conversational contexts. It might be an individual or group interview, or a written narrative telling. Even in the latter, the author of the narrative telling is in conversation with the experience being described. All themes and patterns are constitutively narrative tellings in the context of converging conversations of one kind of another. The following approach presents themes and patterns as they converge in conversations.

---

[8] Themes and patterns reflect recurring concerns. See also Chapters 10, 13 and 14 for discussions of making thematic and converging conversations.

[9] The term narrative telling is an attempt to focus on the conversational aspects of narratives. It is to reflect and embrace a narrative's telling (in all the senses of telling) as the loci of matters of concern. Thereby narratives gather the human being of openness as a call to conversation. For explorations of narrative tellings as method, see Chapter 6.

[10] Patterns are reflected in all themes, but not all themes reflect all patterns. The Concernful Practices of Schooling Learning Teaching are patterns and reflect the highest level of hermeneutic phenomenological analysis. See N. Diekelmann & P. Ironside, 1998a, Hermeneutics. In J. Fitzpatrick (Ed.), *Encyclopedia of nursing research* (pp. 243-245) (New York: Springer), for further discussion of themes and patterns.

[11] The Concernful Practices of Schooling Learning Teaching are co-occurring, are *inter*-related, and belong together. Sidebar commentaries indicate the most compelling practices we have identified but are never meant to tell the whole story. The play of other Concernful Practices can always already be present as possibility.

[12] The practice of questioning is more originary than the question. Questioning is itself a response to the demand that sense makes upon us. See Chapter 9 for explications of teaching and questioning.

"Oh, no! Not another curriculum revision!"

Sarah

Being on the curriculum committee is a real pain. No one wants to volunteer and we tried electing people but *no one* would run. Everyone just moans, "Oh, no, not another curriculum revision!" What does that tell you?

Malala

You got that right! But can't we think outside the box? If you'll allow me that cliché! We are teachers and we have to be involved. We have to pay attention to schooling the students, one way or another. Every nurse must go to some kind of school. But we've got to attend to how we can make curricular revisions better.

Sarah

Yeah, all of us must go to school. But how much can we really change revising the curriculum? Like we must have a curriculum committee for accreditation![13] The funny thing is though, if we'd look at reality, every time we teach a course, it's never quite the same and so the curriculum is revised! And if a new teacher takes over

CP – Assembling: Constructing and Cultivating

Themes:
- Accreditation, Innovation, and Reform: The Curriculum as Tinker-Toy
- Accreditation and Reform: Closing Down or Opening Up Innovation

Questionings:
- Are curriculum committees in existence because accreditation criteria mandate a systematic review of the curriculum?
- Have other ways to revise a curriculum that do not require a curriculum committee been left unexplored?
- Are there other ways to include clinicians and students in curriculum reform than having them represented on the curriculum committee?
- How are innovation and reform in nursing education shaping or shaped by innovation and reform in nursing practice?

---

[13] For a critical hermeneutical analysis of innovation and accreditation criteria for baccalaureate programs, see N. Diekelmann, D. Allen, & C. Tanner, 1989, *The National League for Nursing criteria for appraisal of baccalaureate programs: A critical hermeneutic analysis* (New York: National League for Nursing Press).

my course, changes will be made so the curriculum is always being revised. Right? We equate the curriculum with schooling. But even if you are not "officially" going to school, you are always attending to what life does or does not teach and that's schooling. There is just no getting around this. Malala is right. Schooling of some kind of another is always with us, even if you are not "officially" going to school; even after graduation. To me it seems we're always schooled in a particular time and place. We learn facts are always changing. So schooling is always situated and historical. Yet we act like it's not. We want to get the curriculum revised, have consensus, getting it right for once and for all! Don't we? Yet we know better. The curriculum is always changing so why do we hate doing something that lacks certainty?

CP – Caring: Engendering of Community; Assembling: Constructing and Cultivating

Theme: Revising the Curriculum: Conflating the Documented Curriculum and the Curriculum-as-Experienced

Questionings:
- Do mandated curriculum committees belong to conventional pedagogies?
- How do other pedagogies like Narrative Pedagogy differ on what constitutes the curriculum that would support/negate the need for a mandated curriculum committee?
- Have schools stopped considering other possibilities like all-faculty or all-school curriculum meetings in place of the curriculum committee?

Explicating as identifying, extending understandings, and critiquing presuppositions like "we must have a curriculum committee" is enacting hermeneutic phenomenology. Narrative Pedagogy is enabled as a call to thinking. Hermeneutic phenomenological thinking-saying is thinking "outside the box" or thinking that is called forth as interpreting. It is thinking for its own sake,[14] not necessarily with a goal or purpose in mind. Exploring ways to revise the curriculum without having a curriculum committee, such as all-school or all-faculty meetings in place of the curriculum committee, lets thinking be as thinking-saying. In dialogues that go to the heart of a matter of concern, nothing is dismissed out of hand. In a small school this could be readily explored, but in a large school, where this approach would be impossible, pursuing this idea *for its own sake* frees thinking for alternative thoughts to come along. When thinking is freed in this way, the saying of dialogue enables the identification and explication of presuppositions as a sojourn on the path of enacting hermeneutic phenomenology in order to enable the enacting of Narrative Pedagogy.

---

[14] See Chapter 10 for an explication of hermeneutic phenomenological thinking.

Winona

We hate the whole process of revising the curriculum, don't we? Why don't we just figure out how to manage a constantly *changing* curriculum? Instead we act surprised when it becomes a mess after we've avoided revising it for years.[15] We only really evaluate the curriculum when it's accreditation time. Then we do this massive self-study and as soon as the accreditors leave, we revise the curriculum. We feel compelled to do something about all the problems, gaps, or redundancies we found! But it's not just the evaluation of the curriculum we hate, it's knowing there is going to be such upheaval when it comes time to approve the new curriculum. Coming up with the new curriculum is always incredibly time-consuming and exhausting! After a while, we teachers end up voting to approve certain changes *only* because we're tired of faculty curriculum meetings!

Themes:
- The Nearness of the Near: "On Listening to What Stands In Front of Us!"
- On Listening to What Stands In Front of Us: Changing THE curriculum and the CHANGING curriculum.

Questionings:
- What does the absence of problems, gaps, and redundancies mean for revising the curriculum?
- In conventional pedagogies, is the absence of problems assumed to be an unlikely (or unnecessary) time and place for substantive innovation?
- How can the lack of problems, gaps, or redundancies close down the possibilities for innovation and reform?
- Are there ways to think about innovation and reform that do not rely on breakdown or problems?

CP – Assembling: Constructing and Cultivating; Caring: Engendering of Community; Gathering: Welcoming and Calling Forth; Retrieving Places: Keeping Open a Future of Possibilities

---

For hermeneutic phenomenology, the past as on-coming is always in front of the human being of openness. The human being is always already thrown into on-coming situations. Disclosing and beckoning discloses and beckons the engaged openness of matters of concern. Hermeneutic phenomenology as enacting the engaged openness of matters of concern enables Narrative Pedagogy. It can become an enabling as an enacting of hermeneutic phenomenology.

---

[15] For interpretations of how breakdown influences substantive reform, see N. Diekelmann, 2005c, Engaging the students *and* the teacher: Co-creating substantive reform with Narrative Pedagogy, *Journal of Nursing Education, 44*(6), 249-252.

Sarah

And when we finally come up with a new curriculum, phasing it in requires years.[16] Meanwhile you have to keep the two groups of students separate as the "new" curriculum students and the "old" curriculum students are always after each other. It's a mess and it's our own doing! Why do we keep doing this?

> **Themes:**
>
> • Trying Something New: The Possible, the Familiar, and the At-Hand
> • Solving Problems, Overcoming Tedium, and Innovation

> **CP** – Caring: Engendering of Community; Assembling: Constructing and Cultivating; Gathering: Welcoming and Calling Forth; Retrieving Places: Keeping Open a Future of Possibilities

Julius

The students in the "old" curriculum tell students in the "new" one that they're going to fail Boards[17] because the curriculum has been "watered down" or some other such nonsense. And the "new" students tell the "old" curriculum students they are missing out on important new content and clinical experiences. Faculty then chime in on one side of the other, don't they?

> **CP** – Gathering: Welcoming and Calling Forth; Retrieving Places: Keeping Open a Future of Possibilities; Caring: Engendering of Community

No doubt about it, the transition to the new curriculum is more work for faculty. It's double teaching. New courses to some students and old courses to others! The curriculum committee is overworked and student advisors confused. Everyone hates the curriculum revision, students and teachers.

---

[16] See P. Young, 2004, Trying something new: Reform as embracing the possible, the familiar, and the at-hand, *Nursing Education Perspectives, 25*(5), 124-130, for interpretations of how trying something new is always already embedded in the practice of teaching. See P. Ironside, 2003b, Trying something new: Implementing and evaluating Narrative Pedagogy using a multi-method approach, *Nursing and Health Care Perspectives, 24*(3), 122-128, for an exegesis of the difficulties encountered when teachers attempt to evaluate the changes they make in their courses/curricula. See N. Diekelmann & M. Scheckel, 2003, Teaching students to apply nursing theories and models: Trying something new, *Journal of Nursing Education, 42*(5), 195-197, for a reading of how trying something new shapes and is shaped by instructional strategies.

[17] Refers to the National Council Licensing Examination (NCLEX), a State Board of Nursing requirement that all students must pass in order to obtain licenses to practice. For interpretations of narrative tellings of students who fail NCLEX, see S. Poorman & C. Webb, 2000, Preparing to retake the NCLEX exam: The experiences of graduates who fail, *Nurse Educator, 24*(4), 175-180.

Sarah

A year after the revision we realize our mistakes but we can't. Two curricula are bad, three impossible! Mistakes in revising the curriculum live until they are absolutely intolerable or we are scheduled for an accreditation visit. Whichever comes first!

> These teachers challenge how the curriculum is revised using conventional pedagogies, questioning and explicating how this approach is *dialogically experienced* by teachers and students. When they do this, they are enabling Narrative Pedagogy to show up. Schooling learning teaching, for hermeneutic phenomenology, is a co-occurring, *intra*-related, invisible phenomenon and as such shows itself as a dialogical experience.[18] *Phenomena show up as experiences.* These teachers explore how requirements like accreditation mandates are undergone as periodic experiences of massive curriculum "upheaval" for both students and teachers. Phasing in changes is one common strategy for minimizing this upheaval (although the problems with this approach often go unchallenged).

Winona

Yeah! And it gets worse. Some faculty learn to hide the changes they make when they don't agree with the "new curriculum"! Or some just continue teaching the way they always have in spite of what they put in their syllabi. We really make a lot of messes with curriculum revisions, don't we?[19] In my school, we have faculty

---

[18] See Chapter 4 for exegeses of schooling learning teaching as an intra-related phenomenon.

[19] The background of this converging conversation is a crisis in schools of nursing and clinical settings because of the number of students, and the acuity of patients who often stay in acute care settings for only a short time making safety a constant concern for faculty and clinicians. Calls abound for research-based approaches to nursing education, increasing faculty pedagogical literacy, and addressing a nursing faculty shortage. Conventional pedagogies (outcomes and competency-based nursing education) continue to be the predominant nursing pedagogy in spite of critiques and calls for new pedagogies. In the 1987 National League for Nursing (NLN) Curriculum Revolution Conference, Em Bevis, noted nurse educator, critiqued her conventional pedagogical experiences of evaluating and revising the nursing curriculum, stating, "Usually we negotiate a philosophy or polish up an old one; we reconceptualize, theorize, and agonize over some concepts and theories we want to emphasize; we integrate, irritate, or deteriorate our program objectives; we switch, swap, and slide content around; we rename, malign, and design a new program of studies; we refine and realign our course outlines; and we develop evaluation tools to assess whether or not students have met the designated behaviors. Then we open the champagne and celebrate that it is over—over, that is, until a new curriculum coordinator or dean is hired and we start again. Sometimes I feel much as the great Roman philosopher/orator Seneca

addicted to the notion of critical thinking as a curriculum framework and they constantly complain students can't do it even though they argue all their assignments promote it![20] It seems like anything a student doesn't know or answers incorrectly is taken as evidence they can't think

Theme: The Valorization of Analytic Thinking: Conflating Critical Thinking With Clinical Interpretive Practices

critically![21] Despite our disagreements about what constitutes critical thinking and all the critiques of it in the literature, they still insist all our courses be organized using a critical thinking framework—that the whole point of the curriculum is to teach critical thinking.[22]

Julius

Funny, I thought it was to teach students nursing!

Winona

Right! Some of these faculty will tack on ways of knowing to their critical thinking assignments but *clinical* thinking or "thinking like a nurse" has not entered their vocabulary yet![23]

wrote in his Epistles almost 2000 years ago: 'I was shipwrecked before I got aboard'" (Bevis, 1988, 27). For a contemporary converging conversation on the influence of the Curriculum Revolution, see N. Diekelmann, P. Ironside, & J. Gunn, 2005, Recalling the Curriculum Revolution: Innovation with research, *Nursing Education Perspectives, 26*(2), 70-78. Both the Bevis chapter and the Diekelmann, Ironside, and Gunn manuscript were reprinted in P. M. Ironside (Ed.), 2007, *On revolutions and revolutionaries: 25 years of reform and innovation in nursing education* (New York: National League for Nursing).

[20] In a national study of conceptual frameworks in schools of nursing, "critical thinking was the most frequently emphasized concept by both AD and BSN programs" (M. McEwen & S. Brown, 2002, Conceptual frameworks in undergraduate nursing curricula: Report of a national survey, *Journal of Nursing Education,41*(1), 13). For a review of critical thinking, see W. Cody, 2002, Critical thinking and nursing science: Judgment or vision? *Nursing Science Quarterly, 15,* 184-189. A study of the issues involved in defining critical thinking is reported in Gordon, J. (2000). Congruency in defining critical thinking by nurse educators and non-nurse scholars. *Journal of Nursing Education, 39*(8), 340-351.

[21] See J. Bean, 1996, *Engaging ideas: the professor's guide to integrating writing, critical thinking, and active learning in the classroom* (San Francisco: Jossey-Bass).

[22] For a discussion of mastery learning, problem solving and the conflation of critical thinking and problem solving, see E. Gardner, 2008, Instruction in mastery goal orientation: Developing problem solving and persistence for clinical settings. *Journal of Nursing Education, 45,* 343-247.

[23] See C. Tanner, 2005, What have we learned about critical thinking in nursing? [Editorial], *Journal of Nursing Education, 44*(2), 47-48, for an interpretive exegesis that deconstructs critical thinking and clinical thinking as different constructs. For interpretations of thinking like a nurse, practical knowledge, wisdom, and expertise, see P. Benner, C. Tanner, & C. Chesla, 1996, *Expertise in clinical practices: Caring, clinical judgment and ethics* (New York: Springer) and P. Benner, 2000, The wisdom of our practice: Thoughts on the art and intangibility of caring practices, *American Journal of Nursing, 100*(10), 99-105.

These teachers are in attendance, attending, and listening as they co-respond to one another. As a phenomenon, schooling learning teaching is communal, dialogical experience; that is, schooling as attending, learning as listening, and teaching as co-responding show up as converging conversations. Dialogical experience shows itself anew as an always already back-and-forth calling to which belongs co-responding. The back and forth does not of necessity elevate the calling to some ultimate call (command). It is the reciprocating sharing of the said and the unsaid that offers possibility.

Malala

Most teachers know they have to "go along" once the new curriculum is accepted, at least for a little while. But the more you think about it, the *real curriculum* happens whenever students and the teachers get together, in the kind of experiences they create with one another and the kinds of conversations they have. That's the curriculum that matters! Don't you think? We spend too much of our energy on the written curriculum. Yet few if any students ever read it! Most faculty hardly look at the final product once it's done!

CP – Preserving: Reading, Writing, Thinking-Saying, and Dialogue; Questioning: Sense and Making Meanings Visible; Interpreting: Unlearning and Becoming

Theme: The Curriculum-as-Dialogue: Overcoming the Claims of Epistemologies' Grasp on Schooling, Learning, and Teaching

Questionings:
- How does the curriculum-as-experienced show up as dialogue among students and teachers?
- How might explicating the meaning of the curriculum-as-dialogue point to possibilities, other than curriculum committee, for revising curricula?

Malala describes the *real* curriculum. The *real* can be thought here as the work of the curriculum.[24] While presuppositions, such as defining the curriculum, can never be explicated with certainty, unasked questions can uncover presuppositions enabling Narrative Pedagogy to show up. In this conversation, the question asked is *not* the usual question of how do we define the curriculum, but rather an *unasked question:* How is the work of the curriculum dialogically *experienced* by students and teachers?

Julius

Teachers argue about little things. Does this content belong here or there, when we have taught it equally well in both places! No one wants to really reorganize the curriculum because it's too much work. We tinker with and move stuff around. Then the Dean is told we're ready for our accreditation visit.

---

[24] Consult *QCT,* 167, translation note 19, for discussion of the real.

Sarah

You're right! Funny how little we challenge organizing the curriculum in terms not only of what it should include but also how it should be done. As faculty, we speak up more about issues of teaching and learning, but we seem to just roll over to others like the dean or a professional or specialty organization on curriculum issues.[25] Maybe it's because none of us has ever had a curriculum course.[26] Though I'm not sure the dean has either! For the dean, the curriculum IS accreditation. And for accrediting organizations it often comes down to pushing their particular agenda. Like CCNE[27] or the AACN[28] pushing the "Essentials of Baccalaureate Education." How do we know this list of content is "essential"? I know how these essentials were developed but what if you don't agree with them? What if all the faculty think certain essentials are not important, then what? Our students do well on state board exams and employed everywhere. Makes you start to challenge this whole approach.

> **CP** – Retrieving Places: Keeping Open a Future of Possibilities; Preserving: Reading, Writing, Thinking-Saying, and Dialogue; Questioning: Sense and Making Meanings Visible; Interpreting: Unlearning and Becoming
>
> **Theme:** Accreditation and Reform: Closing Down or Opening Up Possibilities
>
> **Questionings:**
> • What does mandated evaluation and accreditation mean to administrators, faculty, students, clinicians, patients, and citizens?

> **Themes:**
> • Essentials of Baccalaureate Education: "Raising the Bar" for BS Students and AD Faculty, Showing Our Students Are "Just as Good!"
> • Essentials of Baccalaureate Education: Adopting a List and Calling it Essential — Claims and Counter-Claims

---

[25] Understanding the oppressive nature of nursing education is explicated in R. McEldowney, 2003, Critical resistance pathways: Overcoming oppression in nursing education. In N. Diekelmann (Ed.), 2003c, *Teaching the practitioners of care: New pedagogies for the health professions* (Vol. 2, pp. 194-231) (Madison, WI: University of Wisconsin Press).

[26] See S. Bastable, 2003, *Nurse as educator: Principles of teaching and learning for nursing practice* (2nd ed.) (Sudbury, MA: Jones and Bartlett) for descriptions of teaching using conventional pedagogies.

[27] Commission on Collegiate Nursing Education.

[28] AACN refers to the American Association of Colleges of Nursing. See also: American Association of Colleges of Nursing, 1998a, *The essentials of baccalaureate education for professional nursing practice* (Washington, DC: Author); *Revision of the essentials of baccalaureate education for professional nursing practice* (Washington, DC: Author, retrieved 9/1/08 http://www.aacn.nche.edu/Education/pdf/BEdraft.pdf); and American Association of Colleges of Nursing, 1998b, *The essentials of master's education for advanced practice nursing* (Washington, DC: Author).

Where is the research and evidence to support this! Surely there are other ways to do the curriculum than the ones we are using now.[29]

Malala

I know a teacher who went to a faculty meeting where everyone was complaining about having no time or real control of the curriculum to implement innovation. They were upset because all the curriculum committee seemed to do was obsess over proposed course syllabi changes, arguing about assignments and other non-important stuff rather than presenting sorely needed innovation. He said, "I have an idea! What if we just let the BS and MS curriculums lie and agree to not worry about or even discuss them for a year. Wouldn't that allow us time and energy, always an issue for us, to think together and work on the kinds of innovation we're seeking?" There was *dead silence* and then the conversation moved right on to how they could convince the dean they should be able to do something new.

Julius

Well I wish someone could tell our school how to get rid of about half the content in our curriculum! The students are literally suffering from trying to learn and memorize so much stuff.[30] And we spend all our time talking about what students don't know and can't do. We put courses on

> **Theme:** Epistemologies' Grasp and Nursing Education: The Additive Curriculum

line and add more readings. I'm worried about our students. The curriculum has become toxic, even for our best students!

---

[29] See P. Webber, 2002, A curriculum framework for nursing, *Journal of Nursing Education, 41,* (1), 15-24 for an explication of a nursing framework: "It is time that nursing begins to focus more on the profession's epistemological forest than on isolated trees when developing and selecting curricular frameworks" (15).

[30] For exemplars of the additive curriculum, see P. Ironside, 2004, "Covering content" and teaching thinking: Deconstructing the additive curriculum, *Journal of Nursing Education, 43,* 5-12, and N. Diekelmann & E. Smythe, 2004, Covering content and the additive curriculum: How can I use my time with students to best help them learn what they need to know? *Journal of Nursing Education, 43*(8), 341-344, for exemplars of the additive curriculum.

Winona

Ours too! Content just builds up and when the students complain we blame them for "being lazy" or wanting "easy courses." My courses are overflowing.[31] I admit it. It's ridiculous. We had an excellent accreditation visit and showed our site visitors

> **Theme:** "Too Much Content...": Epistemologies' Grasp and Nursing Education

a really tight curriculum. But you can have problems with content *all the while you have* a tight curriculum. For instance, some courses are just too loaded with content that everyone agrees the students need to learn. I mean, when I came here I assumed that since we have a clearly written philosophy and conceptual framework, and have specified outcomes, competencies, learning experiences, and measurable criteria for evaluation for every course, we wouldn't have any redundancy or gaps in what students were learning. All our syllabi even used exactly the same format. The courses had the same percentages for evaluation of student learning—like 80% of student's grades must be test scores and so forth. Now wouldn't you think with that kind of curriculum organization, students and teachers would be happy? But I learned all too quickly that mere organizing does not bring happiness. It's just not the case! We put for student convenience, courses online and then add more readings. Adding content like this has to stop!

> **CP** – Assembling: Constructing and Cultivating; Gathering: Welcoming and Calling Forth; Caring: Engendering of Community; Interpreting: Unlearning and Becoming; Presencing: Attending and Being Open
>
> **Theme:** The Claim of Structuring the Curriculum: Dualistic Thinking and Organizing the Nursing Curriculum
>
> **Questionings:**
> - In what ways does learning as listening call forth organizing the curriculum? How does teaching as co-responding show up as the organization of the curriculum?
> - Is schooling merely an organization and an organizing?
> - How is the play of organizing the curriculum dialogically experienced by students and teachers?
> - Is an unorganized (nonprescriptive) curriculum, developed by students with the guidance of advisors, necessarily unorganized and chaotic?
> - How much organization is too much? How much is just right, or not enough?

---

[31] For hermeneutic phenomenological interpretations of the additive curriculum in full sway, see N. Diekelmann, 2002d, "Too much content . . .": Epistemologies' grasp and nursing education, *Journal of Nursing Education, 41*(11), 469-470.

Conventional pedagogies, such as outcomes or competency-based nursing education, are the signature pedagogies[32] of nursing; that is, they are the predominate pedagogies in schools of nursing. They are based on the Tylerian model of curriculum and instruction.[33] In this model, the processes of revising the curriculum also applies to revising courses. Conventional pedagogies utilize pre-determined, prescriptive, reductionistic approaches to define what should be matters of concern for the curriculum and the processes used to evaluate and revise it.[34] These processes are predetermined, non-site specific, and generalizable. As well, conventional pedagogies reflect the processes used in granting accreditation by agencies and State Boards of Nursing.[35] Evaluating and revising the curriculum as well as preparing for accreditation visits are familiar experiences for most teachers. In this familiar process, the curriculum committee and later faculty meet to review the school's philosophy, vision statements (strategic plan), program or course objectives, and conceptual frameworks. Discussions about problems, such as the additive curriculum and duplication of content or gaps in content among courses, often signal curriculum revisions.[36]

CP – Assembling: Constructing and Cultivating; Gathering: Welcoming and Calling Forth; Caring: Engendering of Community

Theme: Selecting and Sequencing Content: The Tylerian Curriculum Development Model as Experienced

Questionings:

- In conventional pedagogies, the organization, structure, and identification and sequencing of courses, as well as specifying degree requirements, are considered "curricular." Similarly, these concerns at the individual course level are considered "instructional." What are the unasked questions in this approach?

- Does this reduction assume that changes in individual courses can be made that do or do not change the curriculum?

- Can minor course changes enable profound curriculum changes?

---

[32] See L. S. Shulman, 2005, Signature pedagogies, *Daedalus,* 134(3), 52-59.

[33] According to a national study of the conceptual frameworks in undergraduate nursing curricula (baccalaureate, associate degree, and diploma nursing programs), "The curricula of virtually all nursing programs were based on the Tyler Curriculum Development Model published in 1950" (M. McEwen & S. Brown, 2002, Conceptual frameworks in undergraduate nursing curricula: Report of a national survey, *Journal of Nursing Education, 41*(1), 5-14.

[34] For descriptions of conventional pedagogies and organizing curriculums see J. Csokasy, 2002, A congruent curriculum: Philosophical integrity from philosophy to outcomes, *Journal of Nursing Education 41*(1), 32-33; L. Daggett, J. Butts, & K. Smith, 2002, The development of an organizing framework to implement AACN guidelines for nursing education, *Journal of Nursing Education 41*(1), 34-37; and L. Freeman, R. Voignier, & D. Scott, 2002, New curriculum for a new century: Beyond repackaging, *Journal of Nursing Education 41*(1), 38-40.

[35] For a discussion of the history of how State Boards of Nursing and accreditation organizations influence conceptual and organizing frameworks, see M. McEwen & S. Brown, 2002, Conceptual frameworks in undergraduate nursing curricula: Report of a national survey, *Journal of Nursing Education, 41*(1), 5-14.

[36] For elucidations of the ways breakdown shows up as a catalyst for reform, see N. Diekelmann, 2005c, Engaging the students *and* the teacher: Co-creating substantive reform with Narrative Pedagogy, *Journal of Nursing Education, 44,* 249-252.

Julius

We are into competencies and they keep getting broader and more inclusive. Right now my course is overloaded with competencies. Why don't we start thinking about when does a course have too many competencies?[37]

> **Theme:** Competency-Based Nursing Education: The Additive Curriculum in Full Sway

Malala

Previously I taught at a neighboring university and just as I was leaving, an accreditation visit was coming up. We had one of those meetings where faculty were actually asking each other, "Just what framework do we use?" None of us could remember. Then someone said, "You don't need a framework anymore, only outcomes. You can be eclectic." We didn't even know we were eclectic![38] With all the problems we have in our school, like helping students who speak English as a second language (ESL), who have poor writing skills, or who have to work a full-time job to pay their tuition and still be successful in the program, it's ridiculous to use *hours* of the entire faculty's time on stuff like this. We could be using our collective wisdom and expertise to figure out how to help more students be successful and not have to repeat so many courses. Or we could look at how to retain more students in our program or how to better use technology to help students manage the amount of knowledge and skills they are trying to amass in a short time.

> **Theme:** The Long Reach of the Modern Epoch: Technology As Exploitation
>
> **Questionings:**
> * Does instructional technology enframe or command learning?
> * Is instructional technology a "not to be gotten around?"

---

[37] Consult C. Tanner, 2001, Competency-based education: The new panacea? [Editorial], *Journal of Nursing Education, 40*(9), 387-388 for a critical examination of competency-based education; and N. Diekelmann & M. Scheckel, 2004, Leaving the safe harbor of competency-based and outcomes education: Re-thinking practice education, *Journal of Nursing Education, 43*(9), 385-388 for critiques of and possibility that competency-based education is a place of departure rather than arrival.

[38] According to a recent national study of conceptual frameworks in schools of nursing, "The majority of the conceptual frameworks described in nursing programs . . . were eclectic" (M. McEwen & S. Brown, 2002, Conceptual frameworks in undergraduate nursing curricula: Report of a national survey, *Journal of Nursing Education, 41*(1), 10).

Or what about how we keep admitting more students to respond to the nursing shortage during a nursing faculty shortage? Talking about frameworks for organizing the curriculum have little if any bearing on what we do with our students. It's depressing. All of us know these frameworks are meaningless to learning and teaching. We can't remember them, don't use or need them! Don't get me started! In Narrative Pedagogy, this is what you talk about when you learn to listen to what you see all around you. Seeing what stands in front of you for what it is. Challenging it, not fooling ourselves! Not doing things we know are useless or don't work, even when theoretically we are told they do. Theoretically writing the school philosophy together is to help us all get on the same page and think about our values and beliefs. But all we do is come up with small changes we can agree on to show it's been revised and then move on with the substantive things that need our attention! In Narrative Pedagogy, listening to the meaning of experiences, you rethink everything, things the don't work, or are not effective, like organizing frameworks for our courses and the curriculum. Do students not learn without them and do learn with them?

CP – Caring: Engendering of Community; Gathering: Welcoming and Calling Forth; Retrieving Places: Keeping Open a Future of Possibilities; Presencing: Attending and Being Open; Preserving: Reading, Writing, Thinking-Saying, and Dialogue

Theme: Engendering Community: Schooling Learning Teaching as Communal and Collaborative

Questionings:
- How do teachers, students, and clinicians spend their time together?
- In what ways does toxic/supportive community life influence schooling learning teaching?

CP – Creating Places: Keeping Open a Future of Possibilities; Interpreting: Unlearning and Becoming; Assembling: Constructing, and Cultivating

Themes:
- Listening to What You See: Explicating the Familiar and At-Hand
- Listening to What Stands In Front of You: "We All Know . . ."
- The Claim of Structuring the Curriculum: Dualistic Thinking and Organizing the Nursing Curriculum
- Nursing Pedagogies: Gathering the Shared Practices, Common Wisdom, and Expertise of Nurse Teachers and Students

Questionings:
- How are curricular frameworks experienced by faculty and students?
- Is it necessary to create a place in the curriculum for dialogues (discussions) that explicate the meanings of the familiar and at-hand? If so, how? If not, where can/do these dialogues occur?

Conventional pedagogies assume that the curriculum must be "organized" in some way. This necessitates either explicitly or implicitly identifying frameworks or processes for how content is selected and sequenced.[39] Teachers commonly use concepts or theories as organizers, or processes such as the nursing process, critical thinking, caring, and problem solving/decision making.[40] Each of these approaches to organizing contains assumptions about schooling, learning, and teaching. Narrative Pedagogy is enabled through explicating these assumptions (presuppositions). Malala when she enacts a challenge to the worthfulness of conceptual frameworks, begins to make visible the incongruity in the intentions of the faculty using frameworks and the nature of the dialogical experiences as mutually enabled and enacted. The play of disclosing and beckoning turns as the reciprocity of enabling and enacting.

Sarah

The problem with this organizing the curriculum and framework stuff is that they don't work and they aren't helpful, not really, even when they look like they are. And you know that agreement by the faculty is virtually impossible. I've taught a while and I'm up for some real innovation. Maybe we ought to challenge how accreditation and State Boards are holding back innovation, making us do these terribly time-consuming meaningless things![41] I once taught where we used nursing diagnoses as an organizer. There were a few teachers who were gung-ho and had strong opinions about how we should teach and use them. After a lot of debating, or should I say fighting, the rest of us just went along. In our hearts we all wanted to just

[39] McEwen & Brown (2002) reported that the most common frameworks used in schools of nursing were nursing theorists; bio/psycho/social/spiritual model; nursing process; simple-to-complex model; integrated medical model; health promotion/levels of prevention; and other. "The nursing process is the most commonly used component for conceptual frameworks for nursing curricula, reportedly used by 55% of the programs. Simple-to-complex organization, a bio/psycho/social/spiritual model, and nursing theorists were used by at least one third of all programs" (M. McEwen & S. Brown, 2002, Conceptual frameworks in undergraduate nursing curricula: Report of a national survey, *Journal of Nursing Education, 41*(1), 10).

[40] According to McEwen and Brown (2002), the process commonly used in schools of nursing included caring, communication, critical thinking, problem solving/decision making, teaching/learning, therapeutic nursing interventions, values/ethical reasoning/integrity, and other (8). "Critical thinking was the most commonly reported concept/process and was emphasized in 74% of the programs. Therapeutic nursing interventions (64%), problem-solving (53%) and communication (49%) were also mentioned frequently" (11).

[41] The Tyler model mandates a conceptual framework that currently is incorporated into accreditation processes. Many State Boards of Nursing require an organizing framework. For a critical discussion of how accreditation influences schools of nursing, see N. Diekelmann, D. Allen, & C. Tanner, 1989, *The National League for Nursing criteria for appraisal of baccalaureate programs: A critical hermeneutic analysis* (New York: National League for Nursing Press).

organize our individual courses in a way that made sense to us. But once a framework is adopted, it closes down on so many options because it specifies what students must take and when, and what comes first and what comes last and so forth. What would happen if we let that go? I mean, think about how nursing curricula could be different if we got rid of nursing diagnoses and competencies as frameworks, as well as required and elective courses, and just let the students choose their own cur-

> **CP** – Caring: Engendering of Community; Listening: Knowing and Connecting; Presencing: Attending and Being Open
> **Questionings:**
> • Can organizing the curriculum using conventional pedagogies call out conversations that are disaffecting to community life?
> • Is a non-organized curriculum necessarily chaotic?
> • In conventional pedagogies, for the sake of consensus, how are conversations about structure and organization driven by issues of power/control?
> • In what ways is achieving consensus in conventional pedagogies experienced/ not experienced as fair and respectful?

riculum. A lot of majors do that! What courses would all students take? What courses would no one take? That would tell us a lot, wouldn't it? I really think that it gets down to curriculum frameworks don't work like they are theorized to. So why mandate them? Would not using them create chaos? I don't think so. The students can be trusted to put together good curricula with a little guidance from us. And wouldn't that be an interesting discussion to have with the students! They all want to pass Boards anyway. Besides, there's no research on schools that don't use them, so maybe this would really work. We just all assume you can't do without frameworks! Now there's evidence-based nursing education for you![42]

> **CP** – Questioning: Sense and Making Meanings Visible; Preserving: Reading, Writing, Thinking-Saying, and Dialogue; Assembling: Constructing and Cultivating; Interpreting: Unlearning and Becoming
> **Theme:** The Claims of Structuring the Curriculum: Dualistic Thinking and Organizing the Nursing Curriculum

---

[42]   See McEwen & Brown (2002) for a critique of conceptual frameworks. "The challenge that faces faculty from all types of nursing programs is to develop curricula to meet the educational needs of students, while considering changing demographics, trends in health and illness patterns, and a vastly different health care delivery system. A critical review of the conceptual frameworks that direct the curricula of nursing programs is an essential starting place" (13).

Julius

You're right about curriculum frameworks, Sarah, and about teachers not agreeing. But it is in our courses too. Three of our faculty use a nursing theory or model to organize their courses and it drives the students crazy. Just when they learn that language, they take a course that is taught using nursing diagnoses and then there's another language to learn! And all the while we know that the current quality and safety initiatives are emphasizing interdisciplinary communication—so will students ever really *use* all the different languages we teach them, with other healthcare

> **CP –** Questioning: Sense and Making Meaning Visible; Assembling: Constructing and Cultivating; Preserving: Reading, Writing, Thinking-Saying, and Dialogue
>
> **Theme:** On Using Theories as Conceptual Frameworks: The Experiences of Students, Teachers, and Clinicians in Nursing Education
>
> **Questionings:**
> - How do particular theories or models come to be selected?
> - How do curricular frameworks influence student learning?
> - Has outcomes education created outcomes nursing in practice?
> - How do accreditation and certification criteria and State Board requirements influence students' learning? For example, how might certification criteria for nurse practitioners nationalize the nursing curriculum?
> - Does challenging accreditation criteria or the contemporary worthfulness of specialty accreditation itself become unspeakable?
> - Is there any evidence that accreditation of schools ensures a level of safety and preparation of students? That is, do disciplines that do not require disciplinary accreditation have no way to address safety and competence in the entry into practice?

professionals? And so many questions go unasked. Like why are we so focused on diseases instead of prevention. And maybe its because disease is a central part of our lives as nurses that we must attend do and we are necessarily as nurses in attendance with. But maybe the case can similarly be made for prevention. These assumptions we are always making are so invisible. For instance, some people defend our eclectic curricular models using terms like simple to complex as a rationale for organizing the curriculum and courses. But again, no one can agree! Everyone has a different view of what is "simple," what students need before they take "my course," and where students actually learn and who teaches the "complex." I mean, as we persistently add content, we really are at risk of teaching more and more topics in less and less depth! Who knows, maybe we should turn our curricula upside down and start with what is complex! That's a good idea to think about!

> Discursiveness in Narrative Pedagogy is the silence of language speaking. Language as discursiveness commands that it be used and language commends itself to commanding. Converging conversations continually seek to reveal unexplicated presuppositions, for example, What evidence is there that starting with complex content such as beginning at the end of the course is not as efficacious as beginning with simple content? Schooling learning teaching as a co-occurring phenomenon shifts conversational concerns from exclusively teacher-centered concerns about teaching to *schooling learning teaching as a dialogical experience.* Julius, in exploring the assumptions regarding faculty consensus, discusses the meaning of course frameworks for students as they shift from one technical language to another. How, what, and that students and teachers attend to (schooling as calling to attendance), listen to (learning as listening) and co-respond to (teaching as reciprocal listening-to) are embraced in this converging conversation. Julius has neared the essence of language as discursiveness. The unspoken shows itself here as (1) the necessity to learn (in the ontic sense) languages as instruments and (2) the need to be able to communicate (in the ontological sense) matters of concern. Julius listens to what is silent in the saying of language as he calls into question overlooked difference and its concomitant summoning.

Sarah

One of the Narrative Pedagogy pilot schools teaches their research course, usually an upper level course, to beginning students. They introduce students to nursing by teaching them how to do a concept map using evidence-based nursing practice. Students pick a health issue or disease they are interested in and then learn where nursing literature is related to this, how to search for and access it on the Internet, their PDAs, and Web sites, and evaluate the research they find as they write their first concept maps, *before* they go onto the clinical units. The faculty stopped teaching the students the "research process." They decided students don't need to know the process researchers use in conducting studies in order to become good consumers of medical and nursing research or good thinkers. They thought the best way to make students good thinkers is to give them a project that is complex, engaging, and compelling. The students picked diseases for their made-up patients they were interested in and often questions they had about family or friends. And it really works! The faculty challenged a huge number of assumptions about what beginning students can and can't do. If we were honest, we would realize that a lot of time there is no research to support what we currently do or how we do it. And so by default teachers too often overestimate the usefulness of their past experiences. We say things like, "I tried that once and it didn't work," and this suddenly becomes infallible evidence to support their point. Yet there are not many studies in nursing education that are multisite, multimethod, and multipedagogical for us to rely on either.[43]

Themes:
• Conflating Empirical Experience and Evidence-Based Research: Teaching as We Were Taught
• Arrogating Rationality: "I've Tried That and It Doesn't Work!"

The underlying rationale of conventional pedagogies is revealed by Sarah's story. The presupposition challenged is that of logic; specifically, Sarah asks how the assumption that the generalizable process of research followed by researchers is logically necessary for evaluating a research study or learning analytic thinking. This assumption is belied by the complex intangibles of everyday experience and its resistance to being categorized under the aegis of analytical thinking and medical and nursing research. No generalizable process can adequately reflect the complexities embedded in contemporary research. Furthermore, evaluating the efficacy of contemporary studies requires expert knowledge. The assumption that understanding the research process is necessary in order for pre-licensure nursing students to (1) support and appreciate nursing research, (2) learn how to critique research, and (3) learn analytic thinking may be logical, but is no longer necessary or adequate as an approach to learning how to evaluate, or to be a good consumer of medical and nursing research as a student nurse.[44] Students can learn to become intelligent consumers of research through using expert databases that review medical and nursing research, readily available on the Internet.

Winona

We assume that since higher education is research based so too is nursing! Do we really think that research on how students learn chemistry in labs applies equally to learning nursing on the clinical unit? Nursing is slow to do research and challenge assumptions in nursing education. When it comes to curriculum, we have little if any research to back us up!

---

[43] See P. Ironside, 2003b, Trying something new: Implementing and evaluating Narrative Pedagogy using a multimethod approach, *Nursing Education Perspectives, 24*(3), 122-128; P. M. Ironside, 2006a, Reforming doctoral curricula in nursing: Creating multiparadigmatic, multipedagogical researchers [Guest editorial], *Journal of Nursing Education, 45,* 51-52; N. Diekelmann, 2005b, Creating an inclusive science for nursing education [Guest editorial], *Nursing Education Perspectives, 26*(2), 64-65; and N. Diekelmann, (Ed.), 2003c, *Teaching the practitioners of care: New pedagogies for the health professions* (Vol. 2) (Madison, WI: University of Wisconsin Press); and P. Young, 2008, Toward an inclusive science of nursing education: An examination of approaches to nursing research, *Nursing Education Perspectives, 29,* 94-99.

[44] We remind the reader that there is an enigmatic paradox whereby the application of rules exists in the absence of a rule (see Chapter 6).

Julius

We are somehow required to spend all this time making decisions about how to organize the curriculum in the *absence* of nursing education research. Do we even know that organizing the curriculum for or with some kind of consistency or framework, *really is* an effective, let along the only, guide for selecting and sequencing content? Does it really prevent overlap and duplication of content? Does it really enhance learning?

Winona

I sure don't think so! Reorganizing our curriculum to prepare for our accreditation visit turned out to be a big fight. No one was happy. When we collapsed two courses, we fought over a floating credit and

CP – Questioning: Sense and Making Meanings Visible; Interpreting: Unlearning and Becoming; Preserving: Reading, Writing, Thinking-Saying, and Dialogue
Questionings:
- How might we think about designing research studies on various approaches to curricular organization?
- If no consensus on curricular issues were sought, would the curriculum become non-organized and inconsistent? More than it currently is?
- Does more attention to organizing have a positive or negative effect on student learning?
- How is it that so much of what teachers take as a "given" has no basis in research or in experience?
- What does it mean to teachers to admit that their approaches to teaching have no basis in research?
- Have any schools tried "non-organizing" their curriculum?
- How do the signature pedagogies embraced by disciplines influence the ways students are introduced to and practice their disciplines?

who would get it! We went crazy about organizing our courses around a nursing theorist, and I had to spend so much time trying to make it work in places it just didn't. And when we stretch things to make them fit, students see right through that, don't they? I think it's high time we think seriously about how we use nursing theories or nursing process[45] or whatever to organize our curricula! I mean there's not a whole lot of research about their efficacy as organizing frameworks for schools of nursing anyway, not to mention how little they are *really* applied in our rapidly evolving practice settings! Students learn all these different languages, but then it seems that over time they use them less and less, all the while they become more skilled and

---

[45] For a reminder of the historical context in which the nursing process was developed, see: V. Henderson, 1987b, The nursing process in perspective, *Journal of Advanced Nursing, 12*(6), 657-658; V. Henderson, 1987a, Nursing process, a critique, *Holistic Nursing Practice, 1*(3), 7-18.

expert nurses. As teachers we are driving ourselves crazy trying to use the latest framework or theory and to get our curricula all nice and tidy in terms of organization, while our clinical agencies are telling us they need students to be better and better prepared as thinkers. After all, the current practice environments and complex situations our students are going to encounter simply don't fit nicely into a single framework or organizer, if they ever did!

The invisible need to organize the curriculum in the service of teaching and learning can highjack conversations on the *meaning* of students' and teachers' *experiences* of "organizing the curriculum." The presupposition that a curriculum must be or is organized in some consensual way can go unexplored. Through explication of the meaning of organizing-the-curriculum as experienced, what is unearthed is how tenuous the relation is between student learning and organizing frameworks. What is challenged is the worthfulness of spending large amounts of time organizing the curriculum, or trying to make a theory or framework "work" in the curriculum, in every course, content area, and situation. These teachers explore the meaning of having a rationale for sequencing courses in the curriculum. Exploring taken-for-granted assumptions or presuppositions in this way is a converging conversation toward enabling Narrative Pedagogy.

Questionings:

- In what ways does using a nursing theory(ies) help/hinder students as they learn to listen and co-respond to the concerns of particular patients?
- What evidence is there to support this claim?
- Do students oppose or not value theory, evidence-based practice, or nursing science if they have not had experiences in "using or applying" them? And what do students think about these issues after they have been exposed to them?
- How do conventional pedagogies maintain disciplinary boundaries and ensure a place for disciplinary research? What influence does this have on nurses' abilities to work effectively on multidisciplinary teams?

Julius

I realize there is very little research base to what I often get so bothered about and personalize. When I question the positions I so adamantly take, I realize curriculum is not just about me and being right. It's clear we don't know what right is in most situations when it comes to curriculum. Everything we do as teachers is a communal experience. It's easy to forget that! Truthfully, sometimes the positions I take about the curriculum are related to personal things. How should we sequence courses really has more to do with me wanting a lighter teaching load in the spring than in the fall. Sequencing courses calls out the worst in us!

Malala

We go round and round about whether students should have Peds before or after OB, and Community before or after Psych.[46] Finally we'll agree, but if you visit the school across town, they teach it the opposite way using the same rationale! Now is there something wrong with this picture?

Sarah

There are good reasons why we say, "Oh, no! Not another curriculum revision!" But we're all teachers committed to schooling nursing students, so let's work together and make it the best experience for all of us.

> **CP** – Caring: Engendering of Community; Listening: Knowing and Connecting; Presencing: Attending and Being Open; Retrieving Places: Keeping Open a Future of Possibilities
>
> **Themes:**
> - Cartesianism and the Curriculum: Embracing the Rational as the Unexplored Familiar and At-Hand
> - Rationality's Claim on Teachers and Students: "Going Round and Round"
>
> **Questionings:**
> - In discussions about the "rational," is attention paid to the "irrational" and the "non-rational"?
> - Is presupposed agreement better than disagreement among faculty?
> - Is agreement the opposite of conflict? Is there a place for non-agreement in the curriculum?

This conversation has been an attempt to show that schooling is a surplus over mere institutions. Schooling orders its own attendance as tension and contending. Each human being is of the open clearing as a thrown understanding, which as a not-knowing demands that understanding be listened to as the understanding which is listened to. There is no conception of knowing that can do away with or complete this circling. The aspect of revisions, which call out and demand themselves, shows that there is listening.

---

[46] Refers to pediatric nursing, maternal-infant nursing, community nursing, and psychiatric/mental health nursing courses.

Community Interpretive Scholarship: Rethinking Curriculum

Converging Conversation: Scenario 1

"Some of us think the curriculum is just a road map or a railroad track of how the courses and the school are organized. Others of us think it's a legal document, a contract among the students, teachers, and the school. And a lot of us think it's just a political exercise for accreditation. One thing we all agree on is that we hate changing it!"

Questionings:
How are we to "think curriculum"? There are many ways to define the term curriculum; one often overlooked is curriculum as *communal* experiences of students, teachers, and clinicians being attentive, listening, and co-responding to one another. In community interpretive scholarship (putting your heads together), consider experiences of the curriculum and *curriculum experiences.*

- What is a curriculum? How would you know one if you saw it?
- What are the best and the worst things about changing a curriculum?
- What does changing the nursing curriculum mean to you as a teacher, as a student, administrator, hospital and agency, patient, and citizen
- How are we in the attendance of the curriculum?

Converging Conversation: Scenario 2

"Maybe we spend too much time on the documents that define our curriculum and not enough time on how this curriculum we've designed is *experienced* by everyone. Some curricula look very similar, but how they are implemented makes all the difference in how the students and teachers experience them."

Questionings:

If the curriculum is a communal experience attending, listening, and co-responding to one another, the curriculum becomes narrative tellings, dialogues, and conversations among students, teachers, and clinicians.[47]

- What kinds of narrative tellings (stories) show what the curriculum-as-dialogue means to you as a teacher, student, or clinician?
- What kinds of dialogues with peers, students and clinicians do you have (or would you like to have) about the curriculum?
- What would understanding learning as more than a cognitive process under conscious control mean to the curriculum, to students, and teachers?

---

[47] For an explication of pedagogical wayfaring or moving from pedagogies toward schooling learning teaching as a phenomenon, see Chapter 10.

Converging Conversation: Scenario 3

"When we're deciding on the prerequisite courses for nursing I wonder if we too often require certain courses to help them succeed in nursing. Over the years we are piling on more science courses. And that's important, but so is exposing students to different understandings of the world."

Questionings:
A central focus of competency-based education (conventional pedagogies) is discussing pre-requisite courses and what content the nursing curriculum should include.
- Should proficiency in a second language be required?
- What content should the nursing curriculum never include?
- What "counts" as nursing knowledge? Nursing skills? Who decides? Is there a place in the nursing curriculum for that which is currently considered to be not nursing?
- Is the nursing curriculum too human-centered? What does it mean to nursing as a profession to exclude the issues surrounding the well-being of the earth's biota?

Chapter 13

Learning as Listening: *"We learned to listen to what we saw all around us."*

Schools of nursing and clinical settings are in crisis with too many students, a faculty shortage, increases in patient acuity, short hospital stays, and significant concerns about safety.[1] Instructional technology is changing the landscape of learning.[2] A science of nursing education[3] that is inclusive, multimethodological, multipedagogical, and multisite is the contemporary background for reforming nursing education.[4] In response to all these issues, schools are revising their courses and curricula. Calls for reforming nursing education are familiar.[5] Conventional pedagogies (outcomes and competency-based

---

[1] See N. Diekelmann, P. Ironside, & M. Harlow, 2003, Introduction. In N. Diekelmann (Ed.), *Teaching the practitioners of care: New pedagogies for the health professions* (Vol. 2, pp. 3-21). Madison, WI: University of Wisconsin Press for a treatise on the call for new pedagogies in the health and human sciences.

[2] How instructional technology both shapes and is shaped by curricular reform is explicated in N. Diekelmann, R. Schuster, & C. Nosek, 1998, Creating new pedagogies at the millennium: The common experiences of the University of Wisconsin-Madison teachers in using distance education technologies, *Teaching with Technology Today* (Online journal). Available: http://www.uwsa.edu/olit/ttt/98.pdf.

[3] Advocating a science of nursing education is presented in P. Young, 2008, Toward an inclusive science of nursing education: An examination of approaches to nursing research, *Nursing Education Perspectives, 29*, 94-99.

[4] For a discussion of innovation in the *absence* of research and the influence on innovation of developing a science of nursing education, see N. Diekelmann and P. Ironside, 2002, Developing a science of nursing education: Innovation with research [Guest editorial], *Journal of Nursing Education, 41*(9), 379-380.

[5] Twenty years ago the National League for Nursing conferences called for substantive curricular reform in nursing education. One might argue that the Curriculum Revolution was a failure! See these four volumes for conference proceeding publications: National League for Nursing, 1988, *Curriculum revolution: Mandate for change* (New York: Author); National League for Nursing, 1989, *Curriculum revolution: Reconceptualizing nursing education* (New York: Author); National League for Nursing, 1990, *Curriculum revolution: Redefining the student-teacher relationship* (New York: Author); National League for Nursing, 1991, *Curriculum revolution: Community building and activism* (New York: Author); and P. M. Ironside (Ed.), 2007, *On revolutions and revolutionaries: 25 years of reform and innovation in nursing education* (New York: National League for Nursing).

education) remain the dominant or signature nursing pedagogies.[6] Revision of courses and curricula in ways other than those prescribed by conventional pedagogies is slow to occur in nursing education.[7] As long as reform stays within conventional pedagogies, time-consuming[8] experiences like developing curriculum frameworks, organizing courses, and the additive curriculum will obtain.

The interpretive pedagogies (critical, feminist, phenomenological, hermeneutic phenomenological, and postmodern) are meaningful alternatives, and all have particular views of what constitutes a curriculum and the processes of reform.[9] What is neoteric are the substantive *research-based nursing pedagogies,* like Narrative Pedagogy (Narrative Pedagogy), *from* nursing research *for* nursing education.[10] According to Webber, developing *curriculum frameworks for nursing* begins a focus on the profession's "epistemological forest rather than on isolated trees when developing and selecting curricular frameworks."[11] As a research-based hermeneutic phenomenological nursing pedagogy, Narrative Pedagogy proffers possibilities for reforming the curriculum that differ from conventional approaches yet can include them. Narrative Pedagogy challenges the divisions of curriculum and instruction, all the while suggesting that these divisions are necessary but not sufficient.[12]

[6]   A pedagogy is a particular way or approach of schooling, learning, and teaching. For a discussion of signature pedagogies see L. S. Shulman, 2005, Signature pedagogies, *Daedalus,* 134(3), 52-59.

[7]   For a discussion of using new pedagogies to revise courses and curricula, see N. Diekelmann & S. Lampe, 2004, Student-centered pedagogies: Co-creating compelling experiences using the new pedagogies, *Journal of Nursing Education, 43*(6), 245-247.

[8]   Is conventional pedagogy the most time-consuming pedagogy? For a response to this question, see N. Diekelmann, 2005d, Keeping current: On persistently questioning our teaching practice, *Journal of Nursing Education, 44,* 485-488.

[9]   Indeed the term curriculum itself and the division of educational areas of interest into curriculum and instruction belong to conventional pedagogy. P. Ironside, 2001, Creating a research base for nursing education: An interpretive review of conventional, critical, feminist, postmodern, and phenomenologic pedagogies, *Advances in Nursing Science, 23*(3), 72-87.

[10] N. Diekelmann (Ed.), 2003c, *Teaching the practitioners of care: New pedagogies for the health professions* (Vol. 2) (Madison, WI: University of Wisconsin Press); K. Dahlberg, K. Ekebergh, & P. Ironside, 2003, Converging conversations from phenomenological pedagogies: Toward a science of health professions education. In N. Diekelmann (Ed.), 2003c, *Teaching the practitioners of care: New pedagogies for the health professions* (Vol. 2, pp. 22-58) (Madison, WI: University of Wisconsin Press).

[11] Webber, 2002, 15.

[12] The term "sufficient" here is not meant to imply an ultimate completion. In Narrative Pedagogy the play of curricula is always underway. It is not a substitute pedagogy; rather Narrative Pedagogy gathers and keeps in play all pedagogies as possibilities, past, present,

Converging conversations work to demonstrate enacting hermeneutic phenomenology through making thematic or explicating (questioning and interpreting) presuppositions in order to enable Narrative Pedagogy (NP) to show up. The hermeneutic circle as the circle of participating, or cycles of interpretations, is never complete and never-ending.[13] Interpretations reveal the wider play of multiple understandings. There is no one correct interpretation.[14] Correctness is not implicit in interpretations; however, truths can self-disclose. Similarly, there is not one way to present interpretations. In the following converging conversation, cycles of interpretations[15] bring narrative themes and patterns (The Concernful Practices of Schooling Learning Teaching) into dialogue and conversation with one another.[16]

CONCERNFUL PRACTICES OF SCHOOLING LEARNING TEACHING (CP)
• Presencing: Attending and Being Open
• Assembling: Constructing and Cultivating
• Gathering: Welcoming and Calling Forth
• Caring: Engendering of Community
• Listening: Knowing and Connecting
• Interpreting: Unlearning and Becoming
• Inviting: Waiting and Letting Be
• Questioning: Sense and Making Meanings Visible
• Retrieving Places: Keeping Open a Future of Possibilities
• Preserving: Reading, Writing, Thinking-Saying, and Dialogue

and future. Similarly, a reclaiming of completion as an exhaustion of intellectual and practical possibilities is explicated in N. Diekelmann, 1995, Reawakening thinking: Is traditional pedagogy nearing completion? [Guest editorial], *Journal of Nursing Education, 34*(5), 195-196.

[13] See Chapter 3 for discussion of hermeneutic circle as the circle of participating. Interpretations are always already on a background of pre-understandings. In these interpretations, the pre-understanding presupposes hermeneutic phenomenology. For example, in hermeneutic phenomenology, dialogues as they are read (interpreted) are certain paths from thinking as well as in thinking—they take into account the excess of thoughtful interpretation to which interpretation as itself offers itself. The difference between the singular proprieties of voices, ways, modes, is invited as announcement. It is to an announcement and to an opening of the very dialogue of thinking that all are guests—all share in the hospitality/gift/offering of difference. From the temporally particular always already to the on-coming self-presencing of presence—each time the hermeneutical thinking circle does not cease from breaking off.

[14] Refer to Chapter 6 for discussion of how narratives announce, address, and call forth: "There is much to say" as the basic hermeneutical relation. Interpretation can never be a fixing of fleeting meanings (*PH*, 211).

[15] Narrative tellings announce, address, and call forth the saying-relating of a narrative gathering, which distinguishes itself in that it never admits of final understandings. Corresponding asks for the possibility to be allowed such that there may be different answers of each encounter.

[16] See Chapter 11 for hermeneutic phenomenological (ontological) description of each Concernful Practice.

The Concernful Practices of Schooling Learning Teaching were identified in the "data set"[17] of the 20-year longitudinal study of Narrative Pedagogy as reflected in extant research publications and other Narrative Pedagogy studies. They provide a new language for reforming nursing education. Footnotes in this converging conversation link the reader to literature and exegeses in previous chapters to extend interpretations of schooling learning teaching as a co-occurring, intra-related, invisible phenomenon. Sidebar comments address the themes and patterns[18] (Concernful Practices)[19] and reflect questionings[20] that point to the exploration of presuppositions. Boxed commentary, reflecting cycles of interpretations, is given as it arises and occurs within the conversation. This commentary extends the explication of presuppositions and the CP; all the while recurring themes, patterns, and narratives tellings[21] are made thematic,[22] kept in motion, held open and problematic. In this converging conversation, findings from Narrative Pedagogy studies are enacted by teachers and students, from various kinds of schools of nursing, who converse about their experiences of courses and the curriculum revisions. Many narrative tellings of *"We learned to listen to what we saw all around us"* were gathered.[23]

In hermeneutic phenomenological interpretations, the reader is brought into conversation with the text. The thinking of the researcher is made visible so the reader is free to accept or reject the interpretations offered. The intent is to engage conversational thinking between the reader and the text, freeing thinking to reveal otherwise overlooked interpretations.

---

[17] The "data set" of this study (approved by the Institutional Review Board at the University or Wisconsin-Madison) is narrative tellings gathered through group and individual interviews as well as written submissions by students, teachers, and clinicians in nursing education.

[18] Patterns are reflected in all themes, but not all themes reflect all patterns. The Concernful Practices of Schooling Learning Teaching are patterns and reflect the highest level of hermeneutic phenomenological analyses. See N. Diekelmann & P. Ironside, 1998a, Hermeneutics. In J. Fitzpatrick (Ed.), *Encyclopedia of nursing research* (pp. 243-245) (New York: Springer) for further discussion of themes and patterns.

[19] The Concernful Practices of Schooling Learning Teaching are co-occurring, are *inter-*related, and belong together. Sidebar commentaries indicate the most compelling practices we have identified but are never meant to tell the whole story. The play of other Concernful Practices can always already be present as possibility.

[20] The practice of questioning is more originary than the question. Questioning is itself a response to the demand that sense makes upon us. See Chapter 9 for explications of teaching and questioning.

[21] The term narrative telling is an attempt to focus on the conversational aspects of narratives. It is to reflect and embrace a narrative's telling (in all the senses of telling) as the loci of matters of concern. Thereby narratives gather human beings of openness as the call to conversation. For explorations of narrative tellings, see Chapter 6. Themes and patterns reflect recurring concerns.

[22] See Chapters 6 and 11 for discussions of making thematic and converging conversations.

[23] See Appendix A for a narrative telling and guide: Community Interpretive Scholarship: Narrative Pedagogy, Redesigning Courses, and Curricula.

"We learned to listen to what we saw all around us."

Trinity

When we start revising the curriculum, it's amazing how one person, like a dean or curriculum coordinator, can choke out innovation and reform by forcing everyone to do a certain kind of it, even if it doesn't work![24]

Saskia

That's true, but remember we go along with that happening. I used to just assume there were no alternatives and that's why Narrative Pedagogy was so exciting to me—it just plain got us all thinking

> **Concernful Practices (CP)** – Caring: Engendering of Community; Gathering: Welcoming and Calling Forth; Assembling: Constructing and Cultivating
> **Theme:** The Curriculum as Communal: Overcoming Individual-Centered Pedagogies
> **Questionings:**
> - How does assigning roles and responsibilities in pedagogical communities close down/open up possibilities for communal experiences of the curriculum as dialogue?
> - How are conventional pedagogies both teacher centered and individual centered?
> - How have conventional pedagogies shown up for you as a teacher? As a student?

from a different place. Thinking about things like "What are we *not* teaching because of our emphasis on content coverage?"[25] and "How can we create courses that are places for teachers and students to engage with practice in ways that *exceed* learning about content, signs and symptoms, and so forth?" Questions like these got us learning again. Narrative Pedagogy is research based, and right from the start it made sense to me. I had an education course in graduate school but have not kept up with nursing education literature. I knew nothing about the interpretive pedagogies. With Narrative Pedagogy it isn't about all of us teaching the same way, like we do now. Being sure all our course outcomes, objectives, and competencies are clearly spelled out in our syllabi. You can use Narrative Pedagogy and still keep competency-based courses

---

[24] For an exegesis on the cultural and historical perspectives of the curriculum as mirror, see K. Kavanagh, 2003, Mirrors: A cultural and historical interpretation of nursing's pedagogies. In N. Diekelmann (Ed.), 2003c, *Teaching the practitioners of care: New pedagogies for the health professions* (Vol. 2, pp. 59-154) (Madison, WI: University of Wisconsin Press).

[25] For a discussion of covering content and the meaning of curriculum, see C. Tanner, 2004, The meaning of curriculum: Content to be covered or stories to be heard? [Editorial], *Journal of Nursing Education, 43*(1), 3-4.

where they work in the curriculum. We started looking at the silly things we do, just to do them, that are so time-consuming and get us down. Things like all of us using the same clinical evaluation checklist just to ensure we all do everything the same! We learned to think more, look around, and *really* listen. *We learned to listen to what we saw all around us.*

CP – Listening: Knowing and Connecting; Preserving: Reading, Writing, Thinking-Saying, and Dialogue; Questioning: Sense and Making Meanings Visible

Themes:
- Listening as Learning: Preserving the Practices of Thinking-Saying
- Listening to Teach: The Learner as Teacher
- The Nearness of the Near: On Listening to What Is Sighted All Around

Questioning:
- Have conventional pedagogies overtaken thinking as a concept and become only analytic thinking, limiting reform and innovation?
- Is thinking freed as thinking-saying when assumptions of everyday teaching and learning practices are challenged and explicated?
- Where, when, how does listening disclose and beckon?

Trinity

We were hearing in the Teacher Teleconferences[26] that some schools were using Narrative Pedagogy to revise their curriculum from the ground up--one course and one teacher at a time. Is that what your school did?

Saskia

Yep! We revised all our courses using Narrative Pedagogy and the curriculum too, over a year using two-day faculty and student re-

CP – Presencing: Attending and Being Open; Listening: Knowing and Connecting; Caring: Engendering of Community

treats or faculty development days. We started *learning* to really *listen* to one another about what works and what does not work in our school. Listening takes place in many ways. This kind of listening is more than just processing mere sounds or words, though it includes both hearing and seeing. In this listening you try and catch sight of things. When listening is sighting; you work hard to listen, staying engaged and open to the meanings of listenings. You try and catch sight of new possibilities for thinking.

---

[26] Teacher Teleconferences are 90-minute bimonthly conversations of faculty and students among pilot schools in which they share and collectively interpret their experiences using Narrative Pedagogy.

The instantiation of learning as it belongs to schooling learning teaching shows up as the origination and accomplishment of listening in any pedagogical dialogical experiences. Dialogical experiences let learning show itself as itself.[27] Humans can not *not* respond to the call of learning. Not responding is a kind of co-responding. What shows up as a matter of concern is the meaning and significance of attending as listening and co-responding as the call of learning. Listening is not just an aural or oral experience; it is meaningful engagement in situations. To learn means to become knowing (*OWL*, 143), and "to know means to *be able to learn*" (*IM*, 23). Coming into learning is presupposed by listening and understanding, not as a causal chain of events, but as a practical and prudent historically situated belonging-together.[28]

David

We all think we are good listeners until we tune someone out because we know what they are going to say! Or we forget to listen because we are

> CP – Listening: Knowing, and Connecting; Caring: Engendering of Community

so focused on how we will respond to what is being said. When you get right down to it, it is really hard to listen well!

Saskia

And it's very hard not to start revising things by only looking at problems. In my course I started by looking at what the students really liked about the course and learning activities that meant a lot to me, and I tried to build in more of those kinds of activities.

David

You know we really do rush into finding problems and fixing them, don't we? We lose sight of "what is working." No wonder sometimes when we change courses or the curriculum we end up throwing out the baby with the bath water! We are always looking for problems. We become problem-oriented teachers. Our community life suffers when all we do is focus on problems.

> CP – Assembling: Constructing and Cultivating; Retrieving: Keeping Open a Future of Possibilities
> **Theme:** Overcoming Deficit Thinking: "Shifting from what we can't do to what we can!"
> **Questioning:**
> * How would starting every meeting with faculty and students sharing something they were proud of influence the engendering of community?

---

[27] For our discussion of showing showing itself, see Chapter 5.

[28] See Chapter 8 for our discourse on learning as listening.

In conventional pedagogies, curricular or course reform follows evaluation. In this way, problems initiate reform.[29] Preparation of accreditation reports involves the extensive evaluation of the curriculum; it can show where problems lie. Students' performance on NCLEX (National Council Licensing Examination) likewise indicates problems. However, because of the putative association of falling NCLEX scores with reform,[30] schools often delay curriculum revisions until *after* they have received accreditation, since falling NCLEX scores can influence accreditation. Addressing problems is a central area of concern in revising the curriculum using conventional pedagogies.

Conventional pedagogies are claimed by modernity's quest for certainty. The curriculum is thereby organized to prevent students from failing or to ensure some idealized notion of success. Even in the guise of establishing quality education, the quest for certainty resonates. Unexplicated is the assumption that student learning transfers to clinical settings. If students practice and demonstrate their learning in schools of nursing, a context in which their knowledge and skills will never be used, did they learn? Because this assumption has held in the past, it is risky to challenge or change it.

> **Questionings:**
> - How do the pedagogies embraced by practice disciplines influence/ not influence the ways students practice within them? Does a problem-oriented curriculum create problem-oriented nurses?
> - Is there a danger when problem solving is the focus of curricular reform, that what is "good, successful, and working" will be overrun in the revision process?
> - Do conventional pedagogies overemphasize problem solving and analytic thinking? *For a definition of analytic thinking, see DT, on calculative thinking, and ZS, on analysis.
> - Does this approach to curriculum and instruction encourage analytic thinking in students to the detriment or exclusion of other approaches to thinking, such as hermeneutic phenomenological thinking-saying?

In conventional pedagogies, analytic thinking reigns; that is, the analytic is a reduction to constitutive (neutral) parts (science). An enacted questioning of a matter of concern's belonging to engaged openness (hermeneutic phenomenology) is meant to call the answers inherent in analytic thinking into questions and associated rejoinders. Calculative (analytic) thinking in its scientific sense must count on its results. Certainty is sought and assumed. Analytic thinking as calculation, planning, investigating, and computing does not stop to question itself *as* thinking (*DT*, 46). Hermeneutic phenomenological thinking-saying lets the human being be claimed by being engaged "with what at first sight does not go together at all" (*DT*, 53). Thinking-saying can be open for the possibilities of anything to occur. Uncertainty is embraced as the truth of engaged openness.

---

[29] For interpretations of how problems influence reform, see N. Diekelmann, 2005c, Engaging the students *and* the teacher: Co-creating substantive reform with Narrative Pedagogy, *Journal of Nursing Education, 44*(6), 249-252.

[30] For a school-wide remedy to address falling NCLEX scores, see S. Bonis, L. Taft, & M. Wendler, 2007, Strategies to promote success on the NCLEX-RN: An evidence-based approach using the Ace Star Model of Knowledge Transformation, *Nursing Education Perspectives, 28*, 82-87.

Saskia

We also realized right away that as a school everyone needed to behave themselves and work better together to see if we could revise the courses and the curriculum using a different pedagogy. And from the beginning we challenged taken-for-granted assumptions, like do we need a curriculum committee? We did not even assume that everyone knew the entire curriculum, so we made sure we spent time describing our courses to one another.

> CP – Caring: Engendering of Community

In Narrative Pedagogy, schooling learning teaching is an invisible co-occurring phenomenon. As such it is constitutive of the human being. Schooling learning teaching always co-present and arrive together.[31] Gathering the school as a whole during a retreat to conduct revising the curriculum enhances the communal nature of the curriculum-as-dialogue. The gathering begins with sharing "what is." There is structure but only so far as the structure guides the conversations that ensue. This kind of a gathering is in contrast to one typically planned by the curriculum committee with an agenda to be accomplished, like approving new courses or selecting a curriculum framework. Enabling Narrative Pedagogy through enacting hermeneutic phenomenology can occur when teachers and students gather and attend to the curriculum-as-dialogue.[32] This is an emerging example of *community interpretive scholarship,* that is, students and teachers gathering to "put their heads together." Likewise, this approach to revising courses prevents the isolation that can occur when faculty agree as a group to curriculum changes and then individually hide good ideas or changes in their courses or hoard information. Possibility calls forth the human being of openness to its can-be.

> CP – Inviting: Waiting and Letting Be; Assembling: Constructing and Cultivating
> **Theme:** The Curriculum-as-Dialogue: Gathering the Collective Wisdom

> CP – Inviting: Waiting and Letting Be; Assembling: Constructing and Cultivating
> **Note:** Concernful practices are always present and are neither positive nor negative. It is how they are enacted that determines how they are experienced as negative or positive.
> **Theme:** The Curriculum-as-Dialogue: Gathering the Collective Wisdom
> **Note:** Likewise themes can be experienced in negative or positive ways. Gatherings can call forth the best OR the worst in people.

Shireen

I'd love to be at your school! I've heard so much about it.

---

[31] For the to and fro of phenomena, see Chapter 4.

[32] See C. Andrews, P. Ironside, C. Nosek, S. Sims, M. Swenson, C. Yeomans, P. Young, & N. Diekelmann, 2001, Enacting Narrative Pedagogy: The lived experiences of students and teachers, *Nursing and Health Care Perspectives, 22*(5), 252-259.

David

I wish our school would go along with something like that! What a great experience.

Trinity

It wouldn't work at our school, I'm sure of it. There's just no trust. The only way we can get any changes is slowly, one course and one teacher at a time.[33] That's just the way it is. But even thinking about doing curriculum another way helps me. So after everyone learned what the curriculum looked like, then what?

Saskia

Faculty included, in their descriptions of their courses, their assignments, and we learned how many papers students write! And how many pages they have to read each week. It opened my eyes. We forget students don't just have "our" course. There were over 67 papers of one kind or another assigned over the curriculum. So many were redundant. We began to ask ourselves questions like: What is the meaning of these kinds of assignments? You know, lots of them were the "pick a topic" and write about it kind of thing. We started asking ourselves, why are we doing this? Is it so that students can demonstrate they can look up a topic and write it? Now tell me, how many papers does that take? Do we want students to learn how to logically write intel-

CP – Gathering: Welcoming and Calling Forth; Retrieving Places: Keeping Open a Future of Possibilities; Assembling: Constructing and Cultivating; Listening: Knowing and Connecting; Presencing: Attending and Being Open

Theme: Disaffected Learning Communities: Closing Down/Opening Up on Innovation and Reform

Questionings:

- Does listening turn on trust?
- Is a limitation of Narrative Pedagogy that a level of trust is necessary in order for there to be dialogue, conversation, and narrative tellings?
- Is curriculum change as one course at a time a faster way to reform the curriculum because it avoids curricular upheavals and focuses faculty and student energies away from the curriculum and onto reforming courses?

CP – Inviting: Waiting and Letting Be
Theme: Change and Changing: Learning Always Already Discloses and Beckons
Questioning

- Is this approach to change a kind of changing?

---

[33] P. Ironside, 2006b, Using Narrative Pedagogy: Learning and practicing interpretive thinking, *Journal of Advanced Nursing, 55*, 478-486.

ligible sentences, learn APA [style prescribed by the American Psychological Association], or learn to use the library and Internet?[34] If so, what is the best way to teach these skills?[35] What are students *really* learning or not learning? | CP – Preserving: Reading, Writing, Thinking-Saying, and Dialogue

> Community interpretive scholarship takes place as converging conversations that work to demonstrate ways of enacting hermeneutic phenomenology to enable Narrative Pedagogy. Conversation is a "presence-to" as the co-originality of "being able to talk and being able to hear" (*EH,* 57).[36] In contrast to a meaningful conversation for science that is objective, neutral, and fixed in agreement in terms of logically determined utterances, a converging conversation lets co-responding as attending-to show itself as a letting wherein openness is called to listening. The conversation remains engagedly open as on-coming.

Clarence

And besides even writing all these papers, many students still struggle with grammar, punctuation, and writing logically. So maybe assigning tons of papers is not the way learn.[37] I know that practice makes perfect. But sometimes practice makes poor grammar harder to change! And as teachers, we about die trying to grade all the papers we've assigned. Sometimes I spend 45 minutes correcting a paper, and the student doesn't read one word of my online commentary. Once I spent two hours on a paper a student handed in and the student never came by to get it. Why do we do this to ourselves and our students? We teachers are doing to our students, what we hated our teachers doing to us. Talk about teaching as we were taught!

---

[34] See S. McGuire, D. Gerber, & M. Currin, 2001, Helping students use APA format, *Journal of Nursing Education, 40*(9), 414-417.

[35] For integrating writing into learning activities, see J. Bean, 1996, *Engaging ideas: The professor's guide to integrating writing, critical thinking, and active learning in the classroom* (San Francisco: Jossey-Bass) and N. Diekelmann, 2003d, Thinking-in-action journals: From self-evaluation to multiperspectival thinking, *Journal of Nursing Education, 42*(11), 482-484.

[36] Further explication of talking and hearing is presented in Chapter 9.

[37] For an exegesis of writing as learning in the context of nursing practice, see D. Allen, B. Bowers, & N. Diekelmann, 1989, Writing to learn: A reconceptualization of thinking and writing in the nursing curriculum, *Journal of Nursing Education, 28,* 6-10; M. Craft, 2005, Reflective writing and nursing education, *Journal of Nursing Education, 44*(2), 53-57; and N. Diekelmann & P. M. Ironside, 1998b, Preserving writing in doctoral education: Exploring the concernful practices of schooling teaching learning, *Journal of Advanced Nursing, 28,* 1347-1355.

Hayley

I had to write three totally meaningless papers this semester, and after a while you resent doing that kind of thing. Researching the literature, finding a topic and then reporting it in a paper—how boring! Maybe writing one, but not more!

> CP – Preserving: Reading, Writing, Thinking-Saying, and Dialogue; Caring: Engendering of Community; Presencing: Attending and Being Open; Listening: Knowing and Connecting
> **Questioning:** How does the need (call of) writing show up ontically (grammar) and ontologically (interpretation)?

Shireen

I had a course where instead of a final paper, we had to write a one-page discharge referral on one of our patients. It was hard to do, especially short like that, and yet include everything that needed to be there. You had to be clear with every word.

Hayley

Short papers are harder to write. I liked when we had to write a one-page review of an article and include in one paragraph about what were the major points, one paragraph of what the article *meant* to us as junior nursing students in a pediatrics course, and then one paragraph of questions that the article made you ask yourself. And we read these to each other in class, so everyone did a good job writing them. That kind of writing is OK because it's about your thinking or gets you thinking, or something. It's not proving to the teacher you can write a report or library paper. In this short assignment, I *learned* a lot, and you could learn from other students' thinking too.

> CP – Caring: Engendering of Community, Listening: Knowing and Connecting; Interpreting: Unlearning and Becoming; Preserving: Reading, Writing, Thinking-Saying, and Dialogue
> **Theme:** Overcoming Students' Isolation: Assignments That Gather Knowing and Connecting

Shireen

In an online course I took, each week, we had to write down the major points of the unit we were studying in 3 sentences to fit in a box. In another course we had to write dialogues; one-page conversations between patients and nurses, teachers and students. It was hard to do and got you thinking!

Ryan

Don't you like it when you get to hear or read other students' papers? You learn to respect other students more when you hear about how they think or write. I'm a commuting student, so it means a lot to me to get to know the student sitting next to me. Being a commuting student is very lonely.

> **CP** – Caring: Engendering of Community; Preserving: Reading, Writing, Thinking-Speaking, and Dialogue
> **Theme:** Overcoming Students' Isolation: Assignments That Gather Knowing and Connecting

Clarence

I feel the same kind of isolation sometimes. I am around faculty all the time, but how we spend our time together does help me feel connected to them. Most of the times it is either chit-chat or social events. You get to know someone when you have meaningful conversations. I teach a large required class, and there are so many students I don't know.[38] But I found including the students in revising my courses helped me connect with them in new ways. We, as teachers, assume students either are not interested in revising courses or the curriculum or that frankly they just don't know much about either. I guess we just assume courses and the curriculum are faculty's responsibility. Case closed![39] It's a shame, really, because we know teaching and learning is always communal; every class is nothing more than working or not working together.

> **CP** – Caring: Engendering Community; Staying: Knowing and Connecting; Inviting: Waiting and Letting Be
> **Themes:**
> • Overturning Student and Teacher Isolation: Lonely Versus Alone
> • Students as Pedagogical Partners: On Listening to What Stands in Front of Us
> • The Circle of Participation: Students as Pedagogical Partners

---

[38] See N. Diekelmann, 2004a, Class evaluations: Creating new student partnerships in support of innovation, *Journal of Nursing Education, 43*(10), 436-439, and N. Diekelmann, 2002c, "She asked this simple question": Reflecting and the scholarship of teaching, *Journal of Nursing Education, 41*(9), 381-382 for exegeses of students as pedagogical partners.

[39] Explicating students' experiences hermeneutically is discussed in N. Diekelmann & S. Lampe, 2004, Student-centered pedagogies: Co-creating compelling experiences using the new pedagogies, *Journal of Nursing Education, 43*(6), 245-247, and P. Ironside, 2005b, Working together, creating excellence: The experiences of nursing teachers, students and clinicians, *Nursing Education Perspectives, 26*(2), 78-85.

How do students and teachers get to the heart of salient matters of concern? The art of speaking with another shows up as situated in time and place. The non-speaking of one to another is its own way of speaking. The community offers itself as a listening that includes non-listening.

Kwan

I rarely get to know my teachers.[40]

> CP – Engendering of Community
> **Theme:** Listening: Opening Up or Closing Down on Knowing and Connecting

Saskia

It's a shame because when you don't know someone, you still make assumptions about them that influence how you relate. At our school-wide retreat to revamp the curriculum, I was surprised there were several students who were more engaged and knowledgeable about the curriculum issues than some of our faculty. While some of our clinical adjunct faculty and preceptors were our grads, many were not. The clinicians' keen suggestions sometimes "knocked our socks off"! One suggested starting the beginning students off in the ICU where they can be easily mentored and monitored. I've learned students and clinicians are such an amazing resource if teachers would just not assume they're not interested or knowledgeable but reach out and invite them, you know "bring them to the table" and think together in new ways! If students can see how you are including them as pedagogical

> CP – Inviting: Waiting and Letting Be; Caring: Engendering of Community; Gathering: Welcoming and Calling Forth; Assembling: Constructing and Cultivating; Listening: Knowing and Connecting
> **Theme:** The Circle of Participating: Students and Clinicians as Pedagogical Partners

partners in the course, you will be amazed at their participation. I even had a second-degree student who was a school teacher for years, rewrite some of the course objectives! My colleague said I should be ashamed if my objectives were so bad that a student could improve on them. That is the kind of attitude we need to get rid of! The student did some very innovative things!

---

[40] For students and teachers knowing and connecting, see C. Andrews, 1998, Engendering community: Writing a journal to clinical students, *Journal of Nursing Education, 37,* 358-360.

"To speak means to say, which means to show and let [something] be seen. It means to communicate and, correspondingly, to listen. To submit oneself to a claim addressed to oneself and to comply and respond to it" (*ZS*, 215). Responding as such is a fundamental moment of teaching.[41] Saskia describes gathering, welcoming, and calling forth as she invites clinicians and students to become pedagogical partners. To be mindful of collective wisdom can preserve community interpretive scholarship, but collective understanding can in its own way also be a hindrance.

> **Questioning:**
> - How might inviting students as pedagogical partners call out future nurse educators?

David

The other day a clinician pointed out that our school of nursing was doing a good job preparing students for new practice environments.[42] She said, in contrast to another nearby school that prepared students for a healthcare system that no longer exists. These students really struggle! But she also said, our school needed to better prepare students for the future. "Schools of nursing," she said, "should lead reform in practice rather than just follow it!" When I asked her how we were to do that, she said, "Make the students better thinkers than you and I are!" Now that got me thinking! Does what I know and am able to teach hinder students so they can never be any better than I am?[43] This kind of questioning is from a different place. How can the school of nursing lead practice reform when so many teachers are deskilled? And some teachers aren't the best thinkers!

> **CP** – Questioning: Meanings and Making Visible; Preserving: Reading, Writing, Thinking-Saying, and Dialogue; Interpreting: Unlearning and Becoming
>
> **Theme:** Teaching What You Don't Know, Can't Do, or Have Never Seen!
>
> **Questioning:**
> - How is innovation and reform in nursing education shaping or shaped by innovation and reform in nursing practice? (See Diekelmann & Scheckel, 2003.)

---

[41] See Chapter 9 for explication of teaching as co-responding.

[42] The stories of experienced clinicians joining the academic community are interpreted in N. Diekelmann, 2004b, Experienced practitioners as new faculty: New pedagogies and new possibilities, *Journal of Nursing Education, 43*(3), 101-103; M. McAllister, M. Tower, & R. Walker, 2007, Gentle interruptions: Transformative approaches to clinical teaching, *Journal of Nursing Education, 46*, 304-312; and F. Myrick & D. Tamlyn, 2007, Teaching can never be innocent: Fostering an enlightening educational experience, *Journal of Nursing Education, 46*, 299-303.

[43] For interpretive exegeses of teaching thinking in the context of nursing education, see P. Ironside, 2003a, New pedagogies for teaching thinking: The lived experiences of students and teachers enacting Narrative Pedagogy, *Journal of Nursing Education, 42*, 509-516, and P. Ironside, 2006b, Using Narrative Pedagogy: Learning and practicing interpretive thinking, *Journal of Advanced Nursing, 55*, 478-486.

Hermeneutic phenomenological thinking-saying as safeguarding a future as possibilities reveals questionings that call forth sense and making meanings visible. In this situation, the questionings reinterpret the assumption that the best teachers are the most knowledgeable about curriculum and course reform or innovation. David's questionings show how expertise in thinking can be as limiting as a knowledge deficit can be.

Saskia

I learned some awesome new ways to think about my course and content from students. I invited them to join me for coffee in the cafeteria before or after class. It was just an informal thing, and sometimes we just talked about the most recent snowstorm. It gave us a half hour to relax together. Sometimes I learned more about what the students were learning there than I

> CP – Gathering: Welcoming and Calling Forth; Caring: Engendering of Community
> **Theme:** The Teacher as Learner: Listening as Knowing and Connecting

did in class! You know, adding and eliminating assignments and content is always such a big problem. When the students learned I would appreciate their help with the course, one designed a new assignment that was terrific, and several brought me substitute articles that were better than what I had assigned.

Hayley

The articles I like best are ones that make more than one point. If it's research and you can read the abstract and get it all, I'm not too interested. These kinds of readings just pile more facts on top of the textbook and online assignments—more to memorize for the test. And you can tell if the course needs revising by how old some of the readings are and some are just off-point. But it's great when a teacher assigns two readings that disagree and you have to think about what it means for you as a nurse. You realize medical science is not an exact science, no matter how it looks.

> CP – Interpreting: Unlearning and Becoming; Assembling: Knowing and Connecting; Assembling: Constructing and Cultivating; Retrieving Places: Keeping Open a Future of Possibilities; Questioning: Sense and Making Meanings Visible
> **Theme:** Challenging Medical and Nursing Science: The Quest for Certainty

Kwan

One of my teachers asked us each week to rank order the articles. We would talk briefly about which ones should be dropped. Mostly we dropped articles because we thought they were too hard, over our heads. Nothing made sense in them. At midterm she spent time in class reading a difficult article with us, and she showed us how to unpack it. How to skip over some words and be sure and look others up. She showed us where to go to look things up and helped us to see we needed to be able to make sense of this difficult literature to be a safe nurse. She showed us how.

> **CP** – Listening: Knowing and Connecting; Preserving: Reading, Writing, Thinking-Saying, and Dialogue; Interpreting: Unlearning and Becoming; Questioning: Sense and Making Meanings Visible
>
> **Themes:**
> • Teaching Interpretive Thinking: Making Sense of Medical and Nursing Literature
> • Students as Pedagogical Partners: Practicing Reading, Writing, Thinking-Saying, and Dialogue

Trinity

Teachers too often ask students for their evaluations after they can do nothing about it, like at the end of a course.[44] It sounds like your teacher asked you for input and then co-responded to help you learn better while you were still in the course. I know a school that took two whole days during which every class looked at duplication of content and what was missing. It got the students really thinking

> **Themes:**
> • Creating Connecting Conversations: Evaluating as You Go Along
> • Taking Risks: "Dear Teacher" Letters as Ongoing Course Evaluation
>
> **Questionings:**
> • How adequately are schools able to measure and evaluate student learning?
> • What are the assets and limitations of standardized course evaluations?

about how hard it is to drop content. And the faculty were amazed what they learned about the curriculum. Both agreed that some of the redundancy was good and it was planned for. This really helped faculty address the curriculum and course problem of too much content. I think sometimes teachers just assume it's *our* role

---

44　Hermeneutic phenomenological analyses of the narrative tellings of students and teachers as pedagogical partners are presented in N. Diekelmann, 2004a, Class evaluations: Creating new student partnerships in support of innovation, *Journal of Nursing Education,* 43(10), 436-439, and N. Diekelmann, 2003d, Thinking-in-action journals: From self-evaluation to multiperspectival thinking, *Journal of Nursing Education,* 42(11), 482-484.

to find and fix these problems. Working together with students on stuff like this keeps us all learners.

Saskia

Early at our retreat, one student said, "I was thinking it's not that the courses have so much content. I need to know everything there is about nursing. It's that we are tested on content in multiple choice exams, so we have to memorize. In that case, there's too much! But if content were available to us when we need it, like online, when we are preparing for clinical, that's a good way for us to learn things. It's much better than memorizing." That student comment helped us stop worrying so much about redundancies and removing content. Our focus immediately shifted to thinking about what it would be like for us as a school to offer the entire curriculum online to both students and teachers, all the time.

> **CP** – Caring: Engendering of Community
> **Themes:**
> - Keeping Open a Future of New Possibilities: Students and Clinicians as Pedagogical Partners
> - Students as Pedagogical Partners: On Listening to What Stands in Front of Us
> - The Circle of Participation: Students as Pedagogical Partners
>
> **Questionings:**
> - Are students too often involved in unmeaningful ways as pedagogical partners, e.g., at the end of a course or as the one elected member of the class to sit in on curricular committee meetings?
> - In what ways might students become pedagogical partners regarding the curriculum, other than membership on the curriculum committee?

Ryan

Applying helps learning, but so does teachers bringing their stories from nursing practice into class. We get to see our teachers thinking like a nurse—we learn a lot that way.[45] I think there's too much information to be memorized in our courses, like 150 pages on hypertension. We could get by with 50% less. But the stories we discuss in class, I don't want 50% less of that!

---

[45] For teaching and learning with case studies, see T. Delpier, 2006, Cases 101: Learning to teach with cases, *Nursing Education Perspectives, 27,* 204-209; P. Benner, P. Hooper-Kyriakidis, & D. Stannard, 1999, *Clinical wisdom and interventions in critical care: A thinking-in-action approach* (Philadelphia: Saunders) and L. Day, & E. L. Smith, 2007, Integrating quality and safety content into clinical teaching in the acute care setting, *Nursing Outlook, 55,* 138-143.

Shireen

I think we need all the information we can get. The problem is with memorizing. Unless you have a patient that week with that particular disease, you forget it. I always seem to have a patient assignment the week *before* we cover it in class! But I love lectures because the teachers work hard at finding just what is important in all the stuff that is out there. I was thinking, couldn't teachers put all their lectures as podcasts into the online courses for the entire curriculum and then make it available to us from the day we enter? Then we wouldn't have to wait until we get to that course to learn it! It would be available to us from day one when we needed it, even classes we have had and forgotten.

> CP – Inviting: Waiting and Letting Be; Presencing: Attending and Being Open, Assembling: Constructing and Cultivating; Interpreting: Unlearning and Becoming; Questioning: Meanings and Making Visible; Assembling: Constructing and Cultivating
>
> **Themes:**
> • The Circle of Participating: Students and Clinicians as Pedagogical Partners
> • Keeping Open a Future of New Possibilities: Students and Clinicians as Pedagogical Partners

> Conversation is understanding that can be said. It is a narrative telling which can be a dialogue, not as an argument (Palmer, 1969, 199; *TM*, 367) but as a thinking dialogue *with* interpretation itself (Palmer, 1969, 149). Conversations openly hold themselves in convergence as the latter; *converging conversations* show the gatherings/dispersions of conversation, narrative telling, and dialogue.[46]

Kwan

Great idea! I miss face-to-face contact with teachers in online courses and all of the conversations that go along with lectures that are missing in totally online courses. Your idea makes content available when we need it and still teacher contact.

Shireen

I hate all-online courses! Bet a lot of teachers do too! There are no words to describe the learning that was missing. In the online curriculum there's more time to talk and think with teachers.

---

[46] Conversations are described in more detail in Chapter 6.

Clarence

That is an amazing suggestion! Shireen is right. It's not too much content, it's what we do with it![47] All the RNs have PDAs now and look things up as they need it. And yet some of what RNs look up, we require students to memorize and then we test them on it![48] A student often does not learn nursing as nurses learn in nursing practice.

CP – Interpreting: Unlearning and Becoming; Preserving: Reading, Writing, Thinking and Dialogue; Questioning: Meanings and Making Visible; Inviting: Waiting and Letting Be

Themes:
- Explicating the Claims of Epistemology: Experiencing Learning as Listening
- The Call of New Pedagogies: Extending the Unanticipated, Unpredictable, and Immeasurable
- Student Voices: Learning as Listening

Questionings:
- In dialogue, thinking-saying is freed to follow the movement of showing. Can learning be anticipated, predicted, or measured?
- How can converging conversations, and creating a place in the curriculum for community interpretive scholarship, gather the wisdom and expertise of students, teachers, and clinicians, inviting learning and only learning to occur?

Narrative Pedagogy can open the way for students and teachers to bring one another to learning. Matters of concern appear in their own time, as possibilities of conversation, narrative telling, and dialogue. Their on-coming, anticipated movement is whiling as self-disclosedness: conversation as shared appearance; narrative telling as historical movement and the saying/telling of language; dialogue as the always already engaged awakening of the self-presencing of presence.[49] Shireen helps the teachers learn that it is not just the problem of too much content; it is also the issue of how epistemology takes center stage and is experienced by the students as overwhelming memorization.[50] In conventional pedagogies, learning becomes observable behaviors. Testing is the dominant way to assess observable learning. Cognitive gain on tests becomes conflated with learning.[51] But Clarence, a teacher, co-responds, revealing new possibilities for rethinking the additive curriculum and "too much content." Converging conversations show themselves as narrative tellings through and through.

---

[47] P. Ironside, 2004, "Covering content" and teaching thinking: Deconstructing the additive curriculum, *Journal of Nursing Education, 43,* 5-12.

[48] For an exegesis of memorizing content, see P. Ironside, 2005a, Teaching thinking and reaching the limits of memorization: Enacting new pedagogies, *Journal of Nursing Education, 44,* 441-449.

[49] See Chapter 6 for hermeneutic phenomenological interpretations of conversation, narrative tellings, and dialogue.

[50] The additive curriculum-as-experienced is explicated in N. Diekelmann & E. Smythe, 2004, Covering content and the additive curriculum: How can I use my time with students to best help them learn what they need to know? *Journal of Nursing Education, 43*(8), 344-350.

[51] See N. Diekelmann, 1992, Learning-as-testing: A Heideggerian hermeneutical analysis of the lived experiences of students and teachers in nursing, *Advances in Nursing Science, 14,* 72-83 for hermeneutic phenomenological interpretations of learning.

Ryan

Several students told me they wanted to use the time they spend learning the content and preparing for the lecture to better prepare for clinicals.[52] They said loud and clear, *we learn content best when we need it in caring for a patient.*

Trinity

Of course, there is always content you need to know even if you don't ever "use it" in a patient assignment.

CP – Assembling: Constructing and Cultivating; Preserving: Reading, Writing, Thinking-Saying, and Dialogue
Themes:
- Meaning Making: Learning as a Process, Practice, and Phenomenon
- Learning as Experience: Experience as Learning
- "An Ear for the Word": Inviting Learning as Listening
Questionings:
- Converging conversations call students and teachers to attend to the familiar and at-hand that stands in front of them (the nearness of the near). How can what stands in front of them be invisible?
- How do interpretive pedagogies call out thinking-saying from a different place?

Dian

That's true, but if the content is presented in a podcast story, that is, *as if* a nurse were going to take care of a particular patient, it would help. I mean, you could start with a case study, but it has to be real and sometimes with contradicting clinical data or conflicting concerns. I want to be able to see and hear the patient in it![53] I'm a preceptor, so I have current clinical stories to present the realities of the practice world,

Questionings:
- Do conventional pedagogies claim case studies as utilitarian?

even to beginning students! We know as clinicians we can't keep up with the literature like teachers do, but we keep up with clinical practice in ways that few teachers can. Sometimes I co-teach classes where I bring in my clinical practice for the students, but making these narratives available online all at once for the students

---

[52] Explicating preparing for class as a common practice is presented in N. Diekelmann, 2000a, Being prepared for class: Challenging taken-for-granted assumptions, *Journal of Nursing Education, 39,* 291-293.

[53] For interpretive commentary on lecturing with case studies, see N. Diekelmann, M. Swenson, & S. Sims, 2003, Reforming the lecture: Avoiding what students already know, *Journal of Nursing Education, 42*(3), 103-105. Narrative strategies, in the context of clinical education, are explicated in M. Swenson & S. Sims, 2003, Listening to learn: Narrative strategies and interpretive practices in clinical education. In N. Diekelmann, 2003c, *Teaching the practitioners of care: New pedagogies for the health professions* (Vol. 2, pp. 154-193) (Madison, WI: University of Wisconsin Press).

seems like a great idea to me and a way I can contribute to my teaching colleagues.

Kwan

I think a lot of the case studies are boring. The way to get my attention when I'm reading a case study is to make me nervous. Give me parts that are over my head or load it up with complex social or family issues.[54]

David

Sounds like to put lectures online as podcasts for the entire curriculum, you'd need to have a lot of IT [instructional technology] resources.

Saskia

Many schools have that capability now.

Trinity

I think this idea would free up class time to practice thinking, exploring questions, and interpreting stories.[55] When we lecture we spend too much time on problem solving and critical thinking. I want to practice *clinical* thinking with the students, not critical thinking![56] I want to spend more time helping them learn how to

---

[54]   See M. Swenson & S. Sims, 2003, Listening to learn: Narrative strategies and interpretive practices in clinical education. In N. Diekelmann, 2003c, *Teaching the practitioners of care: New pedagogies for the health professions* (Vol. 2, pp. 154-193) (Madison, WI: University of Wisconsin Press); M. Swenson & S. Sims, 2000, Toward a narrative-centered curriculum, *Journal of Nursing Education, 39*(3), 109-115; and P. Ironside, N. Diekelmann, & M. Hirschmann, 2005, Student voices: On listening to experiences in practice education, *Journal of Nursing Education, 44,* 49-52.

[55]   See N. Diekelmann, M. Swenson, & S. Sims, 2003, Reforming the lecture: Avoiding what students already know, *Journal of Nursing Education, 42*(3), 103-105, and P. Ironside, 2003a, New pedagogies for teaching thinking: The lived experiences of students and teachers enacting Narrative Pedagogy, *Journal of Nursing Education, 42,* 509-516.

[56]   For an interpretive exegesis that deconstructs critical thinking and clinical thinking as different approaches to thinking, see C. Tanner, 2005, What have we learned about critical thinking in nursing? [Editorial], *Journal of Nursing Education, 44*(2), 47-48. See M. Scheckel, & P. Ironside, 2006, Cultivating interpretive thinking through enacting Narrative Pedagogy. *Nursing Outlook, 54,* 159-165, for an explication of interpretive thinking and Narrative Pedagogy and C. Tanner, 2006, Thinking like a nurse: A research-based model of clinical judgment in nursing. *Journal of Nursing Education, 45,* 204-211, for a description of clinical thinking as thinking like a nurse.

think like a nurse. The information in my lectures is important, make no mistake about it.[57] But it is how the students make sense of it as a nurse that matters. Does it call out questioning? There is always a lack of answers. We recognize this in clinical thinking. Answering calls out for more questioning.

> **CP** – Questioning: Sense and Making Meanings Visible; Preserving: Reading, Writing, Thinking-Saying, and Dialogue
> **Questioning:**
> * How can hermeneutic phenomenological thinking-saying be taught in online courses?

> Every question is an answer. Every spoken word is an answer, a rejoinder. Critical thinking and analytic thinking sunder, attempting to divide into distinct entities and categories. Hermeneutic phenomenological thinking-saying gathers the seemingly diverse as the same as difference. Thinking-saying works to bring out the strength of a position rather than overcome it.

David

It is exciting! But putting the entire curriculum online with anytime student access is pretty radical. How did you manage this? Were there resisters? I mean, what did you do with students or teachers who did not like this idea at all?

Saskia

People resist in different ways. One teacher who did not like the idea of revising the curriculum slept a lot during the retreat! There were a couple of students and teachers who "talked big" about what they were going to do, but we all knew better. Every community has these kinds of folks. A few teachers and students said online learning was "not for them"

> **CP** – Assembling: Constructing and Cultivating; Presencing: Attending and Being Open; Caring: Engendering of Community
> **Themes:**
> * Being Underway: Unfolding the Possibilities of Instructional Technologies
> * Explicating the Contexts of Learning: Listening to Instructional Technology as Call, Invitation, Path
> * Faculty Development and Increasing Pedagogical Literacy: Recalling Learning to the Lives of Teachers
> **Questioning:**
> * How does instructional technology appropriate schooling learning thinking?

or "their courses," and we all listened respectfully. But they soon got left behind and accepted things were going to change. The online curriculum, accessible from the beginning, was taking on

---

[57] Lecturing as a learning strategy is explicated in N. Diekelmann, 2002b, "Pitching a lecture" and "reading the faces of students": Learning lecturing and the embodied practices of teaching. *Journal of Nursing Education, 41,* 97-99.

a life of its own. We nicknamed it the "All at Once Curriculum"! And the excitement carried us through some horrendous campus administrative hurdles. This was a kind of curriculum revision that was being made doable in a totally different way!

Trinity

There's a problem, though, when teachers just take their lectures and PowerPoints and throw them online but still require students to come to their "mini-lectures" or "reviews," as one of my colleagues calls it! This is adding online learning assignments to an already loaded course! Testing and memorizing remain the same! It's the "same ole" curriculum now online and with more added![58]

> CP – Assembling: Constructing and Cultivating; Preserving: Reading, Writing, Thinking-Saying, and Dialogue
> **Theme:** "Too Much Content . . .": Epistemologies' Grasp and Nursing Education; the Additive Curriculum

> The claim on listening of the familiar and the at-hand is a strong one. Revising courses and the curriculum as well as new strategies can be deeply embedded in conventional pedagogies, such that they can become "the same anew." In this converging conversation, Saskia describes a school that begins revising the curriculum with concerns that reflect conventional pedagogy—the selection of content, namely reducing content and the number of assignments. However, through community interpretive scholarship and converging conversations, thinking-saying was kept in motion, held open and problematic. As students and faculty freed their thinking for challenging their presuppositions, new pedagogies for exploring (thinking about and revising) the curriculum in a different way emerged, revealing the "All at Once Curriculum."

Saskia

We learned from Teacher Teleconference that using new pedagogies means you *teach from a different place,* that you *learn from a different place,* especially with technology.[59] Many things are the

---

[58] For a hermeneutic phenomenological exegesis of the additive curriculum in full sway, see N. Diekelmann, 2002d, "Too much content . . .": Epistemologies' grasp and nursing education, *Journal of Nursing Education, 41*(11), 469-470; P. Ironside, 2004, "Covering content" and teaching thinking: Deconstructing the additive curriculum, *Journal of Nursing Education, 43*, 5-12; and N. Diekelmann & E. Smythe, 2004, Covering content and the additive curriculum: How can I use my time with students to best help them learn what they need to know? *Journal of Nursing Education, 43*(8), 341-344.

[59] For a discussion of touchstones and teaching from a different place, see N. Diekelmann, R. Schuster, & C. Nosek, 1998, Creating new pedagogies at the millennium: The common experiences of the University of Wisconsin-Madison teachers in using distance education technologies, *Teaching with Technology Today* (Online journal). Available: http://www.uwsa.edu/olit/ttt/98.pdf; and N. Diekelmann, 2003a, *Distance desktop faculty development in the new*

same as, but not identical, to conventional pedagogies. The "All at Once Curriculum" helped teachers to not hoard strategies and assignments that worked. With the entire curriculum accessible, some teachers who knew they had too much content were able to compare their courses with others and *see* it for themselves. The most important thing, though, is that if you do not change how you think as a teacher, even in the "All at Once Curriculum," then conventional pedagogies still remain dominant. We had to learn to rethink all the assumptions we make on a day-to-day basis, and that is hard work as well as humbling. Thinking together on a regular basis and talking about our successes and our failures with the students joining us was extremely important. If some teachers or a lot of students stopped coming, we went to them and tried to find out what was going on. This kind of thinking and participation can't be forced or required, only invited. You have to let people come to it, but you can reach out and try and stay connected as you await them to join. And some never do—at least not yet! This curriculum revision meant, for the first time maybe, that we as teachers had more to learn than the students! For us, learning grew to be a path of wondrous, even child-like amazement! We let ourselves be open to sightings as they came along. We realized that we could only let ourselves sight what already let itself be sighted. This was true sharing, not something we made or did ourselves. None of us realized how much we had stopped learning in very important ways!

CP – Caring: Engendering of Community; Listening: Knowing and Connecting; Interpreting: Unlearning and Becoming; Questioning: Sense and Making Meanings Visible; Preserving: Reading, Writing, Thinking-Saying, and Dialogue

Theme: Inviting Reform: The Reaching Out and Letting Be Practices of Students and Teachers

Questionings:

- Are there ways to engender learning communities, perhaps small practices like regular meetings to share "what works and what does not work," that can become a regular part of communal life?
- Do community practices like "blowing your own horn" encourage or discourage engendering of community?
- What is the difference between describing "what works" and "blowing your own horn"?

pedagogies for community-based care (Final Research Report) (Madison, WI: University of Wisconsin-Madison, School of Nursing).

In the rush to redesign courses, teachers can still listen to familiar conventional pedagogical questions, for example, How can I better teach this course or change it to respond to the new curriculum? In Narrative Pedagogy, schooling learning teaching arrive together, belong and show up (co-occur) together. Whenever there is a teaching, there is a learning; and whenever there is schooling, there is teaching and learning. Wherever there is learning, there is a teaching; someone or something, perhaps a situation, is a teaching. There is always already learning; even non-learning is a moment of learning. In conventional pedagogies, teaching can overcome learning. What recedes from view in this approach is that learning is what teaching is all about. Covered over is how teaching and learning arrive together. Rethinking the curriculum retrieves a place for learning to be present as teaching, that is, *learning* as how to teach the new curriculum. Narrative Pedagogy offers a mindfulness to teachers to be *learners as teachers,* rather than teachers as learners.

Trinity

So what happened?

Saskia

We decided to take the next year to improve our online courses and learn some new IT[60] as we got ready. On faculty development days we worked together.[61] We spent time learning how pedagogies influence teaching and learning.[62] We demonstrated to each other what we had developed in our courses as ideas for other faculty. The students joined us, and we talked about what works and what does not. It was really a very different way to revise our courses. Deciding on how to link our courses so the students could find content across the curriculum took a while. Textbooks are available electronically now and there is so much information for students. It was hard organizing and linking everything; the students were invaluable! Our clinical faculty and preceptors were with us at every step.[63] It was easy to admit you were deskilled or didn't know what was happening in clinical. Clinical faculty and preceptors were very

---

[60] For student experiences of using IT simulations for developing clinical judgment skills, see K. Lasater, 2007, High-fidelity simulation and the development of clinical judgment: Students' experiences, *Journal of Nursing Education, 46,* 269-276.

[61] Learning and sharing expertise in the skills and practices of teaching are explicated in N. Diekelmann, 2002a, Engendering community: Learning and sharing expertise in the skills and practices of teaching, *Journal of Nursing Education, 41*(6), 241-242, and N. Diekelmann, 2003b, Engendering community: Learning to live together, *Journal of Nursing Education, 42*(6), 243-244.

[62] Consult Appendix C for Pedagogies: Approaches to Schooling Learning Teaching.

[63] See N. Diekelmann, 2004b, Experienced practitioners as new faculty: New pedagogies and new possibilities, *Journal of Nursing Education, 43*(3), 101-103.

generous with their time and stories. Not fighting over content like we usually do as teachers was such a relief!

Clarence

What I like is how you still had to look at content together but duplication could be avoided with linking. Or that duplication could be seen and planned for—it isn't all bad, is it? While linking is helpful I do think we overplay this sometimes. We think if we make connections obvious for students it will clear up confusion or make everything clear, but we know this really isn't the case. Sometimes I think we spend too much time making links. This approach to the additive curriculum is more thoughtful. It's really another example of listening to what we see around us. You have really got me thinking!

CP – Questioning: Meanings and Making Visible; Interpreting: Unlearning and Becoming; Preserving: Reading, Writing, Thinking-Saying, and Dialogue
Theme: "Too Much Content" and the Additive Curriculum Revisited: Transforming Learning Through Listening
Questionings:
- Is it learning how to access the information needed in patient care situations that matters or memorizing information for recall in patient care situations?
- How can students and teachers learn how to assess the quality and trustworthiness of information accessed online or in articles or textbooks?
- Can teachers and clinicians help students make sense and meanings visible when navigating vast amounts of information in caring for patients?
- What kinds of skills does this require for teachers, students, and clinicians?
- How does listening show up in the above questionings?

Shireen

I sure wish our school would do something like that!

Saskia

Getting ready took us all summer. Then rather than phase in the new curriculum for a few students, we just changed over in the fall. Students and faculty decided we did not want to have this curriculum revision drag on and on like they usually do.[64] So we went with the "All at Once Curriculum" and it worked fine.

---

[64] For including students in negotiated curriculum activities, see R. Thorton & H. Chapman, 2000, Student voice in curriculum making, *Journal of Nursing Education, 39*(3), 124-133.

Clarence

Wow! You did all that in a year and a summer? No problems?

Saskia

That's not true! There were lots and lots of them! But most students and faculty loved the "All at Once Curriculum," so we just pushed ahead and figured out ways to keep working on what was working, and a lot of problems took care of themselves. We are still getting the bugs out of some of the technology and working with clinical preceptors on the clinical courses for students. There's no need to try and link theory and clinical in our courses now, so we separated theory and practice and developed clinical courses that build on each other. That led to looking at distance clinicals. It is very different to provide supervision to clinical students online as some of the courses do, but the teachers say now they know more about clinical thinking in their students than when they did face-to-face supervision with a group of students. And the students love being able to pick their own clinicals rather than having teachers requiring one in each specialty. Before you ask, the students have done progressively better on NCLEX with the new curriculum, every single year.

> **CP** – Assembling: Constructing and Cultivating; Questioning: Meaning and Making Visible; Interpreting: Unlearning and Becoming
> **Theme:** Separating Theory and Clinical Course: Challenging the Corresponding Relationship of Theory and Practice
> **Questionings:**
> - Is there evidence that students learn better when theory presented in class is immediately applied versus applying theory learned online before it is immediately applied?
> - What is the relationship between course learning and clinical practice?
> - Does all learning fall into the linear-corresponding relationship of theory and practice?
> - What are the advantages and limitations when theory and practice are separated/not separated as courses and experiences?
> - Does separating theory and practice into different courses mean that teachers have to "give up" their presentations in class of applying theory in practice?
> - How does modernity's notion of theory relate to practice?

David

That's great! Don't you think any time faculty and students really work together, learning thrives? Did many students resist the new curriculum?

Saskia

At first some did! Some actually wanted lectures back! They didn't want podcasts or like IT. Because of the Narrative Pedagogy approach we really focused on continuing to listen to the students and what we found was that, for some students, the lectures provided them with a way to organize the content they needed to learn.[65] It helped them focus on what was important and it filled in places they were unclear on in their reading. So that has really been helpful to us in creating better podcasts and more diverse media to support students' learning. And of course, each year the students get more sophisticated with technologies. Now they almost all have iPods. But these kinds of conversations keep us thinking. We still have a few faculty who want to require or "strongly suggest" that students buy textbooks instead of using online resources and guides. We try and recruit new faculty who come in with their eyes open, but it is not easy in the faculty shortage.[66]

David

Too many teachers still teach as they were taught.[67] And students learn now differently, using different strategies and tools because of their technology experiences. With instructional technology, teachers need to be learners when they teach so they can learn to see how learning has changed!

Themes:
• Teaching As You Were Taught: Preserving a Healthcare System That No Longer Exists
• Teaching As You Were Taught: Preserving Nursing Practice That No Longer Exists
• Teaching As You Were Taught: Advocating Innovation While Preserving a Healthcare System That No Longer Exists
• Student Learning and Technology: Exploring the Touchstones of Teaching and Learning

---

[65] For another approach to learning about lecturing, see P. Young & N. Diekelmann, 2002, Learning to lecture: Exploring the skills, strategies, and practices of new teachers in nursing education, *Journal of Nursing Education, 41,* 405-412.

[66] A discussion of teacher preparation and the meaning of going back to school while teaching is presented in N. Diekelmann & J. Gunn, 2004, Teachers going back to school: Being a student again, *Journal of Nursing Education, 43*(7), 293-296, and N. Diekelmann, 2004b, Experienced practitioners as new faculty: New pedagogies and new possibilities, *Journal of Nursing Education, 43*(3), 101-103.

[67] For a contemporary converging conversation on teaching as you were taught, see N. Diekelmann, P. Ironside, & J. Gunn, 2005, Recalling the Curriculum Revolution: Innovation with research, *Nursing Education Perspectives, 26*(2), 70-78.

Saskia

You're right, and some faculty are still trying to flee rather than learning the new technologies—how to use them as learning tools and strategies. Using various forms of IT does not mean you stop using class discussions or lectures for learning! Now, even though all our courses are online, even the clinical courses, we still have some courses that meet face-to-face, and others use lots of video conferencing for class discussions.[68] Some of our clinical faculty have learned how to do online supervision. In fact, they say they know more what students are thinking and learning in the online clinical courses with on-site preceptors than the face-to-face clinical courses they teach!

CP – Presencing: Attending and Being Open; Interpreting: Unlearning and Becoming; Questioning: Meanings and Making Visible

Themes:
- On Losing the Familiar and At-hand: Lecturing and Class Discussions as Touchstones in Teaching
- The Absence of Physical Presence: Embodiment and Disembodiment in Instructional Technology

Questionings:
- What are the IT skills and level of expertise required for beginning nursing faculty?
- Does the incompatibility between IT systems preclude learning?
- Is it sufficient that a teacher has been a student and used new IT when preparing to become a teacher?
- Is literacy in both conventional and interpretive pedagogies necessary as background in learning the instructional technologies?

Trinity

You mentioned your dean said she would help people get onboard with their IT skills. Did you lose any faculty?

Saskia

Not that I know of. We try to be really clear when we hire new people, though, what we are about as a school. We let them know that if they don't have the skills they need, there are lots of students

---

[68] See N. Diekelmann, 2000b, Technology-based distance education and the absence of physical presence [Editorial], *Journal of Nursing Education, 39*(2), 51-52; N. Diekelmann, R. Schuster, & C. Nosek, 1998, Creating new pedagogies at the millennium: The common experiences of the University of Wisconsin-Madison teachers in using distance education technologies, *Teaching with Technology Today* (Online journal). Available: http://www.uwsa.edu/olit/ttt/98.pdf; and N. Diekelmann & E. Mendias, 2005, Being a supportive presence in online courses: Knowing and connecting with students through writing, *Journal of Nursing Education, 44*(8), 393-395 for discussions of the absence of physical presence and hermeneutical interpretations of knowing and connecting online among students and teachers.

and teachers around to help them. It's just the way it is now in our school.

David

What I like is how you somehow got everyone or almost everyone onboard over time. I guess I can't imagine our school going along with an "All at Once Curriculum"! We still have faculty who don't even want to share their course syllabi with one another!

Trinity

You remind me, Saskia, of the importance of working on the way we get along, our school of nursing community. It's our neighborhood. The way you describe your curriculum revisions, I find very compelling! This revision must really make your teaching more meaningful and enjoyable. And that's important.

> CP – Caring: Engendering of Community; Retrieving Places: Keeping Open a Future of Possibilities; Interpreting: Unlearning and Becoming
> **Themes:**
> - The Teacher as Learner: The Learner as Teacher
> - Instructional Technology as the "Not to Be Gotten Around"

> CP – Listening: Knowing and Connecting; Retrieving Places: Caring: Engendering of Community
> **Theme:** Academic Misconduct: Closing-Down and Being-Open Practices of Students, Teachers and Clinicians

> CP – Listening: Knowing and Connecting; Retrieving Places: Caring: Engendering of Community
> **Theme:** Schooling Learning Teaching As Communal Attending, Listening and Co-Responding

---

According to Doll, ". . . we are in the midst of radical intellectual, social and political change" (Doll, 1993, 157). A state of uncertainty and disequilibrium in education reigns. But this situation also affords the opportunity to challenge static views of the curriculum. The curriculum-as-dialogue is always underway. *Conversations conduct themselves—"no one knows in advance what will come out of a conversation" (TM, 383).*[69]

David

There are some days when I dread going into the hospital. Teaching and nursing can be such a dangerous practices. Faculty must put their heads together in order to come up with substantive ways to teach students how to be better thinkers. Our curricula need to be in concert with how nurses learn in today's practice environment.

---

[69] See Chapter 6, for discussion of conversation, narrative tellings, and dialogue as method.

Saskia

By the way, in our school, we don't have a curriculum commit-tee any more either.[70] We have gone from "changing THE curricu-lum" to a "changing curriculum."[71]

We didn't throw out conventional pedagogy. We find competency-based approaches very useful. In the areas it is working, we kept it. For example, I have retained my two lectures on neuro (neurologi-cal nursing) that I have worked on for years. I use a systematic approach that I think helps make sense of this difficult content to beginning students, and I inter-weave this content with narratives.

CP – Assembling: Constructing and Cultivating; Caring: Engendering of Community

Theme: Changing THE Curriculum to Changing Curriculum: New Pedagogies for Revising the Curriculum

Questionings:
- Could the curriculum be different every year or with every group of students?
- Is changing the curriculum a recurring theme of conventional pedagogies and a changing curriculum a recurring theme of embracing multiple pedagogical approaches?
- How does an organized and structured curriculum close down/open up making frequent changes?

I can tell from how the conversa-tion moves, how the students are learning. Most of my podcasts are organized around narratives with a lot of content interspersed, but somehow the neuro one needed lecturing. This kind of thing makes me mindful of how the problem isn't lectures. It's that in the past *all* we used was lecturing, in every course, every day, ev-ery semester. Of course that was boring and students were unen-gaged. In class now our time is spent discussing, but I will lecture too, if the occasion arises and when I think it would be helpful. Most of our time is spent interpreting clinical and preceptor stories, answering students' questions if my online FAQ link doesn't do it, and seeing how they are learning to think like nurses.

Clarence

Do you have more time now with the new curriculum and your revised course?

---

[70] For a discussion and critique of using Voices Day as a curricular community experience, see N. Diekelmann, 2003b, Engendering community: Learning to live together, *Journal of Nursing Education, 42*(6), 243-244.

[71] Challenging taken-for-granted assumptions is explicated in N. Diekelmann, 2002c, "She asked this simple question": Reflecting and the scholarship of teaching, *Journal of Nursing Education, 41*(9), 381-382.

Saskia

Yes and no. Some things stay the same. I still have open-door office hours as well as online office hours. And some students call me when they have questions or they leave a message, and some don't call and they should! Yes, I have more time because I don't have students doing boring and meaningless assignments that I have to grade! Students are more engaged now in their own learning, so the amount of time I spend evaluating them is 80% less but 100% better! I am freed from all that preparing the night before for lectures, but then I use that time for reading and keeping current. I am no more or no less busy than I have always been as a teacher. I don't spend time preparing lectures. But I feel more connected to the students, preceptors, and clinical practice than I ever was. I give the same exams now as before, but now they are take-home exams.

Shireen

I think instead of memorizing for tests, when we take exams we should be allowed to work together on answering, consulting with each other like nurses do on the units. Or I like take-home exams where you can work together with other students in answering. You learn more!

> **CP** – Assembling: Constructing and Cultivating; Retrieving Places: Keeping Open a Future of Possibilities; Preserving: Reading, Writing, Thinking-Saying, and Dialogue
>
> **Themes:**
> - The Completion of Conventional Pedagogies: Reaching the Limits of Memorization
> - Learning Is What Teaching Is All About

Trinity

No course or curriculum is perfect, is it? But it sounds like Saskia's brought back excitement into her teaching. It is easy to get stuck in teaching and start feeling either overwhelmed or disengaged.

Saskia

With Narrative Pedagogy, the drudgery seems gone—you know, *the silly stuff that doesn't work and we keep doing it anyway!* Listening to what is all around us has made a big difference. Looking at something and saying, "That is silly!" or "That is really boring. I've got to do something about it." Our curriculum is different, teaching is different, and so is learning. I guess this is what they mean when they talk about applying Narrative Pedagogy. You can't apply Narrative Pedagogy. You can only *enact* it or become it. It's thinking from another place.

Narrative Pedagogy offers thinking-saying from a different locus of meaning. Attending to schooling learning teaching as a co-occurring, intra-related, invisible phenomenon offers hermeneutic phenomenological thinking-saying that is from another place. Traditional analytic thinking in conventional pedagogies arises from the division of schooling, learning, and teaching into the discrete entities of curriculum and instruction. Narrative Pedagogy is a dialogical *experience of thinking-saying* and *not* a particular curricular framework or strategy that can be applied in particular teaching and learning situations. It is an inclusive pedagogy and as such can be engaged with all strategies and frameworks in any pedagogical approach. *Narrative Pedagogy is always already present and familiar, waiting as a possibility to be freed through dialogical thinking-saying experiences as they show up (disclose and beckon) in individual(dyadic) and communal (multiplicate) conversations.* In the above converging conversation, Narrative Pedagogy is initiated and enabled through the exploration of assumptions or presuppositions of what is, namely revising courses and the curriculum using conventional pedagogies. Narrative Pedagogy belongs to listening; as this way. Enabling Narrative Pedagogy can let the widest possibilities for and of reform emerge (be listened to).

Chapter 14

Teaching as Co-Responding:
"Teachers and students are more alike than different."

The hermeneutic circle as the circle of participating, or cycles of interpretations, is never complete and never-ending.[1] Interpretations reveal the wider play of multiple understandings. There is no one correct interpretation.[2] Correctness is not implicit in interpretations; however, truths can self-disclose. Similarly, there is not one way to present interpretations. Cycles of interpretations[3] bring narrative themes and patterns into dialogue and conversation with one another. Converging conversations work to demonstrate enacting hermeneutic phenomenology through making thematic or explicating (questioning and interpreting) presuppositions in order to enable Narrative Pedagogy to show up. The following reenacts a converging conversation among three teachers and three students about the similarities and differences between students and teachers.

---

[1] See Chapter 3 for discussion of hermeneutic circle as the circle of participating. Interpretations are always already of a background of pre-understandings. In these interpretations, the pre-understanding presupposes hermeneutic phenomenology. For example, in hermeneutic phenomenology, dialogues as they are read (interpreted) are certain paths from thinking-saying as well as of thinking-saying—they take into account the excess of thoughtful interpretation to which interpretation as itself offers itself. The difference between the singular proprieties of voices, ways, modes, is invited as announcement. It is to an announcement and to an opening of the very dialogue of thinking that all are guests—all share in the hospitality/gift/offering of difference. From the temporally particular always already to the on-coming self-presencing of presence—each time the hermeneutical thinking circle does not cease from breaking off.

[2] Refer to Chapter 6 for discussion of how narratives announce, address, and call forth: "There is much to say" as the basic hermeneutical relation. Interpretation can never be a fixing of fleeting meanings (*PH*, 211).

[3] Narrative tellings announce, address, and call forth the saying-relating of a narrative gathering, which distinguishes itself in that it never admits of final understandings. Co-responding asks for the possibility to be allowed such that there may be different answers of each encounter.

In converging conversations, themes and patterns co-found one another and arrive together; they do not occur in isolation. Themes and patterns are constitutively narrative tellings in the context of converging conversations. Converging conversations bring the reader into conversational thinking with the text, to free thinking, revealing otherwise overlooked interpretations.

The background of this converging conversation includes the themes and patterns previously identified in Narrative Pedagogy research,[4] a 20-year longitudinal hermeneutic phenomenological program of research in nursing education. Footnotes link the reader to research literature and exegeses in previous chapters that explicate schooling learning teaching as a co-occurring invisible phenomenon. Sidebar comments identify themes and patterns,[5] Concernful Practices of Schooling Learning Teaching[6] and reflect questionings[7] that point to the exploration of presuppositions. Boxed hermeneutic phenomenological commentary is given as it arises and occurs within the conversation; all the while themes and patterns are made thematic, kept in motion, held open and problematic. In the Narrative Pedagogy study, many narrative tellings of *"Teachers and students are more alike than different"* were gathered.

CONCERNFUL PRACTICES OF SCHOOLING LEARNING TEACHING (CP)

- Presencing: Attending and Being Open
- Assembling: Constructing and Cultivating
- Gathering: Welcoming and Calling Forth
- Caring: Engendering of Community
- Listening: Knowing and Connecting
- Interpreting: Unlearning and Becoming
- Inviting: Waiting and Letting Be
- Questioning: Sense and Making Meanings Visible
- Retrieving Places: Keeping Open a Future of Possibilities
- Preserving: Reading, Writing, Thinking-Saying, and Dialogue

---

[4] The "data sets" (approved by the Institutional Review Board at the University of Wisconsin-Madison) of these studies are narrative tellings gathered through group and individual interviews as well as written submissions by students, teachers, and clinicians in nursing education. See N. Diekelmann, 2001, Narrative Pedagogy: Heideggerian hermeneutical analyses of lived experiences of students, teachers and clinicians, *Advances in Nursing Science, 23*(3), 53-71; N. Diekelmann, 1992, Learning-as-testing: A Heideggerian hermeneutical analysis of the lived experiences of students and teachers in nursing, *Advances in Nursing Science, 14,* 72-83.

[5] Patterns are reflected in all themes, but not all themes reflect all patterns. The Concernful Practices of Schooling Learning Teaching are patterns and reflect the highest level of hermeneutic phenomenological analyses. See N. Diekelmann & P. Ironside, 1998a, Hermeneutics. In J. Fitzpatrick (Ed.), *Encyclopedia of nursing research* (pp. 243-245) (New York: Springer) for further discussion of themes and patterns.

[6] The Concernful Practices of Schooling Learning Teaching are co-occurring, are interrelated, and belong together. Sidebar commentaries indicate the most compelling practices we have identified but are never meant to tell the whole story. The play of other Concernful Practices can always already be present as possibility. See Chapter 11 for hermeneutic phenomenological (ontological) descriptions of each Concernful Practice.

[7] The practice of questioning is more originary than the question. Questioning is itself a response to the demand that sense makes upon us. See Chapter 9 for discussion of teaching and questioning.

"Teachers and Students Are More Alike Than Different"

Vontra

With Narrative Pedagogy, I got to thinking about my assumptions, like how different I am from the students. And certainly I am. I'm more experienced as a nurse and know more about nursing. I guess I've never really thought much about how I'm the *same* as the students. Recently, though, I've started listening to myself and paying attention to every time I say something like, the students are "lazy," or the students want to be "spoon-fed." Then I ask myself whether teachers do the same thing. What I am discovering is that *teachers are more like students than they are different!* We have an accreditation visit coming up, and everyone is totally stressed out about what to include in our self-study. Teachers want examples for each required criterion. They want to be told exactly what is required so they can produce it and ensure our success in the accreditation review.[8] Now doesn't that sound just like asking to be "spoon-fed"?

Concernful Practices (CP) – Preserving: Reading, Writing, Thinking-Saying, and Dialogue; Interpreting: Unlearning and Becoming; Questioning: Sense and Making Meanings Visible

CP – Questioning: Sense and Making Meanings Visible

Themes:
- Identifying and Differences: The Grasp of Individualism
- Labeling: Closing Down on a Future of Open Possibilities
- Blaming the Students: Embracing the Claim of Explanation
- The Grip of Utilitarian Individualism: More Different Than Similar

Questioning:
- Does a concern for differences and a belief that no two people are identical overtake concern for how people are similar?
- Do individuals correspond or do they co-respond?

Brandon

And maybe teachers could be labeled "lazy" when they talk like this, until you're in the shoes of a teacher and know how hard we are working teaching. Then "lazy" doesn't fit. Overwhelmed or even desperate maybe, but not lazy! So maybe it's the same with students. From the outside-in perspective, teachers label students

---

[8] For an example of behavioral or conventional pedagogy, see N. Diekelmann, 1993, Behavioral pedagogy: A Heideggerian hermeneutical analysis of the lived experiences of students and teachers in baccalaureate nursing education. *Journal of Nursing Education, 32,* 245-250.

who behave this way as lazy or wanting to be spoon-fed, but from the inside-out with all their competing demands, it looks different too! Then these labels don't work.

Vontra

And *both* teachers and students want to know sometimes "what to say and what not to say" to a site visitor or a patient. When you get down to it, we *all* want to be successful in what we're doing and we *all* want to be sure that we do the "right thing" in terms of what's expected. That's some teachers and students can't also be lazy when they ask these kinds of questions. But time and time again I can see our concerns as teachers and even our responses are the same as the students.

> CP – Preserving: Reading, Writing, Thinking-Saying, and Dialogue; Questioning: Sense and Making Meanings Visible; Interpreting: Unlearning and Becoming
> **Theme:** Embracing the Claim of Certainty: Modernity Reaching Its Culmination
> **Questioning:**
> • Have conventional pedagogies reached their completion with professional specialty accreditation?

> Schooling learning teaching shows up as an invisible phenomenon in every pedagogical dialogical experience. Teaching is not necessarily present in just the dialogues of teachers. That is to say, teaching as co-responding is not bound by pre-established roles, such that the role of the teacher is to teach and the role of the student is to learn. Situations and conversations teach. In Narrative Pedagogy, phenomena call themselves forth in thinking-saying as a surplus. This thinking-saying reaches out/lets/releases/engages the human being for reaching what it is freed to reach, via touching it with matters of concern. The open clearing is not a location; it is a sojourn that gathers.[9]

Brandon

You're right! We even talk alike. I heard one of my colleagues who teaches the first nursing course refer to the students as "newbies," and a few minutes later he called one of our new faculty a "newbie" too! Students too are often aware of who the new teachers are and can put these new teachers through their paces the same as we do to new students—you know, we make them prove themselves a lot!

---

[9] For a discussion of the open clearing, see Glossary.

Connor

That is just *so* disrespectful! Calling me a newbie is demeaning and insulting! I know that sounds critical, but life has not been easy for me. I've managed to stay in school with four kids at home. Newbie sounds like I'm naïve, like I know nothing about anything.[10] Yes, I'm a beginning nursing student, but I know a lot about life and making do, about making

Theme: Labeling: Closing Down on a Future of Open Possibilities **Questionings:** • What day-to-day concernful practices retrieve a place for student, teacher and clinician-friendly curricula? • What learning activities call out the best and the worst in students, teachers and clinicians?

CP – Retrieving Places: Keeping Open a Future of Possibilities; Listening: Knowing and Connecting; Caring: Engendering of Community; Interpreting: Unlearning and Becoming

tough choices, being responsible, and making sacrifices. Using pejorative names to talk about me or my experiences in nursing overlooks all the important things I *bring into* nursing!

> The play of labeling is owed to namings "in which the nameable, the name and the named" (*DT,* 71) disclose and beckon. Labeling as a practice in teaching is critiqued in feminist, critical, and postmodern pedagogies. In Narrative Pedagogy and teaching as co-responding, the issue is not which pedagogy is better for which situation and the kind of learning sought, though that is important. Neither are conventional pedagogies or any pedagogy to be ignored or eliminated. What is called for in Narrative Pedagogy are research-based multipedagogical approaches that are not a polyglot but that rather reflect the contribution of each pedagogy—conventional, feminist, critical, phenomenological, hermeneutic phenomenological, and postmodern. For teaching as co-responding, all these pedagogies are necessary but none is sufficient. Narrative Pedagogy is a research-based nursing pedagogy that brings all extant pedagogies, past, present, and future, into conversation with one another. The issue that calls thinking-saying forth is to follow matters of concern to their heart, their essential unfolding.

---

[10] Concernful Practices are both negative and positive. For example, Retrieving Places: Keeping Open a Future of Possibilities, while stated in the positive, also shows up when possibilities are closed down. The absence or the opposite of a phenomenon shows its presence all the more compellingly. Discussions of presence and absence are presented in J. Diekelmann, 2005, The retrieval of method: The method of retrieval. In P. Ironside (Ed.), 2005, *Interpretive studies in healthcare and the human sciences: Vol. 4. Beyond method: Philosophical conversations in healthcare research and scholarship* (pp. 3-57) (Madison: University of Wisconsin Press).

Brandon

True. I remember what it felt like to be a new teacher and being called a "baby teacher"—it only made me feel more scrutinized, which made my worries worse. Teachers can be as disparaging of students as they are of each other. This became even more apparent to me when I went back for my graduate degree and was a student again after teaching for five years.[11]

> CP – Retrieving Places: Keeping Open a Future of Possibilities; Listening: Knowing and Connecting; Interpreting: Unlearning and Becoming
> **Questioning:** How does labeling influence opening up or closing down on engendering of community and understanding one another?

Teachers have a lot of power, too. [I had] one of those bad teachers [who] has been around for a long time—she's got a lot of big grants and is nationally known. But she would come in with her PowerPoints and stand up in front of us and lecture, basically just reading off her slides. And there were only seven of us in class! We put the chairs in a circle one day to give her the hint, and she asked us to put them back in rows so she could lecture. We all tried to take the readings seriously and to challenge some of the authors' ideas, you know, do some good critiques. But it was clear early on that in this course, "[the teacher's] view was the best!" So then most of us just said "to heck with it" and agreed with her. We would meet in the coffee bar after class and laugh at how we told her the opposite of what we really thought, and she loved it.

> CP – Preserving: Reading, Writing, Thinking-Saying, and Dialogue; Interpreting: Unlearning and Becoming; Caring: Engendering of Community; Inviting: Waiting and Letting Be; Presencing: Attending and Being Open
> **Theme:** The Teacher as Expert and the Expert as Teacher
> **Questioning:**
> • How can the assumption that the teacher is the expert close down on learning? Co-responding?

> CP – Gathering: Welcoming and Calling Forth; Retrieving Places: Keeping Open a Future of Possibilities; Presencing: Attending and Being Open; Caring: Engendering of Community; Inviting: Waiting and Letting Be

---

[11] N. Diekelmann & J. Gunn, 2004, Teachers going back to school: Being a student again, *Journal of Nursing Education, 43*(7), 296.

This got me thinking. I wonder if this was going on in my classroom as well. Do I always try to "clarify comments" in class, but really what I am doing is having the last word? There can be a lot of power plays in classes, not that we mean to do it, and often it can happen when we are trying to do just the opposite! It was being a student again that made me see teaching through a new lens.

Teaching as co-responding shifts the focus from matters of concern like power and control toward Concernful Practices that grant or possibilize them. For example, gathering can show up as the teacher in control of the class co-responding by requesting a placement of seating that granted this teacher even a physical relationship of power over the seated students. Or it can show up as the teacher co-responding and sitting down in a circle of chairs with the students as co-participants. It is not that the issue of power does not matter; rather what matters is the *how* of co-responding of teachers and students in particular contexts and situations, in which gathering as welcoming and calling forth shows up. It is all too obvious (or is it?) that teachers and students belong together as they are of schooling. The Concernful Practices illuminate power and control, mutuality and inclusion. Gathering, welcoming and calling forth, presencing, and attending and being open can show up as situations of power over (power and control) or shared power (mutuality and inclusion). In Narrative Pedagogy as it is in attendance with schooling, the shift is away from analyzing teaching-learning situations for explanations that psychologize or ascribe attributes, such as "a teacher with a high need to control." It is also a shift away from explanations that objectify discrete behaviors into categories, such as a "teacher unable to select among learning strategies (e.g., lecturing vs. class discussion) the appropriate one for a planned learning activity." In enabling Narrative Pedagogy, thinking-saying is freed through enacting hermeneutic phenomenology, as explicating presuppositions of both teachers and the students in particular situations, for similarities and differences. As Brandon explicates his own practices of teaching, the situation he encountered as a student returning to school taught him new ways to co-respond as a teacher. Narrative Pedagogy is a call to mindfulness.

Connor

Teachers have a lot of power. Students can't afford to get off on the wrong foot! You know, once the teacher has a negative view of you, it sticks. But I guess maybe that goes for teachers too, doesn't it?

Brandon

Teachers do worry about getting off on the wrong foot! Students can be very unforgiving if they don't like a course. For me, connecting with a group of students, especially at the beginning of a course, is something I worry about a lot.

Miye

So we're more alike than different. We're all human beings, aren't we? Where does that get us?[12]

> **CP** – Questioning: Sense and Making Meanings Visible
> **Theme:** Identity and Difference: Turning Toward Identifying Practices
> **Questioning:**
> - In what ways are notions of similarities and differences overtaken by concerns for the identical and the different?
> - How are we to think sameness and difference?
> - What matters in naming phenomena the same or different? Does that help?

Miley

Well, I don't know where that gets us, but it's a new idea to me. I never think of my teachers as being the same as me. They don't have to worry about taking a test on Monday, getting an assignment in on time, knowing the right answers, or getting a good grade!

Vontra

But we do! I worry all the time about every test I write and whether one of the questions is going to be bad or if the questions are fairly representative

> **CP** – Assembling: Constructing and Cultivating; Preserving: Reading, Writing, Thinking-Saying, and Dialogue, Caring: Engendering of Community

of what the students need to know. I worry about not knowing the right answer in class and looking unprepared or incompetent if I don't. And I often burn midnight oil to get grades submitted in time, or to get a grant completed by the deadline. Every teacher worries what students will say on the end-of-course evaluations. That's a kind of grade, you know, and it has a huge influence on my merit raises and even contract renewal! The same is true each time I submit a grant, worrying I won't get it in by the due date, or that it won't be well received. That really feels like "getting graded" as well! These kinds of worries show up in different ways and at different times, but they really are the same, aren't they?

Miley

We really don't know much about what teachers go though in teaching. I guess they never show that part to us. It looks easy, but maybe it really isn't?

> **Theme:** Narrative Pedagogy: Teachers and Students Working Together To Bring Teaching Out Into The Open With Each Other

---

12 For a hermeneutic phenomenological interpretation of identity and difference, see *ID*.

Miye

Or maybe we think we shouldn't share these worries with each other. Class time and our interactions together are so minimal that it seems wrong to spend time discussing my worries or concerns as a teacher. It seems like my role should be to use that precious time to talk about student concerns.

> **CP** – Preserving: Reading, Writing, Thinking-Saying, and Dialogue
> **Theme:** Identifying Practices and Differences: The Grasp of Individualism
> **Questionings:**
> - Does treating teaching and learning as separate entities require there to be teachers and learners?
> - If teaching and learning are a co-occurring phenomenon, are the boundaries between/ necessity of teachers and learners lessened? Challenged? Set into motion?

Carla

But that's just the point, isn't it? Maybe we *need* to take time to talk about how we are more alike than different.[13] This would be a good topic for the spring Voices Day.[14] Teachers can look like they have it made until you see that underneath they are just as concerned about succeeding and making the grade as we are! It seems like lots of our problems might be addressed just by talking more about how we are all in this together![15]

> **CP** – Questioning: Sense and Making Meanings Visible, Interpreting: Unlearning and Becoming; Gathering: Welcoming and Calling Forth; Retrieving Places: Keeping Open a Future of Possibilities; Caring: Engendering of Community
> **Theme:** Engendering of Community: Learning to Live Together
> **Questionings:**
> - How is it so little attention is paid to the communal nature of learning communities?—that is, that students are taught/required to learn to work in groups, while teachers are allowed to remain as a group disconnected?
> - How and in what ways does competition among faculty and students erode the engendering of community?
> - How does a disaffected learning community influence (shape and become shaped by) schooling learning teaching?

---

[13] Schooling learning teaching belong together and co-occur as a unitary phenomenon; so too do the Concernful Practices.

[14] Voices Day is an all-school gathering of public storytelling.

[15] See b. hooks, 2003, *Teaching community: A pedagogy of hope.* New York: Routledge Falmer and A. Falk-Rafael, P. Chinn, M. Anderson, H. Laschinger, & A. Rubotzky, 2004, The effectiveness of feminist pedagogy in empowering a community of learners. *Journal of Nursing Education, 43,* 107-115 for the influence of community life on learning.

Schooling learning teaching is communal through and through.

Miley

That sounds like a good idea, but realistically teachers get defensive just like students and these conversations sound simple and straightforward, but they are really difficult! For instance, last Tuesday in class I thought our teacher make a mistake so I asked this question, and the response I got was a snippy, "Let's not get off the topic now!" At first I thought I must have asked a stupid question or that I was simply "out to lunch" because it made sense to me and wasn't off the topic at all. So I asked a classmate and she said it was a good question. She had thought of the same question in her mind too, but hadn't asked it. She said that "[the teacher] knew she made a mistake and just couldn't admit it. You asked her a question she obviously knew she was in trouble so she made it your problem!" But you know, when she asked us a really difficult question at the end of class one day and no one could answer it, Kyle said under his breath but so that every one could hear, "That's a stupid question."

CP – Caring: Engendering of Community; Interpreting: Unlearning and Becoming
Theme: Engendering of Community: Saving Face and Mistake-Making

Connor

But we aren't like teachers! They have all the power, experience, and knowledge and we don't! They can fail us![16]

CP – Caring: Engendering of Community; Listening: Knowing and Connecting
Questionings:
- Whose interests are served by teacher-centered pedagogies?
- How do power and control serve to make egalitarian and emancipatory communities impossible? (For discussion of the subaltern speaking, see Apple & Buras, 2006.)

Vontra

You are certainly right. I guess what I am thinking is that we don't spend enough time looking at *how* we are the same—sharing concerns—and *how* we are different. We are not identical but we are more alike

CP – Caring: Engendering of Community

than different. I might not be so critical of particular students when

---

[16] For discussion and interpretive analysis of faculty abuse of power, see A. McGregor, 2005, Enacting connectedness in nursing education: Moving from pockets of rhetoric to reality, *Nursing Education Perspectives, 26*(2), 90-96.

I see the same behavior in myself. Or I might change my behavior if I am critical of this behavior in students. Sometimes because my intentions are the opposite of how I behave, I let myself off the hook. And really, just like a student who says, "Well, I didn't mean to be disrespectful" or "I didn't know this would be considered disrespectful"—it isn't about the intention, but about how it is actually experienced that matters!

> Teaching as co-responding co-occurs when attendance (schooling) and listening-to (learning) world (matters of concern) demand that something happen. This co-responding is never done in isolation; the human being must always respond to something. World responds by being available.[17]

Carla

This kind of thing helps me see how important it is for students *and* teachers to work together on our community lives—to focus on all the things we do and say to one another that make safe, fair, and respectful communities difficult to come by. Maybe if we would admit how we are more alike than different, it might help us to better understand each other and ourselves in new ways.[18] And what we can do about making our community life better. Focusing on shared community concerns and how these show up in our actions would help. Now the focus is on everyone being treated identically. Teachers think if every student isn't treated exactly the same, it's unfair. Yet teachers try to individualize instruction. How did we ever get to this state of affairs? Focusing on being identical only makes differences more important, discouraging community life. Am I being treated exactly the same way as someone else? Even when I know that is exactly what I do not want! How long has this kind of thinking been around? Historically, where did this kind of relating to one another come from?

---

[17] For a discussion of world, refer to Chapter 2.

[18] An interpretive exegesis of creating new partnerships among teacher, students, and clinicians is portrayed in P. Ironside, 2005b, Working together, creating excellence: The experiences of nursing teachers, students and clinicians, *Nursing Education Perspectives, 26*(2), 78-85.

Have concerns about the identical in pedagogies overtaken the possibility of similarities?[19] Conventional pedagogies are concerned with current notions of objectivity, such as using the identical standards and strategies for every student in the interests of "fairness."[20] Thus in the name of "fairness" (honoring the intention of being a fair teacher), every student is treated in identical ways; all the while, in particular situations, teachers know that treating students identically is the most "unfair" thing to do. Paradoxically, in conventional pedagogies, teachers are also encouraged to "adapt" strategies to conform to the "individual learning needs" of each student as a means to meet the pre-established goals and objectives or competencies.[21] Tensions between these two commitments are great. Competencies define identical outcomes for each student, while using identical strategies with students to meet these competencies is impossible. Is the claim that providing different paths (strategies) for individual students to achieve the identical outcomes skirting the issue of objectivity in instructional strategies? Is it objective to use different strategies with one student and not another? Are competencies, outcomes, and evaluations objective while the selection of strategies to meet them is non-objective? Can a teacher objectively select a strategy for a student? Likewise, when a teacher selects one item from a test bank over another, is the test that is created objective? Is objectivity in conventional pedagogies conflating identical and similar? How is it that concerns about objectivity can influence human comportment, claiming ways of thinking in order to effect control? Pursuing non-objective approaches to grading, even the worthfulness of developing new approaches to testing, can be covered over.

CP – Questioning: Sense and Making Meanings Visible; Presencing: Attending and Being Open; Assembling: Constructing and Cultivating; Caring: Engendering of Community

Themes:

- Reaching the Limits of Objectivity: "Just how objective are teachers when they individualize instruction for particular students?"
- Required Learning Activities: Conformity in the Guise of Fairness
- Exploring the Myths of Objectivity: Tensions in Individualizing Instruction to Achieve Outcomes

Questionings:

- In what ways do learning strategies influence evaluation?
- How is treating/not treating students in identical ways fair/unfair?
- Is not being able to individualize instruction for every student sufficient to warrant treating students differentially, for example by offering tutoring to students who are failing but not to students who are getting A's?
- How do vague notions of objectivity and subjectivity play into each other?

---

[19] A critical pedagogical critique of conventional pedagogies is explicated in C. Mikol, 2005, Teaching nursing without lecturing: Critical pedagogy as communicative dialogue, *Nursing Education Perspectives, 26*(2), 86-89.

[20] A national review of conventional pedagogies is presented in M. McEwen & S. Brown, 2002, Conceptual frameworks in undergraduate nursing curricula: Report of a national survey, *Journal of Nursing Education, 41*(1), 5-14.

[21] Use of competencies in conventional pedagogies is discussed in C. Patterson, D. Crooks, & O. Lunyk-Child, 2002, A new perspective on competencies for self-directed learning, *Journal of Nursing Education, 41*(1), 25-31.

Miley

I had an experience that might be helpful here. You know how over-whelming the week before Thanksgiving is—the semester is coming to a close and all kinds of assignments are due and exams and papers and all—and we're exhausted, really wanting to just skip class and start the holiday? Well, in the pediatrics course I took last semester, the week before Thanksgiving our teacher said, "Thanksgiving is a family holiday and the union says I have to be here for class. But you don't. Many of you live far from your families and want to get home. Others of you may just plain need a break, change in pace, or some time to get ready for the holiday. I will be here and we will have class for whoever comes, but you decide whether you want to come or not." I remember talking all week with my husband about should I or shouldn't I go to class. When he left for work the day before Thanksgiving, I still had not decided. I'm a good student and don't skip classes, but I could really use the time to finish a paper for another class so I could enjoy the holiday. And I wanted to read ahead in the pediatric course so I could listen better in class the next week.

> **CP** – Caring: Engendering of Community; Gathering: Welcoming and Calling Forth; Listening: Knowing and Connecting; Presencing: Attending and Being Open; Inviting: Waiting and Letting Be
> **Theme:** Getting Through to Students: Knowing and Connecting

Well, I sat down that morning and had a cup of coffee. I decided that if my teacher had really wanted us to come to class, she would not have brought up skipping class and there were only optional readings assigned for that day. So first I went and finished my paper and then I read ahead for this class. I did my floors, baked my pies, and got my table all set. It is my son's first year in college, and we were so excited about him coming home for Thanksgiving. When my husband got home, he saw the pies all made, which was something we were going to do that night together. He said, "You stayed home! Good for you!" And about then our son walked through the door and we all went out to dinner and had just the best time! I couldn't have done that if I had gone to class!

I heard later the class she had that week was different. There weren't a lot of students who came, but she called everyone down to the first few rows and sat down herself. She introduced caring for children with long-term illnesses and talked about how "not everyone can be with their family on Thanksgiving." They talked about what it means for patients

> **Theme:** Getting Through to Students: Knowing and Connecting

and their families to be hospitalized over holidays. I heard one of the international students also talked about not celebrating this holiday but missing being around young children. I realized when I heard that, that for these students, not only are they lonely but they miss their family get-togethers with little ones around. During this class they even talked about how some people have a lot of stress and turmoil in their families and so the holidays may not be this wonderful time of togetherness they were initially focusing on. That's really a good thing to be aware of as a nurse, isn't it? Don't assume that everyone's experience is like your own. In an unusual way, this teacher did a lot to help us

> **CP** – Interpreting: Unlearning and Becoming

become more of a community of learners and we learned a lot more about nursing because of it. She made you feel committed to the

> **CP** – Caring: Engendering of Community; Questioning: Sense and Making Meanings Visible

course and learning how to care for each other and our selves. That's nursing.

Schooling learning teaching as a phenomenon is the unfolding of world. It comes from the past and carries us into the future. All that humans have is the present; sojourning as always already becoming.[22] The past, which is in front of us, draws human beings into the future, sojourning as what is, in the present. The future exists only as possibility. The present is situated, particular, and historical. Learning is listening to the world speaking. It is not the listening that humans control—"I listen to this or I listen to that." Rather, it is the listening that arrives with being in the world, attending to matters of concern. To be human is to inhabit a world in which things are always already matters of concern. Schooling as a phenomenon is being in attendance with these matters of concern,[23] and teaching shows itself as co-responding to these matters of concern.

---

22   For a discussion of sojourning/whiling/being drawn, see Chapter 7.

23   Being in attendance is discussed in Chapter 4.

Connor

Personally I think it's dumb to schedule *any* classes Thanksgiving week!

Miley

Remember, though, she did have class, but it wasn't about content or anything that would be on the test. So no one was disadvantaged by not coming. The way this teacher invited us to learn was very caring and engaging at the same time. Those of us who didn't go to class appreciated her generosity. Several of us included in our journal papers what staying home meant to us. This was the first time I ever experienced a teacher who really cared about what was going on in our personal lives, and that's supposed to be what nurses do after all! This was a very engaging class; I will always remember it.

> **Theme**: Requiring Learning: Nearing the Limits of Power and Control

> **CP** – Inviting: Waiting and Letting Be; Listening: Knowing, and Connecting; Presencing: Attending and Being Open; Gathering: Welcoming and Calling Forth; Assembling: Constructing and Cultivating
> **Questioning:**
> • What did coming to class *mean* to those students who chose not to skip class?

Perhaps teachers do not pay sufficient attention to the ways they engage students, the practices of calling out learning and co-responding in their day-to-day lives with students. For teachers, knowing when and how to require class attendance and assignments as evidence of learning is a conundrum. They know full well that learning can never be dictated. Teachers do have the power to fail students who do not achieve the required standard of evaluation. But learning can be dictated only as a narrow range of pre-established parameters. Teachers know full well that learning can never really be ensured, or required, only *invited*. Inviting is of world and is not under the ultimate control of the teacher as agent. Inviting learning lets learning occur as a co-responding in which the human being becomes engaged in learning situations such that learning and only learning occurs. The narrow sense of ontic learning ("cognitive gain") is enriched when we call the sense[24] of learning as learning into question. Miley learned from this teacher and from the situation of not going to class. This teacher's teachings went on in her absence as students learned to listen to this situation speak. Being in attendance with students, engaging in learning as listening to the situation speak, reveals teaching as co-responding. In order for there to be teaching, there must be teachings, teachers, and the teachable. This narrative telling reveals how students and teachers become engaged in their learning as listening to the communal nature of schooling learning teaching. Narrative Pedagogy is enacted schooling learning teaching as a co-occurring phenomenon enabling learning to arrive with and be inseparable from the learnable and learners. Enabling Narrative Pedagogy as the participating of learning, the learnable and learners keeps open ways for students and teachers to co-respond with one another.

---

[24] Sense here does not name sensory perception or intuition but rather learning as held open and problematic. See Glossary for discussion of sense/meaning.

Miye

It was a simple thing this teacher did really. All she did was give the students permission not to come to class, which you already had! It was a little risky because she knows she's supposed to encourage students to attend class, even though we all know attendance is always way down the day before Thanksgiving. And most teachers usually try to cover lighter content because they're probably running around too and students rarely learn this stuff anyway.

The splendor of the simple is what opens possibility as possibility. In this teacher's simple act, multiple meanings are gathered and possibilized.[25] Appreciating how important holidays are to many students and the importance of resting during particularly hectic times of the semester, this teacher *presences* and attends to being open to what holidays mean to her and the students in her course. She co-responds by *listening* to the meaning of a hectic time of the semester and of attending class just before a holiday. She connects with students and their concerns. The teacher *retrieves a place* for them to participate in the holidays without being penalized or feeling guilty about not coming to class. She *gathers* the students who do attend into a conversation that *invites* them to a *questioning* of the *meanings* of holidays made visible when children are hospitalized. The course is *assembled,* constructed, and cultivated in such a way that the student readings for this week are optional. The teacher *invites* storytelling about hospitalized children not being able to be with family during the holidays. As students share their insights and experiences, a *caring* community of learners is engendered. This simple acts *preserves thinking-saying* in students' *questioning* the sense of school policies that conflict with important family gatherings and provide little time for rest or a break from routines. This teacher is of a world of holidays, hectic times, and the need for rest. She chooses to let the self-retrieving of holidays (they come out of the past from the future) show up as a time for the play of decision. Perhaps teachers do not pay sufficient heed to the *sense and making meanings visible* of small acts and the Concernful Practices of Schooling Learning Teaching.

CONCERNFUL PRACTICES OF SCHOOLING LEARNING TEACHING

- Presencing: Attending and Being Open
- Assembling: Constructing and Cultivating
- Gathering: Welcoming and Calling Forth
- Caring: Engendering of Community
- Listening: Knowing and Connecting
- Interpreting: Unlearning and Becoming
- Inviting: Waiting and Letting Be
- Questioning: Sense and Making Meanings Visible
- Retrieving Places: Keeping Open a Future of Possibilities
- Preserving: Reading, Writing, Thinking-Saying, and Dialogue

---

[25] For further discussion of the splendor of the simple as harboring a surplus of meanings, see Chapter 5.

Vontra

We have institutional rules that are uncaring, that are really not student or teacher friendly, don't we? Sometimes I wonder if I am *most* aware of how important caring and being cared for is to learning communities when it is *absent.* I keep thinking back to Miley's story about a teacher who got defensive with a student. This semester I did that and jumped on a student

> **CP** – Questioning: Sense and Making Meanings Visible
> **Themes:**
> - Learning and the Reciprocity of Caring: Caring and Being Cared For
> - Caring: Engendering of Safe, Fair, and Respectful Communities
>
> **Questionings:**
> - Is schooling a surplus over institutions?
> - How do institutions show up in modernity?
> - Do institutions dictate? Co-respond? Listen?

who held a different view than I held of caring for patients using protocols. All week I felt bad, because here I was trying to make the case for multiple ways of providing care and yet when this student stood up for the current protocol, I really cut her off. I was trying to make the point that the current protocols were not bad; they just needed to be considered as one way and there were others. When we met the next week, I began class by publicly apologizing to her for my defensive response. I talked about the danger in my power as teacher, standing in front of the class and leading discussions. As a teacher I realized I was "talking the talk," but not "walking the walk" and began to think more about how I was listening, being open, and responding in safe, fair, and respectful ways to others.

Conventional pedagogies are teacher centered. In this approach, teachers can be overcome by a commitment to achieving their learning objectives. Teaching using conventional pedagogies reduces learning to a rational process that can be pre-specified and observable. In Narrative Pedagogy, learning is an invisible phenomenon that arrives as experience. As such it is historical and situated, ineffably unpredictable, not to be controlled (un-pre-specifiable). While teaching can be defined in ways that are observable (e.g., lecturing, responding to student questions, writing examinations), teaching is always more than can be observed because it is invisible. It is, for example, responding to a student question in a way that calls forth/closes down on thinking. Teaching can be heard/listened to as co-responding.

Teaching is both invisible and silent. In conventional pedagogies, teaching thinking is reduced to a visible process. In Narrative Pedagogy, thinking that accompanies learning and teaching is invisible. Thinking-saying emerges out of co-responding in order to sight the invisible.

Brandon

You must have felt terrible!

Vontra

It was an awful day for me as a teacher. I shared with the students how I had hardly slept that night. I suffered, yet several students wrote in their journey papers at the end of the semester what it meant to them to have a teacher publicly apologize to a student. What impressed me was how grateful they were for my honesty. It was a risky thing for me to do but I will do it again, because I have learned the students never seem to let you down when you are honest with them. We are more alike than different, but it is being honest with one another too. With Narrative

> **Theme:** Risking and Trying Something New: "The students never let you down."

Pedagogy you are always challenging assumptions, such as the assumption that of course I am honest as a teacher, because I always want to be and intend to be! I understand now it is not what I will do, would like to do, or think I should do that matters, though those can be important guides. What matters is what I *do* do and how that, is experienced by others. Thinking about and making the meanings of what I experience with students visible has helped me as a teacher in profound ways. I am trying to make honesty less risky for me, and as I practice honesty, the students are right alongside of me too, taking the same risks.

Brandon

I'm hearing what you're saying! You inspire us to get by our individual concerns and look at others around us, the whole world. Are there better ways of thinking and relating? What you have shown is the real power in our abilities to leave questions open. I know where I am going is my own personal mystery. And this is true for all of us. The best we can do is preserve open questions. You show us how the usual preordained ways of being with one another take over. Students and teachers alike, become who we are, on a day by day basis, as we keep everything open.

Students and teachers are constantly being thrown into situations together as they attend to one another in schools of nursing. This is the phenomenon of schooling as attending in which students and teachers are always already involved with matters of concern.[26] In order for them to be involved, there must be understanding. This is the phenomenon of learning as listening[27]—not the understanding of one person knowing something, but the understanding that comes with listening and attending as being involved in situations with one another.[28] Along with understanding comes discursiveness[29]—not the speaking of vocalization, but the call of language that grants being involved in matters of concern. This is the phenomenon of teaching.[30] To be human is to be involved. Through being in attendance (schooling) with and listening to (learning) the common conversations that students and teacher engender, new possibilities for teaching as co-responding emerge.

Co-responding is of the openness of the open. The open clearing shows itself as a surplus over any assigning of agency, ground, reason, and roles. Teaching as co-responding imparts itself as it unfolds its own overture.

---

[26] For further discussion of schooling and matters of concern, see Chapter 7.

[27] Explications of learning as listening are offered in Chapter 8.

[28] For discussion of understanding see Chapter 3.

[29] An exegesis of discursiveness is described in Chapter 3.

[30] See Chapter 9 for teaching as co-responding.

Community Interpretive Scholarship

Converging Conversation: Exemplar 1

It's like every question I ask I get a defensive response. "The criteria are clear!" It's like she thinks I'm stupid and can't do my work, but I just want to be clear on what is expected. And when I press harder to get a better answer, it gets worse. I would like to just scream, "Just tell me exactly what you are asking me to do and I'll be happy to do it!" But she just seems to think I'm lazy or something and at our last meeting she said something like she was getting tired of "spoon-feeding people." That's so disrespectful!

Is this a conversation between
- A faculty member and a department chair, charged with revising curricular documents for an accreditation visit, and a recalcitrant faculty member?
- A student who is questioning a teacher about an assignment?
- A failing student who is frustrated trying to understand a teacher's expectation?
- A teacher describing negotiating responsibility for a team-taught course with a faculty colleague?

Converging Conversation: Exemplar 2

> On my way to class I was worrying about being asked a question I couldn't answer. I knew I really wasn't prepared for class, but sometimes life intrudes and you just have to do the best you can. Still I was *very worried!*
>
> Is this a teacher or a student?
>
> I'm so far behind I will never get everything I need to do finished by the end of the semester! Every time I'm evaluated I feel like the negatives are focused on while the things I'm doing right are overlooked. I dread getting my evaluations because I always question whether I should keep trying or just give up. I simply can't keep up with all the reading I need to do.
>
> Is this a teacher or a student?

Questionings:

- Just how much do students share in common with teachers? With new teachers? With experienced teachers?

- How do the practices of labeling show up in teachers and students? What are the common ways in which teachers and students label one another? What do such labeling practices mean to teachers? To students? To schools?

- In what ways do institutional practices serve to make the differences between students and teachers central? How are teachers and students treated differently by school policies and institutional rules and practices?

- How does the language used by students and teachers encourage (or discourage) labeling?

- What kinds of language would overcome the practices of identifying differences?

Part IV

Toward Narrative Pedagogy: Openings and Overtures

Chapter 15

Openings and Overtures

> *Hints only remain hints when*
> *thinking does not twist them into*
> *definitive statements and thereby*
> *come to a standstill with them.*
> *POR, 129*

> *An overture—in the active*
> *sense of the term—is neither*
> *interrupted or uninterrupted: it*
> *opens, it discloses itself.*
> *SV, 223*

What remains unthought in schooling learning teaching as it shows up as a matter of concern? We have presented schooling learning teaching as a play rather than as a fixed object in order to follow this intra-related co-occurring phenomenon back to its essential unfolding. We found that following-back-to shows itself as a call that can draw those who listen to it into future possibilities.

Possibility discloses and beckons as possibility. Even if a book such as this ends and is taken as complete, it cannot foreclose on possibility. Possibility as possibility bears and gestures, not to or for something, but simply as an open clearing. The abiding sojourn of hermeneutic phenomenology is claimed by an open clearing that it cannot create. Hermeneutic phenomenology as an illuminating always already presupposes an open clearing which says something. A phenomenon, whether ontic or ontological, sets the human being "the task of learning from it while questioning it, that is, letting it say something" (*BW,* 442) to the interpreter-reader, that is, *all* of us.

Openings and overtures always already call as lacunae, offerings, disclosures, overturnings, opportunities, introductions, and hints. Historicality and temporality are open regions which arrive as they go away.

The Approach of Historicality: Forerunning, Prefiguring, On-Coming

> *There is no "intact matter"; if*
> *there were, there would be*
> *nothing, not one single thing.*
> BP, 203

The tradition of metaphysics is a narrative which tells those who listen to it that "something really is, only when it is finished" (*BH,* 263). But in hermeneutic phenomenology, when possibilities are exhausted (and they cannot be) there can be no understanding human being of openness as such. Likewise, each beginning is a turning back to a matter of concern in order to turn toward its historical, prevailing essence, its provenance (*PM,* 319). To be the temporal-historical human being of openness is to be fated to (thrown as) the endless engagability of given moments. The always already "autonomously initiated self-presentation" (*N,* 301) of matters of concern is "what is *most properly in motion*" (*BCAP,* 150). Narrative telling always already dwells as its ownmost particular historically presented place and time that offers sense as possibility.

Openings are the temporal and historical engagement of humankind that allow the latter to listen to the play of thematicity as it self-retrieves and shows itself. Every human being is granted the play of possibility. Participation with listening to how the human being of openness goes ahead in its singular plurality is the call of schooling learning teaching.

Themes and patterns are herein listened to as a tonal play rather than a static subject or object. The play of making thematic shows itself as a call which is temporal and historical. That call, as a soundless phenomenon, is the issuance of itself. The human being of openness "is its own evocation and provocation: it calls for the responsiveness of concerned (emotionally attuned) thought and action" (Hyde, 2005, 91).[1] The human being of openness and engaged openness can be taken-as themes but cannot be thematized in a mathematical, scientific sense. Schooling learning teaching, insofar as this intra-related phenomenon discloses and beckons itself as a theme to be explicated in the present, is a past which as an already-with is an always already forerunning future. The tonality of themes *is* the actualization of the historicality of the human being of openness (*GBT,* 317-321, 352).

Offerings and Inducements: The Inductive Call

Thinking is thinking only when it pursues whatever speaks for a subject.

WCT, 13

When we follow the calling, we do not free ourselves of what is being asked.

WCT, 168

This book is at once an offering and an inducement. We are offering a way to follow or pursue the call that we see and hear in schooling learning teaching. Our path is not meant to be an induction of a particular into a universal as in the way of inductive logic, or to suggest a universal approach to be applied in each particular. Rather we have attempted to let ourselves be drawn into the magnetic circulation of sighting in terms of re-sighting engaged openness as the possibility of the already seen. This possibility offers itself as a possibility for bringing the already seen into explicit view and interpreting matters of concern in terms of the alreadiness and becoming (on-coming) of each engagement.

Hermeneutic phenomenology as we have articulated it is, in its richest sense, an exposure to an invitation. It is its own open asking-in, asking-after. Practitioners of hermeneutic phenomenology are attendees to their own particular required attendance—Heidegger's temporalized thrownness, disposedness, understanding, and discursiveness as the facticity of finitude and historicality. We submit that this is truth for and of each one of us. Hermeneutic phenomenology listens as "being-with escapes completion and always evades occupying the place of a principle" (*BSP,* 93-94). *Responses and rejoinders are invited when questions are asked that admit of no final, determinable answers.*

What is a fitting response to the question of Jean-Luc Nancy: "How can we be receptive to the [*sense*] of our multiple dispersed, mortally fragmented existences, which nonetheless only make sense by existing in common?" (*IC,* xi). For Schrag (1986, 203), the context turns on the invitation to the question "How does one perform a fitting response?" in a world where ethical questions are no longer "inquiries guided by theories of the moral subject and an inventory of the peculiar properties that constitute moral character" (Schrag, 1986, 202). If the centrality of the Cartesian subject has exhausted its possibilities, responses to the discursive and social practices of the with-world call out with/as their questioning invitations.[2]

Our interpretive reading of Jean-Luc Nancy listens to him say that it is to a disclosing and beckoning announcement of the very text of the with-world that the human being of openness is guest: From thinking-saying to human beings, hermeneutic phenomenological circulation is always already invited to its own surplus of sense (*SV,* 230).

Messengers: Ways of Approach

> *. . . the friend's face looks into the face of the stranger. The radiance of the gathering moment moves the listener's saying.*
>
> *OWL, 191*

> *The voice of each is singular, which speaks the same announcement as the voice of the other.*
>
> *SV, 245*

Hermeneutic phenomenology as it calls into question modernity's subject as the subject *of* modernity can never obtain as a universal particular. The temporal-historical subject is always already other. But not as "a grand other, who will assume the origin of the Discourse-of-the-other in general" (*SV,* 245). The primordial sense of interpreting is the message, heard as the always already on-coming of engaged openness; interpreting *can* listen to and for a message (*OWL,* 29). The proper hermeneutic phenomenological essence of the human being of openness consists in co-responding to and with the claim of the self-presencing of presence (engaged openness) by (1) listening to its messages, (2) announcing the messages that engage as listening, and (3) bringing tidings of the reciprocity of the human being of openness and engaged openness (von Herrmann, 1996, 179). Each and every human being "is in each instance in dialogue with [his or her] forbears, and perhaps even more and in a more hidden manner with those who will come after" (*OWL,* 31). Let us be reminded that disclosing and beckoning plays everywhere as "the veiled engagement of message and messenger's course" (*OWL,* 53). Particular human beings *are* properly as themselves when engaged by the innumerative calls to announce the renewed engaged openness of the human being of openness (*OWL,* 32-33).

The open clearing engages messengers and messaging as the play of political, social, economic, and poetic involvement. As the nonidentifiable, these are always already an other which never reappears as an identical matter of concern. They presence as a dialogue of the same, "the infinite alternative of the other" (*SV,* 246). Narrative pedagogy is a way wherein each "time it is put to an end its announcement is renewed" (*SV,* 246). Its message and its messengers (as announcements) are infinitely claimed by a finitude that cannot be subjected to signification. Narrative pedagogy is engaged as messengers bear and are borne by announcements.

Engaged openness is always already inclusive of the messengers and announcements of social, economic, racial, and gender categories which turn on the subjugation of stereotyped groups in terms of superior-inferior dichotomies. Gadamer has submitted the thought that what humankind "needs is not just the persistent posing of ultimate questions, but the sense of what is feasible, what is possible, what is correct, here and now" (*TM,* xxxviii). For example, that here and now, more often than not, includes the overt issues surrounding global climate change and toxic pollutants, but forgets or overlooks the problems associated with human population expansion in terms of plant and animal extinctions. Forgotten is the spread of invasive plant and animal species and the concomitant degradation of nonhuman habitats. Therefore it should not be overlooked that, for better or worse, the world "is referred back to ourselves" (*N,* 275).

Messages and messengers as they advene (disclose and beckon) do not guarantee either truth or falsity. The reading of messages implies their readability. For Heidegger, the mere dismissal of a message as false does not address the possibility of showing the message in its falsity. For him, one must take over the message "and work it *into* an essential and grounded connection with one's own" (*PM,* 224). Gadamer follows suit as he articulates conversation as other than an argument. He offers the possibility that conversations, which are rooted in available messages, conduct themselves such that putative shortcomings in a given message are worked with in order to bring out their proper and unique temporal-historical essence (*TM,* 367-368). This is done not to effect a fusion or to enforce a mere homogeneous exterior, but obtains as an attempt to share that between which divides (Raffoul, 1997, xxiii). There is always already a co-appearing of singularities, which as the open clearing of the between "renders the separation of the singular from the plural undecidable" (Raffoul, 1997, xxv). Co-appearing is from the surplus of the plural to and through singularities in co-appearings' comings and goings (Raffoul, 1997, xxvi). Co-appearing is a sharing of ways which intersect as a letting of messages and messengers.

Hermeneutic phenomenology is the possibility of dwelling with the con-tension between the claims of achievements and the engaged openness which the human being of openness always already finds itself as — its singular plurality.

Nearness: Meetings, Confluences, and Bonding — the Asymptotic

> *The frantic abolition of all distances*
> *brings no nearness; for nearness does*
> *not consist in shortness of distance.*
> *PLT, 165*

When seen in the light of hermeneutic phenomenology, every available entity as a matter of concern "has a different closeness [nearness], which is not to be ascertained by measuring distances" (*BT,* 135). Nearness is the sense in which the can-be of the human being of openness concerns itself as being claimed and needed (engaged) by engaged openness. Nearer here must be listened to, not as an ontic degree of difference, but as differing pathways (*ZS,* 184). Nearness turns on the meetings, confluences, and bondings of the nearness of the asymptotic which as engaged openness "remains the farthest from the human being" (*PM,* 252).[3]

The above matters of concern are conjoined as temporality wherein disclosing and beckoning as such is enabled as *generation* in the double sense of "bringing-about" and "coming-to-be" (*N,*

289). Matters of concern are discursively and historically available to each finite (mortal) human being such that these matters are always already addressed out of the openness of human finitude. The illusion harbored by modernity is one in which the self (ego) is an atemporal, ahistorical foundation for all that is (*N*, 297-298, fn. 57).[4] Ego-certainty as a methodological rule is called into question by hermeneutic phenomenology's reading of the historicality and temporality of the human experience (*TM*, 265-285). The finite historical existence of the human being "is marked by the fact that the authority of what [is already freed up for it]—and not just what is clearly grounded—always has power over" its disposedness and comportment (*TM*, 280).

The project of hermeneutic phenomenology is to call into question any intellectual position that turns on a return to a subject produced by its own position. Positions (answers) of this sort are engaged by an ahistorical subjecticity (the historically situated subjectivity of the subject) as *the* source of their own authority (Richardson, 1974, 324-330). In order to bring matters of concern into sharper relief, as they show themselves, the task of hermeneutic phenomenology is to let the open clearing that these positions belong to, show itself as the convergence of conversations.

This book has listened to critical theory, feminisms, and science as approaches to the disposition of subjects. The very decidability of critical theory's self-producing subject, feminism's gender subject, and science's objective subject is the limit which grows out of the infinite undecidability of the finite (mortal) subject. This is not to minimize critical theory's exposés of the abuses of various power structures, feminism's articulation of gender bias, and science's demonstration of salient physical characteristics, but go to the heart of their matters of concern as they are revealed in *their* concernful practices.

Preambles and Exordia

> *It is always a past that allows us*
> *to say "I have understood."*
> *PH, 58*

There is a bringing-to-conversation that is not the speaker's invention of language, the author's creation of its textuality, and the performer's production of social practices (Schrag, 1986, 145-157). Hermeneutic phenomenology lets preambles and exordia show themselves as "a discernment of the traces of the coemergence of the subject and the other within the discourse and shared activities of" the practices of communicating (Schrag, 1986, 136). Bringing-to-conversation as a temporal-historical bearing is a calling forth such that "the relation between the speaker and what is spoken, points to a dynamic process, that does not have a firm basis in either member of the relation . . . so the relation between the understanding and what is understood has a priority over its relational terms" (*PH*, 50). Relating relations, as story (narrative) tellings, disclose and beckon, belong to and with, the human being of openness.

Any preamble or exordium as such does not admit of a *(the)* discrete beginning. A reader-interpreter who has read our work to this point finds that food for thought always already arrives at this moment. The presence-to of moments is not the resolution of all that is into some kind of "black hole" where nothing of any kind can escape (*N*, 298, 307). Moments, the instancy of engaged openness, are the specificity of our time, your time; not time as an indifferent universal. *Each* moment of time individualizes all human beings down to their own selves (*RHT*, 277; *EHF*, 89-90).

Preambles and exordia herein become read as the generation of "the unique historical tradition that each generation happens to have inherited" (*RHT*, 266). The above, as it self-retrieves, can only be retrieved as it self-retrieves (ripens) and cannot be subjected to the atemporal singularity of repetition.

The poet Gwendolyn Brooks, who wrote of the African American experience, was called to show this experience and its future of possibilities in her poem "To Black Women" (Brooks, 1994, 502):

> *There have been startling confrontations.*
> *There have been tramplings.*

Her poem shows the situatedness of an always already past. A presence-to a future of becoming as possibility is thought-said by her when she goes on to listen to "large countries" as they remain to be sighted and can show themselves. Preambles and exordia are the unique happenings that allow and enable human beings to come to themselves as the human beings of openness. The poetic work, such as the Brooks poem, shows the unique essence of a path of experience as it gathers reader-interpreters into the experience, as each *of* their own unique yet plural sojourn.

Preambles and exordia are always already with each of us as each of us is always already with them—they cannot be bracketed out in the sense of isolating experiences from each other. They are participated in as the immediate mediating middle ground that each one of us belongs to.

Participation, Cooperation, and the Irenic

> *We can only say "the same" if we think*
> *of difference. It is in the carrying out and*
> *settling of differences that the gathering*
> *nature of sameness comes to light.*
> *PLT, 218-219*

Hermeneutic phenomenology turns on the retrieval of talking with and listening to each other *and* the world. Engaged openness shows itself as the infinite engaging of the open clearing of which this conversation is enabled to take place. Participation, cooperation, and the irenic do not necessarily imply a rapid dissolution of difference wherein the tranquilized disappearance of nonuniformity is effected. Participation, cooperation, and the irenic, when listened to as interpretation, hear "the undecidability of what makes sense, come about" (*DH,* 216).

The decision of choice here is not one of selecting between two binary opposites; it is one of letting the "relative priority of open-endedness over closure in an on-going movement" (*DH,* 214). The human being of openness is the emergence/elusion of lives of always already plurality and as living into the presence of absence.

Therefore participating, cooperating, and comporting oneself irenically means to let oneself as well as one's interpretive readings go along with sense as an issuance rather than choosing one sense to the absolute exclusion of another. This entails a sense of common agreement wherein mutual engagement takes place as an on-coming language game of giving and taking (*PH,* 56-57). In some ways this giving and taking is analogous to the legal procedure of mediation. In this procedure, none of the parties can reasonably expect to get what they want or demand. The focus of an experienced and skilled mediator is always on the possibility of a middle ground acceptable to all parties. Hermeneutic phenomenology is a reading of the middle ground of the open clearing of the human being of openness—that region of infinite availability of matters of concern to finite, temporally situated, and therefore proper selves *of* their unique one-time-only lifetimes (*RHT,* 265).

Experience, time, and historicality do not admit of some idealized consensus based on conceptions of epistemological verity or some empirical datum. Predetermined ideals suppress the performance of discourse as it occurs in its everydayness (Schrag, 1986, 58-63). Humans are engaged by discursiveness as participatory, cooperative, and irenic, not as the ultimately located ground of social-historical processes and action (*PH,* 32). Rather, humans are engaged as the game of interpretation which asks for its *own* conciliation, participation, and cooperation. These practices show up as "that social community with all its tensions [con-tensions] and disruptions [which] ever and ever again leads back to a common area of social understanding through which it exists" (*PH,* 42).

Ritornello

The subject of listening is always still yet
to come, spaced, traversed, and called
by itself, sounded *by itself.*

L, 21

In musical terms, a ritornello is an interlude or prelude especially in a vocal work. Ritornellos sound, as the echo of what has already come and as the calling forth of that which is to come in the work. We have taken our work as an interlude wherein we have endeavored to listen and co-respond with the narrative tellings and conversations we are in attendance with as they always already run ahead of us.

Heidegger's pathway of the always already, Gadamer's experience of undergoing engaged openness as historical play, and Jean-Luc Nancy's participatory passibility all hint of ritornello as the always already involvement of the proper, unique each time of narrative tellings and converging conversations to come. Just as in a symphonic, operatic, choral, or other work, the ritornello of hermeneutic phenomenology involves the totality of the moment. The moment in its singular plurality always already calls as both prelude and retrieval. Musicality in all of its everyday variety can be listened to as narrative telling and converging conversation; everyday conversation can be listened as the narrative unfolding of music. Listening as it belongs to itself as a phenomenon is both an offer and an availability that claims and needs (sights) the human being of openness.

The setting of the conversation *of* hermeneutic phenomenology takes place as the clearing of the offering of the tonal disposedness that matters of concern have about them. This book, if successful, self-performs as an on-coming opened interlude between reaching back into its "motivation and forward into its tendency" (*HWT,* 177). Hermeneutic phenomenology is a telling, and the telling of a silent and invisible call.

Narrative telling is the sojourn all are welcomed unto.

Chapter 15 Notes

1   See also *GBT,* 432-437.

2   See also *BSP,* 93-99.

3   See also Richardson, 1974, 6; *OTB,* 15-16; *PLT,* 165-182.

4   See also *DT,* 77-79.

Appendix A

Community Interpretive Scholarship:[1]
Narrative Pedagogy, Redesigning Courses, and Curricula[2]

The following scenarios reflect the ways Narrative Pedagogy pilot schools have gone about bringing Narrative Pedagogy into revising courses and the curriculum.

Scenario I

The danger in embarking on curricular or course reform with new pedagogies is that new strategies get mistaken for pedagogical reform. Changing pedagogies indicates altering approaches to schooling, learning, and teaching. These changes are reflected in how teachers think and what students will take away from the experiences they together set in motion. In Narrative Pedagogy, curricular reform can begin from the bottom up—redesigning one course at a time, one teacher at a time. Or it can begin at the top, with discussions about how the courses relate to one another. Or teachers and students can together attend to redesigning courses and the curriculum at the same time.

Changing the curriculum in conventional pedagogies is a prescriptive process with particular steps to be followed. These steps begin with discussing curricular concerns such as the philosophy of the school and end with the redesigning of individual courses to be consistent with the structure developed for the curriculum. While student input in any curriculum redesign is always sought, the process is prescribed and students are often invited to respond to proposed changes rather than being part of the reforming process itself.

In Narrative Pedagogy, the structure of the process to be undertaken by both students and faculty is one of together challenging and explicating (interpreting) the assumptions that are encountered in their conversations about redesigning the curriculum and courses. For example, a school-wide meeting might begin with the question, What are the three things every student should take away from each course in the curriculum? Exploring this question in a faculty-student community ensures that as a school, the unique contributions, skills, and abilities of both students and teachers are reflected in the redesigned courses. In addition, working together in community interpretive scholarship (putting their heads together) can avoid reproducing the problems of redundancy, overlapping commitments, and overloading (for teachers *and* students). Teachers discover what is being required of students in other courses. Students discover what is being included in the entire curriculum.

Redesigning courses and the curriculum with Narrative Pedagogy can also begin with students and teachers understanding "what currently *is* the curriculum." In the following narrative telling, Farhad describes his experiences in revising his school curriculum and his course using Narrative Pedagogy.

We started by scheduling a two-day faculty and student retreat. All the students were invited and a good number of them came. We reached out to all our clinical preceptors and clinical adjunct faculty with personal invitations. They actually showed up in larger numbers than we expected. We had an agenda but only a general or open one. It was a time to talk together, put our heads together to create a different kind of nursing program by using Narrative Pedagogy. We focused on listening to each other and not being so addicted to staying on task, finding and solving problems. We tried to let the conversation go where it went, sort of.

We posted on the wall the things we really thought were good about our school and our particular courses, things we wanted to retain. We had talked in the Teacher Teleconferences [90-minute bimonthly teacher-student conversations among Narrative Pedagogy pilot schools] about how we are always looking at problems and we didn't want to dive into them. We tried to keep in front of us the things that mattered . . . the stuff we wanted to hold tight to while we looked at problems.

To get started the first day, beginning with the first course, we each took three minutes to present each of our courses to everyone. You can't assume everyone knows the curriculum! It's easy to forget how courses are sequenced, even what's in them! How many times when we have curriculum meetings do we assume everyone understands what the curriculum is!

Then we took our syllabi and in 20 minutes, individually or in course groups, answered five questions: The three most important things students learn in our course . . . this shifted us away from teaching to looking at learning. We described our course in three sentences and listed how much of the class time allotted to the course was spent delivering content, whether via lectures or podcasts and how many total pages there were of assigned readings. We listed the course pre-reqs [pre-requisite courses] and the required course activities like tests, projects, papers, and concept maps and the like. You had to think fast, but this experience was forcing us to look at what stood out for us as teachers in our courses. Then starting again with the first course, we put up our responses on sheets all around the room so we could "see" our curriculum. Some of the schools did this for all their programs, masters and doctoral, but we just did it for the undergrad curriculum.

Well, we noticed right away two courses could be collapsed. While some of us already thought this was the case, the teachers actually involved brought it up. So that was good. And when we started adding up, literally adding up the pages assigned for students to read, the number was insane! Sure the readings were easily accessible electronically or in textbooks. But, no wonder why, especially some weeks, the students don't read their assignments, some weeks are so loaded with readings that it would be impossible to get it finished!

That afternoon we took our syllabi and tried eliminating 50% of the content, as we all agreed the curriculum was just too stuffed with what we thought was essential content.[3] In small groups we acted like "our lives depended on" removing 50% of the content in our courses and still preparing safe and competent nurses. After 30 minutes, we took each of our syllabi to another faculty unfamiliar with the content area and asked them, how would you teach this course? Like if you were a pediatric nurse and had to teach a psych course, what would you include? We are all prepared with a clinical specialty and it is easy to lose sight of what beginning nurses really need to know and be able to do. So having someone without that specialty knowledge (but obviously prepared as a generalist in their basic nursing education) review the content really showed us a lot! It showed us when we were aiming too high or low, when it wasn't very thought-provoking or when it was unclear what we would be studying. One colleague said to me, "you know, I'm a nurse and I can't understand what you are asking the students to do here." For me this was an eye-opener!

And some students did not offer much but they came and listened. One told me later she had no idea that teachers "do this kind of thing." That taught me how little of our lives as teachers we share or students see.

At the end of the first day, we talked about what kinds of issues we were struggling with. We know the curriculum is stuffed but if we could think of how to unstuff it, we would! That night all of us did more work on our courses. Like how do you create an assignment that students have to go into the literature and learn the content themselves as a part of doing the project. We presented our ideas the next day to each other. The students did the same thing and they totally, totally amazed us by what they came up with.

The dean came to our retreat and was there both days, all day long. And so were our IT staff. The second day we talked about putting the entire curriculum online, all the lectures as podcasts, lists of "frequently asked questions" and links to important resources. And making the entire curriculum available to the students when they entered our program and faculty at all times. The IT staff were there to help us plan how to make this a reality. A few of the faculty started to panic about using IT. Our dean calmed them down by saying, "It's my job to get you access to the resources you need to develop your IT teaching skills." She said, "There's a revolution out there in technology, and it ain't going away!"

Technology was making it possible for our students and

teachers to have access to all the courses at once—an "All at Once Curriculum." Not all schools have a instructional technology support, but we do. This was a simple change for us in a way and nothing new, as all the courses were already online in some form or another. What was different was how talking together about this possibility revealed some teachers who did not want other teachers to see their courses. One teacher said, "I know my course needs a lot of revising but I just do not have the time to update it. I am too busy teaching!" A student responded that maybe one of the assignments next semester could be for a group of students to select a section of the syllabus and update the readings. Another teacher said, "If some of us took over some of your classes for a semester, would that help you be able to update your course? I could do the class on diabetes in children." Some teachers talked about their courses being their intellectual property to be shared with students but not other faculty. Exposing faculty to each other's courses was both risky and enlightening. Students, largely supportive of the new curriculum, were helpful in allaying some teachers' fears that they would be less interested in a course if they had already completed some of the readings and were familiar with the course design and content. We experienced administrative- and university-level quagmires in obtaining students' access to all the courses, all the time. But we just pushed forward, and one thing we all knew was that the "All at Once Curriculum" would unsettle all of us and make us all instant learners—students and teachers.

At another retreat during the year, we realized the problem of linking theory and clinical was gone with the new curriculum. So we started rethinking clinical and theory courses entirely. We challenged the assumption that students need one clinical in each of the major areas of practice, rather than allowing them to stay in one. We decided to quit having a clinical experience attached to each of the theory courses. Instead we developed free-standing clinical courses that built on each other and that students could meet their clinical competencies in any area of specialization or site. Students then could sign up for whatever clinical area they wanted. They could stay on a particular unit in one agency if they wanted. Just think about how much learning time they lose when we bounce students around from site to site. Just *when they get good, and they know their way around, it's time to leave! The only limitations on the students' choices were the number of clinical sites available. They worked with us to develop a fair way for them to sign up each semester.*

One thing that is really different in Narrative Pedagogy is that the students become pedagogical partners. Most of us sort of assumed that students either weren't interested or knew nothing about curriculum or course design. We learned to challenge that assumption along with every other assumption we could find. Sure, some students could care less. But most were incredibly involved once they saw we were serious. Many times they raised the bar in courses that we thought was way too high, only to teach it their way and find out we were 100% wrong! We started revising our masters curriculum a year after the pre-licensure curriculum. We found the courses at the masters level were moving down to the baccalaureate students and masters students were knocking on the door of our doctoral program! Amazing!

I've taught for a while and have been through a lot of new approaches that were supposed to make a difference but just plain didn't. Like teaching using competencies. Not that we don't need some way to guide students to know what they need to be able to know and do. It's just that using objectives and checklists, defining outcomes, and establishing competencies are all conventional pedagogies, just with different names. What Narrative Pedagogy has done is to get me started thinking about are questions that have no answers. If learning is invisible and we know it is, how can I really *measure it? I am thinking more and doing less teaching stuff like constantly testing the students and grading papers. My time with students is entirely different. We think together from all different perspectives and I am learning to not worry when we get into stuff I don't know the answers to. That's nursing too. It really is inviting learning but us putting our heads together. Hard to describe, but you would know it if you came into our classroom. I start class by saying, "You've done a lot of thinking and reading for class today, what caught your gaze? Any thoughts, comments, ideas?" And off we go from there. It's a journey together with the students, every week. [pause] That's it, I guess. I've gone from lecturing to listening to learning showing up.*

Consider the following questionings:[4]
- How are we to think "essential content"? Essential according to whom? In what ways is content deemed essential?
- How significant/insignificant is it that faculty agree or disagree on what constitutes essential content? What would our curriculum look like if we did not identify essential content?
- What is the relationship between (or is there a relationship between) faculty agreeing on essential content and an increase students' learning in practice settings?
- What does disagreement among teachers regarding essential content mean to
  - Students and teachers?
  - Content overlap and duplication?
  - The additive curriculum?
- How much is too much essential content?
- What is the difference between the teacher as learner and the learner as teacher?
- What is the difference between the student as learner and the learner as student?

Scenario II

Community Interpretive Scholarship: Beginning With the Familiar

There is so much to do! Where do we begin?

Consider selecting a particular week in the semester, and at a retreat or school-wide meeting have each faculty member, who has brought one of their syllabi, delineate what students are expected to do that week (readings, assignments, clinical preparation, etc.). Compile the list and, as a group, look at and discuss together the work expected for this particular week. Talk about the meaning and significance of what this "week's assignment" means to you as a teacher or student and what you learned from this experience.
- Compile a list, for each course, of exactly what teachers identify what they would like students to "get" out of their

course. (What are the three most important things in each course?) Together as a group, consider the significance of "these important things" and the current curriculum. How prominent are these things in the current curriculum? How would each course look different if it was constructed around these 3 things as the central foci?

- Make a list of exactly what content is in each course and list what assignments help teachers know how students are doing. For each assignment, list exactly what students should take away from the assignment (the assumption is that assignments should help students learn as well as provide teachers a way to assess what students are thinking and learning). You also might consider having each faculty member do one of the assignments in their course and share it with others as an exemplar. Together consider what can be learned by this experience.

- With a broad understanding of "what is," plan together how students will move through the courses. Consider starting at the senior level—with the most complex courses! Challenging taken-for-granted familiar assumptions like beginning sequencing courses with the first nursing courses, rather than the last, and beginning a course with the most complex content is moving toward enabling Narrative Pedagogies.

Scenario III

"How can teachers teach such that learning and only learning occurs?"

Do teachers have time to attend to their own learning, or are they too busy teaching? Similarly, Do students have time to attend to their own learning, or are they too busy memorizing and doing assignments? Is this how learning comes to be thought of as memorizing or doing what the teachers tell students to do? What are students and teachers actually learning when they are this busy? Likewise, what are students and teachers teaching each other? Can places be retrieved to discuss the learning that is always occurring for both teachers and students? (Not learning is a kind of learning.) As a community of learners, selecting one course at a time, consider exploring the following questions together in relation to each course?

- What are the most meaningful ideas or moments of this courses and why? The most challenging ideas or moments?
- What are the most difficult student and teacher pedagogical problems in this course?
- If it could be perfect, what would teachers and students be able to do as a teacher or student in this course that they are currently unable to do?
- What would most faculty, students, and clinical colleagues like to learn with each other?

Community Interpretive Scholarship: Beginning With the Unfamiliar

Scenario IV

How Can Teachers, Students, Preceptors, Clinicians, Patients, and Citizens Know and Connect as Pedagogical Wayfarers?

When pedagogies cease to become the exclusive domain of students and teachers, they can become *experiences* of schooling learning teaching. Everyone becomes a pedagogical wayfarer. How can everyone connect in pedagogical partnerships? Questionings arise. What does it mean that there is a school of nursing in the neighborhood? How concerned are teachers about their teaching and clinical colleagues, and how willing are they to help them out? What do particular school of nursing courses mean to the preceptors or staff nurses on the particular units or community agencies where students learn nursing practice? How are clinicians, patients, and citizens influenced by school of nursing courses, teachers, and nursing students? *Am I too busy and full with my own responsibilities and in need of help myself that I have neither time nor expertise to share with others?* Narrative Pedagogy attends to how everyone listens and co-responds to one another.

- What does this course or content mean to the students? *Ask them!*
    - o "What does it mean to you as a junior student in [this course] to be studying content like [this]?
    - o Or "What does it mean to you as a senior student to do this kind of assignment?"
    - o Or "What does it mean to you as a beginning student to take this clinical course?"
    - o Or "What does it mean to you as a student to learn in this clinical setting?"
- What would preceptors tell teachers about their students? *Ask them!* "What does it *mean* to you to teach the students in my course?"
- What would preceptors tell teachers about their teaching? *Ask them!*
- What can teachers learn from hospital staff or community nurses about their school? *Ask them!* "What does it *mean* to you to have students from a particular course taking care of the patients or clients in your facility?"
- What does it mean to our citizens and communities that there is a school of nursing in the neighborhood? *Ask them!*

Scenario V

How Can the Assumptions of the Additive Curriculum Be Challenged?

In Narrative Pedagogy a significant commitment is made to dialogue and collectively exploring (interpreting) experiences. When teachers and students "put their heads together," they gather their collective wisdom. This is "community interpretive scholarship." It is often the case that this kind of collective thinking begins with common problems, problems that are very familiar—problems for which many assume there are no alternatives or solutions. For example, one can ask, Has a course become so full of content that there is no time for students and teachers to practice thinking together? Can nothing be done to alleviate this situation? Is there no way to retrieve a place and time for learning together in a "killer course" (a course full of content—often to be memorized and tested on)?

Instead of rushing to answer these kinds of questions with proposed solutions, consider explore the assumptions behind them. For example, is answering a question like "Can nothing be done?" the same as thinking? How can one think about these questions as questionings and not rush to a solution or answer? Perhaps one can begin by looking upstream and considering questions like "If the concern is about too much content in a course, how have information, content, and knowledge come to mean the same thing"? Have words like "essential content," "fundamental," or "core knowledge" taken over thinking such that "without content first, students cannot think," or that "thinking done in the absence of content is dangerous." Is there evidence (research) to show that this is the case? What is the relationship between knowledge (content) and thinking like a nurse?

In community interpretive scholarship, explore (and re-interpret) questions that challenge the assumptions of conventional pedagogical approaches to teaching and learning. Conventional pedagogies assume that students must learn content before they will be able to apply it, and that thinking in the absence of content is dangerous. Teachers define the content that is needed to become a nurse. Students assume that they are prepared to safely practice nursing if they have learned the content and how to apply it to patient care situations. In challenging these assumptions, consider how nurses are called upon to make decisions in current clinical environments with only partial knowledge, and sometimes no knowledge at all, about the situation in front of them. How can students learn this kind of thinking? Other assumptions to explore include assumptions about how students and teachers learn and what the meaning is, to both, of the content that is taught. Can a place be created to focus on the experiences of teaching and learning or the Concernful Practices of Schooling Learning Teaching?

Scenario VI

Can Overcoming Teacher-Centered Pedagogies Reveal the Learner-as-Teacher and the Learner-as-Student?

In Narrative Pedagogy, schooling as attending, learning as listening, and teaching as co-responding cannot be sundered. They are a phenomenon (an experience) that is always already present and invisible. Can you really see teaching? As an experience, schooling learning teaching is communal through and through. In redesigning courses with Narrative Pedagogy, teachers think along with the students and clinicians a lot! Attending to overcoming the teacher-centered assumptions of conventional pedagogy is a matter of concern. Consider how in conventional pedagogies, the role of the teacher in selecting and sequencing content, with responsibility for designing strategies to teach this content, places the major focus on what teachers do rather than on how students learn.

The assumption is made that if students do what teachers say they should, learning will follow. Student-centered pedagogies put students in the center and assume that if students do what they think they need to do to learn, then learning will follow. In Narrative Pedagogy, it is the between that matters. Neither teachers nor students are in the center, but are attending together to move away from roles such that learning and only learning occurs—listening to one another and co-responding in a restless to and fro holding everything open and problematic. This is the learner as teacher, and learning as teaching!

In conventional pedagogies, little attention is paid to teacher learning outside of the assumption that good teachers are current in practice skills and expert in their area of expertise. Questionings arise:

For teachers:
- What is it about [the specialty I'm teaching] that, as the teacher, I would really like to learn? (Consider building this into the course.)

- What will becoming a learner with my faculty colleagues and students mean to our community life in the school? How and in what ways is becoming a learner related to my ability to keep myself (and students) safe?
- How high is my pedagogical literacy in the conventional, critical, feminist, phenomenological. and postmodern pedagogies? (See Appendix B.)
- How willing am I willing to learn new approaches to teaching and learning and use them in my teaching? What worries me most about doing this? What is most exciting?
- What does teaching this course mean to me as a nurse? As a teacher?
- How do I know what I need to learn about teaching and how will this occur?
- Who will teach me, or is it about learning with others? Or both?

For students:
- What does teaching mean to me? How do I know if I'm being "well taught?"
- What does being a learner mean to me? How do I know if I am a good learner? Is there a relationship between how I learn in the school of nursing and how I learn in my life in general?
- What would I like, if anything, to learn about teaching? About learning?
- What kind of learners do teachers appreciate? How so?
- For me, what is the most important thing about learning?
- What does learning mean to teachers and learners?
- How do I know whether a particular teacher is a good teacher or is struggling? In what ways?

- How open can I be with a teacher who is struggling to teach?
- When have you been a teacher? When have you taught a teacher something? If I were struggling as a teacher, how would I want the students to help me be a better teacher?
- Were you the student as learner or the learner as student?

For teachers and students
- In what new ways can students and teachers co-respond to one another and practice reading, writing, dialogue, and thinking-saying?
- How can teachers' and students' *learning* be studied (researched/evaluated) as it shows up in course experiences?
- As teachers and students, how do they know learning and only learning is occurring when it happens?

Notes for Appendix A

1   N. Diekelmann, 2003b, Engendering community: Learning to live together, *Journal of Nursing Education, 42(*6), 243-244.

2   See Chapters 12 and 13 for accompanying converging conversations on revising courses and the curriculum and courses.

3   For interpretations of the additive curriculum, see N. Diekelmann, 2002d, "Too much content . . .": Epistemologies' grasp and nursing education, *Journal of Nursing Education, 41*(11), 469-470, and P. Ironside, 2004, "Covering content" and teaching thinking: Deconstructing the additive curriculum, *Journal of Nursing Education, 43,* 5-11.

4   Questioning is a question that has no answer, but is meant more as a call to thinking.

Appendix B

Community Interpretive Scholarship:
Concernful Practices of Schooling Learning Teaching

How Can Telling Our Stories to One Another Safeguard Our Communal Future?

Concernful Practices of Schooling Learning Teaching reflect the themes and patterns in the narrative tellings (stories) of students, teachers, and clinicians in nursing education. They provide a new language for interpreting narrative tellings.

CONCERNFUL PRACTICES OF
SCHOOLING LEARNING TEACHING

Presencing: Attending and Being Open
Assembling: Constructing and Cultivating
Gathering: Welcoming and Calling Forth
Caring: Engendering of Community
Listening: Knowing and Connecting
Interpreting: Unlearning and Becoming
Inviting: Waiting and Letting Be
Questioning: Sense and Making Meanings Visible
Retrieving Places: Keeping Open a Future of Possibilities
Preserving: Reading, Writing, Thinking-Saying, and Dialogue

Consider sharing a story of what it means to be a student, teacher, or clinician in nursing education. Or perhaps share a story of caring for another or being cared for. Is there a story, an experience that stands out for you because of what it means to return to school or become a nurse or nursing teacher? As a group, reflect on this story and discuss how the concernful practices show up and what the meaning of this experience is to the teller and the listeners. In what ways does this kind of dialogue safeguard the communal future of nursing education?

Appendix C

Pedagogies: Approaches to School Learning Teaching

Conventional Pedagogies (Outcomes and Competency-Based Education)
1. What is essential content?
2. What are essential experiences? How many of these experiences should students have?
3. How can the content and experiences be organized most effectively and efficiently?
4. What are the learning objectives or outcomes or compentencies that are desired?

Critical Pedagogies
1. Whose interests are best served by this (content, experience, course)?
2. Who controls the language and labels being used?
3. What are the issues of power and control that are embedded in the situation?
4. How are power and control serving to reproduce practices that safeguard or overcme the status quo?

Feminist Pedagogies
1. Whose voice is missing or silent?
2. Where are the silent or missing voices to be found?
3. How do language and labels serve to reproduce inequitable relationships?
4. How do power and control serve to make egalitarian and emancipatory communities possible/impossible?

Hermeneutic Phenomenological Pedagogies

1. How can the practical knowledge and wisdom embedded in a situation be made visible, interpreted, and challenged?
2. What are the practices that engender communities that are safe, fair, and respectful?
3. How can the common practices (experiences) of schooling, learning, and teaching be identified and described?
4. What is the meaning and significance of an experience?

Postmodern Pedagogies (Neo-Modern Pedagogies)

1. What are the invisible taken-for-granted assumptions that shape language and understanding in situations?
2. What are the grand narratives embedded within a situation? (What are the questions never asked, e.g., "What does it mean to be white?")
3. Can deconstructing the grand narratives show new ways (practices, approaches) to create communities that simultaneously hold open and problematic creating communities?
4. How can deconstructing situations lead to more thoughtful understanding and avoid pessimism and nihilism?

Bibliography

Allen, D., Bowers, B., & Diekelmann, N. (1989). Writing to learn: A reconceptualization of thinking and writing in the nursing curriculum. *Journal of Nursing Education, 28,* 6-10.

American Association of Colleges of Nursing. (1998a). *The essentials of baccalaureate education for professional nursing practice.* Washington, DC: Author.

American Association of Colleges of Nursing. (1998b). *The essentials of master's education for advanced practice nursing.* Washington, DC: Author.

Andrews, C. (1998). Engendering community: Writing a journal to clinical students. *Journal of Nursing Education, 37,* 358-360.

Andrews, C., Ironside, P., Nosek, C., Sims, S., Swenson, M., Yeomans, C., Young, P., & Diekelmann, N. (2001). Enacting Narrative Pedagogy: The lived experiences of students and teachers. *Nursing and Health Care Perspectives, 22*(5), 252-259.

Apple, M., & Buras, K. (Eds.). (2006). *The subaltern speak: Curriculum, power, and educational struggles.* New York: Routledge.

Aristotle. (1941). *Metaphysics, book 2 (VII),* 1028a10. In R. McKeon (Ed.), *The basic works of Aristotle.* New York: Random House.

Babich, B. (1992). Questioning Heidegger's silence: A postmodern topology. In A. Dallery & C. Scott (Eds.), *Ethics and danger* (pp. 83-106). Albany, NY: State University of New York Press.

Bastable, S. (2003). *Nurse as educator: Principles of teaching and learning for nursing practice* (2nd ed.). Sudbury, MA: Jones and Bartlett.

Bean, J. (1996). *Engaging ideas: The professor's guide to interacting writing, critical thinking, and active learning in the classroom.* San Francisco: Jossey-Bass.

Benner, P. (2000). The wisdom of our practice: Thoughts on the art and intangibility of caring practices. *American Journal of Nursing, 100*(10), 99-105.

Benner, P., Hooper-Kyriakidis, P., & Stannard, D. (1999). *Clinical wisdom and interventions in critical care: A thinking-in-action approach.* Philadelphia: Saunders.

Benner, P., & Sutphen, M. (2007). Learning across the professions: The clergy, a case in point. *Journal of Nursing Education, 46,* 103-108.

Benner, P., Tanner, C., & Chesla, C. (1996). *Expertise in clinical practices: Caring, clinical judgment and ethics.* New York: Springer.

Bevis, E. (1988). New directions for a new age. In E. Bevis, *Curriculum revolution: Mandate for change* (p. 27). New York: National League for Nursing Press. (Pub. No. 15-2224).

Bonis, S., Taft, L., & Wendler, M. C. (2007). Strategies to promote success on the NCLEX-RN: An evidence-based approach using the Ace Star Model of Knowledge Transformation. *Nursing Education Perspectives, 28,* 82-87.

Bonnett, M. (2002). Education as a form of the poetic: A Heideggerian approach to learning and the teacher-pupil relationship. In

M. Peters (Ed.), *Heidegger, education and modernity* (pp. 229-244). New York: Rowan & Littlefield.

Brooks, G. (1994). *Blacks.* Chicago: Third World Press.

Bruns, G. (1997). On the tragedy of hermeneutical experience. In W. Jost & M. Hyde (Eds.), *Rhetoric and hermeneutics in our time: A reader* (pp. 73-89). New Haven, CT: Yale University Press.

Clampitt, A. (2007). *The collected poems of Amy Clampitt.* New York: Knopf.

Cody, W. (2002). Critical thinking and nursing science: Judgment or vision? *Nursing Science Quarterly, 15,* 184-189.

Craft, M. (2005). Reflective writing and nursing education. *Journal of Nursing Education, 44*(2), 53-57.

Csokasy, J. (2002). A congruent curriculum: Philosophical integrity from philosophy to outcomes. *Journal of Nursing Education 41*(1), 32-33.

Daggett, L., Butts, J., & Smith, K. (2002). The development of an organizing framework to implement AACN guidelines for nursing education. *Journal of Nursing Education 41*(1), 34-37.

Dahlberg, K., Ekebergh, K., & Ironside, P. (2003). Converging conversations from phenomenological pedagogies: Toward a science of health professions education. In N. Diekelmann (Ed.), *Teaching the practitioners of care: New pedagogies for the health professions* (Vol. 2, pp. 22-58). Madison, WI: University of Wisconsin Press.

Dahlstrom, D. (2001). *Heidegger's concept of truth.* Cambridge: Cambridge University Press.

Dallmayr, F. (1984). *Polis and praxis.* Cambridge, MA: MIT Press.

David, P. (1995). A philosophical confrontation with the political. *Heidegger Studies, 2,* 191-204.

Day, L., & Smith, E. L. (2007). Integrating quality and safety content into clinical teaching in the acute care setting. *Nursing Outlook, 55,* 138-143.

de Beistegui, M. (2005). *The new Heidegger.* New York: Continuum.

Delpier, T. (2006). Cases 101: Learning to teach with cases. *Nursing Education Perspectives, 27,* 204-209.

Dickinson, E. (1960). *The complete poems of Emily Dickinson* (T. Johnson, Ed.). Boston: Little, Brown.

Diekelmann, J. (2005). The retrieval of method: The method of retrieval. In P. Ironside (Ed.), *Interpretive studies in healthcare and the human sciences: Vol. 4. Beyond method: Philosophical conversations in healthcare research and scholarship* (pp. 3-57). Madison, WI: University of Wisconsin Press.

Diekelmann, N. (1992). Learning-as-testing: A Heideggerian hermeneutical analysis of the lived experiences of students and teachers in nursing. *Advances in Nursing Science, 14,* 72-83.

Diekelmann, N. (1993). Behavioral pedagogy: A Heideggerian hermeneutical analysis of the lived experiences of students and teachers in baccalaureate nursing education. *Journal of Nursing Education, 32,* 245-250.

Diekelmann, N. (1995). Reawakening thinking: Is traditional pedagogy nearing completion? [Guest editorial]. *Journal of Nursing Education, 34*(5), 195-196.

Diekelmann, N. (2000a). Being prepared for class: Challenging taken-for-granted assumptions. *Journal of Nursing Education, 39,* 291-293.

Diekelmann, N. (2000b). Technology-based distance education and the absence of physical presence [Editorial]. *Journal of Nursing Education, 39*(2), 51-52.

Diekelmann, N. (2001). Narrative Pedagogy: Heideggerian hermeneutical analyses of lived experiences of students, teachers and clinicians. *Advances in Nursing Science, 23*(3), 53-71.

Diekelmann, N. (2002a). Engendering community: Learning and sharing expertise in the skills and practices of teaching. *Journal of Nursing Education, 41*(6), 241-242.

Diekelmann, N. (2002b). "Pitching a lecture" and "reading the faces of students": Learning lecturing and the embodied practices of teaching. *Journal of Nursing Education, 41,* 97-99.

Diekelmann, N. (2002c). "She asked this simple question": Reflecting and the scholarship of teaching. *Journal of Nursing Education, 41*(9), 381-382.

Diekelmann, N. (2002d). "Too much content . . .": Epistemologies' grasp and nursing education. *Journal of Nursing Education, 41*(11), 469-470.

Diekelmann, N. (2003a). *Distance desktop faculty development in the new pedagogies for community-based care* (Final Research Report). Madison, WI: University of Wisconsin-Madison, School of Nursing.

Diekelmann, N. (2003b). Engendering community: Learning to live together. *Journal of Nursing Education, 42*(6), 243-244.

Diekelmann, N. (Ed.). (2003c). *Teaching the practitioners of care: New pedagogies for the health professions* (Vol. 2). Madison, WI: University of Wisconsin Press.

Diekelmann, N. (2003d). Thinking-in-action journals: From self-evaluation to multiperspectival thinking. *Journal of Nursing Education, 42,* 484-484.

Diekelmann, N. (2004a). Class evaluations: Creating new student partnerships in support of innovation. *Journal of Nursing Education, 43*(10), 436-439.

Diekelmann, N. (2004b). Experienced practitioners as new faculty: New pedagogies and new possibilities. *Journal of Nursing Education, 43*(3), 101-103.

Diekelmann, N. (2005a). Being a supportive presence in online courses: Attending to students' online presence with each other. *Journal of Nursing Education, 44,* 393-395.

Diekelmann, N. (2005b). Creating an inclusive science for nursing education [Guest editorial]. *Nursing Education Perspectives, 26*(2), 64-65.

Diekelmann, N. (2005c). Engaging the students *and* the teacher: Co-creating substantive reform with Narrative Pedagogy. *Journal of Nursing Education, 44,* 249-252.

Diekelmann, N. (2005d). Keeping current: On persistently questioning our teaching practice. *Journal of Nursing Education, 44,*485-488.

Diekelmann, N., Allen, D., & Tanner, C. (1989). *The National League for Nursing criteria for appraisal of baccalaureate programs: A critical hermeneutic analysis.* New York: National League for Nursing Press.

Diekelmann, N., & Gunn, J. (2004). Teachers going back to school: Being a student again. *Journal of Nursing Education, 43*(7), 293-296.

Diekelmann, N., & Ironside, P. (1998a). Hermeneutics. In J. Fitzpatrick (Ed.), *Encyclopedia of nursing research* (pp. 243-245). New York: Springer.

Diekelmann, N., & Ironside, P. (1998b). Preserving writing in doctoral education: Exploring the concernful practices of schooling teaching learning. *Journal of Advanced Nursing, 28,* 1347-1355.

Diekelmann, N., & Ironside, P. (2002). Developing a science of nursing education: Innovation with research [Guest editorial]. *Journal of Nursing Education, 41*(9), 379-380.

Diekelmann, N., Ironside, P., & Gunn, J. (2005). Recalling the curriculum revolution: Innovation with research. *Nursing Education Perspectives, 26*(2), 70-78.

Diekelmann, N., Ironside, P., & Harlow, M. (2003). Introduction. In N. Diekelmann (Ed.), *Teaching the practitioners of care: New pedagogies for the health professions* (Vol. 2, pp. 3-21). Madison, WI: University of Wisconsin Press.

Diekelmann, N, & Lampe, S. (2004). Student-centered pedagogies: Co-creating compelling experiences using the new pedagogies. *Journal of Nursing Education, 43*(6), 245-247.

Diekelmann, N., & Mendias, E. (2005). Being a supportive presence in online courses: Knowing and connecting with students through writing. *Journal of Nursing Education, 44*(8), 341-344.

Diekelmann, N. & Mikol, C. (2003). Knowing and connecting: Competing demands and creating student-friendly and teacher-friendly nursing curricula. *Journal of Nursing Education, 42*(9), 385-389.

Diekelmann, N., & Scheckel, M. (2003). Teaching students to apply nursing theories and models: Trying something new. *Journal of Nursing Education, 42*(5), 195-197.

Diekelmann, N., & Scheckel, M. (2004). Leaving the safe harbor of competency-based and outcomes education: Re-thinking practice education. *Journal of Nursing Education, 43*(9), 385-388.

Diekelmann, N., Schuster, R., & Nosek, C. (1998). Creating new pedagogies at the millennium: The common experiences of the University of Wisconsin-Madison teachers in using distance education technologies. *Teaching with Technology Today.* Available: http://www.uwsa.edu/olit/ttt/98.pdf.

Diekelmann, N., & Smythe, E. (2004). Covering content and the additive curriculum: How can I use my time with students to best help them learn what they need to know? *Journal of Nursing Education, 43*(8), 341-344.

Diekelmann, N., Swenson, M., & Sims, S. (2003). Reforming the lecture: Avoiding what students already know. *Journal of Nursing Education, 42*(3), 103-105.

Doll, W. (1993). *A post-modern perspective on curriculum.* New York: Teachers College Press.

Dreyfus, H. (1991). *Being-in-the-world: A commentary on Heidegger's Being and time, Division I.* Cambridge, MA: The MIT Press.

Dreyfus, H. (1992). *What computers still can't do: A critique of artificial reason.* Boston: MIT Press.

Eisenstein, G. (1989). The privilege of sharing: Dead ends and the life of language. In D. Michelfelder & R. Palmer (Eds.), *Dialogue and deconstruction: The Gadamer-Derrida encounter* (pp. 269-283). Albany, NY: State University of New York Press.

Eliot, T. S. (1952). *The complete poems and plays 1909-1950.* New York: Harcourt, Brace & World.

Ellsworth, E. (1992). Why doesn't this feel empowering? Working through the repressive myths of critical pedagogy. In C. Luke & J. Gore (Eds.), *Feminisms and critical pedagogy* (pp. 90-119). New York: Routledge.

Emad, P., & Kalary, T. (2006). Translators' foreword. In M. Heidegger, *Mindfulness* (P. Emad & T. Kalary, Trans.) (pp. xiii-xlii). New York: Continuum.

Emad, P., & Maly, K. (1999). Translators' foreword. In M. Heidegger, *Contributions to philosophy (from enowning)* (P. Emad

& K. Maly, Trans.) (pp. xv-xliv). Bloomington, IN: Indiana University Press.

Falk-Rafael, A., Chinn, P., Anderson, M., Laschinger, H., & Rubotzky, A. (2004). The effectiveness of feminist pedagogy in empowering a community of learners. *Journal of Nursing Education, 43,* 107-115.

Falso, N. (1998). *Philip Farkas and his horn.* Elmhurst, IL: Crescent Park Music.

Farkas, P. (1990). My life in music. In M. Stewart (Ed.), *Philip Farkas: The legacy of a master* (pp. 1-33). Northfield, IL: Instrumentalist.

Fiumara, G. (1990). *The other side of language: A philosophy of listening.* New York: Routledge.

Freeman, L., Voignier, R., & Scott, D. (2002). New curriculum for a new century: Beyond repackaging. *Journal of Nursing Education 41*(1), 38-40.

Fynsk, C. (1996a). Foreword to J-L. Nancy, 1991, *The inoperative community* (P. Connor, Ed.; P. Connor, L. Garbus, M. Holland, & S. Sawhney, Trans.) (pp. vii-xli). Minneapolis: University of Minnesota Press.

Fynsk, C. (1996b). *Language and relation.* Stanford, CA: Stanford University Press.

Gadamer, H-G. (1980). *Dialogue and dialectic* (P. Smith, Trans.). New Haven, CT: Yale University Press.

Gadamer, H-G. (1981). *Reason in the age of science* (F. Lawrence, Trans.). Cambridge, MA: MIT Press.

Gadamer, H-G. (1985). *Destruktion* and deconstruction (G. Waite & R. Palmer, Trans.). In D. Michelfelder & R. Palmer (Eds.), 1989, *Dialogue and deconstruction: The Gadamer-Derrida encounter* (pp. 102-113). Albany, NY: State University of New York Press.

Gadamer, H-G. (1987). Hermeneutics and logocentrism (R. Palmer & D. Michelfelder, Trans.). In D. Michelfelder & R. Palmer (Eds.), 1989, *Dialogue and deconstruction: The Gadamer-Derrida encounter* (pp. 114-128). Albany, NY: State University of New York Press.

Gadamer, H-G. (1989a). Reply to Jacques Derrida. In D. Michelfelder & R. Palmer (Trans. & Eds.), *Dialogue and deconstruction: The Gadamer-Derrida encounter* (pp. 55-57). Albany, NY: State University of New York Press.

Gadamer, H-G. (1989b). Text and interpretation (D. Schmidt & R. Palmer, Trans.). In D. Michelfelder & R. Palmer (Eds.), *Dialogue and deconstruction: The Gadamer-Derrida encounter* (pp. 21-51). Albany, NY: State University of New York Press.

Gadamer, H-G. (1990a). Reply to my critics (G. Leiner, Trans.). In G. Ormiston & A. Schrift (Eds.), *The hermeneutic tradition: From Ast to Ricoeur* (pp. 273-297). Albany, NY: State University of New York Press.

Gadamer, H-G. (1990b). *Truth and method* (2nd rev. ed.) (J. Weinsheimer & D. G. Marshall, Trans.). New York: Crossroad.

Gadamer, H-G. (1992). *Hans-Georg Gadamer on education, poetry, and history: Applied hermeneutics* (D. Misgeld & G. Nicholson, Eds.; L. Schmidt & M. Reuss, Trans.). Albany, NY: State University of New York Press.

Gadamer, H-G. (1994a). Foreword (J. Weinsheimer, Trans.). In J. Grondin, *Introduction to philosophical hermeneutics* (pp. ix-xi). New Haven, CT: Yale University Press.

Gadamer, H-G. (1994b). *Heidegger's ways* (J. Stanley, Ed.). Albany, NY: State University of New York Press.

Gadamer, H-G. (1994c). Martin Heidegger's one path. In T. Kisiel & J. van Buren (Eds.), *Reading Heidegger from the start* (P.

Smith, Trans.) (pp. 19-34). Albany, NY: State University of New York Press.

Gadamer, H-G. (1977). *Philosophical hermeneutics* (D. Linge, Trans. & Ed.). Berkeley, CA: University of California Press.

Gadamer, H-G. (1997). Reflections on my philosophical journey (R. Palmer, Trans.). In L. Hahn (Ed.), *The philosophy of Hans-Georg Gadamer* (pp. 3-63). Chicago: Open Court.

Gadamer, H-G. (2001). *Gadamer in conversation* (R. Palmer, Ed. & Trans.). New Haven, CT: Yale University Press.

Gadamer, H-G. (2004). *A century of philosophy* (R. Colman, Trans.). New York: Continuum.

Gadamer, H-G. (2005). Heidegger as rhetor: Hans-Georg Gadamer interviewed by Ansgar Kemmann (L. Schmidt, Trans.). In D. Gross & A. Kemmann (Eds.), *Heidegger and rhetoric* (pp. 47-65). Albany, NY: State University of New York Press.

Gadamer, H-G. (2007). *The Gadamer reader: A bouquet of the later writings* (R. Palmer, Ed.). Evanston, IL: Northwestern University Press.

Gardner, E. (2008). Instruction in mastery goal orientation: Developing problem solving and persistence for clinical settings. *Journal of Nursing Education, 45,* 343-247.

Glazer, R. (2007, February). Business in the nanocosm. *Harvard Business Review,* 44-45.

Gordon, J. (2000). Congruency in defining critical thinking by nurse educators and non-nurse scholars. *Journal of Nursing Education, 39*(8), 340-351.

Grondin, J. (1994). *Introduction to philosophical hermeneutics.* New Haven, CT: Yale University Press.

Grondin, J. (2002). Gadamer's basic understanding of understanding. In R. Dostal (Ed.), *The Cambridge companion to Gadamer* (pp. 36-61). Cambridge: Cambridge University Press.

Groth, M. (2004). *Translating Heidegger.* Amherst, NY: Humanity Books.

Hahn, L. (Ed.). (1997). *The philosophy of Hans-Georg Gadamer.* Chicago: Open Court.

Heidegger, M. (1958). *What is philosophy?* (W. Kluback & J. Wilde, Trans.). New York: Twayne.

Heidegger, M. (1962). *Being and time* (J. Macquarrie & E. Robinson, Trans.). New York: Harper & Row.

Heidegger, M. (1966). *Discourse on thinking* (J. Anderson & E. Freund, Trans.). New York: Harper & Row.

Heidegger, M. (1967). *What is a thing?* (W. Barton & V. Deutsch, Trans.). Chicago: Regnery.

Heidegger, M. (1968). *What is called thinking?* (F. D. Wieck & J. G. Gray, Trans.). New York: Harper & Row.

Heidegger, M. (1971a). *On the way to language* (P. Hertz, Trans.). New York: Harper & Row.

Heidegger, M. (1971b). *Poetry, language, thought* (A. Hofstadter, Trans.). New York: Harper & Row.

Heidegger, M. (1975). *Early Greek thinking* (D. Krell & F. Capuzzi, Trans.). New York: Harper & Row.

Heidegger, M. (1976). *Piety of thinking* (J. Hart & J. Maraldo, Trans.). Bloomington, IN: Indiana University Press.

Heidegger, M. (1977). *Question concerning technology and other essays* (W. Lovitt, Trans.). New York: Harper & Row.

Heidegger, M. (1982a). *Basic problems of phenomenology* (A. Hofstadter, Trans.). Bloomington, IN: Indiana University Press.

Heidegger, M. (1982b). *Nietzsche volume IV: Nihilism* (F. Capuzzi, Trans.; D. Krell, Ed.). New York: Harper & Row.

Heidegger, M. (1985a). *History of the concept of time* (T. Kisiel, Trans.). Bloomington, IN: Indiana University Press.

Heidegger, M. (1985b). *Schelling's treatise on the essence of human freedom* (J. Stambaugh, Trans.). Athens, OH: Ohio University Press.

Heidegger, M. (1991). *The principle of reason* (R. Lilly, Trans.). Bloomington, IN: Indiana University Press.

Heidegger, M. (1992b). *Parmenides* (A. Schuwer & R. Rojcewicz, Trans.). Bloomington, IN: Indiana University Press.

Heidegger, M. (1993a). *Basic concepts* (G. Aylesworth, Trans.). Bloomington, IN: Indiana University Press.

Heidegger, M. (1993b). *Basic writings* (A. Hofstadter, Trans.; D. F. Krell, Ed.). New York: Harper & Row.

Heidegger, M. (1994). *Basic questions of philosophy* (R. Rojcewicz & A. Schuwer, Trans.). Bloomington, IN: Indiana University Press.

Heidegger, M. (1995). *Fundamental concepts of metaphysics* (W. McNeill & N. Walker, Trans.). Bloomington, IN: Indiana University Press.

Heidegger, M. (1996). *Hölderlin's hymn "The Ister"* (W. McNeill & J. Davis, Trans.). Bloomington, IN: Indiana University Press.

Heidegger, M. (1998a). *Pathmarks* (W. McNeill, Ed.). New York: Cambridge University Press.

Heidegger, M. (1998b). Traditional language and technological language. *Journal of Philosophical Research, 23,* 129-145.

Heidegger, M. (1999a). *Contributions to philosophy (from enowning)* (P. Emad & K. Maly. Trans.). Bloomington, IN: Indiana University Press.

Heidegger, M. (1999b). *Ontology—the hermeneutics of facticity* (J. van Buren, Trans.). Bloomington, IN: Indiana University Press.

Heidegger, M. (2000a). *Elucidations of Hölderlin's poetry* (K. Hoeller, Trans.). Amherst, NY: Humanity Books.

Heidegger, M. (2000b). *Introduction to metaphysics* (G. Fried & R. Polt, Trans.). New Haven, CT: Yale University Press.

Heidegger, M. (2000c). *Towards the definition of philosophy* (T. Sadler, Trans.). New York: Continuum.

Heidegger, M. (2001). *Zollikon seminars* (F. Mays & R. Askay, Trans.). Evanston, IL: Northwestern University Press.

Heidegger, M. (2002a). *The essence of human freedom* (T. Sadler, Trans.). New York: Continuum.

Heidegger, M. (2002b). *Identity and difference* (J. Stambaugh, Trans.). Chicago: University of Chicago Press.

Heidegger, M. (2002c). *Off the beaten track* (J. Young & K. Haynes, Trans.). New York: Cambridge University Press.

Heidegger, M. (2002d). *On time and being* (J. Stambaugh, Trans.). Chicago: University of Chicago Press.

Heidegger, M. (2003a). *The end of philosophy* (J. Stambaugh, Trans.). Chicago: University of Chicago Press.

Heidegger, M. (2003b). *Four seminars* (A. Mitchell & F. Raffoul, Trans.). Bloomington, IN: Indiana University Press.

Heidegger, M. (2004). *On the essence of language* (W. Gregory & Y. Unna, Trans.). Albany, NY: State University of New York Press.

Heidegger, M. (2006). *Mindfulness* (P. Emad & T. Kalary, Trans.). New York: Continuum.

Heidegger, M. (2007). *Becoming Heidegger: On the trail of his early occasional writings, 1910-1927* (T. Kisiel & T. Sheehan, Eds.). Evanston, IL: Northwestern University Press. [Note: Some of the material referenced in this publication was not authored by Heidegger.]

Henderson, V. (1987a). Nursing process, a critique. *Holistic Nursing Practice, 1*(3), 7-18.

Henderson, V. (1987b). The nursing process in perspective. *Journal of Advanced Nursing, 12*(6), 657-658.

Hodge, J. (1994). Heidegger, early and late: The vanishing of the subject between ambiguity and duplicity. *Journal of the British Society for Phenomenology, 25*(3), 288-301.

Hogan, P. (2002). Learning as leavetaking and homecoming. In M. Peters (Ed.), *Heidegger, education and modernity* (pp. 211-228). New York: Rowan & Littlefield.

hooks, b. (2003). *Teaching community: A pedagogy of hope.* New York: Routledge Falmer.

Hyde, M. (2005). A matter of the heart: Epideictic rhetoric and Heidegger's call of conscience. In D. Gross & A. Kemmann (Eds.), *Heidegger and rhetoric* (pp. 81-104). Albany, NY: State University of New York Press.

Hyde, M. (2008). *Perfection, postmodern culture, and the biotechnology debate* (Carroll C. Arnold Distinguished Lecture, National Communication Association). Boston: Pearson/Allyn & Bacon.

Ironside, P. (2001). Creating a research base for nursing education: An interpretive review of conventional, critical, feminist, postmodern, and phenomenologic pedagogies. *Advances in Nursing Science, 23*(3), 72-87.

Ironside, P. M. (2003a). New pedagogies for teaching thinking: The lived experiences of students and teachers enacting Narrative Pedagogy. *Journal of Nursing Education, 42,* 509-516.

Ironside, P. (2003b). Trying something new: Implementing and evaluating Narrative Pedagogy using a multimethod approach. *Nursing and Health Care Perspectives, 24*(3), 122-128.

Ironside, P. (2004). "Covering content" and teaching thinking: Deconstructing the additive curriculum. *Journal of Nursing Education, 43,* 5-12.

Ironside, P. (2005a). Teaching thinking and reaching the limits of memorization: Enacting new pedagogies. *Journal of Nursing Education, 44,* 441-449.

Ironside, P. (2005b). Working together, creating excellence: The experiences of nursing teachers, students and clinicians. *Nursing Education Perspectives, 26*(2), 78-85.

Ironside, P. M. (2006a). Reforming doctoral curricula in nursing: Creating multiparadigmatic, multipedagogical researchers [Guest editorial]. *Journal of Nursing Education, 45,* 51-52.

Ironside, P. (2006b). Using Narrative Pedagogy: Learning and practicing interpretive thinking. *Journal of Advanced Nursing, 55,* 478-486.

Ironside, P. (Ed.). (2007). *On revolutions and revolutionaries: 25 years of reform and innovation in nursing education.* New York: National League for Nursing.

Ironside, P. M., Diekelmann, N. L., & Hirschmann, M. (2005). Student voices: On listening to experiences in practice education. *Journal of Nursing Education, 44,* 49-52.

Ironside, P. M., Scheckel, M., Wessels, C., Bailey, M., Powers, S., & Seeley, D. (2003). Experiencing chronic illness: Co-creating new understandings. *Qualitative Health Research, 13,* 167-179.

Iser, W. (2000). *The range of interpretation.* New York: Columbia University Press.

James, I. (2006). *The fragmentary demand: An introduction to the philosophy of Jean-Luc Nancy.* Stanford, CA: Stanford University Press.

Jones, A. (1999). The limits of cross-cultural dialogue: Pedagogy, desire and absolution in the classroom. *Educational Theory 49*(3), 299-316.

Kavanagh, K. (2003). Mirrors: A cultural and historical interpretation of nursing's pedagogies. In N. Diekelmann, *Teaching the practitioners of care: New pedagogies for the health professions* (Vol. 2, pp. 59-153). Madison, WI: University of Wisconsin Press.

King, M. (2003). *History of New Zealand.* Auckland, NZ: Penguin Books.

Kisiel, T. (1985). The happening of tradition: The hermeneutics of Gadamer and Heidegger. In R. Hollinger (Ed.), *Hermeneutics and praxis* (pp. 3-31). Notre Dame, IN: University of Notre Dame Press.

Kisiel, T. (1993). *The genesis of Heidegger's "Being and Time."* Berkeley, CA: University of California Press.

Kisiel, T. (2002a). *Heidegger's way of thought.* New York: Continuum.

Kisiel, T. (2002b). The new translation of *Sein und Zeit:* A grammatological lexicographer's commentary. In T. Kisiel, *Heidegger's way of thought* (pp. 64-83). New York: Continuum.

Kisiel, T. (2006). Recent Heidegger translations and their German originals: A grassroots archival perspective. *Continental Philosophy Review* (formerly *Man and World*) *38,* 263-287.

Lasater, K. (2007). High-fidelity simulation and the development of clinical judgment: Students' experiences. *Journal of Nursing Education, 46,* 269-276.

Lilly, R. (1991). Translator's introduction and Notes on the translation. In M. Heidegger, *The principle of reason* (R. Lilly, Trans.) (pp. vii-xii, 135-138). Bloomington, IN: Indiana University Press.

McAllister, M., Tower, M., & Walker, R. (2007). Gentle interruptions: Transformative approaches to clinical teaching. *Journal of Nursing Education, 46,* 304-312.

McEldowney, R. (2003). Critical resistance pathways: Overcoming oppression in nursing education. In N. Diekelmann, *Teaching the practitioners of care: New pedagogies for the health professions* (Vol. 2, pp. 194-231). Madison, WI: University of Wisconsin Press.

McEwen, M., & Brown, S. (2002). Conceptual frameworks in undergraduate nursing curricula: Report of a national survey. *Journal of Nursing Education, 41*(1), 5-14.

McGregor, A. (2005). Enacting connectedness in nursing education: Moving from pockets of rhetoric to reality. *Nursing Education Perspectives, 26*(2), 90-96.

McGuire, S., Gerber, D., & Currin, M. (2001). Helping students use APA format. *Journal of Nursing Education, 40,* 9, 414-417.

McNeill, W. (1999). *The glance of the eye.* Albany, NY: State University of New York Press.

McNeill, W. (2001). The time of *Contributions to philosophy.* In C. Scott, S. Schoenbohm, D. Vallega-Neu, & A. Vallega (Eds.), *Companion to Heidegger's* Contributions to philosophy (pp. 129-149). Bloomington, IN: Indiana University Press.

Michelfelder, D., & Palmer, R. (Eds.). (1989). *Dialogue and deconstruction: The Gadamer-Derrida encounter.* Albany, NY: State University of New York Press.

Mikol, C. (2005). Teaching nursing without lecturing: Critical pedagogy as communicative dialogue. *Nursing Education Perspectives, 26*(2), 86-89.

Misgeld, D., & Nicholson, G. (Eds.). (1992). *Hans-Georg Gadamer on education, poetry, and history: Applied hermeneutics.* Albany, NY: State University of New York Press.

Myrick, F., & Tamlyn, D. (2007). Teaching can never be innocent: Fostering an enlightening educational experience. *Journal of Nursing Education, 46,* 299-303.

Nancy, J-L. (1990). Sharing voices (G. Ormiston, Trans.). In G. Ormiston & A. Schrift (Eds.), *Transforming the hermeneutic complex* (pp. 211-259). Albany, NY: State University of New York Press.

Nancy, J-L. (1991). *The inoperative community* (P. Connor, Ed.; P. Connor, L. Garbus, M. Holland, & S. Sawhney, Trans.). Minneapolis: University of Minnesota Press.

Nancy, J-L. (1993a). *The birth to presence* (B. Holmes & others, Trans.). Stanford, CA: Stanford University Press.

Nancy, J-L. (1993b). *The experience of freedom* (B. McDonald, Trans.). Stanford, CA: Stanford University Press.

Nancy, J-L. (1997a). *The gravity of thought* (F. Raffoul & G. Rocco, Trans.). Atlantic Highlands, NJ: Humanities Press.

Nancy, J-L. (1997b). *The sense of the world* (J. Librett, Trans.). Minneapolis: University of Minnesota Press.

Nancy, J-L. (2000). *Being singular plural* (R. Richardson & A. O'Byrne, Trans.). Stanford: Stanford University Press.

Nancy, J-L. (2003). *A finite thinking* (S. Sparks, Ed.). Stanford, CA: Stanford University Press.

Nancy, J-L. (2007). *Listening* (C. Mandell, Trans.). New York: Fordham University Press.

Nancy, J-L. (2008). The being-with of being-there. *Continental Philosophy Review* (formerly *Man and World*) 41, 1-15.

National League for Nursing. (1988). *Curriculum revolution: Mandate for change.* New York: Author.

National League for Nursing. (1989). *Curriculum revolution: Reconceptualizing nursing education.* New York: Author.

National League for Nursing. (1990). *Curriculum revolution: Redefining the student-teacher relationship.* New York: Author.

National League for Nursing. (1991). *Curriculum revolution: Community building and activism.* New York: Author.

Nelson, E. (2000). Questioning practice: Heidegger, historicity, and the hermeneutics of facticity. *Philosophy Today, 44,* 150-160.

Ormiston, G., & Schrift, A. (Eds.). (1990). *Transforming the hermeneutic context: From Nietzsche to Nancy.* Albany, NY: State University of New York Press.

Palmer, R. (1969). *Hermeneutics: Interpretation theory in Schleiermacher, Dilthey, Heidegger, and Gadamer.* Evanston, IL: Northwestern University Press.

Park, B. (2004). Differing ways, *Dao* and *Weg:* Comparative, metaphysical, and methodological considerations in Heidegger's *"Aus einem Gesprach von der Sprache."*

Continental Philosophy Review (formerly *Man and World*) *37*, 309-339.

Patterson, C., Crooks, D., & Lunyk-Child, O. (2002). A new perspective on competencies for self-directed learning. *Journal of Nursing Education, 41*(1), 25-31.

Pere, R. (1994). *Ako: Concepts and learning in the Maori tradition.* Wellington, New Zealand: National Library of New Zealand and the Te Kohanga Reo National Trust Board.

Poorman, S., & Webb, C. (2000). Preparing to retake the NCLEX exam: The experiences of graduates who fail. *Nurse Educator, 24*(4), 175-180.

Raffoul, F. (1997). Translator's preface. In J-L. Nancy, *Gravity of thought* (F. Raffoul & G. Rocco, Trans.) (pp. vii-xxxii). Atlantic Highlands, NJ: Humanities Press.

Randall, C., Tate, B., & Lougheed, M. (2007). Emancipatory teaching-learning philosophy and practice education in acute care: Navigating tensions. *Journal of Nursing Education, 46*, 60-64.

Richardson, W. (1974). *Heidegger through phenomenology to thought.* Boston: Martinus Nijhoff.

Rorty, R. (1980). *Philosophy and the mirror of nature.* Princeton, NJ: Princeton University Press.

Schalow, F. (1992). *The renewal of the Heidegger-Kant dialogue.* Albany, NY: State University of New York Press.

Scheckel, M., & Ironside, P. (2006). Cultivating interpretive thinking through enacting Narrative Pedagogy. *Nursing Outlook, 54*, 159-165.

Schoenbaum, S. (2001). Reading Heidegger's *Contributions to philosophy.* In C. Scott, S. Schoenbaum, D. Vallega-Neu, & A. Vallega (Eds.), *Companion to Heidegger's* Contributions to philosophy (pp. 15-31). Bloomington, IN: Indiana University Press.

Schrag, C. (1986). *Communicative praxis and the space of subjectivity.* Bloomington, IN: Indiana University Press.

Sheehan, T. (1978). Getting to the topic: The new edition of *Wegmarken.* In J. Sallis (Ed.), *Radical phenomenology: Essays in honor of Martin Heidegger* (pp. 299-316). Atlantic Highlands, NJ: Humanities Press.

Sheehan, T. (Ed.). (1981). *Heidegger: The man and the thinker.* Chicago: Precedent Press.

Sheehan, T. (1983a). Heidegger's philosophy of mind. In G. Floistad (Ed.), *Contemporary philosophy: A new survey* (pp. 287-318). Boston: Martinus Nijhoff.

Sheehan, T. (1983b). On the way to *Ereignis:* Heidegger's interpretation of *Physis.* In H. Silverman, J. Sallis, & T. Seebohm (Eds.), *Continental philosophy in America* (pp. 131-164). Pittsburgh: Duquesne University.

Sheehan, T. (1985). Derrida and Heidegger. In H. Silverman & D. Ihde (Eds.), *Hermeneutics and deconstruction* (pp. 201-218). Albany, NY: State University of New York Press.

Sheehan, T. (1990, Autumn). Everyone has to tell the truth: Heidegger and the Jews. *Continuum 1*(1), 30-44.

Sheehan, T. (1995a). *Das Gewesen:* Remembering the Fordham years. In B. Babich (Ed.), *From phenomenology to thought, errancy, and desire* (pp. 157-177). Boston: Kluwer Academic.

Sheehan, T. (1995b). Heidegger's new aspect: On *In-Sein, Zeitlichkeit* and the genesis of *"Being and Time." Research in Phenomenology, 25,* 207-225.

Sheehan, T. (1997). Let a hundred translations bloom! A modest proposal about *Being and Time*. *Continental Philosophy Review* (formerly *Man and World*), *30*, 227-238.

Sheehan, T. (1999). Nihilism: Heidegger/Junger/Aristotle. In B. Hopkins (Ed.), *Phenomenology: Japanese and American perspectives* (pp. 273-316). Boston: Kluwer Academic.

Sheehan, T. (2001a). *Kehre* and *Ereignis:* A prolegomenon to introduction to metaphysics. In R. Polt & G. Fried (Eds.), *A companion to Heidegger's introduction to metaphysics* (pp. 3-16, 263-274). New Haven, CT: Yale University Press.

Sheehan, T. (2001b). A paradigm shift in Heidegger research. *Continental Philosophy Review* (formerly *Man and World*), *34,* 183-202.

Sheehan, T. (2002). Nihilism and its discontents. In F. Raffoul & D. Pettigrew (Eds.), *Heidegger and practical philosophy* (pp. 275-300). Albany, NY: State University of New York Press.

Sheehan, T., & Painter, C. (1999). Choosing one's fate: A re-reading of *Sein und Zeit* §74. *Research in phenomenology, 28*, 63-82.

Shulman, L. (2005). Signature pedagogies. *Daedalus, 134*(3), 52-59.

Smith, M. (2008). Translator's introduction to Jean-Luc Nancy, *Dis-enclosure: The deconstruction of Christianity.* New York: Fordham University Press.

Stewart, M. (Ed.). (1990). *Philip Farkas: The legacy of a master.* Northfield, IL: Instrumentalist.

Swenson, M., & Sims, S. (2000). Toward a narrative-centered curriculum. *Journal of Nursing Education, 39*(3), 109-115.

Swenson, M., & Sims, S. (2003). Listening to learn: Narrative strategies and interpretive practices in clinical education. In N. Diekelmann, *Teaching the practitioners of care: New pedagogies for the health professions* (Vol. 2, pp. 154-193). Madison, WI: University of Wisconsin Press.

Tanner, C. (2001). Competency-based education: The new panacea? [Editorial]. *Journal of Nursing Education, 40*(9), 387-388.

Tanner, C. (2004). The meaning of curriculum: Content to be covered or stories to be heard? [Editorial]. *Journal of Nursing Education, 43*(1), 3-4.

Tanner, C. (2005). What have we learned about critical thinking in nursing? [Editorial]. *Journal of Nursing Education, 44*(2), 47-48.

Tanner, C. (2006). Thinking like a nurse: A research-based model of clinical judgment in nursing. *Journal of Nursing Education, 45,* 204-211.

Tanzer, M. B. (1999). Heidegger on being's oldest name: *"To Chreon." Heidegger Studies, 15,* 81-96.

Taylor, C. (1985). *Human agency and language: Philosophical papers 1.* Cambridge: Cambridge University Press.

Taylor, C. (1989). *Sources of the self: The making of the modern identity.* Cambridge, MA: Harvard University Press.

Taylor, M. (1987). *Alterity.* Chicago: University of Chicago Press.

Thompson, I. (2002). Heidegger on ontological education, or how we become what we are. In M. Peters (Ed.), *Heidegger, education and modernity* (pp. 123-150). New York: Rowan & Littlefield.

Thorton, R., & Chapman, H. (2000). Student voice in curriculum making, *Journal of Nursing Education, 39*(3), 124-133.

Trifonas, P. (Ed.). (2003). *Pedagogies of difference: Rethinking education for social change.* New York: Routledge Falmer.

Vallega-Neu, D. (2003). *Heidegger's* Contributions to philosophy. Bloomington, IN: Indiana University Press.

van Buren, J. (1999). Translator's epilogue and Endnotes on the translation. In M. Heidegger, *Ontology—the hermeneutics of facticity* (J. van Buren, Trans.) (pp. 91-125). Bloomington, IN: Indiana University Press.

von Herrmann, F-W. (1989). "The flower of the mouth": Hölderlin's hint for Heidegger's thinking of the essence of language. *Research in Phenomenology 19,* 27-41.

von Herrmann, F-W. (1996). Way and method: Hermeneutic phenomenology in thinking the history of being. In C. Macann (Ed.), *Critical Heidegger* (pp. 171-190). New York: Routledge.

Webber, P. (2002). A curriculum framework for nursing. *Journal of Nursing Education, 41*(1), 15-24.

Williams, B. (2001). Developing critical reflection for professional practice through problem-based learning. *Journal of Advanced Nursing, 34,* 27-34.

Wolin, R. (1991, Spring/Summer). Marcuse and Heidegger: An exchange of letters (R. Wollin, Trans.). *New German Critique 53,* 28-32.

Young, P. (2004). Trying something new: Reform as embracing the possible, the familiar, and the at-hand. *Nursing Education Perspectives, 25*(5), 124-130.

Young, P. (2008). Toward an inclusive science of nursing education: An examination of approaches to nursing research. *Nursing Education Perspectives, 29,* 94-99.

Young, P., & Diekelmann, N. (2002). Learning to lecture: Exploring the skills, strategies, and practices of new teachers in nursing education. *Journal of Nursing Education, 41,* 405-412.

Zarader, M. (1986). The mirror with the triple reflection. In C. Macann (Ed.), *Critical Heidegger* (pp. 7-26). New York: Routledge.

Ziarek, K. (1994). *Inflected language: Toward a hermeneutics of nearness.* Albany, NY: State University of New York Press.

23081775R10317

Made in the USA
Lexington, KY
26 May 2013